M000252017

ROCK CLIMBING

JOSHUA TREE WEST

A FALCON GUIDE®

ROCK CLIMBING
JOSHUA TREE WEST

QUAIL SPRINGS TO HIDDEN VALLEY CAMPGROUND

Randy Vogel

FALCON GUIDE®

GUILFORD, CONNECTICUT
HELENA, MONTANA
AN IMPRINT OF THE GLOBE PEQUOT PRESS

A FALCON GUIDE ®

Copyright © 2006 Randy K. Vogel
Portions of this book were previously published by Chockstone Press © 1992 Randy
K. Vogel and by Falcon Publishing Inc. © 2000 Randy K. Vogel.

All rights reserved. No part of this book may be reproduced or transmitted in any form
by any means, electronic or mechanical, including photocopying and recording, or by
any information storage and retrieval system, except as may be expressly permitted by
the 1976 Copyright Act or by the publisher. Requests for permission should be made
in writing to The Globe Pequot Press, P. O. Box 480, Guilford, Connecticut 06437.

Falcon, FalconGuide, and Chockstone are registered trademarks of Morris Book
Publishing, LLC.

Photos by Randy Vogel (except where otherwise noted).
Spine photo © Brand X Pictures
Maps by XNR Productions Inc. © Morris Book Publishing, LLC

Library of Congress Cataloging-in-Publication Data

Vogel, Randy.
  Rock climbing Joshua Tree West / Randy Vogel.-- 1st ed.
      p. cm. -- (A Falcon guide)
  Includes bibliographical references and index.
  ISBN 0-7627-2965-1
  1. Rock climbing--California--Joshua Tree National Park--Guidebooks. 2. Joshua
Tree National Park (Calif.)--Guidebooks. I. Title. II. Series.
  GV199.42.C2V64 2006
  917.94'97--dc22

                                                                    2005013385

Manufactured in the United States of America
First Edition/First Printing

To buy books in quantity for corporate use
or incentives, call **(800) 962–0973, ext. 4551,**
or e-mail **premiums@GlobePequot.com.**

WARNING:

**Climbing is a sport where you may be seriously injured or die.
Read this before you use this book.**

This guidebook is a compilation of unverified information gathered from many different climbers. The authors cannot assure the accuracy of any of the information in this book, including the topos and route descriptions, the difficulty ratings, and the protection ratings. These may be incorrect or misleading, as ratings of climbing difficulty and danger are always subjective and depend on the physical characteristics (for example, height), experience, technical ability, confidence, and physical fitness of the climber who supplied the rating. Additionally, climbers who achieve first ascents sometimes underrate the difficulty or danger of the climbing route. Therefore, be warned that you must exercise your own judgment on where a climbing route goes, its difficulty, and your ability to safely protect yourself from the risks of rock climbing. Examples of some of these risks are: falling due to technical difficulty or due to natural hazards such as holds breaking, falling rock, climbing equipment dropped by other climbers, hazards of weather and lightning, your own equipment failure, and failure or absence of fixed protection.

You should not depend on any information gleaned from this book for your personal safety; your safety depends on your own good judgment, based on experience and a realistic assessment of your climbing ability. If you have any doubt as to your ability to safely climb a route described in this book, do not attempt it.

The following are some ways to make your use of this book safer:

1. Consultation: You should consult with other climbers about the difficulty and danger of a particular climb prior to attempting it. Most local climbers are glad to give advice on routes in their area; we suggest that you contact locals to confirm ratings and safety of particular routes and to obtain firsthand information about a route chosen from this book.

2. Instruction: Most climbing areas have local climbing instructors and guides available. We recommend that you engage an instructor or guide to learn safety techniques and to become familiar with the routes and hazards of the areas described in this book. Even after you are proficient in climbing safely, occasional use of a guide is a safe way to raise your climbing standard and learn advanced techniques.

3. Fixed Protection: Some of the routes in this book may use bolts and pitons that are permanently placed in the rock. Because of variances in the manner of placement, weathering, metal fatigue, the quality of the metal used, and many other factors, these fixed protection pieces should always be considered suspect and should always be backed up by equipment that you place yourself. Never depend on a single piece of fixed protection for your safety, because you never can tell whether it will hold weight. In some cases, fixed protection may have been removed or is now missing. However, climbers should not always add new pieces of protection unless existing protection is faulty. Existing protection can be tested by an experienced climber and its strength determined. Climbers are strongly encouraged not to add bolts and drilled pitons to a route. They need to climb the route in the style of the first ascent party (or better) or choose a route within their ability—a route to which they do not have to add additional fixed anchors.

Be aware of the following specific potential hazards that could arise in using this book:

1. Incorrect Descriptions of Routes: If you climb a route and you have a doubt as to where it goes, you should not continue unless you are sure that you can go that way safely. Route descriptions and topos in this book could be inaccurate or misleading.

2. Incorrect Difficulty Rating: A route might be more difficult than the rating indicates. Do not be lulled into a false sense of security by the difficulty rating.

3. Incorrect Protection Rating: If you climb a route and you are unable to arrange adequate protection from the risk of falling through the use of fixed pitons or bolts and by placing your own protection devices, do not assume that there is adequate protection available higher just because the route protection rating indicates the route does not have an X or an R rating. Every route is potentially an X (a fall may be deadly) due to the inherent hazards of climbing—including, for example, failure or absence of fixed protection, your own equipment's failure, or improper use of climbing equipment.

There are no warranties, whether expressed or implied, that this guidebook is accurate or that the information contained in it is reliable. There are no warranties of fitness for a particular purpose or that this guide is merchantable. Your use of this book indicates your assumption of the risk that it may contain errors and is an acknowledgment of your own sole responsibility for your climbing safety.

CONTENTS

ACKNOWLEDGMENTS

A guidebook is mostly a compilation of the collective knowledge of the climbing community. Without the contributions of many individuals, this guide would have never been possible. When I asked for help with this new edition, several people really came through and provided a wealth of information, answered multiple questions, and shared their knowledge and opinions.

In particular: Bob Gaines meticulously documented routes and corrections and provided all this information (and more) in a detailed and orderly format; all I can say is wow! Alan Bartlett has tromped and climbed everywhere in Joshua Tree National Park, and then carefully documented all of this in his excellent series of miniguides to the park over the years. Alan has unselfishly shared this knowledge and thus helped immensely in making this guide more complete and accurate. Todd Gordon, the true "Mayor" of Joshua Tree, provided detailed information on literally hundreds of new climbs, then answered questions, and then provided even more information. Todd Swain, as always, provided an amazing amount of information and help. Vernon Stiefel was always providing input, corrections, ratings changes, and gear profiles about every route he encountered. Roger Linfield gave detailed input, corrections, and opinions that helped make this guide far better.

But in the final analysis, this guide simply would not have happened without the support, patience, and help of my wife and climbing partner, Sarah.

Other climbers who provided information and help (including some who contributed to prior editions as well) include: Louie Anderson, Bob Austin, Josh Beck, Tony Bubb, A. J. Burch, Hoffman Cortes, Kevin Daniels, David Evans, Charles Foster, Craig Fry, Dirk Goes, Burton Griffith, Holden Harris, Steve Juhasz, Vaino Kodas, Randy Leavitt, Bill MacBride, Robert Miramontes, Mike Morley, Tom Murphy, Alan Nelson, Chris Owen, Kevin Powell, Tim Powell, Woody Stark, Curt Shannon, Roy Suggett, Steve Sutton, Bob Van Belle, Mike Waugh, Jonny Woodward, and Kai Zinn.

This guide has been built on the 1986 and 1992 editions and without the help of the many people who contributed to these earlier guides, this one would not have been possible. In particular, I would like to thank Matt Cox, whose original compilation of new route information in the early 1970s served as a basis for all my future guidebook efforts. I would like to acknowledge the work of John Wolfe, whose first editions of Josh guidebooks provided the foundation upon which all Josh guides are based. In addition, the following individuals' contributions to prior editions deserve a second thanks: Geoff Archer, Todd Battey, Bill Cramer, Geoff Fullerton, Mari Gingery, Warren Hughes, Mike Lechlinski, Troy Mayr, Dave Mayville, John Mireles, Al Peery, Rex Pieper, Jeff Rhoads, Kelly Rhoads, Aleida Weger, and James Weger.

I would also like to express my sincere appreciation and thanks to George

Meyers, who not only had faith to publish the first two editions of this guide, but went way above and beyond to help me in many ways.

Erik Murdock provided information and many suggestions to make the maps in this edition superior to and more accurate than those in the last edition. Andy Grosvold at XNR Productions then turned these map ideas into reality.

In compiling the history section of this volume, many climbers provided insights, stories, photos, and/or help in tracking people down. All of their contributions have made this guide richer and helped preserve a bit of Josh's climbing legacy. I would like to particularly thank John Ripley for his tremendous help in researching Rock Climbing Section activities in Josh during the 1950s. Special thanks also go to: Mark Powell, Rick Accomazzo, Richard Harrison, John Bachar, Woody Stark, Dick Webster, Bill Briggs, Don McClelland, Tim Powell, Kevin Powell, Mike Waugh, Jon Lonne, Herb Laeger, Spencer Lennard, Dave Houser, Dave Evans, Barbara Lilley, Mike Loughman, Lynn Hill, Craig Fry, Tom Higgins, John Long, Jim Langford, Robert Cates, Royal Robbins, Jerry Gallwas, T. M.

Herbert, Matt Cox, Steve Emerson, Nick Badyrka, Jim Gorin, Bob Kamps, Burt Turney, Mike Sherrick, Don Lauria, Frank Hoover, Mari Gingery, Jean Crenshaw, Rich Wolf, John Wolfe, and Sy Ossofsky.

Through the generosity of several people, a number of early and historic photographs of climbing at Joshua Tree were made available for research purposes and for inclusion in this guide. These contributions have immensely enriched this guide and have changed our understanding of the park's early climbing history. In particular, I would like to thank Barbara Lilley, Don McClelland, Robert Cates, Mike Waugh, Kevin Powell, and Rick Accomazzo for their contributions. I am still seeking photographs of climbing at Joshua Tree for potential future use and research purposes. All help is appreciated.

Lastly, I would like to thank Tracy Salcedo-Chourré, who patiently listened to my frustrations, worked her magic, and transformed raw text, photos, and topos into a well-designed and visually pleasing book.

If I have inadvertently forgotten to thank anyone who has helped, suggested, contributed, or even critiqued, thanks.

Tread lightly and climb safely.

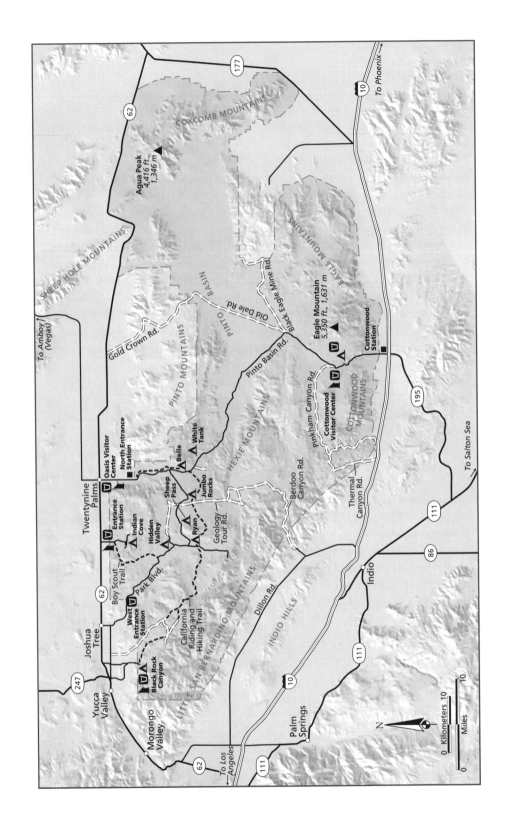

Map Legend

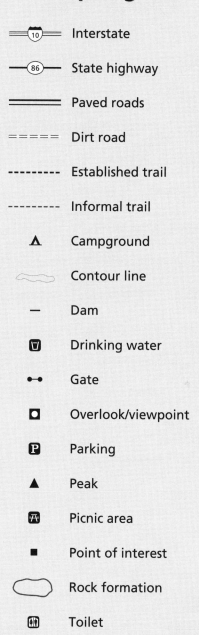

Interstate

State highway

Paved roads

Dirt road

Established trail

Informal trail

Campground

Contour line

Dam

Drinking water

Gate

Overlook/viewpoint

Parking

Peak

Picnic area

Point of interest

Rock formation

Toilet

Visitor Center

INTRODUCTION

This is volume one of a multivolume guide to the rock climbs of Joshua Tree National Park, which contains more than 6,000 established climbs. This volume covers all known routes from the West Entrance to the Hidden Valley Campground and the Outback, including the Quail Springs area (Lizard's Landing, the Negropolis, Vagmarken Hill, Trashcan Rock, APFA Rock); Wonderland of Rocks North, the Lost Horse area, the Hemingway area, Roadside Rocks, Real Hidden Valley, Hidden Valley Campground, and the Outback. Other areas of the park, including the Echo Rock area, the Comic Book area, Barker Dam, the Wonderland of Rocks South and Sheep Pass Area (including Cap Rock, Ryan Campground, the Oyster Bar, Saddle Rocks, Hall of Horrors, Cave Corridor, and Sheep Pass Campground), Queen Mountain, Geology Tour Road, Desert Queen Mine, Jumbo Rocks, Live Oak, Split Rock, Loveland, Belle and White Tank Campgrounds, Stirrup Tank, Oz, Safe Zone, Indian Head, Twentynine Palms Canyon, and Indian Cove will be described in a subsequent volume.

Linh Nguyen soloing The Big Moe *(5.11) in Echo Cove.*   PHOTO: © KEVIN POWELL

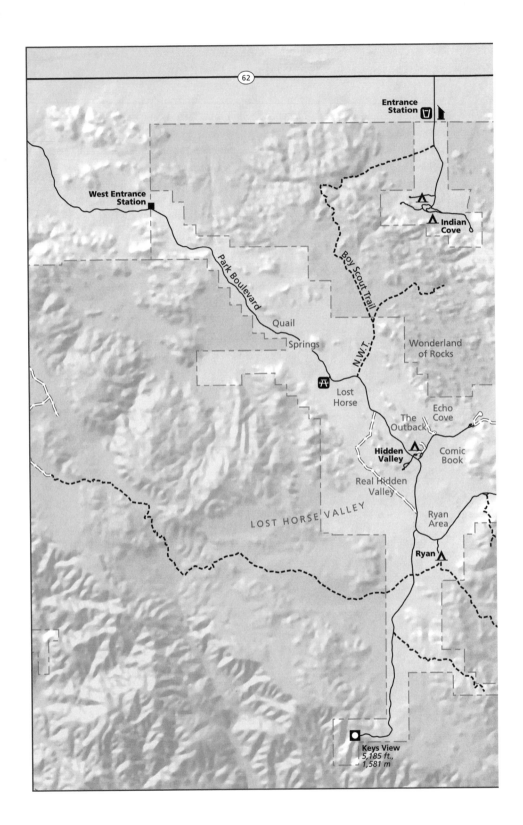

62

Entrance
Station

West Entrance
Station

Indian
Cove

Park Boulevard

Boy Scout Trail

Quail

Springs

N.W.T.

Wonderland
of Rocks

Lost
Horse

Echo
Cove

The
Outback

Hidden
Valley

Comic
Book

Real Hidden
Valley

LOST HORSE VALLEY

Ryan
Area

Ryan

Keys View
5,185 ft.,
1,581 m

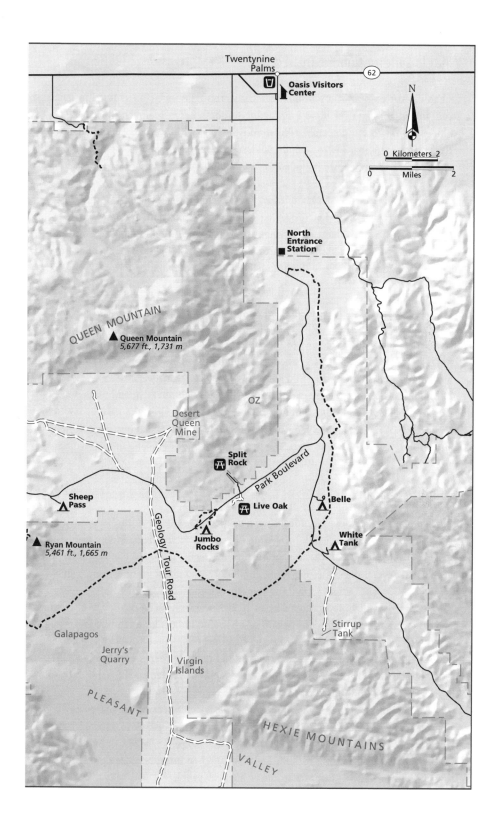

What Is Different about This Edition

Unlike the last edition of the Joshua Tree guide, this edition includes all the known first-ascent information for each and every climb listed. In addition, much more detailed parking, approach, and descent information is included. Maps have been updated to reflect major road changes, to include wilderness boundaries, and to include new crags/areas. Photographs are included for many more rocks, and supplementary topos (as well as photos) are included for a number of the larger rocks. In most cases, suggested gear selections are included. Nearly every route listing includes a short description, notes, and/or comments. Many errors have been corrected (new ones are bound to crop up though). It is hoped that these changes will make the guide more useful for finding the rocks and the climbs. The addition of all this new material (and new climbs) made dividing the guide into several volumes necessary.

Changes at Joshua Tree National Park

Joshua Tree National Park is one of the most popular climbing areas in the world. In 1994, Joshua Tree National Monument was elevated to national park status and its total acreage increased to more than 800,000 acres. Over the past several years, there have been significant changes at the park that directly affect climbers. In addition to new roads, parking areas, and other "improvements," rock climbing in the park is now subject to a number of new rules and regulations (See Rules and Regulations, page 23). Climbers are urged to review and comply with each and every one of these rules.

Minimize Your Impact

Rock climbers constitute a significant percentage of all visitors to this beautiful and often wild part of southern California's high desert. In 1998, the park approved a new General Management Plan that for the first time directly addressed climbing and potential impacts. Several new rules regarding climbing (particularly bolting) were implemented and several studies of climbing impacts commenced.

For this reason climbers must take particular care to insure that their visit to the park has as minimal an impact as possible. Although climbers have tended, as a group, to be some of the more environmentally conscientious users, there has been somewhat of a shift away from this awareness, particularly among new climbers introduced to the sport in climbing gyms. Climbing in a national park requires respect for the natural treasures that are preserved and protected there for future generations.

Virtually none of the bouldering in the park is described in this guide (see Robert Miramontes' *A Complete Bouldering Guide to Joshua Tree National Park*). However, the popularity of bouldering has never been higher and impacts related to bouldering have similarly increased in recent years. Please use care when using bouldering pads, boulder in small groups, and avoid impacts to plant life near problems.

Bart Fay on Sidewinder *(5.10b), Steve Canyon area.*   PHOTO: © KEVIN POWELL

Be responsible: Unfortunately even the thoughtless act of one individual can affect everyone.

In addition to keeping your impacts to a minimum, climbers should contribute back to the park and climber organizations that benefit the park and climbers' interests. I strongly urge every climber to support the Access Fund and the Friends of Joshua Tree, two nonprofit organizations that have worked tirelessly to ensure access to these crags through funding of trails, toilets, environmental studies and brochures, and through advocacy when access is threatened.

Access Fund
P. O. Box 17010
Boulder, CO 80308
www.accessfund.org
(303) 545–6772

Friends of Joshua Tree
P.O. Box 739
Joshua Tree, CA 92252
www.friendsofjosh.org
(760) 366–9699

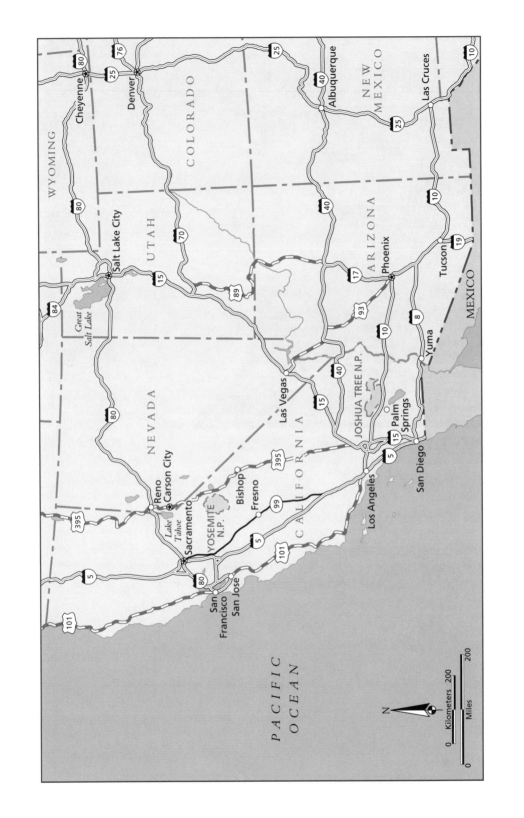

HOW TO GET TO JOSHUA TREE

Joshua Tree National Park is located in the high desert of eastern Southern California, approximately 140 miles east of Los Angeles and about 35 miles northeast of Palm Springs.

From Southern California

Most climbers "approach" the park from metropolitan Southern California. Directions from the various metropolitan areas follow:

- **Los Angeles Area** (plan on 2.5 to 3 hours): Take either Interstate 10 or California Highway 60 east to Beaumont/Banning, where they merge into I–10.
- **Orange County Area** (plan on 2 to 2.5 hours): Take California Highway 91 east to Riverside, then take Highway 60 east to Beaumont/Banning, where it merges into I–10.
- **San Diego Area** (plan on 2.5 to 3.5 hours): Take Interstate 15 East north to Highway 60, then head east to Beaumont/Banning, where it merges into I–10.

From Beaumont/Banning, continue east on I–10 past the Palm Springs exit (California Highway 111), taking the California Highway 62 exit north (toward Twentynine Palms). Several uphill grades take you through Morongo Valley to Yucca Valley. Several miles past Yucca Valley is the town of Joshua Tree. Turn right (south) on Park Boulevard, which leads directly to the park entrance some 5 miles up the road.

From Points North and East

If heading toward Joshua Tree from the north or east, many possible routes (and short-cuts) can be found. Here are a few suggested routes to the routes.

- **From (Through) the Las Vegas Area:** Approximately 55 miles west of Las Vegas (on I–15), there is a particularly good shortcut leading directly to Twentynine Palms via the railroad towns of Cima and Kelso, past the Granite Mountains, across Interstate 40, and past Amboy. However, this road is extremely desolate. The much longer alternative is to take I–15 to Barstow and take California Highway 247 south until it terminates in Yucca Valley (see below).

From the San Francisco Bay Area and Pacific Northwest

From the San Francisco Bay Area and Pacific Northwest, head south via either Interstate 5 or California Highway 99 to Bakersfield. From Bakersfield take California Highway 58 east to Barstow (Highway 58 turns into I–40). From Barstow take Highway 247 south to Lucerne Valley, and continue on to Yucca Valley.

From Yucca Valley take Highway 62 (Twentynine Palms Highway) east for several miles to the town of Joshua Tree. Turn right on Park Boulevard, which leads directly to the park entrance some 5 miles up the road.

From the Southwest

From the southwestern part of the United States (Arizona, New Mexico, etc.), take I–10 west to the park's southern (Cottonwood) entrance near the city of Indio. Alternatively, one can take Interstate 40 west, then head south to Amboy and eventually to Twentynine Palms.

The above are only suggested routes; climbers will undoubtedly find their own shortcuts. A good road map is suggested.

Via Airline or Bus

Some climbers may, for practical reasons, make their initial "approach" via commercial airline to either the Los Angeles area, Palm Springs, or Las Vegas, with Vegas probably having the cheapest airfare. Although a rental car is helpful in getting about in the park, it is, by no means, a necessity.

Bus transport from Palm Springs (about 35 miles southwest of the park) to the towns of Yucca Valley, Joshua Tree, and Twentynine Palms is via Morongo Basin Transit Authority (800–794–6282). The MBTA bus leaves from both Palm Springs International Airport and the Palm Springs bus terminal. Call for specific schedules and cost.

ENTRANCE FEES

As of February 2006, Joshua Tree National Park fees are as follows:

- $5.00 per walk-in visitor, bicycle rider, bus passenger, or motorcycle (one rider); good for seven days.
- $15.00 per vehicle. No limit on occupants; good for seven (7) days.
- $35.00 for a Joshua Tree National Park pass. Good for one year from date of purchase; good only at Joshua Tree National Park.
- $50.00 for a National Parks Pass. Good at all national parks for one year from the date of purchase.
- $65.00 for a Golden Eagle Pass. Good for all federal public lands (Bureau of Land Management [e.g., Red Rock Canyon National Conservation Area], USDA Forest Service, US Fish and Wildlife Service, etc.). Good for one year from the date of purchase.

CAMPING

There are six campgrounds that climbers may want to stay in: Hidden Valley Campground, Ryan Campground, Jumbo Rocks Campground, Belle Campground, White Tank Campground, and Indian Cove Campground. The following information about camping and fees may change; please check with the park to obtain the most up-to-date information by calling (760) 367–5500 or visiting www.nps.gov/jotr.

Hidden Valley, Ryan, Jumbo, Belle, and White Tank Campgrounds work on a first come, first served basis; currently, there are no reservations taken. These campgrounds (particularly Hidden Valley and Ryan) are usually full on weekends. A $5.00 per campsite fee currently is charged for sites in all of those campgrounds. A two-car, six-person limit is also enforced for each site. Money should be placed in an envelope and deposited in the fee collection receptacle for each campground.

Indian Cove Campground and Sheep Pass Group Campground use a reservation system and charge a fee. Sites may be reserved via Biospherics (800–365–2267). Any unreserved sites at Indian Cove may be available on a first come, first served basis. Fees for campsites at Indian Cove are currently $20.00. Due to its remote location, Indian Cove is not convenient to most climbing areas in the park.

Climbers who plan extended stays in Joshua Tree should know that there is a fourteen-day per year camping limit in the park. Because of the popularity of Hidden Valley Campground with climbers, this campground is where most camping limit problems arise. For this reason, it is probably best, if planning a long stay, to make alternative arrangements.

MOTELS AND INNS

Climbers who travel long distances to the park for short visits may find all the campgrounds are full, or may not have all their camping gear with them. Sometimes poor weather may make a retreat to a warm room for the evening very enticing. For these and other reasons it is fairly common for climbers to stay in one of the many reasonably priced motels, inns, and bed-and-breakfasts in the Joshua Tree and Twentynine Palms area. Visit the chamber of commerce Web sites for these towns for specific information. The following establishments are recommended, support the missions of the Access Fund and Friends of Joshua Tree, and welcome climbers' business:

High Desert Motel
61310 Twentynine Palms Highway
Joshua Tree, CA 92252
(760) 366–1978 or (888) 367–3898
www.desertgold.com/highdesert/motel.html
Cable TV, HBO, phones, fresh coffee, refrigerators, microwave ovens, pool, picnic and laundry facilities. Ten percent off if you mention this guide.

Homestead Inn Bed & Breakfast
74153 Two Mile Road
Twentynine Palms, CA 92277
(760) 367–0030 or (877) 367–0030
www.joshuatreelodging.com
Small, select property full of character and charm—only four rooms on fifteen quiet view acres adjacent to Joshua Tree National Park.

ORGANIZATION OF THIS GUIDE

This guide is arranged in the order that you would encounter rock formations as you drive into the park from the West Entrance. Since the park is an incredibly complex area, the guide makes "side trips" into various areas depending on where the nearest approach route is encountered as you drive into the park.

FINDING CRAGS AND ROUTES

To make this guide more useful and accurate, it contains far more information than previous editions about the locations of formations, routes, descents, route descriptions and topos, gear recommendations, and first ascent information.

For nearly every area in this book, there is an overview map showing roads, parking, trails, and the various rock formations, as well as more detailed locator maps for spe-

Chris Miller and Bill Basores on Swept Away *(5.11a).* PHOTO: © KEVIN POWELL

cific formations/climbs. There should always be a reference in the guide to the closest map that covers the area in question.

Parking and mileage directions are given for all formations and areas, though directions to rocks that lie near each other may appear only with the first rock described in that area. These directions are usually given in reference to specific landmarks including:

- The West Entrance
- The four-way intersection of Park Boulevard with the roads to the Intersection Rock and Real Hidden Valley parking areas
- The Park Boulevard-Barker Dam Road intersection.

Photographs and/or topos are provided for many formations in this guide. Route lines are usually drawn on the photo (with the exception of some toprope lines). Climbs are usually described on a cliff from left to right; exceptions should be (it is hoped) obvious. If right or left is used, this always refers to the direction as you face the cliff. The terms north, south, east, and west (or combinations) are only approximations. Likewise, distances between formations and climbs may only be approximate as well.

For nearly every formation and face on a formation, notations are made regarding when (and if) that section of the rock receives sun (e.g., "The face gets morning sun and is shady most of the afternoon"). On hot or cold days, this will help you decide when or whether to climb a particular crag or face.

The guide does not usually refer to individual campsite numbers that may lie adjacent to various rocks in Hidden Valley Campground, Ryan Campground, Indian Cove, Jumbo Rocks, or Belle Campground. The park service has regularly "reformatted" the various campsites and campgrounds and thus changed the campsite numbers, rendering such information less than useless.

Negotiating the Backcountry

Despite all the information provided in this guide, it is very possible to get off track (or even lost) while traveling in Joshua Tree's backcountry. The park features a tremendous amount of backcountry and wilderness climbing and many of these areas feature very complex terrain and may involve arduous and/or complicated approaches and/or descents. Some of the approach and descent descriptions may be wrong or confusing. Even with a detailed approach description, it may take several trips into some of the areas before you find the best way to approach or descend. When time estimates to reach certain crags are included (e.g., in the North Wonderland), these time estimates are based upon correctly navigating to your destination. If you are unfamiliar with where you are going, allow extra time for the approach, descent, and return to your starting point, and take into consideration shorter winter days. In summer or warmer weather, bring sufficient water and protection from the sun. Let others know where you are going and when you expect to return. Sign out at any backcountry boards that request that you do so. Most of all, be self-reliant and self-sufficient.

CLIMBING SEASON

An important reason for Joshua Tree's popularity with climbers lies with its climbing season. When most other areas are covered in snow or rained out, Joshua Tree is often sunny and warm. The season starts in early to mid October and extends to late April or early May.

The best months for climbing are usually from early to mid October to early December, and in March through April. However, there is no such thing as a sure bet with the weather. Some seasons have wonderful Januarys and Februarys and terrible springs. Snow is possible from late November through February. The park receives approximately 7.5 inches of participation per year, with nearly 40 percent falling in thunderstorms during the months of July, August, and September. With the large number of local climbers living near the park, it is not unusual to see climbers in Joshua Tree during the summer months. It is possible (but certainly not a sure bet) that temperatures may be quite reasonable in the shade even during July, August, and September.

For nearly every formation and face on a formation in this guide, notations are made regarding when (and if) that section of the rock receives sun or shade (e.g., "The face gets morning sun and is shady most of the afternoon."). On hot or cold days, this will help you decide when or whether to climb at a particular crag or face.

It is not uncommon for Joshua Tree to experience cold winds, particularly in winter. There are a number of areas listed in this volume that are more sheltered from the wind than others. These include portions of Real Hidden Valley and Steve Canyon.

Current Weather Conditions

It is possible to consult a number of Web sites to get a read on current and predicted weather conditions in the park. For current weather conditions, the following Web sites provide some of the most relevant, useful, and real-time information:

- **Lost Horse Weather Station:** cdec.water.ca.gov/cgi-progs/queryF?LTH
- **Belle Mountain Web Cam** (and weather info): www2.nature.nps.gov/air/WebCams/parks/jotrcam/jotrcam.cfm
- **National Weather Service Forecast:** www.srh.noaa.gov/data/forecasts/ CAZ028.php?warncounty=CAC071&city=joshuatree

ABOUT THE ROCK

The rock formations at Joshua Tree tend to be domelike, and are surrounded by boulders, canyons, flat sandy washes and/or open plains. Some of the rock formations are in fact no more than huge piles of stacked boulders. Other formations lie on hillsides, but still tend to be domelike. Of the many boulders found in the park, many offer excellent boulder problems. There are a number of established bouldering spots and problems in the park, but there remains a tremendous untapped potential for more.

Joshua Tree rock is granitic in origin, of a type called quartz monzonite. The rock is part of a huge underground sea of granite (a batholith) that has pushed its way to the sur-

Brandt Allen on Sail Away *(5.8–), Real Hidden Valley.*   PHOTO: © KEVIN POWELL

face throughout this area of Southern California. Due to the particular way the rock has cooled and was subsequently weathered, it is generally quite rough in texture. This means there is a high friction coefficient and a need to use care to avoid cuts and scrapes.

Fortunately for climbers this translates into a rock surface that is highly climbable. Sections of formations that look hideously hard may be only moderately difficult. Steep faces also often have "plates" that may provide large handholds.

The cracks at Joshua Tree are plentiful and vary from shallow and flared to clean and split. Generally, areas with coarser rock (e.g., Jumbo Rocks) have more flaring cracks, whereas rock of more compact structure tend to have cleaner, deeper cracks (Queen Mountain, etc.). Camming devices are extremely helpful (and often necessary) and provide protection in the flared or horizontal cracks that are commonly seen in the park.

Generally, the western faces of the rock formations tend to be lower angled and rougher in texture. The eastern faces are steeper, often overhanging, and the rock is usually much smoother, even polished. This is a result of the way the rock has faulted and weathered. The rock at Joshua Tree can vary considerably in quality.

Crystalline and other intrusion dikes crisscross many of the formations. In fact, it is possible to trace a single intrusion dike as it crosses various different formations. Such dikes have provided for numerous excellent traversing and vertical face climbs (i.e., *Sidewinder, Pinched Rib, Trespassers Will Be Violated, Sole Fusion,* and *I Can't Believe It's a Girdle*).

EQUIPMENT

Unlike some climbing areas, Joshua Tree is a relatively "traditional" climbing area, although there do exist a large number of "sport" routes. In this guide, sport routes are specifically designated as such after the name and rating (Sport). However, for most climbs in the park, it is necessary to place protection and/or anchors, even at the tops of bolted face routes. Also, many routes with bolt protection may require use of nuts or cams for additional protection.

If you are used to climbing exclusively on sport routes, remember that even fully bolted face climbs at Joshua Tree may not have "sport"-type protection. It may be possible to take long falls. Additionally, because of the short nature of many climbs, and sensitivity about placing too many bolts, many face climbs remain "toprope" problems and should be left that way.

For the purposes of discussion, a "standard Joshua Tree rack" (if there is such a thing) would consist of camming devices (0.5 inch through 3 inches), small to medium wired nuts (0.25 inch to 0.75 inch), micronuts (brass or aluminum), and an assortment of quickdraws and runners. While routes designated (Sport) should only require quickdraws and a sling or two, it is never a bad idea to carry a few extra pieces of gear for anchors, in case bolts are missing.

While there has been an attempt in this guide to list general equipment requirements for routes, these may be inaccurate or incomplete. Each climber should make his or her own judgment call as to what type and amount of gear to bring along on any route.

Fixed Protection

Many of the routes at Josh have fixed protection (bolts, pitons, copperheads, etc.) Some of this fixed protection may be old and/or of dubious nature. While there has been an effort by some climbers and organizations such as the America Safe Climbing Association (ASCA) to replace older bolts, many quarter-inch bolts remain that may be twenty, thirty, or even forty years old.

I strongly encourage climbers to support the work of the ASCA in replacing old and unsafe fixed anchors. ASCA is a 501(c)(3) organization; all contributions are tax-deductible. Members receive the newsletter. To help, send checks payable to ASCA to:

American Safe Climbing Association
P. O. Box 1814
Bishop, CA 93515

You may also donate online by visiting www.safeclimbing.org.

Always treat older fixed protection as suspect and back it up when possible. Never hit bolts with a hammer; this will cause premature failure. However, you may want to test or redrive fixed pins as they tend to loosen over time. Also, fixed protection present at the time this guide was compiled now may be missing, or the guide's information may be in error. Do not rely upon the descriptions of fixed protection in this guide as absolute. Various rules have been instituted in the park regarding placement of new fixed protection: Please read the Rules and Regulations section on page 23.

PHOTO: © KEVIN POWELL

Tony Sartin on Clean and Jerk *(5.10c), Sports Challenge Rock, Real Hidden Valley.*

Toproping

Because most of the climbs at Joshua Tree are relatively short, it is possible to toprope many of these routes. Routes that are commonly toproped (even though they can be led) are usually noted in the guide. You should plan on bringing a good selection of cams and nuts (most in the 1- to 2.5-inch range), a cordelette, and some manner of extendo slings or short rope to extend the toprope point over the edge of the cliff. Some routes have bolts on top; most do not.

The following formations, found in this volume, are popular spots for easy to moderate difficulty toproping and often have easy access to the top for setting up anchors: Trashcan Rock (Quail Springs), Mustang Ranch (North Wonderland approach), Lizard's Hangout (Lost Horse North), Atlantis Area (Lost Horse Area), Dairy Queen Wall— Right Side (Hemingway Area), Playhouse Rock (Hemingway Area), and Locomotion Rock and the Thin Wall (Real Hidden Valley).

Advisory: It is not uncommon for groups and climbing classes to toprope several climbs in an area. If you place a toprope on a route and leave it up for more than a short time, you must be prepared to either share the rope with other climbers, or pull it down. If the route is commonly led, you should offer to pull your rope to allow others to lead the route. Totally dominating a rock or route with topropes and then being unwilling to share or pull your ropes is extremely rude, and might justify the removal of your ropes. Be courteous instead.

RATINGS

Difficulty Ratings

The difficulty rating system used in this guidebook is the Decimal System. Climbers may find the ratings at Joshua Tree harder or easier than to what they are accustomed. **Although the ratings given to routes in the park are generally consistent, the ratings given some routes may just be wrong.** I have not independently verified the ratings of all the routes. Many climbs in the park have seen few ascents and no consensus on its rating has been formed. Some first ascentionists chronically overrate or underrate difficulty. Just as often, climbers have different opinions based upon their own strengths and weaknesses. Keep this in mind, take the ratings as approximates, and use your own judgment.

A **Rating Comparison Chart** has been included in this guide to assist foreign climbers in determining the relative difficulty of the climbs listed.

RATING SYSTEM COMPARISON CHART

YDS	British	French	Australian
5.3	VD 3b	2	11
5.4	HVD 3c	3	12
5.5	MS/S/HS 4a	4a	12/13
5.6	HS/S 4a	4b	13
5.7	HS/VS 4b/4c	4c	14/15
5.8	HVS 4c/5a	5a	16
5.9	HVS 5a	5b	17
5.10a	E1 5a/5b	5c	18
5.10b	E1/E2 5b/5c	6a	19
5.10c	E2/E3 5b/5c	6a+	20
5.10d	E3 5c/6a	6b	21
5.11a	E3/E4 5c/6a	6b+	22
5.11b	E3/E4 6a/6b	6c	22/23
5.11c	E4 6a/6b	6c+	23
5.11d	E4/E5 6a/6b	7a	24
5.12a	E5 6b/6c	7a+	25
5.12b	E5/E6 6b/6c	7b	26
5.12c	E5/E6 6b/6c/7a	7b+	27
5.12d	E6/E7 6c/7a	7c	28
5.13a	E6/E7 6c/7a	7c+	28/29
5.13b	E7 7a	8a	29
5.13c	E7 7a	8a+	30
5.13d	E8 7a	8b	31
5.14a	E8 7a	8b+	32
5.14b	E9 7a	8c	33
5.14c	E9 7b	8c+	33

Quality Ratings

A "star" or "quality" rating is used in this guide. Climbs are given no stars if they are considered just average or less than average in quality, and one through five stars are given (on an ascending scale) if the climb is thought to be a better route. Five-star routes are acknowledged classics. This system is highly subjective. Quality ratings are far less reliable than difficulty ratings and there may be no consensus about certain climbs that deserve stars but have no stars in this guide. Consequently, use the ratings as an indication only, and remember that many routes without stars may in fact be worthy of your attention (and vice versa).

Protection Ratings

This guide gives protection ratings for some poorly protected routes. However, what constitutes good protection to one climber may be poor protection to another. This is especially true for climbers trained on well-protected bolted "sport" climbs. If your protection skills are rusty or undeveloped, you may find some routes very difficult to adequately protect. Little consensus exists for protection ratings. Do not rely on the absence of a protection rating to indicate good protection. Use common sense.

In this guidebook R and X ratings are sometimes given. This guide does not use either the G or PG protection ratings. The protection ratings in this guide are not intended to tell you that a climb is well protected; you should never presume that a route not given a R or X rating is well protected. Further, a long or even deadly fall can occur on almost any route.

- **R Rating:** If a route is poorly protected *at the difficult sections,* but not without some protection, it will be given an R rating. A fall on an R-rated route, at the wrong place, could result in very long or serious fall that results in injury or death.
- **X Rating:** If a climb is essentially unprotected *at the difficult sections,* and a fall would have severe or grave consequences (e.g., hitting a deck is possible), it will be given an X rating. A fall from a route with an X rating could result in severe injury or death if the fall occurred in the wrong place.

The R and X ratings are intended to be used as a guideline only. Only you can judge whether a route is adequately protected for you. Please note that some routes that may deserve an R or X protection rating may not have one. Never assume a route without a protection rating is safe. You alone are responsible for your own safe climbing.

Aid Climbs

The few aid climbs listed in this guide are not given protection or seriousness ratings. Any A3 or A4 routes on such short rocks are by their very nature serious and have a risk of ground fall. Lead aid routes at Josh at your own risk.

PHOTO: © KEVIN POWELL

Scott Cosgrove on G-String (5.13d), Hidden Cliff in the Real Hidden Valley.

FIRST ASCENT INFORMATION

When known, the names of the first ascent party and date (month and year) of the first ascent are listed for climbs. In some instances incomplete information, such as first names, has been provided. Climbers with additional information about first ascents are encouraged to contact the author.

- **FA** means first ascent.
- **FFA** means first free ascent (the FA party used aid).
- **FKA** means first known ascent.
- **FKFA** means first known free ascent.
  (In the case of these last two designations, it is suspected that the route had been climbed or free climbed previously, but no record exists to confirm this.)
- **(TR)** means the first ascent was toproped.
- **(Lead)** means the first party to lead the route (if FA or FFA was on TR).

  In addition to providing historical information about who did what and when, first ascent information can sometimes clue you into other factors about a climb. Individual climbers may tend to establish more runout, well protected, junky, and/or quality climbs. If nothing else, it gives the first ascentionist something to show their parents, spouses, etc. to justify all the time they have been wasting, or perhaps just to remember when.

Mari Gingery on Satanic Mechanic *(5.12a/b), Turtle Rock.*   PHOTO: © KEVIN POWELL

INDEXES

This guide also contains two methods for finding routes, a general alphabetical index and a routes-by-rating index. They cover only routes found in this volume; additional guides will include indexes to the routes contained in those respective volumes only.

The general alphabetical index lists alphabetically all climbs and formations. This index also lists the difficulty ratings, as well as the page numbers. The routes-by-rating index compiles all climbs in this guide by their ratings and provides page numbers. If you are looking for a particular route or formation, find it in the general alphabetical index. If seeking climbs of a particular difficulty, look in the routes-by-rating index.

The routes-by-rating index also serves as a personal checklist to record routes you have climbed. Before each route is a small box that can be used to "check off" the climb. Transferring this info from the last edition and adding newer routes you have done is sure to occupy any number of days of inclement weather.

FOOD, WATER, AND SUPPLIES

No food, water, or supplies are available in the park. Stock up before entering the park or have a car at your disposal for this purpose. The town of Yucca Valley has several well-stocked supermarkets. Yucca Valley, Joshua Tree and Twentynine Palms also sport a virtual swarm of reasonably priced restaurants, as well as "fast food" places.

Climbing and Camping Equipment

The following local businesses sell climbing and camping equipment and support both the Access Fund and the Friends of Joshua Tree. I encourage you to support these establishments.

Nomad Ventures
61795 Twentynine Palms Highway
Joshua Tree, CA 92252
(760) 366–4684
www.nomadventures.com

Coyote Corner
6535 Park Boulevard
Joshua Tree, CA 92252
(760) 366–9683

Equipment Rentals

Many climbers who travel by airline to visit Joshua Tree do not bring their own camping gear, or they leave behind bouldering pads because of security restrictions or space limitations. The following business rents a wide variety of camping and cooking equipment, guidebooks, and bouldering pads. They also offer Internet access. This business also supports the Friends of Joshua Tree and the Access Fund.

Joshua Tree Outfitters
61707 Twentynine Palms Highway
Joshua Tree, CA 92251
(888) 366–1848
www.joshuatreeoutfitters.com

Showers

Showers are not available in the park. A coin-operated shower is available at Coyote Corner (see above) in the town of Joshua Tree.

Guide Services

The following individuals and companies are authorized to offer climbing instruction and guiding in Joshua Tree National Park. They also have supported the missions of the Friends of Joshua Tree and the Access Fund:

Vertical Adventures: Has offered one- to four-day classes, private instruction, and guided climbs since 1983. Contact Bob Gaines, Course Director, at (800) 514–8785; contact him via e-mail at Bgvertical@aol.com; or visit www.verticaladventures.com.

Joshua Tree Rock Climbing School: Locally based guide service; one- to four-day classes and private guiding from September to June. Write to HCR Box 3034, Joshua Tree, CA 92252; call (800) 890–4745; or visit www.joshuatreerockclimbing.com.

Uprising Outdoor Adventure Center: Specializes in individual guiding and group programs; classes for all abilities. Write to P. O. Box 129, Joshua Tree, CA 92252; call (888) Climb–on; e-mail sue@uprising.com; or visit www.uprising.com.

Campfires

If you desire an evening campfire, bring wood with you (it also can be purchased in town). No natural vegetation (dead or not) may be gathered for burning or any other purpose in the park. The desert ecology depends upon natural decay of plant life; the removal of it by visitors is damaging to the delicate balance of life. In addition to being an environmentally unsound practice, it is illegal; you can be cited by the rangers and fined.

Off-Road Travel

Mountain bikes are limited to paved and dirt roads and designated mountain bike trails. In an effort to prevent "braided" trails, the Access Fund has installed, at most popular climbing areas, trail marker signs. Please follow the signed trails, and use only consolidated and established footpaths where possible. Try to follow the footpaths of others so consolidated trails can form. Climbers also can minimize their impact by walking in sandy wash areas whenever possible.

Environmental Considerations

Climbers have become one of the larger user groups of Joshua Tree National Park. The responsibility for lessening environmental impacts rests with each and every climber.

- **Trails:** Use established climbing access trails whenever possible. Travel along sandy streambeds in areas without trails.
- **Plants and Animals:** Do not disturb any plant or animal life encountered while hiking or climbing. Watch where you place bouldering pads, packs, gear, or rope.
- **Trash:** Never leave used tape, cigarette butts, etc., behind. Pick up any litter you see; it will easily fit into your pack or pocket and you will feel better too.

Human Waste

Plan ahead by using toilets before setting out for the day. The park service and the Access Fund have installed toilets near popular climbing areas (Trashcan Rock, Hemingway Buttress, Real Hidden Valley, Echo Rock, North and South Wonderland parking areas, the Hall of Horrors/Saddle Rocks, etc.). Where toilets are not available, use common sense:

1. Do not ever leave human waste anywhere near waterways (i.e., dry streambeds). When it rains in the park, this waste will pollute the valuable and scarce rainwater that is relied upon by many animals in the park.
2. Human waste should never be left on or near the many informal trails that climbers use.
3. Although many climbers make the habit of burying their waste, the fact remains that in desert areas human waste decomposes the quickest when not buried.
4. Soiled paper or tampons always should be carried out in a small plastic zip locked bag; this is the only way to insure that the dry desert environment does not have to struggle for decades to decompose it on its own.

RULES AND REGULATIONS

Occupied Campsite Rule

Any route that begins out of or behind an occupied campsite may not be climbed without the occupants' permission. This rule applies to only a few locations in Hidden Valley Campground, particularly the west face of Chimney Rock from *West Face Overhang* to *Pinched Rib*. Remember, courtesy goes a long way.

Kastle Lund on Pope's Crack *(5.9), Echo Rock.*

PHOTO: © KEVIN POWELL

Dogs

Dogs can have a significant impact on wildlife and plant life. For this reason, the following rules apply to dogs (even poodles) in the park. Dogs must be on a leash, at all times, in developed areas of the park (campgrounds, etc.). Dogs (whether leashed or not) are not permitted in Joshua Tree backcountry areas (not just in designated wilderness). Given these restrictions, perhaps it is better to leave Fifi at home.

Webbing

Nylon webbing (runners) left on fixed protection, anchors, or trees is often an unsightly and unnecessary form of pollution. It is legal to leave only natural (rock-colored) webbing. Never tie slings directly into bolts; it may be impossible for subsequent climbers to clip into the hangers. Loop the sling through the bolt; subsequent parties then can easily remove the sling.

BOLTING REGULATIONS AND GUIDELINES

Wilderness Areas

It is currently not permitted by the park to place new bolt/fixed anchors in designated wilderness areas. It is, however, legal to replace any existing bolt/fixed anchor on a one-for-one basis. No power drills may be used in designated wilderness areas.

As of this writing, a permit process is being developed to allow for placement of a limited number of new bolted routes in wilderness areas. The permit process will take approximately six months from submission to obtain any approval. You should contact the park to obtain a permit application form.

Please see the map on page 2 that shows the general wilderness boundaries in the park. In addition, the detail maps in the guide, together with text for various formations and areas, will indicate the approximate location of wilderness boundaries. Specific formations within wilderness are noted as (Wilderness) after the formation's name.

Non-Wilderness Areas

Bolting of new routes is currently allowed without restriction. However, all new routes that have bolts (protection or anchors) must be reported to the park after they have been completed. A simple route submission form is available at the entrance stations, from the visitor center, and from the park. The form may also be downloaded (pdf format) from the park's Web site: www.nps.gov/jotr; go to activities, then climbing, to locate the form. The reporting of new routes will help the park monitor impacts and climber activity as part of the requirements of its Climbing Management Plan.

Compliance with this new requirement will help assure that more restrictive rules are not implemented.

Motorized Drills

Use of motorized drills to place bolts outside of wilderness areas is by permit only, and generally restricted to ongoing efforts to replace older bolts throughout the park. Motorized drills may never be used in designated wilderness areas.

Bolting Guidelines

It is strongly recommended that the following climber-created guidelines be observed when bolting:

- Buy and install only camouflaged hangers (or chain).
- Use only three-eighths or half-inch diameter bolts (smaller diameter bolts are not permitted in the park).
- Be discreet in where and how you place bolts. Avoid bolting next to public trails, parking areas, or where they would be visually intrusive.
- Do not add bolts to an established route unless belay bolts are inadequate or need reinforcing (belays should always be bomb proof); or when replacing older bolts. Additional protection bolts should generally not be placed on existing routes.

Bolt Belay/Rappel Anchors

Over the last thirty years, climbers have added bolt belay and/or rappel anchors at the tops of many climbs that may not have originally had them. In some cases, anchors are "added" simply because a new route with bolt anchors happens to end near established routes. In some instances, new bolt anchors are added to avoid damage to plant life encountered on a descent. In other cases bolt anchors are added simply as a convenience for belaying, toproping, and descending.

This process has been going on for many years. However, in more recent times, more such anchors have appeared and subsequently disappeared. Controversy over the addition or removal of these anchors has increased.

There are no hard and fast rules for determining whether adding fixed anchors to the top of a route or formation is justified or not. However, some questions to bear in mind before adding such anchors (or removing them) include:

- How good or bad are existing anchors?
- Where are existing natural anchors located?
- How involved and/or technical is the descent?
- Would anchors used for a rappel descent lessen traffic around and disturbance of plants and animals on the downclimb/walk off?
- Would anchors ease or increase crowding on the climb(s)?

Chipping and Gluing

The "chipping" or "improving" of holds should never be acceptable. It is also illegal, and robs future climbers of the ability to establish yet harder and harder routes. Chipping or adding holds to a route or potential route presumes that no one will ever be able to climb at a higher standard. It is illegal within any national park to chip or manufacture holds on rocks.

It is currently illegal in any national park to use epoxy glues for the purpose of attaching or reinforcing natural or artificial holds.

Mari Gingery on Father Figure *(5.13a), Barker Dam area.* PHOTO: © KEVIN POWELL

JOSHUA TREE WEB SITES

The following Web sites provide information about climbing in Joshua Tree National Park and might be a useful resource for up-to-date information, comments, and beta about particular climbs, new route information, and current regulations, permits, fees, etc.

- **www.mountainproject.com:** This Web site provides lots of information about climbing in the park, with listings of established and new routes. All route listings, ratings, action/beta photos, and comments are submitted by climbers. This site also has recommended route lists by ratings and type of climbs, a partner board and a discussion board. An excellent resource for visiting and local climbers alike. No fee to access database. See also www.climbingjtree.com.

- **www.joshuatreeclimb.com:** The newest Josh-specific site has ambitions to cover an incredible array of information about climbing in the park. The site also covers the park's natural history and climbing history, and includes 0action photos, trivia quizzes, climber profiles, new routes, and so much more. Fee charged for access to certain databases.
- **www.nps.gov/jotr:** This is the park's official Web site. You can access new route reporting forms, bolting permit applications, and find out the latest rules and regulations about climbing, as well as current camping and entrance fees.

NEW ROUTE INFORMATION

All new route information to be included in updated printings of this guide should be mailed directly to:

Randy Vogel
P. O. Box 4554
Laguna Beach, CA 92652

Here are a few tips on how to submit new route information:
- If it is a new bolted route, submit a copy of the New Route Reporting form provided by the park service, which you are required to submit. Refer to the section on bolting outside wilderness areas on page 25.

Otherwise:
- Provide the name of the route, the rating (try to use a, b, c, or d rather than plus or minus), the approximate date of the first ascent, and the full names of the first ascent party.
- If the route lies adjacent to an existing route, give directions or reference in relation to the existing route, including the route number. You should also give approximate distances (right or left) in feet or yards.
- A photo of the climb (you may copy the photo in the guide) is extremely helpful in locating the route. You may wish to mark with a pen directly on the photograph the line taken by the route including the location of any bolts or fixed pins.
- A map is always extremely helpful. If a route (or a formation) that you are describing is located somewhere in an area covered by a map in this guide (even if the formation is not specifically shown), you may copy the map from the guide and show on the map where the route or formation lies.

CORRECTIONS

Some information in this guide may not be entirely clear or may be just wrong. Please send any corrections to the author at P. O. Box 4554, Laguna Beach, CA 92652. All corrections and suggestions are welcome.

HISTORY

From Practice Area to Local Sensation (1936 to 1975)

Putting together a history of Josh climbing for this guide seemed a simple enough task. The first-ascent information provided a decent record of who did what when. I decided a few conversations with various climbers would fill in the gaps. The reality proved much more complex and far more interesting.

According to conventional wisdom, Joshua Tree was devoid of any meaningful climbing activity until the mid 1960s, and free climbing standards remained very low until the 1970s. Yet, I have always had serious doubts about this "official" version of Josh's early days. After all, most of the country's best climbers lived in Southern California during the 1950s and some of them climbed at Josh. It seemed implausible that climbers known for pushing the limits of free climbing at Tahquitz and Yosemite would have spent their time in Joshua Tree ambling up 5.1s.

These doubts prompted a bit of research. But the problem with delving into Joshua Tree's early climbing history immediately became apparent: It seemed no one had taken the climbing seriously enough to record routes, ratings, and/or first-ascent parties. In the interest of filling in that piece of Joshua Tree's climbing past, I began a series of telephone conversations with many of the climbers who were active in the 1950s. With their help and ample detective work, I uncovered a variety of reports, photographs, and oral histories that shed light on Josh's formative days.

As of this writing, many unanswered questions remain and research continues. What follows sketches the outlines of an early climbing history that has never been told. It also lays to rest the accepted history of early climbing developments at Joshua Tree.

THE EARLY DAYS

When Joshua Tree National Monument was officially established by Congress in August 1936, technical rock climbing in California was in its infancy. In 1931, East Coast climber Robert Underhill, who had learned belaying techniques while climbing in Europe, visited California and introduced "modern" rope techniques to a few Sierra Club mountaineers. These California mountaineers were so taken with rock climbing that they helped pioneer the formation of "Rock Climbing Sections" (RCS) within several chapters of the Sierra Club. By 1935, members of the Angeles Chapter RCS began conducting an intensive search for promising crags throughout Southern California.

On April 25, 1936, Art Johnson, a member of the Angeles Chapter RCS, made the first recorded "climbing" visit to the Wonderland of Rocks in the then-proposed monument. In a historical context, timing is everything, and Johnson's "visit" did not translate into an immediate interest in Joshua Tree as a climber's destination. His scouting trip was preceded by the discovery of Tahquitz Rock the previous June, and unlike Tahquitz, Joshua Tree's formations were small and the apparent quality of the rock inferior. In addition, 1936 was the height of the Great Depression. Joshua Tree lay at least 60 miles

An early ascent of the popular Toe Jam *(5.7) circa 1954.*   PHOTO: BARBARA LILLEY COLLECTION

farther from Los Angeles than Tahquitz, and was accessible by roads that were often remote and of poor quality. Few climbers had cars, nor the money for gasoline. As a result, Joshua Tree sat all but neglected by climbers. Despite a brightening of the economy during World War II, most active climbers were serving in the military. For the remaining climbers, gas rationing restricted travel to occasional trips.

It was not until Veterans Day weekend in 1949 that the first recorded climbing trip was made to Joshua Tree. Six RCS members spent the long weekend climbing in what is today Hidden Valley Campground. The group climbed several routes including one on Intersection Rock, naming the formation/route *Phil's Folly*. According to a report made in the RCS newsletter, *The Mugelnoos,* a "new climbing area, near Hidden Valley" was "strongly recommended for late fall, early spring and even winter rock climbing." Following this positive report, the RCS began scheduling annual trips to the monument either in the fall or spring, with members of the RCS Angeles Chapter and San Diego RCS present during some of these trips.

These RCS chapters included some of the best rock climbers in the country at the time. In Southern California, RCS members were responsible for most of the new route activity at Tahquitz Rock where free-climbing standards were then at the cutting edge of technical difficulty. A young Royal Robbins participated in several trips to Josh beginning in 1952, the same year he and Don Wilson made the first free ascent of *The Open Book* at Tahquitz, one of the first 5.9 routes in the country. Many other active Tahquitz climbers of the era such as Chuck and Ellen Wilts, Mike Sherrick, Jerry Gallwas, T. M. Herbert, Frank Hoover, Harry Daley, Gary Hemming, Ray Van Aiken, Jim and Roy Gorin, Barbara Lilley, and John and Ruth Mendenhall took part in these early Joshua Tree RCS trips. Still, most RCS members were primarily mountaineers and peak baggers. Only a handful participated regularly in rock climbing trips, and then perhaps only every other weekend. Winters were mostly devoted to skiing.

Almost a year after that first climbing trip, in late October 1950, thirty-eight "would-be desert rats" (as they called themselves) showed up in Joshua Tree, and as the group fanned out many new routes were climbed. The park service had made improvements to Hidden Valley Campground, which included the installation of fire grates and picnic tables. Despite these "developments," camping remained rather primitive throughout the 1950s. According to RCS climber Burt Turney, "You would just pitch your tent wherever you wanted. There was no organized campground." During this period, all the monument's main roads remained unpaved.

By October 1951, Joshua Tree as a climbing destination was gradually becoming legitimate, as the recorded "firsts" reveal. The first foreign climbers had visited Josh (two Swiss climbers), and the first "forced bivouac" atop a formation was recorded. However, there remains some question as to whether the bivouac was really an excuse for a romantic interlude. The record for this October climbing trip noted another first: The first intervention by a park ranger on behalf of climbers, to "a man with a gun [who was instructed] not to shoot the rock climbers."

The formations around Hidden Valley Campground remained the focus of most technical climbing in the monument during the 1950s. By 1952, free and aid routes had been established not only on Intersection Rock, but the Old Woman, the Blob, Outhouse Rock, the Wall, and Chimney Rock. By the mid 1950s, Steve Canyon, the Outback, Real Hidden Valley, Ryan Campground, Saddle Rock, Sheep Pass, and other outlying areas saw route exploration. Bouldering was also a very popular activity on these early trips.

Intersection Rock became a popular formation. *The Upper Right* and *Upper Left Ski Tracks* (via *Zigzag*) were climbed as early as 1950, and within a couple of years perhaps a dozen different routes were established on Intersection Rock alone. The Old Woman was another popular formation, and in November of 1952, Jerry Gallwas, George Scheiff, and Gary Hemming made the first ascent of the now-favorite *Toe Jam* (5.7).

But for the most part, climbers visited Josh when poor weather kept the more alpine areas (Tahquitz and Yosemite) closed. In simple words, climbers bided their time at Joshua Tree until some "real" climbing was in condition. According to former RCS climber Don McClelland, in the 1950s "Nobody thought the climbing was worth keeping track of." Another RCSer, Jim Gorin, remembers, "We went out during times when we weren't going somewhere else. We didn't take it seriously. It was just practice." Other climbers did not like the area due to the rough textured rock. Consequently, routes and formations went largely unnamed and unrecorded.

The climbing activities of these RCS outings were noted by non-RCS climbers drawn to the monument in the early 1950s. Dick Webster, who in the late 1960s would be one of the monument's main activists, first visited the monument with his father

An unknown climber atop Skinny Pin *(5.4) circa 1954.*   PHOTO: BARBARA LILLEY COLLECTION

Harold in 1953. Webster was eleven years old. He remembers that "most of the obvious cracks" on Intersection Rock showed "evidence of pitons"—proof that others had climbed there. However, Webster also recalled that it was rare to see other cars, let alone other climbers in the monument. Hence, communication among the different climbing groups was limited if nonexistent.

As for any official record of who was climbing what in the monument, that task remained the bailiwick of the RCS climbing newsletter *The Mugelnoos*. But it was a task with no formal assignment, and subsequently little consistency. Climbers relied upon the newsletter's infrequent updates about climbing activity in the monument or they heard their "news" firsthand while sitting around the campfire in the evenings after climbing.

By the time Mike Loughman visited Joshua Tree on his first RCS trip on Halloween weekend in 1954 (and watched veteran RCS members free climb *The Orphan* [5.9] on the Old Woman), many crack routes in the campground area up to 5.8 or 5.9 in difficulty had already been climbed. In fact, Loughman was not sure whether the ascent of *The Orphan* he witnessed had been its first. What he did remember "for the record" was the following story shared around the campfire that Saturday night.

"There was a lot of discussion about all the free soloing Royal Robbins had been doing," Loughman says. It was rumored that Robbins had soloed *Lower Right Ski Track* (5.10b), but when asked for the purposes of this history, Robbins admits he had no specific recollection of this event. Some RCS members were very critical of Robbins and his style of climbing. They believed free soloing and pushing climbing beyond the standard of 5.7 were not only dangerous, but damaging to the sport. Most RCS members at the time were college graduates, engineers, and scientists. In contrast, Robbins had dropped out of high school. Although climbers like Wilts and the Mendenhalls were very supportive, others were somewhat outraged by Robbins's attitude toward climbing.

Until 1956 there was no formal numerical rating system for the difficulty of climbs. Routes identified as fifth class were described as being easy, moderate, hard, or very hard. "And one climb might be described as 'a bit harder' than another," T. M. Herbert says. Robbins, Wilson, and Chuck Wilts developed the decimal rating system (later to become the Yosemite Decimal System) in the mid 1950s, which made its first appearance in the 1956 edition of the Tahquitz guidebook, *Climber's Guide to Tahquitz Rock*.

Also active in the 1950s were Don Cornell, Phil Smith, his son Rod, John Merriam, and Bob Boyle. Most had mountaineering background and concentrated their activities on attaining various freestanding "summits." These efforts included: *The Lost Pencil* (A1, 1956; Cornell and Merriam); *The Wedge* (5.5, 1956; Jack Davis, Bruce Fortune, and Rod Smith); *Pope's Hat* (A1, 1956; Cornell and Rod Smith); and *Split Rock* (5.8, 1956; free solo by Bob Boyle). Rod Smith also engineered the first ascent of Headstone Rock in 1956 by throwing twine across the summit to pull a climbing rope over, then prusiking to the top.

During his Easter break in 1956, Loughman, along with fellow high school friend Roger Hope, spent the week at Josh. "My mom drove my buddy and I to Hidden Valley Campground for the week; there wasn't another soul there." In addition to doing the first ascent of the upper half of *Straight Flush* on Outhouse Rock, the pair climbed *Right*

On (5.5), a 3-pitch route on Saddle Rocks. Although this is the first known ascent of this climb, Loughman believes that the route "had probably been climbed before." Dick and Harold Webster established a few first ascents in the later 1950s, including *The Eye* (5.3, 1957) on Cyclops Rock.

In April 1958, another classic route saw its first ascent when Mark Powell and Bill "Dolt" Feuerer climbed the *Southwest Corner* (5.6/5.7) on Headstone Rock near Ryan Campground. Powell named the formation the Can Opener. In early guides, the formation was referred to as Balance Rock; by the late 1970s, its name was changed to Headstone Rock to honor early miners whose graves lay nearby. In 1959, Robbins, Powell, T. M. Herbert, and others climbed several new routes on what is now known as the Cohn Property (closed to the public). These climbs, which were only recently reported, included a 5.9+ crack. Powell, together with Robbins, was one of the great free climbers of the 1950s and perhaps the archetypal climbing bum. Powell is also credited with bringing the decimal system, developed at Tahquitz in the early 1950s, to Yosemite.

Sometime around 1958 Robbins, with the help of Herbert, compiled the first guidebook to known routes in the monument. The guidebook consisted of nine or ten typewritten, mimeographed pages, and a few copies were distributed to other RCS members. Unfortunately, no copies of this guide are known to have survived. Climbing guides are as much repositories of climbing history as they are descriptions of climbs, and much could be learned from this first guidebook.

The climbing activity of the 1950s left little trace. With no widely distributed written record of prior ascents, and no contingent of "local" climbers within which an oral history could survive, the accomplishments of the 1950s were soon lost.

AN AREA REDISCOVERED

During the 1950s and early 1960s, rock climbing was still unfamiliar to the average American. Joshua Tree provided a ringside seat for the curious visitor, on occasion causing traffic jams as cars stopped to watch climbers on the north face of Intersection Rock. (Until 2002, Park Boulevard passed directly under the north face of Intersection Rock; a large parking area is now located here.) As a result, for a few years, climbers were actually banned from climbing the north side of the formation.

By the mid 1960s, climbing was becoming increasingly popular, but members of the Sierra Club RCS were no longer the center of activity and innovation they once were. The RCS still scheduled annual trips to the monument, but its members were generally not climbing at a high standard and little new route activity resulted from these outings.

Of all the top climbers from the 1950s, Mark Powell was one of the few to climb with any regularity in the monument through the 1960s and into the early 1970s. Other preeminent climbers of the 1960s, such as Tom Higgins and the late Bob Kamps—who were, like Powell, pushing standards at Tahquitz—didn't climb much at Joshua Tree. The general perception, just as it had been with the RCS, was that "the rock wasn't very good and that it was just a practice area," recalls Higgins.

The Josh classic, O'Kelley's Crack *(5.10c).*

PHOTO: © KEVIN POWELL

In 1965, Mark and Beverly Powell established *Mama Woolsey* (5.9) on the southeast face of the Blob. The route was named after Mark's then mother-in-law, who was camping with the Powells that weekend. During the mid to late 1960s, Mark established several other routes with Beverly, including *Planet X* (5.8; circa 1966) on the Planet X Pinnacle. About a year later, Mark returned to the Planet X Pinnacle with Frank deSaussure and climbed *Planet Y* (5.10a) via a somewhat easier line than that done today.

It is likely that *Mental Physics* (5.7), a classic two-pitch moderate route in the southern Wonderland of Rocks, was first climbed in the mid to late 1960s. Similarly, the bold *Unknown Route* (5.10a/b) on the North Astro Dome probably dates from this time.

From the mid 1960s to the beginning of the 1970s, several new groups of climbers discovered Joshua Tree. They were not members of the RCS and thus didn't know that Joshua Tree was only a practice area. With fresh eyes, they saw the potential for Joshua Tree to be a serious climbing area and adopted it as their own. These were the monument's first real "locals" and were conspicuous by their regular visits.

The new "local" climbers included members of the Riverside Mountain Rescue Unit (RMRU). Dick Webster had joined the RMRU in 1966 and began climbing with other members including Woody Stark, Bill Briggs, and Jim Foote. Another group called itself "The Desert Rats." It included John Wolfe, Ken Stichter, Dick James, Al Ruiz, Howard Weamer, Rich Wolfe, and Stu Harris. Also active during the mid to late 1960s were Don O'Kelley (of *O'Kelley Crack* fame), Dave Davis, and a bit later Roy Naasz and Chris Wegener.

Stark, Webster, and Briggs were perhaps the most ambitious of the locals. The Desert Rats were, at least initially, far more interested in aid climbing. None of the locals were climbing at a particularly high standard. According to John Wolfe, the Desert Rats harbored the belief that "only dedicated super climbers were capable of climbing 5.7 and harder." And for all any of these climbers knew, the formations around the campground were largely virgin terrain.

Today, it is hard to imagine Hidden Valley Campground as anything but congested. However, during the late 1960s what Stark remembers is the solitude. The campground was never full and most campers were retirees. "They would watch the climbers and sometimes even clap. There was one ranger who lived with his family at Lost Horse. He would often chat with climbers."

Despite the new interest, free climbing standards had regressed. In contrast, at nearby Tahquitz Rock, 5.10 had been firmly established by 1963 and 5.11s were first climbed by 1967. With Joshua Tree off the radar of most climbers, visitation remained sparse. Joshua Tree was being rediscovered, but development proceeded in a much different manner. Though many of the obvious cracks in Hidden Valley Campground had been free climbed years previously, most were "first" climbed again, usually with aid. Later, some of these routes saw their second first free ascents.

In 1966, Jim Foote led a hard-to-protect crack on the right side of Cyclops Rock. Initially rated 5.7, *Leaders Fright* (5.8 R; Foote, Stark, and Webster) was one of the boldest new leads of this era. This fine route's reputation for seriousness remains intact even to this day. According to Stark, "Jim fell a short ways after doing the crux, stopping himself on a small ledge. That is why we called it *Leaders Fright*."

Without a doubt some of the most notable ascents of this time were the 1967 first "known" free ascents of both *Dogleg* (5.9; Webster, Stark, and Briggs) and *Double Cross* (5.7/5.8; Stark, Webster, and Briggs). Though apparently free climbed during the 1950s, *Dogleg* had been "first" climbed on aid in 1965 by John Wolfe and his brother Rich. Webster remembers that a "friendly rivalry" with the Desert Rats was part of the moti-

Matt Cox on the first ascent of Touch and Go *(5.9).*

vation for trying to climb it free. "And," says Webster, "it looked like it should go free."
Stark recalls, "We spent several weekends working on it, getting higher with each effort."
Several falls were taken and the team traded leads a number of times before Webster
finally led *Dogleg* free to the top. "We rated it 5.7 initially because we couldn't do 5.8s,"
says Stark.

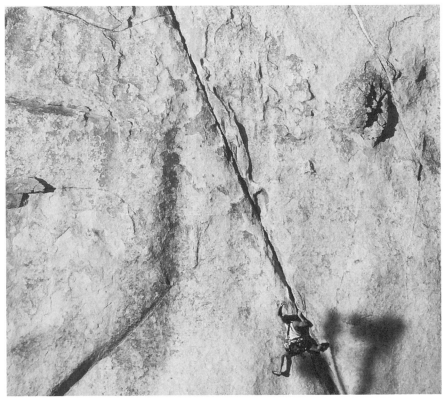

Tony Sartin on Left Ski Track *(5.11a).*

PHOTO: © KEVIN POWELL

In contrast, *Double Cross* was "pretty straight forward. It was a great route," states Webster. Even so, in recent years *Double Cross* has seen more than its share of accidents, as inexperienced climbers are lured into this hand-to-fist crack by its moderate rating.

Yet the most significant first free ascent of the 1960s went all but unnoticed by the locals. In 1968 Tom Higgins on-sighted *Left Ski Track* and established Joshua Tree's first 5.11; a Josh free ascent well ahead of its time. Higgins had not climbed much in Joshua Tree at the time, but he thought the line looked enticing. Higgins was not even sure if *Left Ski Track* had been climbed before. "I was climbing really well at the time. It looked like it had a lot of holds, things I could get my hands and feet in. But it ended up being much harder than it looked. It was very strenuous placing pins for pro."

Sometime around 1967 or 1968 several climbers, including Stark, Briggs, and John Wolfe, had decided to produce a guidebook. They agreed to collaborate on the project. (Wolfe eventually moved forward on his own, completing it in 1970.) The prospect of a new guide spurred some new route efforts. In 1969, Wolfe and Dick James made the first free ascent of *The Flue* (5.8), a fine route on Chimney Rock's east face.

As before, a few adventuresome climbers saw potential for routes outside Hidden Valley Campground. Saddle Rocks saw further exploration at the end of this pre-guide era, with the 1969 ascent of *Orange Flake* (5.8; Roy Naasz and Ron Osborn) followed closely by the 1970 ascent of the popular 2-pitch face climb *Walk on the Wild Side* (5.8-; Naasz and Chris Wegener). With *Walk on the Wild Side* (the title of a Lou Reed tune and one of the first climbing routes named after a rock song), climbers became more imaginative in naming routes.

Powell, Kamps, and Higgins had pioneered bolted face routes at Tahquitz in the 1960s, and by 1969 more bolt-protected face climbs were put up on Suicide Rock. As a consequence, climbers began to look at the many unclimbed faces at Joshua Tree for new route potential, and the large expanse of Saddle Rocks was an obvious objective.

Naasz and Wegener were the first to tackle the large west face of the Sentinel in Real Hidden Valley, climbing a 2-pitch aid line named *Scared Bare* (5.8, A3; 1970). The excellent first pitch was later freed (5.10d) and is now considered part of *Desert Song*.

In 1970 O'Kelley and Davis ventured into the North Wonderland and discovered the Grey Giant formation. Over the next two days they aided the obvious arching crack line of *Hyperion*. This was before designation of the area as federal wilderness, and the pair was able to drive the Old Wonderland Trail for much of the approach. Due to considerable bird feathers and droppings emanating from the crack, their route was named after the Hyperion sewage treatment plant in Redondo Beach.

During the 1970/1971 climbing season, Mark Powell returned to The Can Opener (aka Headstone Rock) and climbed its steep and plated southeast arête. Powell recalls placing only a single bolt on *Cryptic* (5.8), using a piton or two for additional protection. In later years, others have added two more bolts to this route.

Joshua Tree of 1970 was still a place that attracted few visitors, least of all climbers. Campsites were never full. To a novice climber like Richard Harrison, the entire monument "seemed like the most remote spot in the world."

In 1970 Wolfe published the first real guidebook to the monument. This guide contained seventy-eight routes, most located in Hidden Valley Campground. No routes listed were more difficult than 5.9; most routes were 5.7 or under; and many climbs still employed aid. Though this guide may have been mistaken about who did what when, it constituted a huge step forward in giving legitimacy to climbing in the monument.

The first printing quickly sold out. A revised printing in 1973 corrected a notoriously incorrect rating of *The Damper* (5.9) on Chimney Rock. It was rated originally 5.6, causing more than one aspiring leader to be turned away in disgust. But even as the guide was being reprinted so much new route activity had occurred that it was already hopelessly out-of-date.

In addition to finding a ready audience, the effect of this guidebook on Joshua Tree's popularity was immediate. It focused the attention of a large number of climbers on the area. Climbing standards and route development quickly experienced a major boom. Hundreds of new routes were established and many aid routes were freed. The publication of this guide coincided with an increase in the popularity of rock climbing and a revolution in clean climbing equipment. The change in attitude about Joshua Tree was noticeable. "You could tell the difference," says Higgins.

THE NEW GENERATION

In the summer of 1971, John Long was introduced to climbing through a National Outdoor Leadership School (NOLS) course. A natural athlete, Long was immediately hooked, but he needed to find climbing partners. When he returned that fall for his senior year at Upland High School, he started a climbing course. A junior, Rick Accomazzo, was one of the "students" who signed up. Accomazzo recalls Long professing to years of climbing experience. By the time Accomazzo wised up, he was hooked too.

In a few months, Long and Accomazzo met fellow Upland High student Richard Harrison, who had already been climbing for about year and was psyched to climb as much as possible. The three began to climb together regularly.

"We arranged our school schedules so we would have Wednesday off," recalls Accomazzo. "We would drive to Josh for the day on Wednesday, then climb all weekend too. There was something magical about the desert air."

After a few months on this concentrated diet of climbing, Long, Accomazzo, and Harrison improved dramatically. They had soon climbed most of the hardest established routes in the monument. By spring of 1972, Long began establishing new routes and even freeing old aid climbs, including *Judas* (5.10b) and *Candelabra* (5.10a R).

After an intense nine-month apprenticeship, Accomazzo accompanied Long on the first known free ascent of *North Overhang* (5.9) on Intersection Rock. "We were real excited to free such an obvious line. It was a pretty heady thing for a high school student to do something no one had done before," says Accomazzo.

In November 1972, Long pulled out all the stops by leading the first ascent of *Jumping Jack Crack* (5.11a) in Steve Canyon. Gear was still quite primitive by today's standards, with nuts just being introduced. Use of pitons, particularly by older climbers, was still quite common.

Both Accomazzo and Harrison are unequivocal in attributing the drive behind these ascents to Long. "John had endless energy, he always wanted to do something," says Accomazzo. Similarly, Harrison states, "John always had a plan and was the motivating force behind most of the climbs we did. He was hyperactive." Over the next eight years, Long freed or established approximately ninety routes in the monument. The quest for first ascents was often ruthless.

In the fall of 1972, Long made the first lead of an easy but classic face route, and in the process ignited a lingering controversy. The day before, Ken Stichter and John Wolfe had bolted an obvious line up a dark intrusion dike on the west face of Echo Rock. Stichter "ran out of light after placing all the protection bolts." Harrison and Long witnessed the retreat. Long says they knew Stichter wouldn't return to finish the line until later. "[E]arly the next morning, Richard Harrison and I went ahead and led it through," Long says.

The story quickly became campfire fodder and the route became known as *Stichter Quits*. Unaware of the intervening ascent, the next weekend Stichter and Wolfe climbed the route, naming it *Black Tide*. In his later guides, Wolfe listed the route as *Black Tide*,

John Long dynos Saturday Night Live *circa 1982.*

PHOTO: MIKE WAUGH

Richard Harrison on the Aiguille de Joshua Tree.   PHOTO: RICK ACCOMAZZO COLLECTION

crediting Stichter and himself with the first ascent. When corrected in more recent guides, considerable confusion and irritation resulted.

November of 1972 also saw Mark Powell's first ascent of *Papa Woolsey* (5.10b). Up until then, most climbs at Josh followed crack lines. *Papa Woolsey* was a sharp deviation from this precedent. Though Powell's Headstone Rock routes (*Southwest Corner* and *Cryptic*) and Naasz's *Walk on the Wild Side* were bolted face climbs, *Papa Woolsey* was located right in Hidden Valley Campground, where everyone could see it.

"I had done some things at Tahquitz, like *Chingadera,* which were bolted face routes. By then, most routes [at Tahquitz] that used cracks had been done. Faces were the next step," says Powell. Not sure if the line of *Papa Woolsey* would go, Powell first toproped it. About a week later he led it, placing the bolts from the ground up.

Papa Woolsey was far harder and less featured than previous face routes. Though it is perhaps too short to be considered a classic, *Papa Woolsey* was a seminal development in Josh climbing. It caused other climbers to look at otherwise blank-appearing faces, once thought to be unclimbable or too loose. By today's standards, this short slab is essentially "sport" bolted.

Later in the 1970s, the use of bolts as protection on face climbs came into common use. And most of the progeny of *Papa Woolsey* were sparingly bolted. The quarter-inch split shaft Rawl bolt (1 to 1.5 inches long), placed on the lead in a hand-drilled hole, characterized the common "ethic" at Josh until at least the late 1980s.

In December 1972, Chris Wegener made the mistake of commenting to Harrison, Long, Don Watson, and Accomazzo that he had just checked out a good-looking crack line on the formation across the valley. It was, as he naively pointed out, clearly visible from the campground. "As soon as he turned the corner we got racked up and were out there," remembers Harrison. The line, *Comic Book* (5.10a), was quickly sent by the crew, much to the chagrin of Wegener. Another climb that garnered a lot of attention was Long's and Harrison's 1973 first ascent of *Bearded Cabbage* (5.10c) on the Old Woman.

During the early and mid 1970s, John Long had become arguably the single most influential climber in Southern California. It was common to see him making the rounds of the many difficult boulder problems he had pioneered, an entourage of a dozen or so in tow. John's success was born of supreme confidence and the goods to back it up. John had a lot of charisma, and was always spurring others to have fun and try new things.

Long was also well known for helping "direct" the efforts of younger climbers, often suggesting climbs and climbing partners. In 1974 John Bachar remembers Long telling him to lead the as-yet-unrepeated *Bearded Cabbage.* To the astonishment of all, the young Bachar on-sighted the route, in the process becoming the first climber to lieback the crux crack section. "I didn't know how to jam. After that they started calling me 'Laybachar'."

In the early 1970s, it was this new generation of local climbers, including Long, Harrison, Accomazzo, Tobin Sorenson, and Jim Wilson, who applied and honed their talents at Josh. And within a few short years, these self-proclaimed "Stonemasters" had changed Joshua Tree's climbing landscape. Difficult routes (5.10 and 5.11) were no longer mere anomalies, but became common fare. Development began to intensify outside Hidden Valley Campground, and areas like Echo Rock, Rusty Wall, North Wonderland, Saddle Rocks, Hall of Horrors, Conan's Corridor, and Split Rocks saw a rash of new routes.

Illustrative of this rapid change was the 1974 first free ascent of *Hyperion* (5.11) on the Grey Giant (Long, Kevin Worral, Sorenson, and Accomazzo). Located deep in the North Wonderland, *Hyperion* had been discovered and first aid-climbed only few years previously (1970).

Aside from the "big name" climbers, other active climbers in the early 1970s included John Bald, Matt Cox, Spencer Lennard, David Evans, Dean Fidelman (aka "Bullwinkle"), and Gary Ayres. I began climbing in the monument about this time and, along with Matt Cox, began keeping an informal new route guide. Tim Powell (no relation to Mark) says this handwritten guide was copied and "traded around among us. The information about who did a new route also really mattered as some people, like

PHOTO: RICK ACCOMAZZO COLLECTION

Tobin Sorenson on the first free ascent of Hyperion *(5.11d).*

Sorenson or Cox, were notorious for sandbagging or doing runout routes."

John Bachar made his first trip to Josh in 1972 with fellow high school classmate Mike Ransom. Armed with a firm grasp of climbing gained from reading British climbing books and a rack of homemade hexes and machine nuts, Bachar remembers being lured into climbing *The Damper* because of the 5.6 rating in the Wolfe guide (it is actually a 5.9 fist-to-offwidth crack). "It was horrendous and took us forever, going up and down. We were thoroughly depressed. Afterward, we thought: 'If this is 5.6, we're screwed.'"

Whether Tobin Sorenson, one of the mythic climbers of the 1970s, was incredibly bold or totally reckless is subject to debate. But stunts such as climbing with a noose around his neck tend to tilt final judgment toward foolhardy. Still, the handful of routes he established at Josh were big influences on other climbers. Sorenson's lead of *Grit Roof* (5.11a, 1973; Sorenson, Accomazzo, and Wilson) exemplified "typical Tobin style," says Accomazzo. "He was moaning, uncertain, but absolutely going for it." A still-inexperienced John Bachar witnessed Sorenson's lead of this roof to an offwidth crack and came away hugely impressed with Tobin's perseverance and all-out commitment. "It was a huge moment for me."

The following year, Tobin scored a double coup with his first free ascent of the perfect hand-to-fist fissure of *O'Kelley's Crack* (5.10c; FFA: Sorenson, Wilson, Fidelman, and Ayres) and with the first ascent of the adjacent and much more technical thin-hands crack, *Wanger Banger* (5.11c). *Exorcist* (5.10a, 1974; Sorenson, Dick Shockley, Jim Wilson, and Fidelman) is another classic Sorenson route established the same year. Tobin's tenure at Joshua Tree was short; he later excelled at bold alpine climbing, a pursuit that eventually claimed his life.

John Bald, another SoCal climber, was one of the first to explore the Pinto Basin area of the park and is credited with "discovering" Conan's Corridor, Isles in the Sky, and Rubicon (which he aided in 1976) in Split Rocks. Bald shared some of these discoveries with Long and between the two, a number of unclimbed gems were quickly "plucked." These included fine crack climbs in Conan's Corridor: *Spiderman* (5.10b, 1975; Long and Bachar); *Colorado Crack* (5.9, 1975; Billy Westbay, Long, and Hugh Burton); *True Dice* (5.10a R/X, 1974; Bald); and *Gem* (5.8, 1974; Bald, Hugh Burton, and Long).

High school student Matt Cox may have climbed at Joshua Tree for only a few years, but he did so with such intensity and boldness that he established many classic routes and left an enduring reputation in his wake. Spencer Lennard recalls that, "Matt's life was fueled by *Mountain Magazine*," a British publication that was, in the 1970s, the world's premier English-language climbing journal. Cox's resulting approach to climbing was very traditional. "He was one of the best slab climbers of his era," according to Lennard.

In 1973, the fifteen-year-old Cox showed Lennard and Gary Ayers a likely looking crack in Real Hidden Valley, then just headed up. "Gary and I were quivering; Matt was climbing so far beyond what we thought was possible. We were happy to be able to follow it cleanly," remembers Lennard. Located on the west face of the Sentinel, the route was named *Kandy-Kolored Tangerine-Flake Streamline Baby* (5.10a/b). The following year, Sorenson and Wilson climbed the route, thinking it a first ascent and placing a bolt halfway up the pitch (long since removed). They called their new climb *Illusion Dweller*. Even though the first-ascent credit got straightened out a few years later, the second name stuck.

More than any other route, Cox's 1975 first ascent with Lennard of *Trespassers Will Be Violated* (5.10c) typified his "gonzo" style. Cox had spied the new line and with bolt kit in hand started up this rising dike system. But Cox soon came upon a bolt, and two more bolts could be seen higher on the dike. Assuming the route had already been climbed, Cox simply continued on to the top, despite a rather nasty runout at the crux. Only later was it learned that the bolts had been placed on rappel by other climbers planning to add several more before climbing it. Cox's other routes include *Effigy Too* (5.10a, 1975; Cox and Evans); *Touch & Go* (5.9, 1976; Cox, Bobby Kessinger, and Dan Ahlborn), and *Frontal Lobotomy* (5.10a/b, 1975; Cox, Evans, Spencer Lennard, and Alan Lennard).

Although the Desert Rats continued to be active during the early 1970s, their efforts were overshadowed by the large influx of a new generation of young, talented, and ambitious climbers. As Joshua Tree gained more respect, it attracted a wider audience of climbers and standards were soon on par with other major climbing areas.

(The climbing history of Joshua Tree National Park will continue in a subsequent volume of this guide. Stay tuned.)

Quail Springs

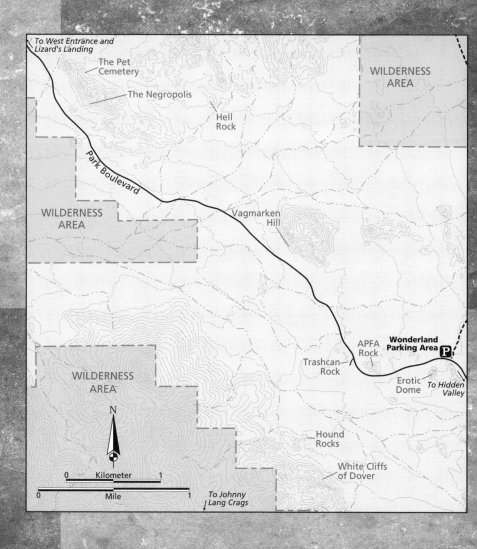

To West Entrance and
Lizard's Landing

The Pet
Cemetery

The Negropolis

Hell
Rock

WILDERNESS
AREA

Park Boulevard

WILDERNESS
AREA

Vagmarken
Hill

APFA
Rock

Wonderland
Parking Area

Trashcan
Rock

WILDERNESS
AREA

Erotic
Dome

To Hidden
Valley

N

Hound
Rocks

White Cliffs
of Dover

0   Kilometer   1

0   Mile   1

To Johnny
Lang Crags

LIZARD'S LANDING

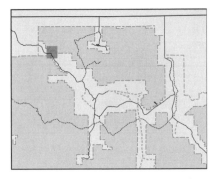

This area lies 0.75 mile northeast of the main road into Joshua Tree National Park (Park Boulevard). Park in a small pullout on the north side of Park Boulevard (1.8 miles from the West Entrance; 6.8+ miles from the Intersection Rock/Real Hidden Valley intersection), just where the road makes a sharp right (southerly) turn at the top of the grade. Several approaches are possible. The best is to hike 100 yards northeast from the parking area along an old road to a gravel pit. From here head east-northeast about 0.5 mile up

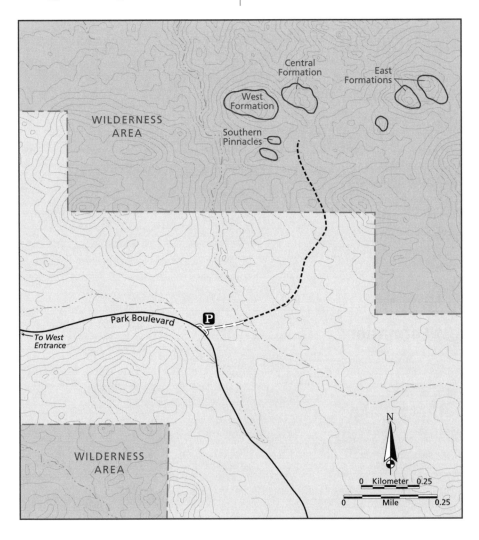

the low hillside, skirting to the east of the hill ahead. Then head roughly north (and slightly west) 0.4 mile over low ridges to the Central Formation. Plan on twenty to thirty minutes for the approach. Map, page 48.

Wilderness Bolting Notice: The entire Lizard's Landing area lies in designated wilderness. The placement of new bolts in wilderness is only allowed by permit. Existing bolts may be replaced on a one-for-one basis. Power drills are not permitted in wilderness areas. For more information refer to the Introduction.

West Formation (Wilderness)

The large western formation has no recorded routes.

Southern Pinnacles

These rocks are located to the left (west) and in front (south) of the Central Formation. The only recorded route lies on the back (north) side of the northern pinnacle. It gets shade most of the day.

1. **Mark of Zorro** (5.11b) ★★ This overhanging thin crack lies on the back side of the small northern pinnacle. The crack has a Z shape to it. **Pro:** Thin to 2 inches. **FA:** Mark Fekkes, Bill Lebans, Chris Krysztofiac; 1984.

Central Formation (Wilderness)

The Central Formation sits lower down and to the north of the end of the approach route. All routes (except *Two Against Everest*) face south and are in sun most of the day.

2. **Last Ticket to Obscuritiville** (5.9) ★ The climb follows a giant flake that starts out of an alcove located halfway up the south face of the central rock formation. Climb up to the alcove, and then up the flake to the summit. **FA:** Craig Fry, Marchello; 2/82.

3. **Maxwell Grunster** (5.10a) Climb the crack/corner about 10 feet right of *Last Ticket To Obscuritiville*. **FA:** Mark Fekkes, Bill Lebans, Chris Krysztofiac; 1984.

4. **John's Ginger Tufties** (5.10a) ★ This
five-bolt route lies on the brown face about
50 feet right of *Maxwell Grunster.* **Pro:** To 2
inches/anchor. **FA:** Todd Gordon, Cyndie
Bransford, Jason Porter; 12/95.

5. **Two against Everest (aka On the
Back)** (5.11c) ★ (not shown on photo) This
steep, quarter-inch crack is on the north
(shady) face of the summit block of the
Central Formation. **FA** (TR): Roy
McClenahan; 1982. **FA** (Lead): Matt
Oliphant.

East Formation (Wilderness)

The East Formation lies on the western edge
of a higher hill about 300 yards to the east of
the Central Formation.

6. **Mimo Provoz** (5.9) This crack lies on
the right side of the buttress below *Jet
Stream.* **Pro:** To 3 inches. **FA:** Todd Gordon,
John "Crimper" Wilson; 11/95.

7. **Lizard's Landing** (5.7) ★ This route follows the west buttress of the East Formation.
Climb ledges and cracks to a chimney that
leads to the summit. **FA:** Craig Fry, Lynn
Hill; 11/79.

8. **Jet Stream (aka Momentary Lapse of Reason)** (5.10b) (R) ★★ This route lies on the right-hand arête of the second terrace of the East Formation; the upper face has two protection bolts. **Pro:** Small to 3 inches, two bolts. **FA** (TR): Craig Fry, Lynn Hill; 11/79. **FA** (Lead): Al Peery, Jim Gregg.

9. **Bighorn Bivy** (5.8+) ★ Start 40 feet right of *Jet Stream;* climb up to and over a roof, then continue up thin cracks above. **FA:** Brendt Allen, Mike Wilson, Sam Waggoner, Alan Bartlett; 5/91.

10. **Canine Crack** (5.9+) (not shown on photo) This right-leaning crack is 150 yards right of *Jet Stream,* on the south face of the rock. **FA:** Brendt Allen, Mike Wilson, Sam Waggoner, Alan Bartlett; 5/91.

11. **The Bone Club** (5.10a) (R) ★★ (not shown on photo) Begin in a left-facing corner *(Little Criminals)* about 30 feet to the right of *Canine Crack,* and on the east face. Climb past three bolts just to the left of the corner. **FA:** Scott Cole, Bruce Morris; 12/88.

12. **Little Criminals** (5.10b) ★★ (not shown on photo) This is the left-facing corner about 30 feet right of *Canine Crack* on the east face. **FA:** Scott Cole, Bruce Morris; 12/88.

13. **Teeter Totter** (5.9) (not shown on photo) Climb the thin, left-facing flake about 10 feet to the right of *Little Criminals.* **FA:** Scott Cole, Bruce Morris; 12/88.

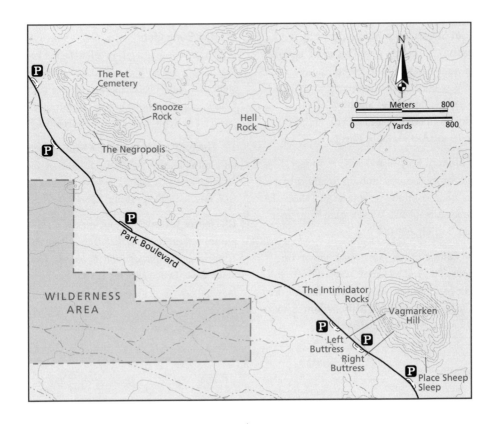

THE NEGROPOLIS AREA

This area encompasses several varied formations that lie about a large hill on the left (east) side of Park Boulevard. The Negropolis Area is approximately 3.4 miles from the West Entrance and 5.2+ miles from the Intersection Rock/Real Hidden Valley intersection. Routes are located on the northern end of the hill (*Sha-Nay-Nay*); on the eastern side of the hill (Pet Cemetery and Snooze Rock); or high on the west side (The Negropolis).

14. **Sha-Nay-Nay** (5.5) (not shown on photo) This route is located on a small brown buttress on the northern end of the Negropolis hill; it starts down low. **FA:** Todd Gordon, Cyndie Bransford, Jason Cushner; 12/94.

The Pet Cemetery

This is a small, shady crag with several overhanging sport routes. The area is actually on the back (east) side of the Negropolis hillside, on the upper part of the northern end of the hill. Park at a pullout on Park Boulevard near the north end of the hillside (3 miles from the West Entrance; 5.6+ miles from the Intersection Rock/Real Hidden Valley intersection). Walk around the northern end of the formation, then up the slope to the Pet Cemetery. Routes face east (in shade all afternoon). There are actually two formations; the left one is the largest. The

routes are described from left to right. Map, page 52.

The Pet Cemetery—Left Formation

This is the larger, left-hand formation. Several fun sport routes can be found here. It's shady; good for warm days.

15. **Skeleton Crew** (5.10d) ★ (Sport) This three-bolt route to a two-bolt anchor/rap lies just left of *Pet Cemetery*. Short, but good rock. **FA:** Don Wilson et al.; 1992.

16. **Pet Cemetery** (5.11a/b) ★★ (Sport) This route follows overhanging rock past five bolts to a lower-angled two-bolt anchor/rap. **FA:** Don Wilson, Karen Wilson; 10/91.

17. **Open Project** (5.12?) (Sport) Begin off a ledge 8 feet right and up from *Pet Cemetery*. Four bolts (the last doubled); may need additional bolt(s). **FA:** Unknown.

18. **Bone Merchant** (5.11b) ★★ (Sport) This five-bolt route lies right of the central crack and left of the right-hand arête *(Bonecrusher Arête)*. Crux is past the first bolt. Two-bolt anchor/rap. **FA:** Mark Bowling, Steve Gerberding, Al Swanson.

19. **Bonecrusher Arête** (5.8) ★ Start in a gully system at the right end of the large formation, step left, and follow the dark arête to the top. **Pro:** Small to 2 inches. **FA:** Don Wilson, Karen Wilson, 10/91.

The Pet Cemetery—Right Formation

This is the smaller, somewhat worthless, right-hand formation. Routes 20 to 22 do not appear on a photo.

20. **Skin and Bones** (5.4) (R) Follow the featured face just left of the crack system on the left side of the smaller (right) formation. **Pro:** To 2 inches. **FA:** Don Wilson; 10/91.

21. **No Bones about It** (5.5) This is the prominent crack in the center of the smaller formation. **Pro:** To 2.5 inches. **FA:** Don Wilson; 10/91.

22. **Bone Up** (5.6) Go up the crack and face to the right of *No Bones About It*. **Pro:** To 2.5 inches. **FA:** Todd Swain, Donette Swain, Marion D-Nittoli; 9/95.

Snooze Rock

Snooze Rock lies on the southernmost part of the east side of the Negropolis hill (away from the road). The best approach is to park as for the Pet Cemetery and walk about 0.25 mile to the south. Snooze Rock is a small formation with excellent rock and a prominent arête. There is no photo.

23. **Naptime for Meggles** (5.9) ★ Follow the left side of the arête past an overhanging start, passing one bolt up higher. **Pro:** To 2 inches. **FA:** Don Wilson, Karen Wilson; 10/91.

The Negropolis

This is the series of brown buttresses and blocks that lie high on the west side of the large hill. Park at one of several small pullouts on the west side of Park Boulevard just south of where the rocks are located (3.4 miles from the West Entrance; 5.2+ miles from the Intersection Rock/Real Hidden Valley intersection). Routes face west and south and see sun most of the afternoon.

24. **Square Dancing** (5.10b) ★ (TR) This route climbs a thin crack left of *Slap Prancing*. Begin from a gully up and left of *Slap Prancing*. **FA:** Bob Gaines; 1/02.

25. **Slap Prancing** (5.8+) ★ A three-bolt route on the pillar to the left of *Dance on Fire*. **Pro:** To 2 inches for anchor. **FA:** Unknown.

26. **Dance on Fire** (5.11a/b) ★★★ This is the three-bolt face climb on the left side of the buttress. Two-bolt anchor/rap. **FA:** Mike Lechlinski, Mari Gingery; 12/87.

27. **Tap Dancing** (5.11a) (R/X) ★★★ Start just right of *Dance on Fire*. Climb a face and thin crack with one fixed pin (one is missing). Two-bolt anchor/rap. **FA** (TR): Bob Gaines, Pat Nay; 10/86. **FA** (Lead): Mike Lechlinski, Mari Gingery; 12/87.

28. **Rap Dancing** (5.10a or c) ★ This two-bolt face route is around the corner and to the right of *Tap Dancing* on the same block. If you stem off the boulder it is 5.10a; it is 5.10c direct. Two-bolt anchor/rap. **FA:** Unknown.

29. **Atrophy** (5.9) ★ The clean, overhanging crack on the left of the upper block of *I Fall Therefore I Am*. **Pro:** To 3.5 inches. **FA:** Cory Zinngrabe; 1989.

30. **I Fall Therefore I Am** (5.10c) This route is on the next pillar to the right of the *Tap Dancing* pillar. Start out of the gully, climb past three bolts, then use the wide crack above, avoiding two bolts on the arête to the left. **Pro:** To 4 inches; two-bolt anchor/rap. **FA:** Larry Kuechlin, Cory Zinngrabe; 1989.

31. **Metal Highway** (5.8+) Go up the face around to the left of *I Fall Therefore I Am*. Two bolts, one fixed pin. **FA:** Todd Gordon, Brian, Jenn, Steve Orr, Rob Raker, Annette Bunge; 5/93.

32. **B for Beers** (5.10b) ★★ (Sport) This is approximately 100 feet right of *Tap Dancing*. Climb a dike system past four bolts. Two-bolt anchor. **FA:** Todd Gordon, Mike Brown, Craig Fry; 10/85.

33. **Girls in the Mist** (5.10d) ★★★ (Sport) This is the big block on the far right side of the Negropolis Area. **Pro:** 4 bolts. **FA:** Todd Gordon, David Evans; 2/90.

34. **Girls in Our Midst** (5.11a) (TR) Start just right of *Girls in the Mist,* up the white dike. **FA:** Bob Gaines; 12/01.

Hell Rock

This formation faces south and is located to the east of the Negropolis Area. It is best approached by parking in a paved turnout on the east side of Park Boulevard 3.9 miles from the West Entrance and 4.7+ miles from the Intersection Rock/Real Hidden Valley intersection. The formation is not visible from the parking area, but can be seen from a point a few hundred yards farther southeast along Park Boulevard. It lies about 0.75 mile to the northeast on the first (southernmost) hillside with rock formations. Hell Rock can be recognized by the large boulder perched on top of its left side. The two bolted routes lie below the boulder. There is no photo.

35. **Route of All Evil** (5.11d) ★★★ The route on the left. **Pro:** To 2 inches; four bolts. **FA:** Jan McCollum, Herb Laeger, Kris Solem; 5/90.

36. **No Rest for the Wicked** (5.12a) ★★★ Just right of *Route of All Evil*. **Pro:** To 2 inches; four bolts. **FA:** Kris Solem, Jan McCollum; 5/90.

37. **Bolters Are Weak** (5.8) (R) Start about 75 feet up and right of *No Rest for the Wicked*. Go up the dike (no pro) to the left end of a roof; go right, then over the roof and up a thin crack. **FA:** Brent Ingram, Karen Tracey, Alan Bartlett, Kris Solem; 3/91.

Intimidator Rocks — Left Buttress — Wrong Buttress — Right Buttress

VAGMARKEN HILL

Vagmarken is a large hill with a variety of crags on its western face located on the east side of Park Boulevard about 4.7+ miles from the West Entrance and 3.9 miles from the Intersection Rock/Real Hidden Valley intersection. The known routes lie on small brown formations on the lower left-hand (northwest) portion of the hillside (the Intimidator Rocks); on the larger buttresses (Vagmarken Buttresses) high on the middle section of the hillside; or on the far right-hand (southern) end of the hill (the Place Sheep Sleep). For Intimidator Rocks and Vagmarken Buttresses, park in a pullout on the west side of Park Boulevard about 5 miles from the West Entrance. For the Place Sheep Sleep, park in a small pullout about on the west side of Park Boulevard about 5.1 miles from the West Entrance and 3.5+ miles from the Intersection Rock/Real Hidden Valley intersection. Map, page 52.

The Intimidator Rocks

These are the small dark formations lying lower down on the northwestern part of Vagmarken Hill. It may be best to park at the farthest north pullout (4.7 miles from the West Entrance and 3.9+ miles from the Intersection Rock/Real Hidden Valley intersection).

38. **Dead Pigeons** (5.11b) (TR) This lies on left skyline of small tower. Face climb past a horizontal and a small roof. **FA:** Mark Wilson; 2/89.

39. **Just Stop It** (5.10b) Climb up and right along a dike past two bolts, then straight up to the top. **Pro:** Small to 3 inches. **FA:** Larry Kuechlin, Mike Humphrey; 2/89.

40. **Bold Is a Four Letter Word** (5.10a) ★ Start near the toe of the buttress; climb past four bolts. **Pro:** Gear for anchors. **FA:** Mark Wilson, Larry Kuechlin, Mike Humphrey; 2/89.

Vagmarken Buttresses

There are several "buttresses" high on the hillside. The known routes are on either the left buttress (up and right from the Intimidator Rocks) or on the right buttress (which is characterized by two long white dike systems). It may be best to park at the parking pullout a little farther south than that used for the Intimidator Rocks (4.8 miles from the West Entrance and 3.8+ miles from the Intersection Rock/Real Hidden Valley intersection). Map, page 52.

Vagmarken Hill—Left Buttress

41. **The Wind Tower** (5.7) ★★ This is the face and crack system on the far left side of the formation, left of the gully that is to the left of route 30. This is a 120-foot pitch. Descend down the back side. **Pro:** To 3 inches. **FA:** Bob Gaines, Yvonne Gaines; 1/96.

42. **The Podium of Indecision** (5.10b) (5.7 var.) This is the bolted face route up the varnished rock left of the *Vagmarken Buttress* route. If you traverse to larger holds in the gully on the left, the route is 5.7. **Pro:** Small to 2 inches. **FA:** Mike Humphrey, Larry Kuechlin.

43. **Vagmarken Buttress** (5.7) Climb the middle of the buttress past one bolt. **FA:** Herb Laeger, Eve Laeger, Dave Houser; 6/80.

44. **Vagabonds** (5.8) (R) A red dihedral rises 50 feet right of the Vagmarken Buttress route. Climb up into the dihedral, then exit (bolt) to the lower-angled face above. **Pro:** Small to 2 inches. **FA:** Todd Swain, Brandt Allen; 9/89.

Vagmarken Hill—Wrong Buttress

This large buttress lies just left of the Right Buttress.

45. **Thin Spin** (5.8) On the left side of this formation is a thin, low-angled crack that ends at a two-bolt belay/rappel anchor. **FA:** Unknown.

46. **Caw Caw** (5.6) This is just right of *Thin Spin*. Climb the face up to a crack that goes through the roof above. **Pro:** To 2.5 inches. **FA:** Todd Gordon, Cyndie Bransford; 1/95.

47. **Unknown** (5.3) (not shown on photo) Start at the right edge of the buttress. Follow an obvious line up and left to finish atop *Thin Spin*. **FA:** Todd Swain; 11/92.

Vagmarken Hill—Right Buttress

This formation is characterized by two long white dikes.

48. **The Great Thief** (5.6) This is on the left side of the Right Buttress, to the right of *James Brown's* . . . Start high in the gully in a crack that slants to the right, then heads back left. **Pro:** To 3 inches. **FA:** Alan Bartlett, Amy Sharpless, Tom Budd; 4/91.

49. **James Brown's Celebrity Hot Tub Party** (5.10b) This route climbs the white dike on the left. **Pro:** To 2 inches, two bolts. **FA:** Geoff Archer, Todd Gordon, Alan Bartlett; 4/91.

50. **The Right-Handed Dyke** (5.10a) This route ascends thin cracks and lieback flakes on the right-hand white dike. **FA:** Todd Gordon, Reggie Thompson, Karen Long, Linda Maron; 10/90.

Vagmarken Hill—Baby Buttress

This small cliff lies about 100 feet downhill and slightly right of *The Right-Handed Dyke* on the Right Buttress. The buttress and routes are not pictured.

51. **Palming the Babyhead** (5.10a) (TR) This route lies on the left edge of Baby Buttress. Go up a steep left-slanting crack/dike to a horizontal; step right and climb a blank face to lower-angled rock. **FA:** Ken Wylie, Nancy Giesmar, Todd Swain, Donette Swain; 3/03.

52. **Betty Spaghetti** (5.8) Begin about 8 feet right of *Palming the Babyhead.* Climb up the face to an obvious vertical crack that is followed to the top. **Pro:** To 4 inches. **FA:** Todd Swain, Donette Swain, Ken Wylie, Nancy Giesmar, Tess Whittlesey; 3/03.

53. **Avalung** (5.7) This route begins about 8 feet right of *Betty Spaghetti* at a right-leaning crack at the right edge of the formation. Go up the face to the crack. **Pro:** To 3 inches. **FA:** Ken Wylie, Nancy Giesmar, Todd Swain, Donette Swain, Tess Whittlesey; 3/03.

Chores of Yore Crag

This small cliff lies about 125 feet up and right of the Right Buttress, and about 100 feet uphill and slightly right of Baby Buttress. Descend to the right. The crag and routes are not pictured.

54. **Stoke the Fire** (5.8) (TR) Begin 15 feet left of *Dig the Well, Build the Cabin* at an overhanging flake/crack. Climb up and left along the flake, then up and right on the slabby face. **FA:** Todd Swain, Donette Swain; 3/03.

55. **Dig the Well, Build the Cabin** (5.9) (not shown on photo) Face climb past one bolt to a thin crack. **Pro:** To 2 inches. **FA:** Todd Gordon, Reggie Thompson; 10/90.

56. **Chop the Wood** (5.8) Begin 15 feet right of *Dig the Well, Build the Cabin,* on the right side of an arête. Climb up and left along dikes out the arête, then up a lower-angled arête to top. **FA:** Todd Swain, Donette Swain; 3/03.

57. **Carry the Water** (5.4) Begin 10 feet right of *Chop the Wood;* go up the obvious vertical crack/flake to a notch in the skyline. **Pro:** To 2.5 inches. **FA:** Donette Swain, Todd Swain; 3/03.

58. **Cook the Dinner** (5.5) Climb the obvious left-facing corner/groove 6 feet right of *Carry the Water.* **Pro:** To 3.5 inches. **FA:** Hanna Mohn, Cooper Mohn, Todd Swain; 4/03.

59. **Eat the Meat** (5.5) The crack/corner just right of *Cook the Dinner.* **Pro:** To 4 inches. **FA:** Tess Whittlesey, Cooper Mohn, Todd Swain; 4/03.

The Place Sheep Sleep

The routes are on an indistinct west-facing wall about 75 yards left of the southernmost point of the Vagmarken hillside. Routes are exposed to morning shade and afternoon sun. Park at a small turnout near the extreme southern end of the Vagmarken hillside (5.1 miles from the West Entrance; 3.5 miles from the Intersection Rock/Real Hidden Valley intersection). Map, page 52.

60. **Where Sheep Sleep** (5.12a) ★ Located on the left side of a split face. Continuous and funky moves; stay right of the crack past four bolts. Bolt anchor. **FA:** Paul Borne.

61. **Where Sheep Shit** (5.10b/c) This is just right of *Where Sheep Sleep,* on right side of split face. A little loose, but you might as well tick it if you're in the area. **Pro:** Three bolts; 2 to 2.5 inch cam; bolt anchor. **FA:** Paul Borne.

62. **Were Sheep Here First?** (5.10c) ★ This is around the corner from *Where Sheep Shit* on the right side of the arête. The crux seems to be getting a draw on the third bolt! **Pro:** Three bolts; bolt anchor. **FA:** Paul Borne.

QUAIL SPRINGS PICNIC AREA

Trashcan Rock

Trashcan Rock is located on the west side of Park Boulevard about 5.8 miles from the West Entrance and about 2.8 miles from the Intersection Rock/Real Hidden Valley intersection. There is a small paved parking area on the east side of the rock, and a very large paved parking area with picnic tables and a toilet on the west side of the rock. No camping is allowed. The park service has designated this area for day use only. This is a fine and popular beginners' area. This area also serves as parking for Hound Rocks and the White Cliffs of Dover, which are located to the southwest. Maps, pages 62 and 63.

Trashcan Rock—East Face

The east side of Trashcan Rock lies adjacent to a small parking area and offers mostly vertical cracks that face Park Boulevard. The face gets morning sun and afternoon shade. The descent is to the right (north) end of the formation.

63. **Filth** (5.8) (R) Begin about 10 feet left of *Filch;* go up the face past a horizontal to a crack. **Pro:** To 3 inches. **FA:** Unknown.

64. **Filch** (5.6) Begin off a boulder; go up the offwidth crack to smaller crack on the right above. **Pro:** To 4+ inches **FA:** Unknown.

65. **Slippery People** (V5) (boulder problem) The mantel and easier upper face (5.10+) between *Filch* and *Ripper.* **FA:** Bob Gaines; 1983.

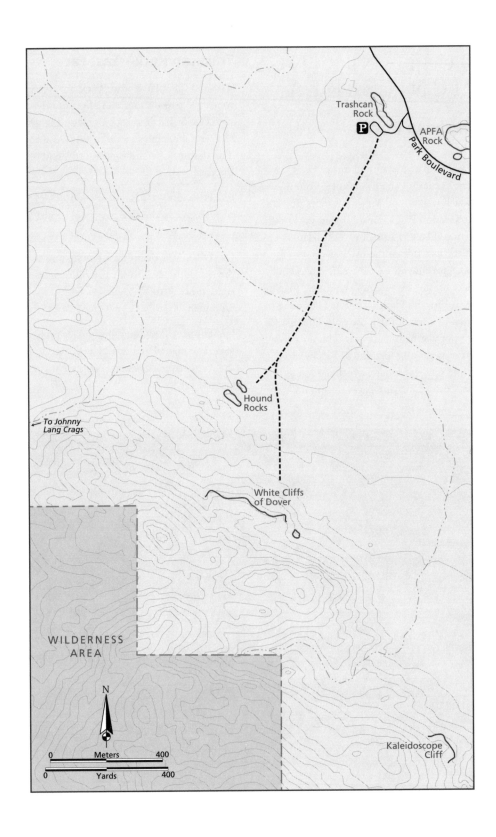

Trashcan
Rock

🅿

APFA
Rock

Park Boulevard

To Johnny
Lang Crags

Hound
Rocks

White Cliffs
of Dover

WILDERNESS
AREA

Kaleidoscope
Cliff

N

| 0 | Meters | 400 |
| 0 | Yards | 400 |

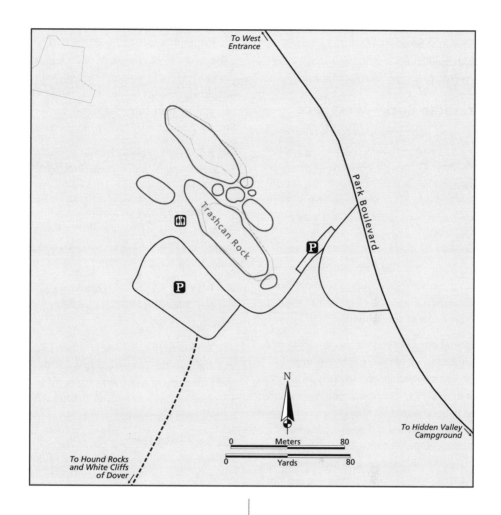

66. **Ripper** (V2) Boulder up into the short crack; escape across the dike to the left. **FA:** Unknown; early 1970s.

67. **Gripper Traverse** (V0+) Boulder problem traverse. **FA:** Unknown.

68. **Wallaby Crack** (5.8) ★ Go up the obvious crack that finishes in a chimney. **Pro:** To 3 inches. **FA:** Unknown.

69. **Hermanutic** (5.10c) (R) ★★ The longest crack on the east face. Easy climbing leads to a thin and hard-to-protect crux high. Rarely lead, easily toproped. **Pro:** Very thin to 2 inches. **FA:** Unknown.

70. **Butterfly Crack** (5.11c) ★★★ This crack begins with a boulder problem-like crux at the bottom, which leads to an easier (5.9) hand crack. **Pro:** Small wired nuts to 3 inches. **FA:** John Bald, John Long; 1973.

71. **Mr. Freeze** (5.12b) ★ (TR) A face climb between *Butterfly Crack* and *Left Sawdust Crack* that joins *Butterfly Crack* near the top. **FA:** Mike Guardino.

72. **Left Sawdust Crack** (5.10c) ★ This is the left-hand of two cracks on the right side of the face. They meet at the top. Usually toproped; the crux is at the top. **Pro:** Small to 2 inches. **FA:** John Long; 1973.

73. **Right Sawdust Crack** (5.8) ★★ The right-hand "hand" crack; begins off a boulder. **Pro:** To 2.5 inches. **FA:** John Long; 1973.

Trashcan Rock—West Face

The west side of Trashcan Rock offers many easy and lower-angled crack and face routes that are popular with novice climbers. A very large parking area lies just west and directly faces this side of the formation. Many of the face routes (with exception of *Tiptoe* and *Profundity*) are unprotected and usually toproped. Medium to 2.5-inch gear, with long slings/cordelette are usually adequate to set up topropes. Descend off the north end of the rock. The rock sees morning shade and is sunny all afternoon.

Note about Courtesy: It is not uncommon for groups and climbing classes to toprope one or more climbs on this rock. If you place a toprope on several routes and leave it up for more than a short time, you must be prepared to either share the rope with other climbers or pull it down. Totally dominating this rock with topropes and then being unwilling to share or pull your ropes is not only extremely rude, but might justify the removal of your ropes. Be courteous instead.

74. **The Trough** 5.0 Begin at the far left side of the west face, just right of a boulder; go up a left-leaning crack to a slot. **Pro:** To 3+ inches. **FA:** Unknown.

75. **Karpkwitz** (5.6) Begin just right of *The Trough;* go up a thin crack. **Pro:** Thin to 2.5 inches. **FA:** Unknown.

76. **B-3** (5.3) This is the large left-slanting crack. **Pro:** To 3 inches. **FA:** Unknown.

77. **Profundity** (5.10a) (or 5.10c) ★ This is a slab route. Begin just right of *B-3,* go up the groove to a face with two bolts. Going straight up past the second bolt is more difficult (5.10c) than going slightly right (5.10a). **Pro:** To 2.5 inches. **FA:** Chris Wegener; 2/73.

78. **B-2** (5.3) ★ This is the wide crack between *Profundity* and *Tiptoe*. **Pro:** To 3 inches. **FA:** Unknown.

79. **Tiptoe** (5.7+) ★★ This fun slab route "tiptoes" up a small vertical dike system past three bolts. **Pro:** To 2.5 inches. **FA:** Dave Stahl, Mona Stahl.

80. **B-1** (5.1) ★ This is the handcrack just right of *Tiptoe*. **Pro:** To 3 inches. **FA:** Unknown.

81. **Walkway** (5.4) R Begin at *B-1*. Go up and right on the face to a thin crack that then traverses up and right on a ramp. Unprotected crux at bottom. **Pro:** To 2.5 inches. **FA:** Unknown.

82. **Baby-Point-Five** (5.8/5.9) (R/X) Begin between *B-1* and the crack/corner of *Tulip*. Crux face moves (unprotected) lead to an easier and unprotected face, then to the easy crack and ramp of *Walkway*. **FA:** Unknown.

83. **Tulip** (5.6) (R) Begin at a short crack/left-facing corner. Higher, climb the face past one bolt. **Pro:** To 2.5 inches. **FA:** John Wolfe, Margie Creed; 10/72.

84. **Bimbo** (5.10a) (R/X) Begin in dark seams to the right of *Tulip* (crux at bottom); join *Tulip* at its bolt. **Pro:** To 2.5 inches. **FA:** Unknown.

85. **Eschar** (5.4) ★ Begin on a small ledge in a recessed area. Go up and left in the left-leaning crack. **Pro:** To 2.5 inches. **FA:** Unknown.

86. **History** (5.11a) (TR) Begin on the small ledge in the recess. Go up the face between *Cranny* and *Eschar*. **FA:** Todd Gordon, Brian Sillasen, Frank Bentwood; 2/88.

87. **Cranny** (5.8) ★★ Begin on the small ledge in the recess. Go up the double cracks. **Pro:** To 2 inches. **FA:** Scott Little; 11/72.

88. **Bloodymir** (5.9) Begin on the small ledge in the recess; go up and right past a bolt, then up a left-slanting crack. **Pro:** To 2.5 inches. **FA:** John Long, John Wolfe; 11/72.

89. **Black Eye** (5.9) R Begin on the left side of a deep recess on the right end of the west face. Go up a flake crack, then exit left, then climb the face past one bolt to a shallow left-slanting crack through a horizontal dike. **Pro:** Thin to 2 inches. **FA:** Unknown.

90. **Simpatico** (5.1) Begin on the left side of the deep recess on the right end of the rock. Go up a curving wide crack/flake, finishing left of a large boulder on top. **Pro:** To 3+ inches. **FA:** Unknown.

91. **Eyesore** (5.4) This is the chimney in the back of the deep recess on the right end of the West Face. **Pro:** To 3+ inches. **FA:** Unknown.

92. **Eyestrain** (5.2) Go up cracks on the easy rib/arête right of *Eyesore*. **Pro:** To 2.5 inches. **FA:** Unknown.

HOUND ROCKS

These rocks (45 to 90 feet tall) are located approximately 0.5 mile southwest of Trashcan Rock. Park in the west (back) side parking area for Trashcan Rock (5.8 miles from the West Entrance; 2.8 miles from the Intersection Rock/Real Hidden Valley intersection). There is a toilet located here; use it before hiking out. From the southwestern part of the parking area, follow a rough trail south-southwest, then down and across a wash, to Hound Rocks. Many fine crack routes are found here. Most of the routes lie on the eastern faces of two principal rock formations (in sun during the morning and in shade all afternoon). Map, page 62.

Baskerville Rock

Baskerville Rock is the first (and smaller) of the Hound Rocks you will encounter. The following routes all lie on the east face (morning sun, afternoon shade). Descend off the back (west) side, behind *Right Baskerville Crack*.

93. **Weathering Frights** (5.9) Go up and right (grainy) to a handcrack. **Pro:** To 3 inches. **FA** (TR): Alan Nelson; 12/81. **FA** (Lead): Roger Linfield, Keith Echelmeyer; 11/83.

94. **Stemulation** (5.9) (R) ★ This is the left-slanting thin crack to the right of *Weathering Frights*. **Pro:** To 3 inches. **FA:** Alan Nelson, Sally Moser; 12/81.

95. **Sound Asleep** (5.10b) Crux moves off the ground lead to a crack and face. **Pro:** To 3 inches. **FA** (TR): Mike Beck, Alan Nelson; 9/82. **FA** (Lead): Roger Linfield, Keith Echelmeyer; 11/83.

96. **Left Baskerville Crack** (5.10b) (R) ★ An unprotected face (crux) leads to a 4- to 5-inch crack. **Pro:** To 5 inches. **FA:** John Long, Dan Dingle; 5/77.

97. **Talking about My Variation** (5.10b) (R) ★ Do the first half of *Left Baskerville Crack,* then take the left-slanting crack to the top. **Pro:** To 4 inches. **FA:** Andy Brown, Jeff Rhoads; 11/89.

98. **Don't Bolt Me** (5.11b) ★★ (TR) **FA:** Roy Haggard; 1991.

99. **Right Baskerville Crack** (5.10a) ★★★ *The* classic climb in this area, on good rock. **Pro:** Small to 2 inches. **FA:** John Long, Janet Wilts; 5/77.

Hound Rock

This is the larger, westernmost of the two main formations. Several good crack routes lie on the east face and are described below. Most of these routes begin down in a small "valley" lying adjacent to the face. The routes get early sun and afternoon shade. Evidence (mostly old trash) still remains of home-steading activity in the area. The west face has a number of crack routes that vary from 5.6 to 5.9 in difficulty; these are not described. Descent options include going down the south end; rappelling from atop *Tossed Green;* or going off the back of the north end (tricky).

100. **Direct Wrench** (5.11a) ★ (TR) Climb straight up to end of *Crescent Wrench.* **FA:** unknown.

101. **Crescent Wrench** (5.10d) ★★ Follow the thin arching crack (crux at end). **Pro:** Many small to 1.5 inches. **FA** (TR): Mike Loughman, Amy Loughman; 10/79. **FA** (Lead): Unknown.

102. **An Eye to the West** (5.9) ★ Start off a boulder; go up the right-hand (thinner) crack. **Pro:** To 2.5 inches. **FA:** Randy Vogel, Lyman Spitzer; 11/79.

103. **Tossed Green** (5.10a) ★★★ This nice straight crack ends at a two-bolt anchor/rap.

Pro: To 2.5 inches. **FA:** John Long, Randy Vogel, Mike Lechlinski, Craig Fry, Mari Gingery; 12/77.

104. **White Powder** (5.7) This is the wide crack just right of *Tossed Green;* two-bolt anchor/rap. **Pro:** To 3.5 inches. **FA:** Janet Wilts, John Long; 5/77.

105. **Over the Hill** (5.9) Start just right of *White Powder;* head up and right to reach a crack. **Pro:** To 3 inches. **FA:** Alan Bartlett, Don Wilson; 5/81.

106. **Animalitos** (5.11b) (R) ★★ Climb up discontinuous thin cracks (crux; hard to protect) to a crack leading to the top. **Pro:** Many thin to 2.5 inches. **FA** (TR): John Long, Eric Ericksson; 1980. **FA** (Lead): Unknown.

107. **Animalargos** (5.11c) (R) ★★★ Go up the face to a small triangular spot, then up (crux) to a thin crack. Above, head left up the crack to join *Animalitos* at the top. **Pro:** Thin to 3 inches. **FA** (TR): John Long, Randy Vogel, Lynn Hill; 1980. **FA** (Lead): Unknown.

WHITE CLIFFS OF DOVER

This northeast-facing band of cliffs is approximately 0.7 mile south of Trashcan Rock, and approximately 0.3 mile south-southwest of Hound Rocks. It sits high on the hillside. The rock tends to be quite excellent. Park at the west (back) parking area for Trashcan Rock (5.8 miles from the West Entrance; 2.8 miles from the Intersection Rock/Real Hidden Valley intersection). There is a toilet located here; use it before hiking out. From the southwestern part of the parking area, follow a rough trail south-southwest (same approach as for Hound Rocks). Just before Hound Rocks, head southwest, then up the hillside to the cliff. While the majority of routes are located near the left end of the outcrop a number of fine routes have been established elsewhere all along the cliff. Map, page 62.

Courthouse Formation

This is a large block (40 feet high) located 100 yards left of the main White Cliffs formation *(Make or Break Flake).* It is about 50 yards up the hillside. The formation and routes are not shown.

108. **In Contempt** (5.11b/c) ★★★ (Sport) A four-bolt sport route on the overhanging south face. **Pro:** One-inch cam; two-bolt anchor/rap. **FA:** Bob Gaines, Dave Evans; 3/96.

109. **Unforgiven** (5.11d/5.12a) ★★ (Sport) A four-bolt sport route on the left side of the block. Two-bolt anchor/rap. **FA:** Steve Sutton; 3/96.

White Cliffs of Dover Left Side

White Cliffs of Dover Right Side

Johnny Lang Crags

Main White Cliffs of Dover Formation

The main White Cliffs formation consists of a band of light-colored cliffs that extend several hundred yards across the hillside. The cliffs are broken in places by small gullies. There is a larger break in the cliffs between *Wokking the Dog* (route 128) and *Wanton Soup* (route 129). Routes to the left of this break are described in "White Cliffs of Dover—Left End"; routes to the right in "White Cliffs of Dover—Right End."

White Cliffs of Dover—Left End

This section of the White Cliffs of Dover covers routes from the far left end (*Make or Break Flake*) to an obvious break in the cliff band just right of *Wokking the Dog*. These routes are best approached by hiking up to the base of the cliffs at the left end (near *Jack of Hearts*), then contouring the base to the right.

110. **Make or Break Flake (aka Later Dude)** (5.10b) ★ This route ascends a flake/crack on a small face on the far left side of the cliff. A bolt protects the entry move. **Pro:** To 4 inches. **FA** (bolt placed on rap): Dan Dingle, Chris Carpenter, Guy Wordsall; 5/77.

111. **Quest for Fire** (5.11b) ★ (not shown on photo) This thin crack is just right of *Make or Break Flake*. **Pro:** Thin to 4 inches. **FA:** Tom Gilje, Dan Osman, Mike Waugh.

112. **Solar Flare** (5.9) ★ (not shown on photo) This is just across the gully from *Make or Break Flake*. Climb an obvious flake, then face climb past a bolt. **Pro:** To 2.5 inches. **FA:** Todd Swain, Dick Peterson; 11/89.

113. **Nolina Crack** (5.10a) ★ (not shown on photo) Start 30 feet right of *Solar Flare* on a block above and left of *Digital Watch*. Climb a crack past a huge nolina plant, joining *Solar Flare* at the bolt. **Pro:** To 2.5 inches. **FA:** Todd Swain, Dick Peterson; 11/89.

114. **Digital Watch** (5.11b) (R) ★★ (not shown on photo) This short, thin finger crack is just left of *Jack of Hearts*. Start out of an ant-covered tree. **Pro:** Small to 1.5 inches. **FA** (TR): Ray Olson; 1985. **FA** (Lead): Paul Craven, Jim Dunn; 1985.

115. **Sen Blen** (5.10c) ★ This route lies on the pillar between *Digital Watch* and *Jack of Hearts*. Approach the route from the high ledges to the left, or climb *Digital Watch* to start. Climb past a fixed (hopefully) RP, then

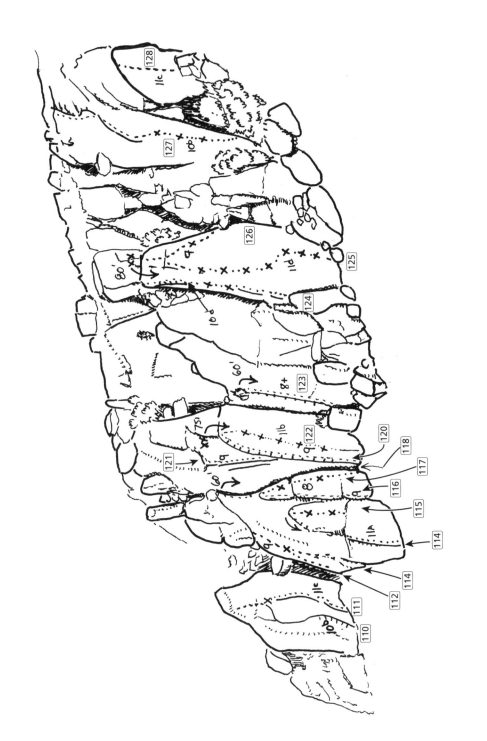

two bolts. There is no fixed anchor; climbers currently must do a simul-rap to get off. **Pro:** Mostly thin. **FA:** Todd Gordon, Tom Michael; 4/89.

116. **Jack of Hearts** (5.9+) ★ This route follows a handcrack on the left side of the tiered pinnacle left of *Popular Mechanics*. **Pro:** To 3 inches. **FA:** John Long, Dan Dingle, Janet Wilts; 5/77.

117. **Scientific Americans** (5.8) (R) ★★ Climb the arête right of *Jack of Hearts* past two bolts. **Pro:** To 3 inches. **FA:** Todd Swain, Peggy Buckey; 1986.

118. **Card Chimney** (5.5) (descent route) The obvious clean chimney right of *Jack of Hearts*. First Descent: John Long, Dan Dingle, Janet Wilts; 5/77.

119. **Conqueror Worm** (A1/A2) (not shown on photo) The seam/thin crack in the right side of *Card Chimney*. **Pro:** Thin stuff. **FA:** Todd Gordon, Dave Vaught.

120. **Popular Mechanics** (5.9) ★★★ This ascends the attractive white dihedral to the right of *Jack of Hearts*. Descend via a two-bolt rappel station at the belay. **Pro:** Thin to 3 inches. **FA:** Mari Gingery, Mike Lechlinski, John Long; 11/77.

121. **Ace of Spades** (5.9) ★★★ This follows the leftmost of two parallel handcracks that are located on the left wall of the *Popular Mechanics* dihedral. **Pro:** Medium to 2.5 inches. **FA:** Mike Lechlinski, John Long, Craig Fry; 12/77.

122. **Good Housekeeping** (5.11b) ★★★ This climbs the crack and arête to the right of *Popular Mechanics* past five bolts. **Pro:** Several to 3 inches; two-bolt anchor/80-foot rap. **FA:** Bob Gaines, Mark Hubbard; 3/96.

123. **Wilted Flower Children** (5.9) Climb the chimney and handcrack in a small right-facing corner 40 feet right of *Popular Mechanics*. **FA:** Todd Swain, Allen Steck, Dick Erbst; 11/89.

124. **High Anxiety** (5.10d) ★ This large, light-colored buttress is 100 feet right of *Popular Mechanics*. It is the largest buttress on the cliff. Scramble up ledges on the left side of the buttress. Climb a thin crack on the left edge of the buttress, face climb past two bolts, then follow the left-hand crack up a steep left-facing corner to the top. **Pro:** Many small to 2.5 inches. **FA:** Todd Swain, Dick Peterson; 11/89.

125. **High Tension** (5.11d) Start atop stacked boulders at the toe of the large light-colored buttress (about 100 feet right of *Popular Mechanics*). Face climb past seven bolts to a thin crack above; go over the headwall to the top. **Pro:** Thin to 2 inches. **FA:** Unknown.

126. **An Officer and a Poodle** (5.9) (R) This is on the right side of the large light-colored buttress. Climb a crack, then up the face past one bolt. **FA:** Ernie Ale.

127. **Search for Chinese Morsels** (5.10b) ★★ This brown wall is 100 feet right of the large light-colored buttress. Climb past three bolts (the third is doubled), then up cracks to top. **Pro:** Thin to 2 inches. **FA:** Glen Pinsoon, Dane Scott, Chris Saltzer.

128. **Wokking the Dog** (5.11c) ★ (TR) Climb the overhanging face just right of *Search for Chinese Morsels.* **FA:** Todd Swain; 9/89.

White Cliffs of Dover— Right End

This section of the White Cliffs of Dover covers routes beginning just right of an obvious break in the cliff band (*Wanton Soup*) to the cliff's far right end (*Karoosh's Wedding Crack*). These routes are best approached by hiking more directly up to the base of the cliffs near *Dover Sole*. Photo, page 69.

129. **Wanton Soup** (5.10a) (TR) Climb the steep rounded arête just left of *Misfortune Cookies,* on the right edge of the wide gully. **FA:** Todd Swain, Brandt Allen; 9/89.

130. **Misfortune Cookies** (5.8) A left-facing dihedral with a left-facing flake rises on the left face directly across the wide gully from *Search for Chinese Morsels.* Climb the flake and the corner. **FA:** Brandt Allen, Todd Swain; 9/89.

131. **Shibumi** (5.10d) ★ This thin, straight-in crack that steepens at the top is to the right of *Misfortune Cookies* (across the wide gully from *Search for Chinese Morsels*). **FA:** Mark Dubae, Alan Roberts, Darrel Hensel; 1/86.

131A. **Skimpy Skampi** (5.10b) Begin in the right-hand of two chimneys. Go up the chimney until you can move right onto the face with a thin crack. Where the thin crack peters out, face climb right and up to a ledge. Downclimb the chimney. **Pro:** Thin to 2 inches. **FA:** Unknown.

132. **Dover Soul** (5.6) This large face with a roof near its bottom is located approximately in the middle of the White Cliffs band of rocks. It is easily distinguished by the thin seam splitting the roof and face above. Climb a right-facing corner system to the right of the face. **FA:** Alan Roberts; 1/86.

133. **Rubber Soul** (5.9) (TR) (not shown on photo or topo) The arête/face just right of *Dover Sole.* **FA:** Bob Gaines; 5/99.

134. **Red Snapper** (5.11a/b) ★★ This ascends a nice piece of rock about 120 feet right of *Dover Sole.* A nice crack system is in the middle of the face. A difficult entry move/overhanging crack leads to a right-facing corner. **Pro:** Fingers to 2.5 inches. **FA:** Kevin Powell, Paul Schweizer, Alan Roberts, Randy Vogel; 1985.

135. **Red Tide** (5.10b) ★★ This climb is just around the corner and right of *Red Snapper* (about 20 feet). Face climb past four bolts to a two-bolt anchor/rap. **FA** (TR): Bill Leventhal, Banny Root; 3/85. **FA** (Lead): Bob Gaines, 5/99.

136. Soviet Union (5.11c) ★★★ The crescent crack on the steep face 100 feet right of *Red Snapper.* **Pro:** Many very thin to 1 inch. **FA** (TR): Ray Olson, John Long; 1985. **FA** (Lead): Paul Craven, Jim Dunn; 1985.

The following two routes lie on the formation just right of *Soviet Union.*

137. Chicken Run (5.7) ★★ (not shown on photo or topo) Go up the crack to the face with three bolts. **Pro:** Thin to 2 inches. **FA:** George Armstrong, Todd Gordon, Suzette Olsen, Karoosh.

138. Karoosh's Wedding Crack (5.9+) ★★ (not shown on photo or topo) This route lies around the corner from *Chicken Run* and faces north. Head up and left on a rail to a crack (white spike to the left) leading to the top. **Pro:** To 2 inches. **FA:** Todd Gordon, George Armstrong, Karoosh, Suzette Olsen.

JOHNNY LANG CRAGS

A high plateau lies above and to the west of the White Cliffs of Dover. The Johnny Lang Crags lie on the hillside to the southwest of that plateau (southwest of the White Cliffs). Though there are a number of crags on this hillside, only four have documented routes. The crags face northwest or west, with morning shade and some afternoon sun.

To approach this area, park at Trashcan Rock (Quail Springs Picnic Area) and head southwest on the trail that heads toward Hound Rocks. A few hundred yards before Baskerville Rock, head right (west) into a wash. The wash narrows into a drainage coming down the hillside, and heads over a short section of water-polished boulders. When the steep section ends, the drainage veers left (south). Follow the drainage toward the Johnny Lang Crags, which are visible high on the hillside slightly left of the wash. When the drainage ends in a small cul-de-sac, climb the steep hillside directly to the crags. Map, page 62.

Wilderness Bolting Notice: The entire Johnny Lang Crags area lies in designated wilderness. The placement of new bolts in wilderness is only allowed by permit. Existing bolts may be replaced on a one-for-one basis. Power drills are not permitted in wilderness areas. See the Introduction for more information.

PHOTO: VERN STIEFEL

Evil Tree Rocks (Wilderness)

These three small crags lie sandwiched together about 60 yards left and slightly uphill from the Fissure King formation. The only recorded route *(Evil Tree)* lies on the middle rock and is characterized by a prominent roof.

139. **Evil Tree** (5.12b/c) ★★★ This three-bolt route is about 35 feet high. **Pro:** To 2 inches, three bolts. **FA:** Mike Lechlinski; 4/91.

Fissure King Formation
(Wilderness)

This is the most prominent crag in the area and has a large rusty streak between white and light brown rock on its left side. The white (left) end is split by a crack *(Fissure King)*. A large block with two bolted routes *(French Roast* and *Doggie Style)* is on the far

right end, split off from the main formation by a gully.

140. **Sideline** (5.11d) (TR) Start in an overhanging bowl left and around the corner from *Fissure King.* **FA:** Mike Lechlinski, Mari Gingery; 4/91.

141. **Fissure King** (5.10a) ★★ The thin crack on the left side of the main face that goes over a small roof near the top. **Pro:** Thin to 2 inches. **FA:** Mike Lechlinski, Mari Gingery; 4/91.

142. **White Trash** (5.11c/d) ★★★★ The five-bolt face 25 feet right of *Fissure King.* **Pro:** To 2 inches, five bolts. **FA:** Mike Lechlinski, Mari Gingery; 4/91.

143. **Gail's Dilemma** (5.10a) ★★ This route lies about 40 feet right of *White Trash,* on the brownish right side of the formation. Go up the face to a left-leaning corner. **Pro:** To 2

inches. **FA:** Janet Wilts, Sam Roberts, Alan Bartlett; 10/91.

143A. My Love Affair with a Wheelbarrow

(5.9) ★★ (not shown) This and the next climb are located on a rock just left of the block with *French Roast* and *Doggie Style*. The left-hand route has three bolts and leads to a two-bolt anchor/rap. **Pro:** Very thin to 1 inch. **FA:** Unknown.

143B. The Hibiscus Shuffle (5.9) ★★ (not

shown) Begin to the right of the last climb; go up the face and crack past two bolts to a two-bolt anchor/rap. **Pro:** Very thin to 1 inch. **FA:** Unknown.

144. French Roast (5.12a) ★★ This six-bolt

route is the leftmost of two bolted routes. It begins at a bulge and veers left up the north-west face. The opening moves are the crux and holds may have broken off; it's a bit loose still. A variation start, up the crack to the left, is a bit easier. **Pro:** To 2 inches for anchors. **FA:** Mike Lechlinski; 4/91.

145. Doggie Style (5.12c) ★★★ The four-bolt

route to the right of *French Roast* on the overhanging west face. **Pro:** To 2 inches for anchor. **FA:** Mike Lechlinski; 4/91.

Tottering Tower (Wilderness)

This larger formation is located about 100 yards above and right of the Fissure King Formation. One route is known.

146. **House of Cards** (5.8) (R) A right-facing chimney leads to face climbing, then a right-facing corner. **Pro:** To 3+ inches. **FA:** Alan Bartlett, Janet Wilts, Sam Roberts; 10/91.

APFA Rock

This nondescript formation faces and lies just north of Park Boulevard about 0.1 mile east of Trashcan Rock. Park on the north side of the road 5.9 miles from the West Entrance and 2.7 miles from the Intersection Rock/Real Hidden Valley intersection. You can also easily park at Trashcan Rock and walk to the rock. Map, page 77.

APFA Rock—South Face

This side of APFA Rock directly faces Park Boulevard and lies only a short distance off the road. It is sunny most of the day. Descend either right or left.

147. **On the Road Again** (5.8) This route climbs a patinaed buttress about 100 feet up and left of *Boulder Crack* and *Boulder Face*. Start at a thin crack, climb over a small roof to a slab, then head up seams over a bulge. **Pro:** To 3 inches. **FA:** Bob Gaines, Patty Klien; 3/99.

148. **Boulder Crack** (5.8+) (not shown on photo) The 20-foot high boulder to the left of the main face has a crack on its west side. **FA:** Unknown.

149. **Boulder Face** (5.7) (not shown on photo) Climb a face and short crack just right of *Boulder Crack*. **FA:** Todd Swain, 4/86.

150. **Zsa Zsa Goes to Jail** (5.7) R Start part-way up the gully, up and left of *Bitch, Bitch*. Climb the face on knobs up and right to a roof. Go up the right side, then up the crack above. **Pro:** Thin to 2 inches. **FA:** Todd Swain; 9/89.

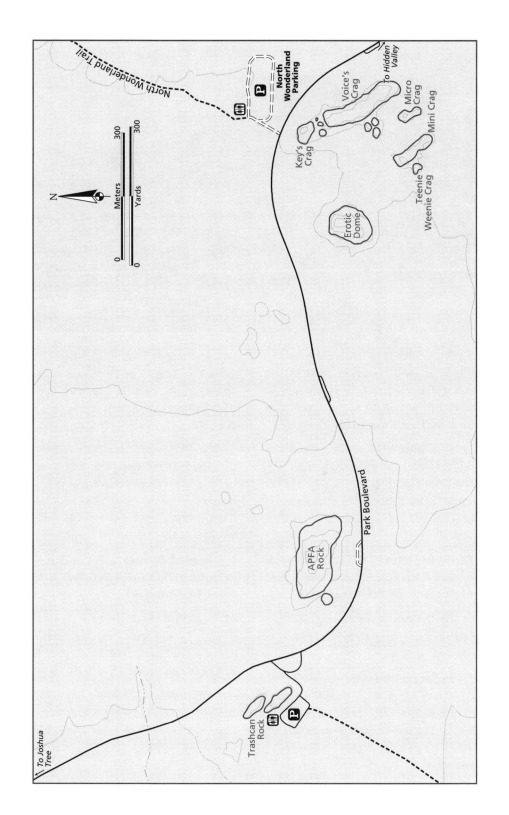

To Joshua Tree

North Wonderland Trail

North Wonderland Parking

P

N

Meters 0 300

Yards 0 300

Key's Crag

Voice's Crag

To Hidden Valley

Micro Crag

Teenie Weenie Crag

Mini Crag

Erotic Dome

Park Boulevard

APFA Rock

Trashcan Rock

P

151. **Bitch, Bitch** (5.7) This is the leftmost obvious line on the main face of APFA Rock. Follow thin cracks and grooves up and slightly left, then up the trough. **Pro:** To 2.5 inches. **FA:** Dave Evans, Marge Floyd.

152. **Sand Witch** (5.10a) Directly above *Bitch, Bitch* is a large, varnished boulder with a short dihedral. Pass a bolt into the corner, then go up the slab and thin crack above. **Pro:** Thin to 2 inches. **FA:** Todd Swain, Kip Knapp; 9/89.

153. **Big Bad Bitch** (5.11d) (TR) This route takes an overhanging thin crack/corner left of *Which Bitch*. **FA:** Bob Gaines; 11/97.

154. **Which Bitch** (5.8) ★ The right-facing corner to the right of *Bitch, Bitch*. **Pro:** To 2.5 inches. **FA:** Unknown.

155. **McDonald–Wilson** (5.10b) (R/X) This begins just right of *Which Bitch*. Go up the face to a right-curving thin crack, exit left, then head up past horizontals and a face. **Pro:** Thin to 2 inches. **FA:** Randy McDonald, Don Wilson.

156. **Andromeda Strain** (5.7) ★ Begin on the face to the right of the obvious crack. Go up the face past bolts (5.7), then left into that crack. Variation: Go straight up the crack (5.8). **Pro:** To 2.5 inches. **FA:** Dave Davis, Don O'Kelley, Bruce Andre; 11/71.

157. **The Terminal Man** (5.8) (R) Climb the face and discontinuous thin cracks/seams on right margin of the face, just left of *Request Chimney*. **Pro:** Thin to 2 inches. **FA:** Todd Swain; 10/91.

158. **Request Chimney** (5.7) The chimney just right of *The Terminal Man*. **Pro:** To 4+ inches. **FA:** Unknown.

159. **Rip Off** (5.6) To right of *Request Chimney*. Go up the face, then up the left side of stacked blocks. **Pro:** To 3 inches. **FA:** Rob Stahl, John Wolfe, Dave Stahl; 11/72.

160. **Which Witch** (5.8) Begin in a blackish crack 10 feet right of *Rip Off*. **Pro:** To 2.5 inches. **FA:** Don O'Kelley, Bill Mikus. **FFA:** John Wolfe; 12/72.

161. **Spaghetti Sauce Sunset** (5.10c) Located just right of *Which Witch*. Go up the thin crack, past a bush, then up the face past one bolt. **Pro:** Thin to 2 inches. **FA:** Tom Weldon; 1981.

162. **Two Our Surprise** (5.8) The crack just right of *Spaghetti Sauce Sunset*. Go up to a chimney. **Pro:** To 3 inches. **FA:** Brad Johnson, Mike Orr; 2/84.

APFA Rock—North Face

The back (north) side of APFA Rock is somewhat broken. The following two routes lie near the middle of this face. They are shady most of the day. The next two routes are not shown.

163. **Hurricane Hugo** (5.10b) This and the following climb lie near the middle of the back side of APFA Rock. **Pitch 1:** Head up two finger cracks separated by a ledge. **Pitch 2:** Climb a small left-facing corner, then go up and right past two bolts. **Pro:** To 2 inches. **FA** (TR): Todd Swain; 9/89. **FA** (Lead): Alan Bartlett, Brandt Allen, Rick Briggs; 9/91.

164. **Sheltered** (5.8) Start about 15 to 20 feet right of *Hurricane Hugo*. **Pitch 1:** Climb a thin crack on a slab to the base of a wide crack. **Pitch 2:** Go left to easy cracks lying right of the finish of *Hurricane Hugo*. **Pro:** To 2 inches, one fixed pin. **FA:** Alan Roberts, Kristen Laird.

Erotic Dome

This formation is 50 yards south of Park Boulevard approximately 0.3 miles past Trashcan Rock. Routes lie on the north face (facing the road) or on the west face. Park at a turnout west of the rock (6.1 miles from the West Entrance; 2.5 miles the from Intersection Rock/Real Hidden Valley intersection); alternatively, park at the Northern Wonderland parking area (6.4 miles from the West Entrance; 2.2+ miles from the Intersection Rock/Real Hidden Valley intersection), and walk back left (west) to the crag. Map, page 77.

Erotic Dome—North Face

The following climbs are on the center and right center of the north side of Erotic Dome. This face gets sun in the morning and shade most of the day.

165. **Erotic City** (5.11b) ★★ Climb a thin crack until it's possible (necessary) to traverse right to a crack that leads to the top. **Pro:** Thin to 2.5 inches. **FA:** Mike Paul, John Mallory, Mike Fogerty; 12/85.

166. **Vulgar Boot Men** (5.8) Climb the wide crack/chimney between *Erotic City* and *Volga Boat Men*. **Pro:** To 4 inches. **FA:** Unknown.

167. **The Leg Lifter** (5.11a) ★ (not shown) Begin around the corner from and about 20 feet to the right of the *Vulgar Boot Men* chimney. Go up past a fixed pin and bolt to "zigzag" thin cracks, then up the face past a bolt. **Pro:** Thin to 2.5 inches. **FA:** Todd Gordon, Steve Strong, Tom Michael; 12/89.

168. **Volga Boat Men** (5.8) (not shown) This less-than-quality route climbs the handcrack on the narrow rib 20 feet right of *The Leg Lifter.* **Pro:** To 3 inches. **FA:** Brian Sillasen, Todd Gordon, Dave Wright; 10/87.

Erotic Dome—West Face

The following climbs lie on the right side of the west face of Erotic Dome, about 150 feet right of *Volga Boot Men.* They get morning shade and are sunny all afternoon. The routes are not shown on photos or topos.

169. **The Awfulwidth** (5.8) (R/X) This nasty, grainy, right-leaning offwidth to chimney is 150 feet to the right of *Volga Boat Men.* **FA:** Unknown.

170. **Wake Me When It's Over** (5.8) (R/X) Climb the thin right-leaning seam just right of *The Awfulwidth.* **FA:** Todd Swain, Patty Furbush; 4/90.

171. **Orgasmatron** (5.?) This four-bolt face route about 75 feet right of *Wake Me When It's Over* may not have been climbed. **FA:** Unknown.

172. **Bald Women with Power Tools** (5.10b) This climb is on the buttress to the right of *Orgasmatron.* Climb a crack to a face with three bolts. **Pro:** To 2.5 inches. **FA:** Tim and Randy.

Wonderland of Rocks North

Holden Harris leads the classic Firewater Chimney (5.10b) in the Valley of Kings.

WONDERLAND OF ROCKS NORTH

The Wonderland of Rocks constitutes the largest concentration of rock formations in the entire park. This area (in excess of nine square miles) is bounded by Indian Cove to the north, Barker Dam to the south, Keys Ranch to the west, and Queen Mountain to the east. Due to its vast size, exploration has been made via three separate points of entry. For this reason, the Wonderland is covered in three different sections. The northern section of the Wonderland of Rocks (Wonderland North) and other areas within the vicinity of the North Wonderland Trail are described in the following section (map, pages 84–85). The southern section (Wonderland South) is approached from near Barker Dam (Wonderland Ranch) and will be described in the Joshua Tree Central volume, and Rattlesnake Canyon and vicinity in Joshua Tree East. A few areas in Wonderland North may actually be more easily approached via Rattlesnake Canyon/Indian Cove; in those instances both the Rattlesnake Canyon and Wonderland North approaches are described.

At Keys Corner, a sharp right turn 0.6+ mile east of Trashcan Rock on Park Boulevard (6.4 miles from the West Entrance; 2.2+ miles from the Intersection Rock/Real Hidden Valley intersection), there is an extremely large parking area (North Wonderland parking area) that serves as the trailhead for the northern portion of Wonderland of Rocks and for the Boy Scout Trail to Indian Cove. Access to Parking Lot Rocks is also from this parking area.

Wonderland North and all other areas in this vicinity (with the exception of Parking Lot Rocks) are approached via the North

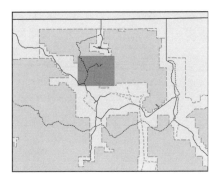

Wonderland Trail, which heads northeast from the North Wonderland parking lot. Parking Lot Rocks are approached via a closed dirt road that heads straight east from just south of the North Wonderland parking area.

Wilderness Bolting Notice: With the exception of Parking Lot Rocks, Wonderland Approach Crags, the Cool and Hidden Domes area, Ellesmere and Gilligan's Islands, and most of the Middle Kingdom, the Northern Wonderland is designated wilderness. The placement of new bolts in wilderness is only allowed by permit. Existing bolts may be replaced on a one-for-one basis. Power drills are not permitted in wilderness areas. (See Introduction for information.)

Dogs Not Permitted: Dogs (whether leashed or not) are not permitted in Joshua Tree backcountry areas (not just wilderness). Dogs are not permitted at any of the areas described in this section of the guide. Dogs can disturb wildlife and plant life, and you can be ticketed. Please keep Fido at home.

A Note about Navigating in the Wonderland: The Wonderland of Rocks,
particularly the North Wonderland, is an extremely complex area that features hundreds of separate rock formations (many with no routes), and boulder-filled valleys and gullies. Even with the very detailed approach

descriptions and maps provided in this guide, unless you are familiar with this area, you can easily get off track. When hiking in the Wonderland of Rocks, make note of formations and features. On your first trip into the deep Wonderland, approaches and return hikes may take longer than indicated in this guide. Leave yourself plenty of time to approach, climb, descend, and return to your car, particularly on short winter days. There are many gems in the deep Wonderland, and there is plenty of adventure too. Be self-sufficient and prepared.

Vern Stiefel leads the technical and excellent Powered by Old English *(5.11d), in the North Wonderland's Valley of Kings.*

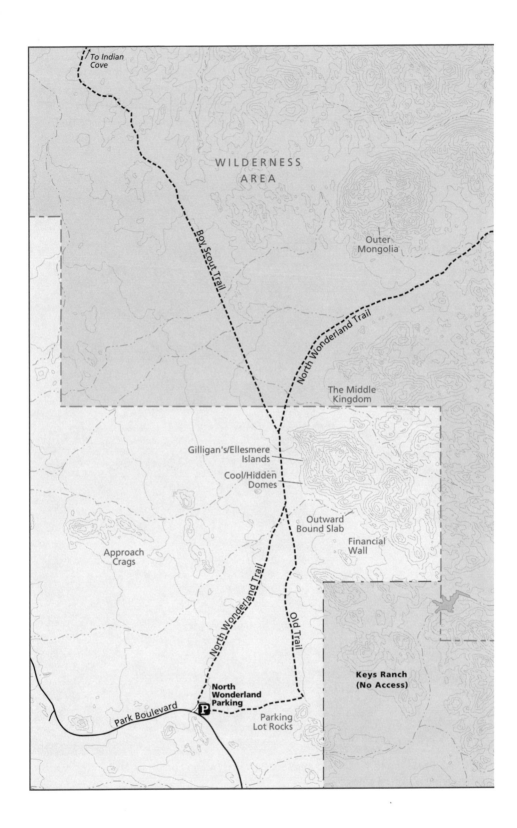

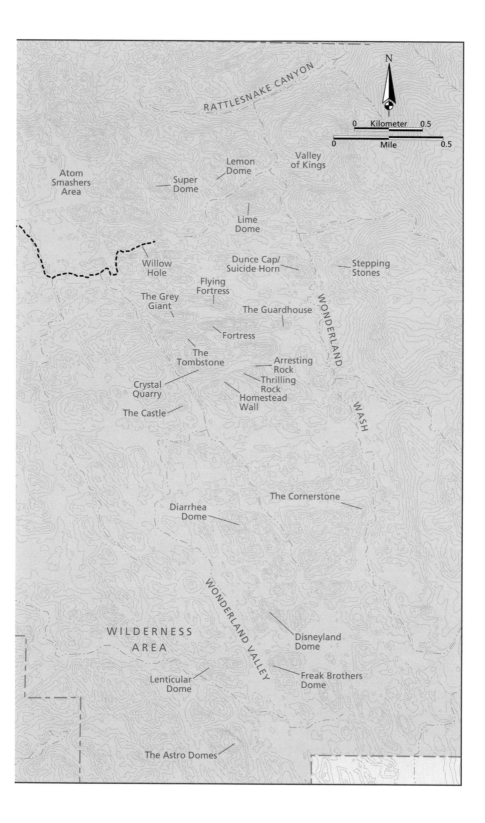

N

0 _____ Kilometer _____ 0.5

0 _____ Mile _____ 0.5

RATTLESNAKE CANYON

Valley
of Kings

Atom
Smashers
Area

Lemon
Dome

Super
Dome

Lime
Dome

Willow
Hole

Dunce Cap/
Suicide Horn

Stepping
Stones

Flying
Fortress

The Grey
Giant

The Guardhouse

WONDERLAND

Fortress

The
Tombstone

Arresting
Rock

Thrilling
Rock

Crystal
Quarry

Homestead
Wall

WASH

The Castle

The Cornerstone

Diarrhea
Dome

WONDERLAND VALLEY

WILDERNESS
AREA

Disneyland
Dome

Lenticular
Dome

Freak Brothers
Dome

The Astro Domes

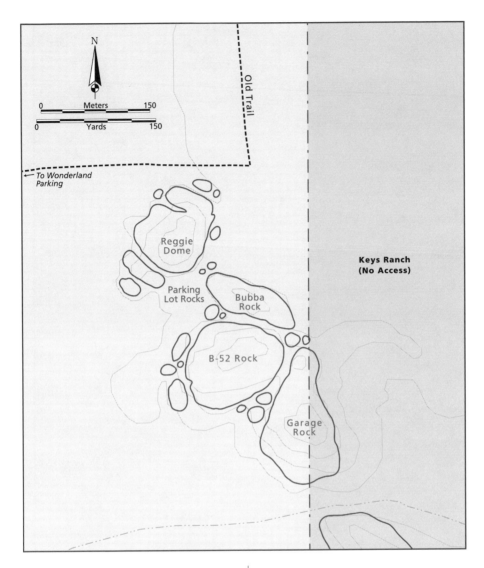

PARKING LOT ROCKS

These formations are located about 0.4 mile directly east from the North Wonderland parking area (See page 82 for driving directions). They can be approached directly via a now-closed dirt road (the Old Trail; being "revegetated") just south of the parking area, which heads straight east. This old road was open until 1991 and these formations are located at the former trailhead/parking area for the north Wonderland (hence the name). A gated fence blocks further progress east (the west border of Keys Ranch). From these formations, a dirt road/trail heads straight north and eventually joins the North Wonderland Trail as it heads northeast from the formal North Wonderland parking area. From Parking Lot Rocks, you can walk straight north to the other Wonderland North areas listed in this section.

Bubba Rock—North Face

The north face of Bubba Rock lies directly south of the "parking area," and left of the northeast face of Reggie Dome. The formation appears to lie partially inside Keys Ranch, access to which is restricted; a fence marks the boundary. Five routes that have been recorded on the northeast face of Bubba Rock may, therefore, not be legally accessible. These routes range from 5.9 to 5.10c, one of which has a single bolt (5.10c R). They climb crack and face lines to the right and left of a big flake, with a (5.10b) toprope beginning from the top of the flake. Map, page 86.

173. **Bubba Takes a Siesta** (5.10a) ★ (not shown) Follow huecos on good rock on the north face of Bubba Rock past one bolt to an arching crack. **Pro:** To 2 inches. **FA:** Don Wilson, Jack Marshall; 2/88.

Garage Rock—Northeast Face

The northeast face of Garage Rock lies directly left (south) of the northeast face of Bubba Rock. This face also appears to lie just inside Keys Ranch (restricted access). Five routes are recorded on the northeast face, two of which have at least one bolt. They range in difficulty from 5.5 to 5.10a.

Reggie Dome

This is the northernmost formation of Parking Lot Rocks, closest to the closed dirt road and former parking lot. As you approach Parking Lot Rocks, Reggie Dome is closest to the road on your right. Map, page 86.

Reggie Dome—East and Northeast Faces

This face gets early sun and afternoon shade. To descend, downclimb the gully/face directly below *Reggie on a Poodle* (Class 4/5).

174. Irresponsibility Lessons (5.9) This crack starts by a pine tree. Go up and right, then up and left, then up to the top. **Pro:** To 2 inches. **FA:** Mark Uphus, Sue Williams et al.; 3/95.

175. The Mole (5.10c/d) ★★ (Sport) Start near the right side of a large roof. Climb up past four bolts to a two-bolt anchor/rap (50 feet). **FA:** Scott Cosgrove, Bob Gaines; 3/01.

176. Thomson Roof (5.8) ★ Climb up and right onto a right-leading ramp, then head back left and climb a finger crack (the left one) over a small roof. **Pro:** To 2 inches. **FA:** Reggie Thomson, Todd Gordon, Scott Gordon, Mike Brown, Howard Boyd; 12/85.

177. Grulcher and Eliza (aka Reggie's Pimple) (5.10c) (TR) Belay from the ground directly below *Reggie On A Poodle*. Go up the face/gully to the base of a thin crack (doesn't quite reach the bottom) just left of *Reggie On A Poodle*. **FA:** Roger Whitehead, Chris French; 1986.

178. Reggie on a Poodle (5.10a) ★ Go up the face/gully, then up the shallow crack just right of *Grulcher and Eliza* to a bolt and face above. Downclimb off the back, then down the gully/face to the base. **Pro:** Thin to 2 inches. **FA:** Reggie Thomson, Todd Gordon, Scott Gordon, Mike Brown, Rick McKay, Howard Boyd; 12/85.

179. Dichotomy (5.10b) This dike with two bolts is down and right of the last two climbs. **Pro:** To 3+ inches. **FA:** Unknown.

Reggie Dome—Northwest Face

The northwest face fronts the approach road/trail. It is characterized by a low-angled slab behind a very large pine tree. Map, page 86.

180. **Sex Farm Woman** (5.7) (R) This route is in a gully-chimney to the left of the low-angled face. Chimney up to a dike on the face. **FA:** Alan Bartlett, Mike Guardino; 2/96.

181. **Speed Bump** (5.6) (R/X) Climb the slab to the left of the pine tree. Two-bolt anchor. **FA:** Unknown.

182. **Fender Bender** (5.8) ★ This is just right of the pine tree. Face climb past two bolts to a two-bolt anchor. **FA:** Unknown.

183. **Thomson's Acne** (5.10b) (R/X) Start about 20 feet right of *Fender Bender* and left of *Ninny's Revenge,* near the right side of the slab. Face climb up to a sloping ledge, then up the face above. **FA** (TR): Nino Botelho, Agust Agustsson; 10/89. **FA** (Lead): Alan Bartlett; 2/96.

184. **Ninny's Revenge** (5.9) This climb begins just left of the deep chimney/gully on the right-hand part of the low-angled slab. Climb a flared crack to join *Thomson's Acne* or *Fender Bender* on the upper face, or just walk off left. **FA:** Don Wilson, Karen Wilson; 3/86.

185. **Pops Goes Hawaiian** (5.7) ★★ This climb is around the corner and 35 feet right of *Ninny's Revenge,* on the left side of a wide gully. Follow a steep dike in brown rock past a bolt to a flake, then move right to rejoin the dike. **FA:** Don Wilson, Karen Wilson; 3/86.

186. **Pop Goes the Weasel** (5.10d) ★ (TR) The face between *Pops Goes Hawaiian* and *The Chief.* **FA:** Bob Gaines; 12/00.

187. **The Chief** (5.5) ★★ Climb the crack 20 feet up and to the right of *Pops Goes Hawaiian.* **FA:** Don Wilson, Karen Wilson; 3/86.

Reggie Dome—Southwest Face, Left Side

This section of Reggie Dome lies just around the corner from northwest face routes. The left end routes are approached by heading right from the northwest face.

188. **Curbside** (5.8) The short left-facing corner. **FA:** Brian Prentice, Bob Gaines; 12/00.

189. **Handicapped Zone** (5.6) Start at a crack just right of *Curbside.* Above, head up then right to another crack. **Pro:** To 2 inches. **FA:** Unknown.

190. **Meter Maid** (5.9) Climb the "X" cracks right of *Handicapped Zone* to eventually join *Handicapped Zone.* **Pro:** Thin to 2 inches. **FA:** Alan Bartlett, Rosanne Gillmore; 1995.

191. **No Parking** (5.10b) (R) Climb the loose-looking face about 15 feet right of *Meter Maid.* **Pro:** Three bolts. **FA:** Unknown.

192. **Short Cuts** (5.10a) ★ (not shown on photo) This short three-bolt climb lies on a boulder to the right and in front of the main face, about 100 feet right of *Curbside.* **Pro:** Three to 4 inches for anchor. **FA:** Steve Sutton, Alan Bartlett; 1/96.

Reggie Dome—Southwest Face, Right Side

This section of Reggie Dome lies a few hundred feet around and right of the north-west face, on the right-hand part of a face to the right of and behind *Short Cuts*. Walk around the west side of the rock to reach these routes. All three routes share the same two-bolt anchor/rappel (70 feet).

193. **Tender Flakes of Wrath** (5.9) This route is the leftmost of the three bolted face routes. Along with the next climb, it finishes in a crack above a horizontal. **Pro:** Two bolts; to 1.5 inches; two-bolt anchor/rap. **FA:** Scott Batie, Kenny Pang; 10/88.

194. **Sunny Delight** (5.9) ★ The middle route with two bolts, finish in same crack as *Tender Flakes of Wrath*. **Pro:** To 1.5 inches, two-bolt anchor/rap. **FA:** Mark Uphus, Sue Williams; 12/94.

195. **Fresh Squeezed** (5.10a) ★★ (Sport) Start just up and right of *Sunny Delight;* go up plates. **Pro:** Seven bolts; two-bolt anchor/rap. **FA:** Bob Gaines, Yvonne Gaines; 2001.

B52 Rock

B52 Rock—Northwest Face

To reach the west face of B52 Rock, either hike around the west face of Reggie Dome and head south, or scramble between Reggie Dome and Bubba Rock. The west face of B52 Rock is what seems to be a continuation of the west face of Bubba Rock. Map, page 86.

B52 Rock—Northwest Slab

The far left side of the west face is a low-angled slab that lies in front of the south side of Bubba Rock. Routes 196 to 198 are not shown.

196. **It's Not Brain Surgery** (5.6) ★ This is the brown face on the left side of the low-angled slab with one bolt. **FA** (TR): Mark Uphus, Sue Williams; 12/94. **FA** (Lead): Phil Bircheff, Tod McFarland, Alan Bartlett; 11/96.

197. **It's Not Rocket Science** (5.10b) (TR) Begin right of *It's Not Brain Surgery*. Climb a right-leaning thin flake to a bulge, head left to a right-leaning crack. **FA:** Bob Gaines; 12/00.

198. **Fine Line between Genius and Insanity** (5.7) (R) Start 25 feet right of *It's Not Brain Surgery;* Go up the slab past one bolt to a right-tending seam. **FA:** Mark Uphus, Sue Williams; 12/94.

B52 Rock—Northwest Face, Upper

The right side of the northwest face has a slab on the left and a steeper face with cracks above and right. The thin crack in the shallow white corner on the left side of the upper face is *Private Idaho*.

199. **Love Shack** (5.8) ★★ This is the right-slanting crack system on the big face left of *Private Idaho*. **Pro:** To 3 inches; two-bolt anchor/70-foot rap. **FA:** Bob Gaines, Yvonne Gaines; 1/01.

200. **Private Idaho** (5.11b) (R)★★★ This climbs the thin crack in the light-colored, left-facing corner. **Pro:** Many thin to 2 inches (fixed pin missing?). **FA:** Mike Paul, Bob Gaines; 1983.

201. **Roam** (5.10b) ★ The three-bolt route up the arête/face 16 feet right of *Private Idaho*. **FA:** Unknown.

202. **52 Girls** (5.9) The left-arching crack just right of *Roam*. **Pro:** To 3 inches. **FA:** Alan Bartlett, Steve Sutton; 1/96.

B52 Rock—South Face

The following climbs lie just around the corner on the southern side of B52 Rock. All start off a ledge system above a slab.

203. **Stem the Tide** (5.11a) Go up an overhanging leaning corner to cracks above. **Pro:** Thin to 2 inches. **FA:** Steve Sutton, Alan Bartlett; 1/96.

204. **Toxic Avenger** (5.11a) ★★ Go up past a fixed head and two bolts to a ledge, then continue up the finger-and-hand crack above. **Pro:** To 2.5 inches. **FA:** Jack Marshall, Don Wilson; 3/89.

205. **Romper Room** (5.11a) ★ Located right of *Toxic Avenger*. Go up the face past three bolts to a ledge, then above a fourth bolt to a small corner. Two-bolt anchor/rap. **Pro:** Thin. **FA:** Justin Sommer, Jim Norton; 1991.

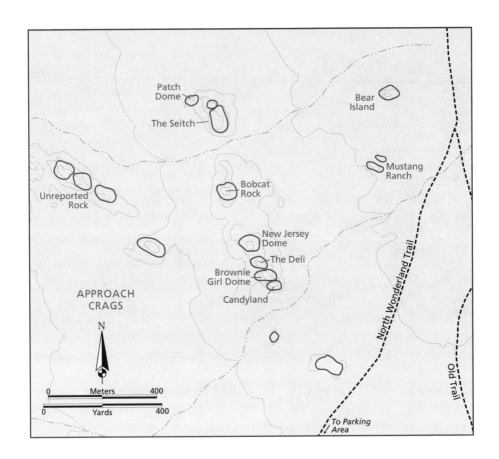

WONDERLAND NORTH— APPROACH CRAGS

The following formations are scattered across the desert to the west of the North Wonderland Trail. Park at the North Wonderland parking area (off Park Boulevard 6.4 miles from the West Entrance and 2.2+ miles from the Intersection Rock/Real Hidden Valley intersection). The North Wonderland Trail heads northeast from the parking area. See the individual crags for specific approach directions. Also, see the map on page 114.

New Jersey Dome, the Deli, Brownie Girl Dome, Candyland

These formations lie about 0.6 mile north of the North Wonderland parking area, and are in plain view from the parking area. They are best approached by taking the Wonderland Trail northeast for about 0.3 mile to a point where the formations lie directly north; this point is before you reach some low rocks on the left (west) side of the trail. Angle off left (north) from the trail for about 400 yards to the southwest faces of, from left to right, New Jersey Dome, The Deli, Brownie Girl Dome, and Candyland. These are nice sunny crags; good for colder days. Map, page 94.

New Jersey Dome

This western/leftmost formation has dark roofs on its southwest face and is about 50 feet tall. It gets sun most of the day.

206. **Jersey Girl** (5.10a) The route is on the southwest corner of the dome, below the dark roof. Climb easy but loose rock up and left of the roofs to an overhanging crack. **Pro:** Very thin to 2 inches. **FA:** Karen Wilson, Don Wilson; 12/85.

The Deli

This is the 55-foot formation up and right from New Jersey Dome. It gets sun most of the day.

207. **Pumpernickel Pickle** (5.9) Begin behind a block. Go up then right on a horizontal, then up. **Pro:** To 2 inches. **FA:** Dave Haber, Sheryl Haber, Mark Hoffman, Alan Bartlett; 1995.

208. **Cold Cuts** (5.9) The right-slanting crack. **Pro:** To 2.5 inches. **FA:** Dave Haber, Sheryl Haber; 1/95.

Brownie Girl Dome

This squarish formation has several diagonal dike systems on its southwest face; it's about 90+ feet tall. Large boulders on top can be slung (30-foot extendo needed) for a toprope anchor. Walk off to the right. The dome is in sun most of the day.

209. **James Brown** (5.6) This is the short crack/corner around and left of *Buster Brown* on the northwest face. **Pro:** To 3+ inches. **FA:** Todd Swain, Gary Garrett; 11/88.

210. **Buster Brown** (5.10a) (R)★★★ Follow a right-slanting dike, with one bolt up high. **Pro:** Thin to 3 inches. **FA:** Kevin Powell, Paula Chambers, Darrel Hensel; 1983.

211. **Brownie Points** (5.9) ★★ (TR) Go up *Buster Brown* to the second horizontal, then up and left on a dike. **FA:** Todd Swain; 11/88.

212. **Brown Sugar** (5.11c) ★★ Go up the left-slanting dike immediately right of *Buster Brown*. **Pro:** Five bolts; to 2 inches. **FA** (TR): Bob Gaines; 3/00. **FA** (Lead): Bob Gaines; 12/03.

213. **Tige** (5.8) (R)★★ Climb the face and discontinuous crack past two horizontals, then go up the dike past a bolt. **Pro:** One bolt; to 2 inches. **FA:** Alan Bartlett, Alan Roberts; 1/88.

213A. **Zonker's Brownies** (5.7) ★ Begin about 45 feet right of *Tige* off a boulder. Head pretty much straight up via discontinuous cracks. **Pro:** To 2.5 inches. **FA:** Dave Haber, Sheryl Haber; 11/91.

213B. **Hole in the Wall** (5.10c) ★ Begin about 35 feet right of *Zonker's Brownies.* Head up the face past four bolts and horizontals to finish past a final bolt. **Pro:** To 3 inches. **FA:** Bob Gaines, Tony Sartin; 12/03.

Candyland

This small formation with a prominent overhang lies down and right of Brownie Girl Dome. The routes are not shown.

214. **Almond Joy** (5.10b) (TR) Climb the overhang to a thin crack on the right. **FA:** Bob Gaines; 4/00.

215. **Milky Way** (5.9) (TR) Climb a left-slanting dike over the roof to an easy face. **FA:** Bob Gaines; 4/00.

Bobcat Rock

This small rock lies about 300 yards north of Brownie Girl Dome, and about 0.7 mile north of the North Wonderland parking area (see page 94). Approach by taking the Wonderland Trail northeast for about 0.3 mile to a point where Brownie Girl Dome lies directly to the north. This point is before you reach some low rocks to the left (west) of the trail. Angle off left (north) for about 400 yards, passing left of the southwest faces of Brownie Girl Dome etc., then continue north for about 300 more yards to this squarish formation sitting on a hill. Map, page 94.

216. **I Taught I Saw a Puddy Cat** (5.9) Go up a left-slanting thin crack just around the corner on the northwest face. A bit contrived since you can stem left and make it easier. **Pro:** Thin to 2 inches. **FA:** Dave Haber, Sheryl Haber; 11/94.

217. **Da Kitty! Da Kitty!** (5.7) Crack on the left end. **Pro:** To 2.5 inches. **FA:** Dave Haber, Sheryl Haber; 11/94.

218. **Bradley** (5.9) ★ A two- bolt face route. **Pro:** For anchors. **FA:** Dave Haber, Sheryl Haber; 11/94.

219. **The Litter Box** (5.8) Crack with bush. **Pro:** To 2 inches. **FA:** Dave Haber, Sheryl Haber; 11/94.

220. **Morris** (5.7) Climb the rightmost thin crack to a face. **Pro:** Thin to 2 inches. **FA:** Dave Haber, Sheryl Haber; 11/94.

The Seitch

This large face lies about 450 yards north of Brownie Girl Dome, and about 0.8 mile north of the North Wonderland parking area (see page 94). Approach by taking the North Wonderland Trail northeast for about 0.3 mile to a point where Brownie Girl Dome lies directly to the north; this point is before you reach low rocks to the left (west) of the trail. Angle off left (north) from here for about 850 yards, passing left of the southwest faces of Brownie Girl Dome (400 yards), and Bobcat Rock (700 yards), then head north for 150 yards to this 100+-foot-tall formation. The Seitch has the potential for some steep face routes. It gets sun most of day. Map, page 94.

221. **Downward Bound** (5.8) ★ Located on the left side of the face. Go up a crack/dike to a ledge, traverse right and go up another crack. **FA:** Unknown.

222. **Gearhart–Spear** (5.10a) (R) Go up *Downward Bound,* but continue up the dike to the top. **FA** (TR): Unknown. **FA** (Lead): Eric Gearhart, Brian Spear.

222A. **Seitch Tactics** (5.11b) ★★ This route lies about 75 feet right of *Downward Bound,* climbing the steep face into a black hole. **Pro:** Six bolts; to 2.5 inches. **FA:** Steve Gerberding, Al Swanson, Cal Gerberding; 12/03.

Patch Dome

This formation lies about 75 yards northwest of the Seitch (see the Seitch for approach directions). It is a lighter-colored rock with three summits. The two known routes are best reached by walking around the left end of the rock and cutting back right. *Cat Walk* lies on the northeast face and is the first route you will reach. The descent is via a two-bolt anchor/rappel (60 feet) from the southwest side. It is shady most of the day. Map, page 94.

223. **Cat Walk** (5.10a) Begin near the northeast corner of the rock. Go up the face with seven bolts. **FA:** Troy Mayr, Amy Sharpless; 1/88.

224. **Climbing Out of Obscurity** (5.10a) Begin up and about 40 feet right of *Cat Walk.* Go up a flake, then face climb past two bolts. **FA:** Terri Peterson, Mike Brown; 9/87.

225. **Smiley Crack** (5.7) (not shown) This route is on the northeast corner of a small

rock just east of Patch Dome. Follow a short finger crack that does not reach the ground. **Pro:** Thin to 2 inches. **FA:** Brandt Allen, Dave Haber, Sheryl Haber; 1995.

Unreported Rock

Unreported Rock is actually the western/ leftmost of the Approach Crags, lying on the right end of a small hillside several hundred yards west of Brownie Girl Dome. It is almost due east from the southern end of Vagmarken Hill. The rock and its neighbors lie about 0.6 mile northeast of Park Boulevard (at its closest point) and 0.75 mile northwest of the North Wonderland parking area (maps, pages 94 and 114). If you approach from Park Boulevard, park along the road about 0.3 mile north of Trashcan Rock (5.5 miles from the West Entrance, 3.1+ miles from the Intersection Rock/Real Hidden Valley intersection). Walk in a northeasterly direction toward the right side of the hill. From the North Wonderland parking area, head northwest, staying left of Brownie Girl Dome.

Unreported Rock—Left End

This is the highest, leftmost end of the cliffs. It gets sun most of the day.

226. **Don't Overlook** (5.8) (TR) Start below a sage bush on a ramp, then go up the obvious chute. **FA:** John Shea, Dave Webster; 1/01.

227. **The Unreported** (5.7) Begin 20 feet left of a small chimney and 30 feet right of *Don't Overlook*. Climb the face up to the ledge, then above past one bolt. **FA:** Unknown.

228. **Boost for the Beginner** (5.4) Go up a small chimney to a face and dike above. **FA:** John Shea, Dave Webster; 1/01.

The following routes either begin or terminate on a large ledge on the upper right side of the rock called the Sundeck.

229. **Bush Driver** (5.6) Go up the wide crack to the left of the gully; above, "dive" under the bush to gully, then up a chimney to the Sundeck. **FA:** John Shea, Dave Webster; 1/01.

230. Plates and Pockets (5.7) (TR) Located to the left of the Sundeck and *Bush Driver* chasm. Face climb up plates, knobs, and flakes. **FA:** Dave Webster, John Shea; 1/01.

231. Squeeze, Pull, and Yank (5.7) ★ The wide crack above the chasm, left of the Sundeck. **FA:** John Shea, Dave Webster; 1/01.

232. Jams, Twists, and Pushes (5.9) ★★ This hand-to-fist crack is to the right of the Sundeck. **FA** (TR): Dave Webster, John Shea; 1/01.

Unreported Rock—Middle Section

This is the more nondescript and shorter midsection of the Unreported Rock. It is sunny most of the day.

233. The Scythe (5.6) The obvious scythe-shaped crack about 40 feet right of a gully separating the Middle Section and the Left End. Where the crack turns horizontal, head up the face. **FA:** John Shea, Dave Webster; 1/01.

234. Butt Print (5.10b) ★ Located on the upper right end of the Middle Section. Climb this face past four bolts to rappel slings. **FA:** John Shea, Dave Webster; 3/01.

235. Dave's Ditch (5.3) The gully to the right of *Butt Print*. **FA:** Dave Webster; 3/01.

Unreported Rock—Right End

The right-end section of Unreported Rock has several face and crack routes. It is sunny most of the day.

236. Where Brownies Dare (5.10a) Go up a left-facing flake near the center of the face to two-bolt face. **FA:** Arnie Ale, Bruce Burns, Kevin Mills; 6/88.

237. Point Break (5.10c/d) ★ The three-bolt face to the right of *Where Brownies Dare*. **FA:** Alan Bartlett, Derek Reinig; 9/96.

238. Breaking Point (5.8+) Follow a crack that splits near the top (go either way). **FA:** Derek Reining, Alan Bartlett; 9/96.

239. Short but Potent (5.9) Follow the left-slanting arch, then go up. **FA** (TR): Dave Webster, John Shea; 3/01. **FA** (Lead): Unknown.

MUSTANG RANCH

The Mustang Ranch consists of two rocks (the West Rock and the East Rock) forming a wide corridor that lies a short distance north of the North Wonderland Trail. Park at the North Wonderland parking area (6.4 miles from the West Entrance; 2.2+ miles from the Intersection Rock/Real Hidden Valley intersection). Follow the North Wonderland Trail for about 0.75 mile, then head left for about 150 yards to these rocks. The larger West Rock is on your left as you approach; the smaller East Rock is on your right. Map, page 94.

Mustang Ranch—West Rock, West Face

These various climbs lie on the west face of the larger West Rock (on your left as you approach). They gets morning shade and sun most of the afternoon. They are not shown on the photo.

240. **Cobs Wall** (5.6 to 5.8) Several leads or topropes near the center of the face. Bolt anchors on top. **FA:** Unknown.

Mustang Ranch—West Rock, East Face

The following climbs lie on the eastern face of the larger West Rock. They get sun in the morning and shade most of afternoon.

241. **Blue Velvet** (5.11d) ★ (TR) This route follows a right-slanting crack/seam that rises 25 feet left of the large crack/break *(The Chicken Ranch)* near the middle of the east face. **FA:** Richard Cilley; 1986.

242. **Game Boy (aka Whips and Grains)** (5.10b) Climb the brown, bucketed face 18 feet right of *Blue Velvet*. Pass one bolt to join *Blue Velvet* near the top. **FA** (TR): Unknown. **FA** (Lead): Dave Wonderly, Don Wilson; 4/91.

243. **The Chicken Ranch** (5.6) ★ This is the crack/chimney that forms a break in the center of the east face. **FA:** Unknown.

244. **Pretty in Pink** (5.11b) (TR) ★★ Follow the leftmost of two thin crack/seams that lie 15 feet to the right of *The Chicken Ranch.* **FA:** Mike Paul, Richard Cilley; 1986.

245. **Women in Cages** (5.11c) (TR) ★ This route is the right-hand crack/seam next to *Pretty in Pink.* **FA:** Mike Paul, Richard Cilley; 1986.

246. **Brotherly Love** (5.10b) (R) Begin at *Women in Cages,* but head up and right to a small bush, then up a crack. **FA** (TR): Unknown. **FA** (Lead): Don Reid; 1996.

247. **Pahrump** (5.4) The chimney just right of *Brotherly Love.* **FA:** Unknown.

248. **Muff Divers** (5.4) Starts 35 feet right of *Pahrump,* to the right of a break in wall. Go up the face. **FA:** Unknown.

249. **Padded Handcuffs** (5.9) (R/X) The very short dike at the very right end of the east face. **FA:** Todd Swain; 10/90.

Mustang Ranch—East Rock, East Face

This is the outer face of the right-hand formation, which gets sun in the morning and shade in the afternoon. The routes are located on the right end of the east face. They are about 25 feet long, and you can boulder as well as toprope them. None of these routes are shown.

250. **Stable Girl** (5.11b/c) (TR) This is the leftmost of two thin cracks/seams. **FA:** Mike Paul, Richard Cilley; 1986.

251. **Viva Las Vegas** (5.11b/c) (TR) The right thin crack/seam; it starts as a left-slanting crack. **FA:** Mike Paul, Richard Cilley; 1986.

252. **Mustang Ranch** (5.10b/c) (TR) Start as for *Viva Las Vegas;* go up the protruding dike to the right of *Viva Las Vegas.* **FA:** Mike Paul, Richard Cilley; 1986.

Bear Island

This formation lies about 150 yards northwest of the Wonderland Trail, just before it joins the larger trail/road running north to south. Park at the parking area (6.4 miles from the West Entrance; 2.2+ miles from the Intersection Rock/Real Hidden Valley intersection). Take the North Wonderland Trail north for about 0.85 mile from North Wonderland Parking area (about 175 yards north of Mustang Ranch), then head left to the rock. Routes all lie on the northwest face, facing away from the North Wonderland Trail. Map, page 94.

Bear Island—Northwest Face

This face gets shade in the morning and gets some afternoon sun.

253. **Shardik** (5.3) Climb the crack on the arête at the north end of the formation. Todd Swain; 3/87.

254. **Shardikawoopoopie** (5.9+) (R) Climb the black-and-white face just right of *Shardik*. **FA:** George Zelenz; 2/92.

255. **Ursa Major** (5.7) Climb the left-hand thin crack to the rounded arête. **FA:** Unknown.

256. **Polar Bears in Bondage** (5.7) Climb the short, right-hand crack through a bulge, then go up the easy gray face. **FA:** Todd Swain; 3/87.

257. **Kodiak** (5.5) This is just left of blocks. Go up the face to a varnished crack; about 7 feet right of Polar Bears In Bondage. **FA:** Todd Swain; 3/87.

258. **My Goose Is Loose** (5.8) (TR) Begin off the ledge up and right of *Kodiak*; go up the face. **FA:** George Zelenz; 1/94.

259. **How Loose Is Your Goose** (5.5) The left-facing dihedral. **FA:** George Zelenz; 1/94.

Bear Island—Southwest Face

This is sunny most of the day.

260. **Ursa Minor** (5.5) (not shown on photo) This route is a right slanting crack above a small roof that leads to a face. **FA:** Alan Bartlett, Karen Tracy; 6/95.

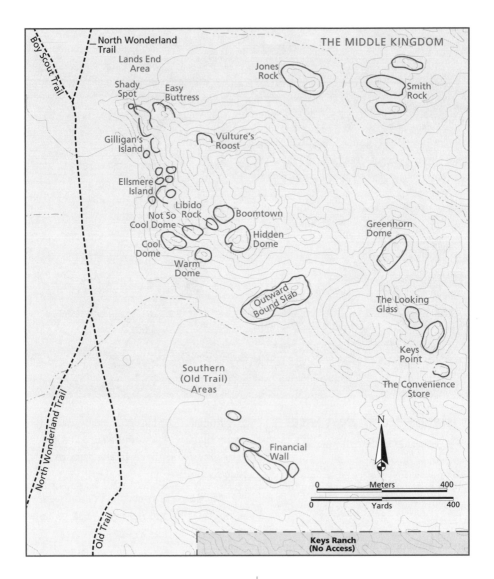

SOUTHERN (OLD TRAIL) AREAS

To reach these areas, park at the Northern Wonderland parking area (on Park Boulevard 6.4 miles from the West Entrance; 2.2+ miles from the Intersection Rock/Real Hidden Valley intersection). Hike nearly 1 mile northeast on the North Wonderland Trail. At

this point, it will join up with a larger trail (a former dirt road) heading straight north. An unused road/trail (the Old Trail) heads straight south from here (there is a sign indicating it is closed). Outward Bound Slab, Financial Wall, the Backstreets, the Convenience Store, and Keys Point all are approached by taking the Old Trail south for about 100+ yards, then angling southeast into an open valley. Outward Bound Slab faces south and is on the left (north) side of the valley, and the Financial Wall faces northeast and is to the south. If you are at the Parking Lot Rocks, you can approach by simply walking north on the Old Trail, and then turning right into the valley. Maps, pages 104 and 114.

Outward Bound Slab

See approach info on page 104. A large open valley is on the right (east) as the North Wonderland Trail joins the Old Trail. Turn right (south) and follow the Old Trail for about 100+ yards, then angle left (southeast) into the valley. On the north side of the valley (the southern side of the hillside holding Cool and Hidden Domes) you will see an obvious south-facing slab. This is Outward Bound Slab. It gets sun most of the day. Map, page 104.

Outward Bound Slab— Northern Side

The following two routes lie on the back (northern) side of Outward Bound Slab.

261. **Duncan Imperial** (5.10a) (not shown on photo) This route is located about 250 feet left of *Oh Pinyon Crack* and reached by heading up a gully on the backside of Outward Bound Slab. It is on the back of the upper right section of Outward Bound Slab. It ascends a crack/flake located right of a roof. **Pro:** To 2.5 inches. **FA:** George Armstrong, Alan Bartlett; 10/95.

262. **Oh Pinyon Crack** (5.9) This is the 40-foot handcrack in a corner near the northwest corner of Outward Bound Slab. You see it as you approach the slab from the Wonderland/Old Trail. It starts behind a pinyon pine. **Pro:** To 2.5 inches. **FA:** Sean Meeham, Pat Kent.

Outward Bound Slab— South Face, Left Side

The following routes lie on the left-hand section of the low-angled slab.

263. **Sandal Crack** (5.4) The leftmost of two slanting cracks on left end of the slab. **FA:** Unknown.

264. **Paint Me Gigi** (5.7) (R/X) ★ Ascend the right-hand of the two left-slanting cracks on left end of the slab. This shares a belay with the last climb. **FA:** Unknown.

265. **Outward Bound Slab Route** (5.8) ★ Climb past three bolts to the right of *Paint Me Gigi*. Two-bolt anchor. **FA:** Mike Brown, Reggie Thomson, Howard Boyd, Scott Gordon, Todd Gordon; 12/85.

266. **Mastering** (5.2) (R)★★ Go up easy scoops and cracks to the right of *Outward Bound Slab Route;* share that route's two-bolt belay. **FA:** Unknown.

267. **Look Mom, No Sweat** (5.4) Go up the right-diagonalling light-colored crack to the face. Bolt belay. **FA:** Unknown.

268. **Look Mom, No Hands** (5.6) Follow the crack to the face just right of *Look Mom, No Sweat,* on the right margin of the lighter rock. Bolt belay. **FA:** Unknown.

269. **Look Mom, No Brains** (5.7+) (R/X) ★ This is to the right of *Look Mom, No Hands.* Go up the face with buckets to a thin crack. Bolt belay. **FA:** Unknown.

270. **Look Mom, No Name** (5.7) ★ Start as for the last climb, but head up and right on a crack, then up the face, eventually working back left to the bolt belay. **FA:** Unknown.

Hidden Dome

Outward Bound Slab—Right End

This section of Outward Bound Slab lies about 200 feet right of the previous routes. A steeper slab with a left-facing dihedral/roof below and straight-in cracks above characterize this section of the formation.

271. **Quo Vadis** (5.6) The corner/ramp just left of *Mom for the Road*. **FA:** Bert Levy (?); 1/01.

272. **Mom for the Road** (5.7) ★ Go up the obvious left-facing corner to the roof, then up to the ledge. **Pro:** To 2.5 inches. **FA:** Alan Roberts, Todd Gordon; 1/89.

273. **One for the Road** (5.10a) ★ A finger crack just right of *Mom for the Road*. **Pro:** Thin to 2 inches. **FA:** Roger Linfield, Dennis Yates; 12/86.

274. **AC/DC** (5.8) The left-hand of two cracks that start off the ledge where the two previous routes end. Starts up a pillar to reach the crack. **Pro:** To 3 inches. **FA:** Alan Bartlett, Cathy McCullough; 1/95.

275. **Tres Fun** (5.10a) ★ The right-hand handcrack above *One for the Road*. **Pro:** To 3 inches. **FA:** Brian Elliott, Cyndie Elliott; 1988.

The Financial Wall

The Financial Wall faces northwest and lies to the south of Outward Bound Slab. Park at the Northern Wonderland parking area (on Park Boulevard 6.4 miles from the West Entrance; 2.2+ miles from the Intersection Rock/Real Hidden Valley intersection). Hike nearly 1 mile northeast on the North Wonderland Trail. At this point, the trail will join up with a larger trail (a former dirt road) heading straight north. An unused road/trail (the Old Trail) heads straight south from here (there is a sign indicating it is closed). The Financial Wall is reached by taking the Old Trail south for about 100+ yards, then angling southeast into an open valley. The Financial Wall faces northeast and is located on a formation in the southern side of the valley. Keep angling southeast until you see a dark overhanging northeast face that contains numerous left-slanting cracks. This is the Financial Wall. You can also reach this area from Parking Lot Rocks by walking north on the Old Trail, then heading right into the valley. It is shady most of the day. Map, page 104.

276. **Taxed to the Limit** (5.12a) ★★ Start at a level area at the base and climb left-slanting thin cracks near the left side of the wall. **Pro:** Many thin to 2 inches. **FA:** Herb Laeger, Bob Yoho; 2/86.

277. **High Interest** (5.11a) ★★★ Starting at a level spot at the base, head up a left-slanting handcrack just right of *Taxed to the Limit;* traverse right about halfway up, then finish up the leftmost of two parallel cracks. **Pro:** To 3 inches. **FA:** Herb Laeger, Bob Yoho; 2/86.

278. **The Speculator** (5.11d) ★ This route follows the obvious central crack. Start off rocks, then move right into the crack. It finishes up just right of the top of *High Interest* in a body slot. **Pro:** Thin to 3 inches. **FA:** Herb Laeger, Bob Yoho; 2/86.

279. **Project** This four-bolt project is found up the center of the wall.

280. **The Crash** (5.12c) ★★ Begin about 30 feet right of *The Speculator. The Crash* follows the left-leaning corner with a fixed pin to a finger crack. **Pro:** Thin to 2 inches. **FA:** Herb Laeger, Bob Yoho; 2/86.

281. **Higher Yield** (5.10d) ★★ Start about 10 feet right of *The Crash.* Climb the thin crack (fixed pin) up and left to cracks/flakes above. **Pro:** To 3 inches. **FA:** Herb Laeger, Eve Laeger, Rich Perch; 11/86.

282. **Capital Gains** (5.8) ★ Climb the crack system about 8 feet right of *Higher Yields.* **Pro:** To 2.5 inches. **FA:** Alan Bartlett, Rosanne Gillmore; 4/95.

The Backstreets

Approach as for the Financial Wall (page 107). The Backstreets lie about 135 yards behind and left (south) of the Financial Wall. The only known route is on the northeast face. It is shady most of the day. The rock and route are not shown. Not shown on map.

283. **Just a Skosh** (5.10a) This route is the left of a break in the east face. Climb over a small slanting roof, then continue up a more moderate crack. **Pro:** To 2.5 inches. **FA:** Don Wilson, Karen Wilson; 4/86.

The Convenience Store

Approach as for Outward Bound Slab and the Financial Wall (page 104). Walk past (to the left of) the Financial Wall, then into a small wash along the base of the hillside. Follow this until you head left (east) up to the high point/highest formation in a rocky gully. Look for a pointed formation (in profile) near the top right of the gully. The Convenience Store is a northwest-facing rock on your right as you reach the top of the gully (the routes are hidden until you reach it). You can also reach this area from Parking Lot Rocks by walking north on the Old Trail, then heading right into the valley. Maps, page 104 and 114.

284. **Corn Dog** (5.9) This is on the northeast face (around the corner from *Big Gulp*). Begin up a steep finger crack. **Pro:** To 2.5 inches. **FA:** Alan Bartlett, Rob Stockstill; 2/98.

285. **Big Gulp** (5.10a) This is on the northwest face, to the left of a chimney. Go up a handcrack, then head right to a wide crack to a dihedral. **Pro:** To 3+ inches. **FA:** Rob Stockstill, Alan Bartlett; 2/98.

286. **Twinkies** (5.8) This route lies on the right side of the northwest face. Go up discontinuous cracks on the slab/face. **Pro:** To 2.5 inches. **FA:** Alan Bartlett, Rob Stockstill; 2/98.

Keys Point

Keys Point lies on the highest point of the hillside to the right (southeast) of Outward Bound Slab. It lies left (north) of the Convenience Store. Approach as for Outward Bound Slab (pages 104 and 105). Walk past (to the right of) Outward Bound Slab, then up the second drainage/gully to that formation's right. Continue up the gully until you reach its top; the Keys Point formation is to your right at the top of the hill. Alternatively, you can head up and left from near the base of the Convenience Store to reach Keys Point. Routes are located on the northwest and southern faces. Maps, pages 104 and 114.

Descents: From top of *The Key Hole* to *The Key Knob,* rappel off a large block and down the face to the right of *The Key Knob.* From the top of *Steeper Than It Looks,* head left to rap slings on a block. From *Broken Plates* and *Cheap Earthenware,* rap from slings atop the routes.

Keys Point—Northwest Face

Routes are described from left to right (from the highest point of the cliff to the right/downhill). The face is shady most of the day, with some afternoon sun.

287. **The Key Hole** (5.4) Begin on the high left side of the northwest face, heading up an easy right-facing crack to a large ledge. Go right, then back left to another ledge. Finish up the chimney/tunnel. **Pro:** To 2 inches, slings. **FA:** Wendell Smith, Ed Gardner, Dean Tower, Tom Martin, Elizabeth Ying; 1998.

288. **The Key Crack** (5.10b) (TR) Begin about 15 feet right of *The Key Hole.* Go up a hand-and-fist crack (5.9) to a platform, then up a thin left-facing corner. Could be led (perhaps with a thin pin). **FA:** Dean Tower, Ed Gardner, Wendell Smith, Tom Martin, Elizabeth Ying; 11/98.

289. The Super Key (5.9+) ★★ Begin down and right of *The Key Crack*. Go up a dark triangular face past two bolts, then up the chimney to two-bolt anchor/rap. **Pro:** Medium gear. **FA:** Wendell Smith, Ed Gardner, Dean Tower; 1/99.

290. The Key Knob (5.6) (R/X) Go up the face around and right of *The Super Key*. A single knob that can be slung provides the only pro until you reach a crack near the top. **Pro:** Slings; to 3 inches. **FA:** Ed Gardner, Wendell Smith, Dean Tower; 1/99.

291. Steeper Than It Looks (5.7) ★★ This route begins about 25 yards down and right of the last routes. It lies on a face that appears to be low-angled with a crack that begins at a horizontal. Go up the face to a crack, then up this to a hole and face past a bolt. **Pro:** To 2 inches. **FA:** Wendell Smith, Ed Gardner, Dean Tower; 1/99.

Keys Point—South Face

This is the lowest section of the formation. It is sunny most of the day.

292. Broken Plates (5.8) (TR) This and the next route lie on the wide face at the far right end of the formation. Begin just above a pinyon pine. Loose and probably not worth climbing. **FA:** Wendell Smith, Ed Gardner, Dean Tower, Tom Martin, Elizabeth Ying, Ed Rivera; 11/98.

293. Cheap Earthenware (5.7) Go up the right-facing corner at the right side of the face; this begins directly behind the pinyon pine. **Pro:** To 2 inches. **FA:** Wendell Smith, Ed Gardner, Dean Tower, Tom Martin, Elizabeth Ying, Ed Rivera; 11/98.

The Looking Glass

This formation lies immediately northwest of Keys Point, straddling the high point of the hillside. Its southwestern exposure is rather small, broken, and unimpressive, but the northeast face is considerably larger and has possibilities for several good climbs other than those described here.

The Looking Glass—Southwest Face

For the southwest face, approach as for Keys Point. From the vicinity of *The Key Crack* and *The Super Key* (routes 288 and 289), head left across the gully/boulders for about 50 yards, and into a narrow corridor between a large boulder and a small face. The sole route recorded begins out of the west end of this corridor. It is sunny most of the day. Map, page 104.

293A. Double Stem (5.11c) ★★ Stem between the boulder and the main face until you can barely reach into a thin crack that begins about 15 feet above the ground. Climb this to the top. **Pro:** Thin cams to 2 inches. **FA:** Tom Murphy, Ben Craft, and Randy Vogel; 1/05.

The Looking Glass—Northeast Face

For the northeast face, approach as for Keys Point. From the vicinity of *The Key Crack* (route 288), head over the crest of the notch between Keys Point and the Looking Glass's southwest side. Head down boulders until you can angle left (north) to the base of the crag. It is distinguished by a large, slabby-looking face bordered on the left side by a nice right-slanting, hand-size crack *(Through the Looking Glass)* and on the right by a very thin parallel crack.

Alternatively, approach as for Outward Bound Slab (page 105), but continue past it until you can head up the largest drainage/gully to that formation's right. When you get near the ridge, head right (uphill), then down the eastern side of the hill. The face is on your left. It gets some morning sun and is shady most of the day. Map, page 104.

293B. Through the Looking Glass (5.10b) ★★★ Go up the right-leaning handcrack on the left side of the slabby face. **Pro:** To 3 inches. **FA:** Ben Craft, Tom Murphy, Jeff Clapp; 12/04.

293C. Pain Is an Emotion (5.10c) ★★ This route lies about 60 yards right of *Through the Looking Glass* on a more broken section of rock/face. Go up a thin finger crack through two tiers, with the crux down low, on the left side of the face. **Pro:** Thin to 2.5 inches. **FA:** Tom Murphy, Ben Craft, Jeff Clapp; 12/04.

Greenhorn Dome

This formation lies on the eastern side of the series of hills containing Keys Point, Outward Bound Slab, the Looking Glass, etc. It overlooks a wash/valley that runs north toward Jones and Smith Rocks in the Middle Kingdom. Although you can reach this formation by heading several hundred yards south from Smith Rock along the wash, it is easier to approach as for Outward Bound Slab (page 105). Continue past Outward Bound Slab until you can head up the largest drainage/gully to that formation's right. When you get to the top of the ridge (a somewhat flat area), you can see the western side of Greenhorn Dome (Greenhorn Alley area) up and slightly to your right (east). Map, page 104.

Greenhorn Dome—West Face (aka Greenhorn Alley)

A fairly narrow gully on the western side of Greenhorn Dome runs uphill in a southerly direction along the base. The following routes all lie on this face, either starting from the toe of the formation or out of the gully. Descend to the right (south) side. The face gets morning shade and is sunny in the afternoon. Map, page 104.

293D. Ignorance Is Bliss (5.10b) ★★ Begin just right of the lowest point (toe) of the west face. Go up the right-leaning crack to a long move where it gets thin. Above, pass the wide crack on the left; follow the edge to the top. **Pro:** Very small brass to 2.5 inches. **FA:** Jeff Clapp, Tom Murphy, Ben Craft; 12/04.

293E. Directionally Challenged (5.10c) ★★ Begin uphill from *Ignorance Is Bliss,* in the gully. Go up the face past a bolt to a very wide crack. Move over the roof to a very thin crack that is roughly followed to the top. **Pro:** Thin to 2.5 inches. **FA:** Tom Murphy, Randy Vogel, Ben Craft; 1/05.

293F. Southern Progression (5.10d) ★★★ Begin about 15 feet right of the previous climb. Go up a flake to a ledge; continue up a thin-hands crack that slants left. **Pro:** To 2 inches. **FA:** Ben Craft, Tom Murphy, Jeff Clapp; 12/04.

293G. Insignificance (5.9) This route begins just east (back) of and a bit down from the point where *Ignorance Is Bliss* and *Directionally Challenged* end. This is a short handcrack on the right wall of a chimney. **Pro:** To 2.5 inches. **FA:** Tom Murphy, Jeff Clapp, Ben Craft; 12/04.

Tom Murphy on the first ascent of A Tenuous Balance *(5.11 b/c) on the east face of Greenhorn Dome.*

Greenhorn Dome—East Face

The eastern side of Greenhorn Dome over-looks the valley/wash that heads north toward the Middle Kingdom. A very promi-nent roof caps the steep face. Descent either down a chimney on the eastern side or down slabs on the southern side. The face gets morning sun and is shady all afternoon. Map, page 104.

293H. **A Tenuous Balance** (5.11b/c) ★★★
Begin up a wide crack/flake to a ledge with loose blocks. Go up and right to the arête and right side of the roof. Above, follow a right-diagonalling thin crack to a ledge, then up a corner to the top. **Pro:** Thin cams to 2.5 inches (optional 3 to 4 inches for the bottom crack). **FA:** Tom Murphy, Ben Craft, Randy Vogel; 1/05.

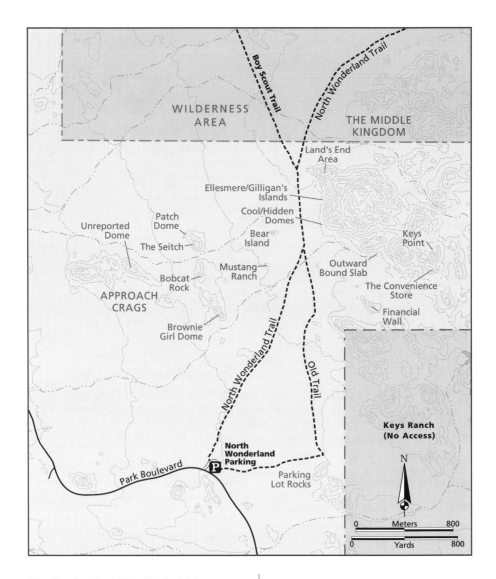

COOL DOME – HIDDEN DOME GULLY AREA

This area consists of several formations that lie adjacent to a gully on the hillside just north of Outward Bound Slab, just east of where the North Wonderland Trail meets the Old Trail. Park at the Northern Wonderland parking area (on Park Boulevard 6.4 miles from the West Entrance and 2.2+ miles from the Intersection Rock/Real Hidden Valley intersection). Hike about 1 mile northeast on the North Wonderland Trail. At this point, it joins a larger trail (a former dirt road) heading straight north; you are below a large hillside with many rock formations. Head east into a gully that leads up to the right of Cool Dome. Cool Dome, Not So Cool

Dome, Libido Rock, and Boomtown lie on the left side of the gully as you ascend. Warm Dome and Hidden Dome lie on its right. Map, page 114.

Peril Rock

This whitish face lies to the left of the approach gully and left of Cool Dome. A large dead tree is below the center of the face.

294. **Finger in a Blender** (5.9) ★★ Go up the face past three bolts to a small ledge, then up and right past two more bolts. Belay at the anchor atop *Women in Peril*. **Pro:** To 2.5 inches. **FA:** Bob Gaines, Todd Gordon, Tucker Tech, F. Laney.

295. **Women in Peril** (5.9) ★★ Climb near the center of the face and cracks. Five bolts. **Pro:** To 2.5 inches; two-bolt anchor. **FA:** Todd Gordon, Tucker Tech; 12/02.

296. **The Booger Man** (5.10a) ★★ The right-most route goes up the crack and face with five bolts; two-bolt anchor. **Pro:** To 2.5 inches. **FA:** Todd Gordon, Tucker Tech; 12/02.

Cool Dome

Cool Dome is on the left side of the gully as you approach from the North Wonderland Trail/Old Trail junction. Cool Dome is the first formation on your left as you head up the gully. Map, page 114.

Cool Dome Pinnacle

This small pinnacle of rock lies on the northwestern flank of Cool Dome. It is obvious as you look at the dome from the vicinity of the junction of the North Wonderland Trail and the Old Trail.

297. **South Arête** (5.?) (not shown on photo) One rusty quarter-inch bolt protects this route. **FA:** Unknown.

Cool Dome—West and South Faces

The west face is shady in the morning, sun in the afternoon. The south face *(Bedtime For Democracy)* receives sun most of the day.

298. **Trash Talk** (5.9) (R) This is 25 feet left of *Bank Note Blues*. **Pitch 1:** Go up a corner with a roof, then up and left on plates and cracks to belay below the headwall. **Pitch 2:**

Go up and right into the slot. **Pro:** To 3 inches. **FA:** Alan Bartlett, Doe DeRoss; 1/94.

299. **Bank Note Blues** (5.9) This route follows the obvious off-width starting with steep twin cracks in a right-facing dihedral. **Pro:** To 4+ inches. **FA:** Alan Roberts, Todd Gordon; 12/85.

300. **Bedtime for Democracy** (5.10b) ★★ This route follows a right-slanting crack on the southwest face of Cool Dome. It is reached via a traverse left from the top of a ramp/corner. **Pro:** Two bolts; two fixed pins; thin to 2.5 inches. **FA:** Tom Addison, Scott Pond; 3/87.

Cool Dome—Northeast Face

To reach this face, go up the gully, past the south face, until you can head left over boulders into a corridor. The left wall of the corridor is Cool Dome's northeast face. It gets some morning sun and shade for the rest of the day. These routes are not pictured.

301. **Take the Money and Run** (5.9) (TR) Begin up the brown, right-facing corner 15 feet left of *Stardust Memories,* then go up the thin seam. **FA:** Todd Swain; 2/98.

302. **Love and Death** (5.9+) (TR) This route starts up a short finger crack to an arête left of *Bananas.* **FA:** Todd Swain; 2/98.

303. **Bananas** (5.9) Begin as for *Stardust Memories,* then move left into an obvious dihedral that is followed to top. **Pro:** Thin to 2 inches. **FA:** Todd Swain; 2/98.

304. **Stardust Memories** (5.9+) ★ This is the face with five bolts on the left side of the wall. Two-bolt anchor/rap (difficult to pull rope). **FA:** Troy Mayr, Steve Anderson, Ed Hunsaker, Steve Axthelm; 2/88.

305. **Boundaries** (5.10c) (TR) This is the face to the right of *Stardust Memories.* **FA:** Al Swanson; 4/96.

306. **Too Silly to Climb** (5.5) Ascend the left-facing dihedral just right of *Stardust Memories*. **FA:** Tom Addison, Scott Pond; 3/87.

307. **Finger Stacks or Plastic Sacks** (5.10b) This is to the right and around the corner from *Too Silly to Climb*. Go up double thin cracks to the face, staying left of a tree. **Pro:** Thin to 2 inches. **FA:** Tom Addison, Scott Pond; 3/87.

308. **Rickets and Scurvy** (5.10a) ★ Two slanting thin cracks are to the right (and through the "notch") from the last climb. Go up the right crack, then switch to the left. **Pro:** To 2 inches. **FA:** Troy Mayr, Steve Anderson, Steve Axthelm; 2/88.

309. **Cool Crack** (5.10a) ★ Start as for *Rickets and Scurvy,* but stay in the right crack to the top. **Pro:** To 2 inches. **FA:** Alan Bartlett, Stephanie Bussell; 4/95.

Not So Cool Dome

To reach this dome, go up gully, past the south face of Cool Dome, until you can head left over boulders into a corridor. The right wall of the corridor (opposite the wall holding the last climbs) is Not So Cool Dome's western face. The climbs get shade in the morning and some afternoon sun. The routes are not shown.

310. **Mussel Beach** (5.11a) (TR) Begin 20 feet left of *Clamming at the Beach*. Go up the face to the obvious crack. **FA:** Todd Swain; 2/98.

311. **Clamming at the Beach** (5.9) ★ This 3-inch crack is on the right end of the wall, roughly opposite *Stardust Memories*. **Pro:** To 3+ inches. **FA:** Tom Addison, Scott Pond; 3/87.

Warm Dome

This small pointed rock lies on the right (south) side of the approach gully, up from and opposite the south face of Cool Dome. The following climb lies on Warm Dome's south face (the opposite side from the gully). The route is pictured on page 115. Map, page 114.

312. **Baffin Crack** (5.8) ★ This is a steep crack on a juggy face. **Pro:** To 2.5 inches. **FA:** Dave Haber, Sheryl Haber; 12/92.

Hidden Dome

This formation lies high up and on the right (northeast-facing) side of the gully you ascend to Cool Dome. See page 114 for approach directions. Routes are described right to left. Map, page 114.

Hidden Dome—Northeast Face

This is shady most of the day.

313. **Calgary Stampede** (5.8) ★★ Climb the farthest left crack up to right-facing corner. **Pro:** To 3 inches. **FA:** Alan Roberts, Pete Charkin, Bruce Howatt; 1985.

314. **Tucson Bound** (5.8) ★★★ This is just right of *Calgary Stampede*. Ascend a thin crack to face climbing. **Pro:** Thin to 1.5 inches. **FA:** Todd Gordon, Alan Roberts; 12/85.

315. **The Screaming Woman** (5.10a) (R) ★★★ Just left of the corner of the rock, go up the crack, right to another crack, then to a face past one bolt. You can also start with *The Screaming Poodle*. **Pro:** Thin to 2 inches; one bolt. **FA:** Dave Evans, Jim Angione, Herb Laeger, Dave Bruckman; 12/86.

316. The Screaming Poodle (5.10c) ★★ Begin behind a tree and to the right of the corner of the rock. Go up cracks then up the face past one bolt. **Pro:** Thin to 2.5 inches. **FA** (TR): Unknown. **FA** (Lead): Kevin Daniels; 1994.

317. Too Secret to Find (5.10b) ★★★ The obvious long, straight crack. **Pro:** To 3 inches. **FA:** Pete Charkin, Alan Roberts, Bruce Howatt; 1985.

318. Balance Due (5.10c) ★★★ Just right of *Too Secret To Find*. Climb thin cracks to the face to cracks. **Pro:** Thin to 2.5 inches; two bolts. **FA:** Herb Laeger, Dave Evans, Dave Bruckman; 12/86.

319. Screaming Cactus (5.7+) (R) Fist/off-width to a chimney. **Pro:** To 5+ inches. **FA:** Todd Gordon, Tony Sartin, Chris Dillon; 1993.

320. Major Creative Effort (5.10a/b) ★ Begin on ledges to the right of *Screaming Cactus*. Climb a thin hands crack to a slab. **Pro:** To 2.5 inches. **FA:** Greg Murphy, Dave Houghton; 2/87.

Hidden Dome—Southwest Face

This is behind and right of *Clamming at the Beach* on Not So Cool Dome. The routes are not shown.

321. Iranian Party Hat (5.6) Dogleg splitter (obvious from below). **Pro:** To 3 inches. **FA:** Todd Gordon, Tucker Tech, Chris Gorky; 2/03.

322. Ass Gasket (5.10a) ★ On the right side of the buttress to right of the *Too Secret to Find* buttress. Pass three bolts, then traverse left to *Iranian Hat Party*. (Would go up with more bolts). **FA:** Todd Gordon, Tucker Tech, Chris Gorky; 2/03.

Libido Rock

This formation lies on the left side of the gully roughly opposite Hidden Dome. See page 114 for approach information. The routes are not shown.

323. Between the Living and the Dead (5.9) (R) This three-bolt slab route is on the southwest face of Libido Rock. **Pro:** To 2.5 inches. **FA:** Walt Shipley, Roy McClenahan; 1987.

324. Too Steep to Climb (5.11b) ★ This is on the southeast side of Libido Rock, around and right of the previous climb. Begin off the left side of the ledge. Face climb past three bolts. **Pro:** To 2.5 inches. **FA:** Walt Shipley, Roy McClenahan; 1987.

325. Cool Jerk (5.10d) Begin on the right side of the ledge, to the right of the last route. **Pro:** To 2.5 inches, 1 bolt. **FA:** Roy McClenahan, Walt Shipley; 1987.

Boomtown

This rock is located across the gully from Hidden Dome, just right of Libido Rock. See page 114 for approach information. Routes are shown on the photo on page 116.

326. Chuckwagon (5.8) ★ A thin crack/corner in the middle of the face. **Pro:** Very thin to 3 inches. **FA:** Bob Gaines, Yvonne Gaines; 3/00.

327. Charley Horse (5.10a) (TR) ★ Begin at *Chuckwagon,* then move left out the undercling flake, over a bulge about 10 feet left of *Chuckwagon.* **FA:** Bob Gaines, Yvonne Gaines; 3/00.

ELLESMERE ISLAND— GILLIGAN'S ISLAND AREAS

These two areas lie on the western flank of the large hillside to the east of the North Wonderland Trail. Park at the Northern Wonderland parking area (on Park Boulevard 6.4 miles from the West Entrance and 2.2+ miles from the Intersection Rock/Real Hidden Valley intersection). Hike about 1 mile northeast on the North Wonderland Trail. At this point, it will join up with a larger trail (a former dirt road) heading straight north. You are below a large hillside with many rock formations. Continue north on the North Wonderland Trail for about 200 yards. The numerous rocks on the hillside to your right are Ellesmere Island. To reach Gilligan's Island, continue about 200 yards farther north; the area consists of two large slabby formations and a smaller formation down and right (the actual Gilligan's Island). Map, page 114.

Ellesmere Island

Ellesmere Island consists of many fairly small crags, rocks, and large boulders that lie on the hillside just east of the North Wonderland Trail. Routes have north, northwest, and/or western aspects and either have shade or see sun most of the afternoon.

Linden–Frost Rock

This slightly overhanging brown block lies directly above Baby Roof Rock. It faces north.

328. **The Linden–Frost Effect** (5.12a) This left-slanting thin finger crack lies on the north face just right of a chimney. **Pro:** Thin to 1.5 inches. **FA:** Robert Alexander, Curt Green; 4/89.

Baby Roof Rock

This rock is characterized by a small roof with a crack on either end about 20 feet up. It faces northwest and west. Descend off to the right.

329. **El Smear or Land** (5.11a) (R) Climb the face left of the roof (*Baby Roof*) past two bolts. **FA:** Andy Brown, Kelly Rhoads; 11/89.

330. **Left Overs** (5.7) (R) Take the thin crack to the roof, then go up the crack around the left side of the roof. **Pro:** Thin to 3 inches. **FA** (TR): Jeff Rhoads, Andy Brown; 11/89. **FA** (Lead): Unknown.

331. **Baby Roof** (5.7) ** Begin just right of *Left Overs*. Go up the crack to and then around the right side of the roof. **Pro:** To 2.5 inches. **FA:** Alan Roberts, Pete Charkin, Bruce Howatt; 1985.

332. **Gail Winds** (5.9) (X) * This is the face 15 feet right of *Baby Roof*. Bolts added after first ascent have been removed. **FA:** Roger Whitehead; 1985.

Baby Face Slab

This is the small face up gully and right from Baby Roof Rock. Rappel from a dead tree (50 feet). The slab faces west.

333. **Baby Face** (5.7) Go up cracks on the left, then up and right on the face past two bolts. **Pro:** To 2 inches. **FA:** John Thackray, Todd Swain; 3/87.

Math Rock

This rock lies directly to the right and some-what in front of Baby Roof Rock. The first three routes end on the highest, left-hand part of the rock; the others are on the lower right-hand summit. Routes face northwest and west.

334. Geometry (5.11a/b) ★ Begin in front of *Baby Face*. Follow a thin crack over a small roof, then go up the face above. **Pro:** Thin to 2 inches. **FA:** Robert Alexander, Eric Fogel, Nick Beer, Ruth Galler; 10/86.

335. Aftermath (5.10a) ★★ Just right of *Geometry* and behind a small pillar. Go up a thin to hands crack, then up and right through two roofs. **Pro:** To 2.5 inches. **FA:** Pete Charkin, Alan Roberts, Bruce Howatt; 1985.

336. Math (5.9) Go up a wide crack to a chimney, beginning off a small block 20 feet right of *Aftermath*. **Pro:** To 3+ inches. **FA:** Robert Alexander, Eric Fogel; 10/86.

337. Foreign Legion (5.10b) ★★ This thin crack begins just right of *Math*. **Pro:** Thin to 2 inches. **FA:** Pete Charkin, Alan Roberts, Bruce Howatt, Shane Swaine; 1985.

338. The Houdini Arête (5.11c) (TR) ★ The face and arête just right of the thin crack of *Foreign Legion*. **FA:** Troy Mayr, John Mallery, Bob Gaines; 1/88.

339. The Great Escape (5.11d) (R) ★★ Follow the left-facing corner to the roof. **Pro:** Many thin to 1.5 inches. **FA:** Bill Meyers; 1985.

340. Made in the Shade (5.9) This is the crack behind the pine tree, right of *The Great Escape*. **Pro:** To 2 inches. **FA:** Bill Meyers; 1985.

341. **Fun in the Sun** (5.9) (TR) Climb the face above the boulder just right of last two climbs. **FA:** Todd Swain, John Thackray; 3/87.

342. **Fright Night** (5.4) Easy crack on face. **FA:** Todd Swain; 3/87.

Napoleon Block

This large boulder lies directly below *Fun in the Sun* and *Fright Night*. Approach from atop *Arms Are for Hugging,* or tunnel through boulders to the right of that route. It faces west.

343. **Able Was I Ere I Saw Ellesmere** (5.7) This is the curving crack on the block below *Fright Night*. Best approached from below and right. **Pro:** To 2.5 inches. **FA:** Randy Vogel, Darrel Hensel, Alan Roberts; 1/86.

Antiwar Block

This square-ish block lies low down on the hillside, below Math Rock and Napoleon Block. The route is on northwest arête.

344. **Arms Are for Hugging** (5.11a/b) ★★★ Go up the left arête past four bolts. Two-bolt anchor. **FA:** Todd Battey, Dave Stahl, Tom Burke, Rob Stahl; 2/87.

Floe Rock

This rock lies about 85 feet right of Antiwar Block. The following routes lie on the north side of the rock, on the right side of a small gully. It is shady most of the day. The routes are not shown.

345. **Lip Service** (5.9) Climb the crack in the right-facing corner near the top of the gully. **Pro:** To 2.5 inches. **FA:** Alan Bartlett, Tom Burke; 5/96.

346. **Go with the Floe** (5.9+) This is the left-slanting crack right and below *Lip*

Service. At the top, you can either go right and up or take the left-slanting traverse crack (original line). **Pro:** To 3.5 inches. **FA:** Pete Charkin, Alan Roberts, Bruce Howatt; 1985.

Gilligan's Island

Gilligan's Island lies about 200 yards north of Ellesmere Island, on the same hillside east of the North Wonderland Trail. It consists of two large slabby formations (Ginger's Face and Mary Ann's Face) and a smaller formation down and right (the actual "Gilligan's Island"). Most of these routes face west and see sun all afternoon. See page 120 for approach instructions. Map, page 114.

Ginger's Face

This is the left-hand large slabby formation. It faces west.

347. **Ginger's Crack** (5.10c/d) ★ This short (20+ feet), overhanging handcrack in a right-facing corner lies about 50 feet down and left of Ginger's Face among the boulders. **Pro:** To 3 inches. **FA:** Unknown.

348. **Little Buddy** (5.9) This route lies on the short steep wall on the far left side of Ginger's Face. Climb a face to a right-slanting crack. **Pro:** To 3 inches. **FA:** Bob Gaines, Yvonne Gaines; 2/99.

349. **Through the Looking Glass** (5.8) ★ (not shown on photo) Go up a flake to a face past four bolts. **Pro:** Thin to 2 inches; 80-foot rappel from slings. **FA:** Bob Gaines, Patty Kline; 2/99.

350. **Guns for Nuns** (5.10a) (TR) Toprope the face just left of *Gun For The Sun*. **FA:** Dick Peterson, Mary Hinson, Todd Swain; 11/96.

351. **Gun for the Sun** (5.9) ★★ Go up the center of the slab, from flakes to face. **Pro:** To 3 inches; two bolts. Rappel from slings atop *Through the Looking Glass* (80 feet). **FA:** Jack Marshall, Don Wilson, Karen Wilson; 3/88.

352. **As the Wind Blows** (5.7) ★★ Follow a left-leaning crack to a left-facing corner. **Pro:** To 2.5 inches; one bolt. **FA:** Unknown.

353. **Tapeworm** (5.3) (R) This route starts in the gully about 30 feet below the diamond shaped chockstone guarding access to Mary Ann's Face. Go up and left to reach a dike system that is followed up to an easy face and cracks. End just left of *Chocolate Decadence.* **FA:** Todd Gordon.

354. **Chocolate Decadence** (5.7) Tunnel under the large diamond chockstone to reach this route on the right side of Ginger's Face. This is the dogleg left-facing dihedral. **Pro:** To 2.5 inches. **FA:** Karen Wilson, Julie White; 3/88.

Mary Ann's Face

This is the right-hand large slabby formation. All the routes are reached by tunneling under a large diamond-shaped chockstone in the gully between this formation and Ginger's Face to the left.

355. **GJOA** (5.9) Start on the first 20 feet of *Northwest Passage,* then climb a flake to a crack and past a roof formed by a huge block. **Pro:** To 2.5 inches. **FA:** Todd Swain; 10/90.

356. **Northwest Passage** (5.10a) ★★ Climb past four bolts (the last with no hanger) on an arête 50 feet left of *Route 66*. **Pro:** 3 to 4 inches for anchor. **FA:** Todd Swain, Patty Furbush; 10/90.

357. **Ape Man Hop** (5.10a) ★★ Begin from boulders up and right of *Northwest Passage*. Go up the face past a bolt to cracks in a corner, then up the face past a second bolt. **Pro:** To 3 inches. **FA:** Ron White, Jack Marshall, Don Wilson, Karen Wilson; 3/88.

358. **Route 66** (5.4) ★ Go up the obvious curving hand-to-fist crack up the slab. **Pro:** To 3.5 inches. **FA:** Unknown.

359. **Hit It Ethel** (5.8) ★★ Begin about 30 feet right of *Route 66*. Go up the flake/corner then up and right past a small roof to a face past three bolts. Rap 100 feet from slings. **Pro:** To 3 inches. **FA:** Don Wilson, Karen Wilson, Jack Marshall; 3/88.

Gilligan's Island Crag

This is the actual "Gilligan's Island" crag. It is the small formation (large block) located below and right of the Ginger and Mary Ann Face slabs. It is mostly sunny in the afternoon.

360. **River Phoenix** (5.9) ★ Begin on the left side of the block. Go up left-slanting thin cracks to a face with two bolts. **Pro:** Thin to 2 inches. **FA:** Todd Gordon, George Armstrong; 10/93.

361. **Roomis E. Gloomis** (5.10d) ★★★ Begin just right of the "corner" of the crag, at its lowest point. Go up the face past five bolts. **Pro:** To 2 inches for anchor. **FA:** Dave Evans, Jim Angione; 1/94.

362. **Lovey (aka Whale of a Time)** (5.8+) ★★ Begin right and up from *Roomis E. Gloomis*.

Go up past a bolt to a curving flake/crack; finish up the face. **Pro:** Thin to 2 inches. **FA:** Dave Wonderly, Jack Marshall, Jennifer Wonderly; 1/88.

363. **Teddy** (5.9) ★★ Start at *G. H. B.* but head up and left, over a roof, to a face past two bolts. **Pro:** To 2 inches. **FA:** Dave Wonderly, Jack Marshall, Jennifer Wonderly; 1/88.

364. **G. H. B.** (5.10a) Begin on the right side of the block. Go up a right leaning crack through flare/chimney. **Pro:** To 3+ inches. **FA:** Todd Gordon, George Armstrong; 10/93.

Techno Block

This small dark-colored rock lies up and right of Gilligan's Island Crag and right of Mary Ann's Face. Approach from the right of Gilligan's Island Crag.

365. **Teckno Sporran** (5.9) The right-leaning crack. **Pro:** To 2.5 inches. **FA:** George Armstrong, Todd Gordon; 10/93.

Vulture's Roost

Easy Buttress

The Shady Spot

366

367

368

370

369

371

LAND'S END AREA

This small area lies just north and around the corner from Gilligan's Island. The various formations lie in or adjacent to a rock-filled canyon/gully on the northern end of the hillside hosting Cool and Hidden Domes, Ellesmere Island, and Gilligan's Island. Approach as for Gilligan's Island (see page 120), and walk farther north on the North Wonderland Trail until you can head right around the end of the hillside. Three crags are found in this area: the Shady Spot, Easy Buttress, and Vulture's Roost. The right side of the gully has a steep wall with several discontinuous cracks (the Shady Spot). The left side of the gully is bordered by a low-angled slab (Easy Buttress). Above and left of Easy Buttress, on the rocky hillside, is a small crag with a left-slanting crack *(Vulture's Roost).* Maps, pages 114 and 127.

The Shady Spot

This formation lies on the right side of the gully (the backside of Gilligan's Island) and is the steep wall with several discontinuous cracks. It gets morning sun and shade in the afternoon.

366. **Landscape Crack** (5.11d) ★★ This route begins on a crack that heads up and right, then heads back up and left through a steep section. **Pro:** Several thin to 2 inches. **FA:** Mike Lechlinski et al.

367. **Land's End** (5.11b) ★ (TR) Begin up *Landscape Crack,* then after about 20 feet, head right to a crack that ends in a small right facing corner. **FA:** Mike Lechlinski et al.

Easy Buttress

This obvious low-angled slab lies on the left side of the gully and is broken by various cracks. It gets shade in the morning and sun in the afternoon.

368. **Easy Buttress, Left** (5.2) This and *Easy Buttress Right* lie on the left section of Easy Buttress. Climb the left side of this section via discontinuous cracks and large face holds. **Pro:** To 2 inches; one bolt anchor. **FA:** Unknown.

369. **Easy Buttress, Right** (5.3) (R) Begin about 12 feet right of the previous route. Go up the face to discontinuous cracks and face. **Pro:** To 2 inches; one bolt anchor. **FA:** Unknown.

370. **Poaching Grain** (5.7) This and the next climb are located on the grainy lower right section of Easy Buttress. This is the route on the left. Go up the face to two rounded flakes, then to a crack and face. **Pro:** To 2.5 inches. **FA:** Todd Swain.

371. **Nothing to Fear but Beer Itself** (5.7) The thin lieback to face climb just right of *Poaching Grain.* **Pro:** To 2 inches. **FA:** Dave Haber, Sheryl Haber; 9/94.

The Vulture's Roost

This formation lies about 175 yards above and right of Easy Buttress on the rocky hillside. The routes are not shown.

372. **Vulture's Roost** (5.9) Climb the most obvious left-slanting crack above a large flake to a ledge. **Pro:** To 2.5 inches. **FA:** Dennis Yates, Roger Linfield; 12/86.

373. **Forget It** (5.10b) (TR) This short thin crack in a corner lies left around the corner and below *Vulture's Roost.* **FA:** Tucker Tech; 1/98.

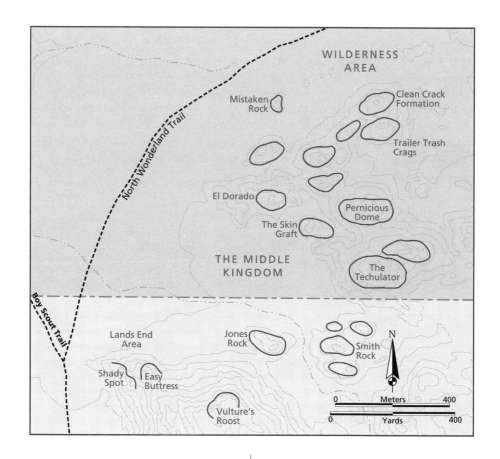

THE MIDDLE KINGDOM

The Middle Kingdom consists of several medium- to larger-size formations that lie on the more level plain just east of the North Wonderland Trail and north of Ellesmere Island/Gilligan's Island. There are a variety of routes, with the quality of both the rock and climbs varying from only fair to very good.

Park at the North Wonderland parking area, which is on Park Boulevard 6.4 miles from the West Entrance and 2.2+ miles from the Intersection Rock/Real Hidden Valley intersection. Hike about 1 mile northeast on the North Wonderland Trail. At this point, it will join up with a larger trail (a former dirt road) heading straight north; you are below a large hillside with many rock formations including Cool and Hidden Domes and Ellesmere and Gilligan's Islands. Continue north on the trail for several hundred yards to where hillside ends; at this point the Boy Scout Trail to Indian Cove heads off to the left (north). Don't take that trail! Instead, follow the North Wonderland Trail as it slowly curves to the northeast (right).

As you walk, you'll see various formations rising to the east (right); this is the Middle Kingdom area. The rest of the northern Wonderland of Rocks is reached by following the North Wonderland Trail to where it ends in a streambed/wash. The northernmost obvious formation in the Middle Kingdom is called El Dorado. It is a brown, square-shaped crag. The other formations are located in reference to El Dorado. Pernicious Dome is the large, rounded, brown dome southeast and back in a wash from El Dorado. The Techulator is a large complex formation that lies south of Pernicious Dome. Several other formations are located nearby. Maps, pages 114 and 127.

Wilderness Notice: All of the crags in the Middle Kingdom, with the exceptions of Smith Rock and Jones Rock, lie in designated wilderness. No new fixed anchors may be placed except by permit (see Introduction). Existing fixed anchors may be replaced on a one-for-one basis. See map (page 84) for the wilderness boundary.

Entering the long dihedral of Bighorn Dihedral *(5.10b/c).*

El Dorado (Wilderness)

El Dorado is the northwestern-most obvious formation in the Middle Kingdom. This brown, square-shaped crag lies about 0.3+ mile northeast of where the Boy Scout Trail leaves the North Wonderland Trail. From that junction, hike out the North Wonderland Trail about 400 yards, then head right (east) for about 350 yards directly to the formation. It is plainly visible from the North Wonderland Trail. Map, page 127.

El Dorado—Northwest Face

This face gets morning shade and some afternoon sun.

374. **Yet Another Cilley Toprope** (5.11c) (TR) This is the thin crack on the extreme left end of the northwest face. Begin by heading over a small roof. **FA:** Richard Cilley.

375. **Mary Decker** (5.11b) ★ (TR) Begin about 8 feet right of *Yet Another Cilley Toprope.* Go up the smooth face. **FA:** Kevin Powell, Darrel Hensel; 1/85.

376. **Zola Budd** (5.10d) ★ (TR) This route lies on the face to the right of *Mary Decker,* and left of the left-slanting crack of *Rob'n the Cradle.* Finish up a seam. **FA:** Alan Roberts, Kevin Powell, Tim Powell, Darrel Hensel; 1/85.

377. **Rob'n the Cradle** (5.10c) ★ The left-leaning crack just right of *Zola Budd.* Start left of the crack; climb the face up and right into it. Follow the crack to a horizontal break (meeting *Zola Budd* briefly). Go right, then up a thin crack. **Pro:** Thin to 4 inches. **FA:** Darrel Hensel, Alan Roberts, Greg Epperson; 12/85.

El Dorado—Southwest Face

This gets some morning shade but is sunny all day.

378. **Frank Shorter** (5.9) Scramble up to a ledge at the base of a large left-facing corner; climb the somewhat loose corner, the most obvious feature on southwest face. **Pro:** To 3 inches. **FA:** Unknown.

379. **Wide World of Sports** (5.10b/c) ★ Begin off the right side of the ledge at the base of *Frank Shorter.* Head up a crack through the overhang, then go up and right to a ledge. Above, follow the right-arching hand-to-fist crack. **Pro:** To 3.5 inches. **FA:** Alan Roberts, Kevin Powell, Tim Powell, Dan Ahlborn, Bobby Kessinger, Darrel Hensel; 1/85.

380. **Agony of Defeet** (5.8) (R) Go up the block, then the thin crack and flakes. Finish up and right. **Pro:** Thin to 2 inches. **FA:** Todd Swain; 9/90.

381. **Tucker's Tick List** (5.3) Begin right of *Agony of Defeet.* Go up easy cracks to a ledge on the right. **Pro:** 2.5 inches. **FA:** Tucker Tech; 1996.

Pernicious Dome

Pernicious Dome lies about 300 yards east of El Dorado and about 150 yards northeast of The Skin Graft; it is the large, rounded, brown dome. The best way to approach this crag is from the vicinity of El Dorado. From the junction of the North Wonderland Trail and the Boy Scout Trail, head north on the North Wonderland Trail for about 400 yards, then turn right (east), passing just south of El Dorado (350 yards). Continue eastward, crossing a wash, for another 300 yards to Pernicious Dome. All the recorded routes lie on the south face, which gets sun most of the day. Map, page 127.

382. **Undercling Bypass** (5.8) Go up the flake, then up and right under a roof. **Pro:** To 2.5 inches. **FA:** Dennis Yates, Roger Linfield; 12/86.

383. **Tail Gunner** (5.11b) ★★★ Begin behind a fallen block. Head up and right in a thin crack/roof/corner (fixed pins?), then go up onto the face above past five bolts. **Pro:** To 2 inches. **FA:** Don Wilson, Karen Wilson, Jack Marshall; 2/90.

384. **Gourmet Sausage** (5.7) ★ This is the small pillar right of *Tail Gunner*. Go up this past three bolts. Two-bolt anchor/rap. **FA:** Todd Gordon, Don Reid, Tucker Tech, Maggie Ross, Uri.

385. **A Little Bit of Magic** (5.10c) ★ Class 3 up a gully to the right of a pine tree. Climb the thin crack that heads up and right to the summit. **Pro:** Thin to 2 inches. **FA:** Roger Linfield, Dennis Yates; 12/86.

386. **Little Brown Jug** (5.7) This and the next climb begin off a ledge atop a block to the right of the gully where *A Little Bit of Magic* begins. Go up a left-arching flake to a straight-in crack. **Pro:** To 2 inches. **FA:** Vince Hernandez, Robert Alexander; 12/88.

387. Dreams of Red Rocks (5.7) Begin just right of *Little Brown Jug*. Go up a left-leaning crack to thin cracks above. **Pro:** Thin to 2 inches. **FA:** Dennis Yates, Roger Linfield; 12/86.

388. Margo's Cargo (5.7) Climb the face to the right of *Dreams of Red Rocks*. **FA:** Todd Swain, Margo Burnham; 1991.

The Skin Graft (Wilderness)

This formation lies about 250 yards southeast of El Dorado and about 150 yards southwest of Pernicious Dome. Its dark brown south face has a large ledge/ramp running along the bottom *(Melanoma)*. From the junction of the North Wonderland Trail and the Boy Scout Trail, head north on the North Wonderland Trail for about 300 yards, then turn right (east) toward this formation, which lies about 600+ yards off the North Wonderland Trail. This formation and its routes are not pictured. Map, page 127.

389. Etiquette Rex, the Well-Mannered Dog (5.8) (R) This route lies on the right end of the northeast face of the Skin Graft (facing Pernicious Dome). Climb up and left to a thin crack, then up the crack to a ledge with bushes. Downclimb right. **Pro:** Thin to 2 inches. **FA:** Chris Miller, Zach Shields, Don Reid, Alan Bartlett; 11/95.

390. Mission Bells (5.7) (R) Climb the low-angled southwest face/slab past two bolts. **Pro:** To 2 inches. **FA:** Todd Gordon, Cyndie Bransford, Steve Orr, Tony Sartin, Elizabeth Brogna, Fonzie; 3/93.

391. Melanoma (5.4) This route climbs the large right-slanting ramp/ledge on the formation's south side. Located about 60 feet right of *Mission Bells*. **Pro:** To 2 inches. **FA:** Todd Swain; 6/92.

392. Tanning Salon (5.7) This route lies about 90 feet right of *Melanoma*. It is a right-facing corner in dark rock. **Pro:** To 2 inches. **FA:** Dennis Yates, Roger Linfield; 12/86.

The Techulator (Wilderness)

The Techulator is the large massif about 100 yards south of Pernicious Dome, 100 yards southeast of the Skin Graft, and about 350 yards southeast of El Dorado. This large formation is easily seen to the east of the North Wonderland Trail just past its junction with the Boy Scout Trail. From that point, head more or less east for about 800 yards to south face of this formation. Map, page 127.

The Techulator—Upper Left End

393. Friendly Fists (5.9) ★ This short, left-arching corner with a fist crack, which then passes through a roof, is on the north face of the Techulator. To locate it, walk around the left end of the formation, then about a hundred yards along the north side of the formation. It faces the west face of Pernicious Dome. **Pro:** To 3.5 inches. **FA:** Roger Linfield, Dennis Yates; 12/86.

394. Hair Line (5.5) (not shown on photo) This route is on a short wall located on the upper left end of the southwest face of the Techulator. It is about 10 feet left of *High and Dry*. Go up and right on the face and very thin crack. **Pro:** Very thin to 1.5 inches. **FA:** Craig Fry; 1985.

395. High and Dry (aka Short but Flared) (5.10b/c) ★ Go up the thin crack in the flare. **Pro:** Thin to 2 inches. **FA:** Alan Roberts, Bill Meyers; 4/85.

The Techulator—Wane's Wall

Wane's Wall is a 60- to 80-foot north-facing huecoed wall in a very narrow corridor on the north side of the Techulator's summit. It has several vertical and overhanging cracks. The corridor looks across to a mushroom-shaped boulder. Two large boulders are wedged in the corridor: one near the lower right end and another near the upper left end of the wall. To reach Wane's Wall, head up toward *High and Dry,* then turn right and up into the narrowing gully/corridor. This wall is shady most of the day. Routes are indicated but not shown on the photo, and are described from left (far end) to right (near end). Map, page 127.

396. **Wren's Nest** (5.11a) (TR) ★ Begin down and left of the upper left-hand boulder. Go up and left on the overhanging face/corner/crack. **FA:** Craig Fry, Alan Roberts; 4/85.

397. **Red Eye** (5.9) (TR) Climb the steep, huecoed face about 12 feet right of *Wren's*

Nest; stay left of the upper boulder/chockstone. **FA:** Craig Fry, Alan Roberts; 4/85.

398. **Now We Know** (5.6) (R) Begin atop the lower, right-hand boulder/chockstone just left of a crack; up and left on the vertical, pocketed face. **Pro:** To 2 inches. **FA:** Robert Alexander, Vince Hernandez; 12/88.

399. **Two Bull Dykes in a Fistfight over the Privilege of Buying a Martini for a Whore** (5.9) (TR) Begin below and right of the lower right-hand boulder/chockstone. Head up, staying right of the chockstone. **FA:** Robert Alexander, Vince Hernandez; 12/88.

400. **The Human Mold** (5.10c) (TR) ★ Begin about 20 feet right of the lower right-hand boulder/chockstone, off a small rock. Head up the face, staying well left of *Jah Loo.* **FA:** Robert Alexander, Eric Fogel; 12/88.

401. **Jah Loo** (5.10c) ★★ Begin about 30 feet right of the lower right-hand boulder/chockstone. Go up the overhanging face left of the left-facing corner, then climb a right-arching crack to a hueco that resembles a

"human mold." **Pro:** Thin to 2 inches. **FA:** Craig Fry, Alan Roberts; 4/85.

402. Cubik's Molecule (5.11b) (TR) ★ Begin about 10 feet right of *Jah Loo*. Go up the overhanging face (variations possible). **FA:** Eric Fogel, Robert Alexander; 12/88.

403. Alexander's Salamander (5.10d) ★ An overhanging finger crack at the right end of the face; about 25 feet right of *Jah Loo*. **Pro:** Thin to 2 inches. **FA:** Robert Alexander 1/89.

The Techulator—Southwest and South Faces

The following routes lie on the southwest and south side of the Techulator. They are sunny most of the day. Routes 404 to 412 are shown on the photo; routes 413 to 415 are not shown. Map, page 127.

404. Science Experiments You Can Eat (5.10b) ★★ Begin on ledges on the left (west) edge of the Techulator. Go up discontinuous cracks on an arête, then up the face past two bolts. **FA:** Todd Gordon, Cyndie Bransford, Steve Orr; 3/95.

405. Muffin Bandits (5.10a/b) ★ Tunnel under blocks to reach the ledge at the base. Follow the thin crack into a left-facing corner. **Pro:** Thin to 2 inches. **FA:** Dennis Yates, Roger Linfield; 12/86.

406. Slow Mutants (5.11a) ★ Tunnel under blocks to reach the ledge at the base. Go up the face just right of *Muffin Bandits*. **Pro:** Four bolts; to 2 inches. **FA:** Don Wilson, Karen Wilson, Jack Marshall; 2/90.

407. E. B. Bon Homme (5.9) ★★ Begin just left of a small tree. Go up a right-leaning corner to a ledge/blocks, then up a thin crack. **Pro:** Thin to 2 inches. **FA:** Todd Gordon; 3/95.

408. Spire Route (5.5) ★ This route climbs the northwest face of the obvious pinnacle 100 feet right and down from *Muffin Bandits*. **Pro:** One bolt; one-bolt anchor/rap! **FA:** Unknown.

409. Tchalk Is Cheap (5.10d) This lies around the corner and uphill from *Spire Route*. Avoid easy cracks to either side and climb past one bolt, then follow cracks above a Gothic arch. **Pro:** Thin to 2 inches. **FA:** Dennis Yates, Roger Linfield; 12/86.

410. Garden Path (5.10a) Climb a chute/crack behind an oak tree 70 feet right of *Tchalk Is Cheap*. **Pro:** To 2.5 inches. **FA:** Roger Linfield, Dennis Yates; 3/87.

411. Under a Raging Moon (5.10b/c) ★ This 20-foot thin crack in a right-facing corner begins at the finish of *Garden Path*. It is located on the summit block. **Pro:** Thin to 2 inches. **FA:** Roger Linfield, Dennis Yates; 12/86.

412. Chute to Kill (5.10c/d) ★ This route lies about 50 feet right of *Garden Path*. Lieback a large flake, then follow three bolts up a loose water chute. **Pro:** To 3 inches. **FA:** Dennis Yates, Roger Linfield; 3/87.

413. Too Thin for Poodles (5.10c/d) ★★ This line lies about 125 feet right of *Chute to Kill*. Climb a thin crack until it forks. Take the left fork, then head up past two bolts. **Pro:** Thin to 2 inches. **FA:** Roger Linfield, Dennis Yates; 12/86.

414. Pillar of Dawn (5.10a) A large pillar rises about 100 yards right and around the corner from the previous routes. This route follows a dihedral on the south face of the pillar. **Pro:** Thin to 2 inches; two-bolt anchor/rap. **FA:** Roger Linfield, Dennis Yates; 12/86.

415. Alcoholic Single Mothers (5.10d) (TR) Toprope the north side of the pillar (the rappel line from *Pillar of Dawn*). **FA:** Phil Bircheff; 10/86.

Jones Rock (Not Wilderness)

This formation lies in the southwestern portion of the Middle Kingdom, directly east of the Lands End Area (Shady Spot, Easy Buttress). See page 127 for initial approach directions. From near the point where the Boy Scout Trail leaves the North Wonderland Trail, head east for about 550 yards to this small formation. It lies about 150 yards southwest of the Skin Graft and about 200 yards west-southwest of the Techulator. It is about 150 yards west of Smith Rock. All recorded routes lie on the northeast face and start off a ledge on the right side of the face. The routes are not shown. Map, page 127.

416. Imgwana Kikbuti (5.10b) The leftmost of two thin cracks that widen at a roof. **Pro:** Thin to 3.5 inches. **FA:** Dave Haber, Sheryl Haber; 3/96.

417. Basketball Jones (5.10a) The rightmost of two thin cracks that widen at a roof. Begin in the left-facing corner to the right *(Tyrone Shoelaces),* then traverse left into the thin crack. **Pro:** Thin to 3.5 inches. **FA:** Dave Haber, Sheryl Haber; 3/96.

418. Tyrone Shoelaces (5.6) This is the left-facing corner that begins off the right end of the ledge; above, head up and right, then back left to the top. **Pro:** To 2.5 inches. **FA:** Dave Haber, Sheryl Haber; 3/96.

419. Tyrone Jones (5.8) The crack right of *Tyrone Shoelaces.* **Pro:** To 2.5 inches. **FA:** Tucker Tech, Todd Gordon, Tom Burke, Maggie Ross, Uri, Andrea Tomaszewski.

Smith Rock (Not Wilderness)

Smith Rock is the southernmost of several rocks that lie about 100 yards south of the Techulator and about 150 yards east of Jones Rock. From near the point where the Boy Scout Trail leaves the North Wonderland Trail, head east for about 550 yards, passing the north side of Jones Rock. From here, follow a wash for about 150 yards as it curves southeast, then back east, until you are below the south side of this small formation. Map, page 127.

420. **The Nuts and Bolts of Climbing**
(5.10c) This route is on the northeast corner of Smith Rock. Climb an overhanging handcrack to a flake, then go up a face past two bolts. **Pro:** To 2.5 inches. **FA:** Roger Linfield, Dennis Yates; 12/86.

421. **Bighorn Hand Crack** (5.7) This is the straight-in handcrack on the south face of Smith Rock. **Pro:** To 3 inches. **FA:** Dennis Yates, Roger Linfield; 12/86.

421A. **Little Bighorn** (5.7) (R/X) (not shown on photo) This is the left-hand crack of two about 30 feet left of *Bighorn Hand Crack*. Begin off a boulder, head up over a roof, then go up and left on the face to a flake. **Pro:** To 3 inches. **FA:** Todd Swain; 6/92.

422. **Riders on the Storm** (5.10a) (not shown on photo) This route lies on the north side of a separate formation southeast of Smith Rock. Two slightly overhanging offwidths are above a slab; this is the right crack. **Pro:** to 4+ inches. **FA:** Roger Linfield, Dennis Yates; 12/86.

Mistaken Rock (Wilderness)

This and the next two formations lie on the northern edge of the Middle Kingdom. This formation is north of El Dorado (see page 127 for initial approach directions). From near the point where the Boy Scout Trail leaves the North Wonderland Trail, follow the North Wonderland Trail for about 0.6 mile as it curves northeast and crosses a small wash. Mistaken Rock is the small solitary formation that lies about 120 yards to the right of the North Wonderland Trail. Map, page 127.

423. **Not the Clean Crack** (5.6) (not shown on photo) A left-slanting hand-to fist-crack facing the North Wonderland Trail (on the right end of the northwest face). **Pro:** To 3+ inches, **FA:** Dave Haber; 9/94.

424. **Excuuuse Me** (5.9) ★ This thin crack lies about 30 feet right and around the corner from *Not the Clean Crack*. **Pro:** Thin to 2 inches. **FA:** Steve Parker, Dave Haber, Sheryl Haber; 9/94.

425. **Blame It on Cain** (5.8) This crack lies just right of *Excuuuse Me*. **Pro:** To 2 inches. **FA:** Dave Haber, Sheryl Haber, Steve Parker; 9/94.

426. **Ben's Magic Weenie** (5.10b) ★ This is the four-bolt face route. **Pro:** Anchors. **FA:** Todd Gordon, Tucker Tech, Mark Synott.

427. **Correct Me If I'm Wrong** (5.6) A flake/crack located about 18 feet right of *Blame It on Cain*. **Pro:** To 2.5 inches. **FA:** Dave Haber; 9/94.

Clean Crack Formation

This formation lies on the northern edge of the Middle Kingdom, about 150 yards south-southeast of Mistaken Rock (see page 127 for initial approach directions). From near the point where the Boy Scout Trail leaves the North Wonderland Trail, follow the North Wonderland Trail for about 0.6 mile as it curves northeast and crosses a small wash. Continue on the North Wonderland Trail for

Mistaken Rock

Clean Crack Formation

428

429

another 100 yards, passing Mistaken Rock (the small solitary formation 120 yards to the right of the North Wonderland Trail. Head south-southeast to this northwest-facing formation; routes are on left side just right of a bush on the face. Map, page 127.

428. **Clean Crack** (5.10a/b) ★★ This route faces north (toward the North Wonderland Trail). This is the right-hand and most prominent left-slanting thin crack. It passes just left of a bush near the bottom and ends on a large ledge. A short direct finish (5.10b/c) heads up the steep thin crack on the headwall above the ledge. **Pro:** Thin to 2 inches. **FA:** Alan Roberts, Bill Meyers; 1987. **FA** (Direct start): Unknown.

429. **Wine of Delusion** (5.8) (R) Begin as for *Clean Crack,* but at the bush head up and right on an unprotected face (5.8) into a right-slanting crack/seam system. **Pro:** Thin to 2 inches. **FA:** Alan Bartlett, Sheryl Haber, Dave Haber; 5/95.

Trailer Trash Crags (Wilderness)

These formations lie about 150 yards to the right and behind the Clean Crack Formation. Approach as for Mistaken Rock (see page 137) but continue south-southeast to this formation. This formation and its routes are not pictured. Map, page 127.

430. **Kletter Rubish** (5.10b) The right-hand crack on the left formation's north-facing rock. **FA:** Dave Haber, Sheryl Haber, Alan Bartlett; 5/95.

431. **You Don't Work and Pat Has Two Kids** (5.8) This route lies around the corner and to the right of *Kletter Rubish* on a separate northwest-facing rock. Go up a crack that widens near top. **Pro:** To 3+ inches. **FA:** Dave Haber, Sheryl Haber, Alan Bartlett; 5/95.

432. **Greek Soldier** (5.9) This thin crack-to-face route lies on the east side of a boulder that is northwest of the last route. **Pro:** Thin to 2 inches. **FA:** Alan Bartlett, Sheryl Haber, Dave Haber; 5/95.

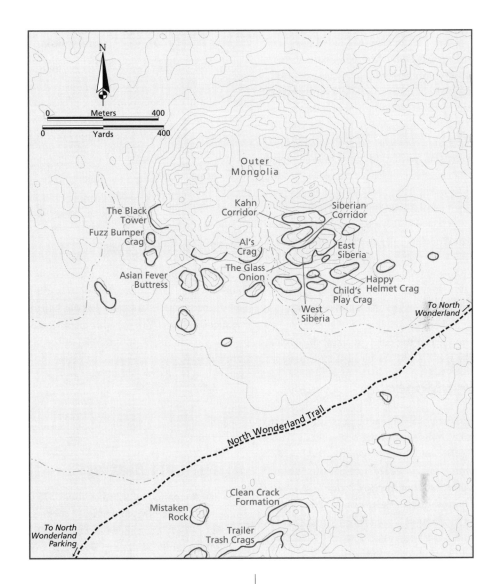

OUTER
MONGOLIA

Wilderness Notice: All of the areas and formations described in the remaining section of Wonderland of Rocks North lie in designated wilderness. No new fixed anchors may be placed except by permit (see Introduction). Existing fixed anchors may be replaced on a one-for-one basis. See map on page 84 for actual wilderness boundary.

Outer Mongolia consists of a large number of small to large formations that lie around a rocky high point about 400 yards north of the North Wonderland Trail and about 2.1 miles from the North Wonderland parking area (about 0.8+ mile past the junction with the Boy Scout Trail). The most prominent of these formations is a large, dark, and slabby formation with several slanting cracks. This formation is called Siberia.

To reach Outer Mongolia, park at the Northern Wonderland parking area on Park Boulevard 6.4 miles from the West Entrance and 2.2+ miles from the Intersection Rock/Real Hidden Valley intersection). Hike about 1 mile northeast on the North Wonderland Trail. At this point, it will join up with a larger trail (a former dirt road) heading straight north. After about 500 yards (just past Gilligan's Island), the Boy Scout Trail to Indian Cove will diverge to the left, and the North Wonderland Trail will begin a slow curve to the right (northeast). Stay right on the North Wonderland Trail for another 0.6 to 0.8 mile. The Mongolia area encompasses many different crags that lie on and about the large and complex hillside to the north. Approaches to the different crags vary. Refer to the specific crag for detailed information.

West Mongolia

West Mongolia consists of various formations that lie to the west of the large hillside that comprises the Outer Mongolia area. Initial approach directions are provided above. From the junction with the Boy Scout Trail, continue northeast on the North Wonderland Trail for about 0.6 mile to where the North Wonderland Trail crosses a wash. Mistaken Rock (a small solitary formation) is about 120 yards right (southeast) of the trail at this point. Head left (north) from here, aiming for a point just left (west) of the formations on the far left end of the Outer Mongolia area. Continue north for about 375 yards until you reach the closest formation. All formations in this area are in designated wilderness. Map, page 139.

The Black Tower (Wilderness)

This dark-colored formation lies on the western side of the Outer Mongolia hillside area, about 225 yards past (north of) the first formation you reach. It is located on the west face of the rock. One route is known; it is not pictured. Map, page 139.

433. **Maisy** (5.7) Climb the arête on the Black Tower with five bolts and one fixed pin. **FA:** Todd Gordon, Suzette Olsen, Tucker Tech.

Fuzz Bumper Crag

This formation lies just south (right about 75 yards) of the Black Tower, 150 yards north of the first formation you reach off the North Wonderland Trail. You pass this formation on the way to the Black Tower. Neither the crag nor the route are pictured. Map, page 139.

434. **The Fuzz Bumper** (5.10a) This is on the north face. Go up the face past two bolts to a slanting crack. **FA:** Todd Gordon, Tucker Tech, K. Burnham, Doug.

Asian Fever Buttress

This white-colored buttress lies about 375 yards west of the obvious and large dark-colored slabs of West Siberia. It faces south and is sunny most of the day. See West Mongolia for initial approach directions. From the junction of the North Wonderland Trail with the Boy Scout Trail, continue northeast on the North Wonderland Trail for about 0.7 mile, about 200 yards past where the North Wonderland Trail crosses a wash near Mistaken Rock (a small solitary formation to the right of the trail). Head left (north) from here aiming for a point just left (west) of the obvious break/gully that is left of the slabs of West Siberia. The buttress and routes are not pictured. Map, page 139.

435. **SARS** (5.7) This and the following route lie left of the obvious handcrack on the face *(Yellow Peril)*. **Pro:** To 2 inches. **FA:** Todd Gordon, Suzette Olsen.

436. **Robitussin** (5.7) **Pro:** To 2 inches. **FA:** Todd Gordon, Suzette Olsen.

437. **Yellow Peril** (5.5) ★★ This route follows an easy handcrack on the slab to the left of *Asian Fever.* **Pro:** To 2.5 inches; rap from the *Asian Fever* anchor. **FA:** Tucker Tech, Todd Gordon.

438. **Asian Fever** (5.8) ★★★ This 120-foot route lies on the right side of the Asian Fever Buttress. Go up the face past seven bolts. A one-bolt/one fixed pin rap anchor is down and left. **FA:** Todd Gordon, Tucker Tech.

Al's Crag (Wilderness)

This small crag lies about 200 yards west of West Siberia's slabs and about 175 yards east of Asian Fever Buttress. It faces south and is sunny most of the day. It is on the right end of the cliffs to the left of the gully/approach to the Siberian and Khan Corridors. It is characterized by darker rock with several right-slanting cracks and small roofs. Approach as for Asian Fever Buttress (see page 140), but angle farther right. Map, page 139.

439. **Twinkle Toes** (5.7) This is the leftmost of three prominent slanting cracks; begin left of a cactus. Go up the right-facing flake to a thin crack. **Pro:** Thin to 2 inches. **FA:** Alan Bartlett, Sheryl Haber, Dave Haber; 11/95.

440. **Oral Sex Bozeman** (5.8) ★ Begin up a right-slanting thin crack about 10 feet right of *Twinkle Toes;* move left to finish in another crack. **Pro:** To 2 inches. **FA:** Dave Haber, Sheryl Haber, Alan Bartlett; 11/95.

441. **Head Room** (5.8) Go up the face into a crack about 15 feet right of *Oral Sex Bozeman;* higher, the crack heads up and left. **Pro:** To 2 inches. **FA:** Dave Haber, Sheryl Haber, Alan Bartlett; 11/95.

The Glass Onion (Wilderness)

This formation lies to the right of Al's Crag and to the left of the main Siberia face. Approach as for Al's Crag and Asian Fever Buttress/Siberian Corridor (see pages 140–141). The formation and routes are not pictured. Map, page 139.

442. **Glass Onion** (5.10b) ★ This route climbs the face of the Glass Onion past six bolts. **Pro:** Anchor? **FA:** Todd Gordon, Tucker Tech.

443. **310 lb. Rosiln Collapses** (5.7+) This is the slanting crack on the left side of the formation. **Pro:** To 2.5 inches. **FA:** Todd Gordon, Tucker Tech, Robert.

444. **Hollywood Diet Disasters** (5.8) Located on the right side of the formation. **Pro:** (?) **FA:** Tucker Tech, Todd Gordon, Robert.

445. **Pregnant Missing Woman** (5.5) Located on the far right side of the Glass Onion. **Pro:** (?) **FA:** Todd Gordon, Tucker Tech, Robert.

Siberian Corridor

This is the east-west corridor formed by the back (north) side of Siberia and the front (south) side of the Khan formation. See page 139 for initial approach. From the junction with the Boy Scout Trail, continue northeast on the North Wonderland Trail for 0.7+ mile to a point about 200 yards past where the North Wonderland Trail crosses a wash near Mistaken Rock (a small solitary formation to the right of the trail; see page 136). Head left (north) from here, aiming for an obvious break/gully left of the slabs of West Siberia. Head up boulders in that gully until you can cut right (east) into this gully "corridor." The routes are not pictured. Map, page 139.

446. **Gengler-Regelbrugge** (5.7) This route is the fairly obvious straight-in crack on the lower-angled south face of the Kahn formation (on your left). **Pro:** To 3+ inches. **FA:** Brian Gengler, Jon Regelbrugge; 2/92.

447. **Mongoloid** (5.9) (R) ★ Continue up the Siberian gully/corridor past the last climb and look right. This route lies on the north side of Siberia and climbs a huecoed wall past two bolts and one fixed pin to a ledge; continue with a leaning thin crack. **Pro:** Thin to 2 inches, two–bolt anchor/80-foot rap. **FA:** Unknown.

Kamchatka Block

This small block lies on the back (north) side of East Siberia, roughly between the tops of Buttress 3 and Buttress 4. It can be approached via the Siberian Corridor, as for *Mongoloid;* from the corridor continue heading east over boulders. A more enjoyable approach would be to climb *George's Route* or *Toby* on East Siberia to the summit, then simply walk around to the base of the route (page 149). There are two recorded routes.

448. **Kublai Corner** (5.8) ★ Lieback up the left-slanting corner system. Begin left of a dead pine. **Pro:** To 2 inches. **FA:** Brian Gengler, Jon Regelbrugge; 2/92.

449. **Broken Dreams** (5.11b) ★★ This route climbs a left-slanting thin-to handcrack on the left side of the face. Begin behind a large pine. A little loose at the top; otherwise excellent climbing. **Pro:** Thin to 2 inches. **FA** (TR): Jon Regelbrugge, Brian Gengler; 2/92. **FA** (Lead): Wally Barker; 12/96.

Broken Dreams 449

448

The Khan Corridor (Wilderness)

This is another east-west corridor formed by the back (north side) of the Khan formation and another formation to the north. See page 139 for initial approach. From the junction with the Boy Scout Trail, continue northeast on the North Wonderland Trail for about 0.7+ mile, about 200 yards past where the North Wonderland Trail crosses a wash near Mistaken Rock (a small solitary formation to the right of the trail; see page 137). Head left (north) from here, aiming for an obvious break/gully left of the slabs of West Siberia. Head up boulders in that gully, staying straight past the Siberian Corridor, then cut right (east) into this "corridor." All routes are on the steep north side of the Kahn formation (shady most of the day). The routes are not shown. Map, page 139.

450. **Kublai Khan** (5.9) This route lies about 15 feet right of *Genghis Kahn*. Head up right slanting cracks that begin under a roof; higher up, finish in another right-slanting crack. **Pro:** To 2.5 inches. **FA:** Wally Barker, Alan Bartlett; 12/96.

451. **Genghis Khan** (5.11b) ★★★★ This steep and excellent route begins off a boulder. Climb 10 feet to a bolt, then up into a finger-to-hand crack. Continue up the face past three more bolts, then go up and left in a crack to a two-bolt anchor/rap. **Pro:** To 2.5 inches. **FA:** Jon Regelbrugge, Brian Gengler, Eric Easton; 2/92.

452. **The Mongolian Lieback** (5.12a) ★★★ This steep route begins about 30 feet left of *Genghis Kahn*. Go up past a bolt, then over a roof, continuing above in a corner past three more bolts to a two-bolt anchor/rap. **FA:** Brian Gengler, Jon Regelbrugge, Eric Easton; 2/92.

Child's Play Crag (Wilderness)

This small crag lies on the right side of the rocky gully on the final approach to Siberia (see the Outer Mongolia approach description on page 139 and the Siberia approach description below). It lies "in front" of Siberia and faces south. It is not visible until you are practically upon it. The crag and route are not pictured. Map, page 139.

453. **Child Proof** (5.10b) ★ Go up a thin crack to a horizontal, then climb a handcrack above. **Pro:** To 2 inches. **FA:** Alan Bartlett, Sheryl Haber, Dave Haber; 11/95.

Siberia (Wilderness)

Siberia encompasses the largest slabby formations in the Outer Mongolia area. The routes are mostly one long pitch with an occasional short second pitch. The left-hand section of Siberia (West Siberia) is very dark patinaed rock with many diagonal cracks; the right-hand section (East Siberia) is lighter-colored rock separated into distinctive "pillars." Many fun, moderate sport-type slab routes are found on the right side.

For initial approach directions, refer to the Outer Mongolia description on page 139). From the junction of the North Wonderland Trail with the Boy Scout Trail, continue northeast on the North Wonderland Trail for about 0.8 mile—about 350 yards past where the trail crosses a wash near Mistaken Rock (a small solitary formation to the right of the trail; see page 137). Head left (north-northeast) from here aiming for the large dark-colored slabs of West Siberia. For either side of the Siberia face, approach via an obvious rocky gully/gap leading straight to the dark face of West Siberia. Map, page 139.

West Siberia—Siberia Left Side

This dark-colored face is characterized by the many diagonal crack systems and a prominent roof on the lower right end. Most routes follow the cracks/seams. Scramble up boulders directly to the base. For most climbs, the descent requires one or more rappels. All routes face south and are sunny most of the day.

A Note about Ratings at West Siberia:

Most of these routes have seen few repeat ascents. Apparently, early reports would seem to suggest that most of the routes here are **conservatively rated** (e.g., potential sandbags).

454. Irish Toothache (5.7) ★★ This route lies on the upper left end of the face. Go up the face past a horizontal (fixed pin) then up past three bolts to top of the "pillar." Two fixed pin anchor/rap. **FA:** Todd Gordon, Tucker Tech, Dara.

455. Daravader (5.9) This is the off-width crack in the right facing corner just right of *Irish Toothache.* **Pro:** To 4+ inches. **FA:** Tucker Tech, Todd Gordon, Dara.

456. Marquess of Lorn (5.7) Begin down and right of *Daravader.* Go up the thin flake to face climbing past one bolt, then to the crack above. **Pro:** Thin to 2 inches. Rap from two-bolt anchor atop *Glen's Crack.* **FA:** Todd Gordon, Tucker Tech, Lori Butts, Dara.

457. Captain Standish (5.6) Begin up the crack just left of *Glen's Crack,* pass a bolt then continue up a seam to the top. **Pro:** Thin to 2.5 inches. Two-bolt anchor/rap. **FA:** Todd Gordon, Tucker Tech.

458. Glen's Crack (5.6) ★★ This is the obvious crack/seam system just left of the left-facing corner of *Jack.* Two-bolt anchor/rap. **FA:** Glen.

459. Jack (5.6) Begin in a left-facing corner up and left from the base of the crag. Pass a fixed pin; above, crack/seams lead to the ledge. Rap from *Glen's Crack* two-bolt anchor. **Pro:** Thin to 2.5 inches. **FA:** Todd Gordon, Tucker Tech.

460. Fixed Bayonets (5.6) Begin just right of *Jack,* heading up and right on a crack that becomes a seam. Where this dies out, head up and left to the belay for *Jack.* Rap from *Glen's Crack* anchor. **Pro:** Thin to 2 inches. **FA:** Todd Gordon, Tucker Tech.

461. Old Hornington (5.10b) Face climb up the slab to the left side of the roof, then go up on thin cracks above to the ledge. **Pro:** Thin to 2 inches; two-bolt anchor/rap. **FA:** Todd Gordon, Tucker Tech.

462. The Bazooka (5.10b) ★★ Go up the slab to the right end of the roof (where it turns into a right-facing corner); go over the roof directly past one bolt, then up thin cracks to the ledge. Two-bolt anchor/rap (as with previous route). **Pro:** Thin to 2 inches. **FA:** Todd Gordon, Suzette Olsen.

463. RPG (Rocket-Propelled Grenade) (5.10d/5.11a) Begin as for *The Bazooka,* but at the roof, head right into the right-facing corner, then go up over the roof via a crack in the corner. **Pro:** To 2.5 inches. **FA:** Unknown.

464. Original Route (aka Jake Off) (5.8) This is the obvious main crack/corner system that goes over the right end of the roof. Above, follow the left-diagonalling crack to the summit. Might be best done in two pitches. **Pro:** To 2.5 inches. **FA:** Unknown.

465. Jake's Route (5.8) (not shown on photo) Begin just right of *Original Route.* Face climb past one bolt to reach a crack system that slants to the right higher up. Rappel from slings. **FA:** Jake Collela.

East Siberia—Siberia Right Side

The routes on the right side of the Siberia formation are mostly sport-bolted face routes on the faces of four main "buttresses" of rock separated by crack systems. The rock is steeper than West Siberia and lighter in color. Large boulders and a tall pillar (Horn Tower) lie at the base of the right side of the face. Approach as for West Siberia (see page 145), but then boulder hop up and right along the base to reach the higher right side. One or more rappels are required for the descent; see topo. All routes face south and are sunny most for the day.

A Note about Ratings at East Siberia: Most of these routes were originally **very conservatively rated** (e.g., potential sandbags). This guide attempts to give more realistic grades, but be advised that some routes may be harder than indicated.

East Siberia—Buttress 1

This is the leftmost buttress of rock. Descent: Make two single-rope rappels down *Love Gas.*

466. Steamy Sluts and Farm Animals (5.7) (R) (not shown on photo) Climb the loose crack to the left of Buttress 1, ending atop the summit of Buttress 1 (170+ feet). Rap down *Love Gas.* **Pro:** To 2.5 inches. **FA:** Tucker Tech, Todd Gordon, Brian Povolny.

467. Randy (5.8) The left-hand seam/crack (fixed copperhead down low) ending with a short face section (two bolts). **Pro:** To 2 inches; two-bolt anchor. An optional short (easy) pitch can be done to the summit (two-bolt anchor) **FA:** Todd Gordon. Tucker Tech.

468. Bull with Gas (5.9) (Sport) ★★ Begin to the right of *Gandy* and climb up past one fixed pin to a face with seven bolts. Angle right to finish at the first belay anchor of *Love Gas.* This route has a large number of loose "plates"; climb with caution. **FA:** Unknown.

469. Love Gas (5.10a) (Sport) ★★★ Located right of the center of Buttress 1. **Pitch 1:** Head up the face past a bolt and several fixed pins, then past seven more bolts to a two-bolt anchor/rap station (5.9). **Pitch 2:** Go up the face past two bolts to another two-bolt anchor (5.10a). An optional short (easy) pitch can be done to the summit (two-bolt anchor). A 60-meter rope required. Rap the route. **FA:** Todd Gordon, Tucker Tech, Tom Burke.

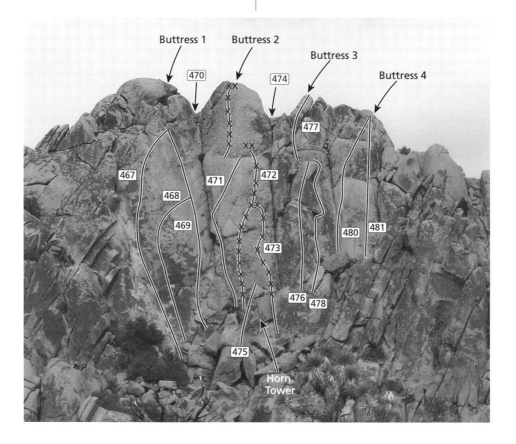

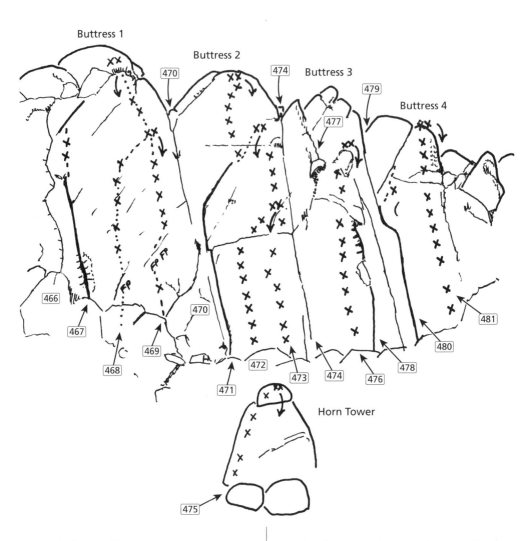

Buttress 1
Buttress 2
470
474
Buttress 3
479
Buttress 4
477
466
470
481
467
469
480
468
472
473 474 476 478
471

Horn Tower

475

470. **Unknown Route** (5.9+) (R/X) This route lies on the right side of Buttress 1. Crack and face climbing (two bolts) leads to the summit of the buttress; two-bolt anchor. **Pro:** Thin to 2.5 inches. **FA:** Unknown.

East Siberia—Buttress 2

The second buttress to the right. Descent: Make three single-rope rappels down *Dos Chi Chis.*

471. **Los Dos** (5.8) This route heads up the crack on the left side of Buttress 2; where the crack dies out, one bolt protects the face to the ledge (two-bolt anchor) atop the first pitch of *Dos Chi Chis.* Two single-rope raps down *Dos Chi Chis.* **Pro:** Thin to 2 inches. **FA:** Todd Gordon, Greg Epperson.

472. **Yasmine Bleath** (5.9/5.10a) (Sport) ★★★ This is the first bolted line right of the crack of *Los Dos.* Go up the face past nine or ten

bolts to join *Dos Chi Chis* at its lowest rap anchor (some loose plates); either finish up the first pitch of *Dos Chi Chis* or rap off from here. **FA:** Todd Gordon, Tucker Tech, Tom Burke.

473. **Dos Chi Chis** (5.10a) ★★★★ (Sport) The rightmost bolted line up the knobby face, this is perhaps the best route on the Siberia face. **Pitch 1:** Go up the face past ten or eleven bolts (the eighth bolt is doubled for rap anchor), and one fixed pin under the roof to a large belay ledge with a two-bolt anchor (5.9+). **Pitch 2:** Move left on the ledge and go up the face past five bolts (5.10a); two-bolt anchor. Make three single-rope raps down the route. **FA:** Todd Gordon, Tucker Tech, Kelsy Burnham, Greg Epperson, Erik Corbin, George Armstrong.

474. **Sheep Shover** (5.7) This is the crack to chimney between Buttress 2 and Buttress 3. Near the top, traverse left to the ledge atop the first pitch of *Dos Chi Chis;* make two raps down that route. **Pro:** To 3+ inches. **FA:** Unknown.

Horn Tower

This is the small pinnacle that lies at the base of the face below Buttress 3.

475. **Gandy** (5.9+) ★ (Sport) Go up the left (southwest) arête of the tower past five bolts. One bolt; one fixed pin anchor/rap. **FA:** Todd Gordon, Tucker Tech.

East Siberia—Buttress 3

476. **George's Route (aka Binder)** (5.8+) ★★ (Sport) This route has two possible finishes: the one described; and via the next route *(Crossroads Finish).* Climb the face up the center of Buttress 3 past six bolts to a ledge;

continue straight up past two more bolts (5.5) to two-bolt anchor. Rap off from here. **FA:** George Armstrong, Todd Gordon, Tucker Tech.

477. **Crossroads Finish** (5.7) (Sport) From the ledge on *George's Route,* head up and left into a shallow corner and discontinuous crack. **Pro:** Six bolts; one fixed pin. Rap from sling to a two-bolt anchor on George's Route, rap from there. **FA:** Unknown.

478. **Britney Spears** (5.7) This route climbs the crack on the right side of Buttress 3 to the ledge on *George's Route.* Finish up either *George's Route* (straight up; two bolts to two-bolt anchor), or up the *Crossroads Finish.* **Pro:** To 2 inches. **FA:** Todd Gordon, Tucker Tech, George Armstrong.

479. **Epperson Groove** (5.3) (R) This is the groove and chimney system between Buttress 3 and Buttress 4. **Pro:** To 3+ inches. **FA:** Greg Epperson.

East Siberia—Buttress 4

This is the far right section of the face that lies above and right of Buttress 3.

480. **Gatorade Boy** (5.7) Located on the left side of Buttress 4. Go up the thin crack that becomes wide corner, then climb the face up and right past one bolt to a ledge. Finish up the thin crack off the left side of the ledge. **Pro:** Thin to 3+ inches. **FA:** Todd Gordon, George Armstrong.

481. **Toby** (5.10a) ★★★ (Sport) Begin on face to the right of *Gatorade Boy.* Go up past nine or ten bolts to the top of the buttress. Two-bolt anchor/95+-foot rap. **FA:** Todd Gordon, Tucker Tech, Mark Hoffman.

East Siberia—Other Routes

482. Weo (5.7) (not shown on topo or photo) Begin down and right of *Gandy* (on Horn Tower). Climb the obvious long arête that leads up to the base of Buttress 4 near *Toby*. **Pro:** Bolts; one fixed pin. **FA:** Todd Gordon, John Middendorf, Grant Hiskes, Tucker Tech.

483. Camp X-Ray (5.8) (not shown on topo or photo) Located about 100 yards to the right of *Toby* is another large formation with dark plates on its lower half. Go up the plates to the obvious crack above. **Pro:** To 2.5 inches. **FA:** Todd Gordon, Tucker Tech, Greg Epperson.

Happy Helmet Crag

This rock lies on the far right end of the smaller formations than lie in front (south) of the main Siberia face. It lies about 100 yards right of the approach gully to Siberia. Several cracks are found on this rock's south face. Map, page 139.

484. Happy Helmet (5.6) (not shown) This route climbs an easy crack on the right side of the south face. It passes a small bush, then splits. Continue up the right crack. **Pro:** To 2 inches. **FA:** Dave Haber, Sheryl Haber, Alan Bartlett; 11/95.

Booty Rock (Wilderness)

This small crag lies about 100 yards south of the North Wonderland Trail. See page 139 for initial approach. From its junction with the Boy Scout Trail, continue northeast on the North Wonderland Trail for about 1.1 mile to where it descends and enters a wash that has numerous oak, juniper, and pine trees. Look right to locate this crag, which has an obvious, vertical crack (*Butt-Headed Stranger*). Map, page 139.

485. Butt-Headed Stranger (5.9+) (not shown) This short vertical crack (25 feet) widens from fingers to hand/fist. **Pro:** To 3.5 inches. **FA:** Don Reid, Alan Bartlett; 11/95.

Three Little Pigs (Wilderness)

These crags lie about 450 yards east of Siberia. See page 139 for initial approach. From its junction with the Boy Scout Trail, continue northeast on the North Wonderland Trail for about 1.3 mile to where it enters the main Wonderland wash, which leads to Willow Hole. The main wash (and trail) heads right (south) here; you should head a bit left. Where the wash heads east through a narrow gap (this leads to the Atom Smashers Area), turn left (north) instead and scramble up slabs to these slabby formations. None of the routes are pictured. Map, page 152.

486. First Little Pig (5.3) This slab/buttress lies to the left of the largest low-angled slab. **Pro:** To 2 inches. **FA:** Jon Regelbrugge, Roberta Straub; 2/92.

487. Second Little Pig (5.7) This route climbs the face up to a thin crack located about 35 feet left of *First Little Pig*. **Pro:** Thin to 2 inches. **FA:** Jon Regelbrugge, Roberta Straub; 2/92.

488. Third Little Pig (5.3) Begin 50 feet left of *Second Little Pig*. Go up dark rock to the right of a crack. Above, go over a block to a ledge, then up and right on the face. **Pro:** To 2 inches. **FA:** Jon Regelbrugge, Roberta Straub; 2/92.

489. Pork Circus (5.5) This is a two-bolt face route in the area. **Pro:** To 2 inches. **FA:** Todd Gordon, Andrea Tomaszewski, Tucker Tech.

The Guardhouse (on back)

The Cornerstone

Poodle Smasher

Lost in the Wonderland

The Inauguron

Diarrhea Dome

Disneyland Dome

Book Of Brilliant Things (on back)

Freak Bros.

Crystal Quarry

The Castle

The Fortress

Lazy Dome

Flying Fortress (on back)

back of Grey Giant

The Tombstone

Hershey Rock

Willow Hole

The Foot

Disappointment Dome

To Wonderland Trail

Hooter Rock

Grinch Rock

PHOTO: DAVE HOUSER

THE ATOM SMASHERS AREA

(Wilderness)

This area consists of a number of formations that lie east of Outer Mongolia and north-west of Willow Hole. The main formation, Timbuktu Towers, is the most prominent in the northern Wonderland. It is easily visible from the North Wonderland Trail as you head past Outer Mongolia and the Middle Kingdom. Here are found some of the most difficult sport routes in the park (on the Ivory Tower), as well as the sharply fractured boulders (the Atom Smashers Boulders) for which this area is named.

Park at the North Wonderland parking area, which is 6.4 miles from the West Entrance and 2.2+ miles from the Intersection Rock/Real Hidden Valley

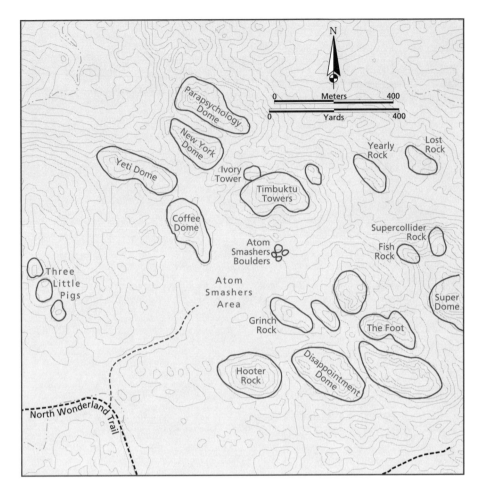

intersection. Hike nearly 1 mile northeast on the North Wonderland Trail; at this point, it will join up with a larger trail (a former dirt road) heading straight north. After another 500 yards (just past Gilligan's Island), the Boy Scout Trail to Indian Cove diverges off to the left and the North Wonderland Trail begins a slow curve to the right (northeast). Stay right on the North Wonderland Trail for about 1.3 miles from the Boy Scout Trail intersection

to where it ends in a sandy wash. The main trail cuts right (south) at a sign, but continue straight ahead for about 90 yards to where the main wash makes a sharp right (south) turn. Head more or less straight ahead (east) into a narrow wash that becomes a bit rocky before reaching a large open valley. The formations lie ahead to the north, east and south. Maps are above and on page 153.

Grinch Rock
The Super Dome
The Foot
Disappointment Dome
Hooter Rock

To Yearly Rock, Lost Rock, Fish Rock, and Supercollider Rock

Atom Smashers

Approach

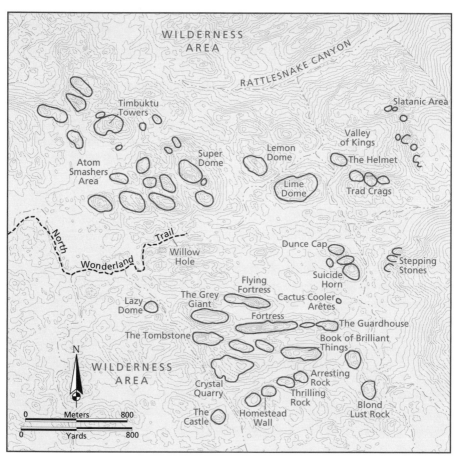

WILDERNESS AREA

RATTLESNAKE CANYON

Slatanic Area

Timbuktu Towers

Valley of Kings

The Helmet

Atom Smashers Area

Super Dome

Lemon Dome

Lime Dome

Trad Crags

North

Trail

Willow Hole

Wonderland

Dunce Cap

Stepping Stones

Suicide Horn

Flying Fortress

Lazy Dome

The Grey Giant

Cactus Cooler Arêtes

Fortress

The Guardhouse

The Tombstone

Book of Brilliant Things

N

WILDERNESS AREA

Crystal Quarry

Arresting Rock

Thrilling Rock

Blond Lust Rock

The Castle

Homestead Wall

0   Meters   800
0   Yards   800

Hooter Rock (Wilderness)

The approach to the Atom Smashers Area is described on pages 151–153. As you enter the open valley, Hooter Rock is the first formation on the right (south). It has a large brownish north face. Map, page 152.

Hooter Rock—East Face

A wash heads eastward and a bit to the right, under the north face. Approach as for the north face, then scramble up around the corner. The face gets morning sun and is shady all afternoon.

490. **KP Corner** (5.10a) ★ This is left of *Earth and Sky* and slightly around the corner. Climb a face to a brown, right-facing corner. **Pro:** To 2.5 inches. **FA:** Kevin Powell, Alan Roberts; 1987.

Hooter Rock—North Face

A wash heads eastward and a bit to the right, under the north face. The following routes lie on the left side of the north face. They are shady most of the day.

491. **Earth and Sky** (5.10d) ★ This route heads up steep huecos on the left side of the north face. Go up past four bolts to a two-bolt anchor/rap. **FA:** Brian Gengler, Jon Regelbrugge; 3/92.

492. **Hooterville Trolley** (5.11a) ★ Begin up a right-leaning crack system that lies just right of *Earth and Sky*. Where this crack ends, head past two bolts (5.11a) to another short crack and ledge above. **Pro:** To 2.5 inches; two-bolt anchor/rap. **FA:** Dave Evans, Brian Sillasen, Dave Stahl; 12/86.

493. **The Crow's Nest** (5.11c/d) ★ Begin about 150 feet right of *Hooterville Trolley,* near the right end of the north face. **Pitch 1:** Go up an easy crack and ledges to a ledge below a left-slanting thin crack. **Pitch 2:** Go up the overhanging face/thin crack, then up and through a roof near the top. **Pro:** Thin to 2 inches. **FA:** Mike Lechlinski; 2/88.

Hooter Rock—West Face

The following climbs lie on a slabby section near the right end of the west face of Hooter Rock. From where you enter the Atom Smashers Area, head toward Hooter Rock, then turn right along a wash that runs south below the west side of the formation. The face is sunny most of the day.

494. **Reverend Blitzo's Hairless Boys Choir** (5.8) ★ Begin near a small corner on the left side of the slabby face. Head up past a bolt, then traverse out right past three more bolts until you can reach a three-bolt belay shared by all five routes on this face. Rap off, or continue up a second pitch. **FA:** Todd Gordon, Tucker Tech.

495. **Blitzo Crack** (5.10a) ★★ Go up the obvious crack to face climbing past two bolts to reach the three-bolt belay. Either rap form here or continue up. **Pro:** To 2.5 inches; three-bolt anchor. **FA:** Todd Gordon, Tucker Tech.

496. **Cora-Door** (5.10c) (TR) This is the crack/left-facing dihedral between *Blitzo Crack* and *Buck.* **FA:** Tucker Tech.

497. **Buck** (5.8) ★ Go up the crack on the slab to the right end of the roof; join *Fake*

Foot and continue up and left to the shared three-bolt belay. **Pro:** Thin to 2.5 inches; three fixed pins; three-bolt anchor. **FA:** Todd Gordon, Bill Sernyk, John, Cora, Suzette Olsen, Chad.

498. **Fake Foot** (5.6) (R) **Pitch 1:** Go up low-angled cracks to the right side of the slab to the right of *Buck,* then angle left to the shared three-bolt belay. **Pitch 2:** Climb the runout face past a two-bolt anchor to the summit. **Pro:** Thin to 2.5 inches. **FA:** Unknown.

Disappointment Dome

This large, southwest-facing face/dome lies immediately east of Hooter Rock and south of Grinch Rock. See pages 151–153 for general approach directions. From where you enter the Atom Smashers Area, head east (a bit right) in a wash past the north face of Hooter Rock (on your right). The routes lie on the southwest face and are easily reached by heading down the notch between this formation and the east side of Hooter Rock. Rock quality is, as the name implies, somewhat less than what would be hoped for. It is sunny most of the afternoon. Descend down a chimney and ramp on the right side of the main face, to the left of *What A Shame.* Map, page 152.

499. **Let's Eat Organ Meat** (5.10a) Begin on the left-center part of the southwest face. Go up past two bolts to a discontinuous crack. **Pro:** Thin to 2 inches. **FA:** Ron White, Jack Marshall, Don Wilson; 3/89.

500. **The Fiasco** (5.10b) (R) Begin on a ledge near the right end of the face, about 80 feet right of *Let's Eat Organ Meat.* Head left

to a left-diagonalling crack to a bolt. Continue up the face, then cracks, to the top. **Pro:** Thin to 2.5 inches. **FA:** Unknown.

501. **The Letdown** (5.8+) Begin as for *The Fiasco,* heading up and left on that route, but instead of continuing left in the leaning crack, head straight up a thin crack to where you can exit right into the descent gully. **Pro:** Thin to 2 inches. **FA:** Kevin Powell, Alan Roberts; 1987.

502. **Roller Coaster** (5.8+) Begin on the same ledge as the last two routes, but head up and right in a finger crack. **Pro:** Thin to 2 inches. **FA:** Kevin Powell, Alan Roberts; 1987.

503. **What a Shame** (5.10a) This route lies on a separate face around to the right and above the start of the previous three routes. It begins out of the bottom of the descent gully. This seam-to-thin crack has two bolts on the bottom section. **Pro:** Thin to 2 inches. **FA:** Unknown.

The Foot (Wilderness)

The Foot lies about 300 yards east of the north face of Hooter Rock. The formation has a feature that looks like a 200-foot-tall "foot" with its "toes" pointing skyward. Routes lie on the northwest face. From where you enter the Atom Smashers Area, head east (a bit right) in a wash, passing the north face of Hooter Rock (on your right) and the north end of Disappointment Dome (also on your right). The Foot can be clearly

seen ahead, and a bit left above a boulder-filled canyon (to the south of the hill with Grinch Rock, on your left). Scramble up the canyon to the base. The Foot is shady in the morning, with afternoon sun. The descent for all the routes is to downclimb left to a small tree, then make a short rap (45 feet) to the ground. Maps, pages 152 and 169.

504. **The New Shoe Review** (5.10a) (R) ★★ This is a two-pitch, six-bolt face route on the left side of the northwest face. **Pitch 1:** Face climb past three bolts, heading up then a bit left to a belay on a ramp. **Pitch 2:** Go up the ramp, then up and right to a face, then straight up past three bolts to ledge. **Pro:** To 2.5 inches. **FA:** Dave Evans, Craig Fry, Todd Battey, Margie Floyd; 9/87.

505. **Dr. Scholl's Wild Ride** (5.9+) ★ This is the long off-width just to the right of *The New Shoe Review.* It is often done in two pitches, but can be done in one very long pitch with a 60+-meter rope. **Pro:** To 4 inches. **FA:** Dave Evans, Margie Floyd, Jim Angione; 12/86.

506. **Mr. Toe's Filed Hide** (5.9) ★ Begin about 15 feet right of *Dr. Scholl's Wild Ride.* Go up the wide crack in the arching left facing corner until it joins *Dr. Scholl's* after about 135 feet; continue up *Dr. Scholl's* to the top. Can be done in one very long pitch with a 60+-meter rope. **Pro:** To 3+ inches. **FA:** Tucker Tech, Alan Bartlett; 10/96.

(Up wide crack; bolts to left)

508

509

X

X

X

X

507

02.GRINCH.eps

Grinch Rock (Wilderness)

This small rocky crag (routes are 40 to 50 feet long) lies on a small hill roughly halfway between Disappointment Dome and the Atom Smashers Boulders. See page 151 for general approach directions. From where you enter the Atom Smashers Area, head roughly straight ahead following a wash, then cut left into another wash that passes under the northeast side of the formation. The only recorded routes are on the northeast face. The most obvious feature is a wide crack in a right-facing dihedral *(The Grinch's Grin)*. The Atom Smashers Boulders lie a short distance to the northeast and are easily visible from below the northeast face of Grinch Rock. It is shady most of the day. Map, pages 152 and 169.

507. **Nonprofit Crack** (5.9+) ★ This route climbs the flake and crack on the large rock below and left of *The Grinch's Grin*. Downclimb to the right. **Pro:** To 3 inches. **FA:** Kastle Lund, Don Reid, Alan Bartlett; 9/96.

508. **The Grinch's Grin** (5.10d) ★★ This is the prominent right-facing dihedral; an off-width crack (6+ inches) lies in the corner. Four bolts on the left wall protect powerful liebacking up this wide crack. Rap from slings (40 feet). **FA:** Jon Regelbrugge, Brian Gengler; 3/92.

509. **Stolen Christmas** (5.9) ★★ This route climbs the handcrack in the left-facing corner about 6 feet right of *The Grinch's Grin*; it becomes fingers near the top (crux). **Pro:** To 2.5 inches. Rap from slings. **FA:** Unknown.

Coffee Dome (Wilderness)

Coffee Dome is the first small formation on your left (northeast) as you enter the open valley of the Atom Smashers Area. See approach directions on pages 151–153. It lies about 200 yards west of the Timbuktu Towers. Routes lie on the south and east faces. From where you enter the Atom Smashers Area, angle left until you can turn left (north) to the south end of the formation. To descend, rap off a tree (80 feet). Map, page 152.

510. **Brown Vibrations** (5.9) (not shown on photo) Begin up the left-hand of two short cracks on the south face, then go right on a horizontal around the corner, then go up a thin crack with a bush to a flake. Head right up to the summit. Maybe best done in two pitches. **Pro:** To 2.5 inches. **FA:** Phil Bircheff, Alan Bartlett; 10/96.

511. **Juan Valdez Chimney** (5.7) (R) (not shown on photo) The obvious chossy chimney about 150 feet right of *Brown Vibrations;* best avoided. **Pro:** To 3 inches. **FA:** Alan Bartlett, Phil Bircheff; 10/96.

Yeti Dome (Wilderness)

This formation lies about 125 yards north of Coffee Dome. Routes are located in the canyon on the formation's northeast side. From where you enter the Atom Smashers Area, angle left until you pass the south side of Coffee Dome. Beyond Coffee Dome, head left (north) between Coffee Dome and Timbuktu Towers. Continue up the rocky, brush-filled gully on the right side of the formation. Temple Balls is near the left end of the northeast face; the remaining routes lie about 250 feet farther right. The dome and routes are not pictured. Map, page 152.

512. **Temple Balls** (5.9+) ★ This route lies on the left end of Yeti Dome's northeast face. It is a finger crack that rises above a large flake at the bottom. **Pro:** Thin to 2 inches. To descend, downclimb the chimney to the left. **FA:** Unknown.

513. **The Grinder** (5.9) This is the leaning left-facing corner with a wide crack. It begins above an easy corner/crack. **Pro:** To 4 inches. **FA:** Jiri Vodrazka, Alan Bartlett, 10/95.

514. **Abdominal Showman** (5.8) This is a short vertical crack that begins down and right of *The Grinder,* ending on loose blocks. **Pro:** To 2.5 inches. **FA:** Alan Bartlett, Jiri Vodrazka; 10/95.

515. **Kathmandu** (5.10a/b) ★ This right slanting crack begins just right of *Abdominal Showman* (to left the of a nolina plant). Rap from a tree atop the crack (90 feet), but apparently care must be taken not to get your rope stuck in the crack. **Pro:** To 2.5 inches. **FA:** Jiri Vodrazka, Alan Bartlett; 10/95.

New York Dome

This formation lies just east of and faces Yeti Dome. The only recorded route lies on the southwest face, opposite the northeast face of Yeti Dome and the routes listed above. Approach as for Yeti Dome. The dome and route are not pictured. Map, page 152.

516. **New York Minute** (5.8) This route is located near the middle of the southwest face. Begin up a crack with a bush at the start; above, head up and right in diagonal cracks to the summit. **Pro:** To 2.5 inches. **FA:** Alan Bartlett, Jiri Vodrazka; 10/95.

Parapsychology Dome

This formation lies northeast of New York Dome and has one recorded route on its northwest end. For initial approach directions, see pages 151-153. The best approach for this route from the valley appears to be boulder-hopping up the gully left of the Timbuktu Towers, then heading north along the gully on the east side of New York Dome. Parapsychology Dome is the formation on the right as you proceed along New York Dome's east side. The dome and route are not pictured. Map, page 152.

517. **Telekinesis** (5.11c or 5.10a) ★★ A large, scoop-shaped boulder is perched at the top of the northwest end of the formation. *Telekinesis* climbs the crack(s) directly below the scoop. **Variation 1** (5.10a): Start from a boulder and undercling the flake up and right to a thin crack. **Variation 2** (5.11c): Start 30 feet down and right of the above variation; climb up and left along double arching cracks to the thin crack. **Pro:** Thin to 2.5 inches. **FA:** Tony Yaniro, Brett Maurer; 1983.

Timbuktu Towers (Wilderness)

Timbuktu Towers are the large and most obvious formations on the hillside to the east of the open valley. They are visible at various points as you approach along the North Wonderland Trail (see pages 151–153 for initial approach). Routes on Timbuktu Towers are found on the west, south, and east sides. The large leaning pillar high on the north side of the Timbuktu Towers is the Ivory Tower, site of several very difficult sport routes. Map, page 152.

Timbuktu Towers—West Face

This is the face that you see as you approach this formation; it gets morning shade and sun all afternoon. The descent for all routes (except *Sine Wave* and the second pitch of *Gravity Waves*) is to rap from the bolt anchor atop the first pitch of *Gravity Waves* (90 feet). Otherwise, downclimb from the summit.

518. **Sine Wave** (5.9) ★ Begin up the right-facing corner, follow this to its end, then go up the face past one bolt until you can move left on a horizontal. **Pro:** To 2.5 inches. **FA:** Tony Yaniro, Brett Maurer; 1983.

519. **Gravity Waves** (5.12a) (R) ★★★★ This was originally rated 5.11a, but several large holds have broken, which has made the route harder and less than ideally protected. **Pitch 1:** Go up the face to the right of *Sine Wave* past five bolts (5.12a past the first bolt), then up and right to a ledge (two-bolt anchor/rap). Either rap off from here (90 feet) or continue. **Pitch 2:** Go up the small corner system (5.10c) and right-leaning crack above. **Pro:** Thin; small cams to 2.5 inches. **FA:** Tony Yaniro, Graham Peace, Bill Leventhal; 2/84.

520. **Gravity Works** (5.11c/d) (R) ★★★ Head up the face to the right of *Gravity Waves* to

reach a thin crack that curves right near the top to just meet *Offshoot*. Next, climb a diagonal crack up and left to reach the belay ledge on *Gravity Waves* (two-bolt anchor/rap). **Pro:** Thin to 2 inches. **FA:** Tony Yaniro, Toivo Kodas; 1983.

521. **Offshoot** (5.10b) ★ This is the obvious off-width to flared chimney right of the center of the west face. **Pro:** To 5 or 6 inches. **FA:** Gib Lewis, Charles Cole; 1982.

Timbuktu Towers—South Face

This wide face has several face and crack routes from 5.10a to 5.12b. The face is sunny most of the day, with some afternoon shade.

Descents: For *The Bates Motel*, you can possibly rap off the *Gravity Waves* anchor; for *The Latex Arête* to *Nuclear Waste*, rap from bolts. Other routes top out and require a downclimb.

522. **The Bates Motel** (5.12b) ★★★ This route follows the right side of the long, obvious arête past six bolts. The first bolt can be clipped from the ground; apparently much to Woodward and Hensel's chagrin. **Pro:** To 2 inches for anchors. **FA:** Jonny Woodward, Darrel Hensel; 2/88.

523. **The Latex Arête** (5.10a) (R) Begin just right of the arête about 25 feet right of *The Bates Motel*. Go up the face past a bolt to a ramp, then up and left, eventually belaying a bolt anchor atop *Polytechnics*. **Pro:** Thin to 2 inches; two-bolt anchor rap. **FA:** Unknown.

524. **Polytechnics** (5.10d) ★★ Begin about 10 feet right of *The Latex Arête;* go up the face and shallow ramp past a copperhead and three bolts to the two-bolt anchor/rap. **FA:** Tony Yaniro, Graham Peace, Toivo Kodas; 2/84.

525. **Nuclear Waste** (5.10a) This route is the off-width crack in the corner about 40 feet right of *Polytechnics*. **Pro:** To 4+ inches. **FA:** Tony Yaniro; 1983.

526. Psychokinesis (aka Missing in Action)
(5.11b) ★★★ Begin about 25 feet right of
Nuclear Waste. **Pitch 1:** Head up the obvious
left-leaning thin crack/ramp into a large
upper dihedral; belay where a diagonal
crack/ramp *(Psychotechnics)* heads up and
right. **Pitch 2:** Continue up the easy
crack/corner to the top. **Pro:** Thin to 2
inches. **FA:** Possibly aided. **FFA:** Either Tony
Yaniro and Ron Carson or Alan Bell and
Vaino Kodas; 1983.

527. Psychotechnics (5.11b) ★★ This route
allows for a better second pitch alternative to
Psychokinesis. Climb that route's first pitch;
from the belay, climb right on a thin crack,
around the corner, then up the exposed arête
past a bolt to the top. **Pro:** Thin to 1.5
inches. **FA:** Jonny Woodward, Darrel Hensel;
1/88.

Timbuktu Towers—East Side Routes

The following routes actually lie on a small
crag just right (east) of Timbuktu Towers
(Pumping Hate) and on an east-facing slab
below Timbuktu Towers' east face *(Psycho* and
Shower Scene). All routes face east, with early
morning sun and shade in the afternoon. The
routes are not pictured

528. Pumping Hate (5.13a) ★★★ (Sport) This
route follows five bolts on the overhanging
east face of the first rock right (east) of the
south face of Timbuktu Towers. Walk past
Psychokinesis, through boulders, then down
and around to this face. **Pro:** To 2 inches for
anchor. **FA:** Randy Leavitt; 4/88.

529. Psycho (5.10d) (R)★ This and the following route lie on slabs just below the east
face of Timbuktu Towers, directly below the
east side of the Ivory Tower. Climb the face
on the left, past three bolts, to the top of a

left-leaning arch. **Pro:** To 2 inches. **FA:** Vaino
Kodas et al.

530. Shower Scene (5.10c) ★ This is the
two-bolt route on the right leading to the
base of the left-leaning arch; belay as for the
above route. **Pro:** To 2 inches. **FA:** Vaino
Kodas et al.

The Ivory Tower (Wilderness)

This is the obvious leaning pillar above and
right (northeast) of the west face of
Timbuktu Towers. *Famous Potatoes* and *This
Spud's for You* are on its east face. Four very
difficult routes (5.13a to 5.13d) have been
done on its overhanging north face, all established by Randy Leavitt in the late 1980s.
The Ivory Tower can be approach from
either side of Timbuktu Towers, but is usually
approached from the left of *Sine Waves.* Both
approaches involve fourth to fifth class
scrambling. Rap anchors/lower-offs for all
routes. See photo on page 162; the routes are
not shown. Map, page 152.

The Ivory Tower—East Face

531. This Spud's for You (5.10c) ★ This six-
bolt face route is left of *Famous Potatoes;* the
crux getting past the first bolt. **FA:**
Unknown.

532. Famous Potatoes (5.11c) ★ This follows
two bolts to the right of *This Spud's for You;* a
little runout. **FA:** Unknown.

The Ivory Tower—North Face

This face offers overhanging face climbing; all are powerful crimp routes. The face is shady most of the day. *Chain of Addiction* is the only route with sport lower-off anchors. It may be climbable in hotter weather, provided you get an early start. The Ivory Tower can be seen in the photo on page 162; the routes are not pictured.

533. The Powers That Be (5.13a) ★★★★ (Sport) This route has five bolts and is near the left edge of the face. There is a "sporty" move at the end of the crux section. **FA:** Randy Leavitt; 4/88.

534. Chain of Addiction (5.13c) ★★★★ (Sport) Climb the center of the face past nine bolts. This has a "sport"-type lower off anchor. **FA:** Randy Leavitt; 10/88.

535. Ocean of Doubt (5.13b/c) ★★★★★ (Sport) This is regarded as the best route on the Ivory Tower, involving classic technical Josh moves. The route is just right of *Chain of Addiction*. **FA:** Randy Leavitt; 1989.

536. La Machine (5.13d) ★★★★ (Sport) This excellent route is the most difficult on the Ivory Tower and lies near the right edge of the north face. Six bolts. **FA:** Randy Leavitt; 8/88.

Atom Smashers Boulders
(Wilderness)

These boulders lie on the valley floor about 125 yards south-southeast and down hill from Timbuktu Towers. They are generally about 50 feet high. Many face climbs are found on the sharp arêtes. To reach the boulders from where you enter the Atom Smashers Area, head more or less directly east until you enter a wash that runs east below the north side of Grinch Rock. Beyond the north side of Grinch Rock, the Atom Smashers Boulders lie on the desert floor a short distance to the northeast (left). The wash passes just south of the boulders. Map, page 152.

537. Nuclear Arms (5.12a) ★★★ Climb the west face of Boulder I, starting above the overhanging bottom via either *Atom Ant* or *Gumshoe*. **FA:** Tony Yaniro, Randy Leavitt; 3/84.

538. Atom Ant (5.11b) ★★ Start left of the northwest arête of Boulder II, and continue up and left past two bolts to the top. Two-bolt anchor/rap. **FA:** Tony Yaniro, Randy Leavitt; 3/84.

539. Gumshoe (5.10d) ★★★ Start as for *Atom Ant*. Traverse up and right around the arête from the second bolt, then past two more bolts to the summit. Two-bolt anchor/rap. **FA:** Gib Lewis, Charles Cole; 1982.

540. Ionic Strength (5.12a) ★★★★ This climbs the steep arête on the southwest corner of Boulder II. There are four bolts and a two-bolt anchor/rap. **FA:** Tony Yaniro, Ron Carson; 1983.

541. Knee Knockers (5.10b) ★ (TR) Climb the face left of *Shin Bashers* on the north face. **FA:** Todd Swain; 12/98.

542. **Shin Bashers** (5.11c) ★ Climb just right of the northeast arête of Boulder III. **FA:** Tony Yaniro, Brett Maurer, Ron Carson; 1983.

543. **Quantum Mechanics** (5.11b) ★★ Climb the center of the north face of Boulder III past two bolts. Two-bolt anchor/rap. **FA:** Tony Yaniro, Ron Carson; 1983.

544. **Isotope** (5.9) ★★ Climb the northwest arête of Boulder III past two bolts. Two-bolt anchor/rap. **FA:** Tony Yaniro, Ron Carson; 1983.

Formations East of the Atom Smashers Area

Several formations have been developed that lie to the east and downhill of the Atom Smashers Area and somewhat northwest of the Super Dome. These formations include Yearly Rock, Lost Rock, Fish Rock, and Supercollider Rock. They are best approached from the Atom Smashers Area, though it is possible to reach them from the vicinity of the Super Dome (but only if you were already at the Super Dome).

To reach these rocks, park at the

Northern Wonderland parking area (6.4 miles from the West Entrance; 2.2+ miles from the Intersection Rock/Real Hidden Valley intersection). Hike nearly 1 mile northeast on the North Wonderland Trail. At this point, it will join up with a larger trail (a former dirt road) heading straight north. After about 500 yards (just past Gilligan's Island), the Boy Scout Trail to Indian Cove diverges to the left and the North Wonderland Trail begins a slow curve to the right (northeast). From where the Boy Scout Trail splits off, stay right on the North Wonderland Trail for about 1.3 miles to where it ends in a sandy wash. The main trail cuts right at a sign, but continue straight ahead for about 90 yards, to where the wash makes a sharp right (south) turn. Head more or less straight ahead (east) into a narrow wash that becomes a bit rocky, then enter a large open valley (the Atom Smashers Area).

The large Timbuktu Towers are more or less straight ahead and a bit to the left, atop a large hillside. From where you enter the Atom Smashers Area, head more or less east along the flats until you enter a wash that runs east, passing below the north side of Grinch Rock. A bit farther the wash passes just right (south) of the Atom Smashers Boulders. From here, continue eastward until you head down into a large valley; the terrain is quite rough through here. Yearly Rock and Lost Rock are located to your left (north), with Fish Rock and Supercollider Rock on your right (south). A large flat boulder on the southern side of the valley provides a good vantage point from which to find Yearly Rock and Lost Rock, as well as Fish Rock and Supercollider Rock. The gully that heads up and right (south) leads to the Super Dome and provides an alternative approach. None of these rocks or routes are pictured. Map, page 152.

Yearly Rock (Wilderness)

Yearly Rock is a small formation about 150 yards east of the Timbuktu Towers. It is located about halfway down the rough hillside described in the approach directions, about 60 yards to your left (north). Look for a right-slanting finger-to-fist crack. Map, page 152.

545. **Year After Year** (5.9) This route lies on the east face of Yearly Rock. It is a finger crack to a hand/fist crack that leads to a flake. **Pro:** To 3+ inches. **FA:** Kevin Zimlinghaus, Brezoczky; 2/90.

Lost Rock (Wilderness)

This rounded formation lies about 100 yards east of Yearly Rock and about 100 yards north of the large flat boulder that lies east of Timbuktu Towers. Map, page 152.

546. **Two Lost Soles** (5.8) This is located on the southwest face of Lost Rock. Climb a semichute with a crack to a flake. Above, climb the fist crack to the top. **Pro:** To 3+ inches. **FA:** Brezoczky, Kevin Zimlinghaus; 2/90.

Fish Rock (Wilderness)

This formation lies on the hillside south of Lost Rock and uphill from the flat boulder. It and Supercollider Rock lie just north of the Super Dome. Maps, pages 152 and 169.

547. **Living in a Fishbowl** (5.10b) (R) This is the thin crack in a distinct right-facing dihedral on the north face of Fish Rock. **Pro:** Thin to 2.5 inches. **FA:** Brezoczky, Kevin Zimlinghaus; 2/90.

Supercollider Rock (Wilderness)

The Supercollider Rock is a small formation located about 75 yards east of Fish Rock at the top of a gully; it lies just north of the Super Dome. Its north side is split by a chimney. The known routes lie on the northwest corner of the rock. Descend via a long rappel (more than 100 feet from bolts), or downclimb to the east. Maps, pages 152 and 169.

548. **Spanking** (5.11c) ★ (TR) Begin in the chimney. Head up and right in a finger crack out a roof that leads to a rounded arête. Climb up *Supercollider* to set up the toprope; two-bolt anchor/100+-foot rap. **FA:** Randy Leavitt, Doug Englekirk; 10/87.

549. **Supercollider** (5.8) ★ Begin on the far right (west) side of the formation. Go up a chimney 80 feet to a long finger crack on the left. Do as one or two pitches. **Pro:** Thin to 2 inches; two-bolt anchor/100+-foot rap. **FA:** Randy Leavitt, Doug Englekirk; 10/87.

THE SUPER DOME AREA

(Wilderness}

The Super Dome is the highest point in the Wonderland of Rocks and a strikingly beautiful rock formation. It is actually visible from Park Boulevard (to the east) at a point between the Negropolis and Vagmarken Hill. Most routes are at least two pitches in length and many sport quarter-inch bolts and runout sections. This is definitely one of the crown jewels of the Northern Wonderland. Plan on one-and-a-half to two hours for the approach. Maps, pages 84 and 85.

Park at the North Wonderland parking area (6.4 miles from the West Entrance; 2.2+ miles from the Intersection Rock/Real Hidden Valley intersection). Hike nearly 1 mile northeast on the North Wonderland Trail; at this point, it will join up with a larger trail (a former dirt road) heading straight north. After about 500 yards (at 1.2 miles, just past Gilligan's Island), the Boy

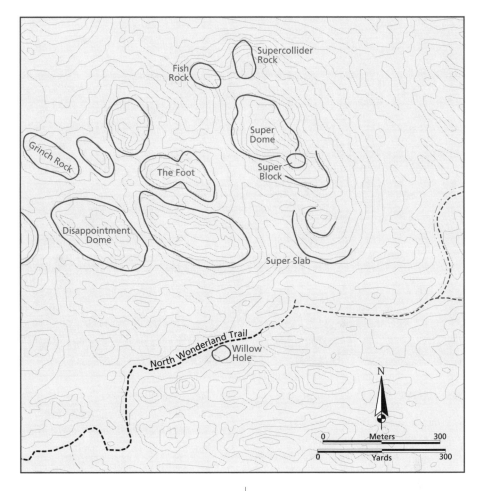

Scout Trail to Indian Cove diverges to the left and the North Wonderland Trail begins a slow curve to the right (northeast). Stay right on the North Wonderland Trail for another 1.4 mile where it joins a large wash (2.6 miles). At a trail marker, head right (south) into the main Wonderland wash system and to where the wash makes a sharp left (east) turn (2.9 miles). Follow the wash east (past a large boulder) where it makes a sharp left (north) turn (3.2 miles). The wash turns east again and leads to a tree- and brush-choked series of shallow water pools (often dry). This

is Willow Hole, a valuable water source for desert bighorn sheep and other animals. From Willow Hole, head over a small rise and down into an open area. The Super Dome and the Super Slab are directly to the north (left). A rocky gully above willow trees leads up to the Super Dome. It is also possible to reach the Super Dome from the Atom Smashers Area by heading toward Lost and Supercollider Rocks, then heading up a small gully to the south; see pages 151–153 for those approach descriptions. See map above and maps on pages 85 and 152.

The Super Slab (Wilderness)

This is the large, south-facing, low-angled slab lying to the right of the bottom of the approach gully to the Super Dome. It gets sun most of the day. All routes have rappel descents. Map, page 169.

550. **Coyote Corner** (5.9) ★ (not shown) This is the left-facing curving corner/flake. Make a 95-foot rappel from trees. **Pro:** To 2.5 inches. **FA:** Unknown.

551. **Dimpled Chad** (5.10c) ★ (not shown) This five-bolt face climb lies to the right of *Coyote Corner,* in the middle of Super Slab. Two-bolt anchor/rap. **FA:** Todd Gordon, Tucker Tech, Mark Synott.

552. **Mike Hunt** (5.9+) ★★ This right-curving crack is to the right of *Dimpled Chad.* **Pro:** Three bolts; three fixed pins; two-bolt anchor/rap. **FA:** Tucker Tech.

553. **Keep the Worm Firm** (5.7) ★★ Go up a crack to the face on the right side. **Pro:** Three bolts, two-bolt anchor/rap. **FA:** Todd Gordon, Tucker Tech, Cora, Bill Sernyk, George Armstrong, John.

The Super Dome (Wilderness)

This formation sits atop a rocky gully. From the open area below the gully, head left of the stand of willow trees, up onto boulders, then back up the right side of the gully until you can head up the steep but more open slopes of the hillside below the dome. It is likely that the Super Dome can be just as easily (maybe more easily) reached by approaching through the Atom Smashers Area and heading east from the vicinity of the Atom Smashers Boulders, then angling southeast to the northwest side of the Super Dome. To descend from the summit, head down and right, then to the top of the Super Block; make a 50-foot rappel from *Lion's Share,* then head back to the base.

554. Stone Hinge (5.11b) ★★ (not shown on picture) This route and the next lie on the north side of the Super Dome, where several "terraces" can be seen. A large block rests against the lower terrace, which sports a finger- to thin handcrack in its right side. These routes are definitely more easily approached from the Atom Smashers Area. **Pro:** To 2.5 inches. **FA:** Tony Yaniro, Vaino Kodas, Dan Michael; 1983.

555. The Bilderberg Conference (5.10c) ★★ Begin just down and left of *Stone Hinge.* Go up the thin handcrack, then reach left into a handcrack leading to the top of a 40-foot pinnacle. **Pro:** To 3 inches. **FA:** A. J. Burch, David Evans; 5/03.

556. The Cole–Lewis (5.10b) ★★ Rope up on a ledge above bushes. **Pitch 1:** Climb a flake/crack to a ledge (5.8; 25 feet). **Pitch 2:** Lieback the crack on the left to a dike; go left, then up past three bolts to a flake. **Pitch 3:** Go up the face past two bolts, then go left (5.10b) into a crack leading to a slab (180-foot pitch). **Pro:** To 3 inches. **FA:** Charles Cole, Gib Lewis; 1983.

557. The Great Unknown (5.10b) ★★ This route climbs the large flake/pillar lying against the southwest face, then heads up face above. Both sides of the pillar have been climbed. **Pitch 1:** Do the first pitch of *The Cole–Lewis* (5.8; 25 feet). **Pitch 2:** Go up the left side of the flake (5.10a). **Pitch 3:** Go up and left past five bolts to a crack then slab to the top (5.10b). **Note:** Two off-route bolts are located up and right of flake's top. **Variation** to pitches 1 and 2: Start right of *The Cole*

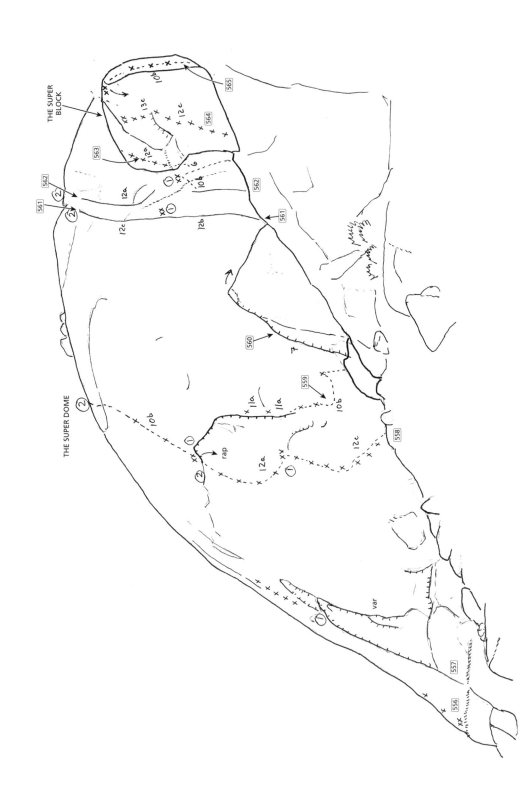

THE SUPER BLOCK

THE SUPER DOME

565

564

563

562

561

562

561

560

559

558

557

556

13c

12c

12a

12b

12c

10b

10b

9

10b

11a

11a

10b

12c

12a

rap

var

2

2

2

2

1

1

1

1

1

The Super Block

The Super Dome

562

563

564

561

560

559

558

12a
rap
11a
12c
10b

556

557

Lewis and head up the right side of flake/pillar (5.10a). **Pro:** Thin to 4 inches. **FA** (Pitches 1 and 2): Mark Bowling, Larry Thaxton, Deborah Boren; 4/76. **FA** (Right side and Pitch 3): Mark Wagner et al.; 1977.

558. **Warpath** (5.12c) ★★★★ (Sport) This climb features excellent position on the center of the face. Begin about 50 feet down and left of *The Last Unicorn*. **Pitch 1:** Go left and up past seven bolts to a two-bolt anchor (5.12c). Some climbers do only the first pitch and rap with a single rope from the anchor. **Pitch 2:** Go left and up past four bolts to the bolt anchor shared with *The Last Unicorn* (5.12a?); 135-foot rappel from here. **FA:** Tony Yaniro, Randy Leavitt; 12/88.

559. **The Last Unicorn** (5.11a) (R) ★★★★★ This takes a striking line up the center of the south face. Begin behind a small oak just left

of the left-facing corner of *Bleed Proof.* **Pitch 1:** Go up 25 feet to a bolt (a sling on a horn might protect), then head down, traverse left, and go up to a second bolt (5.10b/c R). Continue up a shallow corner past three more bolts (5.11a) to a ledge (two-bolt belay; 135-foot rap from here). **Pitch 2:** Go up a steep and a bit loose face past two bolts and a fixed pin to summit (5.10b/c R). **Pro:** Thin to 2 inches. At the time of publication, the old quarter-inch bolts had not been replaced (but they may be replaced in the future). While this is an excellent route, some climbers have been dissuaded from leading due to the runout between the first and second bolts. **FA** (Pitch 1): Dave Evans, Craig Fry, Randy Vogel; 1980. **FA** (Pitch 2): Alan Bartlett, Dan Michael; 4/81.

560. **Bleed Proof** (5.7) (R) Follow the left-facing corner to the top of a small pinnacle

against the face. This is just right of start of *The Last Unicorn*. **Pro:** To 4 inches. **FA:** Dave Evans; 1980.

561. **The Mohawk** (5.12c) ★★★ This two-pitch thin crack begins just right of the *Bleed Proof* pinnacle. **Pitch 1:** Go up the thin crack in the flared corner past two bolts to a two-bolt belay (5.12b). **Pitch 2:** Continue up the very thin crack to the summit; a bit runout at the top (5.12c). **Pro:** Many thin to 2 inches. **FA:** Tony Yaniro, Brett Maurer; 1/82 (with one point of aid on second pitch). **FFA:** Randy Leavitt; 1/87.

562. **Chief Crazy Horse** (5.12a) ★★★ Begin just right of *The Mohawk* in a thin crack. **Pitch 1:** Go up the thin crack til it ends, then go up and right to a two-bolt belay (5.10b R). Alternatively, climb the slab to the right up to the belay (5.6 R/X). **Pitch 2:** Head up and left into a thin crack that leads to the summit (5.12a). **Pro:** Many thin to 2 inches. **FA:** Tony Yaniro, Ron Carson, Brett Maurer; 1/82.

The Super Block (Wilderness)

This large block sits immediately right of the main Super Dome face. Routes here tend to be sheltered from the cold winds that frequent the park. The following routes lie on the west arête and south face. They are sheltered and sunny most of the day.

563. **Sideburn** (5.12a) ★★★ (Sport) To approach, "third class" (5.6 R/X) up the slab to the right of *Chief Crazy Horse* to the two-bolt anchor atop that route's first pitch; belay here. Stem out right, climb over the roof. and continue up the southwest arête past four bolts. Two-bolt anchor. **FA:** Randy Leavitt; 9/89.

564. **Hydra** (5.13c) ★★★★★ (Sport) This excellent steep sport route is located on the south face of the Super Block, to the right of and down from *Sideburn*. Make a series of steep technical face moves (5.12c) to a large jug where you can get a rest. Above, power out the overhanging "wave-like" wall/roof (crux). **Pro:** Nine bolts; two-bolt anchor. **FA:** Randy Leavitt; 2/90.

565. **Lion's Share** (5.10b) ★★ (Sport) This route climbs the arête right of *Hydra* past three bolts. Start by chimneying up, then stemming across to the first bolt. Two-bolt anchor/rap. **FA:** Randy Leavitt, Glenn Svenson; 9/89.

566. **Sitting Bull** (5.10d) ★★ (not shown on photo or topo) This route is located on the back side of the Super Block. To reach it, tunnel through the right side of the block (at *Lion's Share*). This is a classic finger-to-fist crack in a right-facing corner. **Pro:** To 4 inches. **FA:** Randy Leavitt, Rob Slater; 9/88.

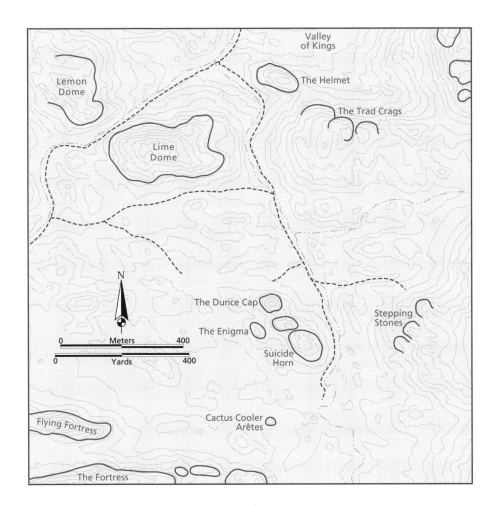

Lemon and Lime Domes

Lemon and Lime Domes are two large formations situated about 0.25 mile east of Willow Hole and Super Dome. Lemon Dome is the smaller northern rock and Lime Dome the larger southern formation. Somewhat broken, they contain little good climbing, but some possibilities on the south side of Lime Dome exist. The wash from Willow Hole down to Rattlesnake Canyon runs between these two formations. Plan on about one-and-a-half to two hours to reach these formations.

To reach the domes, you can head up Rattlesnake Canyon to the Valley of Kings; then head up and right (west) in a rocky canyon between the Lemon and Lime Domes. This may be shorter time-wise, but is certainly more arduous.

Alternatively, park at the North Wonderland parking area (6.4 miles from the West Entrance; 2.2+ miles from the Intersection Rock/Real Hidden Valley intersection). Hike nearly 1 mile northeast on the North Wonderland Trail; at this point, it will join up with a larger trail (a former dirt road) heading straight north. After another 500 yards (just past Gilligan's Island), the Boy Scout Trail to Indian Cove diverges to the left and the North Wonderland Trail begins a slow curve to the right (northeast/1.2 miles. Stay right on the North Wonderland Trail for another 1.4 mile to where it joins a large wash (2.6 miles). At a trail marker, head right (south) into the main Wonderland wash system to where the wash makes a sharp left (east) turn (2.9 miles). Follow the wash east (past a large boulder) to where it makes a sharp left (north) turn (3.2 miles). Soon the wash turns east again and leads to a tree- and brush-choked series of shallow water pools (often dry). This is Willow Hole, a valuable water source for desert bighorn sheep and other animals.

From Willow Hole, head over a small rise and down into an open area. The Super Dome and Super Slab are directly to the north (left). Continue east down the rockier and steeper wash for about 300 yards to a spot where the wash turns left (north); a small drop marks this spot (3.6+ miles). The west side of Lime Dome lies directly ahead to the east. Head north, then east, as the wash leads into a narrower canyon and becomes filled with large boulders. At this point, Lemon Dome is on your left (north) and Lime Dome on your right (south/3.9 miles). These domes and routes are not pictured.

Lemon Dome

567. **The Lemon Head** (5.10b) This route lies on the south face of Lemon Dome. Start up a right-facing flake and chimney to reach the left side of the face and this route (5.2). Above, go up a right-facing corner, then face past four bolts to the middle of the face; slung plates and knobs protect the climbing to the top. **Pro:** To 2.5 inches; slings. **FA:** Todd Gordon, Craig Fry, Marge Floyd; 1/86.

Lime Dome

Lime Dome is the large broken formation south of and across the canyon from Lemon Dome. Map, page 175.

568. **The Lemon Slicer** (5.11a) ★★ This steep thin to handcrack lies on a split boulder low on the right (northwest) side of Lime Dome, directly across from *The Lemon Head*. **Pro:** Thin to 2.5 inches. **FA:** Dave Evans, Craig Fry; 12/85.

569. **Lemon Lemon** (5.10a) This 2-pitch route lies about 150 feet to the left (east) of *The Lemon Slicer.* It is on the north face of Lime Dome.

THE VALLEY OF KINGS

(Wilderness)

The Valley of Kings is a large open valley east of and below Lemon and Lime Domes, near the confluence of the Rattlesnake Wash and the Wonderland Wash. It lies just beyond the ridgeline of Rattlesnake Canyon, behind (south) of Indian Cove. Several formations are located here, including the impressive north and northeast faces of the Helmet, the Arrowhead, the Lynch Crag, Corrugated Wall, and the Trad Crags. Also included in this section is the Slatanic Area, a large pillar of rock normally associated with the Indian Cove-Rattlesnake Canyon areas, but easily approached from and lying adjacent to the Valley of Kings. Map, page 178.

It is definitely faster to reach this area from Indian Cove via Rattlesnake Canyon, though it is often approached from Willow Hole. Both approaches are given here.

Willow Hole Approach: From Lemon and Lime Domes (see page 175 for approach description), continue down the rocky gully of the Rattlesnake Wash into the large open Valley of Kings, where the Wonderland Wash comes in from the right (south). The rounded, isolated dome directly ahead (to the east) is the Helmet (4.2+ miles). Plan on about two hours to reach this crag from the North Wonderland parking area.

Rattlesnake Canyon Approach: From the Park Avenue intersection in the town of Joshua Tree, drive approximately 9.1 miles east on Highway 62 to the Indian Cove Road turnoff (right-hand turn). Drive south on Indian Cove Road for about 2.9 miles (passing the park entrance station at 1 mile) to the Indian Cove Campground, where the campground road forks either right or left. Head left (east) for about 1.2 miles, leaving the campground, then curving south to a parking loop/picnic area (Rattlesnake Canyon Picnic Area). Park on the eastern side of the loop.

Walk east about 100 yards into the Rattlesnake Canyon wash. Head right (south) up the canyon for about 400 yards; at this point the wash has turned right (southwest), and then made an abrupt turn back left (east). The terrain becomes more jumbled from this point. Stay on the right side of the canyon, heading up slabs; higher up, go through a narrow corridor, then drop back into the wash. Continue up a few hundred yards farther until the wash turns right (west) and becomes fairly level.

Continue along this wash for several hundred yards, past some large boulders and trees, until you encounter a very large boulder field on the hillside to your left (south). At this point, the watercourse of the Wonderland Wash descends from your left (south) under these boulders, joining Rattlesnake Canyon (which continues west). Go left (south) up the boulder field, heading for the gap in the hillside where the Wonderland Wash comes down from the North Wonderland. About halfway up, make sure to drop into the main watercourse, following its right side. Once over the gap you will find yourself in a large valley, with the Helmet visible almost directly ahead (to the south-southeast). The Valley of Kings runs east from here. Plan on about one hour to reach the Valley of Kings from Indian Cove. This area is designated wilderness, and bolting restrictions apply.

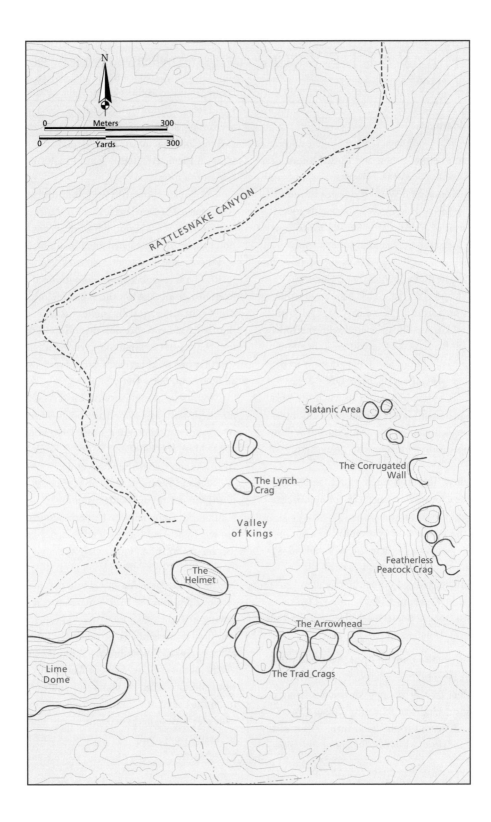

N

0 Meters 300
0 Yards 300

RATTLESNAKE CANYON

Slatanic Area

The Corrugated
Wall

The Lynch
Crag

Valley
of Kings

Featherless
Peacock Crag

The Helmet

The Arrowhead

Lime
Dome

The Trad Crags

The Helmet (Wilderness)

The Helmet is a large isolated dome with an impressive north-northeast face located at the entrance to the Valley of Kings. It is the key reference point and the first formation encountered as you approach this area.

    Descent is via rappel (see route descriptions) or by walking off the southeast side of the rock. Map, page 178.

The Helmet—North and Northeast Faces

The steep north and northeast faces of the Helmet have excellent, clean rock that get early sun and are shady most of the afternoon.

570. **Full Battle Gear** (5.12b) ★★ This obvious vertical, flaring, thin to hand-crack is on the far left side of the northeast face. It is much harder than it looks. Descend off left. **Pro:** Thin to 2.5 inches. **FA:** Steve Sutton, Brian Agnew; 12/92.

571. **The Tomahawk** (5.12a) ★★★★★ This route starts up a left-arching crack 25 feet left of a pine tree at the base of the north face, to the left of an obvious slanting crack with a yucca. **Pitch 1:** Go up and left in the crack, then up past a fixed pin to a bolt; now head up and right past another fixed pin, then traverse right past seven more bolts to a hanging (two-bolt) belay (5.11d/5.12a). **Pitch 2:** Go up the face past nine bolts (5.12a crux past the first bolt) to a two-bolt belay. Either

make two single-rope (100-foot and 70-foot) rappels or one double-rope rappel, or continue up and right on fourth-class ground to a 200-foot rappel from bolts. **FA:** Bob Gaines, Steve Sutton; 10/92.

572. **Open Project** (5.12d/5.13a) This project (not redpointed) goes directly up to the first belay of *The Tomahawk*. Climb up the right side of a flake to the right of a pine tree; off the left end of the flake eight bolts lead to the last two bolts on *The Tomahawk's* first pitch.

The Helmet—West and Southwest Faces

The southwest and west faces of the Helmet are lower-angled and somewhat flaky/grainy. Two routes are known. The faces get morning shade and is sunny all afternoon. The faces and routes are not pictured.

573. **The Regular Route** (5.10b) ★ Begin near the left side of the west face, where a large and very thin flake lies against the face. Climb the flake, then go up the face above. **Pro:** Three quarter-inch bolts. **FA:** Unknown.

574. **Blues for the Red Sun** (5.8) ★ (not shown) An obvious left-facing thin lieback flake in orange rock is on the southwest face is. Begin below and right of this in a 2- to 3-inch right-facing lieback, then make a hand traverse left to the upper flake. This ends on a ledge; walk off left (west). **Pro:** To 3 inches. **FA:** A. J. Burch, Dave Evans, Matt Schubert; 5/03.

The Lynch Crag (Wilderness)

This small brownish crag is located on the left (north) side of the Valley of Kings, about 150 yards east and north of the Helmet. It lies low on the hillside, and is characterized by several vertical crack systems on its south and west faces. Descend from routes via bolted rappel anchors; if you went to the very top of the crag, you could walk off. Map, page 178.

575. **Eraserhead** (5.9) ★★ Go up the crack on west face to join *Wounded Knee* below the horizontal. A little loose at the bottom. **Pro:** To 2 inches; two bolts. Two-bolt anchor/100-foot rappel. **FA:** Steve Sutton, Angie Sutton; 11/92.

576. **Wounded Knee** (5.10a) ★★★ Follow a wide slot to a hand- then finger crack. Go left to another crack, then up the face past two bolts. **Pro:** 0.5 to 2 inches, plus one 4- to 5-inch cam. Two-bolt anchor/100-foot rappel. **FA:** Steve Sutton, Angie Sutton; 11/92.

577. **Mulholland Drive** (5.11c) ★★★ An unprotected seam (a little loose) leads to tips to a finger crack over bulges; traverse right on the crack to finish past the last bolt of *Powered By Old English.* **Pro:** Thin to 1.5 inches. **FA:** Vernon Stiefel, Randy Vogel, Holden Harris; 4/03.

578. **Powered by Old English** (5.11d) ★★★★ The right-hand route. Thin lieback and face climbing past five bolts leads to a crack, then up to a bulge and one more bolt. Two-bolt anchor/85-foot rappel. **Pro:** Six bolts; thin to 0.5 inches. **FA:** Steve Sutton, Angie Sutton; 11/92.

The Trad Crags (Wilderness)

This large and complex formation consists of several 200+-foot, north-facing slabs broken by vertical cracks and ledge systems. The crags lie on the hillside about 250 yards above and left (east) of the Helmet. From the vicinity of the Helmet, head up the wash, staying right where it forks, then angle right, up to the base. Several multipitch routes have been done, but there is no information about these. Map, page 178.

578A. The Sanga's on Fire (5.10b) ★★★
Begin off a large ledge; go up a flake to a finger crack that arches up, ending on a ledge 40 feet below the top. Finish up a handcrack. **Pro:** Thin; several thin cams to 2.5 inches. **FA:** Dave Evans, A. J. Burch, Matt Shubert; 5/03.

579. The Balloon that Wouldn't Die (5.7+)
This climbs the left side of the bowling ball-shaped feature (two roughly parallel crack systems). **Pitch 1:** Go up the corner left of the roof to a ledge (5.7/5.8). **Pitch 2:** Go up easier crack straight to a ledge below a block. **Pro:** To 4 inches. Fixed nut anchor/rap (200+ feet). **FA** (?): Dave Evans, A. J. Burch; 4/03.

580. The Unknown (5.?) This climbs the right side crack system. **Pitch 1:** Climb the face and crack to the right of the large roof to the ledge. **Pitch 2:** Go up the clean right-facing corner to the ledge below block. **Pro:** To 4 inches. Fixed nut anchor/rap (200+ feet). **FA:** Unknown; early 1980s (?).

581. It's Good to Be King (5.8) ★ This is located on the east-facing section of the crag about 20 yards down and right of *The Balloon that Wouldn't Die*. Go up a finger to handcrack that splits at the top; go left at the top past a bush to the face. **Pro:** To 2 inches. **FA:** A. J. Burch, Dave Evans; 4/03.

582. King of Jesters, Jester to Kings (5.10d) ★★ (not shown) This short overhanging crack lies in the back of a flaring left-facing dihedral formed by a block lying against the face. It is above and left of the top of *It's Good to Be King* (which is the best approach to this climb). Stemming, chimneying, and jamming are required. The crack in back is thin hands. Strenuous. **Pro:** Thin to 2 inches. **FA:** A. J. Burch, Dave Evans; 4/03.

The Arrowhead (Wilderness)

A huge flake has exfoliated off the main face of the lower leftmost section of the Trad Crags and lodged itself into the ground. The flake is about 95 feet tall, 65 feet across, and only 2 to 4 feet thick. This flake is the Arrowhead, so named because of its resemblance to an arrowhead thrust point down into the ground. From the vicinity of the Helmet, head up the wash, staying right where it forks, then angle right, up the hillside, to the base. Map, page 178.

583. **Firewater Chimney** (5.10b) ★★★★ This route features exciting and totally classic stemming and chimneying past six bolts between the inside of the flake and the main wall. It's a little runout between some of the bolts, but the climbing is fairly secure, even if moving up may be strenuous. Make a 90+-foot rappel off a two-bolt anchor down the outside of the face. **FA:** Steve Sutton, Karen Roseme; 11/92.

584. The Last Stand (5.12a) ★★★★ (Sport)
Begin on the right side of the outside face of the Arrowhead flake, at a thin crack/seam that runs about halfway up the face. Go up interesting face climbing next to the seam past five bolts (5.10c/d), head left, and then go up past five more bolts to a two-bolt anchor and a 90-foot rappel. The crux is past the sixth bolt, with 5.10+/5.11− climbing above. **Pro:** Ten bolts (optional blue TCU between fourth and fifth bolts); two-bolt anchor. **FA:** Steve Sutton, Karen Roseme; 12/92.

585. Waltz for Debbie (5.10a) ★★★ (not shown) This steep thin crack lies about 30 yards left of the Arrowhead, just right of an overhanging orange wall. The crack angles slightly left and heads over a roof about 50 feet up. Good rock, fun moves. Easy walk off to the left (east). **Pro:** Thin to 2 inches. **FA:** A. J. Burch, Dave Evans, Matt Schubert; 5/03.

Featherless Peacock Crag

This formation lies high on the slopes above the eastern end of the Valley of Kings, to the right (south) of, and up from, the Corrugated Wall. It is most easily recognized by a prominent right-facing dihedral *(My Helmet Is Bigger than Your Helmet)* on the right side of the formation. Neither the crag or the routes are pictured. Map, page 178.

585A. My Helmet Is Bigger than Your Helmet (5.10d) ★★★ Go up the obvious right-facing dihedral. **Pro:** 1 to 5 inches. **FA:** Vernon Stiefel, Holden Harris; 10/03.

585B. White Noise (5.11a) ★★ This and the next route are located in a small "cove" behind *My Helmet Is Bigger than Your Helmet;* it is the off-width crack in the left-facing corner; crux is down low. **Pro:** 3 to 5 inches. **FA:** Vernon Stiefel, Holden Harris; 10/03.

585C. One Size Doesn't Fit All (5.10b) ★★ (TR) This is a narrow chimney to off-width crack. It could be led. **Pro:** Big Bros or equivalent. **FA** (TR): Vernon Stiefel, Holden Harris; 10/03.

PHOTO: VERN STIEFEL

The Corrugated Wall
(Wilderness)

This steep, juggy, dark brown wall lies at the far eastern end of the Valley of Kings. It lies about 400 yards east of the Helmet. From the vicinity of the Helmet, head left (east) up the valley, staying left where the wash splits, then go up boulders to the base. Map, page 178.

586. **Eagle Talons** (5.12a) ★★★★ (Sport) Climb the steep, juggy face on the right-hand section of the upper face past bolts to two-bolt anchor. **FA:** Steve Sutton; 11/92.

The Slatanic Area (Wilderness)

The Slatanic Area lies near the very top of the south ridgeline above Rattlesnake Canyon. This area's main feature is a 100-foot-tall north-facing rectangular monolith. The granite is as solid and smooth as any rock in Josh. Though commonly approached directly from Rattlesnake Canyon (a more direct route to be sure), more than one climber seeking the Slatanic Area has spent hours trying to navigate up the steep, rocky hillside above the canyon. For that reason, and due to the Slatanic Area's location immediately adjacent to the northeastern end of the Valley of Kings, it is recommended, at least on your first visit, to approach the Slatanic Area via the Valley of Kings (see page 177). From the vicinity of the Helmet, head left (east) up the valley, staying left where the wash splits, toward the Corrugated Wall. Turn left (north) into the gully in the ridge that is just north of the Corrugated Wall. The Slatanic Area is just around the corner near the top of the gully/ridgeline. This is probably the best spot to scope (and descend) the direct approach from Rattlesnake Canyon. Map, page 178.

587. **Devil's Advocate** (5.11a) ★★★ This route lies just left of *Witch Hunt,* beginning up an obvious off-width crack (5.10a); the low-angled crack heads up and left and narrows to tips. Above, the crack slants right and steepens (5.10c/d); a final section of face above the crack takes you to the ledge (5.11a). From the belay on the ledge, head up and right to the top of *Witch Hunt* and rap from here (or *South Of Heaven*). **Pro:** Very thin to 4 inches. **FA:** Vernon Stiefel, Holden Harris; 5/03.

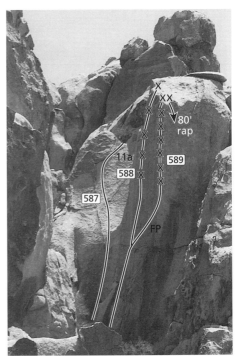

PHOTO: HOLDEN HARRIS

588. **Witch Hunt** (5.10b) ★★★★ Perfect rock with large holds and perfect edges for the entire 100-foot climb. Start in a thin crack on the left (the rightmost of two thin cracks), which leads to the left-hand arête protected by four bolts. **Pro:** Thin to 2 inches; one (⅜-inch) bolt anchor. Either rap from this, or rap off the *South Of Heaven* anchor below. **FA:** Tom Gilje, Mike Lechlinski, Mari Gingery; 1990.

589. **South of Heaven** (5.12d) ★★★★★ One of the most visually enticing lines in the park. This route starts down and right of *Witch Hunt.* Climb thin cracks up and right (fixed pin) to the spectacular right-hand arête. Balancy and technical climbing up the arête past six bolts leads to the top. Two-bolt anchor; 80-foot rap. **Pro:** Thin to 1 inch. **FA:** Tom Gilje, Mike Lechlinski; 1990.

DUNCE CAP, THE ENIGMA, AND SUICIDE HORN ROCK

These three isolated formations lie adjacent to each other in a north-to-south alignment. They lie about 0.7 mile east-southeast of Willow Hole, and about 600 yards east-northeast of The Fortress. Most climbers approach from the Willow Hole vicinity, though it is probably faster to approach up Rattlesnake Canyon. Plan on about one-and-a-half to two hours to reach these formations from the car.

If approaching from Rattlesnake Canyon, refer to the Rattlesnake Canyon approach directions to the Valley of Kings (see page 177). After ascending out of Rattlesnake Canyon, you reach a large wash (right of the Helmet) that continues south. Follow this for about 0.5 mile; you will wind up below the northeast face of the Dunce Cap. Plan on about one-and-a-half hours or so to reach this point from Indian Cove.

If approaching through the Wonderland of Rocks, park at the North Wonderland parking area (6.4 miles from the West Entrance; 2.2+ miles from the Intersection Rock/Real Hidden Valley intersection). Hike nearly 1 mile northeast on the North Wonderland Trail; at this point, it joins a larger trail (a former dirt road) heading straight north. After another 500 yards (just past Gilligan's Island), the Boy Scout Trail to Indian Cove diverges to the left and the North Wonderland Trail begins a slow curve to the right (northeast; 1.2 miles). Stay right on the North Wonderland Trail for another 1.4 miles to where it joins a large wash (2.6 miles). At a trail marker, head right (south) into the main Wonderland wash system to

where the wash makes a sharp left (east) turn (2.9 miles). Follow the wash east (past a large boulder) where it makes a sharp left (north) turn (3.2 miles). Soon the wash turns east again and leads to a tree- and brush-choked series of shallow water pools (often dry). This is Willow Hole.

From Willow Hole, head over a small rise and down into an open area. The Super Dome and Super Slab are directly to the north (left). Continue east down the rockier and steeper wash for about 300 yards to where the wash turns left (north); a small drop marks this spot (3.6+ miles). The west side of Lime Dome lies directly ahead to the east. Here, you want to head somewhat right into an open washy area. From this point, follow the washy area for about 50 yards, then angle to the southeast (right), over a rocky rise and down the other side, into a more open area that leads to the west and northeast faces of the Dunce Cap. Maps, pages, 175 and 192.

The Dunce Cap (Wilderness)

The Dunce Cap has an impressive north-northeast face rising 200 feet up at its highest point. All four of the known routes are found on the northeast face. Descent is a 90-foot rappel off the back (south) side of the formation into a notch, then head west to return to the base. It is shady most of the day. Map, pages 175 and 192.

590. **The Dunce Cap** (5.10c) (R) ★★★ This route begins off the highest leaning pillar on the north face. To reach the start of this route, scramble up ledges (Class 4/5) on the left side. Either stick-clip the first bolt or make very dicey moves (5.10c R) to reach it. Traverse right to a crack that leads to the top. **Pro:** To 2 inches. **FA:** Mike Lechlinski, Mari Gingery, John Bachar, Brenda Bachar, Craig Fry; 1982.

590A. **Spirited Away** (5.11b) ★★★★★ Begin near the center of the northeast face, below and left of a large rectangular block. **Pitch 1:** Go up cracks, then move right to a large ledge atop the block (5.10) **Pitch 2:** Head up and left to a very thin crack with two bolts; move right to a flake. Go up the flake, then up knobs to a third bolt; traverse right and up to a small ledge (5.11b) **Pitch 3:** Move right to, and then up, a finger crack to finish up and left (5.8) **Pro:** Thin to 3+ inches. **FA:** Randy Vogel, Vern Stiefel; 1992.

590B. **Time Out** (5.10b) ★★ Begin on the far right side of the face (V1 boulder problem on right gives access to a large ledge). Go up the long and obvious wide crack; finish to the left. **Pro:** Several to 4/5 inches. **FA:** Randy Vogel, Vern Stiefel; 1992.

590C. **Waltzing in the Wonderland** (5.11b/c) ★★★★ Approach as for *Time Out;* begin below a thin lieback/shallow corner about 25 feet right of *Time Out.* Go up this for about 60 feet to join *Time Out.* **FA:** Vern Stiefel, Randy Vogel; 1992.

The Enigma (Wilderness)

This small, nondescript formation lies just west (in front of) the unnamed larger rock that sits between the Dunce Cap and Suicide Horn Rock. The sole route lies on the east face. Approach it from below the notch between the Dunce Cap and the formation to the south, then head right up boulders to the base. It gets morning sun and afternoon shade. Descend to the left. Neither the formation or route is pictured. Maps, pages 175 and 192.

591. **Hexed and Perplexed** (5.7) ★ This is the right-hand and most prominent of left-diagonalling cracks on the east side. An unknown party may have bailed from high on this route in the early 1990s. **Pro:** To 2 inches. **FA:** Vernon Stiefel, Randy Vogel, Holden Harris; 4/03.

Suicide Horn Rock (Wilderness)

This dome is the most southern of the three main formations. See page 187 for approach directions. *Bighorn Dihedral* is the obvious right-leaning crack leading to the grey dihedral on the west face. *Compact Physical* lies on the northwest side of the summit block, above and left of the finish of *Bighorn Dihedral*. Both are in the sun most of the afternoon. *Rock Lypso* lies on the northeast side of the rock (morning sun, afternoon shade) and is probably best approached from the notch descent or from the vicinity of the

Wonderland Wash to the east. To descend, go right (south) on slabs (Class 4 or 5), or left (north) into the notch. Maps, pages 175 and 192.

Suicide Horn Rock—West Face

This is sunny all afternoon.

592. **Bighorn Dihedral** (5.10b/c) ★★★★ This is located in the center of the west face. Go up the classic, steep, right-leaning crack to a beautiful right-facing corner with a tips crack. Begin atop Class 4 slabs; needs a bit of traffic to clean up the right face. **Pro:** Many thin to 2 inches. **FA:** Mike Lechlinski, Mari Gingery, John Bachar; 1982.

593. **Compact Physical** (5.11a/b) ★★ This is the 30-foot thin tips crack splitting the summit block above and left of *Bighorn Dihedral*. **Pro:** Tiny cams to 1.5 inches. **FA:** Randy Leavitt, Mike Geller; 3/85.

Suicide Horn Rock—Northeast Face

This gets morning sun and afternoon shade.

594. **Rock Lypso** (5.10a) ★★ (not shown) This route lies on the northeast side of Suicide Horn Rock and finishes on the summit block opposite *Compact Physical*. Go up the crack to the wide undercling-lieback curving up and right. **Pro:** To 4+ inches; one bolt. **FA:** Craig Fry, Dave Stahl; 4/86.

Cactus Cooler Arêtes

(Wilderness)

This 30-foot-tall "split" boulder lies about 275 yards south-southwest of Suicide Horn Rock and east of the Fortress valley. If you are at the Fortress, head east and down out the valley to this boulder. If you are near the Dunce Cap/Suicide Horn Rock area, head south. The "arêtes" are formed by the north-south split of the boulder. All of the routes are toprope problems. Not a destination unless you are in the area anyway. There is one bolt atop all four arêtes. **All FAs:** Randy Leavitt, Mike Geller; 1/85. The boulder and routes are not shown. Map page 192.

595. **Arête #1** (5.10a) ★ (TR) This is the northwest arête of the east boulder.

596. **Arête #2** (5.11b) ★ (TR) This is the west side of the southwest arête of the east boulder. It's easy if you stem off the west boulder.

597. **Arête #3** (5.11a) ★ (TR) This is on the south side of the southwest arête of the east boulder.

598. **Arête #4** (5.11a) ★ (TR) This is the southeast arête of the west boulder.

The Stepping Stones

(Wilderness)

This series of cliffs lies about 450 yards east of the Dunce Cap, on the slopes of Queen Mountain. The formations face somewhat north and get morning shade and late afternoon sun. All recorded routes lie on the two leftmost formations (the First Step and Second Step). Approach as for the Dunce Cap (see page 187), either up Rattlesnake Canyon or from the North Wonderland parking lot. From the Wonderland Wash, just east of the northeast face of the Dunce Cap, take another wash to the east that soon heads into a brushy corridor between low rocks. After passing through the corridor, head up and right over boulders to the base of the left-hand formation. Plan on two hours or so to reach this formation. Descend left. Maps, pages 175 and 192.

First Step

This is the leftmost and best looking of the Stepping Stones formations. Three routes are recorded.

599. **Stepping Out of Babylon** (5.9) ★★ This and *Stepping Razor* begin at the same spot, off a large fairly flat boulder. Go up a short wide crack, then go left 12 feet to a crack that heads straight up to the top. **Pro:** To 2.5 inches. **FA:** Craig Fry, Dave Stahl; 4/86.

600. **Stepping Razor** (5.10b) ★★★ This is best done in two pitches (180 feet). **Pitch 1:** Start as for *Stepping Out of Babylon,* but head straight up the thin crack that leads to an obvious hands/off-hands crack (5.10a) that ends on a nice ledge. **Pitch 2:** Go up the steep right-facing dihedral (5.10b), then climb the face and crack to the top. **Pro:** To 3.5 inches. **FA:** Craig Fry, Bob Roback, Dave Stahl; 4/86.

601. **Steps Ahead** (5.10c A1) ★ This route begins about 45 feet right of *Stepping Razor.* **Pitch 1:** Go up the wide crack to where a thin crack cuts straight right below a headwall. **Pitch 2:** Aid right along the horizontal crack, then continue diagonally up and right on a distinctive "wavy" crack. **Pro:** Thin pins to 4 inches. **FA:** Craig Fry, Dave Stahl; 4/86.

Second Step

This formation lies to the right and a bit back from First Step. A large left-facing dihedral with a roof halfway up is the formation's most distinctive feature. The formation and route are not pictured.

602. **First Steps** (5.8) ★ Climb cracks up to join the left-facing corner, then go out left under roof. Above, follow cracks to the top. **Pro:** To 3 inches. **FA:** Craig Fry, Dave Stahl; 4/86.

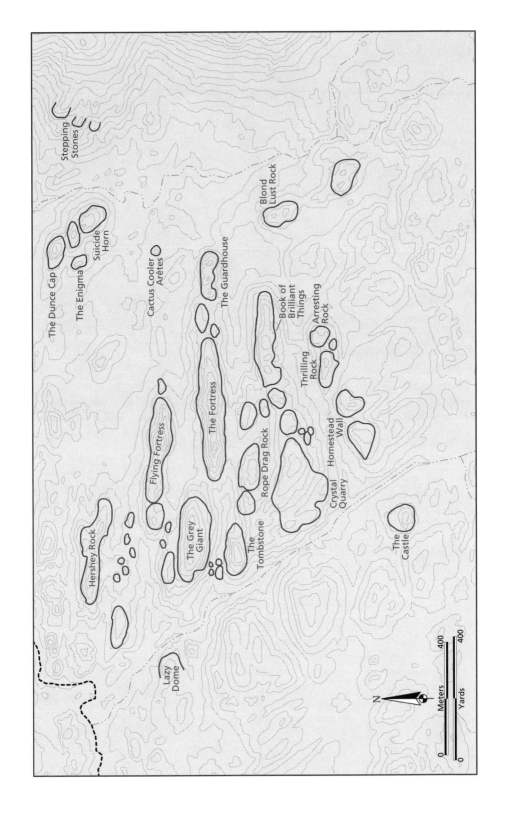

Stepping
Stones

The Dunce Cap
The Enigma
Suicide Horn

Cactus Cooler
Arêtes

The Guardhouse

Blond
Lust Rock

Book of
Brilliant
Things

Arresting
Rock

Thrilling
Rock

The Fortress

Flying Fortress

Hershey Rock

The Grey
Giant

The
Tombstone

Rope Drag Rock

Homestead
Wall

Crystal
Quarry

The
Castle

Lazy
Dome

N

Meters

Yards

0   400

0   400

GREY GIANT, TOMBSTONE, AND FORTRESS AREAS

(Wilderness)

To reach the Grey Giant, Tombstone, and Fortress areas, park at the Northern Wonderland parking area (6.4 miles from the West Entrance; 2.2+ miles from the Intersection Rock/Real Hidden Valley intersection). Hike nearly 1 mile northeast on the North Wonderland Trail; at this point, it joins up with a larger trail (a former dirt road) heading straight north. After about 500 yards (just past Gilligan's Island), the Boy Scout Trail to Indian Cove diverges to the left and the North Wonderland Trail begins a slow curve to the right (northeast/1.2 miles). Stay right on the North Wonderland Trail for another 1.4 mile to where it joins a large wash (2.6 miles). At a trail marker, head right (south) into the main Wonderland wash system to where the wash makes a sharp left (east) turn (2.9 miles). Follow the wash east for about 425 yards and turn right (south) into the second wash you encounter (3.1+ miles). This side wash is about 50+ yards before you pass a very large boulder in the main wash. If you reach the boulder, you've gone too far.

Follow this wash in a southeasterly direction directly toward the Grey Giant. After about 325 yards, a branch of the wash splits left (east), and the way forward involves lots of rock scrambling. If you are heading to the Tombstone, Grey Giant's south face, or Lazy Dome, continue straight (south) over the boulders to the west end of the Grey Giant. If you are heading straight for the Fortress, Flying Fortress, the north face of the Grey Giant, or Hershey Rock, head left (east) in the left-hand wash, which soon becomes blocked by boulders. Maps, pages 84, 85, 192.

Lazy Dome (Wilderness)

This formation lies on your right as you make the rocky approach to the Grey Giant and Tombstone. It lies west and just across the canyon from the Grey Giant. The only known route lies on the northeast face and is not pictured. Map, page 192.

603. Common Law Marriage (5.10c) (R) ★ Begin up a right slanting crack, then go up the face past three bolts to a crack that goes to the top. **Pro:** To 2 inches. **FA:** Mike Lechlinski, Mari Gingery; 1985.

Grey Giant—South Face
(Wilderness)

From the west end of the Grey Giant, head left (east) up boulders to the base of the Grey Giant's south face, which is on your left. Routes receive sun most of the day. Map, page 192.

604. Illusion (5.7) Climb the chimney/gully on the left side of the face. Descend left. **Pro:** To 3 inches. **FA:** Dennis Bird, Chris Wegener; 1/71.

605. Transversal (5.9 A1) Go up *Illusion* for 65 feet, then aid right on the horizontal crack to belay where the first pitch of *Transfusion* ends. Continue across the horizontal crack. Though this was the original line of ascent across the upper south face, it has become an obscure variation. It is unsure if anyone has tried to free it. **FA:** John Wolfe, Bill Mikus; 1/71.

606. Transfusion (5.12a) ★★★ **Pitch 1:** Go up *Illusion* for 40+ feet, then angle up and right in a thin crack/corner (5.12a) to the hori-

zontal crack. **Pitch 2:** Traverse right on the horizontal (5.9) to its end. **Pro:** Many thin to 3 inches. **FA:** Bob Dominick, Mona Stahl; 3/72. **FFA:** Tony Yaniro, Mike Lechlinski, Mari Gingery; 1980.

607. **Lithophiliac** (5.11b) ★★★ **Pitch 1:** Go up *Illusion* for 20+ feet, then up and right along a thin crack (5.11b) to a two-bolt belay. **Pitch 2:** Head up until you go right along a horizontal. Where the crack jogs, go up a vertical crack to the top. **Pro:** Many thin to 3 inches. **FA:** Tony Yaniro, Mike Lechlinski, Mari Gingery; 1980.

608. **Hyperion** (5.11d) ★★★★ **Pitch 1:** Go up the right-arching crack to where you make a move down on the face then back up into the crack (5.11c). Follow the excellent crack (5.10c) to a nice belay ledge (two bolts). You can rappel from here or continue (see the following climbs for variations from this point). **Pitch 2:** Head straight right under the roof (5.10b) and belay. **Pitch 3:** Go up the thin crack a two-bolt belay (5.11d). Head off

the cliff to the right. **Pro:** Thin and many .5 to 3.5 inches. Make two rappels or walk off right. **FA:** Don O'Kelley, Dave Davis; 11/70. **FFA** (First pitch): John Long, Kevin Worrall, Tobin Sorenson, Rick Accomazzo; 2/74. **FFA** (Second pitch): Unknown. **FFA** (Third pitch): Tony Yaniro; 1980.

609. **Slab Start** (Variation) (5.11a?) ★★ Face climb to the right of the initial arch past two bolts to join *Hyperion* after the crux face moves. **FA:** Curt Shannon, Vaino Kodas.

610. **Janus** (5.10d) ★★ From the belay atop the first pitch of *Hyperion,* climb straight up over a roof, following a right-facing flake/corner, then head right to two-bolt anchor. Exit off right. **FA:** John Wolfe, Bill Mikus; 12/70. **FFA:** Unknown; 1979.

611. **Vortex** (5.10a) ★ From the belay atop the first pitch of *Hyperion,* climb left into a chimney/flake (5.10a). At its end, head right to a two-bolt anchor. Exit off right. **FA:** John Long, Tobin Sorenson, Jack Roberts; 6/74.

612. The DMB (5.9) (R) ★★ Go up a gold streak past three bolts, then up and right to two-bolt anchor atop *Two Left Feet* (65-foot rap). You can also head up and left from the last bolt to end at the belay atop the first pitch of *Hyperion* (85 foot rap). **FA:** Randy Vogel, Craig Fry; 1/78.

613. Two Left Feet (5.10a) ★★ Located about 40 feet right of *The DMB*. Go up cracks and face past two bolts to two-bolt anchor/rap. **Pro:** To 2 inches. **FA:** Todd Swain, Peggy Buckey, John Courtney; 2/89.

614. Dimorphism (5.7) (R) Go up a left-diagonalling crack to face past one bolt; end at the *Two Left Feet* belay anchor/rap. **Pro:** To 2 inches. **FA:** Ken Stichter, Rob Stahl; 1/71.

615. The Jewel of Denial (5.9) ★ Begin about 30 feet right of *Dimorphism*. Go up the face (one bolt) to a left-leaning ramp/crack, then face climb up and left past two more bolts. Belay on a ledge with one bolt. Walk off right. **Pro:** To 2 inches. **FA:** Todd Swain, Phil Pearl; 4/90.

616. Heavy Meadow (5.10a) ★ Begin just right of *The Jewel of Denial*. Go up the face past five bolts; belay on a ledge with one bolt (same as *The Jewel of Denial*). Walk off right. **Pro:** To 2 inches. **FA:** Brian Elliot, Cyndie Bransford, Todd Gordon; 1/94.

617. Dawn Yawn (5.11d) ★★★ Begin on the ledge/belay where *The Jewel of Denial* and *Heavy Meadow* end. Go up the right-facing, right-leaning corner to a vertical corner/crack. Walk off right. **Pro:** Thin to 2.5 inches. **FA:** Tony Yaniro; 1981.

The Tombstone (Wilderness)

This large formation lies almost directly opposite the south face of the Grey Giant. Routes are on the north face (facing the Grey Giant), the east face, and the south face. See the general approach description on page 193. From the west end of the Grey Giant, head left (east) up boulders to the base of the Tombstone's north face, which will be on your right. Map, page 192.

The Tombstone—North Face

With the exception of *Turtle Days,* which lies well right of the main north face, routes are two or more pitches in length. Routes are described left to right and tend to be in the shade most of the day. Descend from a two-bolt anchor (needs replacing) atop the east face (*The S Cracker* and *Heaven Can Wait*); 85-foot rappel.

618. Turtle Days (5.8) (not shown on photo) This route lies on the very northwest end of the Tombstone, roughly opposite *Two Left Feet* on the south face of the Grey Giant. Face climb up the slab/buttress past three bolts. Downclimb right. **Pro:** To 2.5 inches. **FA:** Dave Evans, Kelly Carignan, Tom Smith, Crista Smith.

619. Cinnamon Girl (5.11a) ★★ Begin some 175 feet left of *Turtle Days* and 150 feet right and down of The Tombstone. **Pitch 1:** Go up a right-curving finger to handcrack to a ledge (5.10b). **Pitch 2:** Go straight up the crack above, which becomes off-width (5.11a crux) near the top; end at a small tree. Rap from tree (180+ feet) or go up to the anchor

atop the east face. **Pro:** To 4.5 inches. **FA:**
Dan Michaels; 1981.

620. **The Tombstone** (5.11d) ★★★ Begin up
and left on the north side of the rock. **Pitch
1:** Go up and right along the crack/ramp to
a two-bolt belay (5.9, short pitch). **Pitch 2:**
Go up the thin crack above past one bolt and
fixed copperheads (these may have been
replaced with bolts by the time this sees print
per request of FA party) to a belay in the
crack (5.11c/d). **Pitch 3:** Go up the
flake/crack to face on an arête past two bolts
(5.10b). Rap from atop the east face. **Pro:**
Thin to 2 inches. **FA:** Tony Yaniro, Randy
Leavitt, Dan Michael; 1981.

The Tombstone—East Face

Approach the east face by continuing up the
gully/boulders past the north face, then
heading left and up more boulders to the
base of the following two routes. This face
gets morning sun and afternoon shade.
Descend via an 85-foot rappel off a two-bolt
anchor (needs replacing, which may have
been accomplished by the time this sees
print).

The Tombstone

The Grey Giant

XX

80'
rap

X

622   621

621. **The S Cracker** (5.11a) ★★★ The right-hand route. Go up the face past a bolt, then right to reach the S-shaped crack. Two-bolt anchor/rap. **Pro:** Many thin to 1 inch. **FA:** Tim Sorenson, Dan Michael, Alan Bartlett; 3/81.

622. **Heaven Can Wait** (5.10d) ★★★ The left-hand route. Go up the low-angled corner to the steep thin crack/lieback. Two-bolt anchor/rap. **Pro:** Thin to 2 inches. **FA:** Tony Yaniro, Vaino Kodas, 1980.

The Tombstone—South Face

Approach the south face and its only route by continuing up the gully/boulders past the north face, then heading left and up more boulders past the east face, then going left and down on boulders for about 65 yards. It can also be approached by continuing south along the very rocky watercourse past the turn for the Grey Giant, then heading up and left. A unknown and apparently incomplete two-bolt route is found below the left side of the south face. *The Fugitive* is a four-bolt route up and right from there. It is sunny most of the day. The face and route are not pictured.

623. **The Fugitive** (5.10d) ★ This is a four-bolt climb on the south face, 200 feet down and left from *Heaven Can Wait*. **Pro:** To 2.5 inches. **FA:** Dave Evans, Spencer Lennard, Todd Gordon; 11/86.

Rope Drag Rock (Wilderness)

This rock and route face north and lie on the right side of a canyon east of the east end of the Tombstone. See the general approach description on page 193. From the west end of the Grey Giant, head left (east) up boulders past the base of the Tombstone's north face (on your right) and continue up the gully to the west end of the Fortress formation. Rather than heading left into the Fortress valley, go right around the west end of the Fortress into another canyon. Rope Drag Rock is on your right and faces the back side of the Fortress formation. It sees shade most of the day. The rock and route are not pictured.

624. **Rope Drag** (5.10b) This route lies almost directly opposite the west end of the Fortress's south side. Go up a left-facing corner to a thin flake, traverse left beneath a horizontal for 25 feet, then head up a crack. **Pro:** To 2.5 inches. **FA:** Dennis Yates, Roger Linfield; 4/85.

THE FORTRESS AREA

(Wilderness)

The Fortress Area consists of two roughly parallel east-to-west-running ridges of rock with a large, high, flat valley between. It is just east of the Grey Giant. Also covered in this section is the north face of the Grey Giant. The north face of the Fortress is located on the south side of this valley. The north side of the valley is bounded by south face of the Flying Fortress. The north face of the Grey Giant forms the western end of this valley. Though they can be reached from the rock-filled gully between the Grey Giant and the Tombstone by heading slightly left and around the west buttress of the Fortress, this approach should be used only if you are already at either the Tombstone or Grey Giant.

The Fortress Area (and the north face of the Grey Giant) are best approached as follows: From the right-hand turnoff from the main Willow Hole wash (see page 193), follow the side wash in a southeasterly direction directly toward the Grey Giant. After about 325 yards, another wash heads left (east) and the way forward involves rock scrambling. Head left along the second wash until boulders block the way. Scramble along for several hundred yards until you can head up and right toward the notch between the Grey Giant and the Flying Fortress. Descend into the Fortress valley. Map, page 192.

Hershey Rock (Wilderness)

Hershey Rock lies north of the Grey Giant and western end of the Flying Fortress. The sole recorded route is located on the east end of Hershey Rock, facing out on the broad valley containing the Dunce Cap and Suicide

Horn Rock. Approach as for the Fortress valley, but instead of heading up and right over the notch between the Grey Giant and the Flying Fortress, continue up the canyon in an easterly direction, until the north side of the Flying Fortress is on your right and Hershey Rock on your left. Continue to the east end of Hershey Rock. Both the rock and route are not pictured. Map, page 192.

625. **Honorable Hersheys** (5.11a) ★★ (TR) This route lies on the northeast arête on brown-spotted rock. Two-bolt anchor on top. **FA:** Randy Leavitt, Mike Geller; 2/85.

Grey Giant—North Face
(Wilderness)

Unless you are already at the south face of the Grey Giant or the Tombstone already, the north face of the Grey Giant is best approached as for the Fortress Area. From the right-hand turnoff from the main Willow Hole wash (see page 193), follow the side wash in a southeasterly direction directly toward the Grey Giant. After about 325 yards, another wash heads left (east) and the way forward involves rock scrambling. Head left along the second wash until boulders block the way. Scramble along for several hundred yards until you can head up and right toward the notch between the Grey Giant and the Flying Fortress. If you are already at the south face of the Grey Giant or The Tombstone, then head east up boulders past the base of the Tombstone's north face (on your right) and continue up the gully to the west end of the Fortress. Turn left into the Fortress valley. The north side of the Grey Giant is reached easily by walking west from the Fortress valley. The face and routes are not pictured.

626. **The Coliseum** (5.10b/c) ★★ Begin near the right end of the north face. **Pitch 1:** Go up a left-leaning crack to a ledge with a boulder. **Pitch 2:** Follow the obvious flared corner above (5.10b/c). **Pro:** To 3 inches. **FA:** Tony Yaniro; 1983.

627. **Drop Your Drawers** (5.9) Approach from about 50 feet right of *The Coliseum*. Scramble up blocks and cracks to the base of this left-leaning, left-facing dihedral with an off-width. **Pro:** To 5+ inches. **FA:** Brian Povolny, Frith Yazzie; 3/86.

628. **Drop a Frog** (5.9) ★ Approach from about 50 feet right of *The Coliseum*. Scramble up blocks and cracks to the right side of a ledge. Free (5.10d/5.11a) or aid off two bolts to reach a ledge above. Begin from the left end of this second ledge. Go up the off-width/chimney that closes to a finger crack on a slab. At the crack's end, head up and left on the face. **FA:** Randy Leavitt, Mike Geller; 1984.

629. **5 Crying Cowboys** (5.12b) ★★★ Approach from about 50 feet right of *The Coliseum*. Scramble up blocks and cracks to the right side of a ledge. Free (5.10d/5.11a) or aid off two bolts to reach a ledge above. Begin about 75 feet right on the second ledge. Go up the thin left-leaning finger crack for 50 feet to rappel bolts (rock deteriorates above this point). **FA:** Randy Leavitt, Mike Geller; 1984.

The Flying Fortress (Wilderness)

The Flying Fortress—South Face, Left Side

This striking formation is on your left as you enter the Fortress valley. It features several long vertical crack systems. It faces south and is sunny most of the day. This formation is about 100 to 120 feet high. Descent is best made via a 110-foot rappel from slings on top of *No Self Respect*. Either have a 220+-foot rope or bring two ropes; alternatively, it might be possible (but not advisable) to make two shorter rappels via *No Self Respect* to the bolt anchors on *No Self Control*. Map, page 192.

630. **No San Francisco** (5.11b) ★★ (TR) Go up either the face (5.11a) to the thin crack over the roof (5.11a), or begin in the crack/corner to the right and traverse left under the roof, then go up the thin crack above (5.11b). **FA:** Randy Leavitt, Bob Horan; 1984.

631. **Boogs' Route** (5.10c/d) ★★ Go up the thin crack to plates, then continue up the left crack. **Pro:** Thin to 2 inches. **FA:** Dave Bruckman, Todd Gordon, Dave Evans; 11/87.

632. **No Pain, No Grain** (5.10b) (R) ★ The crack about 10 feet right of *Boogs' Route*. **Pro:** Thin to 2.5 inches. **FA:** Tucker Tech, Doe DeRoss; 1995.

633. **No Self Control** (5.12c) ★★★★ Begin on the ledge, just right of a yucca. Go up the thin discontinuous cracks to a bolt belay. Either rap (70 feet) from here, or continue up and right in the chimney. Protection is tricky and hard to place; use many thin to 2 inches. **FA** (TR): Tony Yaniro; 1983. **FA** (Lead): Randy Leavitt, 1984.

634. **No Self Respect** (5.10c) ★★★★ This is the long crack just right of *No Self Control*. **Pro:** Mostly medium to 4.5 inches. Rappel (110 feet) from slings. **FA:** Roger Linfield, Dennis Yates; 1/84.

635. **No Self Confidence** (5.10b/c) ★★★ The other long excellent crack about 15 feet right of *No Self Respect*. **Pro:** Medium to 3.5 inches. Rappel from slings atop *No Self Respect* (110 feet). **FA:** Dennis Yates, Roger Linfield; 12/83.

636. **42N8 One** (5.10a) ★★ This route begins about 35 feet right of *No Self Confidence*. Go up blocks to a right-facing corner, over the roof, then right into a slot. **Pro:** To 3.5+ inches. **FA:** Dennis Yates, Roger Linfield; 1985.

Flying Fortress—Right Side

This section of the Flying Fortress lies about 200 feet to the right and a bit forward of *42N8 One* on the Flying Fortress—South Side. It faces south and is in sun most of the day. Descend via a 100+-foot rappel from trees to the right of the top of *Thumbs Up*.

637. **Hyperventilation** (5.10d) This is on the left side of the face. Go straight up the crack right of the flake, passing a roof about a third of the way up. **Pro:** To 3+ inches. **FA:** Roger Linfield, Dennis Yates; 4/85.

638. **New Day Yesterday** (5.10a) ★★ Begin about 15 feet right of *Hyperventilation*. Go up the obvious crack with an alcove about halfway up. **Pro:** To 3+ inches. **FA:** Dennis Yates, Roger Linfield; 1/84.

639. **Thumbs Up** (5.10a) ★ Head up left–slanting ramps to the base. Go up a curving crack/flake, then face climb left to a corner, then go up. **Pro:** To 3+ inches. **FA:** Dennis Yates, Roger Linfield; 4/85.

640. **Troglodyte Crack** (5.8) (not shown on photo) This wide, left-slanting crack lies about 125 feet right of *Thumbs Up*. It passes a bush near the top. **Pro:** To 4+ inches. **FA:** Roger Linfield, Dennis Yates; 1/84.

The Fortress—North Face
(Wilderness)

This formation lies on the right (south) side of the Fortress valley and faces north. It is riddled with many fine vertical crack systems. Routes are up to 150 feet long. It offers shady climbing; better for warm weather. Map, page 192.

641. **It's Easy to Be Brave from a Safe Distance** (5.12a) (R) ★★★ This route lies near the left-hand end of the Fortress; scramble up to a ledge about 90 feet up to begin this and the next route. Go up a left-facing corner and thin crack to a roof; the crack widens above. Descend left. **Pro:** Thin to 3 inches. **FA:** Randy Leavitt, Mike Geller; 1984.

642. **It's Easy to Be Distant When You're Brave** (Variation) (5.11c) ★★★ Start a bit right of the last route, go up a thin crack, and join the previous route at the roof. **Pro:** Thin to 3 inches. **FA:** Randy Leavitt, Mike Geller; 1985.

643. **Toad Warrior** (5.10b) ★★ This route begins off the desert floor to the right of two obvious wide crack systems. Begin about 15 feet right of a wide crack that heads up to finish between two large summit boulders. Go up and then left on flakes to a ledge, the move left to the previously mentioned crack. Go up this now thin crack to a horizontal; continue up the corner (5.10b) and the crack system above to the top. **Pro:** Thin to 2.5 inches. **FA:** Paul Schweizer, Mike Geller; 1985.

644. Toad Warrior, Direct Start (5.10b) ★★ Climb directly up the wide crack to meet *Toad Warrior* where it comes in from the right at the ledge. **Pro:** Thin to 4 inches. **FA:** Roger Linfield, Dennis Yates.

645. Weekend Warrior (5.11a) ★★ Begin as for *Toad Warrior,* but head straight up thin cracks to the horizontal, then move left and finish up *Toad Warrior.* **Pro:** Many thin to 2.5 inches. **FA:** Mike Lechlinski, Tony Yaniro; 1983.

646. Sublimation (5.10a) ★ Begin about 100 feet right of the last routes, to the right of a pine and a chimney system. Go up boulders, and the right-hand of two cracks (in a corner), passing right of a large roof. Continue up the crack to the top. **Pro:** To 3 inches. **FA:** Roger Linfield, Dennis Yates; 12/83.

647. Grubstake Days (5.9) This route climbs an "obvious break in the wall" located about 40 feet right of *Sublimation.* **Pitch 1:** Go up the crack and blocks to the large ledge. **Pitch**

2: Go up the left side of a pillar into a squeeze chimney (5.9). Make a 165-foot rap from the top just left of *Natural Selection.* **Pro:** To 4+ inches. **FA:** Alan Bartlett, Pat Dennis; 5/97.

648. Natural Selection (5.11a) ★★★★ This route begins just right of *Grubstake Days* and just left of a small pillar of rock. Go up the crack for 50 feet, then move left on a small ledge; head up the right-facing corner to the top. The 165-foot rap is to the left. **Pro:** Mostly small to 2 inches. **FA:** Randy Leavitt, Mike Geller; 1984.

649. Pear-Grape Route (5.10a) This route starts just right of *Natural Selection* from atop the small pillar. Go up the curving left-facing corner to finish with *Natural Selection.* **Pro:** To 2.5 inches. **FA:** Todd Gordon, Tom Michael; 5/87.

650. Grungy (5.10d) The name says it all. This is the large left-facing corner-and-block system about 50 feet right of *Natural Selection*

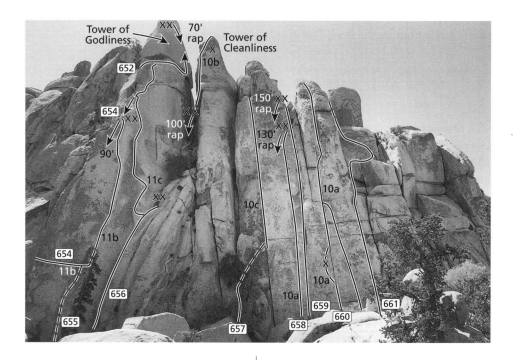

and *Pear-Grape Route*. It lies just left of the start of *Catapult* and ends on a ledge with a dead tree. **FA:** Randy Leavitt, Rob Slater; 1985.

651. Tower of Godliness—East Side (5.6) This "tower" is the left-hand of two small summit pinnacles (the other being *Tower of Cleanliness*) on the right portion of the Fortress. They are separated by a large chimney. Begin where *Grungy* and *Arms Control* finish (the ledge with the dead tree). Go up the chimney on the east side of the tower "summit block." Rap off a two-bolt anchor to the notch between the two towers, then one or two raps to the ground from there. **Pro:** To 4+ inches. **FA:** Unknown.

652. Tower of Godliness—Original Route (5.10a) ★ Begin off the ledge with the dead tree where *Grungy* and *Arms Control* end. **Pitch 1:** Head straight right on a horizontal crack around to the right (west) side of the tower. **Pitch 2:** Go up a chimney past one

bolt. Two-bolt anchor; 70-foot rap into the notch between *Tower of Godliness* and *Tower of Cleanliness*. Make one or two more raps down from the notch. **Pro:** To 3+ inches. **FA:** Randy Leavitt, Rob Slater; 1985.

653. Tower of Cleanliness (5.10b) ★★ Probably the best way of to approach this route is to climb *Tower of Godliness* and rap into the notch; a two-bolt anchor is found here. Go up past a bolt to a crack in a corner, then up the face above past a second bolt. **Pro:** To 2 inches. **FA:** Randy Leavitt, Rob Slater; 1985.

654. Catapult (5.11b) (R) ★★★★★ Begin just right of the start of *Grungy;* go up a crack until you can traverse straight right in a horizontal thin crack to a flake/crack. Go up and left along the crack/flake to a two-bolt anchor/90-foot rap. **Pro:** Several thin to 2.5 inches. **FA:** Tony Yaniro, Brett Maurer, Suzanne Sanbar; 1984.

655. Wheresabolt? (5.11c) ★★ (TR) This is a direct start to *Catapult* that heads straight up the face to the upper flake/crack and avoids the long traverse. **FA:** Mark Robinson, Will Chen; 10/86.

656. Arms Control (5.11d) ★★★ This route begins in the wide crack/chimney just right of *Wheresabolt*. **Pitch 1:** Go up the chimney for 50 feet to a two-bolt anchor. **Pitch 2:** Move left to a thin flake/crack that angles up and left until you can move left to meet *Grungy*. **Pro:** Thin to 3+ inches. **FA:** Randy Leavitt, Rob Slater; 1985.

657. Roark (5.10c) ★ Begin at a pine about 50 feet right of the chimney of *Arms Control* and to the left of a left-facing corner system. Go up past the pine then up and right to meet the corner system. Above, go up cracks to the top. Make a 150-foot rappel from above the next two climbs. **Pro:** To 2.5 inches. **FA:** Roger Linfield, Dennis Yates; 5/85.

658. New Hampshire, Naturally (5.10c) ★ Begin in the left-hand of two parallel crack systems; go up this for 130 feet to two-bolt anchor/rap. **Pro:** Thin to 2.5 inches. **FA:** Todd Swain, John Courtney; 2/89.

659. The Old Man Down the Road (5.10a) ★ Begin in the right-hand of two parallel crack systems; go up this for 130 feet to a two-bolt anchor/rap. **Pro:** To 2.5 inches. **FA:** Roger Linfield; 4/85.

660. The Man Who Cried (aka Julius Seizure) (5.10a) ★ Begin just right of *The Old Man Down the Road* in either of the two crack systems (that merge higher up). The left crack has a bolt partway up. Go up the cracks then finish on the face. There is no anchor on top of this 165-foot pitch. **Pro:** To 2.5 inches. **FA** (left start): Unknown. **FA** (right start; bolt added later): Dave Evans, Craig Fry; 4/85.

661. Ganado (5.10b) Begin in double cracks right of *The Man Who Cried*. Go up the hand-and-fist crack to a ledge, then up the corner. **Pro:** To 3+ inches. **FA:** Todd Gordon, Sharon Sadlier, Dave Evans, Craig Fry, Marge Floyd; 3/86

The Guardhouse (Wilderness)

This is a formation on the east end of the Fortress. The Guardhouse can be approached as for, and from the vicinity of, Suicide Horn Rock and the Cactus Cooler Arêtes by heading southwest around the left (eastern) end of the Fortress cliff band and just around the corner to the south side of the formation (for initial approach directions, see page 193). Alternatively, from the Fortress/Flying Fortress, head east and down the rocky valley/slope, and then around the east end of the Fortress band of rock.

This area can also be approached from the southern Wonderland from the vicinity of the Cornerstone by heading north in the main Wonderland Wash for about 600 yards to where the valley opens up. Rather than following the wash down the rocky drop, head right (east) and contour the bottom of the slope of Queen Mountain into a broad valley. Suicide Horn Rock lies directly north, the Guardhouse (the southeastern end of the Fortress) lies off to the northwest.

It is a pretty long walk (two-plus hours) no matter how you approach. It is sunny most of the day. The formation and routes are not pictured. Map, page 192.

662. Dihedralman (5.13a) ★★★ Begin on the left side of the south face of the Guardhouse. Go up past a bolt into the left-facing dihedral with a thin crack. At the top of this, head up and right past more two bolts to the top. **Pro:** Very thin to 2 inches, and some fixed wired nuts. **FA:** Randy Leavitt; 1987.

663. **Avante Guard-Dog** (5.11d) ★★ Begin below and left of a double roof just right of *Dihedralman*. Go up past a bolt to a roof into a corner, then past another bolt and over the second roof into cracks above. **Pro:** Thin to 2 inches; two fixed pins. **FA:** Randy Leavitt and Glenn Svenson; 10/88.

Blond Lust Rock

This formation lies about 300 yards south-southeast of the Guardhouse and about 600 yards south of Suicide Horn Rock. Either approach this rock from one of those formations, or alternatively you can approach it from the vicinity of the Cornerstone in the southern Wonderland; it is located on your left (west) after dropping down into the broad valley (see approach description for the Guardhouse from the Cornerstone on page 205). Routes are located on the east face. It receives morning sun and afternoon shade. The rock and routes are not pictured. Map, page 192.

664. **Lusting CLH** (5.8) Climb a left-slanting flake/crack on the upper left side of the east face. **Pro:** To 2 inches. **FA:** Rob Slater.

665. **Blonde Eyebrow Fetish** (5.10c) ★★★ This is the thin-hands crack about 30 feet right of *Lusting CLH*. **Pro:** To 2 inches. **FA:** Randy Leavitt, Rob Slater.

Book of Brilliant Things (Shining Dome)

666. **Book of Brilliant Things** (5.12d) ★★★★ This route is located in the eastern end of the Southern Canyon. Its description will be found there. See page 214.

THE FAR SOUTH CRAGS

The following formations lie to the south of the Tombstone/Grey Giant/Fortress area and involve a long approach to reach. Though there are a few good routes (e.g., *Warrior Eagle*), most of the routes are not major attractions. Consequently, few people venture out to these crags, though there are prospects for new routes (subject to wilderness bolting restrictions). There are three ways to reach these crags: heading south from the Grey Giant; the Middle Kingdom approach; and heading north from the southern Wonderland. The Middle Kingdom approach (and variations) is certainly the quickest and easiest means of reaching this area. However, it is more devious and a good sense of direction is necessary. It also could be used to access to other remote crags in the central Wonderland. All three approaches are given below. Map, page 192.

The Grey Giant (Standard) Approach: Park at the North Wonderland parking area. Hike northeast on the North Wonderland Trail for about 1 mile and join up with a larger trail heading straight north. After about 500 yards, the Boy Scout Trail to Indian Cove diverges to the left and the North Wonderland Trail begins a slow curve to the right (northeast/1.2 miles). Stay right on the North Wonderland Trail for another 1.4 miles to where it joins a large wash (2.6 miles). At a trail marker, head right (south) into the main Wonderland wash system and proceed to where the wash makes a sharp left (east) turn (2.9 miles/see Middle Kingdom approach below). Follow the wash east for about 425 yards and turn right (south) into the second wash heading right that you encounter. This side wash is about 50+ yards before you pass a very large boulder in the main wash. If you reach the boulder, you went too far (3.1+ miles).

Follow the side wash in a southeasterly direction directly toward the Grey Giant. After about 300 yards, the way forward involves rock scrambling; continue straight ahead (south) to the west end of the Grey Giant (3.4+ miles). Continue south along the rocky valley for another 600 yards of pretty rough going until you suddenly drop into a sandy wash (3.8 miles). The Castle is just ahead to your right, the slabby southwest face of Crystal Quarry to your left and the rocky canyon leading to the Homestead Wall, Thrilling Rock, and Arresting Rock to your left (east). Plan on one-and-a-half to two hours.

The Middle Kingdom Approach: Park at the Northern Wonderland parking area. Hike northeast on the North Wonderland Trail for about 1 mile, and join a larger trail heading straight north. After about 500 yards, the Boy Scout Trail to Indian Cove diverges to the left and the North Wonderland Trail begins a slow curve to the right (northeast/1.2 miles). This is just beyond Gilligan's Island, and the Middle Kingdom lies to the east and northeast of this point.

Head straight east (don't contour the hillside), reaching a large wash after about 550 yards. Follow this wash east then south as it heads up a small rise. The wash wanders in a southeasterly direction in a valley. Head more or less straight southeast, leaving and following the wash for about 600 yards and eventually passing through a gap between hills into another open valley. Continue southeast for about 350 yards, staying right where the main wash heads more to the east and heading for another gap in the hillside. On the other side of the gap, pick up another wash descending to the southeast.

Follow this for about 600 yards, eventually encountering old metal fence posts marking the northern margin of Keys Ranch, and entering the northern end of a open basin.

Follow the wash until it joins a much larger wash running from north to south. Turn left here and follow this larger wash in a northerly direction into another large open valley, where this wash dies out. Continue north for about 900 yards until you finally reach another large wash that heads straight north and descends through a gap (this wash joins the Grey Giant approach at the 2.9-mile point; see above). At this point, turn right (east) and follow the left branch of the wash "upstream," tending left at any obvious "forks." After 700 yards or so, the wash disappears and you will see an obvious pillar of rock atop a hill to your right (southwest). (If you don't . . . well, you're lost, aren't you?) Another large valley runs south from here.

Now head directly east, passing over the rocky "low point" and going down and slightly right (southeast) into yet another small wash. Follow this down a small and slightly rocky canyon until you join a nice sandy wash that you can follow east and then a bit north. This wash eventually turns north, joining another large wash. At this point, the Castle should be on your left (northwest), and Crystal Quarry along the wash to the north. A rocky canyon to your right (east) leads to the Homestead Wall, Thrilling Rock, and Arresting Rock. Plan on about one-and-a-half hours if you stay on course; variations are possible.

Southern Wonderland Approach: From Park Boulevard, take Barker Dam Road east for 1.4+ miles; the Barker Dam parking area is located to the left. Don't turn here; continue straight ahead as the road becomes dirt. After only about 150 yards, a dirt road (Big Horn Pass Road) splits off to your left;

turn left here. Follow the road as it curves around to the right to a large dirt parking area (South Wonderland parking area). A toilet is located here.

From the South Wonderland parking area, head east past a gate on a old dirt road that soon curves left toward the ruins of a house (Uncle Willie's Health Food Store). Just past Uncle Willie's, head left under trees into the wash (0.1+ miles), then turn right (north). Hike north along the wash for about 875 yards to where the wash opens up (with a good view of the Astro Domes to the northwest/0.6+ miles). Continue straight ahead along the valley for another mile; you will have to veer a bit left around low forma-

tions (1.6+ miles). Pick up a wash heading north-northwest from this point. Follow it until it curves right (north) and drops between some low rocks, then proceed north again. Eventually, this wash turns sharply right, and winds through some low formations. The wash becomes more open and sandy, then joins another wash heading directly north. At this point, the Castle will be on your left (west) and the large slabby south side of Crystal Quarry will be directly north. A rocky canyon to your right (east) leads to the Homestead Wall, Thrilling Rock, and Arresting Rock. Plan on about one-and-a-half to two hours.

The Castle (Wilderness)

The Castle lies on the west side of the wash/valley and contains two short routes on its north face. A left-facing dihedral is on the left *(Warrior Eagle)*, and a thin crack on the right *(Knight in Shining Armor)*. The face is shady most of the day. Map, page 192.

667. **Warrior Eagle** (5.12b) ★★★ This is the left-facing corner. Stem the corner with a very thin crack for protection. **Pro:** Many thin to 1.5 inches. **FA:** Tony Yaniro et al.; 1981.

668. **Knight in Shining Armor** (5.11b) ★★★ Begin about 25 feet right and around from *Warrior Eagle.* Go over a roof and up the finger crack that widens to 2 inches. **Pro:** To 2 inches. **FA:** Tony Yaniro et al.; 1981.

Crystal Quarry (Wilderness)

This large, slabby formation lies northeast of the Castle, roughly opposite and across the gully/valley. The three known routes lie near the center of the southwest face. It is sunny most of the day. See pages 206 and 207 for approach information. Map, page 192.

669. **Sack in the Wash** (5.10b) Approach this and the following route by third-classing up slabs. This is a 45-foot right-facing dihedral on the upper left side of the face. **Pro:** To 2.5 inches. **FA:** Rob Stahl, Dave Stahl, Craig Fry, Todd Battey; 1987.

670. **Hands of Fire** (5.11c) (TR) Begin just right of *Sack in the Wash*. Go up and left in an overhanging wave-shaped flake/crack, then right and up to top. Two-bolt anchor on top. **FA:** Dave Stahl; 2/87.

671. **Crystal Deva** (5.10a to 5.10c) Begin about 45 feet down and right of the last two routes, from atop a boulder. Go up discontinuous cracks and face (5.10a R to right, or 5.10c to left). **Pro:** Thin to 2 inches. **FA:** Craig Fry, Dave Stahl; 2/87.

THE SOUTHERN CANYON

The following formations and routes lie in an east-west canyon that begins below the south side of the Crystal Quarry. It is filled with numerous boulders.

The Homestead Wall

(Wilderness)

From the vicinity of the Castle and Crystal Quarry (see pages 206 and 207 for approach directions), head east in the Southern Canyon for about 350 yards. The Homestead Wall will be the second (or third, depending on what you count) north-facing formation on your right. The routes are on the lower left side of the north face and are fairly short. Descend to the right. It is shady most of the day. Map, page 192.

The Homestead Wall— Northwest Face

The following four routes lie on the lower left side of the north face of the formation, on your right as you approach from the Crystal Quarry. They climb vertical well-patinaed rock and get morning shade and some afternoon sun.

672. **Mercy Road** (5.11a) ★ This is a five-bolt face route on the left side of the north face. **Pro:** To 2 inches. **FA:** Randy Leavitt, Glenn Svenson; 1988.

673. **Looking for Mercy** (5.11a) ★ Begin just right of *Mercy Road*. Go up the face past three bolts, then join *Mercy Road* past the last two bolts. **Pro:** To 2 inches. **FA:** Randy Leavitt, Glenn Svenson; 1988.

674. **Empty Street** (5.10c) ★ Begin about 12 feet right of *Looking For Mercy*. Go up the face past four bolts. **Pro:** To 2 inches. **FA:** Randy Leavitt, Glenn Svenson; 1988.

675. **Moonstruck** (5.10b) This route is on the right side of the north face, about 30 feet right of *Empty Street*. Go up the face to a small roof, then up a hairline crack. **Pro:** Thin pins; thin to 2 inches. **FA:** Randy Leavitt, Glenn Svenson; 1988.

The Homestead Wall—Northeast Face

The next two routes lie on the northeast side of the Homestead Wall, around the corner, up and to the left of the previous routes. They are shady most of the day. Descend to the left. The routes are not shown.

676. **The Mistake** (5.9) Begin about 25 feet left of a pine tree at a crack; go up the crack(s) past a bush. **Pro:** To 2.5 inches. **FA:** Tucker Tech, Alan Bartlett; 10/96.

677. **Bloodsucker** (5.10c) This crack begins about 60 feet left of *The Mistake*. **Pro:** To 2.5 inches. **FA:** Alan Bartlett, Rich Wachtel; 10/96.

Thrilling Rock

This north-facing formation lies about 75 yards east of the Homestead Wall, on the right, about 425 yards into Southern Canyon. Routes are located on the north and southwest sides of the rock. Descend by rapping from a pine tree on the west side of the rock. Map, page 192.

Thrilling Rock—Southwest Face

This side of Thrilling Rock faces the northeast face of the Homestead Wall. Approach via the gap between these two formations.

678. **5 Crying Sportclimbers** (5.10c) (not shown) This climb faces (and is right of) the route *Bloodsucker* on the Homestead Wall. Go up a low-angled shallow crack that deepens into a handcrack higher. **Pro:** To 3 inches. **FA:** Alan Bartlett, Tucker Tech; 10/96.

Thrilling Rock—North Face

The following route lies near the left side of the north face of the formation. Several other crack route possibilities lie on the face to the right.

679. **The Thrill of Desire** (5.12c) ★★★★ Begin off a ledge. This is an obvious, steep, left-facing corner with a very thin crack and some bolts in its lower section. **Pro:** Thin to 1.5 inches. **FA:** Randy Leavitt; 1987.

Arresting Rock (Wilderness)

This small formation lies on the right-hand side of Southern Canyon (facing north), near the eastern end and about 100 yards east of Thrilling Rock. It lies just south and west of *Book of Brilliant Things. Book of Brilliant Things* could be easily approached from here, if you were in the area. The rock and routes are not pictured. Map, page 192.

680. **B.A.S.E. Arrest** (5.10c) This is a short left-slanting thin-hands crack on the west face of the summit block. It is easily seen from near the vicinity of *The Thrill of Desire*. **Pro:** To 2.5 inches. **FA:** Randy Leavitt, Rob Slater; 3/85.

681. **Bailey's Foster** (5.10b) This is on the upper left end of the north face of the formation about 175 feet left (east) of, and around from, *B.A.S.E. Arrest*. Climb a chimney/off-width leading to a handcrack in a corner. **Pro:** To 5+ inches. **FA:** Brian Bailey, Randy Leavitt.

Shining Dome

Shining Dome is a large formation that lies on the north side of the Southern Canyon near its eastern end. It lies roughly opposite Arresting Rock and is a bit farther east. The best approach is to follow the Southern Canyon east from near Castle Rock until you reach Arresting Rock. From here, continue east and down a bit, then scramble north up boulders to the base of the orangish-colored dihedral to the left of a notch high on the left side of the otherwise slabby Shining Dome.

Alternatively, and if you are already near the west end of the Grey Giant, head left (east) up boulders past the base of the Tombstone's north face (on your right), and continue up the gully to the west end of the Fortress formation. Rather than heading left into the Fortress valley, go right, around the west end of the Fortress, into another canyon. You will then pass Rope Drag Rock on your right. Continue about 400 yards down the rocky valley until you can head up and right toward a "V" notch near the east end of a north-facing formation on your right. Tunnel under a large boulder and you will be on the south face of this formation. *Book of Brilliant Things* (route 666) is just to your right (west) on the south side of the formation.

To reach Shining Dome from the Guardhouse, head south, then turn right (west) and up a rocky canyon (the Southern Canyon) to a point just before Arresting Rock. From here, head up and right to the route.

666. **Book of Brilliant Things** (5.12d) ★★★★
Go up the clean, short, orangish-colored right-facing corner. **Pro:** Many thin to 1.5 inches. **FA:** Randy Leavitt; 1985.

Lost Horse Area

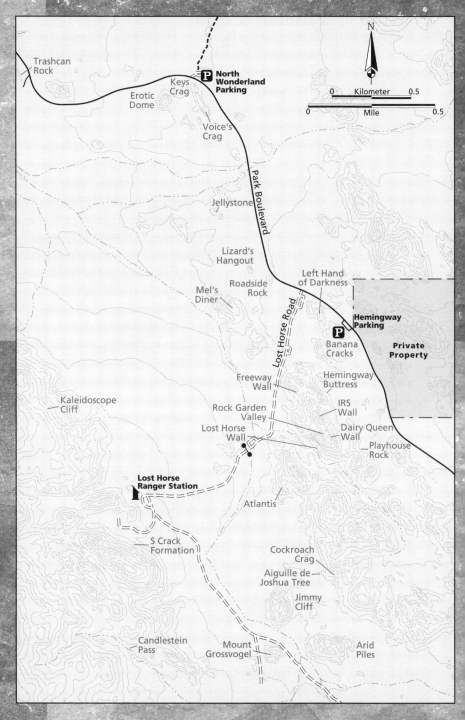

Trashcan Rock

Keys Crag

Erotic Dome

Voice's Crag

P **North Wonderland Parking**

N

0 Kilometer 0.5

0 Mile 0.5

Park Boulevard

Jellystone

Lizard's Hangout

Left Hand of Darkness

Mel's Diner

Roadside Rock

Lost Horse Road

Hemingway Parking P

Banana Cracks

Private Property

Freeway Wall

Hemingway Buttress

Kaleidoscope Cliff

Rock Garden Valley

IRS Wall

Lost Horse Wall

Dairy Queen Wall

Playhouse Rock

▲ **Lost Horse Ranger Station**

Atlantis

S Crack Formation

Cockroach Crag

Aiguille de Joshua Tree

Jimmy Cliff

Candlestein Pass

Mount Grossvogel

Arid Piles

LOST HORSE AREA

The Lost Horse Area covers the well developed crags and formations lying west of Park Boulevard and between the North Wonderland parking area to the north and Playhouse Rock to the south, together with areas adjacent to and approached from the unpaved Lost Horse Road. There is a high concentration of climbing on these formations, with many very popular routes and crags. These areas see a lot of traffic, so please stay on established trails and keep your impacts to a minimum.

The Lost Horse Area is divided into several subsections:

- **Lost Horse North,** covering the formations west of Park Boulevard from the North Wonderland parking area to Lost Horse Road;
- **Lost Horse Road,** covering all the formations lying adjacent to Lost Horse Road;
- **Atlantis–Jimmy Cliff,** covering the formations lying south of the end of Lost Horse Road;
- **Lost Horse West,** covering crags lying near the Lost Horse Ranger Station and in the hills to the south;
- **Hemingway Buttress,** covering Hemingway Buttress, IRS Wall, Copenhagen Wall, Dairy Queen Wall, Playhouse Rock, and adjacent crags.

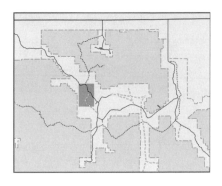

LOST HORSE NORTH

The following crags lie in the northern part of the Lost Horse valley area, encompassing the sparsely scattered formations adjacent to Park Boulevard from the North Wonderland (Keys Corner) parking lot to Lost Horse Road, 0.9 mile to the south. All formations described lie to the west of Park Boulevard.

Parking mileage references are generally given in distance relative to both the West Entrance and the four-way intersection of Park Boulevard with the road to Intersection Rock and Real Hidden Valley to the south.

Keys Crag

This small tower is located almost directly across Park Boulevard from the North Wonderland parking area. It is actually the very northern end of Voice's Crag. Park in the large North Wonderland parking area (6.4 miles from the West Entrance; 2.2+ miles from the Intersection Rock/Real Hidden Valley intersection). The crag and routes are not pictured. Map, page 217.

682. **Mush Puppies** (5.8+) ★ This lies on the left side of the northeast face, facing Park Boulevard. It connects several right-slanting cracks. **Pro:** Thin to 2 inches. **FA:** Unknown.

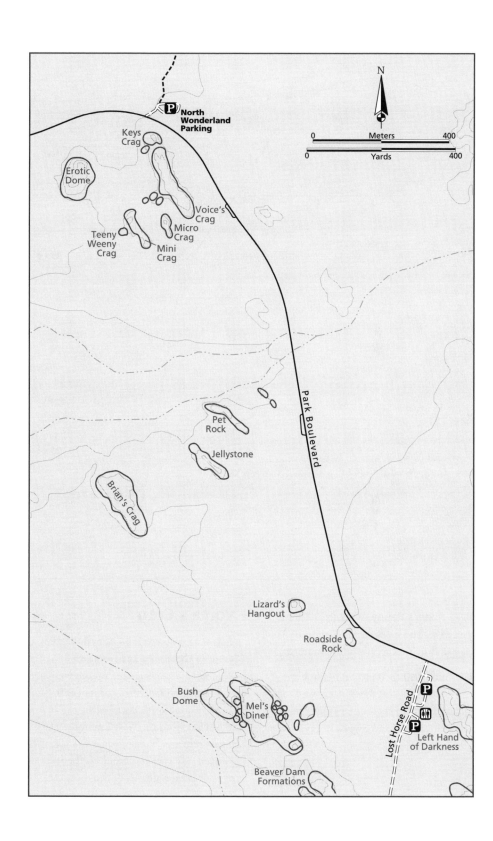

North
Wonderland
Parking

Keys
Crag

Erotic
Dome

Voice's
Crag

Micro
Crag

Teeny
Weeny
Crag

Mini
Crag

N

Meters
0   400

Yards
0   400

Park Boulevard

Pet
Rock

Jellystone

Brian's Crag

Lizard's
Hangout

Roadside
Rock

Bush
Dome

Mel's
Diner

Lost Horse Road

Left Hand
of Darkness

Beaver Dam
Formations

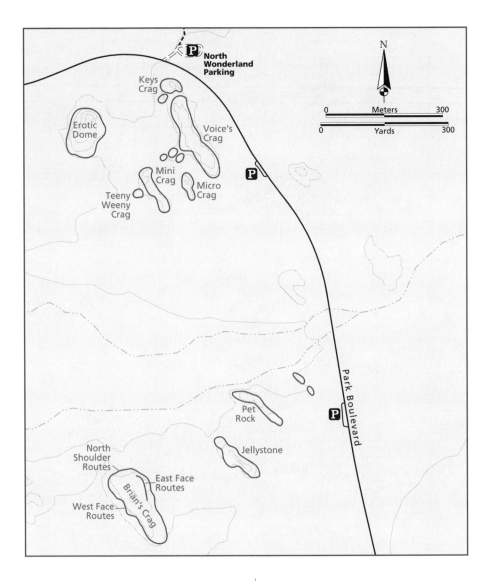

682A. **Adam's Happy Acres** (5.7) Climb steep flakes and cracks 15 feet right of *Mush Puppies*. **Pro:** To 2 inches. **FA:** Unknown.

683. **Gibberish** (5.10c) (TR) Climb the brown streak on the short, steep, west face up right and around the corner from *Adam's Happy Acres*. **FA:** Todd Swain, Peggy Buckey; 4/90.

Voice's Crag

This long, low, reddish–colored crag lies just south of the Keys Corner–North Wonderland parking area on the west side of Park Boulevard. A small turnout is 0.2 mile south of the North Wonderland parking area (6.6 miles from the West Entrance; 2.0+ miles from the Intersection Rock/Real Hidden Valley intersection) on the west side of Park Boulevard. All of the routes are

located on the east face. The crag was named for Alan Roberts, who was affectionately known as "the voice of the crags" for his ability to give beta on nearly any route. The routes are in sun in the morning and afternoon shade. Routes are described from left to right. Map, page 218.

684. B Flat (5.7+) Begin in the right of two slots on left end of crag; at a horizontal, move right then up the crack. This is located about 35 feet left of *C Sharp Roof.* A direct finish (5.9 TR) has been done. **Pro:** To 2 inches. **FA:** Todd Swain; 6/90.

685. Lean-To (aka B Sharp) (5.7) Begin about 10 feet right of *B Flat;* go up the right-tending thin cracks (two possible starts). **Pro:** To 2.5 inches. **FA:** Dave Haber; 4/89.

686. C Sharp Roof (5.10c) This low overhang that leads to a thin crack is near the left (south) end of Voice's Crag. **Pro:** Thin to 2 inches. **FA:** Herb Laeger, Rich Smith; 3/79.

687. Ironsides (5.9) This route begins right and up from *C Sharp Roof.* Go up a greyish right-facing dihedral. **Pro:** To 2 inches. **FA:** Alan Bartlett, Dave Bengston; 2/90.

688. Alto (aka Blonde Bombshell Babylon) (5.8) This route lies about 90 feet right of *Ironsides.* Begin just right of a small roof, up

the leftmost of several cracks. **Pro:** To 2.5 inches. **FA:** Dave Haber; 4/89.

689. Hot Cross Buns (5.7) Begin about 8 feet right of *Alto,* in the right-hand crack. **Pro:** To 2.5 inches. **FA:** Alan Bartlett, Katie Wilkinson; 11/89.

690. Friday Afternoon Fix (5.9) The straight-in crack between *Hot Cross Buns* and *Life in the Fat Lane.* **Pro:** To 3 inches. **FA:** Brian Moore; 4/98.

691. Life in the Fat Lane (5.9) Begin on the right side of the brownish face, about 30 feet right of *Hot Cross Buns;* go up the right-tending crack. **Pro:** To 3 inches. **FA:** Todd Swain; 6/90.

692. War Crimes (5.10a) This is located about 60 feet right of *Life in the Fat Lane* on a dark rib of rock just left of a small tree. Go up cracks on the rib. **Pro:** To 4 inches. **FA:** Alan Roberts, Don Reid, Shari; 4/85.

693. Dwindling Greenbacks (5.10d) ★★ The best route on Voice's Crag is about 30 feet right of *War Crimes,* on the right side of a small face. Go up a left-tending thin crack. **Pro:** Many thin to 1 inch. **FA:** Alan Roberts, John Mattson.

Micro Crag

This small crag lies about 75 yards west of Park Boulevard, just south and slightly behind Voice's Crag. Park at a small turnout 0.2 mile south of the North Wonderland parking area (6.6 miles from the West Entrance; 2.0+ miles from the Intersection Rock/Real Hidden Valley intersection) on the west side of Park Boulevard. Map, page 218.

Micro Crag—East Face

The east face of Micro Crag faces Park Boulevard and gets sun in the morning and afternoon shade.

694. **The Todd Couple** (5.10c) ★ This is the left-slanting crack on the left end of the east face. The crux is a steep section low down. **Pro:** To 2.5 inches. **FA:** Todd Swain, Peggy Buckey; 4/91.

695. **The Confessional** (5.10b) (R) ★ This is the obvious left-facing corner system with a ledge midway up; the crux is the upper corner. **Pro:** Very thin to 2 inches. **FA:** Robert Hynes, Dave Wonderly; 1/89.

696. **Wired** (5.10b) ★★ Go up the thin crack beginning just right of *The Confessional*. **Pro:** Many very small to 2 inches. **FA:** Alan Roberts, Don Reid, Bob Harrington; 1985.

697. **Snicker Biscuit** (5.11b) ★ Begin below and right of a thin crack above a horizontal; go up and left on a ramp/face to the horizontal, then up a thin crack. **Pro:** Thin to 2 inches. **FA** (TR): Robert Hynes; 3/89. **FA** (Lead): Todd Swain; 4/91.

698. **Direct Start** (Variation) (5.12c) (TR) Climb straight up to the thin crack of *Snicker Biscuit*. **FA:** Scott Cosgrove; 1/96.

699. **Mitigating Damages (aka O. W.)** (5.11c) (TR) This is the wide crack just right of *Snicker Biscuit*. **FA:** Scott Cosgrove; 1/96.

Micro Crag—West Face

This faces Mini Crag's left end and gets shade in the morning and afternoon sun.

700. **The Inseam** (5.7) This is on the wall just left of the dihedral of *The Hem*. Go up a straight-in crack to a bulge with jugs to a face

with one bolt (added after first ascent). **Pro:** To 2 inches. **FA:** Todd Swain; 1992.

701. **The Hem** (5.7) Climb the dihedral with a bush partway up. **Pro:** To 2 inches. **FA:** Dave Haber, Sheryl Haber; 10/91.

Mini Crag

This little outcrop rises just west of Micro Crag. Several routes lie on the east face at the northern and southern sections (the middle section is fairly nondescript). *Opus Dihedral* lies on the west face. Park at the North Wonderland parking area (6.4 miles from the West Entrance; 2.2+ miles from the Intersection Rock/Real Hidden Valley intersection), or for Voice's Crag (6.6 miles from the West Entrance; 2.0+ miles from the Intersection Rock/Real Hidden Valley intersection). Map, page 218.

Mini Crag—East Face, Left Side

This gets morning sun and afternoon shade. The routes are not pictured.

702. **Steeped T** (5.8) Located at the far left end of the east face, this 25-foot route climbs twin cracks just right of a gully. **FA:** Todd Swain; 6/90.

703. **Model T** (5.7) Start 10 feet right of *Steeped T*. Face climb up and right to a crack; tunnel under a block at the top. **FA:** Todd Swain; 6/90.

704. **Mr. T** (5.9+) Begin 10 feet right of *Model T*. Go up the face to a crack to an arête. Above, cut right and up the face. **Pro:** To 2 inches. **FA:** Unknown.

Mini Crag—East Face, Right Side

This face gets morning sun and afternoon shade.

705. **Cats Claws** (5.11a/b) ** Climb a right-slanting crack past two bolts on far right end of east face. **Pro:** Thin to 2 inches. **FA:** Dave Bengston, Alan Bartlett; 2/90.

706. **Arête Buster** (5.11b/c) (R) * This arête split by a diagonal crack is 15 feet right of *Cats Claws.* Start on the leftmost of two possible bouldery starts, then follows the crack left around the arête and up. **Pro:** Thin to 2 inches. **FA:** Dave Bengston; 2/90.

707. **Piddle Pug** (5.8) (R) Start just right of *Arête Buster* in a flare, then head straight up. **Pro:** To 2 inches. **FA:** Dave Bengston; 2/90.

Mini Crag—West Face

The back side of the formation receives morning shade and sun all afternoon. Routes are located near the center of the west face. The face and routes are not pictured.

708. **Opus Dihedral** (5.9) * A 35-foot right-facing dihedral is high on the west face (near the middle of the formation). **Pro:** To 2.5 inches. **FA:** Alan Roberts, Don Reid, Shari Schubot; 1985.

709. **Bloom County** (5.8) The crack/corner just right of *Opus Dihedral.* **FA:** Todd Swain; 6/90.

Teeny Weeny Crag

This very small rock lies west of the west face of Mini Crag. The one known route lies on the west side. It receives shade in the morning, sun all afternoon. The crag and route are not pictured. Map, page 218.

710. **Moderate Man** (5.5) This is a right-leaning wide crack on the west face. **FA:** Brian Moore; 4/98.

Pet Rock

This is the small (and fairly forgettable) formation midway between Voice's Crag and Lizard's Hangout. The routes lie on the west face. Park at a turnout on the west side of Park Boulevard (7 miles from the West Entrance and 1.6 miles from the Intersection Rock/Real Hidden Valley intersection). The crag is about 150 yards northwest of Park Boulevard. It gets morning shade and is sunny all afternoon. The rock and routes are not pictured. Map, page 218.

711. **Penthouse Pet** (5.6) Begin about 10 feet left of *Excitable Boy.* Go up thin right-slanting cracks to a ledge, then join *Excitable Boy* near its end. **Pro:** Thin to 2 inches. **FA:** B. Guccione.

712. **Excitable Boy** (5.9) Climb the short, shallow left-facing corner (it doesn't reach the ground) near the middle of the west face. **Pro:** To 2 inches. **FA:** Todd Swain, Peggy Buckey; 3/86.

713. **Pet Project** (5.4) Begin on the left (southern) end of the west face about 150 feet right of *Excitable Boy.* Go up flakes and a face. **FA:** Todd Swain; 11/89.

714. **She's So Unusual** (5.7) Climb thin seams in brown rock 6 feet right of *Pet Project.* **Pro:** Thin to 2 inches. **FA:** Todd Swain, Peggy Buckey; 3/86.

715. **Pet Shop Girls** (5.8) (R) Climb the face past a horizontal about 10 feet right of *She's So Unusual.* **Pro:** To 2 inches. **FA:** Unknown.

Jellystone

This so-so formation lies about 350 yards
west of Park Boulevard and 175 yards southwest of Pet Rock. Routes are located on the
northeast face (facing Park Boulevard) and
on the southwest face. Park at a small
turnout on the west side of Park Boulevard
(same as for Pet Rock) located 7 miles from
the West Entrance and 1.6 miles from the
Intersection Rock/Real Hidden Valley intersection. Map, page 218.

Jellystone—Northeast Face

These routes all face Park Boulevard and get
early sun and afternoon shade.

716. **Yogi** (5.10c) ★ This is the obvious, left-
facing corner on the upper left side of the
northeast face. It will get better (clean up)
with a little traffic. **Pro:** To 2.5 inches. **FA**
(TR): Todd Swain; 4/91. **FA** (Lead):
Unknown.

717. **Boo Boo** (5.9) (R) Begin down and
right from the *Yogi* dihedral. Climb thin
cracks past a bush to a ledge, move right,
then go up the slot. **Pro:** To 2.5 inches. **FA:**
Todd Swain; 4/91.

718. **Mr. Ranger Sir** (5.7) Climb the thin
crack to the left side of the roof to the ledge;
finish up the slot. **Pro:** Thin to 3 inches. **FA:**
Todd Swain; 4/91.

719. Smarter Than the Average Ranger
(5.11a) ★ Climb the thin crack 7 feet right of
Mr. Ranger Sir to a ledge; finish up and right.
Pro: Very thin to 3 inches. **FA:** Randy Vogel,
Todd Gordon; 1989.

720. Pick-a-Nick Baskets (5.9) (R) Begin 6
feet right of *Smarter than the Average Ranger.*
Go up twin seams, then over a roof. **Pro:**
Thin to 3+ inches. **FA:** Todd Swain; 4/91.

721. The Bear Necessities (5.7) Climb the
left-facing corner, go over the roof, then up
and right. **Pro:** Thin to 3 inches. **FA:** Todd
Swain; 4/91.

722. Hiding from the Rangers (5.8+) Start
10 feet right of *The Bear Necessities.* Head up
a diagonally cut bulge to a handcrack, then
up the bulge to a wide crack. **Pro:** To 3
inches. **FA:** Brian Moore; 4/98.

723. Scrabble Marathons (5.8+) (not shown
on photo) Begin 30 feet right of the chimney in the center of the east face. Go up a
left-leaning crack, then over the bulge. **Pro:**
To 3 inches. **FA:** Brian Moore; 4/98.

Jellystone—Southwest Face

One recorded route has been established on
the southwest face; it gets morning shade and
afternoon sun.

724. Toiling Midgets (5.10b) ★ Climb a face
with three bolts to two-bolt anchor/rap. **FA:**
Unknown.

Brian's Crag

This large broken formation lies about 375
yards west of Jellystone (700 yards west of
Park Boulevard). Park at a turnout on the
west side of Park Boulevard (7 miles from
the West Entrance; 1.6 miles from the
Intersection Rock/Real Hidden Valley intersection). It is pretty nondescript-looking
from Park Boulevard (and otherwise); most
routes are short and lie on the western side.
The crag and routes are not pictured. Map,
page 218.

Brian's Crag—East Face

This is the short upper wall on the right
hand section of the east face; it gets shade in
the afternoon.

725. Swain Tradition (5.7) This handcrack
passes through horizontals and lies 20 feet
right of a chimney with large chockstone.
Pro: To 3 inches. **FA:** Brian Moore; 4/98.

726. Fool's Progress (5.9/5.10) ★ Follow a
flaring dihedral to a wide crack on the far
lower right end of the wall. There is a large
bush at the base. **Pro:** To 4 inches. **FA:** Brian
Moore, Tucker Tech; 4/98.

Brian's Crag—North Shoulder

The following climbs are extremely short
(20+ feet) and lie on the north end of the
formation. They are in shade most of the day.

727. Windy Corner (5.4) The left edge of the
face. **FA:** Brian Moore; 4/98.

728. Right Crack (5.4) Go up past a bush,
then left up the face. **FA:** Brian Moore; 4/98.

Brian's Crag—West Face, Left End

Most of the climbs on Brian's Crag lie on the west face. It is sunny all afternoon. These routes are on the left end.

729. **Junior Well's** (5.9/5.10a) ★ This route lies just around the corner from the north shoulder routes. Go up cracks, traverse right at a horizontal/small roof, then go up a crack. **Pro:** To 2.5 inches. **FA:** Brian Moore, Tucker Tech; 4/98.

730. **Juanita** (5.7) Climb the face and crack left of detached flake. **Pro:** To 2.5 inches. **FA:** Brian Moore; 4/98.

731. **14 Day Limit** (5.7) Climb through overlapping bulges and up through broken rock and discontinuous cracks. **Pro:** To 2 inches. **FA:** Brian Moore; 4/98.

732. **Cat Claw Corner** (5.7) This is the 20-foot brown dihedral right of *14 Day Limit*. Go up past a cat's claw bush to the dihedral. **Pro:** To 2 inches. **FA:** Brian Moore; 4/98.

733. **Buzz, Buzz** (5.8+) ★ The hand-to-fist crack just right of *Cat Claw Corner*. **Pro:** To 3 inches. **FA:** Brian Moore; 4/98.

734. **Lalapoluza** (5.11b) (TR) Climb thin seams right of *Buzz, Buzz*. Two-bolt anchor. **FA:** Raleigh Collins, Lisa Thompson; 4/98.

735. **Spanuerism** (5.11a) Start right of *Lalapoluza*. Go up past a bolt to a crack. **Pro:** To 2.5 inches. **FA** (TR): Raleigh Collins, Lisa Thompson; 4/98. **FA** (Lead): Unknown.

736. **Unknown** (5.7+) The rack right of *Spanuerism*. **FA:** Raleigh Collins, Lisa Thompson; 4/98.

737. **Assholes and Elbows** (5.10b) Start right of the last climb, just left of a prominent roof. Go up the face past a knob to a groove and crack. **Pro:** To 2.5 inches. **FA:** Alan Bartlett, Mike Wilson; 6/98.

738. **El Nino Special** (5.7) Begin right of *Assholes and Elbows;* face climb to the crack then go right and up to a handcrack. **FA:** Brian Moore; 4/98.

Brian's Crag—West Face, Right End

These routes are located on the right end of the west face, to the right of a slabby area that separates the west face.

739. **Unknown** (5.9+) (TR) Go up a flaring crack above bushes on the left side of the right end. **FA:** Raleigh Collins, Lisa Thompson; 4/98.

740. **Unknown** (5.7) **FA:** Raleigh Collins, Lisa Thompson; 4/98.

741. **Escape from Wyoming** (5.6) The crack/leaning pillar on the right end. **FA:** Brian Moore; 4/98.

Roadside Rock

Roadside Rock lies a few yards west of Park Boulevard and is 7.2 miles from the West Entrance and 1.4+ miles from the Intersection Rock/Real Hidden Valley intersection. A turnout is located here, on the west side of Park Boulevard. The rock is about 60 feet high. Descend off to the south (the left side if you are facing the rock from the road). This turnout also serves as parking for Mel's Diner and Lizard's Hangout. Map, page 227.

742. **Just Another Roadside Attraction** (5.7+) ★ Begin up the right-hand of two obvious converging cracks. **Pro:** To 2 inches. **FA:** Unknown.

743. **Cheap Thrills** (5.11b) ★(TR) Start just right of *Just Another Roadside Attraction*. Go up a very thin crack, then right, then back left to a wide crack. **FA:** Bart Groendycke.

744. **Restaurant at the End of the Universe** (5.10c) ★ Start on the upper tier of rock around the corner from the above routes. Climb a thin arch to a roof, then past two bolts. **Pro:** To 2.5 inches. **FA:** Todd Swain et al.

745. **Stains of the Stars** (5.10a) This right-slanting undercling leading to a off-width crack is to the right of the previous route. **Pro:** To 4+ inches. **FA:** Todd Gordon, Todd Swain, Derrick; 3/86.

746. **Roy's Solo** (5.7) Follow the diagonalling crack 6 feet right of *Stains of the Stars*, then go up and left in thin cracks. **Pro:** To 3.5 inches. **FA:** Roy McClenahan; 3/86.

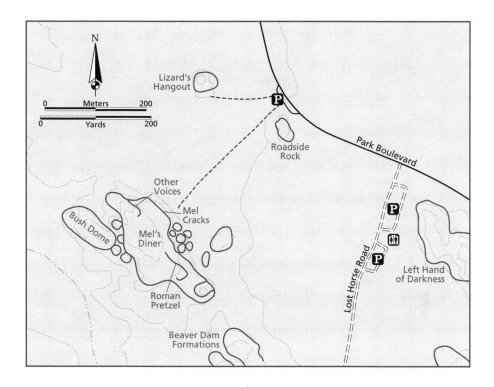

Lizard's Hangout

This small, popular rock (about 40 feet high) is located just west of Park Boulevard about 7.2 miles from the West Entrance and 1.4+ miles from the Intersection Rock/Real Hidden Valley intersection. A turnout is on the west side of Park Boulevard (same as for Roadside Rock). Lizard's Hangout lies approximately 75 yards to the northwest. Nearly all routes are located on the back (west) side of the rock. This is a nice sunny crag on colder days. Map is above.

A Note about Courtesy: It is not uncommon for groups and climbing classes to toprope several climbs in this area. If you place a toprope on several routes and leave them up for more than a short time, you must be prepared to either share the ropes with other climbers, or pull them down. Totally dominating this crag with topropes

and being unwilling to share or pull your ropes is not only extremely rude, but might justify the removal of your ropes. Be courteous instead.

Lizard's Hangout—West Face

747. **Into You Like a Train** (5.11c) (TR) (not shown on photo) This 20-foot high thin overhanging seam/crack is on the extreme left end of the rock, about 40 feet left of *Lizard Taylor* (and on a slightly separate section of rock). **FA:** Dick Cilley, Mike Paul.

748. **Off to See the Lizard (aka Komodo Dragon)** (5.5) (R/X) (not shown on photo) This is on the left side of the main face. Go up buckets just right of a left-slanting ramp/crack. **FA:** Todd Swain; 11/89.

749. **Lizard Taylor** (5.5) (R/X) (not shown on photo) This face is 10 feet right and around corner from *Off to See the Lizard;* past

two horizontals. **FA:** Todd Swain, Peggy
Buckey; 3/86.

750. **Lizard Breath Arden** (5.5) This is a
hand-to-fist crack in a right-facing corner to
a small roof. **Pro:** To 3+ inches. **FA:** Todd
Swain; 11/89.

751. **Chicken Lizard** (5.10b) ★ Follow a left-
slanting crack/seam. **Pro:** Thin to 2 inches.
FA (TR): Kevin Powell, Darrel Hensel; 4/83.
FA (Lead): Unknown.

752. **Progressive Lizard** (5.9) ★ The obvious
crack. **Pro:** To 2 inches. **FA:** Kevin Powell,
Darrel Hensel; 4/83.

753. **Lizard in Bondage** (5.11a) ★ This is the
crack/seam just right of *Progressive Lizard.*
Thin moves (5.11a) lead to an easier crack.
Pro: Thin to 1.5 inches. **FA:** Unknown.

754. **Left Lizard Crack** (5.10d) ★ The left-
slanting crack; it has a height-dependent start
(crux). **Pro:** Thin to 1.5 inches. **FA:**
Unknown.

755. **Right Lizard Crack** (5.9) ★ Start at the
same place as *Left Lizard Crack,* but go up
and right. **Pro:** To 2 inches. **FA:** Unknown.

756. **Lizard Skin (aka Blue Belly)** (5.9) ★
Climb a right-slanting crack, then go straight
up. **Pro:** To 2 inches. **FA:** Unknown.

757. **Wally Gator** (5.11c) ★ This is a hard
direct bouldering start to the upper part of
Lizard Skin. **FA:** Darrel Hensel.

758. **Alligator Lizard** (5.10a) (R) ★ Begin
just right of *Wally Gator.* Go up the face and
arch to the top. **Pro:** To 2.5 inches. **FA:** Kevin
Powell, Darrel Hensel; 4/83.

759. **Poodle Lizard** (5.7) Climb an easy face
on large holds to the right of *Alligator Lizard.*
FA: Unknown.

Lizard's Hangout—East Face

This faces Park Boulevard and gets morning sun and shade in the afternoon. The route is not pictured.

760. **Goeb's Goes Gecko** (5.2) ★ Located around the corner from *Poodle Lizard*. Go up the left side of the east face on plates. **FA:** Jason Goebel; 8/96.

Mel's Diner

This formation lies about 250 yards southwest of Park Boulevard about 7.2 miles from the West Entrance and 1.4+ miles from the Intersection Rock/Real Hidden Valley intersection. A turnout is located on the west side of Park Boulevard, also used for Roadside Rock/Lizard's Hangout. Mel's Diner is also about 300+ yards north of Lost Horse Road near the Filipino Wall (page 241). All of the routes face east (morning sun, afternoon shade). Map, page 227.

Mel's Diner—Left End

All of the following routes lie on the upper left (southern) end of the east face of Mel's Diner.

761. **Shamrock Shooter** (5.11c) This is a 30-foot overhanging crack/flake on a boulder. **Pro:** Thin to 2 inches. **FA** (TR): Kevin Powell; 4/83. **FA** (Lead): Mike Lechlinski.

762. **Roman Pretzel** (5.8+) This is the crack and knobby face in the left-facing corner. **Pro:** To 2.5 inches. **FA:** Todd Swain, Alan Roberts; 12/88.

763. **Fusion Punk** (5.9) Start just left of *Modern Jazz,* but head up and bit left. **Pro:** To 3 inches. **FA:** Unknown.

764. **Modern Jazz** (5.10b) Start in thin cracks, then head up and right to a hand-crack. **Pro:** Thin to 2 inches. **FA:** Alan Nelson, Karl Mueller; 12/81.

765. Rock & Roll Girl (5.9) Go straight up the handcrack. **Pro:** To 2.5 inches. **FA:** Alan Nelson; 12/81.

766. Kickin' Bach (5.10a) ★ Start 3 feet right of *Rock & Roll Girl*. Follow a thin crack up and right. **Pro:** Thin to 1.5 inches. **FA:** Alan Nelson, Karl Mueller; 12/81.

Mel's Diner—Center

The two routes for which the crag is named (*Right* and *Left Mel Cracks*) lie on lower center of the formation's east face and are easily discerned as two parallel thin cracks. Descend the chimney to the left of *Right Mel Crack*. A two-bolt anchor is on top of *Right Mel Crack*.

767. Right Mel Crack (5.10c) ★★ Actually, this is the left crack (climber humor); the short thin crux is down low. **Pro:** To 1 inch; two-bolt anchor. **FA:** Kevin Powell, Mike Waugh, Darryl Nakahira; 4/83.

768. Left Mel Crack (5.10b/c) ★★★ Yes, it's the right crack; and the better of the two. **Pro:** To 2 inches. **FA:** Darryl Nakahira, Alan Roberts, Mike Waugh, Kevin Powell; 4/83.

Mel's Diner—Right End

The following routes lie well to the right of the Mel Cracks on a section of the formation that is somewhat set back from the previous climbs.

769. I Love Brian Piccolo (5.8+) ★ This and *Other Voices* lie on the east-facing wall around the corner and right of the *Mel Cracks*. This is the right-hand of two steep cracks high on the left part of the face; you will need to scramble up to the base. **Pro:** To 3 inches. **FA:** Todd Gordon, Quinn McCleod, Brian Sillasen; 9/86.

770. Overheard (5.10a) (TR) Face climb up huecos and a flake left of *Other Voices*. **FA:**

Todd Swain, Donette Swain, Teresa Malone; 1993.

771. **Other Voices** (5.7) ★ This crack lies near the right end of the lower section of the right end of Mel's Diner; down and right of the previous climbs. Start at a block on the left, then go up a widening crack through a small roof. **Pro:** To 3 inches. **FA:** Kevin Powell, Darrell Hensel; 4/83.

Bush Dome

Park at a large turnout on the west side of Park Boulevard located 7.2 miles from the West Entrance and 1.4+ miles from the Intersection Rock/Real Hidden Valley intersection (same as for Mel's Diner). This dome is located behind (west) of the right (northern) end of Mel's Diner. Walk around the right end of Mel's Diner (past *Other Voices*), then head west and back left to the base. All

but one route is located on the formation's east face, and most of these may be more easily done in two pitches. Map, page 227.

Bush Dome—East Face

The east face gets morning sun and is shady in the afternoon.

772. **Chestwig** (5.10a) ★★ Begin in a thin crack left of the center of the crag. **Pitch 1:** Go up the thin crack to a large ledge. **Pitch 2:** Go up the left-hand thin crack above the ledge. **Pro:** Many thin to 3 inches. May have a fixed pin. **FA:** Dave Evans, Margie Floyd, Jim Angione, Scott Gordon, Eric Charlton, Todd Gordon; 9/86.

773. **Lean on Me** (5.10a) ★ This starts in the crack just right of *Chestwig*. **Pitch 1:** Go up the thin crack, then pass a couple of bushes ending on the large ledge. **Pitch 2:** Go up the right-hand wide crack. **Pro:** Thin to 4 inches.

FA: Jeff Rhoads, Kelly Rhoads, Todd Gordon; 11/89.

774. Kate's Bush (5.8) ★ Begin about 30 feet right of *Lean on Me*, in an obvious hand-crack. **Pitch 1:** Go up the handcrack 30 feet to a ledge/block. **Pitch 2:** Follow the corner, then go up a crack to the top. **Pro:** To 3 inches. **FA:** Todd Gordon, Dave Evans, Margie Floyd, Deanne Gray, Jim Angione, Eric Charlton, Scott Gordon; 9/86.

775. The Camel (5.7) A pillar is left of *The Raccoon*. **Pitch 1:** Chimney up inside the right side of the pillar and climb to a ledge on the northwest side of the face. **Pitch 2:** From the right end of the ledge, gritty friction leads up and right past a horizontal to the top. **FA:** Alan Bartlett, Laurel Colella; 9/98.

776. The Raccoon (5.9) This route lies on a shorter, inset wall to the right of *Kate's Bush*. This is the left-hand (and "best"-looking) of several short cracks. **FA:** Todd Gordon, Brandt Allen; 5/95.

Bush Dome—West Face

This face sees morning shade and afternoon sun. The face and route are not pictured.

777. Beanie Babies (5.5) This route lies on the west corner of Bush Dome. Start amid boulders, chimney up and climb a crack that heads up, then right, then up to the top. **FA:** Alan Bartlett, Laurel Colella; 7/98.

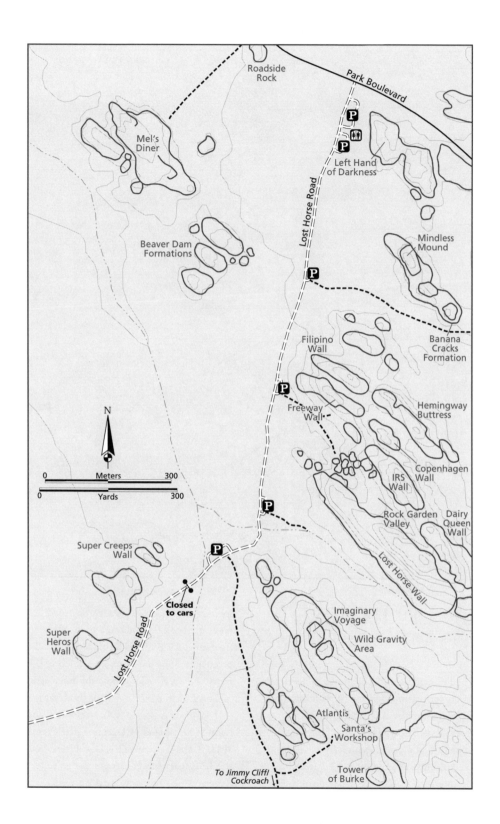

Roadside
Rock

Park Boulevard

Mel's
Diner

P

P

Left Hand
of Darkness

Lost Horse Road

Beaver Dam
Formations

Mindless
Mound

P

Banana
Cracks
Formation

Filipino
Wall

Hemingway
Buttress

N

P

Freeway
Wall

Copenhagen
Wall

Meters   300

IRS
Wall

Yards   300

P

Rock Garden
Valley

Dairy
Queen
Wall

Super Creeps
Wall

P

Lost Horse Wall

Closed
to cars

Imaginary
Voyage

Super
Heros
Wall

Wild Gravity
Area

Lost Horse Road

Atlantis

Santa's
Workshop

To Jimmy Cliff/
Cockroach

Tower
of Burke

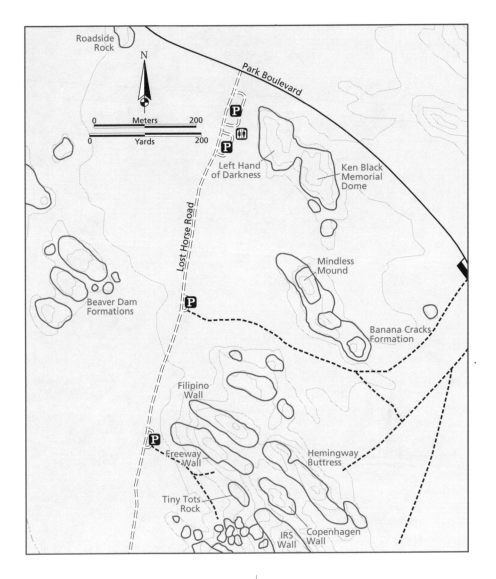

LOST HORSE ROAD

The following section of the Lost Horse area covers formations that are either located off of, or are initially approached from, Lost Horse Road. Lost Horse Road intersects Park Boulevard at a point about 7.3+ miles from the park's West Entrance and 1.3 miles from the Intersection Rock/Real Hidden Valley

intersection. This well-graded dirt road heads west for about 0.6 mile to a point where further vehicular traffic is forbidden. A number of small parking areas are located along Lost Horse Road. A toilet is near the intersection of Lost Horse Road and Park Boulevard.

Popular crags along Lost Horse Road include Left Hand of Darkness, the Freeway Wall, Rock Garden Valley, Lost Horse Wall, the Imaginary Voyage area, and the Super Creeps Wall. Overview map, page 233.

Left Hand of Darkness

This formation is located at the southwest corner of the junction of Park Boulevard and Lost Horse Road (7.3 miles from the West Entrance; 1.3+ miles from the Intersection Rock/Real Hidden Valley intersection). Several parking spots and a toilet are located off Lost Horse Road. Map, page 234.

Left Hand of Darkness—
East Face

This side of the formation is just south of Lost Horse Road and directly faces Park Boulevard. It gets morning sun and is shady in the afternoon.

778. **Aleister Crowley (aka Brew 102)** (5.8) Climb the grainy corner on the left side of the rock. **Pro:** To 2 inches. **FA:** Todd Swain, Jim Browning; 10/89.

779. **Route 152** (5.10a) (R) Begin just right of *Aleister Crowley.* Face climb into a crack; higher, join *Aleister Crowley.* **Pro:** Thin to 2

inches. **FA** (TR): Unknown. **FA** (Lead): Todd Swain, Jim Browning; 10/89.

780. **Left Route** (5.10a) (R) ★★★ Climb the left of two thin cracks on the main face. **Pro:** Thin to 2 inches. **FA:** Chick Holtkamp, John Lakey; 2/78.

781. **The Omen** (5.10b) ★ (TR) Begin at the *Left Route,* then move right and climb a flake (it shares a few feet with *Right Route* here), then go straight up the face above. **FA:** Bob Gaines; 5/01.

782. **Right Route** (5.10b/c) ★★ Start right of the right-hand crack system, then go up and on the left flake/face to the roof. Go left, then back right, then continue up the crack to the top. **Pro:** Thin to 2 inches. **FA:** Chick Holtkamp, John Lakey; 2/78.

783. **Variation** (5.11c) ★★ (TR) Avoid the jog to the left and back on *Right Route;* instead climb straight up the crack. **FA:** Unknown; 1979.

784. **The Uh Cult** (5.10a) Go up the crack right of *Right Route,* then left and up the face. **FA** (TR): Todd Swain; 10/89. **FA** (Lead): Tom Michael.

785. **Mandarina** (5.11b) ★ (TR) The arête/face left of *To Air Is Human;* leads to a hole near top. **FA:** Bob Gaines, Todd Gordon, D. Reinich; 9/96.

786. **To Air Is Human** (5.10d) (R) ★★ Climb the right side of the upper arête. **Pro:** Three bolts; anchors. **FA:** Herb Laeger, Eve Laeger, Rich Perch; 11/87.

787. **Uncle Fester** (5.10d) ★★ Go up the very thin crack (crux) to the ledge and upper dihedral. **Pro:** Thin to 2 inches. **FA:** Kevin Powell, Randy Vogel, Rob Raker, Darryl Nakahira; 5/83.

788. **Whistling Sphincter** (5.11c) ★ (TR) This is the face of the upper block, right of the upper dihedral of *Uncle Fester.* **FA:** Kevin Powell; 5/83.

789. **Jane Pauley** (5.8) Go straight up the crack to the ledge; move right to a short flake/crack. **Pro:** To 2 inches. **FA:** Tom Michael, Todd Gordon; 10/86.

790. **Bryant Gumbel** (5.8) Begin as for *Jane Pauley,* but go right where the crack splits. **Pro:** To 2 inches. **FA:** Todd Gordon, Cody Dolnick; 10/86.

791. **Pump Up the Volume** (5.11a/b) ★ Start off blocks, then go up the left side of the slabby face past three bolts. **Pro:** Anchors. **FA:** Todd Gordon, Cyndie Bransford; 3/90.

792. **Grandpa Gander** (5.10c) (R) ★ Begin down and right of *Pump Up the Volume,* angle left to finish as for that route. **Pro:** Three bolts; gear for anchor. **FA:** Herb Laeger, Andy Brown, Lotus Brown; 10/86.

793. **Granny Goose** (5.7) Begin on the right side of the face; undercling left and finish up a handcrack. **Pro:** To 2.5 inches. **FA:** Fred East, John Edgar; 1973.

794. **Mother Goose** (5.4) (R/X) Begin as for *Granny Goose,* but face climb up the arête. No pro. **FA:** Todd Swain; 1990.

Left Hand of Darkness— West Face

The west side of the Left Hand of Darkness has several faces, the most prominent being a steep orange-colored face that is located about 100 yards south of Lost Horse Road's intersection with Park Boulevard. Park in the second parking area, just past the toilet. The face sees morning shade and sun all afternoon.

795. **Bamboozled Again** (5.11b/c) ★ (not shown on photo) This is on the back side of the actual Left Hand of Darkness rock, approximately 100 feet left of routes 797 to 801. There are three bolts on the brownish face. **FA:** Dave Mayville; 1990.

796. **Billy Barty Crack** (5.10a) (not shown on photo) This short thin crack starts over small roof about 45 feet right of *Bamboozled Again.* **Pro:** Thin to 2 inches. **FA:** Alan Bartlett, Brandt Allen, Dave Mayville; 9/90.

797. **White Dopes on Punk** (5.10a) ★ Climb the face and double thin cracks on the left side of the face to a small left facing corner. The climb lies left of *Baby Huey* . . . **Pro:** Thin to 2 inches. **FA:** Todd Swain; 11/89.

798. **Baby Huey Smokes an Anti-Pipeload** (5.11d) (R) ★★ Begin just left of the pillar; go up left-slanting seams/cracks past one bolt. **Pro:** Thin to 2 inches. **FA** (TR): Unknown. **FA** (Lead): Kurt Smith.

799. **Anti-Gravity Boots** (5.11c) (R) ★★
Begin behind the pillar. Go up double left-
leaning seams. **Pro:** Thin. **FA** (TR):
Unknown. **FA** (Lead): Dave Schultz.

800. **Gomma Cocida** (5.10d) (R) ★ Follow
the discontinuous crack straight up, beginning just right of *Anti-Gravity Boots*. **Pro:**
Thin to 2 inches. **FA:** Dave Schultz.

801. **Potato Masher** (5.12b) (R) ★ This is
the seam with one bolt right of *Gomma
Cocida*. **Pro:** Thin to 2 inches. **FA** (TR): Tom
Herbert; 12/87. **FA** (Lead): Kurt Smith; 1/88.

802. **The Nose in a Day (aka Mano Negra)**
(5.9) Begin about 50 feet right and below
the previous routes on a separate face; go up
the obvious crack into a corner. **Pro:** To 4
inches. **FA:** Unknown.

803. **Salathe Free** (5.7) The crack just right
of *The Nose in a Day*. Even though this and
the previous climb are quite forgettable, you
can amaze and amuse your friends by naming
off these ascents. **Pro:** To 3 inches. **FA:** Todd
Swain.

Ken Black Memorial Dome

This formation is just south of the Left Hand of Darkness (7.4 miles from the West Entrance and 1.2 miles from the Intersection Rock/Real Hidden Valley intersection). It is just west of Park Boulevard. A small turnout off Park Boulevard, 0.1 mile southeast of Lost Horse Road provides easy access; alternatively, you can walk south from the Left Hand of Darkness parking area (on Lost Horse Road next to the toilet). Routes face south (sunny most of the day) and east (shady in the afternoon). Map, page 234.

Ken Black Memorial Dome— Left Side

The following climbs lie on the left side of the formation. Most routes face in a southerly direction and are sunny much of the day.

804. **Blackheart** (5.10b) ★ Go up the face with two bolts left of *Blackout*. **Pro:** Small cams to 2 inches; two-bolt anchor/80-foot rap. **FA:** Bob Gaines, Alan Bartlett; 3/97.

805. **Blackout** (5.11a) (R) ★ This route heads up the center of the face past two bolts and horizontals. **Pro:** Small cams; two-bolt anchor/80-foot rap. **FA:** Todd Swain, Rick Guerrieri, Dave Evans; 10/89.

806. **Black Magic** (5.10b) (TR) Climb the face just right of *Blackout*. **FA:** Bob Gaines, Alan Bartlett; 3/97.

807. **Pitch Black** (5.10a) Begin up and left on a ramp/ledges, then move up the ledgy face to the left side of the arch/roof. Go up the corner/roof and cracks above; finish as for *Blackjack*. **Pro:** To 3 inches; two-bolt anchor/rap. **FA:** Todd Swain, Dave Evans, Marge Floyd; 10/89.

808. **Blackjack** (5.11a) ★★★ (Sport) This is a fine seven-bolt sport route. Two-bolt anchor/70-foot rap. **FA:** Bob Gaines, Todd Gordon, Yvonne Gaines, Cyndie Bransford; 12/95.

809. **Holiday in the Sun** (5.10a) (R) ★★ Go up the arête (right at the roof) on excellent rock to a bolt; it's runout above the bolt. **Pro:** Small cams; two-bolt anchor. Rap from *Blackjack*. **FA:** Ken Black; 1983.

Ken Black Memorial Dome— Right Side

The following climbs lie to the right of the arête of *Holiday in the Sun* and face more or less east. Morning sun, afternoon shade.

810. **My Friends Treat Me Like a Mushroom** (5.8+) ★ Go up the gully to the right of *Holiday in the Sun,* then up the face past two bolts. **Variation:** Go right after the first bolt and join the upper part of *Chicken Mechanics.* **Pro:** To 3 inches. **FA:** Bill Cramer, Michelle Cramer, Mike Shacklett; 11/92.

811. **Chicken Mechanics** (5.9) ★ Best done as two short pitches. **Pitch 1:** Go up to a small roof, then take the left-slanting crack to a ledge. **Pitch 2:** Move left, then up easy climbing to the top. **Pro:** To 2 inches. **FA:** Brian Sillasen, Todd Gordon; 5/86.

812. **Poultry Pilots** (5.7) This is the light-colored widening crack right of *Chicken Mechanics*. **Pro:** To 3 inches. **FA:** Todd Swain; 10/91.

813. **Powdered Toast Man** (5.10a) This is the arête left of *Fryer Flyers*. **Pro:** To 2 inches; one bolt. **FA:** Todd Gordon, Cyndie Bransford; 10/92.

814. **Fryer Flyers** (5.5) Follow the left-tending hand-to-fist crack around the corner *Powdered Toast Man*. **Pro:** To 3 inches. **FA:** Todd Swain; 10/91.

815. **Pacific Ave. Dorm** (5.7) ★ This is a three-bolt face route located on the face to the right of the second pitch of *Chicken Mechanics*. Approach from that route or up the gully right of *Fryer Flyers*. **FA:** Warren Hughes, Mike Van Volkem; 10/90.

816. **Pacific Heights** (5.8) (X or TR) Climb the face 10 feet right of *Pacific Ave. Dorm*. **FA** (TR): Warren Hughes; 10/90. **FA** (Lead): Todd Swain; 10/91.

Mindless Mound

Though described on page 317, Mindless Mound is most easily approached, and lies only about 100 yards, from the parking area on the east side of Lost Horse Road (0.2 mile south of Park Boulevard). It is easily seen to the southeast from here and is actually the northern end of the Banana Cracks Formation. Maps, pages 234 and 313.

Banana Cracks Formation

This formation is perhaps most easily approached, and is visible, from the parking area on the east side of Lost Horse Road, 0.2 mile south of Park Boulevard. The marked climbers' trail heading south from the parking area leads directly to the base. Described on page 314. Maps, pages 234 and 313.

Beaver Dam Formations

These small formations lie about 100 yards west of Lost Horse Road, almost directly north of the west face of Freeway Wall and Filipino Wall. Lost Horse Road intersects Park Boulevard 7.3 miles from the West Entrance and 1.3+ miles from the Intersection Rock/Real Hidden Valley intersection. The crags are best approached from the small turnout on the east side of Lost Horse Road 0.2 mile west of the Park Boulevard intersection. They lie south of Mel's Diner, and can be approached from there as well. The formations and routes are not pictured. Map, page 234.

817. **Busy Beaver** (5.10a) ★ This thin crack (a fixed pin may be present) to a dogleg roof crack lies on the east face of the middle formation. **Pro:** To 4 inches. **FA:** Bob Gaines, Todd Gordon; 3/95.

818. **Manicured Bush** (5.10d) Climb the thin crack to an easy chimney right of *Busy Beaver*. **Pro:** Thin to 2 inches. **FA:** Bob Gaines, Todd Gordon; 3/95.

819. **Daddy's Long Leg** (5.10c) ★ A short stemming corner with two bolts on the east face of the formation is just west of the above two routes. **FA:** Bob Gaines, Yvonne Gaines; 5/95.

820. **Unnamed** (5.10a) This route lies on a short wall on a formation left and slightly behind the Beaver Dam Formations. It climbs a left-slanting thin crack about 25 feet long. **Pro:** Thin to 2 inches. **FA:** Don Reid, Todd Gordon, Alan Bartlett; 3/96.

Filipino Wall

This "wall" is actually the extreme right (northern) extension of Hemingway Buttress where it reaches Lost Horse Road. It is located just north of the Freeway Wall. Routes face northeast (morning sun, afternoon shade). The wall is located a short distance east of (and is easily seen from) Lost Horse Road. Lost Horse Road intersects Park Boulevard 7.3 miles from the West Entrance; and 1.3+ miles from the Intersection Rock/Real Hidden Valley intersection; the best approach is from a small turnout on the east side of Lost Horse Road about 0.2 miles south of the Park Boulevard intersection. Map, page 234.

821. **Imelda's New Shoes** (5.10a) This is the leftmost route. Take the left of two thin cracks that eventually join. **Pro:** Thin to 3 inches. **FA:** Todd Gordon, Todd Swain, Eric Anderson, Alan Bartlett; 6/90.

822. **The Orgasmatron** (5.10b) Start 12 feet right of *Imelda's New Shoes.* Take the flared crack up and left to a small right-facing corner. Continue up a handcrack. **Pro:** Thin to 3 inches. **FA:** Eric Anderson, Todd Gordon, Todd Swain, Alan Bartlett; 6/90.

823. **Summer School** (5.10a) Start as for *The Orgasmatron,* but stay in thin cracks to the right. **Pro:** Thin to 2 inches. **FA:** Alan Bartlett, Eric Anderson; 7/90.

824. **The Granulator** (5.10c) (R) This is about 20 feet right of *Summer School.* Take

the right-hand of two cracks, over a small roof, then go up discontinuous cracks and the face. **Pro:** To 2 inches. **FA:** Eric Anderson, Alan Bartlett; 7/90.

825. **Aquino** (5.8) This handcrack is 35 feet right of *The Granulator* on the right-hand buttress. Best approached up ledges. **Pro:** To 2.5 inches. **FA:** Todd Gordon, Dave Evans; 2/86.

826. **Exiled** (5.10a) ★ This is located directly under *Marcos,* 25 feet down and right of *Aquino.* Two bolts lead to a thin crack to the ledge where *Marcos* starts. **Pro:** Thin to 2 inches. **FA:** Richard Shoup, Bart Groendycke, Todd Alston.

827. **Marcos** (5.10a) ★ This is the high, right-facing dihedral that starts on the ledge where *Exiled* ends. **Pro:** Thin to 2.5 inches. **FA:** Dave Evans, Todd Gordon; 2/86.

828. **Yvonne's Arête** (5.10a) ★ This is a two-bolt arête left of the *Marcos* dihedral. Rap 80 feet from a tree. **FA:** Todd Swain, Jeff Rickerl; bolts added later.

829. **Planetary Motion** (5.8) Climb a hand-crack to a small roof/horizontal, go right, then head back left to an upper thin crack. This route is about 150 feet right of *Marcos/Exiled.* **FA:** Alan Roberts, Lyman Spitzer; 89.

830. **False Smooth as Silk** (5.5) (not shown on photo) This faces Lost Horse Road and is 35 feet right and around the corner from *Planetary Motion.* Climb the low-angled thin cracks. **Pro:** To 2 inches. **FA:** Unknown.

The Freeway Wall

Located immediately east of the Lost Horse Road, the "toe" of this long southwest-facing wall nearly reaches the road. Lost Horse Road intersects Park Boulevard 7.3 miles from the West Entrance and 1.3+ miles from the Intersection Rock/Real Hidden Valley intersection; the best approach is from a small turnout on the east side of Lost Horse Road about 0.3+ miles south of the Park Boulevard intersection. Routes face south-west (morning shade, sunny all afternoon). The upper (right-hand) portion ends just north of Copenhagen Wall, and it is possible to walk through a narrow corridor behind (west of) the Copenhagen Wall to reach the IRS Wall. Map, page 234.

Lower Freeway Wall

This section of the Freeway Wall lies just east of Lost Horse Road. It gets morning shade and afternoon sun.

831. **Silkworm** (5.6) This is the left-facing corner with a thin crack on the right wall. It is 100 feet around the corner (left) of, and up a gully from, *Smooth as Silk.* **Pro:** thin to 2.5 inches. **FA:** Todd Swain; 9/89.

832. **Smooth as Silk** (5.8) ★ This is the smooth, low-angled slab with a finger crack; it faces Lost Horse Road. **Pro:** Small to 2 inches. **FA:** John Bald, John Edgar; 1973.

833. **Thigh Master** (5.9) ★ Climb the but-tress to the right of *Smooth as Silk* past two bolts. **Pro:** To 2 inches. **FA:** Tucker Tech, Todd Gordon, Tom Burke; 12/99.

834. **Stop Making Sense** (5.11a) This route begins just left of *Stop Trundling.* Go up the face and thin crack to finish on the upper

part of *Thigh Master.* **Pro:** Very thin, one bolt. **FA:** Unknown.

835. **Stop Trundling** (5.10a) ★ Begin off the lower left of a slab; go up a left-facing corner. **Pro:** To 2.5 inches. **FA:** Todd Gordon; 3/86.

836. **Start Trundling** (5.10a) ★ Begin about 10 feet up and right of *Stop Trundling.* Go up a thin crack into a shallow leaning corner. **Pro:** To 2.5 inches. **FA:** Darryl Nakahira, Randy Vogel, Maria Cranor; 1980.

837. **Start Fumbling** (5.10c/d) (R) Begin about 15 feet up and right of *Start Trundling.* Go up the crack past a fixed pin. **Pro:** Thin to 2 inches. **FA:** Roy McClenahan; 1987.

838. **Stop Grumbling** (5.8) This wide crack begins right of the slab and 20 feet right of a tree. **Pro:** To 3 inches. **FA:** Unknown.

839. **Barney Rubble** (5.1) Begin to the right of *Stop Grumbling;* go up this gully and loose blocks. **FA:** Unknown.

840. **Wilma Rubble (aka Guide's Crack)** (5.7) This route begins about 60 feet to the right of *Barney Rubble,* to the left of a tree, and below and right of the obvious roof/block. Go up the crack, passing to the right of the roof. Rap 80 feet from slings over a horn. **Pro:** To 3 inches. **FA:** Unknown.

841. **S'nose of Winter** (5.8) Start as for *Wilma Rubble,* but at the roof traverse left, moving under it and around the corner to a steep face. Rap off the previous route. **Pro:** To 3 inches. **FA:** Bill Cramer, Gregg Bruno; 3/90.

842. **Death on the Pile** (5.7) (R) (not shown on photo) Begin right of *Wilma Rubble,* behind the tree. **Pitch 1:** Go up a left-facing corner to a right-leaning ramp. **Pitch 2:** Go up cracks above the right end of the ramp, right of the face. **Pro:** To 2.5 inches. **FA:** Unknown.

The Freeway Wall—Upper Face

A popular southwest-facing crag, the Freeway Wall—Upper Face is shady in the morning, but gets sun most of the afternoon. The best approach is from a small turnout on the southeast side of Lost Horse Road about 0.3+ mile south of the Park Boulevard/Lost Horse Road intersection (7.3 miles from the West Entrance; 1.3+ miles from the Intersection Rock/Real Hidden Valley intersection).

Routes are located either on a lower face (Upper Face—Left End, all of which are reached from near the start of Freeway at a large pine tree), or on the Upper Face—Right End. The Upper Face—Right End faces Tiny Tots Rock. The Upper Face—Right End has a number of good crack routes and ends just north of Copenhagen Wall. It is also an easy walk through a narrow corridor behind (west of) the Copenhagen Wall to reach the IRS Wall. To descend,

downclimb off the back (east) face of the formation, then head right and around the southern end.

The Freeway Wall—Upper Face, Left End

843. **Sweet Transvestite** (5.8) (R) Begin as for Freeway, but head up and left in slanting cracks to the plate-covered buttress. **Pro:** To 2 inches. **FA:** Roy McClenahan, Helga Brown; 1988.

844. **Freeway** (5.7) (R) ★ Start below a large pine tree; head up a slab and thin cracks, then up and right along the obvious ramp. **Pro:** To 2 inches. **FA:** John Wolfe, Chris Gonzalez; 11/74.

845. **Passing Zone** (5.8) (R) Start up *Freeway*, but continue up the face (three bolts), then left up the crack. **Pro:** To 2.5 inches. **FA:** Todd Swain, Nina Burnell; 2/91.

846. Sigalert (Variation) (5.11a) (TR) Climb *Passing Zone,* then head up and right after the last bolt. **FA:** Alois Smrz, Miguel Carmona; 1/90.

847. Totally Nuts (5.9) (R) Climb *Freeway.* About 30 feet from the top of the ramp, climb a discontinuous crack and face straight up. **Pro:** Thin to 2 inches. **FA:** Gib Lewis, Charles Cole; 1981.

848. Padded Cell (5.9) (R) This route is on the extreme right end of the headwall near the end of *Freeway.* **Pro:** Thin to 2 inches. **FA:** Todd Swain.

The Freeway Wall—Upper Face, Right End

849. Road Rage (5.9) The crack 30+ feet left of the next route (*Sig Alert*). **Pro:** To 3 inches. **FA:** Alan Bartlett, Don Reid, Tucker Tech; 2/98.

850. Sig Alert (aka Cast Up a Highway) (5.10b/c) ★★★ (Sport–ish) Start just left of *Nobody Walks in L. A.* Head up, then left, to a steep enjoyable face past five bolts. This essentially takes the line of *Cast Up a Highway* in the 1992 edition of this guide, but avoids the bottom (left-hand) rotten section. **Pro:** 0.5 to 1 inch; two-bolt anchor/80-foot rap. **FA** (TR): Eric Rasmussen, Rob Segger, Matt Shubert; 4/88. **FA** (Lead): Bob Gaines, Bill Russell; 12/97.

851. Gridlock (5.10a/b) ★★ (TR) (not shown on photo) Climb the arête between *Sig Alert* and *Nobody Walks in L. A.* **FA:** Ron Herschberg, Bob Gaines; 9/02.

852. Nobody Walks in L. A. (5.9) ★★ This is the crack system just right of *Sig Alert.* It is

possible to traverse left near the upper part of this route to reach the rap anchor on *Sig Alert.* **Pro:** Thin to 2 inches. **FA:** Charles Cole, Steve Anderson, Marjorie Shovlin; 1981.

853. Pretty Gritty (5.10a) Begin between yuccas. Go up a grainy crack to a roof, then up a wider crack above. **Pro:** Thin to 2.5 inches. **FA:** Gib Lewis, Charles Cole; 1981.

854. Anacram (5.10c) ★★★ This challenging thin crack and lieback is well worth doing. Go up past one bolt to a flake/corner, then left to a second bolt and the steep thin crack. **Pro:** Thin to 2 inches. **FA:** Charles Cole, Gib Lewis, R. Smith; 1981.

855. Cake Walk (5.8) ★★★ Begin about 20 feet right of *Anacram.* Go up the crack, traverse left (5.8), then go up an easier crack. **Pro:** To 2 inches. **FA:** Chick Holtkamp, John Lakey; 2/78.

856. The Talking Fish (5.10c/d) ★★★ Begin about 8 feet right of *Cake Walk.* Go up the face past three bolts and a fixed pin to a left-leaning crack, then up a crack back right. **Pro:** Thin to 2.5 inches, three bolts. **FA:** Todd Gordon, Tom Beck; 9/88.

857. Junkyard God (5.9) This route is on the far right side of the upper Freeway Wall, about 25 feet right of *The Talking Fish.* Go up cracks and corners to a crack. Go up this, then move right to another crack. **Pro:** To 2 inches. **FA:** Gib Lewis, Charles Cole; 1981.

858. Unknown (5.10b?) (not shown on photo) This is two bolts to a crack on the back side of the upper Freeway formation. **Pro:** To 2 inches. **FA:** Unknown.

Descent

859

860

861

862

863

864

865

Tiny Tots Rock

This pillar of rock lies just west of (opposite) and faces the upper Freeway Wall. It gets morning sun and shade in the afternoon. Park at the small turnout 0.3+ mile down Lost Horse Road (same as for Freeway Wall) and walk up the rocky gully. Descend off to the left (class four). Map, page 234.

859. **Date Rape** (5.9) ★ The left thin crack. **Pro:** To 2 inches. **FA:** Unknown.

860. **Tinker Toys** (5.10b) ★★ The thin crack just right of *Date Rape.* **Pro:** To 2 inches. **FA:** Unknown.

861. **Dinkey Doinks** (5.8) ★★ Climb the handcrack up the center of the east face. **Pro:** To 2 inches. **FA:** Unknown.

862. Who'da Thought (5.11c) ★ (TR) Thin seams to face between *Dinkey Doinks* and the *Cole–Lewis*. **FA:** Eric Rasmussen, Rob Segger, Matt Shubert; 4/88.

863. Cole–Lewis (5.8) Crack that goes over roof on right end of east face. **Pro:** To 3 inches. **FA:** Charles Cole, Gib Lewis; 1981.

864. Spontaneous Human Combustion (5.11c) ★ Go up the face past four bolts, then right to join *Fatal Flaw*. **Pro:** To 2 inches; four bolts. **FA:** Dave Evans, Jim Angione; 10/88.

865. Fatal Flaw (5.8+) ★★ Climb the crack on north face, in the corner, going over a small overhang. **Pro:** To 2 inches. **FA:** Randy Vogel, Charles Cole; 1982.

Copenhagen Wall

You can easily reach this formation from the vicinity of the Upper Freeway Wall–Tiny Tots Rock, and it is common to climb routes on it if you are in this area. It is just southeast of the upper end of the upper Freeway. Described on page 329. Map, page 234.

IRS Wall

The IRS Wall also can be reached easily from the upper Freeway Wall–Tiny Tots Rock area. Head up (south) from Tiny Tots Rock, and walk through the narrow passage behind the Copenhagen Wall, passing under a large wedged block. IRS Wall will be immediately on your right. Described on page 327.

Rock Garden Valley

Rock Garden Valley is formed by the back (west) side of the IRS Wall on the left, and the back (east) side of the Lost Horse Wall on the right. All but two of the recorded routes lie on the right-hand side and face east, though other route possibilities exist on the upper western face. The rock gets morning sun and afternoon shade. Park at the turnout on the southeast side of Lost Horse Road; 0.3+ mile from its junction with Park Boulevard (same as for Freeway Wall). Lost Horse Road intersects Park Boulevard 7.3 miles from the West Entrance and 1.3+ miles from the Intersection Rock/Real Hidden Valley intersection. A short trail heads southwest from the parking area; from its end, scramble up boulders, staying near the right side of the huge boulder-filled gully. Map, page 253.

Rock Garden Valley—West Face

Though the upper left side of Rock Garden Valley has several possible routes, only two are known. It is west-facing, with shade in the morning, sun in the afternoon. Descend left. The face and routes are not pictured.

866. Watch Out for the Wet Spot (5.8) This route is located directly across the "valley" from *Young Lust* (route 879 on the middle section of Rock Garden Valley). Climb an overhang to gain a right-traversing wide crack. Then head straight up a short hand-crack to easier climbing. **Pro:** To 4 inches. **FA:** Tim Schneider, Sandy Draus; 2/95.

867. **MZM** (5.8) Begin about 10 feet left of a large chasm with a nolina at its base. Face climb up to a short right-facing corner, then up a finger-to-hand crack ending in a "pod." Exit the pod and continue to the top. **Pro:** 1 to 3 inches. **FA:** Richard Adler, Dan Zacks; 3/04.

Rock Garden Valley—Upper End

The following climbs lie at the very upper end of Rock Garden Valley. Descend left. The rock sees sun in the morning and is shady all afternoon.

868. **Pop Rocks** (5.10c) ★★ This and the next four routes lie at the very upper end of the Rock Garden Valley. Begin left of a yucca. Face climb (one bolt) to a crack, then go left, then climb the face (one more bolt) to a

crack over a roof. **Pro:** To 2 inches. **FA:** Mike Hord, Mike McMullen.

869. **Sugar Pops** (5.10c) (TR) ★ Start as for *Pop Rocks.* At the first bolt, head left to a groove/face, then go up to join *Pop Rocks* at the second bolt. **FA:** Bob Gaines, Yvonne Gaines; 11/02.

870. **Top of the Pops** (5.10d) ★★★ This is 15 feet right of *Pop Rocks;* follow six bolts to a crack. **Pro:** To 2 inches. **FA:** Todd Swain, Debbie Brenchley, Kip Knapp; 8/91.

871. **Silent but Deadly** (5.9) (R) Start up the low-angled crack just right of *Top of the Pops,* then go up the arête. **Pro:** To 3+ inches. **FA:** Alan Bartlett, Katie Wilkinson; 4/88.

872. **On the Side** (5.10a) ★ (TR) Go up the right-facing corner just right of *Silent but Deadly*, then head up the steep face right of the arête. **FA:** Bob Gaines, Yvonne Gaines; 11/02.

873. **Holly Device** (5.10c) ★ This is a narrow buttress with four bolts 50 feet right of *Silent but Deadly*. **FA:** Todd Gordon, Tom Michael, Mark Walters, Jeff Jarvi; 3/87.

874. **The Griffin** (5.10a) (R) Climb the double crack 30 feet right of *Holly Device* to the face (two bolts). **Pro:** Thin to 2 inches. **FA:** Jim Kominski, Ann Kominski; 3/89.

875. **Fortune Cookie** (5.10a) Follow a short crack, 20 feet right of *The Griffin*, then go up the face (three bolts). **Pro:** To 2 inches. **FA:** Jim Kominski, Ann Kominski; 3/89.

Rock Garden Valley—Middle Section (aka Shorter Wall)

This section of Rock Garden Valley features some of the most popular routes in the area. Your scramble up the boulders is rewarded by the relatively level, hidden high valley for which the area was named. Descend via rappel from anchors atop *Young Lust, Rock Candy,* or *Split Personality*. It sees sun in the morning and is shady all afternoon.

876. **Spitwad** (5.9) ★★ Go up the face to a crack that goes left and up, stem back right near the top. **Pro:** Thin to 2 inches. **FA:** Keith Cunning et al.; 1979.

877. **Euthyphro** (5.8) ★ Start as for *Spitwad*, but take the handcrack straight up. **Pro:** To 2 inches. **FA:** Keith Cunning et al.; 1979.

878. **Euthenics** (5.8) This is the chimney between *Euthyphro* and *Young Lust*. **Pro:** To 4 inches. **FA:** Unknown.

879. **Young Lust** (5.8) ★★★ This thin crack is 10 feet right of *Euthyphro*. **Pro:** Thin to 1.5 inches; two-bolt anchor/rap. **FA:** Keith Cunning et al.; 1979.

880. **Lewd and Lascivious Conduct** (5.10c) (R) ★ Climb the thin seam between *Young Lust* and *Smithereens*. **Pro:** Very thin to 2 inches. **FA** (TR): Todd Gordon, Todd Swain. **FA** (Lead): Jeff Rhoads, Stan Brown, David Lambert; 11/89.

881. **Smithereens** (5.8+) ★★★ This thin crack is 10 feet right of *Young Lust* (at the right-hand section of the wall). **Pro:** Thin to 1.5 inches; two-bolt anchor/rap. **FA:** Keith Cunning et al.; 1979.

882. **Yi** (5.6) Climb the thin cracks just right of *Smithereens*. **Pro:** To 2 inches. **FA:** Chinson Yi, Benjamin Lowe; 3/96.

883. **Rock-a-Lot** (5.7) ★★ **FA:** Keith Cunning et al.; 1979.

884. **Candyman** (5.9) ★ (TR) (not shown on photo) Face climb between *Rock-A-Lot* and *Rock Candy*. **FA:** Bob Gaines, Yvonne Gaines; 5/02.

885. **Rock Candy** (5.9) ★★★ This is the steep face left of *Double Dogleg*. **Pro:** Thin; four bolts; two-bolt anchor/rap. **FA:** Keith Cunning et al.; 1979.

886. **Rock Dog Candy Leg** (5.11c) ★★ (TR) (not shown on photo) Climb the face between *Double Dogleg* and *Rock Candy*. **FA:** Jeff Rhoads; 10/88.

887. **Double Dogleg** (5.7) ★★★ This is the dogleg crack in the middle of the brown-and-white pocketed face. **Pro:** To 2.5 inches. **FA:** Kevin Powell, Dan Ahlborn, Tim Powell; 4/76.

888. **Split Personality** (5.9) ★★★ Start up *Double Dogleg*, but stem out right to a very thin crack. **Pro:** To 2.5 inches; bolt anchor/rap. **FA:** Unknown.

889. **Personal Space** (5.10c) ★★ (TR) (not shown on photo) Climb the face between *Split Personality* and *Beck's Bet*. **FA:** Jeff Rhoads, David Lambert; 11/89.

890. **Beck's Bet** (5.8) ★ This handcrack is 20 feet right of *Double Dogleg*. **Pro:** To 2.5 inches. **FA:** Tom Beck et al.

Rock Garden Valley— Swiss Cheese Wall

This is the left section of the lower right part of Rock Garden Valley. It is characterized (as the name might suggest) by a steep dark section of rock riddled with huecos and jugs. Descend to the left. This route gets morning sun and shade all afternoon.

891. **Single Cat Leg (aka Why Does It Hurt When I Pee?)** (5.10b) ★ These thin cracks are 10 feet left of *What's Hannen*. **Pro:** Thin to 2 inches. **FA:** Vaino Kodas, Diana Leach.

892. **What's Hannen** (5.10b) ★ This starts in a chimney/alcove, then goes up right-facing corner. **Pro:** To 4 inches. **FA:** Jack Roberts, Kevin Powell, Alan Roberts; 1981.

893. **Swiss Cheese** (5.6 to 5.8) ★ Start 6 feet right of *What's Hannan*, just right of pine tree. Go up a crack to a ledge, then up the pocketed face to a bolt high up. Finishing straight up is 5.8, left is 5.6. **FA:** Tom Beck et al.

894. **The Treat** (5.7+) ★ Start right of the beginning of *Swiss Cheese*. Go up a right-facing lieback flake; move right on a ledge then up the pocketed face above past four bolts. **Pro:** To 2.5 inches. **FA** (TR): Ellen Holden, Pete Werren, Tom Beck; 6/98. **FA** (Lead): Tom Beck, Ellen Holden; 7/98.

Swiss
Cheese Wall

Rock Garden Valley
Lower Section

Rock Garden Valley— Lower Section

All these routes climb the far right and lowest section of Rock Garden Valley. Most of these routes begin off a ledge system that is reached from its left end. The easiest descent is to rappel off anchors near the top of *Bolivian Freeze Job* (at the right end of the face). This sees sun in the morning and shade in the afternoon.

895. Mr. Michael Goes to Washington (5.7/5.8) ★ Pillar to cracks. **Pro:** To 2.5 inches. **FA:** Tom Michael, Alan Bartlett; 4/88.

896. I Wish I Knew Josh Mac (aka Wack) Was Going to Steal the Money Then (Variation) (5.10a) (TR) Climb *Mr. Michael* ... to where it jogs left, then head out right and up the face past two horizontals. **FA:** Tom Correa, Jacob Colella; 9/99.

897. Blue Sky, Black Death (5.5) Take the hand-to-fist crack left and out of the gully. **Pro:** To 3 inches. **FA:** Unknown.

898. Hear My Grain a'Comin' (5.11b) (TR) Start up *Barn Door Left*, then head up and left, staying on left side of a small face. **FA:** Unknown.

899. Unknown (5.10b) (TR) Start as for route 898, but stay right. **FA:** Unknown.

900. Barn Door Left (5.9) This route lies 15 feet left of *Barn Dance* and starts off stacked ledges left of that route. Go up the ramp, then right diagonalling crack. **Pro:** Thin to 2 inches, one bolt. **FA** (TR): Unknown. **FA** (Lead): Chris Miller; 1998.

901. Barn Dance (5.10a) ★ Start in a short crack that heads up and left past a hole in the rock; go up the face and discontinuous crack above past two bolts. **Pro:** To 2 inches (4 inch for anchor) **FA:** Chris Miller, Karen Roseme; 1998.

902. Barn Door Right (5.10a) ★ Begin near the left end of the ledge; go up a slightly right leaning thin crack with three bolts. **Pro:** Thin to 2.5 inches (4 inch for anchor). **FA** (TR): Unknown. **FA** (Lead): Chris Miller; 1998.

903. Born in a Barn (5.10a/b) ★ Go up to a small overlap, then continue up the face and seams with three bolts just right of *Barn Door Right*. **Pro:** Thin to 2.5 inches (4 inch for anchor). **FA** (TR): Unknown. **FA** (Lead): Chris Miller; 1998.

904. Amber Waves of Grain (5.9) ★ This is a four-bolt face route just left of *Bolivian Freeze Job*. **Pro:** Four bolts. **FA:** Chris Miller; 1998.

905. Bolivian Freeze Job (5.9+) ★ This is the thin crack on the right end of the wall. **Pro:** Thin to 1.5 inches; two-bolt anchor/rap. **FA:** Kelly Rich and others; 1/80.

906. Chasin' the Grain (5.10b) (TR) ★ Start as for *Chile Willie*, but head up and left on face between *Bolivian Freeze Job* and *Chile Willie*. **FA:** Chris Miller; 1998.

907. Chile Willie (5.8) ★ Climb the first crack right of *Bolivian Freeze Job*. **Pro:** Thin to 2 inches. **FA:** Todd Swain; 1/89.

908. Grain Splitting (5.9+) This is the crack immediately right of *Chile Willie*. **FA:** Unknown.

909. Barn Stormer (5.7+) (TR) Toprope the arête right of *Grain Splitting*. **FA:** Unknown.

The next three routes lie on a small crag down from *Chile Willie* (north of/toward Lost Horse Road). They are not pictured.

910. Training for Patagonia (5.10b) (R) Climb the left crack past two ceilings. **FA:** Todd Swain; 1/89.

911. Cold Columbian (5.9) The right-hand crack/arête. **FA:** Todd Swain; 1/89.

912. Peruvian Power Layback (5.9) Climb the clean right-facing corner 20 feet right of *Cold Columbian*. **FA:** Todd Swain; 1/89.

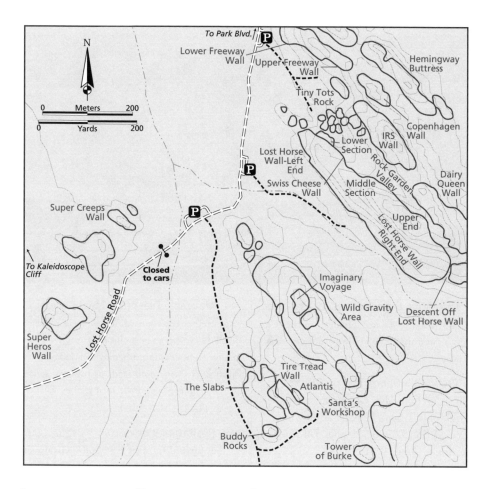

Lost Horse Wall

This large, west-facing formation (which doubles as the backside of Rock Garden Valley) is located just southeast of Lost Horse Road about 0.5 mile from the Park Boulevard junction. Lost Horse Road intersects Park Boulevard 7.3 miles from the West Entrance and 1.3+ miles from the Intersection Rock/Real Hidden Valley intersection. A small parking lot is on the southeast side of Lost Horse Road.

The left side of the formation contains several one- to two-pitch routes; the middle section is quite broken and has a few moderate multipitch routes; the right section is clean and contains many excellent multipitch climbs. The valley/wash below the formation originates to the south in Real Hidden Valley. It is shady in the morning and gets sun all afternoon. Map is above.

Lost Horse Wall—Left End

This section of the rock lies closest to Lost Horse Road. *Enos Mills Glacier* through *Moveable Feast* end atop the far right, lower end of Rock Garden Valley; you can rappel from anchors atop *Bolivian Freeze Job* (page 252) and walk around. Other routes have rappel anchors or downclimbs to the right.

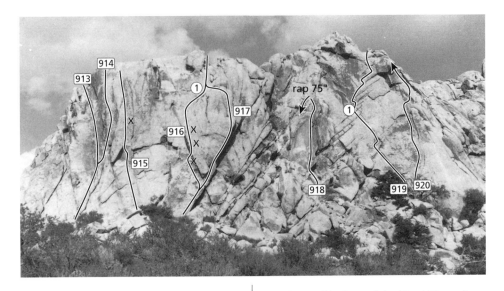

913. **Enos Mills Glacier** (5.11a) (R) ★★ This is the obvious left-facing dihedral on the left margin of the face. **Pro:** Thin to 2 inches. **FA:** Unknown.

914. **Cretin Bull Dancer** (5.11b) (R) ★★★ Begin as for *Enos Mills Glacier,* but head up and right into a small dihedral leading to a thin crack. **Pro:** Thin to 2 inches. **FA:** Tom Gilje, Alison Osius; 1981.

915. **Are You Experienced?** (5.11a) ★★ (TR) This route begins about 20 feet right of the previous two routes. Go up a thin left-leaning seam (5.11a) to a ledge, then follow a handcrack past one bolt. **FA** (Aid/5.10b/A3): John Long, Rick Accomazzo, Richard Harrison; 12/73. **FFA** (TR): John Bachar, Mike Lechlinski, John Yablonski, John Long, Lynn Hill; 1979.

916. **Terror in de Skies** (5.10a) Begin about 35 feet right of *Are You Experienced?,* below a large V-shaped roof. **Pitch 1:** Go up the left side of the roof to a bolt, then up and right near the left arête past two more bolts to a ledge. **Pitch 2:** A short pitch to the top. **Pro:** To 3 inches; three bolts. **FA:** Todd Swain, Kip Knapp; 1/89.

917. **Moveable Feast (aka Meat Wagon)** (5.9) Begin just right of *Terror In De Skies.* **Pitch 1:** Go up to and climb the right-facing, right-leaning dihedral to a ledge. **Pitch 2:** A short pitch leads to the top (same as *Terror in de Skies*). **Pro:** To 4 inches. **FA:** Kevin Powell, Alan Roberts; 1987.

918. **Hesitation Blue** (5.10b) ★ Begin about 90 feet up and right of last climbs. Go up the thin crack above a cave; stay right where it splits, to a ledge. Rap 75 feet. **Pro:** Thin to 3 inches. **FA:** Alan Roberts, Eric Gompper; 1987.

919. **Happy Landings, Linda** (5.11b) Start by a dead tree. **Pitch 1:** Go up left-slanting cracks to where they meet a series of right-slanting cracks. **Pitch 2:** Go up the right-slanting cracks. **Pro:** Thin to 2.5 inches. **FA:** Ken Black, Mike Law; 1983.

920. **Just Another Crack from L. A.** (5.9) ★ Start at a dead tree (just right of *Happy Landings, Linda*). Head up and right into an obvious crack. **Pro:** To 2.5 inches. **FA:** Dave Evans, Jim Angione; 1/79.

Lost Horse Wall—Middle Section

This large, broken wall has two recorded multipitch routes. Other routes may have been done here and are possible. On occasion, the middle section may be closed due to the presence of nesting raptors. Please respect all closures. Descend off the very right end of the Lost Horse Wall.

921. Gossamer Wings (5.10a) Start at the high point of the slope/boulders about 150 feet left and up from *The Swift*. **Pitch 1:** Go up the left-facing corner, then up right to a belay alcove. **Pitch 2:** Climb the left side of the plated face to a big ledge. **Pitch 3:** Go up slabs to the final right-facing corner (5.10a). **Pro:** To 3 inches. **FA:** Alan Bartlett, Alan Roberts; 4/88.

922. Wilson Regular Route (5.5) Climbers regularly get off-route on this long, easy, and fairly worthless climb. Care should be taken due to loose rock on the upper part of this climb. Begin about 25 feet down and right of the high point of the slope/boulders (where *Gossamer Wings* begins). **Pitch 1:** Go up the easy and fairly obvious left-slanting cracks/ramp, then up to a big ledge. *Do not continue up the ramp.* **Pitch 2:** Move left, then up plates on the right side of the steep dark face; belay on the large right-leaning ramp/ledge (short pitch). **Pitch 3:** Go up and right via ramps and ledges. **Pro:** To 3 inches. **FA:** Don Wilson et al.; 1979.

923. Wilson Irregular Route (Variation) (5.9) (not shown on photo) **Pitch 1:** Same as *Wilson Regular Route*. **Pitch 2:** Head up and right on right-slanting cracks to finish just left of *Altitude Sickness*. **Pro:** To 3 inches. **FA:** Unknown.

Lost Horse Wall—Right End

The right-hand section of Lost Horse Wall is a sunny, west-facing crag with some of the longer routes in the park. A large ledge system cuts across most of the lower face (the "Ledge"); many of the routes begin off of, and are accessed by, the Ledge. Easiest access to the Ledge is via a left-slanting crack below its left end. Descend by walking off the right end of the wall. Map, page 253. Topo, page 258.

924. **Altitude Sickness** (5.8+) Begin near the left side of the main face, just left of a pillar-shaped boulder and right of bushes. **Pitch 1:** Head up a left-slanting crack to the left end of the Ledge (5.5); traverse right to a protruding block and crack on the block's right side. **Pitch 2:** Go up the right side of the block, then continue up and left on a slanting crack (5.5), then up a crack to a belay at bushes. **Pitch 3:** Head straight up a left-facing corner, pass a small roof (5.8/5.9), and continue up easier ground to the top. **Pitch 3 variation:** Go slightly right, and then up and right in right-slanting cracks (5.10a). **Pro:** To 3 inches. **FA:** Tom Bombaci, Chet Wade; 11/87.

925. **The Swift** (5.7) ★★ This is a popular longer moderate climb. **Note:** It is not uncommon for parties to get off-route where the climb exits the corner system near the beginning of Pitch 3. Begin near the left side of the main face, just left of a pillar-shaped boulder and right of bushes. **Pitch 1:** Head up a left-slanting crack to the left end of the Ledge (5.5); traverse right to a protruding block and crack on the block's right side. **Pitch 2:** Go up the right side of the slot and crack above; then up and right on the face (5.6) to a left-facing corner that you climb to a belay stance. **Pitch 3:** Continue up the cor-

ner until you are about 15 feet below a small overhang at the top of the corner, then traverse right on face (5.7). Go up to cracks that join with the finish of *Dappled Mare.* **Pitch 3 variation:** Continue straight up over the small roof (5.9) and up cracks above (5.10a). **Pro:** To 3 inches. **FA:** Bob Dominick, John Wolfe; 4/76. **FA** (Var.): Unknown.

926. **Bird on a Wire** (5.10a) ★★★ **Pitch 1:** Do the first pitch of *Dappled Mare,* but move a bit left on the Ledge. Alternatively, start below and right of the route, just left of a large boulder, and climb a left-arching flake to the Ledge (5.10a R). **Pitch 2:** Follow thin cracks up and slightly left, past a bolt, then continue up the thin crack as it curves to the right. Belay in this area; do not belay higher, where you cross *Dappled Mare,* to avoid conflict with climbers on that route. **Pitch 3:** Continue up the crack as it curves right and crosses *Dappled Mare,* then go up. **Pro:** Thin to 2.5 inches. **FA:** Dave Evans, Kevin Powell, Dan Ahlborn; 1977.

927. **Hairline Fracture** (5.10a) (R) ★ **Pitch 1:** Do either the first pitch of *Bird on a Wire* or *Dappled Mare;* belaying on the Ledge about 20 feet right of *Bird On A Wire.* **Pitch 2:** Go up blocks, then up the face past a horizontal to a short crack. Move left to a very thin crack (the hairline fracture) that leads to the traversing pitch of *Dappled Mare.* **Pitch 3:** Finish up *Dappled Mare.* **Pro:** Thin to 2.5 inches. **FA:** Charles Cole, Gib Lewis, Darryl Nakahira, Jessica; 1980.

928. **City Slickers** (5.11b) ★★ This is a five-bolt face between *Hairline Fracture* and *Dappled Mare.* Either continue up *Dappled Mare* or *Roan Way,* or make a 150-foot rappel to descend. Two-bolt anchor. **Pro:** To 3 inches. **FA:** Bob Gaines, Billy Merritt; 5/01.

929. **Dappled Mare** (5.8) ★★★ Begin below the Ledge. **Pitch 1:** Go up left-slanting cracks to the Ledge, and move right to the base of the main crack (5.7). **Pitch 2:** Go straight up cracks (5.8) to a bolt belay just above a slanting crack system. **Pitch 3:** Traverse left and down the slanting crack, then up and left along a crack/corner (5.8); where this ends, head up and a bit right on a crack and face to the top. **Pro:** To 2.5 inches. **FA:** John Long, Richard Harrison, Rick Accomazzo; 1/73.

930. **Roan Way** (5.8+) ★★ This is a spicier and bit more difficult finish to *Dappled Mare*. Climb Pitch 2 of *Dappled Mare* to the bolt belay. Head straight up the crack above to the summit (5.8+). **Pro:** To 2.5 inches. **FA:** Chris Gonzalez, John Wolfe; 5/75.

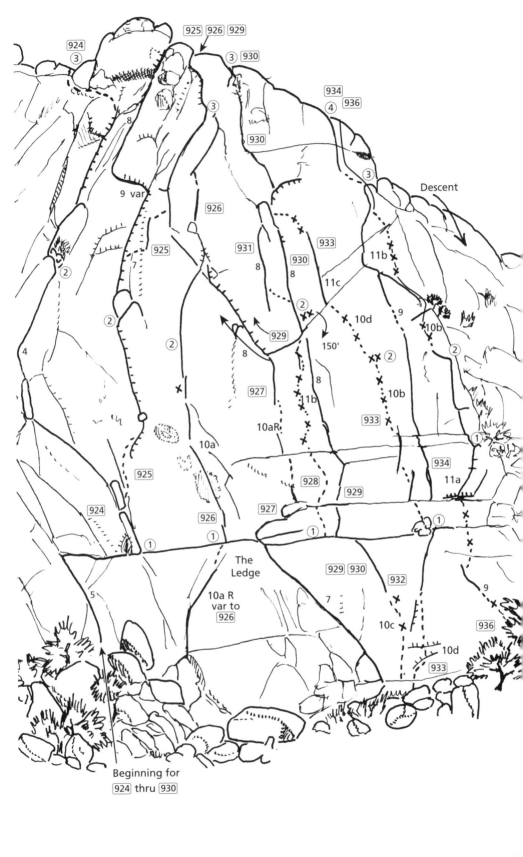

931. Billy the Kid (Variation) (5.8) From the bolt belay on *Dappled Mare,* head up *Roan Way* for 15 feet, then move left to a thin flake system. Eventually rejoin *Roan Way.* **Pro:** To 3 inches. **FA:** Bob Gaines, Erik Kramer-Webb; 2/02.

932. Edgar Rice Burros (5.10c) Begin about 15 to 20 feet right of the beginning of the first pitch of *Dappled Mare.* **Pitch 1:** Go up the face past two bolts to a left-leaning seam to the Ledge (5.10b/c). **Pitch 2:** Go up Pitch 2 of *Dappled Mare* (5.8). **Pitch 3:** Head right and up along a crack/break to the far right side of the summit (5.10b). **Pro:** Thin to 2 inches. **FA:** Todd Swain, Dick Peterson; 11/91.

933. Headbangers' Ball (5.11c) ★ Begin just right of *Edgar Rice Burros.* **Pitch 1:** Undercling an arch to the right, then go over it (5.10d) to reach a thin crack leading to the far right end of the Ledge. **Pitch 2:** Move left, then up thin cracks, to face past three bolts to a two-bolt belay (5.10b/c). **Pitch 3:** Go left and up past two bolts to a diagonal crack (*Edgar Rice Burros*); continue up past a fixed pin (5.11c) to a face with two more bolts. Move left to finish the last bit of *Roan Way.* **Pro:** Thin to 2 inches. **FA:** Roy McClenahan, Alan Bartlett; 4/88.

934. Mare's Tail (5.9) ★ Begin on the far right end of the Ledge (up the first pitch of *Dappled Mare*) and traverse right. **Pitch 2:** Go straight up the crack, past several undercuts, for about 80 feet to a horizontal break on the right (5.7/5.8). **Pitch 3:** Move up to a seam (5.9), then continue up the crack system past the next horizontal, where the crack widens. Then, to the top. **Pro:** To 3 inches. **FA:** Paul Neal, Charlie Saylan; 12/76.

935. Lost in Space (Variation to *Mare's Tail*) (5.8) ★ From belay at the end of Pitch 2 of *Mare's Tail,* head right on a crack system for about 20 feet, then up to the top. **Pro:** To 3 inches. **FA:** Dave Evans, Jim Angione; 3/77.

936. Lost and Found (5.11b) ★★ This route lies on the far right side of Lost Horse Wall. Begin about 50 feet right of *Headbangers' Ball* at a fixed RURP. **Pitch 1:** Go up and left past a bolt (5.9) to a crack, then up an easy slab above past two more bolts to an awkward roof crack (5.11a/b); belay on ledge. **Pitch 2:** Go straight in a finger crack (5.7) to a small ledge. **Pitch 3:** Head off the left side of the ledge, slab past two bolts (5.10b), traverse right, then back left on ledges, finishing on thin slab moves (5.11b) past three bolts to roof. Belay about 20 feet higher. **Pitch 4:** Class 4 to the top. **Pro:** To 3 inches; extra 0.4 to 1 inch. **FA:** Bob Gaines, Erik Kramer-Webb; 5/03.

Wild Gravity Formation

This formation lies opposite the south end of the Lost Horse Wall and faces east (shady in the afternoon). The cliff is characterized by numerous vertical crack systems and many large roofs. Several routes have been done on this wall. Park at the Lost Horse Wall parking area, 0.5 mile down Lost Horse Road from Park Boulevard. Lost Horse Road intersects Park Boulevard 7.3 miles from the West Entrance and 1.3+ miles from the Intersection Rock/Real Hidden Valley intersection. Routes 937 to 942 are not pictured. Map, page 253.

937. Top Flight (5.10a) Located near the left (southern) end of the cliff, this route takes the second crack to the left of *Wild Gravity.* A Top-Flight golf ball may be lodged at the base. **FA:** John Sherman, Todd Skinner, Kelly Rich; 1983.

938. **Wild Gravity** (5.9) This is the crack directly under the left side of the largest, highest roof on the wall. Go up an incipient crack to a right-facing corner, then over the left side of the roof. **Pro:** Thin to 3 inches. **FA:** Kelly Rich, John Sherman, Todd Skinner; 1983.

939. **Psycho II** (5.9) Found near the middle of the cliff, this is 250 feet right of *Wild Gravity*. Climb a loose crack into a left-facing corner. **Pro:** To 2 inches. **FA:** Ken Black; 1983.

940. **Psycho No More** (5.8) The rack immediately right of *Psycho II* becomes wide. Rap/belay from a tree. **Pro:** To 4 inches. **FA:** Ken Black; 1983.

941. **Chocolate Mob Nobs** (5.10a/b) Left of *Moon Your Neighbor,* this is the crack in the arête with an undercut start. Finish up a knife-edge, stem right into a chimney. **Pro:** To 1.5 inches. **FA:** M. Hind, George Armstrong; 11/98.

942. **Moon Your Neighbor** (5.10a) Located 50 feet right of *Psycho No More,* this crack gets wider and wider; starts with a roof. **Pro:** To 4 inches. **FA:** Todd Gordon, Steve Parker, Alan Bartlett; 8/91.

Imaginary Voyage Formation

This formation consists of a 50-foot summit block lying atop the northern end of the Wild Gravity face. A large cave/crack is on its west side. Approach the routes along the large ledge from the left.

Park at either the Lost Horse Wall or Super Creeps parking areas, 0.5 or 0.6 mile down Lost Horse Road from Park Boulevard, respectively. Lost Horse Road

intersects Park Boulevard 7.3 miles from the West Entrance and 1.3+ miles from the Intersection Rock/Real Hidden Valley intersection. Map, page 253.

943. **Dead Man's Party** (5.10b) (R) Begin on the left side of the north face of the block; left of the wide crack of *Journey Into Intoxica.* Go up the face past three bolts. **Pro:** Thin to 2 inches. **FA:** Don Wilson, Jack Marshall; 4/89.

944. **Journey into Intoxica** (5.8+) Climb the very wide crack in the right-facing corner that splits the north face. **Pro:** Big stuff! **FA:** George Armstrong, M. Hind; 11/98.

945. **Black Plastic Streetwalker** (5.10c) (R/X) ★★★ Begin just right of *Journey Into Intoxica.* Go up and a bit left on the face. **Pro:** Many thin to 1 inch. **FA:** Mike Lechlinski et al.

946. **Lessons from Laeger** (5.10b/c) ★★★ The arête right of *Black Plastic Streetwalker* with four bolts. **Pro:** To 2.5 inches. **FA:** Unknown.

947. **Imaginary Voyage** (5.10d) ★★★★ This unique route is located on the west side of the block and climbs out of a large cave-like feature; traverse into the cave from the left (the base of the previous routes). Lieback up a crack in the back of the cave to a roof, then hand-traverse right, then up and left to a bolt over the roof. Finish up the wide crack above. **Pro:** 1 to 5 inches. **FA:** John Long, Richard Harrison; 11/77.

948. **Layback and Groove on a Rainy Day** (A2) (not shown on photo) This is the 10-foot roof crack that lies on the north side of the formation right of *Imaginary Voyage.* **FA:** M. Hind, George Armstrong; 11/98.

Lost Horse Wall

945
946
943 944
947
950
949

949. **Gravel Shower** (5.10b) (TR) Begin below the cave of *Imaginary Voyage;* go up the recess and face up to the start of *Imaginary Voyage.* **FA** (TR): Hans Florine, Mike Lopez, Phil Requist; 3/88.

950. **The Gap** (5.0) (R) ★ The clean chimney splits the formation right of *Imaginary Voyage.* **FA:** Bob Gaines; 5/93.

Super Creeps Wall

This small formation (about 45 feet tall) lies just north of the Lost Horse Road, approximately 0.6 mile from its junction with Park Boulevard. The Super Creeps Wall faces east (shade in the afternoon) and is plainly seen from the parking area at the end of Lost Horse Road. Routes are 35 to 50 feet long.

Lost Horse Road intersects Park Boulevard 7.3 miles from the West Entrance and 1.3+ miles from the Intersection Rock/Real Hidden Valley intersection. The parking area is located on the right (north) side of Lost Horse Road. Lost Horse Road is closed to the public vehicular traffic from this point to Lost Horse Ranger Station. Map, page 253.

951. **Tales of Powder** (5.10b) ★ A short, clean handcrack. **Pro:** To 2 inches. **FA:** Randy Leavitt, Tony Yaniro; 1980.

952. **Scary Monsters** (5.12a) ★★★ A difficult, clean stemming corner. **Pro:** Many thin to 1.5 inches. **FA:** Tony Yaniro, Randy Leavitt; 1980.

953. **Young Frankenstein** (5.11a) ★★★ Climb a flake to a nice thin crack. **Pro:** Thin to 1.5 inch. **FA:** Randy Leavitt, Tony Yaniro; 1980.

954. **Waltzing Worm** (5.12a) ★★★ This is a thin finger crack; the crux is getting over a bulge near the bottom. **Pro:** Several 0.5 to 1.5 inch. **FA:** Tony Yaniro, Randy Leavitt; 1980.

Super Creeps Wall

951

952 953 954

Super Heros Wall

This formation lies about 150 yards west of Super Creeps Wall and faces northwest (sun in the afternoon). It is the westernmost of several small formations that include Super Creeps Wall. Park as for Super Creeps Wall, on the right 0.6 mile down Lost Horse Road (see Super Creeps Wall approach on page 261). Walk west on Lost Horse Road until you can turn right to the west face. The center of the northwest face has two cracks next to each other in the desert-varnished rock/buttress. The right-hand crack in the center is *Mr. Magoo*. Map, page 253.

955. **Elmer Fudd** (5.11b) ★★ (TR) This is the left-hand crack/shallow dihedral system that

ends with face climbing. It is near the center of the face, just left of *Mr. Magoo*. **FA:** Todd Swain; 11/88.

956. **Captain Kangaroo** (5.9) ★ (TR) Begin up *Elmer Fudd*. After about 15 feet, move right to, then up, a right-slanting crack. **FA:** Bob Gaines; 5/02.

957. **Mr. Magoo** (5.10a) (R) ★ The right-hand S-crack near the center of the face. **Pro:** To 2 inches. **FA:** Todd Swain; 11/88.

958. **Yosemite Sam** (5.4) ★ Climb the cracks/flakes 15 feet right of *Mr. Magoo;* join that route near the top. **FA:** Todd Swain; 11/88.

Super Heros
Wall

Kaleidoscope Cliff

This formation lies on the hillside about 0.6 mile northwest of Super Creeps Wall and south of the White Cliffs of Dover. Though it could be reached from the vicinity of Trashcan Rock, it is more easily reached from the Super Creeps parking area. Park as for Super Creeps Wall (on the right 0.6 mile down the Lost Horse Road; see Super Creeps Wall approach on page 261). Hike along a trail around the right side of the Super Creeps Wall, then head west (cross-country) to an old dirt road. Head northwest on this old road about 0.4 mile. Head left (west) to the base of the hillside, and up the hillside about 100 yards to the crag. Descent is via an 80-foot rappel off the top of *The Reach Around*. The cliff faces east and gets sun in the morning, shade in the afternoon. Map, page 215.

959. **Skeleton in My Closet** (5.8) ★ The left-most route, beginning at a flake. Head up and left past two bolts. **Pro:** To 2.5 inches. **FA:** Bob Gaines, Yvonne Gaines; 5/97.

960. **Mrs. Magoo** (5.10a) ★ Start as for the previous route, but head up discontinuous thin cracks. **Pro:** Thin to 2.5 inches. **FA:** Bob Gaines, Yvonne Gaines; 5/97.

961. **The Reach Around** (5.10c) ★ This starts off the block 15 feet right of *Mrs. Magoo*. A bolt protects moves into the crack. **Pro:** To 3 inches. **FA:** Bob Gaines; 5/97.

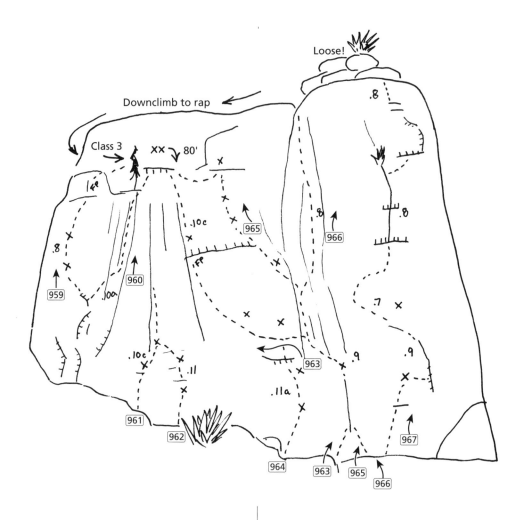

962. **Acrobat's Overhang** (5.11a/b) ★★ Start right of *The Reach Around;* three bolts protect climbing up and left to the crack on that route. **Pro:** To 3 inches. **FA:** Bob Gaines; 5/97.

963. **Technicolor Yawn** (5.10c) ★★★ Start up thin crack about 60 feet right of *The Reach Around,* then head up and left past bolts. **Pro:** To 2 inches; four bolts. **FA:** Bob Gaines, Yvonne Gaines; 5/97.

964. **Lemon Lime** (Variation) (5.11a) ★ This is a two-bolt direct start to *Technicolor Yawn.* **FA:** Bob Gaines; 5/97.

965. **Magnetic North** (5.10a) ★★ Start as for *Technicolor Yawn,* but continue up and then slightly left past bolts. **Pro:** To 2 inches; five bolts. **FA:** Bob Gaines, Yvonne Gaines; 5/97.

966. **Treasure Island** (5.9) ★ Climb *Magnetic North* until you can head more or less straight up cracks. **Pro:** To 3 inches; one bolt. **FA:** Bob Gaines, Yvonne Gaines; 5/97.

967. **Dead Reckoning** (5.9) ★★★ Face climb to cracks systems just right of the start of the previous routes. **Pro:** To 3.5 inches; two bolts. **FA:** Bob Gaines, Yvonne Gaines; 5/97.

ATLANTIS— JIMMY CLIFF AREA

The following formations and crags all lie south of the parking area at the end of Lost Horse Road (0.6 mile from Park Boulevard) and are best approached from that parking area. The Park Boulevard/Lost Horse Road junction lies 7.3+ miles from the West Entrance and 1.3 miles from the Intersection Rock/Real Hidden Valley intersection. Beyond the parking area Lost Horse Road, which leads to Lost Horse Ranger Station (and to Jimmy Cliff, Arid Piles, and Mount Grossvogel), is closed to public vehicle traffic. From the parking area, walk south, along a well-defined trail, skirting along the base of the rocks below Imaginary Voyage. Arid Piles may be also approached from the Real Hidden Valley parking area by walking west past Houser Buttress, then northwest. Popular areas here include Atlantis, Uncle Remus, the Aiguille de Joshua Tree, Cockroach Crags, Jimmy Cliff, and Arid Piles. Maps, pages 215, 233, 253, and 266.

Atlantis Area

This area is located in a hidden canyon southwest of and below Imaginary Voyage. It is best approached by parking about 0.6 mile down Lost Horse Road from its junction with Park Boulevard (see approach directions above). Cross the road and head south along a well-defined trail, skirting along the base of the rocks below *Imaginary Voyage*. Map, page 266.

Atlantis Approach Routes

The following lie on the rocks left of the Atlantis approach trail. They are not shown.

The Slabs

968. **Sparky** (5.10a) Climb a crack to three bolts on a small slab on the north face of the first rocks you come to on the left during the Atlantis approach. **FA:** Todd Gordon, Brian Stokes; 4/93.

Buddy Rocks

This small rock lies immediately on your right at the left (east) turn off the main trail to get to Atlantis. It is about 400 yards directly south of the parking area. The following route lies on the northwest and west faces (morning shade, afternoon sun).

969. **Buddy Rocks** (5.8) Begin in the right-hand crack; go up this to a horizontal. Traverse right until you can head up the face of the upper block past one bolt. **Pro:** To 2 inches. **FA:** Darryl Krieghoff, David Pylman, Phil Spinelli.

Atlantis and Tire Tread Walls

These formations are quite popular due to the presence of many easy to moderate short climbs, most of which can be toproped. From the parking area 0.6 mile down Lost Horse Road, cross the road and walk south along a well-defined trail. Skirt along the base of the rocks below Imaginary Voyage for about 400 yards until you can turn left (east). Proceed

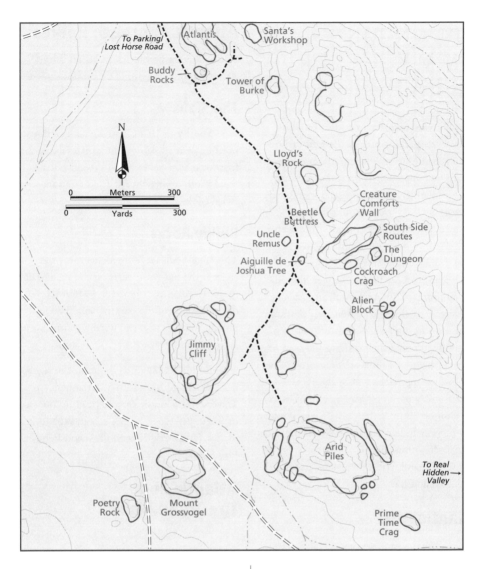

east for about 50 yards, then make another left (north) turn to reach the base of the left end of the east-facing Atlantis Wall. Routes are short (35 to 50 feet). The face sees shade in the afternoon. Also, several crack routes have been done on the east facing wall behind the main Atlantis Wall (behind *Wet Pigeon*); none are recorded here. Map, page 253 and above.

Atlantis Wall—Left

This is the main east-facing cliff on the west side of the canyon, with many vertical crack systems (morning sun and shade in the afternoon. Photo on page 268; topo on page 269.

970. **Neptune** (5.8) Climb the left-leaning crack on a pillar on the far left side of the wall (35 feet left of *Vorpal Sword*). **Pro:** To 2 inches. **FA:** Todd Swain, Andy Schenkel; 3/89.

971. **Trident** (5.10c) ★ Begin in the left-slanting crack about 30 feet right of *Neptune;* above, head right past one bolt . **Pro:** To 2 inches. **FA:** Andy Schenkel, Todd Swain; 3/89.

972. **Vorpal Sword** (5.9+) ★ Begin about 5 feet right of *Trident.* Go up the left-leaning thin crack. **Pro:** Thin to 2 inches. **FA:** Todd Gordon, Brian Sillasen, Tom Atherton; 3/88.

973. **Galumphing** (5.10a) ★ (TR) Toprope the face between *Vorpal Sword* and *Grain Surplus.* **FA:** Bob Gaines; 5/03.

974. **Grain Surplus** (5.8) Go up cracks located about 10 feet right of *Vorpal Sword.* **Pro:** To 2 inches. **FA:** Alan Bartlett, Todd Gordon, Brian Sillasen; 3/88.

975. **Grain for Russia** (5.7) This is the crack in the corridor about 10 feet up and right of *Grain Surplus.* **Pro:** To 2 inches. **FA:** Todd Swain; 3/89.

Minotaur Wall

This small face lies just in front of the left side of the main Atlantis Wall. It gets morning sun and is shady all afternoon.

976. **Mystic Knights of the Sea** (5.9) Go up the face to double thin cracks on left side of wall. **Pro:** Thin to 2 inches. **FA:** Dave Haber; 5/91.

977. **Devine Wind** (5.10a) (TR) Toprope the face between *Mystic Knights of the Sea* and *Minotaur.* **FA:** Larry LeVoir, Phil, Mogge; 4/98.

978. **Minotaur** (5.7) ★ The obvious crack to the right of *Mystic Knight of the Sea* that turns wide at the top. **Pro:** To 3 inches. **FA:** Todd Gordon, Alan Bartlett; 3/88.

979. **Fantasy of Light** (5.10a) ★ Begin just right of *Minotaur;* go up the face (5.10a) to reach a crack. **Pro:** To 2 inches. **FA:** Brian Sillasen, Todd Gordon, Alan Bartlett; 3/88.

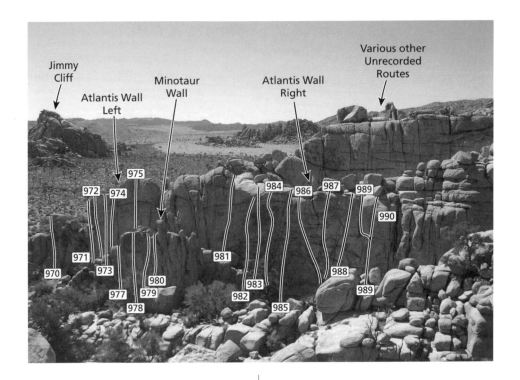

980. **Nittany Lion** (5.10b) Begin just right of *Fantasy of Light;* go up to and then over a small V-shaped roof. Above, stay right of the last climb. **Pro:** To 2 inches. **FA:** Unknown.

Atlantis Wall—Right

These routes are located on the section of the Atlantis Wall that lies right of the Minotaur Wall, though the first few routes begin out of a small corridor between Minotaur Wall's right end and the Atlantis Wall. The routes get morning sun and afternoon shade.

981. **Self Abuse** (5.6) Begin on the far left side of the wall, just left of a large chockstone bridging the corridor between Minotaur Wall and Atlantis Wall. Go up the obvious crack. **FA:** Alan Bartlett, Todd Gordon; 3/88.

982. **Hot Crystals** (5.9) ★ Begin on the far left side of the wall, just right of the large chockstone bridging the corridor between Minotaur Wall and Atlantis Wall. Go up the double cracks, then right to another crack above a final horizontal. **FA:** Brian Sillasen, Todd Gordon, Tom Atherton; 3/88.

983. **Pocket Pussy** (5.11b) (R) ★ This starts off a big block 10 feet right of *Hot Crystals.* Go up the face and thin cracks. **FA:** Brian Sillasen, Todd Gordon, Tom Atherton; 3/88. **FA** (Lead): Unknown.

984. **Anointed Seagull** (5.8) ★ Begin about 8 feet right of *Hot Crystals,* off a big block. Go up the crack that arches left near the top. **Pro:** To 2.5 inches. **FA:** Todd Gordon, Tom Atherton; 3/88.

985. **Ceremony** (5.10c) ★ Begin about 10 feet right and down from *Anointed Seagull.* Go up the face past one bolt to a thin crack.

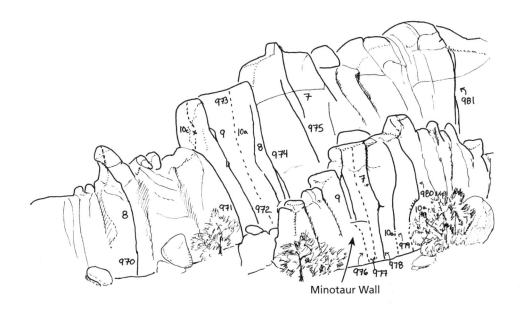

Minotaur Wall

Pro: Thin to 2 inches. **FA:** Dave Evans, Craig Fry, Jim Angione, Brian Sillasen, Todd Gordon, Alan Bartlett, Cyndie Bransford; 3/88.

986. **Solar Technology** (5.6) Start as for *Men With Cow's Heads,* but after a few feet take the crack that slants up and left. **Pro:** To 2.5 inches. **FA:** Craig Fry, Dave Evans, Jim Angione, Brian Sillasen, Todd Gordon, Alan Bartlett, Cyndie Bransford; 3/88.

987. **Men with Cow's Heads** (5.5) Start as for *Solar Technology,* but go straight up. **Pro:** To 2.5 inches. **FA:** Brian Sillasen, Todd Gordon, Tom Atherton; 3/88.

988. **Wet Pigeon** (5.8) ★ Begin about 6 feet right of the last two routes. Go up a crack, past a small ledge, then straight to the top. **Pro:** To 2 inches. **FA:** Brian Sillasen, Todd Gordon, Jim Angione, Dave Evans, Alan Bartlett; 3/88.

989. **Unwiped Butt** (5.4) This begins in the last crack on the right side of the wall before the chimney. Go up the crack, then at the horizontal move left, then go up another crack to the top. **Pro:** To 2.5 inches. **FA:** Todd Gordon, Brian Sillasen, Alan Bartlett, Craig Fry, Cyndie Bransford; 3/88.

990. **Taurus** (5.7) Start as for *Unwiped Butt,* but go straight up. **Pro:** To 2.5 inches. **FA:** Todd Swain; 10/89.

Tire Tread Wall

This steep wall, with a weird black tread-like stain on it, is located up and right from the main Atlantis Wall. It gets morning sun and shade in the afternoon. Large pine trees are located at the base of the wall. Map, page 253.

991. **Mental Retread** (5.9) (R) Begin on the left side of the face, just right of the left-hand pine tree. Go up and left past horizontals, then move right and up into left-facing corner systems. **Pro:** To 2 inches. **FA:** Todd Swain; 10/89.

992. **Don't Tread On Me** (5.10b) (TR) Begin just right of *Mental Retread*. Go straight up the face and horizontals to meet *Mental Retread* in the final corner. **FA:** Todd Swain; 10/89.

993. **Treadmark Left** (5.10a) Begin at the right-hand pine tree. Go up the face to the ledge, move left, then up cracks. **Pro:** To 2.5 inches. **FA:** Alan Bartlett, Todd Gordon; 3/88.

994. **Treadmark Right** (5.9) Begin as for *Treadmark Left*. At the ledge go up cracks on the right; move right at the top. **Pro:** To 2.5 inches. **FA:** Todd Gordon, Alan Bartlett; 3/88.

995. **Flat Tire** (5.8) Begin about 15 feet right of the right pine tree. Go up thin cracks and horizontals; finish left at the top of *Treadmark Right*. **Pro:** Thin to 2 inches. **FA:** Alan Bartlett, Todd Gordon; 3/88.

Santa's Workshop

This formation lies on the right corner of the hill just east of (facing) Atlantis. The routes lie on the west face (sun all after-noon). Park about 0.6 mile down Lost Horse Road from its junction with Park Boulevard (this junction is 7.3 miles from the West Entrance and 1.3 miles from the Intersection Rock/Real Hidden Valley intersection). Walk south, along a well-defined trail, skirting the base of the rocks below Imaginary Voyage for about 400 yards, until you can turn left (east). You will see the Santa area directly to your east, high on the hillside. Map, page 253.

996. **Santa's Magic Lap** (5.10a) ★ Climb the handcrack just around the left side of forma-tion, then go right across the slab to join the upper wide section of *Hot Buttered Elves*. **Pro:** To 4 inches. **FA:** Chris Miller, Todd Gordon; 12/94.

997. **Hot Buttered Elves** (5.10c/d) This is on the left side of west face. Go up a seam past a fixed pin, one bolt, and another fixed pin to a wide, shallow crack. **Pro:** Thin to wide. **FA:** Todd Gordon, Chris Miller; 12/94.

998. **Grab My Sac for a Toy** (5.8) Climb the crack over a small roof between *Hot Buttered Elves* and *The Backdoor Santa*. **Pro:** To 3

inches. **FA:** Tucker Tech, Tom Burke, Todd Gordon, Andrea Tomaszewski.

999. The Backdoor Santa (5.7) Climb a low-angled crack to a face with three bolts on the right side of the west face. **Pro:** To 2 inches. **FA:** Todd Gordon, Jason Cushner, Chris Miller; 12/94.

Tower of Burke

This pinnacle of rock lies south of the Atlantis Area. Park 0.6 mile down Lost Horse Road from its junction with Park Boulevard. Walk south along a well-defined trail, skirting below *Imaginary Voyage* for about 400 yards (where you can turn left/east to get to Atlantis). From here, the Tower of Burke is about 175 yards to the southeast. The tower and route are not pictured. Maps, pages 253 and 266.

1000. Burkulator (5.10a) ★ Go up the crack on the west face of this pointed tower, past a fixed pin, then up and left on the face past two bolts. **Pro:** Thin to 2 inches; two-bolt anchor/rap. **FA:** Todd Gordon, Tucker Tech, Tom Burke; 12/99.

Lloyd's Rock

Lloyd's Rock is located about 250 yards southeast of the Atlantis area, just northeast of Uncle Remus. It is part of the toe of the hillside and faces west (afternoon sun). It is best approached by parking 0.6 mile down Lost Horse Road from its junction with Park Boulevard (same as for Atlantis); this junction is 7.3 miles from the West Entrance and 1.3 miles from the Intersection Rock/Real Hidden Valley intersection. Walk south along a well-defined trail, skirting the base of the rocks below *Imaginary Voyage* (400 yards).

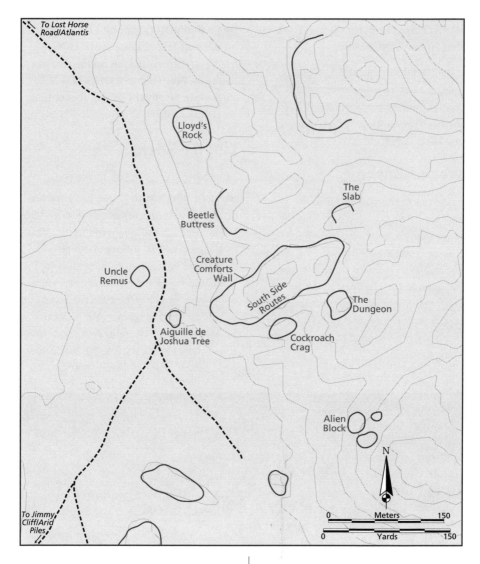

Continue south on the trail past the turn for Atlantis and across more open flats for another 250 yards (650 yards total). Head a bit left (east) to the base of the rock. The descent is a walk-off to the right. Maps, pages 266 and above.

1001. Flawless Fissure (5.9) ★ Begin on the left in a wide lieback, then stay right up a thin crack that heads left around a roof. **Pro:** Thin to 3 inches. **FA:** Don Wilson, Karen Wilson; 4/86.

1002. Lizard of Ahhs (10c/d) ★★ Start on *Flawless Fissure,* but move right on the ramp, then up the clean arête past four bolts. **Pro:** To 2 inches. **FA:** Don Wilson and others.

1003. Friend Eater (5.9) ★ Start on *Flawless Fissure,* but move right on the ramp near the bottom, then up and right on a right-slanting crack system. **Pro:** To 2.5 inches. **FA:** Don Wilson, Karen Wilson; 4/86.

1004. **RR Does It Again** (5.10d) (TR) ★
Begin directly below the upper crack of
Friend Eater. Go up a thin right-leaning seam
and face to join *Friend Eater.* **FA:** Alan
Roberts, Don Reid; 1/88.

1005. **Micronesia** (5.10d) ★ Begin in a right
slanting thin crack about 6 feet right of *RR
Does It Again.* Go up and right in the crack,
then up and finally back left in cracks to join
Friend Eater near the top. **Pro:** Thin to 2
inches. **FA:** Don Reid, Alan Roberts; 1/88.

1006. **Borneo** (5.4) This is the short crack in
the gully about 25 feet up and right of
Micronesia. **Pro:** To 3 inches. **FA:** Todd Swain;
1/89.

Uncle Remus

This small boulder/pillar lies about 75 yards
southwest of Lloyd's Rock and 100 yards
north of a finger of rock known as the
Aiguille de Joshua Tree. Park about 0.6 mile
down Lost Horse Road from its junction
with Park Boulevard (same as for Atlantis);
this junction is 7.3 miles from the West
Entrance and 1.3 miles from the Intersection
Rock/Real Hidden Valley intersection. Walk
south along a well-defined trail, skirting the
base of the rocks below Imaginary Voyage
and across more open flats for 725 yards. A
two-bolt anchor/rap is located on top. Maps,
pages 266 and 272.

Uncle Remus

Aiguille de Joshua Tree

1007
1008
1009
1010

1007. **Uncle Remus** (5.11b) ★★★ A three-bolt route on the south face and arête. A sling is useful between the second and third bolt. Two-bolt anchor/rap. **FA** (TR): John Bachar. **FA** (Lead): Kurt Smith.

1008. **Up the Ante** (5.11d) ★★ (TR) Begin immediately right of *Uncle Remus.* Go up the short crack to face climbing. **FA:** Jonny Woodward, Kevin Powell, Darrel Hensel; 2/89.

1009. **Man from Uncle** (5.10b) ★ A two-bolt face route on the east side of the block. **Pro:** Bring tie-offs for knobs; two-bolt anchor/rap. **FA:** Bob Gaines, Yvonne Gaines; 12/94.

Aiguille de Joshua Tree

This 30-foot, ultrathin finger of rock is a must-do, if for the photo opportunities alone. It is located among boulders about 100 yards south of Uncle Remus (see approach directions for Uncle Remus) and 350 yards northeast of Jimmy Cliff. Maps, pages 266 and 272.

1010. **Aiguille de Joshua Tree** (5.6) (X) ★★★ Standing up can be quite exhilarating, reversing down even more so. No pro. **FA:** Unknown (perhaps Richard Harrison); mid 1970s.

Beetle Buttress

This west-facing rock (afternoon sun) lies about 100 yards south of Lloyd's Rock and directly east of a point about halfway between Uncle Remus and Aiguille de Joshua Tree. It's also about 100 feet above the valley floor and a rocky slope. The rock is good, but the routes are rather short. Park about 0.6 mile down Lost Horse Road from its junction with Park Boulevard (same as for Atlantis et al.); this junction is 7.3 miles from the West Entrance and 1.3 miles from the Intersection Rock/Real Hidden Valley intersection. Walk south along a well-defined trail skirting the base of the rocks and hillside, then across open flats, for about 750 yards. The buttress is to your left (and up). Maps, pages 266 and 272.

1011. **Beat 'Til Soft** (5.9) (TR) Climb the crack and corner on the far left side of the formation. **FA:** Unknown.

1012. **Let It Be** (5.10c) ★★★ Climb the prominent roof crack on the left side of the formation, then diagonal up and right on

the face past horizontals. **Pro:** To 4 inches. **FA:** Bob Gaines; 12/94.

1013. **Direct Start** (Variation) (5.10d) ★ (TR) (not shown on photo) This is the face to the right of the roof crack start.

1014. **The Beatles** (5.4) The leftmost right-facing chimney. **FA:** Todd Swain; 1/89.

1015. **Beatle Bailey** (5.4) The blocky ramp/corner just right of *The Beatles*. **FA:** Todd Swain; 1/89.

1016. **Left Beetle Crack** (5.10b) This short, overhanging handcrack is on the left side of the corner with *Beetle Corner*. **FA:** Todd Swain; 1/89.

1017. **Beetle Corner** (5.11a) This is the obvious short corner near the right edge of the cliff. **FA:** Todd Swain; 1/89.

1018. **Right Beetle Crack** (5.10b) This finger crack is just right of *Beetle Corner*. **FA:** Todd Swain; 1/89.

COCKROACH CRAG AREA

This area consists of a buttress of rock almost directly above and east of the Aiguille de Joshua Tree and a small rock below and right of the south side of the buttress (this small brown rock is Cockroach Crag proper). Routes are on both the north side (Creature Comforts Wall) and south side (Classic Corner Wall) of the buttress.

To reach Cockroach Crags, park 0.6 mile down Lost Horse Road from its junction with Park Boulevard (same as for Atlantis, Uncle Remus/Aiguille de Joshua Tree et al.). The Lost Horse Road/Park Boulevard junction is 7.3 miles from the West Entrance and 1.3 miles from the Intersection Rock/Real Hidden Valley intersection. From the parking area, walk south along a well-defined trail, skirting the base of the rocks then across open flats, for about 825 yards. Alternatively, it is possible to reach Cockroach Crag and the Creature Comforts Wall from the vicinity of Czech Dome in Real Hidden Valley by heading a short distance west over the hill from Czech Dome. Maps, pages 266 and 272.

Creature Comforts Wall

These routes lie on the north side of the buttress. It is easily seen from the vicinity of Uncle Remus. Scramble up boulders to the base. Routes are located on a left-hand Upper Tier and a right-hand Lower Tier. They are shady most of the day.

Creature Comforts Wall— Upper Tier

1019. **Little Big Horn** (5.5) The hand-and-fist-crack starting just left of *Snap Crackle & Pop* heads up and left, then back right. Downclimb the chimney to left. **Pro:** To 3 inches. **FA:** George Armstrong, Matt Hind, J. Parker, F. Kirsten; 11/98.

1020. **Snap Crackle & Pop** (5.11a) ★★ This is a four-bolt route that heads up the dark-colored arête. Downclimb the chimney to left. **Pro:** To 2 inches (anchors). **FA:** Matt Hind, George Armstrong; 11/98.

1021. **If 6 Were 9** (5.10c/d) ★★★ This four-bolt route lies on the left side of the grey-colored block near the middle of the wall. It is perhaps best approached from the left; from near the base of the *Snap Crackle & Pop,* walk and tunnel right. Downclimb to the left. **Pro:** To 2 inches for anchor. **FA:** Matt Hind, George Armstrong, 11/98.

1022. **Grand Day Out** (5.9) Go up the face to reach this hand-and-fist-size crack, which is around the corner and right of *If 6 Were 9.* Descend right to the ramp. **Pro:** To 3 inches. **FA:** Matt Hind, George Armstrong; 11/98.

1023. **Yank Yer Knob** (5.10a) Go up a flake/crack to a bolt then face climb to a roof with a fixed pin. Traverse left under the roof. Descend right to the ramp. **Pro:** Very thin to 1 inch. **FA:** Matt Hind, George Armstrong; 11/98.

1024. **Kinder Surprise** (5.9) Follow the crack to the right of *Yank Yer Knob* to the roof, then go up. Descend right to the ramp. **Pro:** To 3 inches. **FA:** Matt Hind, George Armstrong; 11/98.

Upper Tier

1020 1021 1022 1023

Lower Tier

1024

1025

1026

Creature Comforts Wall— Lower Tier

1025. **Weener Dude** (5.10a) This is a left-leaning hand-to-finger crack on the left end of the Lower Tier. Descend left to the ramp between the Upper and Lower Tiers. **Pro:** To 3 inches. **FA:** Todd Gordon, George Armstrong, Matt Hind; 11/98.

1026. **Shagadelic** (5.5) The right-facing corner on the lower right section of the Lower Tier. **Pro:** To 3 inches. **FA:** George Armstrong, Todd Gordon, Matt Hind; 11/98.

1027. **Shagaholic** (5.6) (not shown on photo) Climb a crack to a flake to a tree on the far lower right section of the Lower Tier. **FA:** Todd Gordon, George Armstrong, Matt Hind; 11/98.

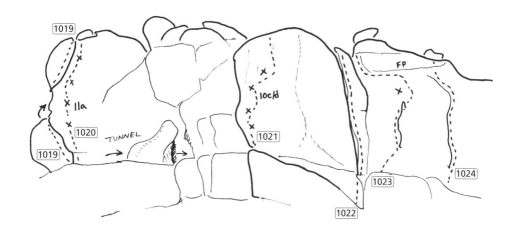

The Slab

This north-facing slab lies just east of and over the rise from the left (east) end of the Creature Comforts Wall. The Slab and route are not pictured. Map, page 272.

1028. Unknown (5.10c?) ★ This route lies on a slab about 75 feet down and left of *Little Big Horn*. **Pro:** Three bolts; gear for anchors. **FA:** Unknown.

Classic Corner Wall

These routes lie on the south side of the buttress of rock almost directly above and east of the Aiguille de Joshua Tree (the north side of this buttress is the Creature Comforts Wall). Descent for first three routes is to the left. The wall is sunny most of the day. Maps, pages 266 and 272.

1029. False Classic Corner (aka Nolina Crack) (5.6) ★★ The clean crack in the left-facing corner is often mistaken for *Classic Corner*. **Pro:** To 3 inches. **FA:** Unknown.

1030. The Leatherhead Arête (5.11b) ★★★ Begin just left of *Classic Corner*, then head up and left past four bolts on the arête. **Pro:** Gear for anchor. **FA** (TR): Pat Nay, Karen Roseme, Derek Rednig, Mark Rosner. **FA** (Lead): Chris Miller et al.

1031. Classic Country (5.10b) ★ (TR) Climb *Classic Corner*, then head straight left on a horizontal crack (crossing *The Leatherhead Arête*), then go up a thin crack. **FA:** Pat Nay.

1032. Classic Corner (5.7) ★★ Climb the clean right-facing dihedral to the right of the above routes. **Pro:** To 2 inches. **FA:** Scott Cosgrove; 1/88.

1033. Arms for Hostages (5.11b) ★ (TR) This is the overhanging brown wall about 100 feet right of *Classic Corner*. Two-bolt anchor. **FA:** Tom Gilje, Mike Lechlinski, Scott Cosgrove; 1/88.

Cockroach Crag Routes

All of the following climbs lie on the actual Cockroach Crag, a small brownish block that lies below the south side of the buttress. Downclimb off the back. See page 276 for approach directions. Maps, pages 266 and 272.

1034. R. S. Chicken Choker (5.11b) ★★ This finger crack over a roof lies on the southwest (left) side of Cockroach Crag. **Pro:** Thin to 1.5 inches. **FA:** Mike Lechlinski, Tom Gilje, Mari Gingery, Todd Gordon, Scott Cosgrove; 1/88.

1035. The Fabulous T. Gordex Cracks (5.8) This crack lies immediately right of *R. S. Chicken Choker*. **Pro:** To 2 inches. **FA:** Todd Gordon; 1/88.

1036. Roach Motel (5.10a) (R) This is located around the corner and to the right of the two previous routes, on the left end of the southeast face. The route ascends thin cracks and passes several horizontals. **FA:** Tom Gilje; 1/88.

Classic Corner Wall

Around corner

1031 1032

1033

Cockroach Crag

1029 1030

1034 1035 1036 1037 1038

1037. **Climb of the Cockroaches** (5.8) (R)
Ascend a big flake leading to face moves 15
feet right of *Roach Motel*. **FA:** Todd Gordon,
Mike Lechlinski, Mari Gingery, Cyndie
Bransford, Jennifer Wonderly; 1/88.

1038. **Roach Roof** (5.6) Climb the short,
right-facing corner leading to a roof. This is
to the right of *Climb of the Cockroaches*. **FA:**
Todd Gordon, Mike Lechlinski; 1/88.

The Dungeon

This rock is about 100 yards up and right of Cockroach Crag proper. All routes face roughly west, but are mostly hidden from view behind a boulder in front, and lie in a deep pit. Approach as for the Cockroach Crag (see page 276 for approach directions). The rock sees morning shade and afternoon sun. Maps, pages 266 and 272.

1039. **Mike Fink** (5.9) Located on the far left of the face. Go up the face past one bolt, then up and right to a thin hands crack. **Pro:** To 2 inches. **FA:** Dana Adler, Todd Gordon, Tom Burke, Cyndie Bransford, Dave Evans, Derrick Reinich, Jim Reinich, Mike Rossner, Jackeline Rossner; 3/96.

1040. **I-Go-Go-E** (5.8) ★ Climb the dike between *Mike Fink* and *The Dungeon,* up and right past two bolts. The first ascent party must get points for being one of the largest recorded. **FA:** Todd Gordon, Cyndie Bransford, Pat Nay, Dana Adler, Derrick Reinich, Jim Reinich, Karen Roseme, Mike Rossner, Mark Rossner, Jackeline Rossner, Tom Burke, Dave Evans, Kastle Lund; 3/96.

1041. **The Dungeon** (5.9+) ★ This is a slanting thin crack that starts in the pit, then goes up a more distinct handcrack. **Pro:** Thin to 2 inches. **FA:** Kevin Powell, Alan Roberts.

Alien Block

A steep, fractured block with two bolted face routes is about 250 yards right of, and up from, Cockroach Crag. Park about 0.6 mile down Lost Horse Road from its junction with Park Boulevard (same as for Atlantis, Uncle Remus/Aiguille de Joshua Tree et al). The Lost Horse/Park Boulevard junction is 7.3 miles from the West Entrance and 1.3 miles from the Intersection Rock/Real Hidden Valley intersection. Walk south along a well-defined trail, skirting the base of the rocks and hillside for about 1,000 yards, then angle up the hillside to the rock. Maps, pages 266 and 272.

1042. **Green Visitor** (5.11d) ★★★ Begin near the center of the north side of the block; go up the center of the face past two bolts. **FA:** Tom Gilje, Mari Gingery, Scott Cosgrove; 1/88.

1043. **Third Bolt from the Sun** (5.11a) ★ Start as for *Green Visitor,* but after the first bolt head right to the arête and up past two more bolts. A direct start (three bolts) has not been free climbed. **FA:** Mike Lechlinski, Mari Gingery; 1/88.

JIMMY CLIFF AREA

This area is comprised of three major formations (Jimmy Cliff to the north, Arid Piles to the south, and Mount Grossvogel to the west). To reach it, park about 0.6 mile down Lost Horse Road from its junction with Park Boulevard (same as for Atlantis, Uncle Remus/Aiguille de Joshua Tree et al). The Lost Horse Road/Park Boulevard junction is 7.3 miles from the West Entrance and 1.3 miles from the Intersection Rock/Real Hidden Valley intersection. Beyond this point, Lost Horse Road is closed to public vehicular traffic (bicycles are OK); this is unfortunate because the closed dirt road passes just west of Jimmy Cliff and Arid Piles. This area lies about two-thirds of a mile south of the parking area.

The easiest approach is to walk directly south from the parking area on a well-established trail (passing Atlantis and Uncle Remus, etc.). When you get to the Aiguille de Joshua Tree (a 30-foot thin needle), head west to Jimmy Cliff. Arid Piles lies to the southwest, and Mount Grossvogel is best reached by walking west between Jimmy Cliff and Arid Piles. Maps, pages 266 and 282.

Arid Piles, Prime Time Crag, and Mount Grossvogel are actually quite close to Real Hidden Valley (which lies to the east). As a result, these crags can be just as easily approached from the Real Hidden Valley parking area. To approach from Real Hidden Valley, take Park Boulevard from the West Entrance for 8.6+ miles and turn left (west) on the Hidden Valley Picnic Area road. This road lies opposite the Intersection Rock parking area and 0.1 mile north of the T intersection with Barker Dam Road (which provides access to Hidden Valley

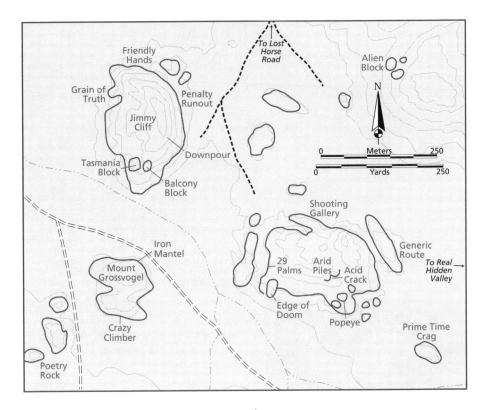

Campground). A few hundred yards down the Real Hidden Valley road, a large parking area is adjacent to (and south of) the trailhead for Real Hidden Valley proper. From this main parking area, head west on a climbers' trail leading toward Houser Buttress. Continue past Houser Buttress into more open desert, then head a bit right (northwest) toward a very large pile of rocks; this is Arid Piles. See the map on page 369 (Real Hidden Valley).

Jimmy Cliff

This is the northernmost of three large formations rising from the otherwise level desert floor. It is west of the Uncle Remus and Cockroach Crag areas. It has a complex topography and multifaceted faces. Approach information is on page 281. Descents vary. Map is above.

Jimmy Cliff—East Face

This faces Uncle Remus and Cockroach Crags; it gets morning sun and shade in the afternoon. Descent: For routes *I Forgot* (1046) to *Fiendish Fists* (1059), the easiest descent is to rap off the bolted anchor atop *Dick Van Dyke*.

Jimmy Cliff—East Face, Left

1044. **Secret Sauce** (5.11b) (not shown on photo) This route lies among boulders just east of the southeast corner of Jimmy Cliff; it is on the west side of these boulders. Go up a left-slanting undercling/lieback, then face climb past one bolt. **Pro:** Thin to 2 inches. **FA:** Mike Lechlinski, Mari Gingery, Tom Gilje, John Yablonski; 1/88.

1045. **Bad Boy Club** (5.9) (R) A wall with several horizontal cracks is located about 150 feet down and left from *I Forgot*. Climb the central seam/flake past the horizontals. Downclimb to the right. **Pro:** Thin to 2 inches. **FA:** Alan Bartlett, Geoff Archer; 5/91.

1046. **I Forgot** (5.10a) Begin up and right of *Bad Boy Club*, atop large blocks (about 50 feet left and above *Last Minute Additions*). Go up the crack and corners. **Pro:** To 2.5 inches. **FA:** Unknown.

1047. **Last Minute Additions** (5.6) Go up the right side of several blocks, climbing the various right-facing corners to a ledge and the top. **Pro:** To 2.5 inches. **FA:** Alan Bartlett, Alan Roberts; 11/82.

1048. **Wandering Swain** (5.7) This route wanders around connecting cracks between *Last Minute Additions* and *Chilly Willy*. **Pro:** To 2.5 inches. **FA:** Todd Swain; 1991.

1049. **Chilly Willy** (5.10c A1 or 5.11a variation) Start about 40 feet right of *Last Minute Additions* and just left of *Penalty Runout*. Go directly up the face to the upper corner of *Penalty Runout* past three bolts. Aid (A1) past the first bolt or traverse left 6 feet off the deck from *Penalty Runout* (5.11a). **Pro:** To 2 inches. **FA:** Dave Evans, Brad Singer, Dale Chocker; 2/88. **FA** (free variation): Dave Evans; 5/89.

1050. **Penalty Runout** (5.9) (R) ★★ This is just right of *Chilly Willy;* it's best done in two short pitches. **Pitch 1:** Go up the face past one bolt (5.8) to a horizontal; head left to a ledge below a left-facing corner. **Pitch 2:** Go up the dihedral (5.9). **Pro:** Thin to 2 inches. **FA:** Randy Vogel, Maria Cranor, Alan Roberts; 1980.

1051. **Sudden Death** (5.10a) Begin from a ledge atop the first pitch of *Penalty Runout;* go right around the corner and up the arête, then face climb past bolt and go up thin cracks. **Pro:** Thin to 2 inches. **FA:** Dave Katz, Jack Roberts, Bob Gaines; 11/82.

Jimmy Cliff—East Face, Right

1052. **The Harder They Fall** (5.10a) ★★ Begin near the high point along the base, just right of *Penalty Runout*. Go up cracks and a right-facing corner to a roof; go left out the roof and up discontinuous cracks above. **Pro:** Thin to 2 inches. **FA:** Alan Bartlett, Alan Roberts; 11/82.

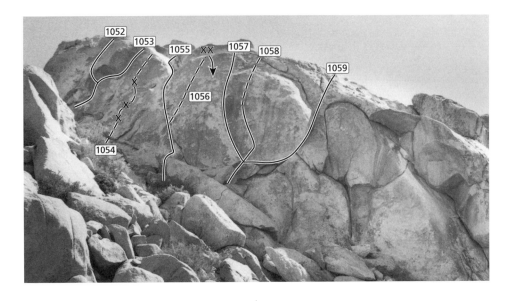

1053. **Third World** (5.9) Begin up *The Harder They Fall,* but head right under the roof and up the corner above. **Pro:** Thin to 2 inches. **FA:** Mike Paul, Jeff Elgar; 1980.

1054. **The Brontos or Us** (5.11a) ★★ Climb the steep face just right of *Third World* past three bolts. **Pro:** To 2 inches. **FA:** Gordon Brysland, Eric Easton.

1055. **The Dike** (5.10b) (R) ★★ Climb the obvious left-slanting dike system between *The Brontos or Us* and *Friendly Hands.* **Pro:** To 3.5 inches. **FA:** Mike Paul and others; 1980.

1056. **Dick Van Dyke** (5.10b) (TR) Start up *The Dike,* then head up and right on the face to bolt anchors. **FA:** Chris Miller, K. Jameson; 3/89.

1057. **Friendly Hands** (5.10b) ★★★ This is the obvious, clean, thin crack that slants up and left. **Pro:** To 2.5 inches. **FA:** Kevin Powell, Alan Roberts; 1981.

1058. **Cliff Hanger** (5.10b) (R) ★★ Begin as for *Friendly Hands,* but go up small corner and the face past one bolt. **Pro:** Thin to 1.5 inches. **FA:** Andy Brown, Lotus Steele; 4/87.

1059. **Fiendish Fists** (5.9) ★ Begin at the start of *Friendly Hands,* but take the wide crack that heads up and right. **Pro:** To 3.5 inches. **FA:** Unknown.

Jimmy Cliff—West Face

This wide and complex side of Jimmy Cliff has routes scattered mostly on the right (north) and left (south) ends of the face.

Descent: For *Hueco Thanks* through *The Lone Ranger,* downclimb the gully between *Grain of Truth* and *GS-5.* Other routes have walkoffs or rappel anchors. The face gets morning shade and sun all afternoon.

1060. **Hueco Thanks** (5.4) (R/X) This route heads up the low-angled, very huecoed face on the extreme left end of the west face. **Pro:** To 2.5 inches. **FA:** Todd Gordon; 1990.

1061. **Grain of Truth** (5.10d) ★ Begin off a small pillar just left of the descent gully. Go up the right hand of twin thin cracks on the dark rock. **Pro:** To 3 inches. **FA:** Charles Cole, Maria Cranor; 1982.

1062. **GS-5** (5.9) (TR) This and the next route lie just right of the descent gully, about 50 feet right of *Grain of Truth*. Go up the face left of *The Lone Ranger,* joining that route at its last bolt. **FA:** Todd Swain; 11/88.

1063. **The Lone Ranger** (5.9) ★★ Go up the bucketed face about 50 feet right of *Grain of Truth,* passing three bolts. **Pro:** To 2.5 inches. **FA:** Todd Swain; 11/88.

1064. **Tasgrainian Devil** (5.9) This and the next climb lie about 100 feet left of *Live from Tasmania.* Begin in an alcove below a chimney; climb a hidden finger crack to varnished lieback flakes. This climb is only visible from (and is best approached from) *Live from Tasmania.* **Pro:** To 2 inches. **FA:** Todd Swain, Gary Garrett; 11/88.

1065. **Live from Tasgrainia** (5.8) The two-bolt route just right of *Tasgrainian Devil.* **Pro:** To 2 inches. **FA:** Mike Shacklett, Mitch Shacklett.

Tasmania Block

The following routes lie near the right end of the west face, on a block of rock above the desert floor that lies just down and left of the large Balcony Block. Scramble up to the base.

1066. **What a Riot** (5.7) The two-bolt arête left of *Live From Tasmania.* **Pro:** To 2 inches. **FA:** Mike Shacklett, Mitch Shacklett, Bill Cramer, Michelle Cramer; 5/92.

1067. **Live From Tasmania** (5.9) ★ This is the handcrack that starts in a small left-facing corner. **Pro:** To 2.5 inches. **FA:** Kevin Powell, Alan Roberts; 1981.

1068. **Bad Czech Girl** (5.11a) Begin about 25 feet to the right and around from *Live From Tasmania;* go up the face past three bolts. **Pro:** To 2 inches. **FA:** Todd Gordon, Radim Bedin; 4/91.

1069. **Lurleen Quits** (5.8) This is the right-slanting crack just right of *Bad Czech Girl.* **Pro:** To 2.5 inches. **FA:** Darryl Nakahira; 1982.

1070. **Lurleen Never Tried It** (5.7) (not shown on photo) This is a direct start to *Lurleen Quits,* starting to that route's right and climbing up to meet it where it curves right. **Pro:** To 2.5 inches. **FA:** Bill Cramer; 5/92.

1071. **Seismo** (5.7) Go up and right, then up the face (past a fixed pin) to the right of *Lurleen Quits.* **Pro:** To 2 inches. **FA:** Bill Cramer, Michelle Cramer, Mike Shacklett, Mitch Shacklett; 5/92.

1072. **Quit Doing Czech Girls** (5.9) (TR) (not shown on photo) I am unsure of where this route lies. **FA:** Todd Swain, 11/91.

The Balcony Block

This is the large steep block on the upper right end of the west face of Jimmy Cliff. Rap off *The Balcony* anchor.

1073. **Peanut Gallery** (5.11a) ★★★ This is a steep, bolted climb on the backside of the block. The third bolt may be missing a hanger; one-bolt anchor. Rap from *The Balcony.* **FA** (TR): John Mallery; 1987. **FA** (Lead): Alfred Randell, Dave Tucker; 1988.

1074. **The Balcony** (5.11b) ★★★ (Sport) This fun, steep face route with 6 bolts is on the northwest side of the large block. The crux at the sixth bolt. Two-bolt anchor/65-foot rappel. **FA:** Bob Gaines, Yvonne Gaines; 11/97.

Jimmy Cliff—South Face

Routes generally are sunny most of the day. Descents vary.

1075. **Hot Cross Bunnies** (5.10a) (TR) (not shown on photo) Begin just left of *The Velveeta Rabbit* then go up the face. **FA:** Todd Swain; 11/89.

1076. **The Velveeta Rabbit** (5.7) (not shown on photo) This climb is located about midway between *Lurleen Quits* and *Downpour,* at the point where Jimmy Cliff is closest to the road. It is the leftmost crack in a slab that goes over a small roof. **Pro:** To 2 inches. **FA:** Kelly Carignan, Marge Floyd; 4/86.

1077. **They Found Hitler's Brain** (5.12b) ★ This is located on the southwest face about 50 feet right of *The Velveeta Rabbit,* off the desert floor. Climb past two bolts on a small face. Two-bolt anchor. **FA:** Unknown.

1078. **Short Stop** (5.10a) This thin crack lies about 70 feet to the right and around from *They Found Hitler's Brain.* Go up the crack to a small roof. **Pro:** Thin to 2 inches. **FA:** Unknown.

1079. **Downpour** (5.8) ★ This and the following two routes lie up off the desert floor on a section of Jimmy Cliff that is characterized by a large, low-angled corner system and buttress to the right. Go up the obvious left-facing corner. **Pro:** Thin to 2 inches. **FA:** Randy Vogel, Craig Fry, Steve Quinlan; 1975.

1080. **Thin Flakes** (5.9+) ★ Begin on *Downpour,* but climb a thin flake on the right wall of the corner. **Pro:** Thin to 2 inches. **FA:** Tom Gilje; 1982.

1081. **Ratrace** (5.11a) (R) ★★ This route heads up the arête to the right of the last two routes. It's runout between the second and third bolts. **Pro:** Three bolts; gear for anchor. **FA:** Tom Gilje; 1982.

Arid Piles

This large formation lies south of Jimmy Cliff and consists of a complex series of faces, corridors and large blocks. Many fine and difficult routes are found here. Approach either from the parking area at the end of Lost Horse Road (0.6 mile from its junction with Park Boulevard) or from the Real Hidden Valley parking area by heading past Houser Buttress. See page 281 for detailed approach directions. This was named to poke fun at the much more famous (and better) crag, Arapiles, in Australia. Map, page 282.

Arid Piles—Northeast Face

The northeast face of Arid Piles faces Cockroach Crags, and on its right section presents the tallest face on the entire formation. A separate short rock left of the main northeast face has several climbs (the Short East Wall). The face gets some morning sun, afternoon shade.

Arid Piles—Short East Wall

The following three routes lie on the smaller wall separated from the main formation by a boulder-filled corridor that sits in front of the east face of Arid Piles. The wall and routes are not pictured.

1082. **Barley, Wheat or Rye (It's All Grain)** (5.10a) Begin on the left end of the wall, just left of a chimney. Go up a right-leaning ramp to a bolt, past horizontals, move left 15 feet, then go up an easy crack. **Pro:** To 2.5 inches. **FA:** Todd Swain, Bill Friesen, Jim Schlinkmann; 1/89.

1083. **Generic Route** (5.8) Begin just right of the chimney (right of the last route). Face climb up to a right-slanting crack that peters out into face climbing. **Pro:** Thin to 3 inches. **FA:** Alan Bartlett, Dave Black; 1/83.

1084. **Elbow Room** (5.10d) This route is about 120 feet right and around the corner from *Generic Route.* It is the right-hand off-width/fist crack. **Pro:** To 4+ inches. **FA:** Todd Swain; 9/91.

Arid Piles—Main Northeast Face

The main northeast face of Arid Piles is the tallest section of the formation and is characterized by a large steep face crossed by several horizontal crack systems.

1085. **Weasel Woof** (5.7) Begin off a boulder up the small talus slope on the left end of the main northeast face. Go up a handcrack over a roof, then jog right and up a thin crack to a ledge/ramp. Either downclimb left or finish up *Hip, Hip Belay.* **Pro:** To 2.5 inches. **FA:** Brian Boyd, Gary Jones; 2/90.

1086. **Hip, Hip Belay** (5.7+) (R) Either do *Weasel Woof* (5.7), or traverse up and right on a chimney/ramp to a belay ledge above *Weasel Woof.* Head up and left from the belay, then climb discontinuous cracks to a short

corner. **Pro:** To 2 inches. **FA:** Todd Swain, Cyndie Bransford; 10/91.

1087. **Night Gallery** (5.8+) Go up and left in a right-facing corner, move right on a horizontal, then go up the upper crack. **Pro:** To 2.5 inches. **FA:** Todd Gordon, Marge Floyd, Jim Angione, Dave Evans; 9/86.

1088. **Shooting Gallery** (5.10b) (R) ★ Begin below and right of the obvious left-facing corner crack (5.10b) on the upper face (right of the top of *Night Gallery*). Go up and right, then back left, to reach the upper corner. Alternatively, you can climb directly up the face and horizontals (5.10a/b) to reach the upper crack. **Pro:** Thin to 2 inches. **FA:** Alan Bartlett, Alan Roberts; 11/82. **FA** (Direct): Dave Evans.

Descent
1090
1091
1092
1093
1094 1095
and
1098 thru 1102
(hidden)
1103

Arid Piles—Northwest Face

The northwest face of Arid Piles is quite complex. The main face lies in a corridor of sorts formed by a ridge of rocks lying below and in front of it (the 29 Palms Corridor). Most routes are found in the 29 Palms Corridor, both on the main northwest face, but also on the inside of the ridge of rocks. Easiest entrance into the 29 Palms Corridor is from the east, though you can also access it from the west end. It receives morning shade and some afternoon sun.

1089. **Nice and Steep and Elbow Deep** (5.10b) (not shown on photo) This is a north-facing, overhanging fist crack on a separate ridge of rock north of *The Outsiders*. **Pro:** To 4 inches. **FA:** Dennis Yates, Roger Linfield; 4/86.

1090. **The Outsiders** (5.11a) (R) ★ This route lies high on the left end of the main northeast face. Go up the face into a small left-facing corner, then up and left to top. **Pro:** Two bolts; thin to 2 inches. **FA:** Russ Raffa, Paul Trapani, Laura Chaiten, Iza Trapani; 1983.

1091. **Quarter Moon Crack** (5.10a) Begin on the face to the right and down from *The Outsiders* (right of the descent gully). Go up to a small curving corner, then face climb past the horizontal. **Pro:** To 2 inches. **FA:** Alan Bartlett, Alan Roberts, Sally Moser; 11/82.

1092. **Napkin of Shame** (5.10b) ★ This is the right-tending thin to wide crack just right of *Quarter Moon Crack*. **Pro:** To 3 inches. **FA:** Charles Cole, Jim Ducker, Maria Cranor, Randy Vogel; 1982.

1093. **Quickstone** (5.12c) (R) ★★★ This four-bolt face route lies left of *29 Palms* on

the main northwest face. Begin by stemming off a small pinnacle in the *29 Palms Corridor* (the Pinnacoid; 5.7/5.8; no anchor). **Pro:** Very thin to 2 inches. **FA:** Jonny Woodward, Darrel Hensel; 1/88.

1094. **29 Palms** (5.11d/5.12a) ★★★★ (not shown on photo) This route takes the beautiful, curving, left-facing dihedral on the right end of the main face. Stem and palm your way up. A classic. **Pro:** Many thin to 1.5 inches. **FA:** Tony Yaniro, Mike Lechlinski, Vaino Kodas, Alan Nelson; 1981.

1095. **The 39 Slaps** (5.11c) (R) ★★ (not shown on photo) This is the face just right of the arête formed by *29 Palms.* Poorly protected for the second. **Pro:** Three bolts, to 2 inches. **FA:** Darrel Hensel, Jonny Woodward; 12/87.

1096. **U. B. Kool** (5.10d/5.11a) Begin right and around the corner from *The 39 Slaps.* Face climb up to a crack and roof, then up and left in a flake/crack to the top of *29 Palms.* The crux is at the bottom where a large flake has come off. **Pro:** To 2.5 inches. **FA:** Gordon Brysland, Dan Sullivan; 4/85.

1097. **Edge of Doom** (5.10c) ★★★ This route lies on a large block sitting high on the western shoulder of Arid Piles, found about 100 feet right of *U. B. Kool.* A height-dependent crux getting started leads to face climbing up the arête. **Pro:** Three bolts; two-bolt anchor/rap. **FA:** Charles Cole, Marjorie Shovlin; 1982.

The following routes lie on the inner faces of the rocks that lie in front of the northwest face and form the 29 Palms Corridor.

1098. **Tower of Babel** (5.10d) (R) ★ (not shown on photo) This route lies down and right of *Napkin of Shame* on the east-facing side of rocks forming the narrow corridor with the main northwest face. **Pro:** Three bolts; two-bolt anchor/rap. **FA:** Bill Leventhal, Dave Katz.

1099. **Baggage Claim** (5.9) Start in a chimney right of *Mr. Bunny Quits;* go up the finger crack, then up and left to the *Mr. Bunny Quits* slings/rap. **Pro:** Thin to 2 inches. **FA:** Bill Leventhal, Mike Guardino; 12/82.

1100. **Mr. Bunny Quits** (5.10a) ★ This is the finger crack facing *29 Palms;* above, move right to rap slings at a block or continue to the summit to a two-bolt anchor/rap. **Pro:** Thin to 2 inches. **FA:** Darryl Nakahira, Rob Raker, Dan Leichtfuss.

1101. **Spinner** (5.6) (R) Go up the southwest face of the very tiny spire of rock that lies at the southwestern end of the 29 Palms Corridor. **Pro:** A sling can be used for the dicey rap anchor, but most treat this as a solo and downclimb it. **FA:** Alan Nelson, Scott Loomis; 1981.

1102. **Spooner** (5.7) (R) Go up the varnished east face of the spire with *Spinner.* **FA:** Todd Swain; 1992.

The following route lies on the outer faces of the crags/boulders that form the 29 Palms Corridor.

1103. **The Jackalope (aka Secret Sauce)** (5.11b) This route lies about 100 feet left of *Spinner* and is more or less "in front of" *29 Palms.* Go up and left via an undercling/lieback, then up the face past one bolt (photo on page 289). **Pro:** To 2 inches. **FA:** Mike Lechlinski, Mari Gingery, John Yablonski, Tom Gilje; 1/88.

Arid Piles—Southwest Face

The southwest face (or rather "side") of Arid Piles is comprised mostly of large boulders and small faces above the desert floor. *Swift* and *The Acid Crack* lie high on the southwest side of Arid Piles noticeable for a large, overhanging, right-facing corner. These routes are all best approached from Real Hidden Valley by walking west past Houser Buttress, then northwest to the southern end of Arid Piles.

See approach directions on pages 281 and 282. They are sunny most of the day.

1104. Swift (5.11a) ★ Begin atop a ramp/slab and climb the overhanging corner. **Pro:** Thin to 2 inches. **FA:** John Bachar; 1982.

1105. The Acid Crack (5.12d) ★★★★ This overhanging finger to very thin crack was discovered by Josh locals while wandering the desert under the influence of LSD. It was later toproped, then led. A nice choice on colder days. **Pro:** Many thin to 1.5 inches. **FA** (TR): John Bachar; 1982. **FA** (Lead): John Bachar; 1983.

1106. Just Another New Wave Route (5.9) This is the short thin crack on the right side of a boulder near the desert floor, down and right of *The Acid Crack*. **Pro:** Thin to 2 inches. **FA:** Unknown.

1107. I'd Slap You but Shit Splatters (5.9+) Begin in a chimney right of *Just Another New Wave Crack Route*. Go up a left-leaning crack on the right side. **Pro:** To 2 inches. **FA:** Todd Gordon, Deanne Gray.

1108. Popeye (5.11a) ★★ This route climbs the left side of the hourglass formation facing *The Taming of the Shoe*. **Pro:** To 4 inches. **FA:** Alan Bartlett; 11/82.

1109. The Taming of the Shoe (5.11a) (R) ★★★ Go up a thin crack that thins to a seam; from the crack's end, face climb (5.11a R) up and somewhat right. **Pro:** Very thin to 1 inch. **FA:** John Bachar, Mari Gingery, Randy Vogel; 1981.

Prime Time Crag

This small rock lies about 100 yards south of Arid Piles. The only known routes are two cracks on the west side. Approach as for Arid Piles; coming in from Real Hidden Valley is probably best (approach described on pages 281 and 282). Not a destination crag; it gets morning shade and afternoon sun. The crag and routes are not pictured. Maps, pages 266 and 282.

1110. My Three Sungs (5.10b) The wider left-hand crack. **Pro:** To 3+ inches. **FA:** Todd Swain; 1992.

1111. The Ming Dallas (5.10b) The right-hand crack; crux at the bottom. **Pro:** To 2.5 inches. **FA:** Randy Vogel, Charles Cole; 1983.

Mount Grossvogel

This fairly nondescript formation lies just across an old dirt road and west of Arid Piles and Jimmy Cliff. A branch in the dirt road to the north heads to the west of (behind) this rock as well. Approach from the parking area at the end of Lost Horse Road (0.6 mile from junction with Park Boulevard) by heading south toward the Aiguille de Joshua Tree, then walking southwest between Jimmy Cliff and Arid Piles. Alternatively, head west from the Real Hidden Valley parking area, past Houser Buttress, then northwest around the west side of Arid Piles. See pages 281 and 282 for detailed approach directions. It was named to poke fun at this guidebook author, but roughly translates to mean "Big Bird." Maps, pages 266 and 282.

Mount Grossvogel— Northeast Face

This face lies adjacent to the old road running between Arid Piles/Jimmy Cliff and Mount Grossvogel. It gets some morning sun but is shady most of the day.

1112. **Blind Me with Science** (5.10b) This route follows a thin right-leaning crack on the very left end of the face. Continue up easy ground to the summit. **Pro:** Thin to 2 inches. **FA:** Todd Swain, Kip Knapp; 4/85.

1113. **Ranger Danger** (5.8) Begin in a right-facing corner located about 12 feet right of *Blind Me With Science;* go up the thin crack. Continue up easy ground to summit. **Pro:** Thin to 2 inches. **FA:** Todd Swain, Kip Knapp; 4/85.

1114. **Dr. Seuss Vogel** (5.7) This route lies just right of *Ranger Danger*. Go up a right-slanting crack to a flake that is passed on the right. **Pro:** Thin to 2.5 inches. **FA:** Todd Gordon, Cathy Boyd; 4/86.

1115. **Iron Mantel** (5.10c) (R) Begin right of center below a "gull wing"-shaped roof. Go up over the roof, then face climb past a bolt to reach a flake and discontinuous thin cracks. **Pro:** Thin to 2 inches. **FA:** Charles Cole, Darryl Nakahira, Steve Anderson et al.; 10/82.

1116. **Big Bird** (5.7+) Begin off a boulder to the right of *Iron Mantel,* below a roof. Go up the left side of the roof, then head up and left on flakes and cracks. **Pro:** Thin to 2.5 inches. **FA:** Todd Gordon, Cathy Boyd; 4/86.

1117. **Roboranger** (5.5) Begin as for *Big Bird,* but stay right until you can finish up a low-angled right-facing corner. **Pro:** Thin to 2.5 inches. **FA:** Todd Swain; 11/88.

1118. **Robaxol** (5.3) Begin just right of the block where *Big Bird* and *Roboranger* start. Go up and right on various broken crack systems. **Pro:** To 2.5 inches. **FA:** Susan Ducker, Jim Ducker et al.; 1982.

Mount Grossvogel— Northwest Face

1119. **Ohm on the Range** (5.4) (not shown on photo) Start in the chasm between the northeast and southwest faces of Mount Grossvogel, on the back (northeast) side of the *Chaffe N' Up* summit block. Climb a short, right-leaning finger crack, then move left and follow a vertical handcrack to the top. **Pro:** To 2.5 inches. **FA:** Todd Swain; 11/88.

Mount Grossvogel— Southwest Face

This side of Mount Grossvogel is rather wide, with routes located at both the right and left ends. It is sunny most of the day.

1120. **Killer Bees** (5.10a) Begin on the far left end of the face, off a boulder behind a "gotcha" bush. Go up the steep short crack. **Pro:** To 3 inches. **FA:** Charles Cole; 1983.

1121. **Chaffe n' Up** (5.8) (R) Begin about 40 feet right of *Killer Bees* below the left side of a roof. Go up thin cracks to a right-slanting crack/ramp; near the end of the ramp, go up the face of the summit pinnacle (5.8 R). **Pro:** Thin to 3 inches. **FA:** Steve Anderson, Charles Cole; 1983.

1122. **The Maritimer** (5.10d) (TR) This route lies on the right side of the face, about 20 feet right of a pine tree. Go up the obvious crack that reaches the ground. **FA:** Todd Swain; 1/89.

1123. **Lazy Rhymer** (5.10c) (TR) This is the crack system about 15 feet right of *The Maritimer.* **FA:** Alan Roberts, Todd Swain; 1/89.

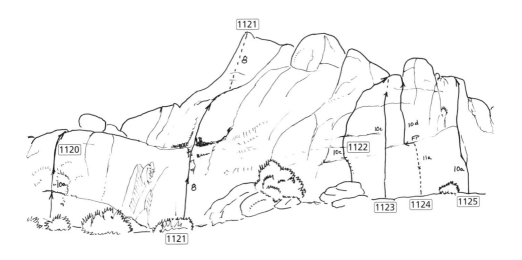

1124. **Crazy Climber** (5.11a) ★★★ Begin about 15 feet right of *Lazy Rhymer.* Go up the face past a bolt, then up and left to a crack system above a horizontal (one fixed pin in the horizontal). **Pro:** Thin to 2 inches. **FA:** Dave Wonderly, Charles Cole, Steve Anderson; 1983.

1125. **Berserk** (5.10a) ★ This route lies about 20 feet right of *Crazy Climber.* Go up twin cracks on dark rock past a horizontal. **Pro:** Thin to 2.5 inches. **FA:** Charles Cole; 1983.

Poetry Rock

This small formation rises across the branch in the road on the western side of Mount Grossvogel (to the west). The rock and route are not shown. Maps, pages 266 and 282.

1126. **Poetry in Motion** (5.9) ★ This route lies on the west side of a small pinnacle. Begin in a left–diagonalling crack, then go up past two bolts (no hangers; wired stoppers over bolts). No fixed anchor on top; simul-rap to descend. **Pro:** Thin to 2 inches. **FA:** Todd Swain, Kip Knapp; 4/85.

LOST HORSE WEST

The following areas and crags generally lie west of the dirt road that runs south from the Lost Horse Ranger Station. All are best approached by parking about 0.6 mile down Lost Horse Road from its junction with Park Boulevard. The Lost Horse/Park Boulevard junction is 7.3 miles from the West Entrance and 1.3 miles from the Intersection Rock/Real Hidden Valley intersection. A small parking area is located on the right (north) side of the road. The road beyond, which leads to Lost Horse Ranger Station, is closed to public vehicle traffic; continue on foot for about 0.5 mile. Popular crags include Ranger Station Rock, S Cracks Formation, and Candlestein Pass area. Maps, pages 215 and 297.

Ranger Station Rock

This formation lies behind the Lost Horse Ranger Station. Park about 0.6 mile down Lost Horse Road from its junction with Park Boulevard. The Lost Horse/Park Boulevard junction is 7.3 miles from the West Entrance and 1.3 miles from the Intersection Rock/Real Hidden Valley intersection. Continue west on foot for approximately 0.5 mile along the Lost Horse Road to the ranger station. This is the large formation above and to the right of the ranger station. It is easily seen from the road as you walk. Scramble up boulders to the base. The rock gets sun in the morning and shade in the afternoon. Map, page 298.

Ranger Station Rock— Northeast Face

The photo of this cliff is on page 299.

1127. **Barbara Bush** (5.10b) ★ Climb the face with two bolts. **Pro:** To 3 inches for anchor. **FA:** Sam Owing, Jack Marshall, Don Wilson; 1988.

1128. **Bush Crack** (5.7) ★ The obvious thin handcrack on the slab. **Pro:** To 2.5 inches. **FA:** Unknown.

1129. **Open Casket Funeral** (5.11a) (TR) The arête to the right of *Bush Crack*. **FA:** Sam Owing, Jack Marshall, Don Wilson; 1988.

1130. **Hercules** (5.11c/d) ★★★★ This excellent, overhanging hand-to-finger crack curves up and right. Nice and pumpy. **Pro:** To 2.5 inches, with several three-quarters to 1 inch. **FA** (TR): John Long; 10/76. **FA** (Lead): Dale Bard; 11/79.

Ranger Station Rock— North Face

This is the larger face of Ranger Station Rock; it lies to the right and around the corner from the northeast face. It is hidden from view from the ranger station and gets sun in the morning and shade in the afternoon. Either approach from the vicinity of the northeast face or, from the ranger station, head right (north) along a wash, then left (west) up a small canyon, then up boulders to the base. Map, page 298.

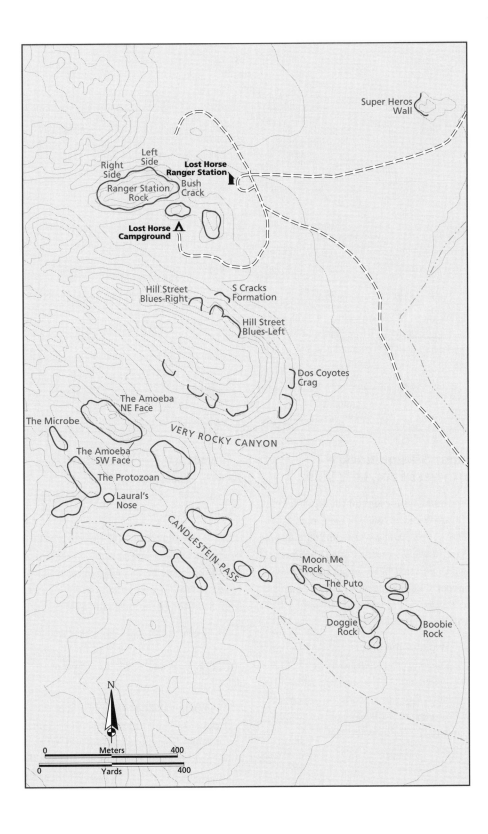

Super Heros
Wall

Left
Side
Right
Side
**Lost Horse
Ranger Station**
Ranger Station
Rock
Bush
Crack

**Lost Horse
Campground**

Hill Street
Blues-Right
S Cracks
Formation

Hill Street
Blues-Left

Dos Coyotes
Crag

The Amoeba
NE Face
VERY ROCKY CANYON

The Microbe

The Amoeba
SW Face

The Protozoan

Laural's
Nose

CANDLESTEIN PASS

Moon Me
Rock

The Puto

Doggie
Rock

Boobie
Rock

N

0   Meters   400

0   Yards   400

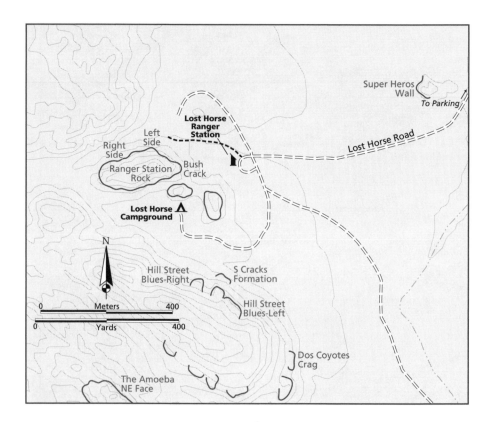

Ranger Station Rock—Northwest Face, Left Side

These routes are located on the left side of the northwest face. *Swain in the Breeze, 4U2DO2,* and *Owatafooliam* climb the upper left face, above a "sunken garden" behind a ledge. A ramp that heads up and right below the upper wall provides easy access. *Swain Lake, Ranger Rendezvous,* and *Swain Song* lie on the lower left face.

1131. **Swain in the Breeze** (5.6) ★★ Go up a slanting crack to the ledge, then up the face above the left side of the sunken garden. **Pro:** To 2 inches; four bolts (without hangers; stopper cables can be used) placed after the first ascent. **FA:** Todd Swain; 1985.

1132. **4U2DO2** (5.5) (X) Climb the face between *Swain in the Breeze* and *Owatafooliam,* starting in the sunken garden. **FA:** Todd Swain; 1991.

1133. **Owatafooliam** (5.8) Begin right of *Swain in the Breeze;* go up a flake/crack to the sunken garden. Above, follow a left–facing flake to a yucca, then go left up the face. **Pro:** To 2.5 inches. **FA:** Todd Swain; 1985.

1134. **Swain Lake** (5.5) (R) The short dirty finger crack on the left side of the lower left wall. **Pro:** To 2 inches. **FA:** Todd Swain; 10/89.

1135. **Ranger Rendezvous** (5.7) Start 30 feet right and down from *Swain Lake* (same as for *Swain Song*) but climb up and left to a thin crack in a slab. **Pro:** Thin to 2 inches. **FA:** Todd Swain, Maria Gillett, Dan Wirth; 4/89.

1136. Swain Song (5.11a) ★★ Begin at same spot as *Ranger Rendezvous,* but head up and right on flakes and cracks to a steepening face with four bolts (some may not have hangers). Descend to the right. **Pro:** To 2 inches. **FA:** Todd Swain, Peggy Buckey; 4/89.

Wall of 10,000 Holds

This aptly named wall lies on the upper right section of the northwest face of Ranger Station Rock. One route is recorded. It is best approached by taking the ramp up to the "sunken garden" on the left-side wall. From there, tunnel through the groove and chimney on the right of the sunken garden to a 20-by-100-foot ledge at the base of this "Swiss cheese" wall.

1137. Wall of 10,000 Holds (5.4) (R) ★ This climb follows a "Swiss cheese" wall above a block that is just right of the approach chimney. **Pro:** Cams in pockets are helpful. **FA:** Todd Swain; 4/85.

Ranger Station Rock— Northwest Face, Right Side

The following five routes are on a wall in front and slightly right of Wall of 10,000 Holds. Rap 75 feet from a bolt anchor on top of *Pirates of the Carabiner.*

1138. Pegleg (5.7) Begin off a boulder on the left side of the face, then face climb up and right to the ledge; above, go up the slot then left below the block. **Pro:** To 3 inches. **FA:** Peggy Buckey, Randy Schenkle, Andy Schenkel, Todd Swain; 3/89.

1139. Polly Wants a Crack (5.10a) ★ Start off a pointed boulder and climb past three bolts to join and finish on *Pegleg.* **Pro:** To 3 inches. **FA:** Tad Walch, Peggy Buckey, Todd Swain; 3/86.

1140. Scaried Treasure (5.10b) ★★ Begin just right of *Polly Wants A Crack*. Go up past a small roof to a bolt, up a rib/arête, over a boulder, then past one more bolt. **Pro:** To 2 inches. **FA:** Todd Swain, Andy Schenkel; 3/89.

1141. Pirates of the Carabiner (5.10b) ★ Start right of *Scaried Treasure*. Follow horizontals to a bolt, then go up a flake and past two more bolts to a right-leaning offwidth. **Pro:** To 4+ inches. **FA:** Todd Swain, Tad Welch, Peggy Buckey; 3/86.

1142. Swatchbuckler (5.8) This is the left-facing crack/corner right of *Pirates of the Carabiner*. **Pro:** To 2.5 inches. **FA:** Todd Swain, Randy Schenkel; 3/89.

Lost Horse Campground

The following routes are in the ranger campground/picnic area at the end of a service road behind and left of Lost Horse Ranger Station. Other routes have been done in the campground area, but no information is available; it isn't really a destination anyway. Park about 0.6 mile down Lost Horse Road from its junction with Park Boulevard, which is 7.3 miles from the West Entrance and 1.3 miles from the Intersection Rock/Real Hidden Valley intersection. Continue west on foot for approximately 0.5 mile along the Lost Horse Road toward the ranger station. Head south from the station, taking the right-hand fork in the dirt road, which winds around west into a small valley and the campground. None of the routes are pictured. Maps, pages 215 and 298.

1143. **When Two Become Three** (5.8) This is the obvious south-facing dike near the end of the service road. **FA:** Don Wilson, Karen Wilson, Meg Wilson; 2/89.

1144. **Josar Crack** (5.8+) ★ This and the next route lie on a northwest-facing wall located in the back of the campground; a picnic table is near the base. The route climbs the central handcrack. **Pro:** To 2.5 inches. **FA:** Unknown.

1145. **Mosar** (5.9+) Begin about 18 feet right of *Josar Crack;* go up the face to a horizontal, then discontinuous cracks to a final horizontal where you head left to finish as for *Josar Crack*. **Pro:** Thin to 2 inches. **FA:** Unknown.

1146. **RMRU Crack** (5.8) This route lies about 75 feet right and around from *Mosar,* on the south face of the rock. Go up a thin dike to a crack. **Pro:** Thin to 2 inches. **FA:** Unknown.

1147. **How Spoilers Bleed** (5.10d) This right-leaning ramp is directly opposite (faces) *Josar Crack* and *Mosar,* high on what is actually the back side of the Wall of 10,000 Holds. It begins just left of a tree. Class 4/5 scrambling up and right leads to the start. **Pro:** Very thin to 2 inches. **FA:** Geoff Archer, Alan Bartlett; 5/91.

S Cracks and Hill Street Blues

These formations lie on the northeast-facing hillside that lies just south of the Lost Horse Campground. Park about 0.6 mile down Lost Horse Road from its junction with Park Boulevard; the junction is 7.3 miles from the West Entrance and 1.3 miles from the Intersection Rock/Real Hidden Valley intersection. After parking, continue west on foot along the Lost Horse Road toward the ranger station. From the station, head south, taking the right-hand fork in the dirt road, which winds around to the west into a small valley and the campground. Just before you get to the campground, where the road bends to the right, you can walk directly to these cliffs. Maps, pages 215 and 298.

S Cracks Formation

This rather small, dark rock sits at the base of the hillside. The first three routes actually lie on a small pinnacle of rock about 40 feet left of the main S Cracks Formation.

1148. **Vogels Are Poodles Too** (5.11) (TR) Toprope the face just left of *Android Lust,* avoiding the easy arête (a bit contrived). **FA:** Mark Robinson, Will Chen; 10/86.

1149. **Android Lust** (5.11a) (R) ★★ Thin cracks go up the face. **Pro:** Thin to 2 inches. **FA** (TR): Todd Swain; 4/85. **FA** (Lead): Mark Robinson; 10/86.

1150. **Robotics** (5.8) The thin crack around the corner from *Android Lust*. **Pro:** Thin to 2 inches. **FA:** Todd Swain, Kip Knapp; 4/85.

1151. **Left S Crack** (5.8) ★ Go up a right-tending crack/flake, then up a left-leaning crack. **Pro:** To 2.5 inches. **FA:** Dave Ohlson, Jon Lonne; 4/76.

Hill Street Blues—
Left Formation

Hill Street Blues—
Right Formation

S Cracks
Formation

To Campground ⟶

1152. **Middle S Crack** (5.11a/b) (R) ★★★
The S-shaped crack in the middle of the
face. **Pro:** Thin to 2 inches. **FA:** Dave Ohlson,
Jon Lonne; 4/76.

1153. **Right S Crack** (5.9) ★ The vertical
crack 12 feet right of *Middle S Crack*. **Pro:** To
2.5 inches. **FA:** Dave Ohlson, Jon Lonne;
4/76.

1154. **Jingus Con** (5.11c) ★★ Start up *Right
S Crack;* after about 15 feet, head right onto
the face, then up the seam past two bolts.
Pro: To 2.5 inches. **FA:** John Yablonski, Mike
Lechlinski, Mari Gingery, Tom Gilje; 1/88.

1155. **Furthest Right S Crack** (5.8) Begin
off a boulder about 20 feet right of *Right S
Crack*. Head up then left into a left-slanting
crack. **Pro:** To 2.5 inches. **FA:** Unknown.

Hill Street Blues

This is actually two separate formations that
lie uphill and left of the S Cracks Formation.
See approach information on page 301. An
additional route photo is on page 304. Map,
page 298.

Hill Street Blues—
Left Formation

1156. **Once in a Blue Moon** (5.4) (R) This
route heads up a low-angled bucketed face
around and left of *Blue Nun*. **FA:** Patty
Furbush, Todd Swain; 4/85.

1157. **Blue Nun** (5.8) Climb the zigzag crack
20 feet left of the obvious corner system
(Blue Bayou) and just left of an off-width
crack. **Pro:** To 3 inches. **FA:** Todd Swain, Patty
Furbush; 4/85.

1158. **Blue Bayou** (5.4) This right-facing, exfoliated corner system is on the left side of the formation. **Pro:** To 3 inches. **FA:** Patty Furbush, Todd Swain; 4/85.

1159. **Blues Brothers** (5.10a) ★★★ Climb the obvious thin crack that runs up the center of the slab. To descend, move left and rappel 80 feet from a tree atop *Blue Monday*. **Pro:** Thin to 2.5 inches. **FA:** Todd Swain, Kip Knapp; 4/85.

1160. **Bluebelly** (5.10c) (TR) ★★ The clean slab between *Blues Brothers* and *Blue Monday*;

use the tree atop *Blue Monday* for an anchor. **FA:** Bob Gaines; 3/96.

1161. **Blue Monday** (5.10b) ★ This is a thin crack 30 feet right of *Blues Brothers*. Rappel 80 feet from the tree. **Pro:** Thin to 2.5 inches. **FA:** Darrel Hensel, Alan Roberts, Dave Evans.

1162. **Rhythm and Blues** (5.10b) ★ This short thin crack/flake system lies uphill and right of *Blue Monday*. **Pro:** Thin to 2.5 inches. **FA:** Todd Swain, Patty Furbush; 4/85.

80'
rap

1156 1158 1157 1162 1159 1160 1161

Hill Street Blues— Right Formation

This formation lies roughly above the S Cracks Formation. Other routes may have been done on this formation, but information is not available. The routes are not pictured.

1163. **Black and Blue** (5.6) This starts atop a boulder 100 feet right of *Rhythm and Blues,* and follows a thin crack that leads to boulders at the top. **FA:** Todd Swain, Patty Furbush; 4/85.

1164. **Baby Blue Eyes** (5.10b) (R) Begin right of *Black and Blue.* Go up a left-leaning arch, then up the face past small roofs. **Pro:** Thin to 2 inches. **FA:** Dave Evans, Darrell Hensel, Alan Roberts.

Dos Coyotes Crag

This formation lies about 300 yards left of the S Cracks Formation. Three crack routes are recorded on its northeast face. Approach as for Hill Street Blues (page 302). Information on first ascents and protection is not known. The crag and routes are not pictured. Map, page 298.

1165. **A Taste of Blood** (5.7) The left crack.

1166. **Dances with Coyotes** (5.7) The middle crack.

1167. **Dance without Sleeping** (5.7) The right crack.

CANDLESTEIN PASS

This area is located south of the large hillside containing the S Cracks Formation, Hill Street Blues and Dos Coyotes Crag, in a canyon/wash that runs northwest. Approach this area from either from the end of Lost Horse Road (0.6 mile from Park Boulevard), or from the Real Hidden Valley parking area.

The Lost Horse/Park Boulevard junction is 7.3 miles from the West Entrance and 1.3 miles from the Intersection Rock/Real Hidden Valley intersection. The Real Hidden Valley parking area is located at the western end of the Hidden Valley Picnic Area road, which heads west from Park Boulevard 8.6 miles from the West Entrance.

Lost Horse Road approach directions:
From the parking area at the end of Lost Horse Road, head west on foot for approximately 0.5 mile along the Lost Horse Road

toward the ranger station. From the station head south, taking the right-hand fork in the dirt road, which winds around to the west into a small valley and the campground. Just before you get to the campground, where the road bends to the right, head more or less south toward the base of the hillside. Head left along the base of the hill for several hundred yards until you enter a small valley. At this point you should be able to spot a formation up and right (the back of the Amoeba). If you wish to approach the Amoeba, the Protozoan, or Laural's Nose directly, continue up the valley, then up the hillside above toward the formation.

Alternatively, and to reach Boobie Rock, Doggie Rock, the Puto, and Moon Me Rock (as well as the other upper formations), it is probably better to stay on the main (left-hand) dirt road heading south toward Jimmy Cliff and Mount Grossvogel from the Lost Horse Ranger Station. The road splits just before Mount Grossvogel; take the right-hand fork. Follow this farther south until you can head right (west) into a gentle valley (the Candlestein Pass main wash) that heads northwest. Boobie Rock, Doggie Rock, the Puto, and Moon Me Rock are on the right side of the lower valley; Laural's Nose and the Protozoan are on the left side of the upper valley, with the Amoeba on the upper right. Map, page 215.

Real Hidden Valley approach directions:
From the Real Hidden Valley parking area, walk west on a well-marked trail past Houser Buttress, then head a bit northwest toward the southern end of Arid Piles. Stay south of Arid Piles, cross the dirt road and continue west toward the gentle valley heading northwest into the hills. Before reaching the valley, you will cross another dirt road. Make sure you stay south of Mount Grossvogel. Boobie Rock, Doggie Rock, the Puto, and Moon Me Rock are on the right side of the lower valley; Laural's Nose and the Protozoan are on the left side of the upper valley, with the Amoeba on the upper right. Map, page 369.

Boobie Rock

This formation lies at the base of the hillside on your right just before you enter Candlestein Pass's main wash. The rock and routes are not shown. Map, page 305.

1168. **Overbite** (5.7) This is a somewhat loose crack in white rock located on the north side of Boobie Rock. **Pro:** To 2 inches. **FA:** Todd Gordon, Karlis Ogle, Tucker Tech; 12/99.

1169. **Karl's Crack** (5.8) This crack lies on the south face of Boobie Rock, in a corridor of sorts. **Pro:** To 2 inches; one fixed pin. **FA:** Karlis Ogle, Todd Gordon, Tucker Tech.

Doggie Rock

This formation is near the start of the valley, on the right (north) side of the wash. Map, page 305.

1170. **A Dog in Heat Is Hard to Beat** (5.10b) ★ This overhanging handcrack is

Doggie Rock

1170

located on the right side of the west face of Doggie Rock. **Pro:** To 2.5 inches. **FA:** Todd Gordon, Tucker Tech, Karlis Ogle; 12/99.

The Puto

This reddish-colored tower is located on the right side of the canyon about 150 yards past Doggie Rock. Map, page 305.

1171. **Puto de Yo Yo** (5.10a) ★★ The face/crack on the south face of the Puto. **Pro:** One bolt; three fixed pins; two-bolt anchor. **FA:** Todd Gordon, Tucker Tech, Mark Synott; 12/00.

Moon Me Rock

This is the white face on right side of canyon 100 yards up from the Puto. Map, page 305.

1172. **Karl's White Ass** (5.10a) ★ This four-bolt face route lies on the south side of Moon Me Rock. **FA:** Todd Gordon, Andrea Tomaszewski; 1/00.

Laural's Nose

This small spire lies in the upper section of the Candlestein Pass canyon, to the left and below the Protozoan. Descend via a two-bolt anchor/rappel. Map, page 305.

1173. **Nose Goblin** (5.7) This is the hand-crack leading to face climbing on left (east) side of spire. **Pro:** To 2.5 inches. **FA:** Todd Gordon, Brandt Allen, Tucker Tech; 12/99.

1174. **The Incredible Shrinking Nose** (5.7) (not shown on photo) This is the obvious crack on the north (front) face of the spire. **Pro:** To 2.5 inches. **FA:** Todd Gordon, Tucker Tech; 12/99.

The Protozoan

This formation lies high on the left (south) side of the Candlestein Pass canyon; it is split by a large right-slanting chimney/gully on the left side of its northeast face. The Protozoan roughly faces the Amoeba, which lies above the right (north) side of the

Laural's Nose

The Protozoan

The Microbe

1173 1175

1176

canyon. One route has been recorded on the Protozoan, though a bolt to the right of the one recorded route marks the start of an abandoned route. It is shady most of the day. Map, page 305.

1175. **13-Year-Old Death Trap** (5.7) ★ Begin in the chimney/gully on the left side of the north face, then move up and left into cracks in dark rock in a right-facing corner. Descend via the gully/chimney. **Pro:** To 3 inches. **FA:** Don Wilson, Karen Wilson, Chris Wilson, Doug Munoz; 10/87.

The Microbe

This small formation lies about 100 yards right of the Protozoan on the left (south) side of the Candlestein Pass canyon. It is shady most of the day. Map, page 305.

1176. **The Toothpick** (5.11c) ★ (TR) This is the leftmost of two cracks on the north side of the formation; it begins behind boulders. Go up the thin overhanging crack that narrows to a seam. **FA:** Mike Lechlinski, Mari Gingery.

The Amoeba

The Amoeba lies on the right (north) side of the upper part of Candlestein Pass canyon, roughly opposite the Protozoan formation. Most of the routes lie on the northeastern side of the rock. Map, page 305.

The Amoeba—Southwest Face

This is easily seen on your right as you reach the upper section of Candlestein Pass. The following two routes lie on the right (southern) end of the southwest face and are sunny most of the day.

1177. **Hollow Dreams** (5.11c/d) ★ This ascends a difficult, friable flake on the south side of the formation. Go up the face past three bolts to a crack; head right of a roof. **Pro:** Thin to 2.5 inches. **FA** (Led on aid, followed free): Dave Evans, Craig Fry, Todd Battey.

1178. **The Amoeba** (5.10a) (R) Begin about 35 feet right and around from *Hollow Dreams*. Go up the thin flake; higher are two bolts and one fixed pin. **Pro:** To 3 inches. **FA:** Unknown.

The Amoeba—Northeast Face

The northeast face of the Amoeba is divided by a right-slanting gully system. Routes lie on both sections of rock. From the Candlestein Pass wash area, head through the gap to the right of the south end of the formation, then boulder-hop down and left into a small canyon running along the base of the northeast face. The northeast face can also be reach directly via the rocky canyon approach from Lost Horse Ranger Station, but it is probably easier to take the regular approach up the Candlestein Pass wash. The face is shady most of the day.

1179. **Small Business** (5.11a) (R) This is leftmost route on the northeast face. Climb a crack past a bush into a shallow, left-facing corner (crux). **Pro:** Thin to 2 inches. **FA:** Mark Bowling, Alan Bartlett; 9/91.

1180. **Chamber of Commerce** (5.10c) ★
Begin about 10 feet right of *Small Business*, on the left side of the face. Go up a loose pillar to a thin crack; higher, move right into another crack with a small yucca plant. **Pro:** Thin to 2 inches. **FA:** Craig Fry, Dave Bruckman; 2/88.

1181. **The Skeptic** (5.10c) Go up the gully and right of *Chamber of Commerce* to two arching cracks; this is the left-hand crack. Go up the crack, then stay right under the roof and finish as for *Peruvian Princess.* **Pro:** To 2 inches. **FA:** Jack Marshall, Ron White, Sam Owing, Robert Carrere; 10/87.

1182. **Peruvian Princess** (5.10c) (R) This is the right-hand of the two right-arching cracks; the routes join at the top. **Pro:** To 2 inches. **FA:** Jack Marshall, Ron White, Sam Owing, Robert Carrere; 10/87.

1183. **City Council** (5.9) ★ This and *Illicit Operations* lie on the right-hand section of the northeast side of The Amoeba, to the right of the central gully that divides the face. Climb a thin crack/ramp out left and around the corner; continue up a fist crack to a chimney. **Pro:** To 4+ inches. **FA:** Craig Fry, Dave Bruckman; 2/88.

1184. **Illicit Operations** (5.11c) ★ Begin at same spot as *City Council;* take a wide, low-angled lieback up and right to a ledge, then go up a thin crack in a rust-colored wall. **Pro:** Thin to 2.5 inches. **FA:** Craig Fry, Dave Bruckman; 2/88.

Lower Life-Form Rock

This formation lies about 225 feet right of the northeast face of the Amoeba. The rock and route are not pictured. Map, page 305.

1185. **Lower Life Forms** (5.10b) ★ Begin behind a tree; go up a steep finger-and-hand crack that splits higher up. **Pro:** To 2.5 inches. **FA:** Don Wilson, Karen Wilson, Ron White, Sam Owing, Doug Munoz; 10/87.

1186. No route.

John Bachar on the first lead of The Acid Crack *(5.12d).*

Hemingway Area and Roadside Rocks

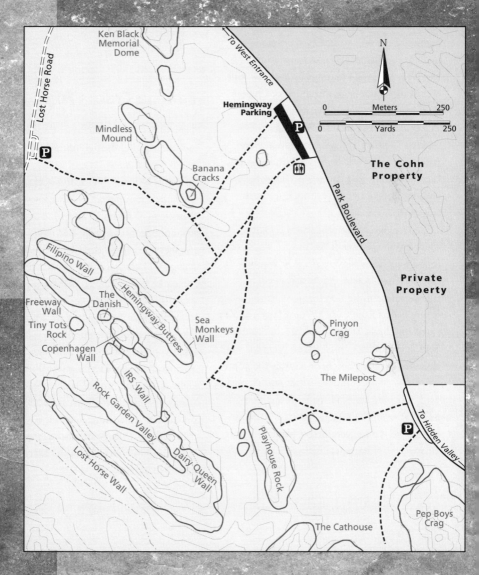

Ken Black Memorial Dome

Lost Horse Road

To West Entrance

Hemingway Parking

N

Meters 0 250

Yards 0 250

The Cohn Property

Mindless Mound

Banana Cracks

Park Boulevard

Private Property

Filipino Wall

Freeway Wall

The Danish

Hemingway Buttress

Sea Monkeys Wall

Pinyon Crag

Tiny Tots Rock

Copenhagen Wall

IRS Wall

The Milepost

Rock Garden Valley

To Hidden Valley

Lost Horse Wall

Dairy Queen Wall

Playhouse Rock

Pep Boys Crag

The Cathouse

HEMINGWAY AREA

The Hemingway Area encompasses the crags and rocks that lie west of Park Boulevard and south of Lost Horse Road beginning with the long east-facing Hemingway Buttress and ending at the Milepost. Crags covered include the Banana Cracks Formation, Mindless Mound, Hemingway Buttress, the IRS Wall, Copenhagen Wall, Dairy Queen Wall, Playhouse Rock, the Milepost, and Pinyon Crag. For nearly all of these areas, parking is either at the large Hemingway parking lot off Park Boulevard or at various turnouts along Park Boulevard. Detailed parking directions are described for each crag. Map, page 313.

Hemingway Buttress and the Dairy Queen Wall are two of the most popular crags in the park. Hemingway Buttress was one of the first crags outside Hidden Valley Campground to be developed, with routes dating back to the early 1970s. Many good to excellent climbs from 5.6 to 5.11 are found here. Expect other climbers; be prepared with alternative route choices or to wait for popular climbs. Most climbs face east and receive early morning sun and shade in the afternoon. Stay on the established trails to reduce damage to the delicate desert plant life.

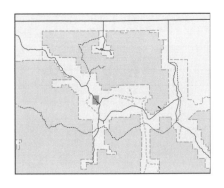

Banana Cracks Formation

This formation lies between Park Boulevard and the right end of Hemingway Buttress. The actual Banana Cracks lie on the west side of the formation's summit block. Park at the large Hemingway parking lot off Park Boulevard (7.6+ miles from the West Entrance and 0.9+ mile from the Intersection Rock/Real Hidden Valley intersection). There is a toilet located here. From the parking lot's right (north) end, head straight and a bit right on a marked trail toward a small formation that lies forward and to the right of Hemingway. The trail takes you directly to the Banana Cracks Formation. From Hemingway Buttress, turn right north on a signed trail to reach the formation. Alternatively, park at small turnout on the left (east) along Lost Horse Road 0.2 mile west of Park Boulevard; a marked trail leads southeast, straight to the base. Map, page 313.

Banana Cracks—West Face

The following routes start off a sloping ledge area some 35 feet off the ground. Approach up class 4 slabs to the left and traverse right to the base. To descend, downclimb left or behind, and then right. A rappel anchor (slings under a block) is off the back (northeast side), directly above *Rotten Banana*. The face gets shade in the morning and is sunny in the afternoon.

1187. **Papaya Crack** (5.11a) ★★ This fun thin crack lies left of the two arching *Banana Cracks;* take care with the rotten flake near the bottom. **Pro:** Thin to 2 inches. **FA:** Robert Finley; circa 1985.

1188. **Left Banana Crack** (5.10b/c) ★★ The left-hand, left-leaning crack. Another classic Jon Lonne crack discovery. **Pro:** To 3 inches. **FA:** Jon Lonne, Dave Ohlson, Martin McBirney; 4/76.

1189. **Right Banana Crack** (5.11b) ★★★ The right-hand, right-curving crack; the crux is near the top. Excellent liebacking and jams. **Pro:** To 3 inches. **FA:** Jon Lonne, Dave Ohlson, Martin McBirney; 4/76.

1190. **Banana Peal** (5.11b) ★★ Climb the face right of *Right Banana Crack,* past two bolts, then join that route at its crux. **Pro:** To 3 inches. **FA:** Peter Hayes, Dave Tidwell, Jeff Constine; 11/90.

1191. **Unknown** (5.12?) This four-bolt route climbs the steep southwest corner. **FA:** Unknown.

rap anchor

1193 thru 1195

1196

1192. **Tails of Poodles** (5.10b) ★ This wide crack lies on the south face, about 25 feet right and around the corner from the previous climbs. A rather bold free solo. **Pro:** To 2.5 inches. **FA:** Charles Cole; 1982.

Banana Cracks—Northeast Face

The following routes lie on the northeast face (facing Park Boulevard) of the Banana Cracks Formation. Descend to the left or rap from slings atop *Rotten Banana*. It sees sun in the morning and is shady in the afternoon.

1193. **Baby Banana** (5.7) This left-slanting crack can be started two ways. **(A):** Begin behind a tree to the left; go up into a left-facing corner, then traverse right to reach the upper part of the crack. **(B):** Begin directly up the crack (in the same spot as *Rotten Banana*). **Pro:** To 2.5 inches. **FA:** Don Wilson, Karen Wilson; 11/86.

1194. **Rotten Banana** (5.7) (R) Go up flakes to a right-facing flake just right of *Baby Banana,* then go up grainy face. It finishes at rap slings. **Pro:** To 2.5 inches. **FA:** Unknown.

1195. **Barfing at Zeldas** (5.10d) (R/X) This is the face and thin crack just right of *Rotten Banana*. Two fixed pins have been removed (either toprope or 5.10d R/X). **Pro:** Many thin to 2.5 inches. **FA:** Todd Gordon, Tom Michael, Mark Walters; 4/89.

1196. **Red Bull** (5.11b) (R) ★★ This thin crack with one bolt and a fixed pin is about 200 feet right (north) and in front of (east) the northeast face of the Banana Cracks Formation (and right of a steep wall with a horizontal crack). **Pro:** Thin to 2 inches. **FA:** Roy McClenahan, Dave Evans, Jim Angione.

Mindless Mound— West Face

This rock (really a continuation of the Banana Cracks Formation) lies about 175 feet left (north) of the *Banana Cracks* and slightly farther back (east). Routes are on the west face (afternoon sun). It can be recognized by a crack/vaguely rounded dihedral leading to a block/roof (*Don't Think Twice*). Though you can park at the Hemingway parking area, it is far closer to park at a small turnout on Lost Horse Road 0.2 mile south of the Park Boulevard junction. Map, page 313.

1197. **Rainy Day Women** (5.7) Start by a bush on the far left end of the cliff; diagonal cracks lead right to a handcrack. It's about 75 feet left of *Don't Think Twice*. **Pro:** To 3 inches. **FA:** Unknown.

1198. **Maggie's Farm** (5.7) This lies 15 feet right of *Rainy Day Women*. Go up a crack to a clean, small, brown dihedral. **Pro:** To 2.5 inches. **FA:** Unknown.

1199. **Don't Think Twice** (5.9) ★ The rounded corner to the roof/block. **Pro:** To 3+ inches. **FA:** Herb Laeger, Eve Laeger, Patrick Paul, Rich Smith; 11/82.

1200. **Shake the Monster** (5.11d) A three-bolt face just right of *Don't Think Twice*. **Pro:** To 2 inches. **FA:** Dave Mayville, Alan Bartlett; 6/90.

1201. **Idiot Wind** (5.8) Begin about 65 feet right of *Don't Think Twice* in a left-facing corner system; at the top move left, then back into a chimney. **Pro:** To 4 inches. **FA:** Bob Gaines, Keith Brueckner; 1/96.

Hemingway Buttress

Hemingway Buttress—East Face

This east-facing wall faces, and lies about 275 yards west of, Park Boulevard. It receives early morning sun and afternoon shade. It is one of several parallel "walls"—formations that include the IRS Wall, Rock Garden Valley, and Lost Horse Wall, etc. Hemingway Buttress has one of the highest concentration of routes in the park. Classics such as *Overseer, White Lightning, Poodles Are People Too,* and *Prepackaged* are often crowded.

To reach the buttress, park at the large parking area on the west side of Park Boulevard 0.2 mile southeast of the Lost Horse Road junction (7.6+ miles from the West Entrance; 0.9+ mile from the Intersection Rock/Real Hidden Valley intersection). A toilet is located here; the trail starts south of the toilet. Please stay on the established trails. Map, page 313.

Hemingway Buttress— Lower Left End, Sea Monkeys Wall

The following six routes lie on a small face about 150 feet left and a bit down from the left end of the main wall. They see morning sun; shade in the afternoon. Map, page 313.

1202. **Us versus Them** (5.7) Start behind the left side of a tree; go up a left-slanting crack/ramp that goes over a roof. **Pro:** To 2.5 inches. **FA:** Alan Bartlett, Dave Mayville, Laurel Colella; 6/00.

1203. **Still Pumpin'** (5.11a) This starts right of *Us Versus Them,* just left of a right-facing corner and wide crack/chimney (*Slander Master*) and behind the right side of the tree. This overhanging crack curves up and right to meet *Slander Master* at midheight. **FA:** Dave Mayville; 7/00.

1204. **Slander Master** (5.9+) This is the right-facing corner with a wide crack/chimney on the left side of the Sea Monkeys Wall. **Pro:** To 4+ inches. **FA:** Alan Bartlett; 7/00.

1205. **Sea Monkeys** (5.10c) (R) Start at *Ant Farm,* undercling left, go over the roof, then go up the left-slanting crack. **Pro:** To 2 inches. **FA:** Todd Swain, Debbie Brenchley; 11/91.

1206. **Ant Farm** (5.8) Climb flakes up to a ledge, then go up a brown left-facing corner. Rap from a tree 20 feet right of the finish. **Pro:** Thin to 2 inches. **FA:** Alan Bartlett, Rick Briggs; 7/90.

1207. **Horn Dog** (5.10c) ★ The face right of *Ant Farm.* **Pro:** Fixed pin; three bolts. **FA:** Dave Evans, Margie Floyd, Brian Polvony, Randy Perez, Cyndie Bransford, Todd Gordon; 10/91.

Hemingway Buttress—Left End

The following climbs lie on the left end of the main upper Hemingway Buttress. The face gets morning sun and is shady all afternoon. Map, page 313.

Descents:

- 60-foot rappel off the top of *Roadrunner;*
- 110-foot rappel right of the top of *Poodles Are People Too;*
- 80-foot rappel from the top of *The Importance of Being Ernest;*
- Downclimb left of *Poodle Jive* (5.6/5.7);
- Downclimb the left end of the rock.

1208. **More Funky Than Junky** (5.10a) Climb a slab to a small square roof; go up a crack in corner above the right side of the roof. **Pro:** To 2 inches. **FA:** (TR) Roger Whitehead, Mike Ayon, Mike Wolfe, Ed White; 3/85. **FA** (Lead): Unknown.

1209. **The Roadrunner** (5.11c) ★★★ Face climb along the thin left-arching crack on the south-facing wall, just right of *More Funky Than Junky.* A little loose at the bottom, but good patina above; sustained. **Pro:** Thin to 1.5 inches; four bolts; one fixed pin; two-bolt anchor/60-foot rap. **FA:** Bob Gaines; 11/95.

1210. **Smoke-a-Bowl** (5.9) ★ This is right of *The Roadrunner* and just left of the arête. Head up the corner/ramp to a bolt, then right around the corner and up cracks. **Pro:** To 2 inches; two-bolt anchor/rap. **FA:** Mike Ayon, Roger Whitehead; 3/85.

1211. **Rock Wren** (5.10a) ★★ Start up *Smoke-A-Bowl,* but move left up the arête past three bolts to *The Roadrunner* anchor. **Pro:** To 2 inches; two-bolt anchor/60-foot rap. **FA:** Bob Gaines, Yvonne Gaines; 11/95.

1212. **Hernie, Hernie, Hernie** (5.8) ★ Go up the fin to the left of *Funky Dung,* then right, crossing that route. Go up and right on the face (one bolt) to cracks. **Pro:** To 2.5 inches. **FA:** Todd Gordon, Cyndie Bransford; 5/93.

1213. **Funky Dung** (5.8) ★ Go up the crack in the right-facing corner to a large roof; move left and up, avoiding the roof, then up the crack above. This route follows the left-hand of three large crack systems (*Funky Dung, Dung Fu,* and *White Lightning*). **Pro:** To 2.5 inches. **FA:** John Long, Kevin Worrall; 12/74.

1214. **Overseer** (5.9) ★★★ Go up cracks in a shallow left-facing corner, then move right until you can head over the upper right side of the roof/headwall in a nice crack. **Pro:** To 2.5 inches. **FA:** Dan Ahlborn, Tim Powell; 4/77.

1215. **Overseer Direct Start** (5.10a) (R) ★★ Begin just right of the corner system (regular

start of *Overseer*); follow thin discontinuous cracks straight up to meet *Overseer* just below the roof/headwall. **Pro:** Thin to 2.5 inches. **FA:** Jonny Woodward; 1/83.

1216. **Dung Fu** (5.7) ★★ This route follows the middle of three large crack systems (*Funky Dung, Dung Fu,* and *White Lightning*). It begins in a right-facing corner, becoming wide about halfway up. **Pro:** To 4+ inches. **FA:** John Long, Rick Accomazzo, Richard Harrison; 2/74.

1217. **Pig in Heat** (5.9) (R) ★★ Start up *White Lightning* for 15 to 20 feet, then move left and up on the face to a bolt; continue up past various flakes. **Pro:** Thin to 1.5 inches. **FA:** Matt Cox, Randy Vogel, Jim Dutzi; 2/76.

1218. **Pig in Heat Direct Start** (5.10b/c) (R) ★ Climb an unprotected face (crux is the first 10 feet) straight up past a large loose flake to join *Pig in Heat.* **FA:** Unknown.

1219. **White Lightning** (5.7) ★★★ This prominent straight crack was the first route on Hemingway and is perhaps the most obvious line on the entire face. It is also very popular. It follows the rightmost of three large crack systems (*Funky Dung, Dung Fu,* and *White Lightning*). The crux is about 15 to 20 feet up. Take the left crack at the top. It is wide in places. **Pro:** To 4 inches. **FA:** Chris Wegener; Roy Naasz; 3/73.

1220. **Poodles Are People Too** (5.10b) ★★★★ A Hemingway classic; more of a face climb with excellent crack pro. Go up the thin crack on the face just right of *White Lightning* (5.10b); where the routes meet near the top, take the right-hand crack (5.8). This is the first "Poodle" route at Josh; it was named after Charles Cole's very large standard poodle, Gus. The "poodle" thing just got out of hand after that. **Pro:** Several thin to 2 inches. **FA:** Randy Vogel, Charles Cole; 2/80.

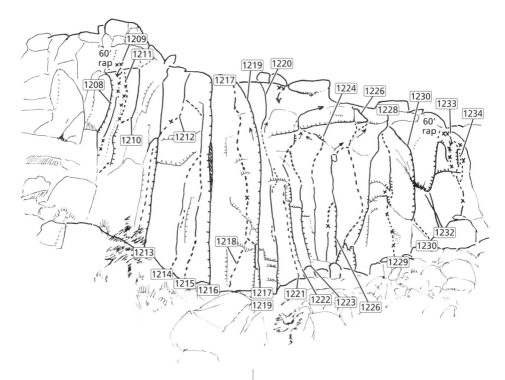

1221. **Man's Best Friend** (5.9) (TR) The arête left of *Poodlesby;* it joins that route above the roof. **FA:** Todd Swain, Linda Maron; 10/90.

1222. **Poodlesby** (5.6) Go up the crack in the right-facing corner, over a small roof, then continue up the face until you can head back right to finish over a small roof. Like *Solosby* (and numerous other Josh routes), it was established free solo. **Pro:** To 2.5 inches. **FA:** Darryl Nakahira; 11/82.

1223. **Coyote Bait** (5.7+) Begin just right of *Poodlesby.* Head up the left-facing corner, over the right side of the roof, then join *Poodlesby.* **Pro:** To 2.5 inches. **FA:** Dave Evans, Margie Floyd, Jim Angione; 4/89.

1224. **Such a Poodle** (5.8+) (R) ★ Begin in a thin crack to the right of *Coyote Bait;* follow this straight up. When the crack ends continue up and a bit right on a face and cracks. **Pro:** Thin to 2.5 inches. **FA:** Darryl Nakahira, Randy Vogel; 11/82.

1225. **Golden Years** (5.9+) ★ Go up a very thin seam just left of *Feltoneon Physics* past a fixed pin and bolt, then move left to join *Feltoneon Physics.* **Pro:** To 2 inches. **FA:** Todd Gordon, Cyndie Bransford, Jim Angione, Dave Evans, Margie Floyd; 6/89.

1226. **Feltoneon Physics** (5.8) ★★ Start off a block into a small right-facing corner. Above continue in the crack, which tends up and right. **Pro:** Thin to 4 inches. **FA:** Randy Vogel, Charles Cole; 2/80.

1227. **Gift Wrapped** (5.10d) ★★ (TR) Begin just right of *Feltoneon Physics.* Head up and right to the arête of *Prepackaged,* then left on the face to finish up *Feltoneon Physics.* **FA:** Bob Gaines; 4/00.

1228. Prepackaged (5.10a) ★★★ This is a good crack route, though pro may be a little tricky at the beginning. Start off a boulder/flake against the face, go up the right-slanting thin crack in a corner (5.9/5.10a), then up over a bulge. Higher, head up and right. **Pro:** To 2.5 inches. **FA:** John McGowen, Rick Smith, Herb Laeger; 2/77.

1229. The Sun Also Rises (5.12b) Begin right of *Prepackaged*. Climb the face (5.11c), then go up over an overhang (5.12a/b) into a crack system; loose and funky. **Pro:** Thin to 3 inches; four bolts. **FA:** Bob Gaines, Dave Mayville, Tommy Romero; 5/95.

Hemingway Buttress—Center

The following climbs lie on the center section of the main upper Hemingway Buttress. The face gets morning sun and is shady all afternoon. Map, page 313.

Descents:

- 80-foot rappel from the top of *The Importance of Being Ernest;*
- 120-foot rappel off the top of *Moveable Feast;*
- Downclimb just left of *Poodle Jive* (5.6/5.7);
- Downclimb the left end of the rock;
- Downclimb the gully left of *The Old Man and the Poodle.*

1230. Spoodle (5.9) ★ Go up the somewhat unattractive crack in a corner, then up a wide crack over a roof/bulge. **Pro:** To 2.5 inches. **FA:** Brian Povolny, Steve Strong, Tom Michael, Todd Gordon; 10/86.

1231. To Have and Have Not (5.11b) ★ (TR) The face between *Spoodle* and *The Importance of Being Ernest.* **FA:** Bob Gaines, Erik Kramer-Webb; 4/01.

1232. The Importance of Being Ernest (5.10c/d) (R) ★★★ One of the best routes on Hemingway Buttress, but a bit sporty. Go up the left-slanting X crack (5.10c/d), then right and over a roof. Finish up a thin crack/face (5.10c; tricky thin pro) to a final bulge. **Pro:** Several very thin and small cams to 2 inches; two-bolt anchor/rap. **FA:** Darryl Nakahira, Randy Vogel; 1982.

1233. Death in the Afternoon (5.11b) ★★ Start right of *The Importance of Being Ernest,* atop the highest boulders. Make a "bouldery" move off the block (5.11b; height-dependent), then go up past a bolt. Above, head left and over a roof; then stay right of *The Importance Of Being Ernest* (5.11a) past three more bolts. Either stick clip the first bolt or use small gear to protect the crux move getting off the block. **Pro:** Medium; four bolts; two-bolt anchor/rap. **FA:** Bob Gaines, Tommy Romero; 4/96.

1234. The Bullfighter (5.11b) ★★ Start as for *Death in the Afternoon* (5.11b; height-dependent), but above the first bolt go right over the roof into a small right-facing corner (5.11a), passing two more bolts. **Pro:** To 1.5 inches; three bolts; two-bolt anchor/rap. **FA** (TR) upper crux (aka *Frank and Ernest*): Todd Swain; 10/90. **FA** (Lead): Bob Gaines, Tommy Romero, Todd Gordon; 5/96.

1235. Poodle Jive (5.9) The short left-leaning crack. **Pro:** To 3 inches. **FA:** Dave Evans; 1989.

1236. Scary Poodles (5.11b) ★★★ Another classic Hemingway route; more pumpy to lead than really hard. Go up the lower left diagonal crack, then up to a second thin diagonal crack. Follow this past a fixed pin (5.11a/b), finishing up a tricky shallow arch (5.10d). **Pro:** Thin to 1 inch. **FA:** Darryl Nakahira, Randy Vogel; 11/82.

1237. **Poodle in Shining Armor** (5.8) Begin just right of a large chimney. Go up a loose crack to blocks where you can move left into a crack splitting the right side of the summit block. **Pro:** To 2 inches. **FA:** Randy Vogel, Darryl Nakahira, Charles Cole; 11/82.

1238. **This Ain't the Poodle-Oids** (5.8+) (R) Start up the loose chimney just left of *Poodle-Oids from the Deep,* join *Poodle-Oids from the Deep* where that route slants back to the right. **Pro:** To 3+ inches; two-bolt anchor/120-foot rappel. **FA** (by mistake): Alan Bartlett, Johnny Gibson; 9/97.

1239. **Poodle-Oids from the Deep** (5.10b) Go up the central crack that slants left and passes a small roof before heading back to the right and over another roof/bulge. **Pro:** To 2.5 inches; two-bolt anchor/120-foot rappel. **FA:** Dave Evans, Todd Gordon; 5/86.

1240. **Moveable Feast** (5.10d) ★★ Begin up the crack of *Poodle-Oids from the Deep,* but where the crack leans left, head right and up

on the plated face past four bolts. **Pro:** To 2.5 inches; two-bolt anchor/120-foot rappel. **FA:** Roy McClenahan, Helga Brown; 3/88.

1241. **On the Nob** (5.10b) Follow a left-slanting thin crack, then go right up a crack that widens to become wide slot near the right margin of the face; finish up to the summit. **Pro:** To 3.5 inches; two-bolt anchor/120-foot rappel. **FA:** Scott Erler; 1981.

1242. **976** (5.9+) (R) The short crack beginning just right of *On the Nob.* **Pro:** To 3 inches. **FA:** Dave Evans, Margie Floyd, Jim Angione, Cyndie Bransford, Todd Gordon; 6/89.

Hemingway Buttress— Right End

The following climbs lie on the less-crowded right section of Hemingway Buttress. The routes see morning sun and are shady all afternoon. Map, page 313.

Descents:

- Downclimb gully left of *The Old Man and the Poodle;*
- 60-foot rappel from atop *Astropoodle;*
- Downclimb the leftmost gully off the back (west) side (class 3) and return in the notch to the right of *Head Over Heals* etc. by tunneling in through the lowest inconspicuous tunnel to the base.

1243. **The Old Man and the Poodle** (5.8) Begin just right of the gully; head up and right to this handcrack. **Pro:** To 2.5 inches. **FA:** Randy Vogel, Darryl Nakahira, Maria Cranor; 11/82.

1244. **For Whom the Poodle Tolls** (5.9) ★ Begin down and right of last route. Head straight up a thin to handcrack. **Pro:** To 2.5 inches. **FA:** Randy Vogel, Maria Cranor, Darryl Nakahira, Marjorie Shovlin; 11/82.

1245. **A Farewell to Poodles** (5.9) The obvious crack system to the right of *For Whom the Poodle Tolls.* **Pro:** To 2.5 inches. **FA:** Charles Cole, Marjorie Shovlin, Maria Cranor; 11/82.

1246. **Head over Heals** (5.10a) ★★★ Definitely the best route on the right end of Hemingway. Begin down near the corner of the rock. Go up to the roof near the corner, then head left and up left-leaning cracks to the top. **Pro:** Thin to 2 inches. **FA:** Herb Laeger et al.; 1979.

1247. **Astropoodle** (5.10c) ★★ Climb *Head Over Heals* around the roof, then go straight up, encountering a bolt at the next roof. Head up and a bit right past the roof and another bolt to meet *Space Walk*. **Pro:** To 2 inches. **FA:** Herb Laeger, Bob Kamps, Kevin Wright; 10/88.

1248. **Mind over Matter** (5.10a/b) (R) ★★ (not shown on photo) Start as for *Head Over Heals,* but turn the roof on the right and climb past a bolt directly up. Finish on *Space Walk.* **Pro:** To 3 inches. **FA:** Bob Gaines, Yvonne Gaines; 3/96.

1249. **Space Walk** (5.8) ★ (not shown on photo) Start 25 feet right of *Head Over Heals* and climb a handcrack that leads left around a corner to a large ledge. **Pro:** To 3 inches. **FA:** Herb Laeger, Eve Laeger, Mike Jaffe, Rich Smith; 1/80.

1250. **Mind over Splatter** (5.10a) (not shown on photo) This route starts just right of the start of *Space Walk;* go up a thin flake/crack to the obvious clean dihedral. Follow that to the top. **Pro:** Thin to 2 inches. **FA:** Todd Swain; 4/85.

Hemingway Buttress— Far Right End

The following climbs lie on the far right end of Hemingway Buttress. This section of cliff is separated from the rest of the right end by a deep cleft/gully located just right of *Head Over Heals* et al. To descend, downclimb off back (west) side (class 3), and return in the notch to the left of *Suspect Rock* etc. by tunneling through the lowest inconspicuous tunnel to the base. The routes get morning sun and are shady all afternoon. Map, page 313.

1251. **Suspect Rock** (5.9) (not shown on photo) The two-bolt route on the far left of the right wall of the gully, left of *Puzzlin' Evidence*. **Pro:** To 3 inches. **FA:** Bob Gaines, Keith Brueckner; 3/96.

1252. **Puzzlin' Evidence** (5.11b) This is near the left side of the right wall of the gully. Go up the face past one bolt to a curving crack (fixed pin), then to the face (one bolt). Pro To 2 inches. **FA:** Dave Evans, Todd Gordon, Craig Fry; 10/87.

1253. **Fusion without Integrity** (5.10b) Face climb past two bolts to a thin crack; begins 15 feet right of *Puzzlin' Evidence*. **Pro:** Thin to 2 inches. **FA:** Pat Brennan, Todd Gordon, Dave Vaught, Frank Bentwood, Quinn McCleod; 1/81.

1254. **Route 182** (5.9) Begin about 12 feet right of *Fusion Without Integrity*. Go up cracks and flakes to a brown right-facing corner. **Pro:** To 3 inches. **FA:** Unknown.

1255. **Ravens Do Nasty Things to My Bottom** (5.9) Begin behind trees about 25 feet right of *Route 182*. Head up discontinuous cracks and flakes to a ledge/ramp, then go up and left. **Pro:** To 3 inches. **FA:** Dave Evans, Todd Gordon; 5/86.

1256. **Easy as Pi** (5.7) Start by a pine tree about 15 feet right of *Ravens Do Nasty Things to My Bottom*. Go up the left-leaning handcrack to a ledge/ramp, then up and left to the top. **Pro:** To 2.5 inches. **FA:** Todd Swain; 1985.

Filipino Wall

This "wall" is the distinct, separate, and extreme right extension of Hemingway Buttress. Since it lies adjacent to Lost Horse Road and is best (easily) approached from a parking area 0.2 mile down Lost Horse Road, it is described in the Lost Horse Road section of the guide (see page 241).

Hemingway Buttress— West Face

This seldomly visited side of Hemingway Buttress faces the IRS/Copenhagen Walls. Park at a large parking area on the west side of Park Boulevard 0.2 mile southeast of its intersection with Lost Horse Road (7.6+ miles from the West Entrance; 0.9+ mile from the Intersection Rock/Real Hidden Valley intersection). Take the trail toward Hemingway Buttress, but after nearly 100 yards, take a left-hand branch. This trail terminates at a large boulder field lying below the IRS/Dairy Queen Walls. Head up and right along the west face of Hemingway. You could also approach from vicinity of the Freeway Wall (page 242). The face gets morning shade and afternoon sun. Descend the south end of Hemingway.

1257. **Execution Time** (5.11d) ★★★ Climb the face with seams, left of *American Express*. **Pro:** To 2 inches; four bolts; two-bolt anchor (70-foot) rap. **FA:** Bob Gaines; 4/01.

1258. **American Express** (5.9) ★ This crack lies near the center of the west face; it leans slightly left and leads to the summit block. **Pro:** To 2.5 inches. **FA:** John Yablonski, Mike Lechlinski; 12/79.

1259. **Layaway Plan** (5.11a) ★★ (TR) This crack is 5 feet right of the last route. It first leans a bit right, then heads back a bit left. **FA:** John Bachar, John Yablonski, Mike Lechlinski; 12/79.

1260. **Cash and Carry** (5.9) Start 10 feet right of *Layaway Plan,* then traverse up and right to a crack that curves all the way back left to meet the upper part of *Layaway Plan.* **Pro:** To 2.5 inches. **FA:** Unknown.

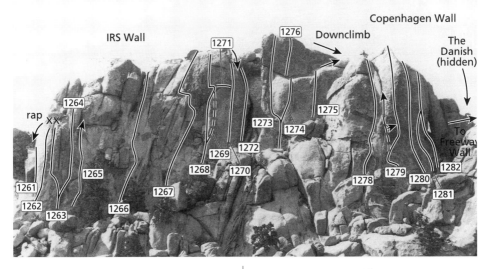

The IRS Wall

The IRS Wall—East Face

This wall faces east and lies behind (west) and left (south) of Hemingway Buttress. It receives morning sun and afternoon shade. The wall classic, *Tax Man,* is quite popular. Park at a large parking area on the west side of Park Boulevard 0.2 mile southeast of Lost Horse Road (7.6+ miles from the West Entrance; 0.9+ mile from the Intersection Rock/Real Hidden Valley intersection). A toilet is located here; the trail starts south of the toilet. Take the trail toward Hemingway Buttress, but after nearly 100 yards, take a left-hand branch. This trail terminates at a large boulder field below the IRS/Dairy Queen Walls. Head up and right from here. You can also approach from vicinity of the Freeway Wall (see page 242) by walking behind Copenhagen Wall. Map, page 313.

Descents:

- 70-foot rappel from atop *Alf's Arête;*
- Downclimb the back side and left end;
- 85-foot rappel from atop *Tax Man;*
- Downclimb right, then down the block/gap between Copenhagen Wall and IRS Wall.

1261. **Squatter's Right** (5.10d) ★★ The clean, but very short, overhanging corner at the far left end of the IRS Wall, just left of *Alf's Arête.* Jon Lonne was known for ferreting out hard crack problems. **Pro:** To: 3+ inches. **FA:** Jon Lonne, Dave Ohlson; 2/76.

1262 **Alf's Arête** (5.11a/b) ★★★★ (Sport) The excellent, rounded arête on the left end of the IRS Wall. This classic line was discovered and begun by Alf Randell, who relinquished the lead to Alan Nelson who proceeded to drill and climb nearly to the top. According to Alan, Alf would not pay out any more rope unless Alan came down and let Alf top out first, which Alan reluctantly did. **Pro:** Seven bolts; two-bolt anchor/rap. **FA:** Alan Nelson, Alf Randell; 12/87.

1263. **Nuclear Waste** (5.10b) Just left of a right-facing corner, Go up past one bolt to thin cracks. You might be able to rap from Alf's Arête. **Pro:** Thin to 2 inches. **FA:** Mike

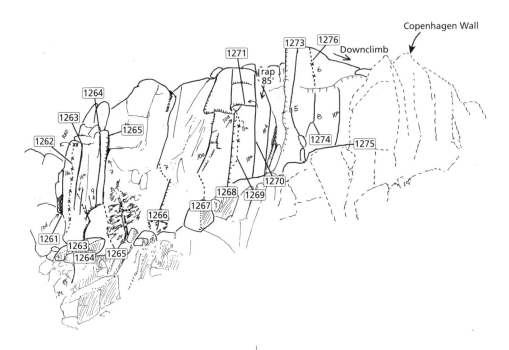

Lechlinski, Mari Gingery, Randy Vogel, Maria Cranor; 1982.

1264. Atomic Pile (5.9) Go up a right-facing corner and cracks just right of *Nuclear Waste.* **Pro:** To 2 inches. **FA:** Randy Vogel, Maria Cranor; 4/80.

1265. The Loophole (5.7) (R) Begin off a flake just right of *Atomic Pile.* Go up buckets and cracks to an overhanging dihedral; avoid this by tunneling through a hole at its base. **Pro:** To 3 inches. **FA:** Alan Bartlett, Laurel Colella; 6/00.

1266. Commander Cody (5.7) Climb cracks and the plated face midway between *Atomic Pile* and *Tax Free.* **Pro:** To 2.5 inches. **FA:** Todd Gordon, Cody Dolnick; 11/86.

1267. The Thing (5.10a) Go up a plated face to a right-slanting crack, then up and around the left side of a roof. **Pro:** To 3 inches. **FA:** Pol Anderson, Chris Breemer, Ola Nilsson; 1/90.

1268. Tax Free (5.10d) (R) Go up the left-facing dihedral to a roof; head a bit right, then left and up the crack above. **Pro:** To 2.5 inches. **FA:** Tom Gilje et al.; 1982.

1269. Bullet Head (5.11a) (R) Begin as for *Tax Free,* then go up the arête to the right, past two bolts, joining *Tax Free* at the roof. **Pro:** To 2 inches. **FA:** Chris Breemer, Pol Anderson, Bill Willey, Ola Nilssan; 1/90.

1270. Tax Man (5.10a) ★★★★ A nice, straight, thin crack (crux near the bottom). The first route on the formation and an obvious "plum" found by early activists. **Pro:** Thin to 2 inches; two-bolt anchor/rap. **FA:** Tim Powell, Dan Ahlborn; 4/76.

1271. Tax Evasion (Variation) (5.10a) ★★ Climb *Tax Man* to a horizontal, then traverse left to the last crack of *Tax Free.* **Pro:** To 2.5 inches. **FA:** Mike Lechlinski et al.; 1982.

1272. Bloody Tax Break (5.10b) ★★ The thin crack about 6 feet right of *Tax Man.* Would be nicer if the crack wasn't so close to the chimney on the right. **Pro:** Thin to 2 inches. **FA:** Steve Gerberding, Jay Punkman; 2/83.

1273. **Mr. Bunny's Tax Shelter** (5.5) Begin off a boulder on the left end of the higher right-hand section of IRS Wall, about 30 feet right of *Tax Man*. Take the crack up and left, then up. **Pro:** To 4 inches. **FA:** Alan Bartlett; 5/88.

1274. **Mr. Bunny versus Six Unknown Agents** (5.8) ★★ Start in same spot as *Mr. Bunny's Tax Shelter*, but climb the right-slanting thin cracks to a large ledge. **Pro:** Thin to 2 inches. **FA:** Unknown.

1275. **Mr. Bunny's Refund Check** (5.10a) ★★ Climb the straight-up thin crack 20 feet right of *Mr. Bunny Versus Six Unknown Agents*. **Pro:** Thin to 2 inches. **FA:** Randy Vogel, Maria Cranor; 4/80.

1276. **H & R Block** (5.6) ★ The upper juggy face begins where the last two routes finish. **Pro:** Two bolts, to 2 inches. **FA:** Warren Hughes, Mike Van Volkem; 10/90.

1277. **Hidden Taxes** (5.6) (not shown on photo) This short finger crack is in the corridor just right of the descent for the preceding routes. **Pro:** Thin to 2 inches. **FA:** Warren Hughes; 10/90.

Copenhagen Wall

This wall faces east (early sun, afternoon shade) and lies behind and left of Hemingway Buttress and just right and slightly in front of the IRS Wall. Park at a large parking area on the west side of Park Boulevard 0.2 mile southeast of Lost Horse Road (7.6+ miles from the West Entrance; 0.9+ mile from the Intersection Rock/Real Hidden Valley intersection). A toilet is located here; the trail starts south of the toilet. Take the trail toward Hemingway Buttress, but after nearly 100 yards, take a left-hand branch. This trail terminates at a large boulder field below the IRS/Dairy Queen Walls. Head up and right, staying right of the base of the IRS Wall.

Copenhagen Wall is also commonly approached from Lost Horse Road, as it lies just beyond the upper end of the Freeway Wall formation (see page 242). Downclimb off the back and chimney down. Map, page 313.

1278. **It Satisfies** (5.7) Begin near a tree; go over a small arch, then up the obvious crack. **Pro:** To 3 inches. **FA:** Alan Bartlett, Katie Wilkinson; 5/88.

1279. **Quantum Jump** (5.10c/d) ★★★ Go up the right-slanting thin crack to the straight-up crack (tricky thin pro), finishing with the face near the top. **Variations: (A)** Exit the right-slanting crack early, go up a thin crack, then move back right on the face (5.10b/c) to rejoin the straight crack; or **(B)** Exit as for variation (A), but go up, then left, into another crack system altogether to the left (5.10a/b). **Pro:** Very thin to 2 inches. **FA:** Herb Laeger et al.; 2/77.

1280. **The Schrodinger Equation** (5.10b) (R) ★★ Go up a left-slanting thin crack to the face (5.10b R), then past one bolt to another thin crack. **Pro:** Very thin to 2 inches; one bolt. **FA** (TR): Dave Evans, Mike Lechlinski, Craig Fry, John Long; 11/79. **FA** (Lead/without protection; bolt added later): Johnny Woodward; 1985.

1281. **Heavy Mettle** (5.10d) ★★ Start just right of *The Schrodinger Equation*. Go up discontinuous thin cracks and three bolts to join the upper crack on *Heavy Water*. **Pro:** Thin to 2 inches. **FA** (TR): Alan Roberts, Todd Swain; 1/89. **FA** (Lead): Herb Laeger, Bob Yoho; 2/89.

1282. **Heavy Water** (5.10a) (R) Begin off the ledge up and right, then go up and left in a crack. **Pro:** To 2 inches. **FA:** John Bachar, Mike Lechlinski; 4/82.

1283. **Perhaps the Surgeon General** (5.8) (not shown on photo) This face climb with one bolt is on the back side of Copenhagen Wall, up and right through the tunnel from *Heavy Water*. **Pro:** To 2.5 inches. **FA:** Alan Bartlett, Todd Gordon; 10/88.

The Danish

The next two routes are located on the east face of a small rock just right (north) of the main Copenhagen Wall. They get early sun and are shady all afternoon. The Danish is easily approached from vicinity of the upper Freeway Wall (see page 242). Neither the crag or routes are pictured. Map, page 313.

1284. **Limpy Grandma** (5.8) ★ Located on the left-hand arête. Go up the crack (fixed pins) to two bolts. Two-bolt anchor/rap. **FA:** Todd Gordon, Tom Burke, Andrea Tomaszewski; 5/00.

1285. **Dial-a-Pile** (5.5) This is right of *Limpy Grandma*. Go up a crack right of a tree, then traverse right to another crack leading to the top. **Pro:** To 2.5 inches; rappel off *Limpy Grandma*. **FA:** Alan Bartlett, Katie Wilkinson; 5/88.

Dairy Queen Wall

This east-facing formation lies to the left
(south) of the IRS Wall and left and behind
Hemingway Buttress. Routes receive morning sun and afternoon shade. Park at the
Hemingway parking area (7.6+ miles from
the West Entrance; 0.9+ mile from the
Intersection Rock/Real Hidden Valley intersection). Follow the trail that starts just south
of the toilet; then take the left-hand split
toward the formation. Scramble the last bit
up boulders to the base.

Alternatively, park at the small Playhouse
Rock turnout on the west side of the road
7.9 miles from the West Entrance and 0.7
mile from the Intersection Rock/Real
Hidden Valley intersection and follow a
clearly marked trail that heads around the
right end of Playhouse Rock and ends below
Dairy Queen Wall. Scramble the last bit up
boulders to the base. The rock is named after

the old Dairy Queen fast-food stand in what
was the far eastern edge of Yucca Valley that
was a favorite of Kevin and Tim Powell's and
their friends (now a Mexican restaurant
named Santana's). Map, page 313.

Dairy Queen Wall—Left Side

The left section of the formation has slab
routes below and steep, overhanging climbs
to the upper left (the Upper Tier). The leaning and overhanging right-facing corner at
the upper left is *Pat Adams Dihedral*. You can
approach the Upper Tier routes via a class 4
crack/gully directly below the rappel at the
base of *Chili Dog*. The wall faces east, and
receives morning sun and afternoon shade.

Descents:

- Rappel off top of *Norm;*
- 80-foot rappel off the base of *Chili Dog;*
- Downclimb off to the left;
- Downclimb off to the right.

Dairy Queen Wall—Left Side, Lower Left End

All these routes begin from the base of the left end of the left side of Dairy Queen Wall. All routes lie to the left of a fourth-class gully that heads up right of center of the left end, terminating on a large ledge about halfway up the face.

1286. **Blizzard** (5.10a) (TR) This wide crack lies up the gully on the left end. Loose. **FA:** Unknown.

1287. **Foot Massage** (5.10b) ★ Climb the face to the right of *Blizzard* past four bolts to a crack, then over roof. **Pro:** To 2.5 inches. **FA:** Todd Gordon, Dana Adler, Richard White, Cyndie Bransford, Pat Nay, Karen Roseme; 3/95.

1288. **Karl's Magic Goggles** (5.9+) (TR) (not shown on photo) Go up the face left of *Norm,* starting in the gully. **FA:** J. Hammerle; 4/95.

1289. **Norm** (5.10a) ★★★ Go up the face/arête on the left side of face. **Pro:** Five bolts; two-bolt anchor/rap. **FA:** Todd Gordon, Dana Adler, Cyndie Bransford, Jim Angione, Brian Haslam, Susan Alford; 3/95.

1290. **Snake Oil** (5.7) The long crack system just right of *Norm.* **Pro:** To 3 inches. **FA:** Unknown.

1291. **Faith Healer** (5.6) The crack system to the right of *Snake Oil.* **Pro:** To 3 inches. **FA:** Unknown.

1292. **Look Before You Leap** (5.8) Begin as for *Faith Healer,* but continue up and right on a thin flake, then goo right to join *Leap Erickson* for the last two bolts. **Pro:** To 2.5 inches. **FA:** Bob Gaines; 4/03.

1293. **Leap Erickson** (5.10b) ★ The seven-bolt face route up the center of the clean face. **Pro:** 1.5 to 2.5 inches for the anchor. **FA** (TR): Todd Swain; 10/89. **FA** (Lead): Unknown.

1294. **Leap Year Flake** (5.7) ★★★ Go up the thin crack to the right of *Leap Erickson,* then up and left on a thin flake. **Pro:** Thin to 2.5 inches. **FA:** Todd Gordon, Cyndie Bransford; 2/88.

1295. **Look Before You Leap** (Variation) (5.7) (R) Instead of following *Leap Year Flake* as it moves left out the flake, climb straight up the arête. **FA:** Todd Swain; 10/89.

Dairy Queen Wall—Left Side, Upper Tier Routes

All of the following routes begin from near a large ledge system above the center part of the crag. They are most easily approached via a class 4 crack/gully to the right of *Leap Year Flake.*

1296. **Brother from Another Planet** (5.11a) (R) ★★ The left of two bolted routes around left of *Pat Adams Dihedral.* **Pro:** Three bolts, to 2.5 inches for anchor. **FA:** Dave Evans, Todd Gordon.

1297. **Electric Free Gordon** (5.12a) (R) ★★ The right of two bolted routes around and left of *Pat Adams Dihedral,* on the arête. **Pro:** Four bolts; to 2.5 inches for anchor. **FA:** Tom Gilje, Mike Lechlinski.

1298. **Pat Adams Dihedral** (5.11b/c) ★★★★ The obvious, strenuous, and overhanging corner system on the upper block. **Pro:** To 2 inches, with several in the 1- to 2-inch range. **FA:** Pat Adams; 1979.

1299. **Toxic Waltz** (5.12a) ★★★ This climbs the arête 15 feet to the right of *Pat Adams Dihedral.* **Pro:** Four or five bolts. **FA:** Tom Gilje, Mike Lechlinski.

1300. **Tofutti** (5.8) The crack right of *Toxic Waltz,* finishing up through the summit block. **Pro:** To 2.5 inches. **FA:** Unknown.

1301. **Double Delight** (5.7) Start as for *Tofutti,* but climb the right-leaning crack ending just right of the summit block. **Pro:** To 3 inches. **FA:** Unknown.

1302. **Chili Dog** (5.6) Start to the right of *Tofutti* and *Double Delight* in a left-facing corner; go up this to the end as for *Double Delight.* **Pro:** To 2.5 inches. **FA:** Unknown.

1303. **Brazier Food** (5.6) This is the very thin flake and crack to the right of *Chili Dog.* **Pro:** Thin to 2.5 inches. **FA:** Todd Swain; 10/89.

Dairy Queen Wall—Left Side, Lower Right Routes

The following climbs lie on the right end of the left side of Dairy Queen Wall and begin from the ground. All lie to the right of a fourth-class gully that leads to the ledge halfway up the center of the left end of the crag.

1304. **The Mojus (aka Slushie)** (5.10c) ★ This route lies on the large slab to the right of the class 4 gully. Face climb past nine bolts to short crack and a two-bolt belay below the summit blocks. Rappel (100+ feet) or descend to the right. **FA:** Rondo Powell, Jo Bently.

1305. **Addams Family (aka Get Right or Get Left)** (5.9) ★ Begin up the thin crack just right of *The Mojus;* follow this to the ledge below the blocks. **Pro:** Thin to 2 inches. **FA:** Tom Beck, Tim Ramsey; 1982.

1306. **Gomez** (5.10a) ★ Go up the face to the right of *Addams Family* to a crack system. **Pro:** Thin to 2.5 inches; three bolts. **FA** (TR): Todd Swain; 10/89. **FA** (Lead): Unknown.

1307. **Lurch** (5.8) Begin off a sloping ledge up and right of *Gomez*. Go up a left-facing corner, then up a thin crack and corner. **Pro:** Thin to 2.5 inches. **FA:** Unknown.

Dairy Queen Wall—Right Side

The right side of Dairy Queen Wall is steep, very knobby, and has several cracks of varying widths. This section of the wall has many easy to moderate routes on good rock. It is quite popular (expect crowds).

Park at the Hemingway parking area (7.6+ miles from the West Entrance; 0.9+ mile from the Intersection Rock/Real Hidden Valley intersection). Take the trail that starts just south of the toilet, then take the left-hand fork toward the formation. Scramble the last bit up boulders to the base. Alternatively, park at the small Playhouse Rock turnout on the west side of Park Boulevard (7.9 miles from the West Entrance; 0.7 mile from the Intersection Rock/Real Hidden Valley intersection) and follow a clearly marked trail that heads around the right end of Playhouse Rock, ending below Dairy Queen Wall. Scramble the last bit up boulders to the base. The wall gets morning sun and afternoon shade. To descend, down-climb to the right. Map, page 313.

Advisory: It is not uncommon for groups and climbing classes to toprope one or more climbs in this area. If you place a toprope on a route and leave it up for more than a short time, you must be prepared to either share the rope with other climbers, or pull it down. Totally dominating this crag or these climbs with topropes and then being unwilling to share or pull your ropes is not only extremely rude, but might justify the removal of your ropes. Be courteous instead.

1308. **Possum Pie** (5.8) (not shown on photo) This route lies on a block down and left of *I Forgot to Have Babies*. Go up twin cracks, then left on the face to a crack through a roof. **Pro:** To 2.5 inches. **FA:** Todd Gordon, Brian Haslan; 3/95.

1309. **Unknown** (5.9) The crack and arête left of *I Forgot to Have Babies*. **Pro:** To 2.5 inches. **FA:** Unknown.

1310. **Squirrel Attack** (5.6) This crack lies 8 feet left of *I Forgot to Have Babies;* a number of variations on the exact line of this route have been done. **Pro:** To 3 inches. **FA:** John O'Connor, Dawn Rawlins; 4/96.

1311. **I Forgot to Have Babies** (5.10b) ★ (TR) Climb cracks on the arête on the left end of the wall, then up the face above. **FA:** Darrel Hensel, Dave Evans, Kate Duke, Todd Gordon; 5/88.

1312. **Airy Scene** (5.11b) ★★ Go up the face past several small bulges/horizontals. **Pro:** To 2.5 inches; four bolts. **FA:** Jeff Rhoads, Kelly Rhoads, Bobby Knight; 10/88.

1313. **Scrumdillyishus** (5.7) ★ The crack just right of *Airy Scene;* it slants left at start, then goes up in corners. This is the first route on the face. **Pro:** To 2.5 inches. **FA:** Tim Powell, Dan Ahlborn; 1976.

1314. **Frosty Cone** (5.7) ★★★ Begin immediately right of *Scrumdillyishus,* and head straight up the crack and juggy face. **Pro:** To 2.5 inches. **FA:** Unknown.

1315. **A Hot Fudge** (5.9) (R) ★ Go up the pocketed face with thin pro in discontinuous cracks on the right. **Pro:** Small wires to 2 inches. **FA:** Dave Wonderly, Jack Marshall; 12/86.

1316. **Dilly Bar** (5.5) The break/chimney near the center of the wall. **Pro:** To 2.4 inches. **FA:** Tim Powell; 4/76.

1317. **Mr. Misty Kiss** (5.7) ★★★ The obvious left-slanting crack just right of the break/chimney of *Dilly Bar.* **FA:** Dan Ahlborn, Tim Powell; 4/76.

1318. **Double Decker** (5.7) ★ Go up the thin crack (*Nuts and Cherries*) 12 feet right of *Mr. Misty Kiss,* then traverse left on jugs to a wide crack that goes to the top. **Pro:** To 3+ inches. **FA:** Unknown.

1319. **Bill's Nuts** (5.7) ★★ Begin as for *Double Decker,* but head up and left on big holds to a thin crack between the finish of *Double Decker* and *Nuts and Cherries.* **Pro:** Thin to 2 inches. **FA:** Bill MacBride, Amanda Bedoy; 3/99.

1320. **Nuts and Cherries** (5.6) Go up the thin crack 12 feet right of *Mr. Misty Kiss* to the top. **FA:** Dave Wonderly, Jack Marshall; 12/86.

1321. **Date Shake** (5.6) (not shown on photo) Go up twin cracks and big holds just right of *Nuts and Cherries.* **FA:** Dave Wonderly, Jack Marshall; 12/86.

1322. **Biological Clock** (5.9+) ★ (not shown on photo) This route is on the small wall right of Dairy Queen Wall, facing south. Climb a handcrack, then go over a roof and up plates past one bolt. **Pro:** To 2.5 inches. **FA:** Todd Gordon, Dave Evans, Kate Duke, Darrel Hensel, Alan Bartlett; 4/86.

Playhouse Rock

This nondescript east-facing formation lies about 175 yards west of Park Boulevard 0.6 mile southeast of Lost Horse Road (7.9 miles from the West Entrance; 0.7 mile from the Intersection Rock/Real Hidden Valley intersection). A turnout on the west side of the road is just south of the Milepost (a 50-foot pillar next to the road). This is a popular toprope and moderate lead area that gets sun in the morning and shade in the afternoon. Map, page 313.

Advisory: It is not uncommon for groups and climbing classes to toprope one or more climbs in this area. If you place topropes on routes and leave them up for more than a short time, you must be prepared to either share the ropes with other climbers or pull them down. Totally dominating this crag with topropes and then being unwilling to share or pull your ropes is not only extremely rude, but might justify the removal of your ropes. Be courteous instead.

1323. **Short and Scrappy** (5.8) (not shown on photo) This route is located in a chimney/alcove about 150 feet up and left of *Balancing Act;* it starts on a block. **Pro:** Thin to 3 inches. **FA:** Bob Gaines, Brian Prentice; 2/99.

1324. **Balancing Act** (5.10) ★ (TR) The face with three distinct ledges just left of *Final Act.* **FA:** Brian Prentice, Bob Gaines; 2/99.

1325. **Final Act** (5.4) ★ The left-facing corner on left side of the cliff. **Pro:** To 2.5 inches. **FA:** Dave Davis, Don O'Kelley; 3/76.

1326. **Break a Leg** (5.9) (R) ★ Climb the arête and face right of *Final Act* to a thin crack over a roof. Most will toprope. **Pro:** Thin to 2 inches. **FA** (bottom section, aka *Fighting the Slime*): Mike Law. **FA** (entire route): Jack Marshall, Dave Wonderly, A. Avarado; 11/86.

1327. **Curtain Call** (5.6) ★ Thin cracks beginning just right of *Break A Leg*. **Pro:** Thin to 2 inches. **FA:** Don O'Kelley, Dave Davis; 11/76.

1328. **Psycho Groove** (5.9) ★ Begin in the crack/groove with one bolt just right of *Curtain Call;* join *Curtain Call* higher. **FA:** Ken Black; 1983.

1329. **I'm So Embarrassed for You** (5.7) ★ Start just right of *Psycho Groove.* Go up the short right-facing corner to a left-facing dihedral, then go over the headwall. **Pro:** To 2 inches. **FA:** Randy Vogel, Charles Cole; 2/80.

1330. **Leading Lady** (5.9) (R) ★ Go up a left-slanting crack to the right of *I'm So Embarrassed for You,* then back right over a corner. **Pro:** Thin to 2 inches. **FA:** Jack Marshall, Dave Wonderly, A. Avarado; 11/86.

1331. **Beck's Bear** (5.7) ★ Climb the left-facing corner up to a crack. **Pro:** To 2.5 inches. **FA:** Tom Beck, Tim Ramsey, Curt Shanebeck; 11/78.

1332. **Stucca by a Yucca** (5.7) The twin crack right of *Beck's Bear,* then up and right from a pine tree. **FA:** Rachel Dobrotin, R. Shull; 9/89.

1333. **Kline's Incline** (5.10a) ★ (TR) Go up the face to cracks between *Stucca by a Yucca* and *Practice Rehearsal.* **FA:** Bob Gaines, Patty Kline; 5/98.

1334. **Practice Rehearsal** (5.7) Climb the left-tending crack to bushes, then go right and up the crack on the arête. **FA:** Chris Miller, Jan Margett; 11/89.

1335. **The Irritators** (5.7+) Take the crack just right of *Practice Rehearsal,* then go up the brown face. **FA:** Tom Michael, Vicki Michael; 4/89.

1336. **The Playwright** (5.6) A right-tending crack that heads up and then back left. **FA:** Unknown.

1337. **Anthrax** (5.8) Begin about 25 feet right of *The Playwright* (left of the tree near the top of the crag), in a vertical crack system. Begin off a large dead manzanita. **FA:** Woody Stark, Bill Briggs, Karen Briggs; 11/01.

The Cathouse

This seldom visited crag lies a short distance to the left (south) and behind (west) of Playhouse Rock. It faces southeast (sun most of the day, shade late in the day) and looks out into the long north-south valley running from Lost Horse Wall in the north to Real Hidden Valley in the south (Land That Time Forgot; see page 397). Park at a turnout on the west side of Park Boulevard 0.6 mile southeast of Lost Horse Road (7.9 miles from the West Entrance; 0.7 mile from the Intersection Rock/Real Hidden Valley intersection). This turnout is just south of the Milepost (a 50-foot pillar next to the road). From the parking area you will see the Cathouse in profile; a tree is growing out of its right side. Walk toward the left side of the crag, over a rocky notch. Poon Tang Rock lies just left of the Cathouse. Map, page 343.

The Cathouse—Left Side

This formation has distinct left and right sections divided by a low-angled broken area. The following routes lie on the left-hand section.

1338. **Felix** (5.4) Begin near the pine tree at the left side of the main face; head up and right via cracks and ledges. **FA:** Todd Swain; 10/91.

1339. **Little Brown Jug** (5.7) Go up and right on a seam/crack, then up the face and cracks. **Pro:** To 2 inches. **FA:** Alan Bartlett, Amy Sharpless; 1/90.

1340. **Limited Partnership** (5.8) Climb double thin cracks, then go up the face. **Pro:** Thin to 2 inches. **FA:** Alan Bartlett; 2/90.

1341. **Marmac's Crack** (5.6) Follow the handcrack up the center of the face with a

ledge halfway up. **Pro:** To 3 inches. **FA:** Alan Bartlett, Amy Sharpless; 1/90.

1342. **Tourette's Syndrome** (5.10c) Climb thin seams to the ledge, then go right up a thin crack. **Pro:** Thin to 2 inches. **FA:** Jack Roberts, Pam Ranger, Alan Bartlett, Bob Harrington; 1/90.

1343. **Garfield** (5.7) (X) The right arête of the left-hand formation. **FA:** Todd Swain; 10/91.

The Cathouse—Right Side

This formation has distinct left and right sections divided by a low-angled broken area. The following routes lie on the right-hand section. Descend to the right.

1343A. **Feline Pine** (5.6) ★ Go up the crack through a small roof on the far left side of the right hand section of the Cathouse. **Pro:** To 2 inches. **FA:** Unknown.

1344. **Heathcliff** (5.8) Go up large flakes to a crack/corner on left side of the right-hand section of the rock. **Pro:** To 2 inches. **FA:** Todd Swain; 10/91.

1345. **Hello Kitty** (5.9+) ★ Go up the face to the crack, then face climb past four bolts to the right of *Heathcliff*. **Pro:** To 2 inches. **FA:** Unknown.

1345A. **Feed the Kitty** (5.9) (TR) Toprope the face between *Hello Kitty* and *Nine Lives*. **FA:** Unknown.

1346. **Nine Lives** (5.8) ★ Go up the center of the right-hand face to a bolt, then left into a crack. **Pro:** To 2 inches. **FA:** Unknown.

1347. **Cat Scratch Fever** (5.9+) ★ Go up the face with two bolts to the right of *Nine Lives* and left of the *San Rio Crack*. **FA:** Unknown.

1348. **San Rio Crack** (5.6) The corner/crack on the right end of the face. **Pro:** To 2.5 inches. **FA:** Todd Swain.

Poon Tang Rock

This formation lies just south of The Cathouse. It is a large, low-angled gray slab that faces southwest into the Land That Time Forgot (see page 397). Park at the Playhouse Rock turnout on the west side of Park Boulevard 0.6 mile southeast of Lost Horse Road (7.9 miles from the West Entrance; 0.7 mile from the Intersection Rock/Real Hidden Valley intersection). This turnout is just south of the Milepost (a 50-foot pillar next to the road). From the parking area you can see the Cathouse formation in profile. Walk toward the left side of that crag, over a rocky notch. Poon Tang Rock lies just left of the Cathouse.

If you are in the Real Hidden Valley area, head to the northernmost apex of the Nature Trail (near the Brown Wall) and head north about 300 yards in the wash; Poon Tang Rock is on your right just a bit north and opposite of Short Rock. Map, page 343.

1349. **Spoonful** (5.9) (R/X) Begin by a dead tree on the left side of the face at a right-facing corner. Go up and right, then up. **FA:** Todd Swain.

1350. **Poon** (5.10a) (R/X) Begin in the middle of the face; go up the left-hand of two seams, then move right to the other seam. **Pro:** Thin to 2 inches. **FA:** Todd Gordon, Alan Roberts; 1/88.

1351. **Tang** (5.5) (R) The left-angling crack/seam to the right of *Poon*, joins *Poon* after about 50 feet. **Pro:** Thin to 2 inches. **FA:** Todd Gordon, Alan Roberts; 1/88.

The Cohn Property

The various large and inviting domes and rocks located across Park Boulevard from the Hemingway Buttress and the Milepost, and north of the Aviary and Watts Towers, are privately owned. Though a few routes were established here in the 1970s, the owners/caretakers historically have been extremely unfriendly; climbers have actually been shot at for trespassing here. Unless or until this situation changes, all climbers are advised to stay off this property. It is clearly posted NO TRESPASSING.

The Milepost

This large pinnacle of rock lies about 50 feet west of Park Boulevard (7.9 miles from the West Entrance; 0.7 mile from the Intersection Rock/Real Hidden Valley intersection). Park at a long pullout on the west side of the road just south of the formation (the same pullout as for Playhouse Rock). Map, page 313.

1352. **Scrambled Leggs** (5.10c) ★ Climb a crack on the southwest corner of the forma-tion to its end. A bolt protects face moves up and right to another small crack. **Pro:** Thin to 2 inches. **FA** (TR): Todd Swain, Dana Bartlett; 10/89. **FA** (Lead): Eric Anderson, Alan Bartlett; 8/90.

1353. **The Gettysburger** (5.10b/c) ★★ Start right of *Scrambled Leggs,* near the center of the southwest face. Climb a leaning crack up and right past three bolts to a crack leading to the top. **Pro:** Thin to 2 inches; three bolts. **FA:** Todd Gordon, Kevin Sisler, Tom Atherton; 2/89.

1354. **French Flies** (5.7) (not shown on photo) This is located on the northwest face of the Milepost. Climb up to a halfway ledge, then up the left crack to the top. **Pro:** To 2.5 inches. **FA:** Todd Swain, Patty Furbush; 10/89.

1355. **Chocolate Snake** (5.6) (not shown on photo) Start as for the previous route, but take the right crack and face to the top. **Pro:** To 2.5 inches. **FA:** Todd Swain, Patty Furbush; 10/89.

Pinyon Crag

This small, broken rock lies about 150 feet northwest of the Milepost and about 200 feet west of the road. Park at the long pullout on the west side of Park Boulevard 7.9 miles from the West Entrance and 0.7 mile from the Intersection Rock/Real Hidden Valley intersection (same as for Playhouse Rock). The crag and routes are not pictured. Map, page 313.

1356. **Pinyon Crack** (5.10b) This short (25-foot) climb is on the east side of Pinyon Crag near a pinyon pine. Go up a short finger crack to a horizontal, then up the widening handcrack. **Pro:** Thin to 2.5 inches. **FA:** Brandt Allen, Tom Atherton; 9/90.

1357. **The Satchmo** (5.10a) ★ Another very short route is located left of *Pinyon Crack* (on the south face). Climb a left-leaning crack to a face with one bolt. **Pro:** Thin to 0.5 inch. **FA:** Unknown.

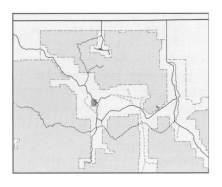

ROADSIDE ROCKS AREA

The Roadside Rocks Area covers a variety of crags that lie adjacent to Park Boulevard between the large Playhouse Rock turnout to the north and the Intersection Rock Parking/Real Hidden Valley intersection to the south. The Playhouse Rock turnout is located on the west side of Park Boulevard 7.9 miles from the West Entrance and 0.7 mile from the Intersection Rock/Real Hidden Valley intersection. Crags in this section of the guide include Pep Boys Crag, Dihedral Rock, Glory Dome, Summit or Plummet Rock, The Aviary, , X-Factor Dome, Lost in the Shuffle and Found in the Duffle Crags, Jam or Slam Rock, Red Burrito, Wall Street, Slump Rock, and the Foundry. The Roadside Rocks Area does not include coverage of Cereal Rock, the Hot Tub, or Watanobe Wall, which are found in the Outback Area (after Hidden Valley Campground). Map, page 343.

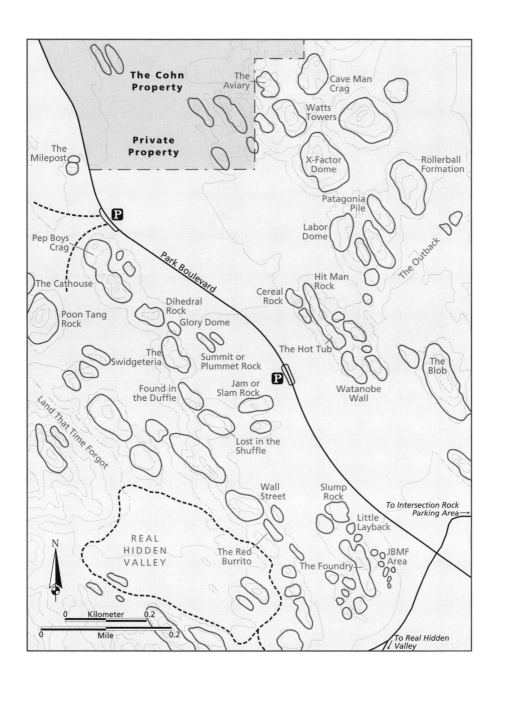

The Cohn Property

The Aviary

Cave Man Crag

Watts Towers

Private Property

The Milepost

X-Factor Dome

Rollerball Formation

Patagonia Pile

Labor Dome

The Outback

Pep Boys Crag

Park Boulevard

Hit Man Rock

The Cathouse

Cereal Rock

Dihedral Rock

Poon Tang Rock

Glory Dome

The Hot Tub

The Blob

The Swidgeteria

Summit or Plummet Rock

Found in the Duffle

Jam or Slam Rock

Watanobe Wall

Land That Time Forgot

Lost in the Shuffle

Wall Street

Slump Rock

To Intersection Rock Parking Area →

Little Layback

JBMF Area

REAL HIDDEN VALLEY

The Red Burrito

The Foundry

N

0   Kilometer   0.2

0   Mile   0.2

To Real Hidden Valley

The Pep Boys Crag

This formation lies just west of Park Boulevard 0.1+ mile southeast of the Milepost. Park at the long Playhouse Rock turnout on the west side of Park Boulevard 7.9 miles from the West Entrance and 0.7 mile from the Intersection Rock/Real Hidden Valley intersection. Walk south. Routes on the left end, just north of Dihedral Rock, face the road (morning sun, afternoon shade). Right-end routes lie on the northern and western faces and are reached by walking southwest from the pullout. Map, page 343.

Pep Boys Crag—East Side, Left End

This section of this complex formation lies immediately to the right (north) of Dihedral Rock as viewed from Park Boulevard. Routes 1359 to 1362 are pictured with Dihedral Rock routes on page 346.

1358. **Arturo's Arête** (5.8) (not shown on photo) This route actually lies on the southwestern end of Pep Boys Crag left and around the corner from *Yabo Phone Home* (about 200+ feet right of *Poison Hamburger* on the west side). Follow cracks up the arête to two bolts, then traverse across on the ridge. **FA:** Todd Gordon, Arturo; 1998.

1359. **Yabo Phone Home** (5.10c) ★ A right-facing corner, off-width to stemming. **Pro:** Thin to 4 inches. **FA:** Darryl Nakahira, Mike Waugh, Kevin Powell; 1983.

1360. **Yaborrhea** (5.8) ★ Ramp to a corner/thin crack. **Pro:** To 2 inches. **FA:** Alan Bartlett, Brandt Allen, Laurel Colella; 11/00.

1361. **Dos Perros Negros** (5.9) From the gully on the left, go up and right to a corner, to flakes, to a face with one bolt. **Pro:** To 2 inches. **FA:** Todd Gordon, Pat Brennan, Dave Evans.

1362. **The Three Best Friends You Ever Had** (5.10c) ★ From the gully between the two towers, go up and right past a bolt to a crack heading around right to a face with two more bolts. **Pro:** To 2 inches; one-bolt anchor. **FA:** Todd Gordon, Randy Vogel, Jim Angione; 10/85.

Pep Boys Crag—Middle East

The next two routes lie about 75 feet down and right of *The Three Best Friends You Ever Had*. They are not pictured.

1363. **Grease Monkey** (5.9+) Start in a chimney leading to a left-leaning offwidth; above, go up an overhanging hand/fist crack. **Pro:** To 4 inches. **FA:** Alan Bartlett, Alexis Sonnenfeld; 6/00.

1364. **Gas Jockey** (5.9) ★ Begin off a boulder up and right of *Grease Monkey*. This is the right-facing corner with a thin crack; go through a bulge at the top. **Pro:** Thin to 3 inches. **FA:** Alan Bartlett, Laurel Colella; 6/00.

Pep Boys Crag— North and West Faces

The following routes lie on the more jumbled northern and western faces of Pep Boys Crag.

1365. **Two Guys on the Wrong Climb** (5.10c) Begin in an easy right-leaning arch left of *Fingertip Traverse of Josh,* then go up the seam to bolt anchors. **Pro:** Thin to 2 inches. **FA:** Eric Odenthal, Anthony Scalise; 4/02.

1366. **Fingertip Traverse of Josh** (5.8) ★ This route is down low and on the right side of the Pep Boys Crag massif. It is close to the road and faces the Milepost. Go up to and follow the left side of a short Gothic arch; traverse right from its top, then go up the short left-facing corner. **Pro:** To 2.5 inches. **FA:** Alan Roberts, John Hayward.

1367. **Strain Gauge** (5.10b) ★ This lies about 160 feet around and right from the

previous route, facing west. Go out of an alcove/roof via a finger crack that widens to thin hands. **Pro:** To 2.5 inches. **FA:** Alan Roberts, Alex.

1368. **Flim-Flam Man** (5.11c) ★★★ This three-bolt route is just right of *Strain Gauge.* **FA:** Don Wilson et al.; 1992.

1369. **We Must Improve Our Bust** (5.11b/c) ★ This bolted face route lies on the northeast corner of the block 40 feet up and left (south) of *Strain Gauge.* **Pro:** One fixed pin; two bolts. **FA:** Dave Evans, Reggie Thomson, Todd Gordon; 2/89.

1370. **Poison Hamburger** (5.8) (not shown on photo) This right-facing corner to a flake lies about 50 feet right of *Strain Gauge.* **Pro:** To 2.5 inches. **FA:** Alan Bartlett, Tucker Tech, Phil Bircheff; 3/00.

1371. **Tainted French Fries** (5.8) (R) (not shown on photo) Begin in the obvious dihedral left of *Poison Hamburger;* after 15 feet, traverse right across a loose flake, then head up and right. **Pro:** Thin to 2 inches. **FA:** Dave Haber, Sheryl Haber; 8/01.

Dihedral Rock

This formation lies about 50 yards west of Park Boulevard 0.8 mile southeast of Lost Horse Road (8.1 miles from the West Entrance; 0.5+ mile from the Intersection Rock/Real Hidden Valley intersection). The characteristic large left-facing dihedral on its left side (the classic *Coarse and Buggy,* 5.11a/b) can be seen easily from the road. Park at the turnout either 0.2 mile north of the formation (Playhouse Rock parking) or 0.2 mile south of the formation (Jam or Slam Rock parking), on the west side of the road, and walk. Map, page 343.

Dihedral Rock—East Face

The routes get sun in the morning and afternoon shade.

1372. **Happy Happy, Joy Joy** (5.9) The wide crack left of *Coarse and Buggy.* **Pro:** To 4 inches. **FA:** Todd Gordon, Tom Michael, Stacey Bocks, Dave Dixon, Jeff; 10/92.

1373. **Coarse and Buggy** (5.11a/b) ★★★★ A Josh classic, involving stemming to liebacking up the obvious left-facing dihedral. You can start from the ground (loose) or traverse in

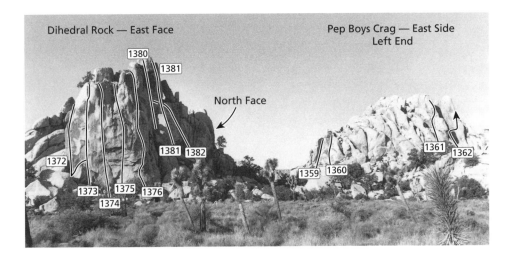

The Road Block

1372
1373
1374 1375 1376
1380 1381 1382

from the left up off the block. Named for the fact that at the time of the first free ascent the right side of the dihedral was fairly loose; but after many ascents it is now perfectly clean. **Pro:** Several thin to 2 inches. **FA** (former name *Left Out*): Bill Mikus, Bob Dominick; 12/70. **FFA:** Spencer Lennard, Randy Vogel; 2/78.

1374. **Rots o' Rock** (5.12c) (TR) An unattractive overhanging crack about 15 feet right of *Coarse and Buggy*. **FA:** Bill Mikus, Steve Godshall; 11/70. **FFA** (TR): Scott Cosgrove.

1375. **Tons of Junk** (A3) Aid up the face and rotten cracks right of *Rots O'Rock*. **FA:** Unknown; 1982.

1376. **The Sowsuckle** (5.12a/b) ★★★ Go up discontinuous cracks and the face on right side of the east face about 50 feet right of *Coarse and Buggy*. This has gotten harder as a key hold broke off. **Pro:** Thin to 2 inches; four bolts; fixed pin. **FA** (TR): Craig Fry,

Mike Lechlinski; 4/84. **FA** (Lead): Paul Borne.

1377. **Hazing Incident** (5.7) Begin on ledges up and right of *The Sowsuckle*. Go up the left-leaning crack to the face, and then to another crack. **FA:** Alan Bartlett, Tucker Tech; 10/00.

1378. **Fire Escape** (5.9) Begin up the descent gully to the left of *Limp-Wristed Faggot*. Go up the crack on the right side of a block, then go left and up a finger crack and buckets. **Pro:** To 3 inches. **FA:** Tucker Tech, Alan Bartlett; 10/00.

1379. **Ohhh Dude** (5.10c/d) Begin on *Fire Escape,* but where that route goes left, step right up a steep arching crack. **FA:** Steve Gerberding, Mark Bowling; 12/00.

1380. **Limp-Wristed Faggot** (5.11a) ★★ This route follows the right-hand of two thin diagonalling cracks that face the road, but lies in the descent gully. (The left crack has two

bolts, but has apparently not been climbed.)
Pro: Thin to 2 inches. **FA:** Roy McClenahan; 1984.

1381. **How 'bout It** (5.10d) ★★ Go up the face past two bolts just right of *Limp-Wristed Faggot* to cracks/flakes. Go up and right, then back left past four more bolts. **Pro:** To 2 inches. **FA:** Mark Bowling, Steve Gerberding; 10/00.

1382. **Couldn't Wait** (5.10a) Climb left-slanting cracks up and right of *How 'Bout It*. Go left across that route to a wide crack/chimney. **Pro:** To 5+ inches. **FA:** Steve Gerberding, Mark Bowling; 10/00.

Dihedral Rock—North Face, The Road Block

The next five routes are on the north face of the Dihedral Rock formation, referred to as the Road Block. Gear is needed for belay anchors on all routes. Shady most of the day.

1383. **Midnight Oil** (5.11a) The leftmost line, with two bolts. Move a bit left at the first bolt (5.11c, straight up). **Pro:** To 2 inches. **FA:** Michael Paul, Paul Borne; 3/88.

1384. **Ramming Speed** (5.11d) ★ The next line to the right, also with two bolts (first bolt doubled). The crux is past the first bolt. **Pro:** To 2 inches. **FA:** Paul Borne; 3/88.

1385. **Vanishing Point** (5.12b) ★ Just right of *Ramming Speed*. Go up small corner to a face with four bolts. **Pro:** Thin to 2 inches. **FA:** Paul Borne; 3/88.

1386. Immaculate Conception (5.9+) ★ Go up a right-facing dihedral right of *Vanishing Point*. **Pro:** To 2 inches. **FA:** Charles Cole, Dave Evans, Dave Wonderly.

1387. Crotch Putty (5.10b/c) (not shown on photo) The crack between *Immaculate Conception* and *Far Side of Crazy*. **Pro:** To 2 inches. **FA:** Todd Gordon, Tucker Tech, Sean; 1999.

1388. Far Side of Crazy (5.10b) (R) (not shown on photo) Begin about 30 feet right and around the corner from *Immaculate Conception*. Climb the low-angled face with seams and one bolt. **Pro:** Thin to 2 inches. **FA:** Paul Borne; 2/88.

Dihedral Rock—West Face

The following climbs lie on a brown slab on the west face of Dihedral Rock. They are best approached by walking around the left (south) side of the formation. Walk off to the right (south). They get morning shade and are sunny all afternoon. The face and routes are not pictured.

1389. Carlos (5.9) ★ The left-hand three-bolt route. **Pro:** To 2 inches for anchor. **FA:** Todd Gordon, Cyndie Bransford; 5/94.

1390. Smears of Joy (5.10b/c) (TR) The face between *Carlos* and *Slabulous*. **FA:** Chris Miller; 1999.

1391. Slabulous (5.9) ★ The right-hand bolted slab route. **Pro:** Four bolts; to 2 inches for anchor. **FA:** Chris Miller; 1999.

The Swidgeteria

1395

Glory Dome

1397

1396 1398 1399 1400 1401

1392

1393

1394

Glory Dome

This little slabby rock lies about 150 feet left of Dihedral Rock on the west side of Park Boulevard. Park at the turnout for Jam or Slam Rock (8.3 miles from the West Entrance; 0.3 mile from the Intersection Rock/Real Hidden Valley intersection) and walk about 0.1+ mile north. The dome gets morning sun and afternoon shade. Map, page 343.

1392. **Glory Days** (5.10b) (TR) Climb the seam 10 feet right of a pine tree on the left end of the rock. **FA:** Todd Swain; 11/89.

1393. **Glory Road** (5.11d) ★ Climb the slab on the right center face of Glory Dome. **Pro:** Five bolts; one fixed pin. **FA:** Mike Paul, Paul Borne; 3/88.

1394. **Hope and Glory** (5.8) The finger crack to the right of the flake on the right side of the rock. **Pro:** Thin to 1.5 inches. **FA:** Unknown.

The Swidgeteria

This formation faces east and lies about 150 left (southwest) and farther from the road than Glory Dome. It is just northwest of Summit or Plummet Rock. Park at the Jam or Slam Rock turnout (8.3 miles from the West Entrance; 0.3 mile from the Intersection Rock/Real Hidden Valley inter-section) and walk about 0.1+ mile north. It sees morning sun and afternoon shade. Map, page 343.

1395. **Gordo Started It** (5.10c) Climb the thin crack to the face with three bolts on the left side of the rock. **Pro:** Thin. **FA** (retro-bolted later): Todd Swain, Dave Mayville; 9/90.

1396. **Three Swidgeteers** (5.2) The easy right-angling ramp. **FA:** Unknown.

1397. **For a Few Swidgets More** (5.9) This is right (30 feet) of *Gordo Started It*. Climb thin cracks up to and then join the easy ramp of the last route. **Pro:** Thin to 2 inches. **FA:** Todd Swain; 10/90.

1398. **Calling All Swidgets** (5.10a) Just right of *For a Few Swidgets More.* Start on a ledge, climb up a crack, then up a face. **Pro:** Thin to 2 inches. **FA** (TR): Todd Swain; 10/91. **FA** (Lead): Alan Bartlett; 2/92.

1399. **The Swidgeteria** (5.9) This is a crack-to-arête climb located 50 feet right of *Gordo Started It.* **Pro:** Thin to 2 inches; one bolt. **FA:** Todd Swain, Dave Mayville, Bill Donnelly; 9/90.

1400. **Still Life** (5.10b) (R) A straight crack 15 feet right of *The Swidgeteria.* **Pro:** Thin to 2 inches. **FA:** Mike Paul, Dave Titus.

1401. **Fidget with Swidgets** (5.9) (R) Climb a face to a crack/flake 10 feet right of *Still Life.* **Pro:** Thin to 2 inches. **FA:** Todd Swain; 10/91.

Summit or Plummet Rock

This rock is about 150 yards southeast of (left and closer to the road than) Dihedral Rock. Park at the Jam or Slam Rock turnout on west side of Park Boulevard (8.3 miles from the West Entrance; 0.3 mile from the Intersection Rock/Real Hidden Valley inter-section) and walk about 0.1+ mile north. The routes are on the left-hand part of the east face, and face the road. They get sun in the morning and afternoon shade. Map, page 343.

1402. **Three Dorks on Dope** (5.10a) The left-hand of two thin cracks (with lots of holes) 18 feet left of *Light Touch.* **Pro:** To 2 inches. **FA:** Dave Mayville, Brandt Allen, Tom Burke; 1999.

1403. **Light Touch** (5.12a) ★★ Face climb past two bolts (crux) to a thin crack on left. **Pro:** Several thin to 2 inches; two bolts. **FA:** Herb Laeger, Bob Yoho; 3/89.

The Aviary   Watts Towers   X-Factor Dome

To Cave Man Crag and Resolution Rock

1404. **Kodas Silence** (5.11b) ★★ Begin 10 feet right of *Light Touch*. Go up a crack to the height-dependent face crux (two bolts) to a thin crack. **Pro:** Several thin to 2 inches; two bolts. **FA:** Vaino Kodas, Rich Perch, Herb Laeger, Bob Yoho; 11/87.

1405. **Laeger Domain** (5.10b/c) ★★ This is a discontinuous crack to the right of *Kodas Silence* with one bolt. **Pro:** Thin to 2 inch; one bolt. **FA:** Herb Laeger, Rich Perch, Vaino Kodas, Bob Yoho; 11/87.

1406. **Three Friends and a Baby** (5.9) Climb a right-facing corner past two large holes immediately right of *Laeger Domain*. **Pro:** To 2 inches. **FA:** Todd Swain, Patty Furbush, Donette Smith; 6/93.

1407. **Split Shift** (5.9) This is the face to handcrack line just right of the above route. **Pro:** To 2.5 inches. **FA:** Todd Swain; 10/91.

Roadside Rocks—East Side

The following formations lie east of Park Boulevard opposite the Milepost, Pep Boys Crag, and Dihedral Rock. Map, page 343.

The Aviary

This formation is the northernmost of the east side rocks; it lies about 150 yards east of Park Boulevard, roughly opposite the Milepost/Playhouse Rock. The property immediately to the north (the Cohn Property), as shown on the map, is private. Avoid crossing this private land in approaching the Aviary. Park at a turnout on the west side of Park Boulevard about 7.9 miles from the West Entrance and 0.7 miles from the Intersection Rock/Real Hidden Valley intersection (same as for Playhouse Rock). Map, page 343.

Easy
5th

1408. **Birdman from Alcatraz** (5.10a) ★
Begin from a ledge and bush about 20 feet
below the roof. Go up and left on a ramp,
then up the finger crack over a small roof.
Pro: Thin to 2 inches. **FA:** Mike Law, Bob
Gaines; 1983.

1409. **Studebaker Hawk** (5.10c) ★★ Begin
as for *Birdman from Alcatraz,* but head up and
right into a hand-to-fist crack in the corner.

Pro: To 3+ inches. **FA:** Mike Paul, Jim May,
Bob Gaines; 1983.

1410. **Soul Research** (5.9) This straight
crack is on a wall directly opposite and facing the Aviary; it begins as a thin groove. **Pro:**
Thin to 2 inches. **FA:** Brian Sillasen, Todd
Gordon; 3/87.

Watts Towers

This formation is the middle of the East Side rocks, and lies about 150 yards east of Park Boulevard roughly opposite Pep Boys Crag. It appears as a large rocky hill with an elevated and squarish summit formation featuring a number of vertical crack systems. Routes lie high on the upper west-facing section of the formation (the vertical crack systems) and gets shade in the morning and sun in the afternoon.

There is private property just northwest of the crag; avoid this when approaching from Park Boulevard. Park at a turnout on the west side of the road 7.9 miles from the West Entrance and 0.7 mile from the Intersection Rock/Real Hidden Valley intersection (same as Playhouse Rock), and head east. Alternatively, park on the east side of

Park Boulevard at a turnout 8.3 miles from the West Entrance and 0.3 mile from the Intersection Rock/Real Hidden Valley intersection (near Watanobe Wall) and walk north along the road until you can head northeast. Approach the upper face from the right (via the canyon left of X-Factor Dome), then go left up boulders. Map, page 343.

1411. **Infectious Smile** (5.9) (R) (not shown in photo) This climbs a narrow, northwest-facing arête with one bolt near the bottom. Begin about 100 feet down and left of *Jemimagina*. **Pro:** To 2.5 inches. **FA:** Alan Nelson, Ken Black; 3/83.

1412. **Watt's a Matter** (5.7) (X) (not shown on photo) Begin atop *Infectious Smile*, left of *Watt's Wrong*. Go up the big face holds on the northwest side of the summit block. **FA:** Donette Smith, Todd Swain; 1/95.

1413. **Watt's Wrong (**5.11a) (TR) Begin about 25 feet left and around from *Jemimagina.* Go up a short crack to a horizontal, then back left on a dike to a ledge; go up the face above. **FA:** Todd Swain; 1/95.

1414. **Jemimagina** (5.10b) This is the leftmost crack/deep slot on the west face, and it goes over a roof formed by a huge block. **Pro:** To 3 inches. **FA:** Alan Bartlett, Alan Roberts; 11/82.

1415. **Watt, Me Worry** (5.5) ★ Begin left of *Sole Food;* go up a left-facing dihedral, then up a crack on the right. **Pro:** To 2 inches. **FA:** Todd Swain, Donette Smith; 1/95.

1416. **Sole Food** (5.10a) ★★ An extremely thin, right-slanting crack that disappears after 40 feet is left of the center of the west face (about 20 feet right of *Jemimagina*). Go up this crack, then move right to another crack (*Urban Redevelopment*) that is followed to the top. **Pro:** Very thin to 2 inches. **FA:** Alan Bartlett, Alan Roberts; 11/82.

1417. **Urban Redevelopment** (5.10a) ★ Begin about 10 feet right of *Sole Food* and climb a thin seam past one bolt, then go up the crack to the top (shared with *Sole Food*). **Pro:** Very thin to 2 inches. **FA:** Dave Evans, Jim Angione; 12/86.

1418. **James Watt** (5.8) (R) Begin left of *Talus Phallus;* go up a right-facing dihedral. **Pro:** To 2 inches. **FA:** Todd Swain, Donette Smith; 12/94.

1419. **Talus Phallus** (5.6) There are two cracks right of *Sole Food* (a roof lies between them). This is the right crack. **Pro:** To 2.5 inches. **FA:** Todd Gordon, Cody Dolnick, 6/88.

1420. **Bandersnatch** (5.10b) ★ This is a steep fist crack to the right of *Talus Phallus* (tricky crux near the bottom); above, go up and left under the roof/arch. **Pro:** To 3 inches. **FA:** Todd Gordon, Cody Dolnick; 6/88.

1421. **Plunger-Faced Mutant** (5.7) Begin as for *Bandersnatch,* but head up and right, past a bush, to the right side of a roof. Go up the crack to the left through the roof. **Pro:** To 2 inches. **FA:** Don Reid, Alan Bartlett; 10/00.

1422. **Adult Books** (5.11a) ★ Begin on the right end of the west face. Go up cracks and a right-facing corner (5.9) to a ledge; move right and up the upper corner (5.10d). **Pro:** To 2.5 inches. **FA:** Roy McClenahan, Alan Bartlett; 11/82.

Cave Man Crag

This small cliff lies to the east of (behind) Watts Towers. The best approach is to park on the east side of Park Boulevard at a turnout 8.3 miles from the West Entrance and 0.3 miles from the Intersection Rock/Real Hidden Valley intersection (near Watanobe Wall). Walk north along Park Boulevard until you can head northeast. Take the canyon between X-Factor Dome and Watts Towers, then head up and left. It can also be approached from the gap between the Aviary and Watts Towers. The following routes are on the formation's northeast face. The crag and routes are not pictured. Map, page 343.

1423. **Cave Man Crack** (5.11a) This thin arching crack lies on the left side of the face and begins up a roof. Very short. **Pro:** Thin to 2 inches. **FA:** Ken Black, Alan Nelson; 1983.

1424. **Pterodactyl Crack** (5.9) Begin about 8 feet right of *Cave Man Crack;* this crack is steep at the bottom. **Pro:** Thin to 2 inches. **FA:** Ken Black; 1983.

1425. **Monster Mash** (5.10a) This is the overhanging and longer crack about 8 feet right of *Pterodactyl Crack.* **Pro:** To 2 inches. **FA:** Ken Black, Alan Nelson; 1983.

Resolution Rock

This small face on the south side of the Watts Towers formation is on the left side of the gully between Watts Towers and X-Factor Dome, past the routes on the north face of X-Factor Dome (*Runaway Truck Ramp* etc.) and on the opposite side of the canyon/gully. The wall faces southeast and gets sun most of the day. The rock and routes are not pictured. Map, page 343.

1426. **Off Night Backstreet** (5.11a) (TR) ★ Climb thin seams/cracks on the left side of the face. **FA:** Kevin Powell, Dan Ahlborn; 1979.

1427. **Get Smarter** (5.10a) (TR) Climb the left-facing corner, then go left to a finger crack. This begins about 12 feet right of *Off Night Backstreet.* **FA:** Donette Smith, Todd Swain; 1/95.

1428. **Do Better Routes** (5.9) (TR) Go up the corner of *Get Smarter,* but then go right up the face. **FA:** Donette Smith, Todd Swain; 1/95.

X-Factor Dome

This formation is the southernmost of the east-side formations, lying about 150 yards east of Park Boulevard roughly opposite Dihedral Rock. It is very complex (broken) and has several crack systems that lead through roofs on its upper west face. Several crack and face routes are to be found on the far right, on the south buttress.

The closest parking is from one of these turnouts along Park Boulevard:

- A large turnout on the west side of the road 7.9 miles from the West Entrance and 0.7 mile from Intersection Rock/Real Hidden Valley intersection (same as for Playhouse Rock);
- Large turnouts on both the west and east sides of road 8.3 miles from West Entrance and 0.3 mile from Intersection Rock/Real Hidden Valley intersection (same as for Jam or Slam and Watanobe Wall).

Note: There is private property (the Cohn Property) northwest of this formation. Avoid crossing it when approaching from the Playhouse Rock turnout. Like many of the other crags nearby, it is an easy walk from Hidden Valley Campground and the Intersection Rock parking area. Map, page 343.

X-Factor Dome—North Face

The following routes are located on the lower north side of X-Factor Dome, below Freeway Jam and adjacent to the rocky gully on the north side of the formation. They are shady most of the day. These routes are not pictured.

1429. **Runaway Truck Ramp** (5.9) ★ The left-facing dihedral on the left. **FA:** Chris Miller; 4/00.

1430. **Dump Truck** (5.11b/c) ★ (TR) Climb up to and over the roof to the right of *Runaway Truck Ramp.* **FA:** Steve Gerberding; 10/00.

1431. Indecision 2000 (5.8) This route lies on the right side of the wall with (and right of) the previous routes. Go up past an inverted V, then up the right-hand crack. **FA:** Mark Bowling, Steve Gerberding, Alan Bartlett; 10/00.

X-Factor Dome— Upper West Face

These routes are located high up on the west face of the northern end of the formation, facing Park Boulevard. They get morning shade and afternoon sun.

1432. Freeway Jam (5.10c) ★ This route lies on the north side of X-Factor Dome, around the corner and left of the main upper west face. It is the farthest right of several cracks. **Pro:** To 2 inches (several 1 to 1.5 inches). **FA:** Roy McClenahan, Alan Roberts, Alan Bartlett; 11/82.

1433. Child's Spray (5.10a) (TR) The crack left of *False TKO*. Lieback to a horizontal; traverse right. **FA:** Tucker Tech et al.

1434. False TKO (5.10d) Begin left of a tree; go up a crack that goes through the roof. **Pro:** To 2.5 inches. **FA:** Roger Linfield.

1435. Death Before Lycra (5.10a) Just right of *False TKO*. Go out of a tree and up an arête past three bolts. **Pro:** To 2.5 inches. **FA:** Alan Bartlett, Dave Haber; 2/92.

X-Factor Dome—South Buttress

The following routes lie on the far right (southern) end of X-Factor Dome, a rounded buttress of rock. This is about 50 yards north of Labor Dome in the Outback Area behind Hidden Valley Campground (see page 483); it could be easily approached from Hidden Valley Campground and the Intersection Rock parking area.

1436. Whoville (5.8+) The obvious crack with a boulder at the base; left of *Max Factor* and *Charles Who?* More difficult (5.11a?) if you do not stem off the boulder to start. **Pro:** To 2 inches. **FA:** Randy Vogel, Dave Evans, Rob Raker; 2/87.

1437. Max Factor (5.11c) ★★ A five-bolt face route between *Whoville* and *Charles Who?* **Pro:** To 1.5 inches for anchor. **FA:** Bob Gaines; 3/96.

1438. Charles Who? (5.11b) ★★ Climb a thin flake to the face past three bolts at the extreme south corner of the dome. **Pro:** Thin to 1.5 inches. **FA:** Randy Vogel, Dave Evans, Rob Raker; 2/87.

1439. Give a Hoot (5.11c) ★ Climb a very thin seam 10 feet to the right of *Charles Who?*, just left of a pine tree. **Pro:** Thin; fixed pins? **FA** (TR): Todd Swain; 12/91. **FA** (Lead): Unknown.

1440. Charles Chips (5.9) This is the very thin, right-facing flake 20 feet right of *Charles Who?* **Pro:** To 2 inches. **FA:** Randy Vogel, Dave Evans, Rob Raker; 2/87.

1441. Charles in Charge (5.10a) This is the thicker, left-facing flake 8 feet farther right of *Charles Chips*. **Pro:** To 2 inches. **FA:** Randy Vogel, Dave Evans, Rob Raker; 2/87.

Lost in the Shuffle Crag

This formation is on the west side of Park Boulevard, directly west of Jam or Slam Rock and almost directly across from Watanobe Wall and Steve Canyon. Park at either of the large turnouts on the west and east sides of Park Boulevard 8.3 miles from the West Entrance and 0.3 mile from the Intersection Rock/Real Hidden Valley intersection. This is the same parking area as Jam or Slam Rock and Watanobe Wall. Like many of the other crags nearby, it is an easy walk from Hidden Valley Campground and the Intersection Rock parking area. It gets morning sun and is shady in the afternoon. Map page 343.

1442. **Blair's Flake** (5.9+) Begin on the upper left side of the crag. Go up a thin flake to a roof; go left then up over the roof. **Pro:** To 3 inches. **FA:** Paul Borne.

1443. **Impulse Power** (5.11a) (R) ★ Begin up the left-hand of two left-slanting crack, past a bolt; above a small roof, head up the face past a second bolt (stay left of last bolt; going right of it is 5.11c). **Pro:** To 3 inches. **FA:** Paul Borne.

1444. **Daddy Long Legs** (5.11a) (R) ★★ Begin up the left leaning crack just right of *Impulse Power*. Go up the crack, past a bolt, and join *Impulse Power,* then cross that route to finish far left (atop *Blair's Flake*). **Pro:** Thin to 3 inches. **FA:** Mike Waugh, Darryl Nakahira, Kevin Powell, Dan Leichtfuss; 1983.

1445. **Black Hole** (5.11d) (R) ★★★ Begin in the crack/seam to the right of *Daddy Long Legs.* Go up this past three bolts, then up and left on flakes, then over the right side of the roof. **Pro:** Thin to 2 inches. **FA:** Paul Borne.

1446. **Warp Speed** (5.11d) (R) ★ This seam lies to the right of *Black Hole* and also has three bolts near the bottom; above, head up and left in a crack system. **Pro:** Thin to 2 inches. **FA:** Paul Borne.

1447. **Sugar Daddy** (5.7) Begin atop a pointed block on the right-hand side of the main face (about 10 feet right of *Warp Speed*). Go up the left-slanting crack. **Pro:** To 3 inches. **FA:** Unknown.

Several easier routes have been done on the more broken face to the right of *Sugar Daddy.*

Found in the Duffle Crag

This is the crag just right of Lost in the Shuffle Crag on the west side of Park Boulevard, to the west and a bit north of Jam or Slam Rock and across from Watanobe Wall and Steve Canyon. Park at either of the large turnouts on the west and east sides of Park Boulevard 8.3 miles from the West Entrance and 0.3 mile from the Intersection Rock/Real Hidden Valley intersection. This is the same parking area as for Jam or Slam Rock and Watanobe Wall. Like many of the other crags nearby, it is an easy walk from Hidden Valley Campground and the Intersection Rock parking area. It gets morning sun and is shady in the afternoon. Map page 343.

Found in the Duffle Crag— East Face

1448. **Twins** (5.7) This short fist crack lies on the very left edge of the east face. **Pro:** To 3.5 inches. **FA:** Todd Swain, Kip Knapp; 9/89.

1449. **Separated at Mirth** (5.9+) (R) Begin abut 6 feet right of *Twins,* off a small pointed boulder. Go up the right-facing corner to a thin crack. **Pro:** Thin to 2.5 inches. **FA:** Todd Swain, Kip Knapp; 9/89.

1450. **Double Impact** (5.10a) (R) ★ Begin about 15 feet right of *Separated at Mirth,* just left of yuccas and bushes. Go up and right to thin, left-slanting cracks to a sloping shelf. Above, take a thin crack up the steep headwall. **Pro:** Thin to 2 inches. **FA:** Paul Borne.

1451. **The Magic Touch** (5.9) ★ Begin about 20 feet right of *Double Impact* and just left of *The Gauntlet.* Go up a right-facing corner to a left-slanting crack. **Pro:** Thin to 2 inches; one fixed pin. **FA:** Herb Laeger, Eve Laeger; 11/80.

1452. **The Gauntlet** (5.12a) ★★ Go up the face in center of the formation past four bolts to a thin crack that heads up and a bit left. **Pro:** Thin to 2 inches. **FA:** Paul Borne.

1453. **Heavy Handed** (5.10c) Begin off a boulder just right of *The Gauntlet.* **Pitch 1:** Go up a right-facing corner, then up and right on the face to a left-facing corner to a small ledge. **Pitch 2:** Go up right to a left-slanting crack. Two short pitches. **Pro:** Thin to 2.5 inches. **FFA:** Todd Swain, Paul Borne; 1989.

1454. **Life without TV** (5.9) (not shown on photo) This is a grainy, right-slanting fist crack on the small formation right (north) of Found in the Duffle Crag. It is visible from the road. **Pro:** To 3 inches. **FA:** Alan Bartlett, Tom Atherton, Vicki Pelton, Todd Gordon; 3/88.

Found in the Duffle Crag— Southwest Face

The following routes lie on the back (southwest face) of Found in the Duffle Crag. They get morning shade and are sunny all afternoon. Approach from the right side of the east face. The routes are not pictured.

1455. **Bummerang** (5.8) Climb a right-slanting crack on a separate rock down and left of the main southwest face. **FA:** Tucker Tech, Mark Senyk, Eileen Coleman; 1/00.

1456. **Bung Hole** (5.10a) A chimney, stem, face to crack climb on the left end of the main face. **Pro:** To 2.5 inches; one bolt. **FA:** Mark Senyk, Tucker Tech; 1/00.

1457. **Raunchy Bung** (5.8) Start just right of *Bung Hole;* climb cracks and over a small roof to the summit. **Pro:** To 2 inches; two-bolt anchor/rap the northeast face. **FA:** Mark Senyk, Eileen Coleman, Tucker Tech; 1/00.

1458. **Sore Loserman** (5.10a) The right-leaning crack right of *Raunchy Bung;* passes through an alcove. **Pro:** To 3 inches. **FA:** Steve Gerberding, Cal Gerberding, Mark Bowling; 10/00.

1459. **Boomerang** (5.7) A large, right-slanting ramp to the right of the above routes. **Pro:** To 2 inches. **FA:** Alan Roberts, Alex; 1/88.

1460. **Comes Around** (5.8) The right-tending crack right of *Boomerang;* step right and back halfway up. **Pro:** To 2.5 inches. **FA:** Todd Swain; 2/95.

Jam or Slam Rock

This small rock is just west of Park Boulevard, to the west and a bit south of two large turnouts on both the west and east sides of Park Boulevard. Park at one of these turnouts, which are located 8.3 miles from the West Entrance and 0.3 mile from the Intersection Rock/Real Hidden Valley intersection. This formation is almost directly across the road from Watanobe Wall. Like many of the other crags nearby, it is an easy walk from Hidden Valley Campground and the Intersection Rock parking area. The south face is sunny much of the day; the north face is mostly shady. Descend either by rapping off *Fire or Retire* (two bolts) or by downclimbing to the east. Map, page 343.

Jam or Slam Rock—South Face

This face is not visible from the road. Walk south and then west into a small canyon filled with boulders to reach the south face. A sunny and warm crag for most of the day.

1461. **Cranking Skills or Hospital Bills** (5.10d) (R) ★ Go up the very thin crack on the left side of the face, then up an unprotected face (5.10b R) above. **Pro:** Thin to 2 inches. **FA:** Unknown; 1984.

1462. **Fire or Retire** (5.10b/c) ★★★ Go up the obvious left-facing dihedral, then up the face above past two bolts. **Pro:** Thin to 1 inch. **FA:** Randy Vogel, Randy McDonald; 1979. **FA** (Direct finish): Chris Miller; 1999.

1463. **Amionit** (5.12a/b) (TR) ★★ Climb the face and arête just right of *Fire or Retire*. **FA:** Peter Hayes et al.; 1991.

1464. **Crimp or Wimp** (5.10d) (TR) Begin off a round boulder about 25 feet right of *Fire or Retire;* Go up the face to a seam. **FA:** Todd Swain; 10/91.

1465. **Free Bubba John** (5.10d) (R) Begin just right of *Crimp or Wimp;* go up and right on right-slanting leaning seams. **Pro:** Thin; one bolt. **FA:** Tom Atherton, Todd Gordon.

1466. **Grip or Whip** (5.11b) (TR) (not shown on photo) This is the thin seam located about 8 feet right of *Free Bubba John*. **FA:** Todd Swain; 10/91.

Jam or Slam Rock—North Face

Routes are located on the upper summit block of the formation and face Park Boulevard and the parking turnout. They are shady most of the day. Scramble up to the base. The routes are not pictured.

1467. **No Perch Is Necessary** (5.10d) ★★ This route is located on the right side of the summit block and is visible from the road. Face climb past two bolts to a thin crack. **Pro:** Thin to 2 inches. **FA:** Rich Perch, Vaino Kodas, Bob Yoho, Herb Laeger; 11/87.

1468. **Usual Suspects** (5.10c) ★★ This is on the arête to the right of *No Perch Is Necessary;* go up a thin crack to the arête with three bolts. **Pro:** Thin to 2 inches. **FA:** Chris Miller, Chuck Scott, Loren Scott, Tyler Logan; 3/00.

The Red Burrito
(aka The False Great Burrito)

This is a short, steep, brown wall located about 200 yards west of Park Boulevard between Jam or Slam Rock and Slump Rock (8.4 miles from the West Entrance and 0.2 mile from the Real Hidden Valley/Intersection Rock junction). Park either at the large Intersection Rock parking area or at one of two large turnouts (on both the west and east sides of Park Boulevard) that are located 8.3 miles from the West Entrance and 0.3 mile from the Intersection Rock/Real Hidden Valley intersection.

From the turnouts, walk south along Park Boulevard until you can head in a west-ward direction to the formation. It is also an easy walk from Hidden Valley Campground and the Intersection Rock parking area. The formation to the right and slightly behind the Red Burrito is Wall Street. To descend, downclimb *California Burrito.*

1469. **California Burrito** (5.3) (descent route) (not shown on photo) Climb corners on the south side. **FA:** Unknown.

1470. **Burrito Crossing** (5.10b) ★ Start left of *Tuna and Cheese,* then climb a horizontal all the way right to the end of the formation. **FA:** Chris Miller.

1471. **Tuna and Cheese** (5.8) This is at the extreme left side of the formation. Climb a short crack to a horizontal, then go up an arête. **Pro:** To 2 inches. **FA:** Todd Swain; 4/90.

1472. **Spam and Bean** (5.10d) (R) ★ Start 6 feet right of *Tuna and Cheese.* Go up the crack, then the face. **Pro:** Thin to 2 inches. **FA** (TR): Todd Swain; 4/90. **FA** (Lead): Todd Swain; 8/93.

1473. **Red Chile** (5.10d) ★ (TR) The face between *Spam and Bean* and *Beef and Bean*. **FA:** Rick Cashner; 1979.

1474. **Beef and Bean** (5.10a) ★ The central crack. **Pro:** To 2.5 inches. **FA:** Roy McClenahan, Alan Roberts.

1475. **Green Chile** (5.11a) ★ (TR) The face 4 feet right of *Beef and Bean*. **FA:** Rick Cashner; 1979.

1476. **Cheese** (5.11a) ★ (TR) The face 10 feet right of *Beef and Bean*. **FA:** Todd Swain; 4/90.

1477. **Jalapeno** (5.10b) ★ (TR) The thin, vertical crack 20 feet right of *Beef and Bean*. **FA:** Todd Swain; 4/90.

1478. **Chicken** (5.10a) (TR) The short crack on the right; finish at a small pine tree. **FA:** Todd Swain; 4/90.

Wall Street

This large, low-angled dome, just right and slightly behind the Red Burrito, is actually the back side of Elephant Dome. Approach as for Red Burrito. Like many of the crags nearby, it is an easy walk from Hidden Valley Campground and the Intersection Rock parking area. Map, page 343.

1479. **Buyer Beware** (5.10a) (R) The upper left-hand arête. Steep buckets; one bolt. **Pro:** To 2 inches. **FA:** Todd Swain, Peggy Buckey; 10/90.

1480. **Wall Street** (5.9) (R) ★ Start 25 feet down and right of *Buyer Beware*. Climb up and right to a ledge. **Pro:** Thin to 2 inches; fixed pin. **FA:** Alan Roberts, John Hayward; 2/88.

1481. **Wunsch's Electronic Trading** (5.10b) (TR) This is the thin seam between *Wall Street* and *Lost My Shirt*. **FA:** Todd Swain; 8/93.

1482. **Lost My Shirt** (5.9) ★ This three-bolt slab lies just left of *Insider Information*. **Pro:** To 1.5 inches; two-bolt anchor/80-foot rap. **FA:** Bob Gaines, Patty Kline; 5/01.

1483. **Insider Information** (5.7) ★ Start off the flake, then go up and over a small roof. **Pro:** Thin to 2 inches; two-bolt anchor/80-foot rap. **FA:** Roy McClenahan.

1484. **Power Lunch** (5.10b) (TR) Located 10 feet right of *Insider Information;* go over the roof at an orange stain. **FA:** Todd Swain; 9/90.

1485. **Lunch Is for Wimps** (5.9) (R) ★ Just right of *Power Lunch* (one bolt at start); stay right. **Pro:** To 2 inches. **FA:** Alan Roberts, John Hayward; 2/88.

1486. **Walrus-Like and Wimpy** (5.8) (R) This is the right-facing corner right of *Lunch Is for Wimps.* **Pro:** To 2 inches. **FA:** Todd Swain, Kip Knapp, Patty Furbush, Peggy Buckey; 9/89.

Slump Rock

This rock lies just west of Park Boulevard at a point 8.5 miles from the West Entrance and 0.1+ mile from Intersection Rock/Real Hidden Valley intersection. It is probably best approached from the large Intersection Rock parking area (8.6+ miles from the West Entrance). It faces northeast and is shady most of the day. Map, page 343.

1487. **Look, but Don't Touch** (5.7) This and the next two routes lie on a separate block/face to the left of the main Slump Rock face. Go up a chimney to twin cracks, around to the right of *Touchy Feely.* **Pro:** To 3 inches. **FA:** Todd Swain; 3/92.

1488. **Touchy Feely** (5.10b) Begin to the left of *No Touchee Wallee;* go up the face past two

bolts. **Pro:** To 2 inches. **FA:** Todd Swain, Todd Gordon, 3/92.

1489. **No Touchee Wallee** (5.8 or 5.11b/c) Begin to the left of a chimney, then head up and right past three bolts. If you use the right wall of the chimney past the third bolt it is only 5.8; it is 5.11b/c if you don't. **Pro:** To 2 inches. **FA:** Herb Laeger, Bob Kamps, et al.

1490. **Cheese Nip** (5.11a, A0) Begin to the left of *Nip and Tuck;* aid off a bolt, then face climb past two more. **Pro:** To 2 inches. **FA:** Todd Swain, Mike Van Volkem; 3/92.

1491. **Nip and Tuck** (5.10c) Traverse in from the left, then go up the flake and face past two bolts. **Pro:** To 2 inches. **FA:** Todd Swain, Patty Furbush; 5/90.

1492. **Have a Nip** (5.7) Traverse in from left (or go up 5.10d), then go up the obvious wide crack. **Pro:** To 4 inches. **FA:** Unknown.

1493. **Nip in the Air** (5.10b) (R) ★ Start off a boulder on the right side of the face; face climb up and left to a thin crack, then up the face past one bolt near the top. **Pro:** To 2 inches. **FA:** Charles Cole, Darryl Nakahira, Randy Vogel; 1981.

1494. **The Pile** (5.5) (R) Climb the second crack to the right of *Nip in the Air,* then go up the left end of the roof. **Pro:** To 4 inches. **FA:** Unknown.

The Foundry

This complex "broken rock" formation lies just west of Park Boulevard just south of Slump Rock. It is located directly behind the JBMF bouldering area. Two routes are located on its west (back side) face. Park at the Intersection Rock Parking area (8.6+ miles from the West Entrance) and walk west. Map, page 343.

The Foundry—East Face

These routes see morning sun and are shady all afternoon.

1495. **Hash Brownies** (5.10b) This route is located high on the far left end of the formation. Go up the right-facing corner. **Pro:** To 4 inches. **FA:** Todd Swain, Patty Furbush; 6/93.

1496. **Hashish Crack** (open project) This is the thin seam on the smooth face (with one bolt down low) between *Hash Brownies* and *Hashish Corner.*

1497. **Hashish Corner** (5.7) This is the left-facing corner to the right of the smooth face. **Pro:** To 3 inches. **FA:** Alf Randell, Dave Paul.

1498. **Stainless Steel Rat** (5.10c) Go up the thin right-slanting crack on the left side of the lower face; finish up and right in a slot. **Pro:** Thin to 3 inches. **FA:** Jack Roberts, Greg Soneger et al.; 1981.

1499. **Steel Pulse** (5.12a) ★ (TR) Begin about 15 feet right of *Stainless Steel Rat;* go up a thin seam to the face to finish on that route. **FA:** Michael Paul.

JBMF Boulders

1500. **Metal Shop** (5.11a) (R) ★ Begin about 15 feet right of *Steel Pulse;* go up the left-leaning thin crack. Finish as for the last two routes. **Pro:** Many thin to 2 inches. **FA:** Mike Lechlinski.

1501. **Full Metal Jacket** (5.11a) (R) ★ Climb *Metal Shop* for 25 feet, then face climb up and right past one bolt. **Pro:** Thin to 2 inches. FA: Michael Paul, Paul Borne.

1502. **Vaino's Crack** (5.7) This is the short handcrack to the right of *Full Metal Jacket.* **Pro:** To 3 inches. **FA:** Vaino Kodas.

1503. **Molten Mettle** (5.11a) ★ From the base of *Vaino's Crack,* head up and right past a bolt to a thin crack, then face climb past a second bolt. **Pro:** Thin to 1 inch. **FA:** Todd Swain, Patty Furbush; 5/90.

1504. **Little Lieback** (5.10a) This short route lies about 125 feet right of the Foundry (just around the corner from Slump Rock). Climb a wide lieback to a roof; go right at the corner of the roof. **Pro:** To 3.5 inches. **FA:** Matt Cox; 1973.

The Foundry—West Face

1505. **Jumar of Flesh** (5.9+) ★ (not shown on photo) This is the left of two off-width/chimney routes on the west face. **Pro:** To 5 inches. **FA:** Todd Gordon, Alan Roberts, Brian Sillasen, Bob; 1/88.

1506. **Six-Pack Crack** (5.10b) ★ (not shown on photo) The right route. **Pro:** To 5 inches. **FA:** Alan Roberts, Todd Gordon, Brian Sillasen, Bob; 1/88.

Mike Waugh on The Chameleon *(5.12b), on the west face of the Sentinel.* PHOTO: © KEVIN POWELL

Real Hidden Valley

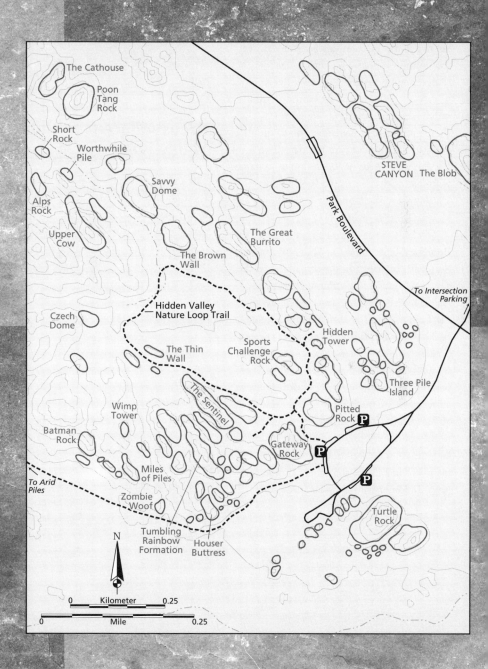

The Cathouse

Poon Tang Rock

Short Rock

Worthwhile Pile

Savvy Dome

Alps Rock

Upper Cow

The Brown Wall

The Great Burrito

Czech Dome

Hidden Valley Nature Loop Trail

The Thin Wall

Sports Challenge Rock

Hidden Tower

The Sentinel

Wimp Tower

Three Pile Island

Batman Rock

Pitted Rock

To Arid Piles

Miles of Piles

Gateway Rock

Zombie Woof

Tumbling Rainbow Formation

Houser Buttress

Turtle Rock

STEVE CANYON

The Blob

Park Boulevard

To Intersection Parking

N

Kilometer   0   0.25

Mile   0   0.25

THE REAL HIDDEN VALLEY AREA

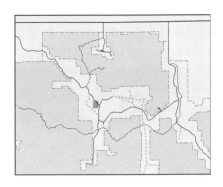

The Real Hidden Valley (National Park Service name: Hidden Valley Picnic Area) is the location of many good to excellent routes ranging from 5.3 to 5.14. Because of its easy accessibility and its location within walking distance of Hidden Valley Campground, it has become one of the most popular climbing areas in the park. The Real Hidden Valley Area includes climbs contained within and adjacent to the Real Hidden Valley proper, including the Turtle Rock and Houser Buttress areas.

From the park's West Entrance, take Park Boulevard 8.6+ miles to a four-way intersection, with Intersection Rock parking to the east, and Hidden Valley Picnic Area to the west. This intersection lies 0.1 mile north of the T intersection of Park Boulevard and Barker Dam Road (which provides access to Hidden Valley Campground). Turn west on the Hidden Valley Picnic Area road. A large parking area a few hundred yards beyond is adjacent to the trailhead for Real Hidden Valley proper (to the north). A picnic area is to the south and directly behind it is the large mass of Turtle Rock. To the west of the main parking area is a climbers' trail leading toward Houser Buttress. Map, page 369.

Areas Adjacent to Hidden Valley Road

The following climbs lie just north of the Real Hidden Valley road, just before you get to the main parking area. Park in the main parking lot and walk back up the road to the fork, then directly to the crags. Map, page 374.

Three Pile Island

Bite Rock
1511

1507

1508   1509   1510

Three Pile Island

A blocky crag known as Three Pile Island lies just north of the Real Hidden Valley road, near where the road splits. Rappel from slings.

1507. **Rhoid Warrior** (5.10c) (R) Traverse in from the left to reach the first bolt, then go up past the second bolt and horizontals. **Pro:** To 3 inches; two bolts. **FA:** Todd Swain, Dick Peterson; 10/91.

1508. **The Colossus of Rhoids** (5.11a) ★★★ Climb overhanging twin cracks; finish in the right crack. **Pro:** To 2.5 inches. **FA:** Perry Beckham, Bill Ravitch; 1/84.

1509. **Hold Your Fire** (5.13a) ★★ This is a two-bolt face up to a thin crack 15 feet right of *The Colossus of Rhoids*. Holds may be missing; the rating has not been confirmed since the first ascent. **Pro:** Thin to 2 inches. **FA:** Kurt Smith; 1/88.

Bite Rock

This small tower-like formation lies about 40 yards northeast (right of and behind) Three Pile Island. Map, page 374.

1510. **Acupuncture** (5.8) ★ This is an obvious handcrack facing the road. **Pro:** To 3 inches. **FA:** Earl Philips, George Zelenz, Dean Rosnau; 12/86.

1511. **The Wolfman** (5.10d) ★★ Follow the face past four bolts 12 feet right of *Acupuncture*. **Pro:** To 2 inches for anchor. **FA:** Todd Gordon, Alan Bartlett, Brandt Allen, Mike Wilson, Tom Atherton; 6/90.

1512. **Jerry Smith Memorial Route** (5.12a) ★ (TR) (not shown on photo) Toprope the face about 25 feet right of *The Wolfman*. **FA:** Raleigh Collins.

The Green Room

This rock is on a brown buttress facing east, located a short distance up the canyon/wash on your left (west) left of Three Pile Island. It can also be reached from the vicinity of Hidden Tower and the Sand Castle by walking southwest in the wash/canyon; it will be on your right just past Fissura Crag. The rock and route are not pictured. Map, page 374.

1513. **Vicki the Visitor** (5.10b) Begin up a crack with a few small holes at its base. Connect cracks by moving up and right to reach a cleft near the summit. **Pro:** To 3 inches. **FA:** Todd Gordon, Alan Bartlett, Vicki Pelton; 2/88.

Fissura Crag

This small formation lies just north of the Green Room on the left (west) side of the wash as you approach from the parking area. It lies south of Hidden Tower. The crag and route are not pictured. Map, page 374.

1514. **Fissura** (5.10b) Go up past two bolts into a crack. **Pro:** To 2.5 inches. **FA:** Todd Gordon, Luis from Spain; 8/99.

Pitted Rock

This large formation lies up and right of the trail into the Real Hidden Valley (pretty much above the toilets). It faces the main parking area. Map, page 374.

1515. **Pete Foundation Crack** (5.10b) Located up and left of *Pitfall,* this is a thin right-slanting crack to a handcrack. **Pro:** To 3 inches. **FA:** Todd Gordon, Alan Bartlett, Paul Johnston; 5/92.

1516. **Pitfall** (5.11c) ★★ This is a four-bolt face climb on the steep (brown) south face of Pitted Rock, facing the parking area. Two-bolt anchor/rap. **FA:** Herb Laeger, Rich Perch, Jim Beyer; 11/86.

1517. **Over-Powered by Hootch** (5.12c) (TR) This and the next route (a variation) lie on the large boulder to the right and in front of *Pitfall.* Go up the block, traversing left and up the corner near the top. **FA:** Doug McDonald.

1518. **Reefer Madness** (Variation) (5.12c) (TR) Same as above, but go straight up at the top. **FA:** Scott Cosgrove.

1519. **Chuckles** (5.7) Climb the handcrack in a right-facing corner, then go up the chimney. Belay at *Pitfall* bolt anchor/rap. **Pro:** To 3 inches. **FA:** Mary Ann Kelly, Alan Bartlett; 9/00.

1520. **Hurricane** (5.10c) Climb thin cracks to the right of *Chuckles,* then go left to finish up the chimney of that route. **Pro:** Thin to 3 inches. **FA:** Dave Mayville, Alan Bartlett; 8/00.

1521. **The Pit Slut** (5.12a) ★★ This and *The Gash* lie around the corner (on the east face of Pitted Rock), about 60 right of *Pitfall*. A thin crack leads to a slightly overhanging face. These may be more easily approached from the vicinity of Locomotion Rock. **Pro:** Four bolts; to 3 inches. No fixed anchors. **FA:** Dave Bengston; 1991.

1522. **The Gash** (5.10a) ★ This is the left-leaning crack that meets the top of *The Pit Slut*. **Pro:** To 3 inches. **FA:** Dave Bengston, Bill Russell; 1991.

1523. **Betty Gravel** (5.9) This left-leaning hand rack lies about 80 feet up and right of *The Gash,* on the summit block of Pitted Rock facing Locomotion Rock. **Pro:** To 2.5 inches. **FA:** Todd Swain, Peggy Buckey; 5/85.

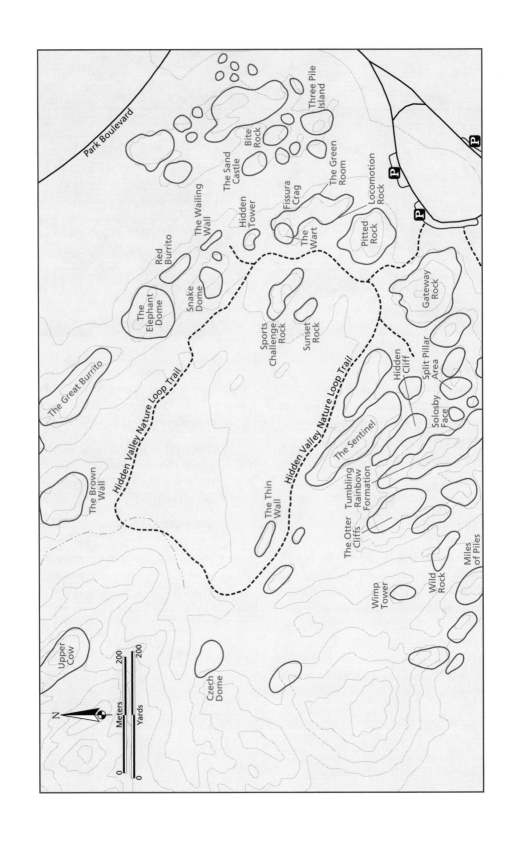

THE REAL
HIDDEN
VALLEY

The following routes lie in and around Real
Hidden Valley proper, a rock-enclosed valley
accessed by a trail that heads north through
boulders from the main parking area. Once
you enter the Hidden Valley, the trail makes a
loop of about 1 mile around the valley
(Hidden Valley Nature Loop Trail). The formations are described in order you would
encounter them going clockwise around the
loop trail (begin by heading left on the loop
trail).

From the park's West Entrance, take Park
Boulevard 8.6+ miles to a four-way intersection, with Intersection Rock parking to the
east, and Hidden Valley Picnic Area to the
west. This intersection lies 0.1 mile north of
the T intersection of Park Boulevard and
Barker Dam Road (which provides access to
Hidden Valley Campground). Turn west on

the Hidden Valley Picnic Area road. After a
few hundred yards, you will find a large
parking area adjacent to the trailhead for
Real Hidden Valley proper (which lies to the
north). Take this nature trail north, up steps
and between boulders, until it drops you in
to the southern end of the Real Hidden
Valley; here the trail splits (it forms a loop).
This point will be used as the reference for
approach descriptions to the various formations in the Real Hidden Valley.

It is reputed that during the 1880s and
1890s, the Real Hidden Valley was used by
the McHaney Gang to hide stolen horses and
cattle until they could be rebranded. Jim
McHaney ran a large-scale "rustling" opera-
tion, and was generally involved in various
unsavory activities during this period of time.
Willie Button is often credited with discovering the present-day entrance to Real
Hidden Valley. Gang members, Button, and
his brother Charley met their end in a bar-
room fight.

Betty Jo Yablonski VI

Gateway Rock

This is the large formation on your left as you walk up the nature trail into the Real Hidden Valley. Routes are on the east and north faces. An interesting cavern/cleft runs through the entire formation (north to south), beginning in the cleft where *In the Pit* begins and running south to the desert floor on the south side of the rock. This cleft can be used (with scrambling) to reach *False Tumbling Rainbow*. Map, page 374.

Gateway Rock—East Face

This side of the formation faces the parking area and nature trail heading up into the Hidden Valley. It gets sun in the morning and shade in the afternoon.

1524. False Tumbling Rainbow (5.8) This is the left-arching corner high on the east face. It bears a passing resemblance to *Tumbling Rainbow.* Approach is best made up the cavern/cleft beginning by *In the Pit,* and climbing this to the ledge at the route's base. **Pro:** To 2.5 inches. **FA:** Dave Evans; 1977.

1525. Hands Away (5.9) The very clean-looking, left-slanting handcrack just left of the trail into the Hidden Valley. **Pro:** To 2.5 inches. **FA:** Steve Anderson et al.; 1980.

1526. Lay Back and Do It (5.11a) (TR) This thin lieback flake lies just right of *Hands Away.* **FA:** Dale Bard, John Yablonski; 1980.

Gateway Rock—North Face

The north face of Gateway Rock is comprised of several blocks facing into Real Hidden Valley. Just as you enter Real Hidden Valley (where the trail splits), two obvious cracks can be seen on the northeast corner of Gateway Rock. These are *Solo* and *Broken Glass*. To the right of this is a narrow crevice/gully/tunnel (which tunnels under the entire formation, emerging on the floor of the desert on its south side). *In the Pit* lies in the lower end of this crevice system. *Semi Tough* is the left-hand of two cracks on the face to the right.

1527. **Solo** (5.9) ★ On the northeast corner of the rock, climb a thin crack to a ledge, then go up a wider crack in a corner above. See photo on page 378. **Pro:** To 3 inches. **FA:** Tobin Sorenson; 1976.

1528. **Broken Glass** (5.10a) ★ The dogleg crack on the east side of the block to the

right of *Solo*. See photo on page 378. **Pro:** To 2.5 inches. **FA:** Charles Cole, Gib Lewis, Randy Vogel; 12/79.

1529. **In the Pit** (5.10a) ★ The thin hand-crack on the right side of the crevice/gully. Tunnel through boulders to reach the base. Descend back and downclimb right. **Pro:** To 2 inches. **FA:** Dan Michael; 1980.

1530. **Pit Bull Attack** (5.10d) ★ Stem off a boulder to begin a thin crack leading to a ledge; above climb the face/arête past one bolt. Descend back and downclimb right. **Pro:** Thin to 2 inches. **FA:** Bob Gaines, Dwight Brooks; 1/88.

1531. **Semi Tough** (5.10d) ★★★ A balancy entry move leads to a finger-to-hand crack. Descend back and downclimb right. **Pro:** Thin to 1.5 inches. **FA:** Mike Lechlinski, Mari Gingery, Charles Cole, John Yablonski, Dean Fidelman; 10/79.

Gateway Rock — North Face

Split Pillar Area

Split Pillar Area

This area is composed of a group of large blocks and an obvious pillar/tower (Split Pillar) about 70 yards west of Gateway Rock *(Semi Tough)*. For parking/approach directions, see page 375. From the point the trail enters the valley and forks, take the left trail for about 120 feet until you can turn left into a trail/small wash (some remnants of asphalt are here). The trail heads more or less straight; angle up boulders to Split Pillar. For routes ending on Split Pillar, there may (or may not) be fixed anchors. If not, a simul-rap may be necessary to descend. Map, page 374.

1532. **Martin Quits** (5.10c) ★★ This short, thin crack lies on a small east-facing rock below and in front (east) of Split Pillar. **Pro:**

Thin to 2 inches. **FA:** Jon Lonne, Dave Ohlsen; 9/76.

1533. Death Blow to the Uninitiated

(5.12b) ★ This three-bolt route is on the south side of the Split Pillar. **Pro:** For anchor (fixed anchor may not be present). **FA:** Eric Anderson, Herm Harrison; 1/91.

1534. **The BMW Route** (5.9) (R) Climb a wide crack to a flake to a face past one bolt on the east face. **Pro:** To 3+ inches. **FA:** Alan Bartlett, Paul Miller, Marcel Wolf; 11/90.

1535. **The Cheese Grater** (5.10c) (R) Begin right of *The BMW Route*. Head right under a roof to a wide crack and face climbing past a bolt. Join *The BMW Route* at the last bolt. **Pro:** To 3+ inches. **FA:** Eric Anderson, Alan Bartlett; 8/90.

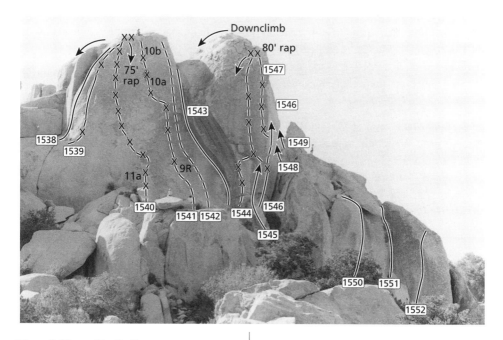

Tumbling Rainbow Formation

This is the highest formation in the Real Hidden Valley area, rising up to your left (west) as you enter the valley. The following routes lie on the east face (sun in the morning, shade in the afternoon). The rock tends to be better than average, with the main face having a hard grayish patina.

For parking and approach directions, see page 375. From the point the nature trail enters the valley and forks, take the left trail for about 120 feet, until you can turn left into a small wash with a side trail (some remnants of asphalt will be found). The trail heads more or less straight (southwest), then heads toward the formation through boulders. Class 3 scrambling takes you to the base of the main upper face. Map, page 374.

Descents:

• Rappel 75 feet from atop *Runaway/Run For Your Life,* etc.

• Downclimb left to the base of Solosby Face, then tunnel through the cave back left (east), and scramble back to the base (original descent).

• Rappel 80 feet from the top of *Rainy Day Dream Away/Tic Tic Boom* etc.

1536. Run from Your Mother-in-Law (5.10a) ★ (not shown on photo or topo) This route lies about 110 feet left of the main Tumbling Rainbow Formation, to the left of the approach to the Solosby Face. This is a hand-to-off-width crack that starts in a cave/pit. **Pro:** To 4 inches. **FA:** Alois Smrz, Miguel Carmona; 12/89.

1537. Army Armstrong (A2+) ★ (not shown on photo or topo) Aid up large roof to the right of *Run from Your Mother-in-Law.* **Pro:** Thin pins to 1-inch angles; large hook. **FA:** Unknown.

1538. Two Stage (5.10a) Start on a ledge up and left of the main face; climb a crack to a right-facing corner. **Pro:** To 2 inches. **FA:** Roger Linfield; 11/86.

1539. Run from Your Wife (5.10b) ★ Start on the ledge up and left of the main face. Face climb past a bolt to a crack, then to a face past a second bolt. **Pro:** Thin to 2 inches; one fixed pin. **FA:** Charles Cole, Troy Mayr; 12/87.

1540. Runaway (5.11a) ★★★★ (Sport) Another great face climb on grey patina. Hard moves at bottom past two bolts (5.11a), lead to easier (5.10b/c) but sustained fun moves up and right. **Pro:** Ten bolts; two-bolt anchor/rap (this anchor has been removed and replaced; a few nuts can be used for an anchor if it's not present). It is also possible (original line) to bypass the crux and first two bolts by beginning up *Run For Your Life* and traversing straight left from that route's first bolt to the third bolt on this route. Done this way, the route is 5.10c. **FA:** Bob Gaines, Dana Adler, Yvonne Gaines; 10/97.

1541. Run for Your Life (5.10b) ★★★★ A classic Josh face route, with excellent grey patina. Begin right of *Runaway*. The first few moves (5.9) are unprotected, but soon ease to the first bolt; above, fun climbing leads to the crux above the last bolt. **Pro:** Six bolts; two-bolt anchor/rap; optional medium pro for anchor. **FA:** Charles Cole, Dave Houser, Herb Laeger; 1978.

1542. S. D. R. (5.10d) ★★ (TR) Toprope the face between *Run For Your Life* and *Tumbling Rainbow*. **FA:** Bob Gaines, Scott Steele, Paul Cooper, Scott Cosgrove; 11/99.

1543. Tumbling Rainbow (5.9) ★★ The obvious left-curving widening crack. **Pro:** To 4 inches. **FA:** John Long, Richard Harrison, Rick Accomazzo, Ging Gingrich; 3/73.

1544. Tonic Boom (5.12d) ★★ Begin just right of *Tumbling Rainbow*. Go up the face past two bolts to a roof (crux), then easier face climbing above. **Pro:** Five bolts; two-bolt anchor/rap. **FA:** Russ Walling; 1990.

1545. Tic Tic Boom (5.12a) ★★★ Begin up *Rainy Day, Dream Away*, then head up and left, then up on the face. **Pro:** Thin to 0.75 inch; four bolts; two-bolt anchor/rap. **FA:** Roy McClenahan; 1989.

1546. Rainy Day, Dream Away (5.11b/c) ★★★ Begin on the block below the arête with finger cracks. Go up finger cracks to a bolt, then up (5.11b/c) and right into a shallow corner/crack system. **Pro:** Thin to 2.5 inches. The bolt was added when *Tic Tic Boom* was established (1989); prior to that, the crux was very poorly protected by a fixed RURP. **FA:** Dave Evans, Jim Angione; 1979. **FFA** (TR): John Bachar, Kevin Powell, Mari Gingery; 1979. **FFA** (Lead): Russ Raffa; 1979.

1547. Days of Thunder (5.11b/c) ★★★ (Variation finish to *Rainy Day, Dream Away*) Go up *Rainy Day, Dream Away* to the beginning of the dihedral/shallow crack, then move left around the arête and up an easier face (5.10a/b) past three bolts. **Pro:** Thin to 0.75 inches; four bolts; two-bolt anchor/rap. **FA:** Bob Gaines, John Mallory; 11/99.

1548. White Room (5.9) Begin about 30 feet up and right of the arête of *Rainy Day, Dream Away;* either go up a nasty gully or climb *Don't Look a Gift Frog in the Mouth/Handcuffs* to reach base of this and the next route. Go up a white-featured face to a crack and tree. **Pro:** To 2.5 inches. **FA:** Bob Gaines, Alan Bartlett; 2/92.

1549. Tales of Brave Ulysses (5.9) Begin up and right of *White Room;* climb a finger crack to a tree on the right arête (*White Room* joins this route). **Pro:** To 2.5 inches.

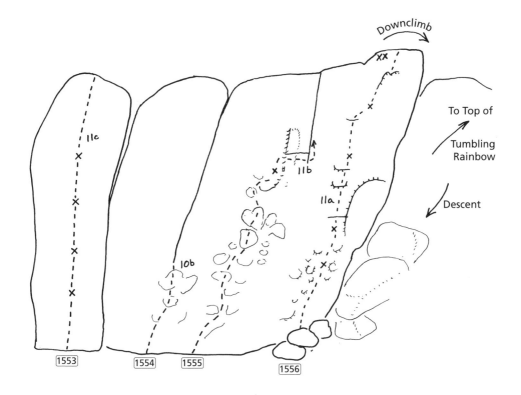

1550. Don't Look a Gift Frog in the Mouth
(5.9) Follow the right-facing corner to a
roof, tunnel through to ledges; descend right.
Pro: To 3 inches. **FA:** Unknown.

1551. Handcuffs (5.9) The handcrack in the
left-facing corner. **Pro:** To 3 inches. **FA:** Bob
Gaines, Alan Bartlett; 2/92.

1552. Fisticuffs (5.10b) ★★★ This is the short
but clean hand-and-fist crack splitting the
right side of the rock. **Pro:** To 4 inches. **FA:**
John Long, Rick Accomazzo; 3/73.

Solosby Face

This overhanging, knobby, orange-colored
face lies to the left (south) and behind (west
of) the Tumbling Rainbow Formation,
behind a series of blocks that hide it from
view from the trail. The downclimb from
Tumbling Rainbow leads past this face. The

"best" approach is to climb one of the routes
on the main Tumbling Rainbow formation
and then downclimb left to reach the base of
this face.

For parking and approach directions, see
page 375. From the trail fork, take the left
trail for about 120 feet, until you can turn
left into a small wash with a side trail (some
remnants of asphalt will be found). The trail
heads more or less straight (southwest), then
heads toward the Tumbling Rainbow
Formation through boulders. Stay left of the
base of the Tumbling Rainbow Formation,
and tunnel through boulders next to a large
roof to reach the base of this shady, east-facing
wall. Downclimb right. Map, page 374.

1553. Slam Dance (5.11c) ★ A four-bolt
route on a small face left of the main Solosby
Face; the first bolt may be missing a hanger.
Pro: Wired stopper for hangerless first bolt;

to 2.5 inches for anchor. Walk off left. **FA:** Paul Turecki, Dave Griffith, Chris Schneider, Jordy Morgan, et al.

1554. **Solosby** (5.10b) (R) ★ Face climb up huecos to a crack on the left side of the main face. **Pro:** To 3 inches. **FA:** Rick Cashner; 1979.

1555. **Latin Swing** (5.11b) ★★ This route ascends the center of the main face on large huecos (5.8 R) to a bolt, then traverse right to a thin crack. **Pro:** Thin to 2 inches; one bolt. **FA** (TR): Rick Cashner, John Yablonski, Dale Bard; 1979. **FA** (Lead): Unknown.

1556. **Bebop Tango** (5.11a) ★★★ (Sport) Climb overhanging buckets and rails on excellent orangish rock on the right side of the face; reachy crux. **Pro:** Four bolts; two-bolt anchor. **FA** (TR): John Bachar, John Yablonski, Mike Lechlinski; 1979. **FA** (Lead): Paul Borne; 1990.

The Sentinel

This large formation lies on the west side of the Real Hidden Valley and sports a large east face (with easy to moderate routes) and an even larger west face (with moderate to difficult routes).

For parking and approach directions, see page 375. From the trail fork, take the left fork for about 100 yards. The east face lies just left of the nature trail at this point; the west face lies in a hidden canyon.

The Sentinel—East Face

Routes on the east face range from 5.6 to 5.10 in difficulty and, in most cases, are two pitches in length. They get sun in the morning and afternoon shade. Descend down easy slabs to the left (southern end).

1557. **Climb of the Sentry** (5.5) (R/X) This route starts off a boulder and heads up a slab to a right-facing flake near the top. It lies about 45 feet left of *Sentinel Beach.* **FA:** Todd Swain; 1989.

1558. **Watch Dog** (5.7) (R) Roughly halfway between *Climb of the Sentry* and *Sentinel Beach,* head up past several horizontals and a hole in the rock. **FA:** Todd Swain; 1989.

1559. **Sentinel Beach** (5.8) (R) Begin left of a pine; head up a crack/seam to a right-facing corner. **Pro:** Thin to 2 inches. **FA:** Alan Bartlett, Katie Wilkinson; 5/88.

1560. **Me Mum Shit the Bed** (5.11a) Start up the face about 12 feet left of the flake at the beginning of *Beauty and the Beach.* Face climb up and left past three bolts to a left-slanting seam/crack. **Pro:** Thin to 2 inches. **FA:** Nic Conway, Todd Gordon; 5/91.

1561. **Beauty and the Beach** (5.9) Go up and right on a big flake (35 feet right of *Sentinel Beach*) to a bolt, then move up and left to an obvious crack. **Pro:** To 2.5 inches. **FA:** Todd Swain, Dick Peterson, Peggy Buckey; 11/89.

1562. **Life's a Beach** (5.10a) (R) Begin as for *Beauty and the Beach,* but head straight up from the bolt. **Pro:** To 2.5 inches. **FA:** Todd Swain, Dick Peterson, Peggy Buckey; 11/89.

Solosby Face

Tumbling Rainbow Formation

Sentinel—East Face

1546 1540 1541 1543 1552 1557 1558 1559 1561 1560 1564 1563 1564 1567 1570

1563. **Be Good or Be Gone** (5.10d) ★ The left-leaning crack system that begins at ground level; this passes left of the roof higher up. **Pitch 1:** Go up the crack to belay on a midway ledge. **Pitch 2:** Go up a left-facing corner past two bolts, and then up a crack. **Pro:** To 2.5 inches. **FA:** Dave Mayville, Brandt Allen; 7/91.

1564. **Ball Bearing** (5.10a) ★★★ A worthy climb; begin up the crack just right of *Be Good or Be Gone.* **Pitch 1:** Head up a crack, move right at a horizontal, then go up a thin crack (5.9) to a two-bolt belay below a roof. **Pitch 2:** Head around the right side of the roof, and up a left-leaning crack (5.9); where the crack splits, go either way. **Pro:** To 2.5 inches. **FA:** Herb Laeger, John McGowen; 11/76.

1565. **Hog Heaven** (5.9) ★★ Located near the center of the face. Go up a left-leaning ramp to a small tree (same as *Fote Hog*). Either begin or belay here. Go left on a crack, then straight up a thin crack, staying right of the second pitch of *Ball Bearing.* **Pro:**

Thin to 2.5 inches. **FA:** Don Reid, Alan Bartlett, Derek Reinig; 7/98.

1566. **Look Ma, No Bolts** (5.7) (R) Located near the center of the face. Go up a left-leaning ramp to a small tree (same as *Fote Hog*). Either begin or belay here. **Pitch 1:** Head up the face above, passing bulges on big holds to a small tree. **Pitch 2:** Head up and left in a crack to the top. **Pro:** To 2.5 inches. **FA:** Bob Gaines, Kurt Stitz; 1/92.

1567. **Fote Hog** (5.6) ★★ This is a popular, easy, multipitch route. Begin near the center of the face. Go up a left-leaning ramp to a small tree (either begin or belay here). **Pitch 1:** Head up the face, traverse right on big holds, then head up and right to a ledge. **Pitch 2:** Go up a flake (left of a finger crack), go right, then up a left-facing corner to a ledge. **Pitch 3:** Class 3 to the top. **Pro:** Thin to 2.5 inches. **FA:** Bob Dominick, John Wolfe; 9/76.

1568. **Hog Trough** (5.10a) ★★ Begin to the right of the ramp at the bottom of *Fote Hog.*

Head up to a cave-like feature, then up on big holds to join *Fote Hog* at end of the first pitch. **Pro:** Thin to 3 inches. Alan Bartlett, Mary Ann Kelly; 7/98.

1569. **Warthog** (5.9) ★★ (Variation to *Hog Trough*) (not shown on topo) Head up *Fote Hog's* ramp for about 30 feet, then undercling right out a small flake, then go up the flake to the cave and big holds on *Hog Heaven*. **Pro:** 0.5 to 3 inches. **FA:** Bob Gaines, Ron Herschberg; 4/03.

1570. **Western Saga** (5.9) ★★ Characterized by the large right-facing corner capped by a roof. **Pitch 1:** Climb up a crack to a ledge at the base of the corner. **Pitch 2:** Go up the corner, over the roof, to easier climbing above. **Pro:** To 3 inches. **FA:** Dan Ahlborn, Maria Cranor; 12/76.

1571. **Celebrity Death March** (5.10a) (R) ★ Begin about 40 feet right of *Western Saga*, behind bushes. **Pitch 1:** Go up to "orange"–

colored depressions, then up and left to a ledge. **Pitch 2:** Go up to a left-slanting groove/crack; where this ends, head left and then up to a headwall passed on the left. **Pro:** Thin to 2.5 inches. **FA:** Alan Bartlett, Todd Gordon, Don Reid, Kastle Lund, Derrick Reinich, Laurel Colella, Mary Ann Kelly; 7/98.

1572. **Guard Duty** (5.7) The wide crack–chimney to the right of *Celebrity Death March*. **Pro:** To 4+ inches. **FA:** Unknown.

1573. **Beefeater** (5.10a) (not shown on topo) Climb an obvious crack to thin cracks in a gray slab, then over a bulge (5.10a) and cracks to top. **Pro:** To 2.5 inches. **FA:** Todd Swain, Donette Smith; 11/00.

1574. **Western Omelette** (5.7) (not shown on photo) Located on right end of the east face. Go up horizontals to a left-facing flake, then up cracks past another horizontal. **Pro:** To 2.5 inches. **FA:** Unknown.

The Sentinel—West Face

The west face of the Sentinel offers some excellent vertical moderate to difficult routes up to 200 feet in length. Routes are 1 and 2 pitches long.

For parking and approach directions, see page 375. From the trail fork, take the left fork for about 150 yards, until you are past the northern end of the Sentinel. Here, it is possible to cut left (west) across rocks and pick up the climbers' trail that runs south along the western face of the Sentinel, entering a narrow

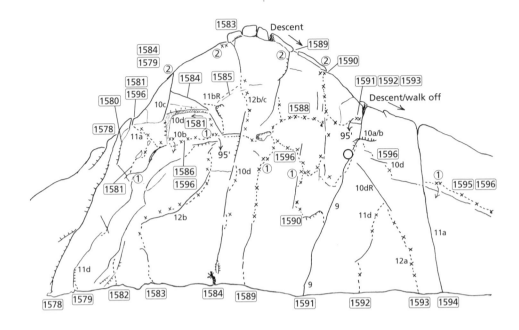

canyon. It is also possible to reach the west face from the southern end of the formation, but this involves fourth to fifth class down-climbing into the narrow southern end of the canyon along the base. A 60-meter rope is recommended. For routes that top out, descent is down right (south) on easy slabs.

1575. The Butt Buttress (5.10b) ★ (not shown on photo or topo) This is a four-bolt climb on the far left side of the face (facing north), starting from ledges about 45 feet off the ground. **Pro:** To 2 inches. **FA:** Dave Evans, Todd Gordon, Marge Floyd, Mike Brown, Terry Peterson; 1/88.

1576. Flared Bear (5.10b) (not shown on photo or topo) This route takes the right-arching, chimney-wide crack at the extreme left side of the west face. It leads into a vertical chimney system (*Where Janitors Dare*).

Follow that route up or rappel from a horn below a cubbyhole. **Pro:** To 4+ inches. **FA:** James Barnett, Ted Doughty; 5/75.

1577. Great White Buffalo (5.12a) ★ (not shown on photo or topo) Begin about 12 feet right of *Flared Bear*. Go up a face past two bolts, cross *Flared Bear*, face climb past two more bolts to meet *The Butt Buttress* at its second bolt. **Pro:** To 3+ inches; seven bolts. **FA:** Charles Cole.

1578. Where Janitors Dare (5.7) This is the obvious, right-slanting chimney. **Pro:** To 4+ inches. **FA:** Unknown.

1579. Where Eagles Dare (5.11d) ★★★ This right-leaning crack system about 12 feet right of the chimney of *Where Janitors Dare* begins with a short vertical thin crack. **Pitch 1:** Go up the thin crack (5.11d), then up and right, switch to a higher crack, then go up and right past one bolt to a bolt belay at a ledge below the left side of a roof. **Pitch 2:** Go up past three bolts to the left side of the roof, then up the crack above. **Pro:** Thin to 3 inches. **FA:** Kevin Powell, Dan Ahlborn; 1/76. **FFA** (First pitch): John Long; 12/79. **FFA** (Second pitch): Jonny Woodward; 4/84.

1580. **Crystal Keyhole** (5.9) From the point on the first pitch of *Where Eagles Dare* where a crack angles up and left, set up a belay. From here, head up and left on this crack, then straight up a right-facing corner/crack to the top. **FA:** Unknown; 12/81.

1581. **Medicine Man** (5.11b) ★ From the point on the first pitch of *Where Eagles Dare* where a crack angles up and left, set up a belay. Go up past plates to a face with three bolts, moving left to finish in the last bit of *Crystal Keyhole*. **Pro:** To 2.5 inches. **FA:** Bob Gaines, Alan Bartlett; 2/92.

1582. **Not for Loan** (5.10c) ★★ Begin off a ledge about 30 feet up and right of *Where Eagles Dare*. Go up right-leaning cracks to belay on a ledge. **Pro:** To 2.5 inches. **FA:** Jeff Morgan, Tony Zeek; 1975. **FFA:** Gib Lewis, Charles Cole; 12/79.

1583. **Some Like It Hot** (5.12c) ★★★★ **Pitch 1** (Sport): Go up and left to reach the traversing (5.12b), then upward-arching thin crack/seam. Go up (5.11c/d) to two-bolt belay shared with *Desert Song;* 100-foot rappel. **Pitch 2:** Traverse right, then go up a flare/seam (5.12c) to the top; two-bolt anchor. Though the first pitch is sport-bolted, it is necessary for someone to clean it due to its traversing nature. **Pro:** (first pitch) draws; (second pitch) to 3 inches; 5 bolts. **FA** (first pitch): Todd Gordon, Jim Murray; 2/86. **FA** (second pitch, formerly *Nameless A3*): Unknown. **FFA** (Entire route): Dave Mayville, Paul Borne; 1989.

1584. **Desert Song** (5.11b) (R) ★★★ This route used to start off a large yucca, which has since fallen down. Now either use a shoulder stand or make difficult moves (5.12+;V6/V7) to get started. **Pitch 1:** Go up a difficult flare to a crack/seam system. Follow the seam up past two bolts and some fixed copperheads (5.10d) to a good flake/crack. From here, traverse left to a two-bolt belay on a ledge below the right side of a large roof. **Pitch 2:** Go up the crack/flake on right, then face climb up and left (5.11b R) above the lip of the roof to a slanting crack. Many people do the easier (better, but still spicy, protected) first pitch and rappel (100+ feet). **Pro:** First pitch to 2 inches, two bolts, two fixed copperheads; second pitch to 2.5 inches. **FA** (first pitch): Roy Naasz, Chris Wegener; 2/70. **FFA** (first pitch) and **FA** (second pitch): John Bachar; 1977.

1585. **Desert Long** (Variation) (5.11b) (R) Climb pitch two of *Desert Song* past the crux, then head up and right along a seam to join pitch two of *Some Like It Hot* at the second to last bolt. **FA:** Dave Mayville, Peter Croft; 12/00.

1586. **I Can't Believe It's a Girl** (5.10b) From the two-bolt belay atop the first p of *Desert Song,* traverse left past three b a two-bolt belay in the corner (on the part of *Where Eagles Dare*). Rap or co up *Where Eagles Dare,* or climb the l of *New Latitude.* **FA:** Bob Gaines, M Loeher, Todd Gordon; 4/98.

1587. **Scared Bare** (5.10d) (R) T and rarely done. From the belay a pitch of *Desert Song,* go up to, the under, the large roof; join *Where I* turning the left end of the roof. F Naasz, Chris Wegener; 2/70. **FFA:**

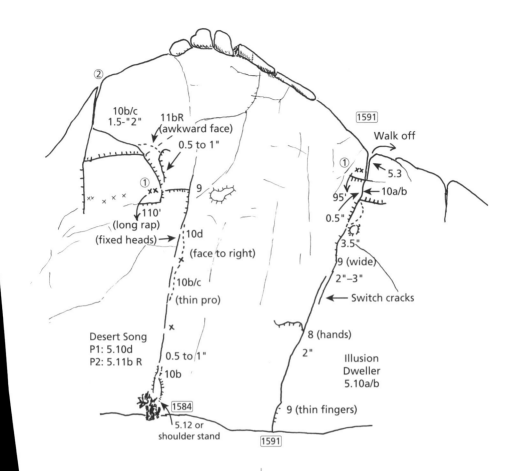

② 10b/c
1.5-"2"   11bR
          (awkward face)
          0.5 to 1"

① xx
110'
(long rap)
(fixed heads) →

9

10d
(face to right)
x

10b/c
(thin pro)

x

Desert Song
P1: 5.10d
P2: 5.11b R

0.5 to 1"
10b

1584

5.12 or
shoulder stand

1591

Walk off

① xx ← 5.3
95' ← 10a/b
0.5"
3.5"
9 (wide)
2"-3"
← Switch cracks

8 (hands)
2"

Illusion
Dweller
5.10a/b

9 (thin fingers)

1591

1588. Desert Tortoise (5.12a/b) ★★★
Though this traversing route can be climbed
in either direction, left to right is probably
best. Begin atop the first pitch of *Desert Song.*
Head back right, and continue right past a
bolt into a hueco, then head up and right past
eight more bolts, one fixed pin, and one fixed
nut. You end up briefly joining, then crossing
both *The Scorpion* and *The Tarantula* until you
reach the bolt belay atop *Illusion Dweller.* **Pro:**
To 3 inches. **FA:** Bob Gaines; 9/99.

1589. The Scorpion (5.13c) ★★★ This two-
pitch route begins about 20 feet right of
Desert Song, in the next crack/seam system.
Pitch 1: Go up the crack and seam past some
bolts to a bolt belay (5.12c). **Pitch 2:** Go up

then right past bolts until you can head back
left to a crack that is followed to the top
(5.13c). **Pro:** To 3 inches. **FA:** Paul Borne,
Dave Mayville; 1989.

1590. The Tarantula (5.12c) ★★★ This route
takes various cracks/seams on the open face
between *The Scorpion* and *Illusion Dweller.*
Begin at *Illusion Dweller.* **Pitch 1:** Go up
Illusion Dweller for about 25 feet, then go left
on a flake, then go up a face to a vertical
seam/crack and a bolt belay on the right.
Pitch 2: Head right to another vertical
crack/seam with several bolts and fixed gear,
then go up the open face to the top. **Pro:** To
2 inches. **FA:** Dave Evans, Charles Cole. **FFA:**
Paul Borne; 1989.

1591. Illusion Dweller (aka Kandy-Kolored Tangerine-Flake Streamline Baby) (5.10a/b) ★★★★★ This very popular and classic route climbs the extremely obvious and inviting right-slanting crack near the right-hand section of the main west face. Go up thin fingers to the right-diagonalling hand- to off-hand-size crack system (5.9), then up to and over a small roof (5.10a/b) near the top.

Two-bolt anchor on a ledge; 95+ foot rappel. Or, you can head up a wide crack to top and walk down to the right. *Kandy-Kolored Tangerine Flake Streamlined Baby* was the name given the route by the first-ascent party; *Illusion Dweller* was the name given by the second-ascent party. **Pro:** To 3 inches. **FA:** Matt Cox, Spencer Lennard, Steve Emerson; 1973.

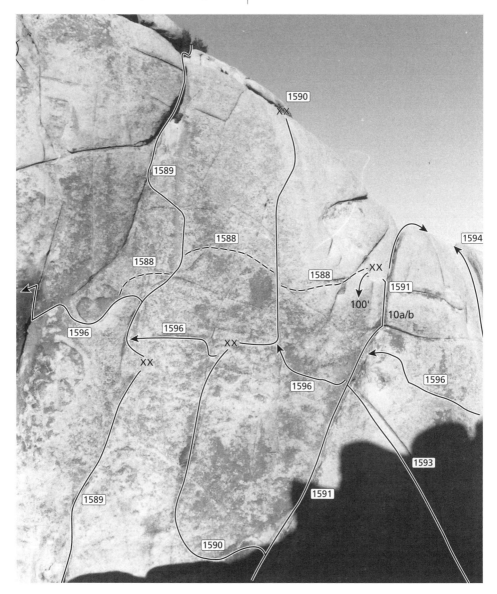

1592. The Centipede (5.11d) ★★ Begin about 30 right of *Illusion Dweller*. Go up the face past a bolt to a short right-leaning thin crack, then past two more bolts (5.11d) to join *The Chameleon* as it heads up and left (5.10d R) to meet Illusion Dweller. **Pro:** Thin to 3+ inches. **FA:** Dave Mayville, Paul Borne; 1989.

1593. The Chameleon (5.12b) ★★★★ Begin in a left-leaning seam about 60 feet right of *Illusion Dweller*. Follow the seam past four bolts (5.12b) to where it becomes a difficult-to-protect crack/flare (5.10d R), ultimately joining *Illusion Dweller* below its crux roof. **Pro:** To 3+ inches. **FA** (TR): John Bachar, Mike Lechlinski; 12/79. **FA** (Lead): Dave Mayville, Paul Borne.

1594. The Rubberfat Syndrome (5.11a) (TR) This route climbs the straight-up, shallow off-width crack right of the start of *The Chameleon.* Named for Gaston Rebuffat, who popularized the "gaston" technique used to climb this shallow crack. **FA:** John Bachar, Mari Gingery, John Yablonski; 12/79.

1595. Worms in Your Brain (5.11c) ★★ This right-to-left traversing route begins opposite *Bikini Whale* (on Hidden Cliff) on the far right end of the west face (80 feet right of *The Rubberfat Syndrome*). It can be done as a separate route or as the first pitch of the next route (*New Latitude,* a six-pitch girdle traverse of the west face). Head left on a horizontal crack, then up and left past two bolts and a fixed copperhead to a horizontal with three bolts, to a two-bolt belay/rap. **Pro:** To 3 inches. **FA:** Todd Gordon, Jim Angione; 11/93. **FFA:** Bob Gaines, Dave Mayville; 11/93.

1596. New Latitude (5.12a) ★★★★ This is an amazing six-pitch girdle traverse of the entire west face of the Sentinel; one of the longest climbs in Josh. It is climbed as a right-to-left traverse. Begin in the narrow corridor opposite *Bikini Whale* (on Hidden Cliff), on the far right end of the Sentinel's west face. **Pitch 1:** Climb *Worms in Your Brain* (5.11c) to a two-bolt anchor. **Pitch 2:** Walk left on a ledge, then go up the face past one bolt; angle left to a hanging belay (gear) below the crux roof on *Illusion Dweller* (5.10d). **Pitch 3:** Downclimb *Illusion Dweller* about 15 feet, then head left past two bolts to three-bolt belay on *The Tarantula* (5.11b). **Pitch 4:** Go up, then left, past three bolts to a thin face traverse left to reach a groove on *The Scorpion;* go up the groove past two bolts, then left to a flake and one more bolt to finish atop the first pitch of *Desert Song* (5.12a). (See *Desert Tortoise* as a 5.12a/b alternative to pitches 3 and 4.) **Pitch 5:** Climb left past three bolts to a two-bolt belay in a corner (5.10b; this is a "route" called *I Can't Believe It's A Girl*). **Pitch 6:** Traverse left past a bolt to reach last two bolts (up and left) of *Medicine Man,* finishing atop *Crystal Keyhole*. **Pro:** To 3 inches. **FA:** Bob Gaines, Dave Mayville; 5/99.

The Hidden Cliff

This aptly named, overhanging cliff faces the far right end of the Sentinel's west face, forming the right side of a narrow corridor. For parking and approach directions, see page 375. From the trail fork, take the left route for about 150 yards, until you are past the northern end of the Sentinel. Here, it is possible to cut left (west) across rocks and pick up the climbers' trail that runs south along the western face of the Sentinel, entering a narrow canyon. Follow this to its very end. *Bikini Whale* lies on your right about 20 feet to the right of the end of the corridor. It is also possible to reach this wall from the southern end of the Sentinel, but this is more involved and involves fourth to fifth class downclimbing into the narrow southern end of the canyon along the base. Descend down this southern end of the corridor. The cliff and its routes are not shown. Map, page 374.

1597. **Bikini Whale** (5.12a/b) ★★★★ (Sport) This excellent route begins about 20 feet right of the end of the corridor. A powerful lockoff move (crux) past the first bolt leads to climbing straight up knobs and horizontal bands to a seam. A second crux is past the last bolt. Shorter climbers may want to stick clip the first bolt. **Pro:** Five bolts; two-bolt anchor; extendo needed to lower or toprope. **FA:** Unknown French climbers; 1984. **FA** (Lead): Kurt Smith; 1988.

1598. **Railer** (5.12c) ★★ Climb *Bikini Whale* past two bolts and then work out left in a horizontal crack, which is followed to the top. **Pro:** To 2.5 inches. **FA:** Scott Cosgrove.

1599. **Bikini Beach** (5.12b) ★★ (TR) Climb *Bikini Whale* to where *Railer* splits off left.

Move right in the diagonalling/horizontal crack, then up to the top of *Against the Grain*. **FA:** Scott Cosgrove.

1600. **G String** (5.13d) ★★★ (Sport) This unrepeated route begins with the first two bolts of *Bikini Whale* to a horizontal crack (*Railer*); go left a short distance, then up a thin flake/corner and face, eventually finishing at the top of *Bikini Whale*. **Pro:** Seven bolts. **FA:** Scott Cosgrove.

1601. **Against the Grain** (5.10a) ★ This climb is located about 25 feet right of *Bikini Whale*. Climb knobs past two bolts up to a crack, thin at first, that gradually widens. **Pro:** To 2.5 inches; two-bolt anchor. **FA** (TR): Charles Cole, Gib Lewis, Randy Vogel; 12/79. **FA** (Lead): Tracy Dorton et al.

The Otter Cliffs

These indistinct and jumbled rocks are actually the north and northwestern extension of the Tumbling Rainbow Formation. For parking and approach directions, see page 375. From the trail fork, take the left fork for about 150 yards, until you are past the northern end of the Sentinel. Here, it is possible to cut left (west) across rocks; cross the climbers' trail that runs south (to the west face of the Sentinel) and continue west over some boulders and down into a wash.

To reach the west face, it may be easier to approach as for Wimp Tower (page 395), but continue southwest in the small wash until you are directly below the west face. Alternatively, if you are near Zombie Woof or Miles of Piles, you can follow the wash north. Map, page 374.

The Otter Cliffs—North End

The following climb is on the somewhat broken northern end of the Otter Cliffs.

1602. **Roberts Crack** (5.11a) ★ This route is located on your left on the northern apex of the formation as you scramble over the boulders. This is the overhanging finger-to-hand crack. It begins with a small roof. **Pro:** To 3 inches. **FA:** Alan Roberts.

The Otter Cliffs—West Face

The west face of the Otter Cliffs is a varied face with several large crack and chimney systems. It lies above a small wash that flows southwest between Wild Rock and Miles of Piles' east face into a small dam near Zombie Woof Rock. It is sunny most of the afternoon, with more shade for routes on the right section. It lies about 100 feet east of Wild Rock (page 440).

1603. **The Joker** (5.12c) ★★ This steep, three-bolt route is high up on the far left end of the west face of the Otter Cliffs, on a brownish wall that is around and right of *Roberts Crack*. **Pro:** Gear for anchor. **FA:** Dave Bengston, Paul Borne, Dave Mayville; 1991.

1604. No route.

1605. **Out of Shape** (5.9) Begin about 100 feet down and right of *The Joker.* Go up a left-facing dihedral to a ledge, then up past a block and a dike-like scooped-out section. Go right and up to the top of a left-facing corner and past a small bush. **Pro:** To 2.5 inches. **FA:** Mark Bowling, Alan Bartlett; 8/94.

1606. **Otter Pops** (5.10b) (R) ★ This is the right-slanting thin crack just right of *Out of Shape.* Go up this to the same ledge, up the thin crack above, then up the left-leaning dihedral with a wide crack to meet *Out of*

Shape at the bush. **Pro:** Thin to 3.5 inches. **FA:** Mark Bowling, Steve Gerberding, Alan Bartlett; 11/00.

1607. **Goofy Grape** (5.9) Begin right of *Otter Pops.* Go up a trough past a bush to the ledge. Move up and right in discontinuous cracks, left to another crack, then up the face. **Pro:** Thin to 3 inches. Alan Bartlett, Steve Gerberding, Mark Bowling; 11/00.

1608. **Leopold Lime** (5.10c) (TR) This is the left-slanting crack that begins up and right of *Goofy Grape.* **FA:** Alan Bartlett, Steve Gerberding, Mark Bowling; 11/00.

The Otter Cliffs—West Face, Right Section

The following four routes lie on a black/face to the right of the previous climbs. A large right-slanting groove *(Fascist Groove Thing)* marks the left side of the face. A large pine is below the face.

1609. **Fascist Groove Thing** (5.12a) (TR) Go up the thin crack over a small roof to a right-leaning groove. Exit left at the top. **FA:** Russ Walling, Mari Gingery.

The following routes lie right of *Fascist Groove Thing* and are reached by tunneling right under large boulders.

1610. **Welfare Trough** (5.7) Go up to a chimney/trough that leans left, then head straight up. **FA:** Ernie Ale, Laurel Colella, Alan Bartlett; 11/00.

1611. **Chemical Imbalance** (5.10d) ★ Start up *Welfare Trough,* then head straight up a small right-facing corner/thin crack. **Pro:** Thin to 3 inches. **FA:** Steve Gerberding, Mark Bowling, Alan Bartlett, Cal Gerberding; 11/00.

1612. **Barracuda** (5.10a) ★ Begin at *Welfare Trough,* but head more or less straight up to a thin handcrack in a right-facing corner over a small roof. **Pro:** Thin to 2.5 inches. **FA:** Alan Bartlett, Cal Gerberding, Steve Gerberding, Mark Bowling; 11/00.

The Thin Wall

This narrow and short formation is very popular due to the large number of easy to moderate routes on its east face. The Thin Wall lies just north of the Sentinel, to the right of the nature trail. For parking and approach directions, see page 375. From the trail fork, take the left fork for about 150 yards and past the northern end of the Sentinel. The southern end of the Thin Wall is directly ahead. To reach the east face, head slightly right off the nature trail (there is a pretty obvious path here) directly to the base of the east face. Map, page 374.

The Thin Wall—East Face

This crag has numerous easy to moderate routes on its right end, and a couple of harder climbs on the taller left section. Several sets of fixed anchors are found atop the routes on the left. Descend right. The face gets morning sun and is shady all afternoon.

Advisory: It is not uncommon for groups to toprope one or more climbs in this area. If you place topropes on routes and leave them up for more than a short time, you must be prepared to either share the ropes with other climbers, or pull them down. Totally dominating this crag with topropes and then being unwilling to share or pull your ropes is not only extremely rude, but might justify the removal of your ropes. Be courteous instead.

1613. **Child's Play** (5.10c/d) (R) ★★ Go up the shallow right-facing corner, then over the roof. Both this and *Congratulations* are usually toproped from a two-bolt anchor on top (slings advised). **Pro:** Thin to 1.5 inches. **FA** (TR): Mike Tupper, Greg Mayer; 12/82. **FA** (Lead): Unknown.

1614. **Congratulations** (5.10d) (R) ★★ Go up the brown face past horizontals, then left and over the roof, finishing as for *Child's Play.* Both this and *Child's Play* are usually toproped from a two-bolt anchor on top (slings advised). **Pro:** Thin to 2 inches. **FA** (TR): Unknown; 1979. **FA** (Lead): Jonny Woodward.

1615. **No Calculators Allowed** (5.10a) ★★ Take the thin crack up to a bulge at the top (crux). **Pro:** Thin to 2 inches; two-bolt anchor. **FA:** Craig Fry, Dave Evans, Mari Gingery; 1979.

1616. **Count on Your Fingers** (5.9) ★ Climb thin cracks just left of a small right-facing corner and arête. **Pro:** Thin to 2 inches; two-bolt anchor. **FA:** Todd Swain, Ned Crossley; 3/86.

1617. **Peculiar Taste Buds** (5.8) The right-facing corner. **FA:** Todd Swain; 9/89.

1618. **Conservative Policies** (5.8) The crack just right of the right-facing corner; move right at the top. **Pro:** To 2 inches. **FA:** Alan Bartlett, Debbie Daigle; 3/88.

1619. **Butterfingers Make Me Horny** (5.8) The crack about 8 feet right of *Conservative Policies.* **Pro:** To 2 inches. **FA:** Todd Gordon, Cyndie Bransford; 5/88.

1620. **Chocolate Is Better Than Sex** (5.9+) Follow double cracks to a thin crack left of corner/blocks *(Square Root).* **Pro:** To 2 inches. **FA:** Todd Gordon, Cyndie Bransford; 5/88.

1621. **Square Root** (5.8) The right-facing corner/blocks. **Pro:** To 3 inches. **FA:** Todd Swain; 9/89.

1622. **Almost Vertical** (5.7) Climb the crack off the ledge, about 8 feet right of *Square Root*. This is the left-hand of two obvious cracks. **Pro:** To 2.5 inches. **FA:** Alan Roberts, Kristen Laird; 12/87.

1623. **The Face of Tammy Faye** (5.8) ★ Go up the face past horizontals between the two obvious cracks (*Almost Vertical* and *Ain't Nothing but a J-Tree Thing*), with one bolt near the very top. **Pro:** Thin cams to 2 inches. **FA:** Jeff Rhoads, Tim from Atlanta; 11/89.

1624 **Ain't Nothing But a J-Tree Thing** (5.6) ★ The right-hand of two obvious cracks. **Pro:** To 2.5 inches. **FA:** Steve Shearer; 7/87.

The Thin Wall—West Face

The west face of the Thin Wall is reached by staying on the nature trail past where you exit right to reach the east face. The nature trail passes just west (left) of the west face. The face gets morning shade and afternoon sun. The face and routes are not pictured.

1625. **Sandbag** (5.10c) (R) ★ Begin off a boulder. Follow a thin crack near the middle of the face, staying in the right crack higher up, which leads to the summit block. **Pro:** Thin to 2 inches. **FA:** Mike Beck et al.; 1979.

1626. **Keith's Work** (5.11a) (TR) Begin about 18 feet right of *Sandbag*. Go up to a ledge, then up thin diagonal cracks that lead to a V handcrack near the top. **FA:** Hans Florine, Phil Requist; 3/88.

The Wimp Tower

This east-facing formation lies about 100 yards northwest of the Otter Cliffs and about 75 yards west of the Thin Wall. It is distinguishable by a thin crack on the east face that leads to a large crystal dike.

For parking/approach directions, see page 375. From the trail fork, take the left route. About 50 yards past the northern end of the Thin Wall, head sharply left (southwest) across flat ground, then down into a small gully/wash. At this point, the Wimp Tower is on your right (west). It gets morning sun and is shady in the afternoon. The tower and route are not pictured. Map, page 374.

1627. **Magnetic Woose** (5.10b) ★ This is on east face. Go up a thin crack to a dike, go right, then up the crack above as it diagonals left. **Pro:** To 2 inches. **FA:** John Long, Lynn Hill, Randy Vogel; 1/80.

Czech Dome

This is the whitish/grey face to the north of the Thin Wall. For parking and approach directions, see page 375. From the trail fork, take the left fork for about 300 yards, until you are about 100 yards past the northern end of the Thin Wall and the nature trail begins to curve right (east). From this point, head off left (northwest) to the formation, which is more or less directly ahead. The sole route lies on the east face (morning sun, afternoon shade). The dome and route are not pictured. Map, page 374.

1628. **Ahoj** (5.10c) This route follows a thin seam/crack up the middle of the Czech Dome past one fixed pin and two bolts. **Pro:** Thin to 2 inches. **FA:** Todd Gordon, Raim Bedin, Betsy Dolge, Tom Atherton, Phil, Beth; 5/91.

The Brown Wall

This chocolate-brown formation lies approximately 500 yards north of Sports Challenge Rock; just east of the northern terminus of the nature trail. For parking and approach directions, see page 375. From the trail fork, take the left fork for 400+ yards as it heads north, then cuts east. At the apex of the trail, proceed north along a wash, then right (east) up to the base of this obvious formation. It faces west (morning shade, sunny all afternoon). Descend on either end of rock. Map, page 374.

1629. **Sgt. Saturn** (5.9) This is just left of *Brown and Serve.* Start in a small right-facing corner, then traverse right into an obvious left-facing corner. **Pro:** To 2 inches. **FA:** Todd Swain, Donette Smith; 4/95.

1630. **Brown and Serve** (5.11a) ★ Begin about 15 feet down and left of *Captain Kronos.* This is the thin crack beginning from flat ground. **Pro:** Thin to 2 inches. **FA:** Chris Miller; 1995.

1631. **Captain Kronos** (5.9+) ★ Begin off a block, then move left (5.9+) into a right-leaning handcrack. **Pro:** Thin to 2 inches. **FA:** Howard King, Rob Fainberg; 1977.

1632. **Brownian Motion** (5.10b) ★ Begin off a block about 10 feet right and up from *Captain Kronos;* move left into a right-slanting finger crack. **Pro:** Thin to 2 inches. **FA:** Steve Bartlett, Steve Untch; 3/84.

1633. **Mr. Hankey** (5.10d) (TR) ★ The crack between *Brownian Motion* and *Jerry Brown.* **FA:** Chris Miller; 1995.

1634. **Jerry Brown** (5.10b) ★★★ Climb a thin crack to the roof, move left and up the crack over the center of the roof. **Pro:** Thin to 2 inches. **FA:** Randy Vogel, Mari Gingery, Mike Lechlinski, John Yablonski; 12/79.

1635. **James Brown** (5.11b) ★ (TR) Start up *Jerry Brown,* but head up the crack over the right side of the roof; join *Brown 25* higher up. **FA:** Matt Dancy; 12/85.

1636. **Brown 25** (5.11a) (R) ★★★ Begin about 5 feet right of *Jerry Brown;* go up the crack that converges with *James Brown.* **Pro:** Many thin to 2 inches. **FA** (TR): Unknown. **FA** (Lead): Unknown.

1637. **Skid Mark** (5.12c) ★ (TR) The face between *Brown 25* and *If It's Brown, Flush It.* **FA:** Scott Cosgrove; 3/00.

1638. **If It's Brown, Flush It** (5.11c/d) ★ (TR) Climb the seam to thin crack on the right end of the face. **FA:** Steve Bartlett; 1983.

THE LAND THAT TIME FORGOT

This canyon and wash runs northwest from the northern apex of nature trail (near the Brown Wall) and eventually leads to the Lost Horse Wall. The following routes/formations are described as though you are coming from Real Hidden Valley, but they could be approached (in some cases more easily) from Park Boulevard by walking around the north side of Pep Boys Crag (south of Playhouse Rock), then south on an old road until you can drop into the canyon. Map, page 398.

Fingertip Rock

This small formation (and several adjacent to it) lie about 100 feet up and left of the Brown Wall. Approach as for the Brown Wall (see page 396). The rock and routes are not pictured.

1639. **Peggy Fleming** (5.10b/c) (TR) This route lies about 20 feet left and across from *Fingertip Pleasure* on a steep brown wall. **FA:** Todd Swain; 1/98.

1640. **Chexquest Flemoids** (5.3) (R) This route climbs a juggy face out of a gully on the back side of Fingertip Rock. **FA:** Todd Swain; 1/98.

1641. **Fingertip Pleasure** (5.10c) (TR) This route lies on the north side of Fingertip Rock. It is a finger crack that begins above yuccas. **FA:** Brian Elliot; et al.

1642. **Cough Up Phlegm** (5.7) This crack and juggy face is located about 20 feet right and around the corner (on the west face) from *Fingertip Pleasure.* **Pro:** To 2.5 inches. **FA:** Brian Elliot et al.

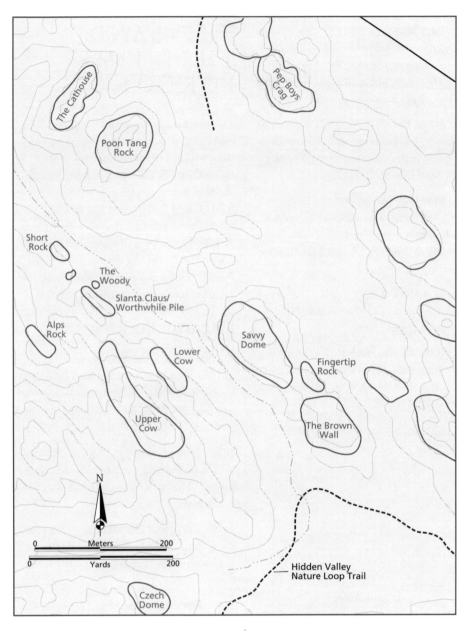

The Cathouse

Pep Boys Crag

Poon Tang Rock

Short Rock

The Woody

Slanta Claus/
Worthwhile Pile

Alps Rock

Lower Cow

Savvy Dome

Fingertip Rock

Upper Cow

The Brown Wall

N

| 0 | Meters | 200 |
| 0 | Yards | 200 |

Hidden Valley
Nature Loop Trail

Czech Dome

1643. **False Scent** (5.8) This route lies on a separate wall about 75 feet above and left of *Peggy Fleming*. It is the left-hand of two thin V cracks. **Pro:** Thin to 2 inches. **FA:** Alan Bartlett, Bruce Hawkins; 10/00.

Savvy Dome

This formation lies about 100 yards left of the Brown Wall. For parking and approach directions, see page 375. From the trail fork, take the left fork for 400+ yards as it heads north, then cuts east. At the apex of the trail, proceed north along a wash until you reach this buttress, which falls almost straight into the right (east) side of the wash. The dome and routes are not pictured. Map, page 398.

1644. **7** (5.10a) This route is located on a shorter section of rock about 75 feet left of the main Savvy Dome formation. Climb the seam to the 7-shaped crack. **Pro:** Thin to 2 inches. **FA:** Randy Vogel, Todd Swain; 10/91.

1645. **Miss Steak (aka Flare)** (5.7) This lies about 20 feet right of 7; go up and left in a flare on scoops. **FA:** Todd Swain; 10/91.

1646. **Tube Steak** (5.10c) ★ The left-leaning "tube" with a finger-and-hand crack in its back, just right of *Miss Steak*. **Pro:** To 2.5 inches. **FA:** Alan Roberts, John Hayward.

1647. **Savwafare Ist Everywhere** (5.8+) ★★ The route takes a direct line up the left-hand crack system on the main Savvy Dome formation. **Pro:** To 2.5 inches. **FA:** Steve Untch, Steve Bartlett; 3/84.

1648. **Shame** (5.10c) (R) ★ Begin about 8 feet right of *Savwafare Ist Everywhere*. Go up a seam to a horizontal, then right and up a thin crack with one fixed pin. **Pro:** Thin to 2.5 inches. **FA:** Jonny Woodward, Darrel Hensel; 1/87.

1649. **Satyriasis (aka Chimney)** (5.7) This thin crack to a cleft/chimney begins about 10 feet right of *Shame*. **Pro:** Thin to 4+ inches. **FA:** Todd Swain; 11/79.

The Cow Formations

These two formations (Upper Cow and Lower Cow Rocks) face east and lie high above the canyon/wash, about 150 yards north of the apex of the nature trail. The rocks (and others in the vicinity) can be reached via two different approaches:

- Park at the large turnout on the west side of Park Boulevard 7.9 miles from the West Entrance and 0.7 miles from the Intersection Rock/Real Hidden Valley intersection. This is the parking area for Playhouse Rock. Head south-southwest from the parking area, staying right of Pep Boys Crag, following a trail and bits of an old road that head due south. Then head southwest over boulders and down into the canyon/wash.

- Alternatively, park at the Real Hidden Valley parking area (for parking/approach directions, see page 375). From the trail fork, take the left fork for 400+ yards as it heads north, then cuts east. At the apex of the trail, proceed north along a wash into a wide canyon (past the Brown Wall and Savvy Dome). The Cow Formations lie high on the left (west) side of the canyon. Map, page 398.

Upper Cow Rock

This is the higher, larger (rectangular-shaped), and east-facing formation high above the wash.

Upper Cow Rock—East Face

This is the main aspect of the rock, seen from the wash below. It gets morning sun and is shady all afternoon.

Upper Cow Rock — XX — 1655 — Lower Cow Rock
1651 — 1652 — 1657 — 1658 — 1659
1653 — 1654 — 1656
1650
1663
1664 — 1666
1665

1650. **Prime Real Estate** (5.12d) ★★★
(Sport) This six-both route lies on a separate
dark-colored face about 150 feet down and
left of *Cowabunga.* Two-bolt anchor; walk off.
FA: Tony Sartin; 10/05.

1651. **Cowabunga** (5.10c) ★ This is located
on a separate section of the formation to the
left of the main face. Go up cracks on the
right side, over a roof, then up a face past
one bolt. **Pro:** To 3 inches. **FA:** Bob Gaines,
Lou Langlais; 9/94.

1652. **Hollywood and Bovine** (5.10d) ★★
The left-hand five-bolt route; move right at
the top to belay/rap from the *Udder Chaos*
two-bolt anchor. **FA:** Bob Gaines, Yvonne
Gaines; 6/93.

1653. **Udder Chaos** (5.10c) ★★ The right-
hand five-bolt route, beginning just left of an
obvious crack in the center of the face
(Upper Cow). Two-bolt anchor/rap. **FA:** Bob
Gaines, Yvonne Gaines; 6/93.

1654. **Upper Cow** (5.10a) (R) ★ The obvious
crack in the center of the face. **Pro:** Thin to
2 inches. Todd Gordon, Alan Roberts; 1/88.

1655. **Milkman (aka Reach for a Peach)**
(5.10a) ★ Begin 15 feet right of *Upper Cow.*
Go up to a bolt, then go right and up to a
second bolt. **Pro:** To 2 inches. **FA** (TR): Alan
Roberts, John Hayward. **FA** (Lead): Bob
Gaines, Lou Langlais; 9/94.

1656. **Cottage Cheese** (5.9) ★ Begin as for
Milkman, but go left after the first bolt. **Pro:**
To 2 inches; two bolts. **FA:** Bob Gaines, Lou
Langlais; 9/94.

1657. **Cow Pie Corner** (5.6) The right-
facing corner. **FA:** Alan Roberts, John
Hayward.

1658. **One Bolt Jolt** (5.11a) Located about
150 right of *Cow Pie Corner* on a shorter,
lower section of Upper Cow Rock. Climb
past an eyebolt to a handcrack. **Pro:** To 2.5
inches. **FA:** John Bachar; 1987.

1659. **Super Quickie** (5.12b) ★ Located 50
feet right of *One Bolt Jolt.* Follow a thin
crack/flair with three bolts. Two-bolt anchor.
FA: John Bachar; 1987.

1660. **Denali Solo in Winter** (5.5) (not
shown on photo) This climbs a right-facing
flake on the northwest end of the rock, about
100 feet right of *Super Quickie* and near a
pine tree. **FA:** Karlis Ogle; 2/00.

Upper Cow Rock—West Face

Only a couple of fairly forgettable routes lie on the west face, which gets morning shade and afternoon sun. This face and its routes are not shown.

1661. **Don't Have a Cow** (5.9+) This route is on the back (west) side of the Upper Cow, near the left side. Climb past a fixed knife blade, then up thin cracks and over a small roof. **Pro:** Thin to 2 inches. **FA:** Alan Bartlett, Brandt Allen; 3/90.

1662. **Stress Fracture** (5.9+) This is located on a short dark-colored tower facing *Don't Have a Cow.* It is the rightmost of several cracks on the tower. **FA:** Alan Bartlett, Katie Wilkinson; 11/91.

Lower Cow Rock

This rock is below and right of Upper Cow. It has a summit feature that, from some angles, resembles a cow. It sees morning sun and afternoon shade. Map, page 398.

1663. **Mad Cow Disease** (5.10b) ★ Go up to and over a large roof, which is trivialized by the fact that you can climb to the left, avoiding much of the route. **Pro:** To 3 inches. **FA:** Terry Olsson, Todd Swain; 3/98.

1664. **Sacred Cow** (5.10a) ★ The obvious crack up the center of the formation. **Pro:** To 3 inches. **FA:** Alan Roberts, Todd Gordon; 1/88.

1665. **Devine Bovine** (5.10b) (TR) ★ Climb the face up and right to a flake then to an arête. **FA:** Bob Gaines, Yvonne Gaines; 5/93.

1666. **Variation** (5.11a) (TR) ★ Start farther right and go straight up to the flake. **FA:** Todd Swain; 3/98.

Slanta Claus Rock, Worthwhile Pile, and The Woody

These three small formations lie low on the west side of the large wash that proceeds north from the apex of the Hidden Valley Loop Nature Trail. Worthwhile Pile is a small formation with many cracks on the lower left; Slanta Claus Rock is just up and right with several diagonalling cracks; the Woody is the phallic-shaped spire on Slanta Claus Rock's right side. These rocks (and others in the vicinity) can be reached via two different approaches.

- Park at the large turnout on the west side of Park Boulevard 7.9 miles from the West Entrance and 0.7 miles from the Intersection Rock/Real Hidden Valley intersection. This is the parking area for Playhouse Rock. Head south-southwest from the parking area, staying right of Pep Boys Crag, on a trail and bits of an old road that heads due south. Then head southwest over boulders and down into the canyon/wash. This is a much shorter and more direct approach.
- Alternatively, park at Real Hidden Valley parking area (for parking/approach directions, see page 375). From the trail fork, take the left fork for 400+ yards as it heads north, then cuts east. At the apex of the trail, proceed north along a wash into a wide canyon (past Brown Wall, Savvy Dome and the Cow formations). The Slanta Claus, etc. lie about 175 yards farther down the wash from Savvy Dome and 125 yards past Lower Cow Rock. Map, page 398.

Worthwhile Pile   Slanta Claus Rock

The Woody

Worthwhile Pile

This is the lower left-hand section of rock, with lots of cracks on the left end, some thin seams and slab in the middle, and thin cracks on the right. It gets morning sun and afternoon shade.

1667. **Pile It Higher and Deeper** (5.7) Begin in gully; go up left-leaning crack to a left-facing corner. **Pro:** To 2 inches. **FA:** Todd Swain; 10/91.

1668. **Ernie Pyle** (5.7) Start bout 6 feet right of *Pile It Higher and Deeper*. Go off a small boulder, up a handcrack, then up and right to finish in another crack. **Pro:** To 2 inches. **FA:** Todd Swain; 10/91.

1669. **Worthless Bile** (5.7) Crack just right of *Ernie Pile*. **Pro:** To 2 inches. **FA:** Tucker Tech, Alan Bartlett, Laurel Colella; 3/00.

1670. **Not Worth Your Pile** (5.4) The next crack right of *Worthless Bile*. **Pro:** To 2 inches. **FA:** Tucker Tech; 1994.

1671. **Holden On** (5.10a) ★ Go up the face to a bolt and thin seams. **Pro:** Thin to 2 inches. **FA:** Mark Holden, Karl Pearson, Todd Swain; 11/89. **FA** (Lead): Unknown.

1672. **Overlooked** (5.10a) ★★ Begin just left of *Worthwhile Pile* and head up and left in thin seams to a bolt, then up a left-slanting thin crack. This ends in the same spot as *Holden On*. **Pro:** Thin to 2 inches. **FA:** Bob Gaines, Brian Prentice; 4/01.

1673. **Worthwhile Pile** (5.7) ★ This is the left-curving thin crack on the right side of the face. **Pro:** Thin to 2 inches. **FA:** Todd Gordon, Alan Roberts; 1/88.

1674. **Holden Out** (5.10a) (R) Begin up a seam 5 feet right of *Worthwhile Pile*. **Pro:** Thin to 1.5 inches. **FA:** Todd Swain, Mark Holden, Karl Pearson; 11/89.

1675. **Holden Hands** (5.8) Begin 10 feet right of *Worthwhile Pile,* just right of a yucca. Go up cracks. **Pro:** To 2 inches. **FA:** Todd Swain, Mark Holden, Karl Pearson; 11/89.

Slanta Claus Rock

Slanta Claus Rock is located just right of and behind Worthwhile Pile, and as the name would suggest, is characterized by several left-leaning cracks. It gets morning sun and afternoon shade.

1676. **Return of the Mimmster** (5.8) The left-slanting crack just left of *Slanta Claus Left*. **Pro:** To 2 inches. **FA:** Brandt Allen, George Burton; 1993.

1677. **Slanta Claus Left** (5.7) The left-slanting handcrack. **Pro:** To 2.5 inches. **FA:** Alan Roberts, Todd Gordon; 1/88.

1678. **Slanta Claus Center** (5.10a) ★ Begin about 18 feet right of *Slanta Claus Left* off a boulder. Go up thin cracks and a juggy face. **Pro:** Thin to 2 inches. **FA:** Alan Roberts, Todd Gordon; 1/88.

1679. **Slanta Claus Right** (5.8) Start as for *Slanta Claus Center,* and head up cracks and the face right of that route. **Pro:** To thin 2 inches. **FA:** Alan Roberts, Todd Gordon; 1/88.

The Woody

The Woody is a small leaning pinnacle to the right and in front of Slanta Claus Rock. The rock and routes are not shown.

1680. **The Woody** (5.5) (R/X) From near the start of *Slanta Claus Right,* traverse right, then up a grainy face. Rap from the summit. **FA:** D. B. Cooper; 2/92.

1681. **The Stiffy** (5.6) Go up the outer face of the Woody, climbing crack to face with one bolt. Rap from the summit. **FA:** Todd Gordon, Cyndie Bransford, Randy Vogel, Sarah Vogel, Tom Burke, Maria, Linda, Kevin Bransford, Harry Star; 9/94.

The Alps Rock

A wall with many cracks (the Bread Loaves), which bears some resemblance to a loaf of sliced bread, is about 200 feet right of the far right end of the Upper Cow formation. The following routes are on a wall about 100 feet right of the Bread Loaves, and about 200 yards behind Worthwhile Pile. It faces east, with morning sun and afternoon shade. Approach as for Worthwhile Pile (see page 401). Map, page 398.

1682. **North Face of the Eiger** (5.10a) This is the leftmost of two cracks, and starts just left of a pine tree. **Pro:** To 2.5 inches. **FA:** Alan Roberts, Todd Gordon; 1/88.

1683. **Formic Acidhead** (5.10b) This is the face between the two cracks (*North Face of the Eiger* and *Walker Spur*). Stem off an ant-infested tree, then go up the face past two bolts. **Pro:** Thin to 2 inches. **FA:** Alan Bartlett, Brandt Allen; 3/90.

1684. **Walker Spur** (5.10a) The straight right-hand of the two cracks. **Pro:** To 2.5 inches. **FA:** Todd Gordon, Alan Roberts; 1/88.

1685. **Bonatti Pillar** (5.10b) (TR) Begin at a crack on the right side of the face, then go up the face staying right of *Walker Spur.* **FA:** Chris Miller, Karlis Ogle; 1/00.

Short Rock

This small formation lies about 50 yards

north of Worthwhile Pile/Slanta Claus Rock, on the west side of the wash (facing east). It has a roof on the east face. Approach as for those formations (see page 401). It gets morning sun and afternoon shade. Map, page 398.

1686. **Clive Live** (5.10d) ★ This thin crack lies to the left of *Coming Up Short.* **Pro:** Thin to 2 inches. **FA:** Todd Gordon, Richard White, Derek Reinig; 10/95.

1686A. **Coming Up Short** (5.10a) Climb over a roof to a handcrack above. **Pro:** To 2.5 inches. **FA:** Alan Roberts, John Hayward.

Poon Tang Rock

This large, low-angled gray slab faces west. It lies about 300 yards north of the Brown Wall. You can approach it from the vicinity of Slanta Claus Rock, but it is far more easily approached from the turnout for Playhouse Rock on Park Boulevard. See page 340.

The Great Burrito

This west-facing, light-colored face lies about 50 yards east of the Hidden Valley loop trail, roughly 200 yards north of Elephant Dome and 100 yards southeast of the Brown Wall. Routes are either full rope-length or broken into two shorter pitches. A bit loose (but cleaning up), and worth a visit.

For parking and trailhead location information, see page 375. From the trail fork, take the right fork for 300+ yards as it heads north, then descends into the fairly level valley floor. The formation is visible to the right (east), about 60 yards east of the trail. Head right (east) up to the base of this obvious formation. It faces west and gets morning shade and afternoon sun. Map, page 374.

1687. **Scamp** (5.3) Start in a low-angled crack just left of *Quesadilla;* the farthest left crack on the formation. **FA:** Alan Bartlett, Al Swanson; 11/00.

1688. **Quesadilla** (5.7) (R) The crack between *Scamp* and *Carne Asada.* **FA:** Todd Swain; 1/98.

1689. **Carne Asada** (5.10a) (R) Start in the left-hand of twin cracks/seams; left of *Stood Up.* **Pro:** Thin to 2.5 inches. **FA:** Stuart Wagstaff, Todd Swain; 12/97.

1690. **Stood Up** (5.8) ★ Climb a groove/crack to the horizontal/roof; then go left to a crack. **Pro:** Thin to 2 inches. **FA:** Jim Boone, Ellen Dempsey; 11/79.

1691. **Desperado** (5.10a) ★ This is just left of a big corner. Climb a face (one bolt) to parallel cracks; go right to a crack through a break/roof. **Pro:** Thin to 2.5 inches. **FA:** Jim Boone, Ellen Dempsey; 11/79.

1692. **Kemosabe and Tonto** (5.9+) ★★ Start near yuccas; go straight up a crack system. **Pro:** To 2.5 inches. **FA:** Ted Chapin, Jim Boone; 11/79.

1693. **Tonto and the Great White Leader** (5.9) Climb *Kemosabe and Tonto* for 45 feet to an alcove; move left to a crack and then up. **Pro:** To 2.5 inches. **FA:** Jim Boone, Ellen Dempsey; 12/79.

1694. **Non-Decumbent Destiny** (5.8) Start 30 feet right of the yuccas; go up and slightly left. At a horizontal/roof, either go straight up (5.10a R), or right for 15 feet to finish up *Three Burner Stove* (5.8). **Pro:** To 2.5 inches. **FA:** Ted Chapin, Ellen Dempsey, Jim Boone; 11/79.

1695. **Three Burner Stove** (5.10c) (R) Start on *Non-Decumbent Destiny;* after 25 feet, go up and right (one bolt) to a crack. **Pro:** To 2 inches. **FA:** Jim Boone, Ted Chapin; 11/79.

1696. **One Pot Meal** (5.9) (TR) Start atop a pillar to the left of *Learn Quick or Die.* Go up the right side of an alcove; finish in a thin crack. **FA:** Todd Swain; 1/98.

1697. **Learn Quick or Die** (5.9) Start left of the pillar; climb the crack to the face (two bolts), then go up cracks. **Pro:** Thin to 2 inches. **FA:** Jim Boone, Ted Chapin; 11/79.

1698. **Out, Out, Brief Candle (aka Thinning the Herd)** (5.10a/b) (R) The seam just right of *Learn Quick or Die.* **Pro:** Many thin to 2.5 inches. **FA** (TR): Todd Swain; 1/98. **FA** (Lead): Woody Stark, Sam Chang; 12/05.

1699. **Genetic Culling** (5.10a) (TR) The next seam right of *Thinning the Herd.* **FA:** Todd Swain; 1/98.

1700. **Fat Free** (5.9+) ★ The face route on the right side of the face. **Pro:** To 2 inches; four bolts; one fixed pin. **FA:** Todd Gordon, Cyndie Bransford, Tony Sartin, Ann Rogers; 1/94.

The next five routes lie up and right of the above. Routes 1702 to 1705 are not shown.

1701. **Tostada Supreme** (5.7) A slanting crack just left of the next route. **FA:** Todd Swain; 1/98.

1702. **Fish Taco** (5.5) Climb a right-facing corner to a bulge. **FA:** Todd Swain; 1/98.

1703. **Drop the Chalupa** (5.8) (R) The left-facing corner (wide crack) right of *Fish Taco.* **FA:** Tucker Tech, Alan Bartlett, Grant Hiskes; 10/00.

1704. **Up the Down Staircase** (5.4) Climb buckets on a block to cracks; this is right of *Drop the Chalupa.* **FA:** Alan Bartlett, Grant Hiskes, Tucker Tech; 10/00.

1705. **Vanderklooster's Stinky Wet Kitty** (5.9) Climb a crack to horizontals to a slab about 30 feet right of *Up the Down Staircase.* **FA:** Ben Vanderklooster, Tucker Tech; 11/00.

Elephant Dome

Elephant Dome, a rock with an elephant-shaped flake on the southwest face, is located 100 yards north of Sports Challenge Rock. From the trail fork, take the right fork for about 200+ yards as it heads north and begins to descend toward the flatter valley ahead. Elephant Dome is just left (north) and farther off the trail (east) than a smaller brownish rock on your right (Snake Dome); it is about 25 yards off the trail. It faces southwest and is sunny for the bulk of the day. Map, page 374.

1706. **Pachyderms to Paradise** (5.9) Go up a thin crack on the left side of the face that heads up to the left side of the "elephant's trunk." **Pro:** To 3 inches. **FA:** Robert Fainberg, Howard King; 1977. **FFA:** Randy Vogel, Dave Evans; 12/79.

1707. **Dumbo Drop** (5.11b) ★ This five- bolt face route lies on the slab on the right side

of the southwest face. **Pro:** To 3 inches. **FA:** Bob Gaines, Troy Trimmer; 2/95.

Snake Dome

This is the smaller brownish and blocky formation to the right (south) of Elephant Dome, closer to the trail. It has several vertical cracks on its southwest face. Approach as for Elephant Dome, but cut off the nature trail earlier. Map, page 374.

1708. **Rattlesnake Roundup** (5.10c) (TR) Go up the steep face that is 30 feet left and around the corner from *Handlin' Snakeskin*. **FA:** Bob Gaines; 1/96.

1709. **Handlin' Snakeskin** (5.10c) ★ Climb thin cracks on the left side of the southwest face, then go up and left on the face. **Pro:** Thin to 2 inches. **FA:** Alan Bartlett, Dave Evans; 2/88.

1710. **I Love Snakes** (5.10a) This follows seams to cracks that head up to the split in the summit block. Either begin on *Handlin' Snakeskin* and traverse right (5.9), or go directly up seams (5.10b R). **Pro:** Thin to 3 inches. **FA:** Todd Gordon, Vicki Pelton, Marge Floyd; 2/88.

1711. **Black Todd** (5.10b) Start from boulder right of *I Love Snakes;* go up a right-leaning crack, then up the face past horizontals and one bolt. Finish up and right in a short arch/crack. **Pro:** To 2 inches; one bolt. **FA:** Dave Evans, Alan Bartlett; 2/88.

Hidden Tower

This small but very popular tower lies about 50 yards east of Sports Challenge Rock and just east of the nature trail. For parking and approach directions, see page 375. From the trail fork, take the right fork for about 60 yards to where it ascends some rocky steps, then descends. At this point, the west face of Hidden Tower lies directly ahead (east). Where the nature trail turns left (north), cut off right (northeast) along a faint trail that heads up to a notch to the left (north) of Hidden Tower. All routes except *Not Forgotten* (on the west face) are reached by heading right after passing over the notch. To descend, make a 70-foot rappel from a two-bolt anchor; alternatively, downclimb *Splotch* (5.6). Map, page 374.

1712. **Splotch** (5.6) This route lies on the southeast end of Hidden Tower. Face moves at the bottom (crux) lead to an easy chimney that splits the formation. This also serves as a potential downclimb route. **FA:** Unknown.

1713. **Split** (5.6) This route lies 10 feet right and around the corner from *Splotch* (around and left of *Wild Wind*); go up the corner to a handcrack. **FA:** John Wolfe, Rich Wolfe, Stu Harris; 1966.

1714. **Wild Wind** (5.9) ★★ The left-hand of two obvious cracks on the east face. Near the top, head up and right on thin cracks to finish as for *Sail Away* (or just go straight up). This often overlooked route is worth doing, particularly if *Sail Away* is otherwise engaged. **Pro:** Thin to 2 inches. **FA:** John Lakey, Chick Holtkamp, Randy Russell; 2/78.

1715. **Sail Away** (5.8–) ★★★ This is the right-hand of the two obvious cracks on the east face. This route is extremely popular, well protected, and ends atop a nice pinnacle; hence it is often crowded. Begin off boulders, heading up and left until you can reach the crack that at first angles right, then proceeds straight up. Where the crack thins, exit left, then go up to another crack/flake. **Pro:** To 2 inches, with several 0.5 to 1.5 inch. **FA:** Chick Holtkamp, Randy Russell, John Lakey; 2/78.

Hidden Tower—West Face

This route lies near the left end of the west face (facing Sports Challenge Rock). The face and route are not pictured.

1716. **Not Forgotten** (5.10a) ★ Climb a thin crack/lieback on the west face until you can reach left to another crack that leads to the top. **Pro:** Thin to 2 inches. **FA:** John Wolfe; 1966; **FFA:** John Long et al.; 1979.

The Perch (aka The Rhino Horn)

This is the small tower immediately northwest of, and joined with, Hidden Tower. The notch where Hidden Tower and the Perch are joined is where *Not Forgotten* begins. There is no anchor on top. Descend down *The Perch Crack* (5.3) or do a simul-rappel. The formation and routes are not pictured.

1717. **The Perch Crack** (5.3) This 30-foot-long wide crack begins on the east face,

forming the notch between Hidden Tower and the Perch. It is the easiest way down. **FA:** Todd Swain, Donette Swain, 11/00.

1718. **Budgie** (5.7) Go up the crack 15 feet right of *Sail Away* to the saddle between Hidden Tower and the Perch, then up the north face of the Perch up a right-leaning wide crack. **Pro:** To 5 inches. **FA:** Todd Swain, Donette Swain; 11/00.

1719. **Catbird Seat** (5.9) Start about 20 feet right of *Budgie* at the northwest corner of the rock. Go up a crack to a right-facing flake. **Pro:** To 3 inches. **FA:** Todd Swain, Donette Swain; 11/00.

The Wailing Wall

This extremely narrow wall with several large summit blocks is approximately 65 yards north of Hidden Tower. For parking and approach directions, see page 375. From the trail fork, take the right fork for about 60 yards to where it ascends some rocky steps, then descends. At this point, the west face of Hidden Tower lies directly ahead (east). Where the nature trail turns left (north), cut off right (east) along a faint trail that heads up to a notch to the left (north) of Hidden Tower. Continue over a small "pass," then down until you can turn left (north) to the easily seen west face of the Wailing Wall. You can also reach this crag from Park Boulevard from a point just north of Slump Rock. The east face has a ramp system that provides the easiest descent; *Decent Buckets* (5.2) on the west face is also commonly downclimbed. Map, page 374.

The Wailing Wall—West Face

The west side of the Wailing Wall has a number of short routes. The west face is north of Hidden Tower, on the right side of a small canyon/corridor. It gets morning shade and is sunny all afternoon.

1720. **Decent Buckets** (5.2) This is the crack that splits (take right split) on the far left end of the west face. This may be used for descent, although it's a bit loose. **FA:** Unknown.

1721. **Burn Out** (5.10b) ★ Go up thin cracks about 6 feet right of *Decent Buckets*. **Pro:** Thin to 2 inches. **FA:** Chick Holtkamp, Randy Russell; 2/78.

1722. **Good Grief** (5.10c) (R) ★ Go up the face past horizontals to two-bolt anchor. **Pro:** Thin to 1 inch. **FA** (TR): Karl Mueller, Alan Nelson; 12/81. **FA** (Lead): Dave Mayville.

1723. **Comic Relief** (5.11a) (R) ★ Go up the face and horizontals 5 feet right of *Good Grief* to a thin crack leading to the summit. **Pro:** Thin to 2 inches. **FA:** Chick Holtkamp; 2/78.

1724. **Pussy Galore** (5.10d) (R/X) ★★ Go up the center of the west face on the face and discontinuous cracks to a crack splitting the summit block. **Pro:** Thin to 2 inches. **FA:** Chick Holtkamp, Bob Yoho; 2/78.

1725. **Legal Briefs** (5.9) ★ Climb a seam and finger crack up to the right shoulder. **Pro:** Thin to 2 inches. **FA:** Bob Yoho, Chick Holtkamp; 2/78.

1726. **Brief Case** (5.10c) (TR) Climb the face and discontinuous seams/cracks about 8 feet right of *Legal Briefs*. **FA:** Michael Paul; 1981.

1727. **Liquid Confidence** (5.11a) ★ Climb the face past two bolts to a thin crack/seam on the right end of the west face. **Pro:** To 2 inches. **FA** (TR): John Heiman, Dave Robinson; 3/89. **FA** (Lead): Paul Borne.

The Wailing Wall—East Face

This is the "back" side of this formation, facing Park Boulevard; it gets morning sun and afternoon shade. The face and route are not pictured.

1728. **Joshua Judges Ruth** (5.10c) Climb the left-leaning thin crack that overhangs and doesn't quite reach the ground. **Pro:** Thin to 2 inches. **FA:** Don Reid, Alan Bartlett; 4/96.

The Sand Castle

This tower is located about 70 yards southeast of Hidden Tower, in the middle of a wash/canyon. For parking and approach directions, see page 375. From the trail fork,

take the right fork for about 60 yards to where it ascends some rocky steps, then descends. The west face of Hidden Tower lies directly ahead (east). Where the nature trail turns left (north), cut off right (east) along a faint trail that heads up to a notch to the left (north) of Hidden Tower. Head over the notch and down into the wash below; turn right (south) to reach the north side of this tower.

This formation can also be reached by following the wash/canyon containing *Vicki the Visitor* (on the Green Room; see page 372) north toward Hidden Tower; the Sand Castle will be on your right. You can also reach it from Park Boulevard from a point north of Slump Rock. Descend steep ledges off the back (south) side or by making a short rappel. The formation and route are not pictured. Map, page 374.

1729. **My First First** (5.9+) On the north face, go up a smooth face past one bolt to a short curvy crack near the top. **Pro:** To 2.5 inches. **FA:** Alan Bartlett, Todd Gordon, Tom Atherton, Vicki Pelton; 2/88.

1730. **Bivy at Gordon's** (5.6) Go up rotten flakes and cracks 10 feet right of *My First First*. **Pro:** To 3+ inches. **FA:** Alan Bartlett; 2/88.

1731. **Under 6′2″, Don't Know What You'll Do** (5.11a to 5.12a) (TR) (height dependent) This climb is located 25 feet right of *Bivy at Gordon's* on the west side. Climb the crack on the arête to a ledge; above the ledge. Go up and right (crux). **FA:** Todd Swain; 10/89.

1732. **Fingerstack or Plastic Sack** (5.9+) A short, slanting, and overhanging crack on the east face. **Pro:** To 2.5 inches. **FA:** Todd Swain; 10/89.

Sports Challenge Rock

This excellent formation lies roughly in the center of Real Hidden Valley, and is one of the best (and most popular) rock formations in this area. Most routes on Sports Challenge Rock are easily (and commonly) toproped. Nevertheless, almost all the routes may be led. If you do toprope routes, be prepared to share your rope or take it down if someone wants to lead a route.

The formation is located about 100 yards north of the fork in the nature trail. For parking and approach directions, see page 375. From the trail fork, take the right fork for about 30 yards to where a climbers' trail leads north to the west face. For the east face, take the right trail fork for about 50+ yards, then head north to the base of the east face. Map, page 374.

Sports Challenge Rock— West Face

The west face sports mostly vertical crack and face routes on solid dark-brown rock. For the shorter, left-hand part of the formation (the first three routes listed), descend down a crack on the west face, then right into a chimney system. For all other routes, descend to the right, down the southern end of the rock. The face gets morning shade and is sunny all afternoon. Named by Tim Powell, Kevin Powell, and Dan Ahlborn with the idea that all route names would have a "sports" theme to them (e.g., *Championship Wrestling, Dick Enberg,* and *Clean and Jerk*). Routes 1733 to 1735 are not pictured.

1733. **Chick Hern** (5.8) This is near the left end of the shorter section of the cliff, left of the main face. Go up left-leaning cracks to a bulge. **Pro:** Thin to 2.5 inches. **FA:** Alan Bartlett, Tucker Tech; 11/00.

1734. **Ankle Breaker** (A3) Go up thin cracks and seams past one bolt between *Chick Hern* and *Spring Cleaning*. **Pro:** Thin aid stuff. **FA:** Spencer Pfingsten, Jesse Ortega; 1994.

1735. **Spring Cleaning** (5.10a) (TR) Climb the large left-leaning dihedral located about 40 feet left of *Sphincter Quits*. **FA:** Tucker Tech, Ben Vanderklooster; 11/00.

1736. **Alligator Tears** (5.9) This is located directly below the start of *Ride a Wild Bago*. Start in a 10-foot dihedral, go over a roof, then up to top. **Pro:** To 2 inches. **FA:** Unknown.

1737. **Sphincter Quits** (5.9+) ★★★ A fun and popular crack. Go up the right-slanting handcrack to a ledge; move right into a very thin crack (5.9+). Go up this to a large ledge, finish up and right in the corner. **Variation:** After the initial handcrack, move left and up the face past one bolt to the large ledge. **Pro:** Several thin to 2 inches. **FA:** Dave Evans, Randy Vogel; 12/78.

1738. **What's It to You** (5.10d) ★★★ Begin atop a block at the base of *Ride a Wild Bago/Rap Bolters Are Weak*. Go up, then traverse left (first bolt of *Rap Bolters Are Weak* helps protect) on a horizontal crack to reach a vertical thin crack that ends on a large ledge; finish up the corner. **Pro:** Thin to 1.5 inches. **FA** (TR): Maria Cranor, Randy Vogel; 11/79. **FA** (Lead/without bolt): Tom Gilje; 1992.

1739. **Rap Bolters Are Weak** (5.12a) ★★★ (Sport) Excellent thin cranking. Begin atop a block at *Ride a Wild Bago*. Go up, traverse a bit left, then up a thin face that moves past

five bolts. The bottom crux can be avoided by moving right to *Ride a Wild Bago,* then back left to the second bolt. Two-bolt anchor. **FA:** Paul Borne, Dave Mayville; 1989.

1740. **Ride a Wild Bago** (5.10a) ★★ Begin atop the block. Go up the face and thin cracks to a wider crack above. **Pro:** To 3 inches. **FA:** Randy Vogel, Dave Evans; 12/78.

1741. **Don't Be Nosey** (5.10d) ★ (TR) Begin just right of *Ride a Wild Bago*. Head up and right on diagonal cracks, then up the face to finish as for *None of Your Business*. **FA:** Jonny Woodward, Maria Cranor; 11/87.

1742. **None of Your Business** (5.10c) (R) ★★ Begin about 10 feet right of *Ride a Wild Bago*. Go up a right-slanting crack, then up the face past several horizontals. Finish up and right into an easier crack. **Pro:** Thin to 2 inches. **FA** (TR): Randy Vogel, Maria Cranor; 10/79. **FA** (Lead): Gib Lewis, Charles Cole, 12/79.

1743. **I Just Told You** (5.10a) ★ Begin about 10 feet down and right of *None of Your Business;* head up a right-slanting crack system to the right shoulder of the formation. **Pro:** Thin to 2 inches. **FA:** Gib Lewis, Charles Cole; 12/79.

1744. **Ranger J. D.** (5.6) The left-hand of two converging cracks on the right side of the formation. **Pro:** To 2+ inches. **FA:** Randy Vogel, Maria Cranor; 10/79.

1745. **Ranger J. B.** (5.6) The right-hand of the two converging cracks on the right side of the formation. **Pro:** To 2+ inches. **FA:** Unknown.

1746. **Itty Bitty Buttress** (5.11a) (TR) ★ Toprope the face between *Ranger J. B.* and *Eddie Haskell Takes Manhattan*. **FA:** Bob Gaines, Yvonne Gaines; 1/92.

1747. Eddie Haskell Takes Manhattan (5.10c/d) ★ Begin on the right-hand arête of the west face; go up the face, then head up and around the corner to finish. **Pro:** Two bolts; nuts to 2 inches. **FA:** Eric Rasmussen, Bob Hines.

1748. Mortal Thoughts (5.11b) ★ This is a girdle traverse of the west face of the rock, traversing right to left on a prominent horizontal crack. Use the third bolt on *Rap Bolters Are Weak*. **Pro:** To 3 inches. **FA:** Rex Pieper, Brent Brown; 4/91.

Sports Challenge Rock— East Face

The east face of Sports Challenge Rock is continuously overhanging and has many excellent crack and face climbs. It is divided into two sections: the Main East Face (the larger left-hand section) and the shorter Right End. It is not uncommon for people to toprope popular routes here, such as *Clean and Jerk, Leave It to Beaver,* and *Cool but Concerned.* However, if you set up a toprope, be prepared to share it with others, or to remove it if people want to lead a route. Good boulder problems are located on the face below *Leave It to Beaver.* The face gets early sun and is shady all afternoon. Descend to the left (south) for *Triathlon* through *Leave It to Beaver*. Descend right and around to the west face for *Cool but Concerned* et al. (see East Face—Right End description).

Sports Challenge Rock— Main East Face

The Main East Face of Sports Challenge Rock is about 70 feet tall, with excellent brown- and gold-colored rock. It is home to the classics: *Clean and Jerk, Leave It to Beaver,* and *Cool but Concerned*. The easiest approach to, and descent from, the top is down the southern shoulder of the formation (class 4/5). It is not uncommon for many of the routes to be toproped, but they are (for the most part) well protected leads. If a party is waiting to lead a route, don't monopolize it with a toprope. The face gets morning sun and is shady all afternoon.

1749. **Blue Jean Crack** (5.9) (not shown on photo) The obvious wide crack on the left end of the face. **Pro:** To 4 inches. **FA:** Alan Bartlett, Brandt Allen; 4/92.

1750. **Triathlon** (5.11c) (TR) Start 10 feet right of *Blue Jean Crack*. Climb straight up to the right-slanting crack system. Head right about 15 feet, then up when possible. **FA:** Bob Gaines; 4/88.

1751. **Cool but Not Too Concerned** (5.12c) (TR) Start right of *Triathlon,* eventually joining the slanting crack on that route. **FA:** Scott Cosgrove.

1752. **Clean and Jerk** (5.10c) ★★★★ One of the most popular 5.10s in the park; many find it stiff for the grade. Go up horizontals on an overhanging face (5.10c off the deck) to a nice overhanging crack (5.10a). Originally finished up a right-slanting chimney; the direct finish is now the standard route. A good spot is advisable for the leader

as the crux moves are getting to the first horizontal, where a cam can be placed. **Pro:** To 3 inches. **FA:** Tim Powell, Kevin Powell, Dan Ahlborn; 4/77.

1753. **Dick Enberg** (5.11c) ★★ (with tree) Climb and stem off the pine tree until you can climb the crack above. Not an easy lead. **Pro:** To 2 inches. **FA:** Dan Ahlborn; 4/77. **FFA:** Jeff Elgar; 1979.

1754. **The Lobster** (variation) (5.12a) (R) ★★★ (no tree) Start up *Leave It to Beaver* to the ledge, then go left to, then up (5.12a R), the *Dick Enberg* crack. **Pro:** Pins; thin to 2 inches. Usually toproped. **FA** (TR): John Bachar, Mike Lechlinski. **FA** (Lead): Tony Yaniro.

1755. **Leave It to Beaver** (5.12a) ★★★★★ This Josh classic requires using a wide variety of techniques on superb overhanging rock. Go up horizontals to a ledge, then up to the block (5.12a), finishing on the face past horizontals above (5.11b/c). Though commonly toproped, it is a well protected lead. Bring a 20+-foot extendo (and 2- to 3-inch cams) if you want to toprope this. **Pro:** 0.5 to 2.5 inch cams. **FA:** Dave Evans. Jim Angione; 1/78. **FFA:** John Bachar; 3/78. **FA** (Lead): John Bachar; 1979.

Sports Challenge Rock— East Face, Right End

The following climbs lie (or end) on the shorter Right End of the east face of Sports Challenge Rock. Many of these climbs are commonly toproped. To approach the top, begin up the left face of the chimney left of *Sphincter Quits* on the west face, then traverse left and up to a ledge. Go up a crack in a corner, then around right. Descend the same route; a sling rap anchor also exists atop *Disco Decoy/Hang and Swing*. The face gets morning sun and is shady all afternoon.

To downclimb

rap

1756 1757 1758 1759 1760 1761

1756. Championship Wrestling (5.10a) ★
The off-width to narrow chimney. **Pro:** To
5+ inches. **FA:** Dan Ahlborn, Kevin Powell;
1/77.

1757. Cool but Concerned (5.11d) (R) ★★★
Climb the steep face that roughly follows a
thin crack on the left side of the lower right
section of the rock. At the last horizontal,
either head up a seam on the left or move
right, then up a crack/lieback. Usually
toproped as the crux is difficult to protect.
Pro: Many very small to 2 inches. **FA** (TR):
John Bachar, Mike Lechlinski, Lynn Hill,
John Yablonski; 1980. **FA** (Lead): Jonny
Woodward.

1758. Slightly Sweating (5.12a/b) ★★ (TR)
Climb the seam to the right of *Cool but
Concerned,* joining it for the right-hand crack
finish. **FA:** Unknown.

1759. Fun Loving Criminal (5.13a/b) ★★
(TR) Begin about 15 feet right of *Cool but
Concerned.* Go up the overhang near the bottom to a right-slanting thin crack, then up
the face to a big horizontal; finish left to
Cool but Concerned. This was originally a
bolted/lead route, but the bolts were
removed by the first ascensionist as they were
unsightly on a wall free of any bolts. **FA**
(Lead and TR): Matt Beebe.

1760. **Disco Decoy** (5.11b) (R) ★★ Begin to the right of a large slanting roof; go up horizontals (5.11a/b R) to a crack system that splits the block. **Pro:** Thin to 2.5 inches. **FA** (TR): John Bachar, Mike Lechlinski, Lynn Hill, John Yablonski; 1980. **FA** (Lead): Jonny Woodward.

1761. **Hang and Swing** (5.10d) ★★ This is near the right end of the rock. Head up and left on horizontals and cracks to a crack over a small roof. **Pro:** To 3 inches. **FA** (TR): John Bachar, Mike Lechlinski, Lynn Hill, John Yablonski; 1980. **FA** (Lead): Charles Cole, Gib Lewis; 1981.

Sunset Rock

This small formation is located on the northern end of the rocks in front (just west) of the west face of Sports Challenge Rock. Routes are on the west face and get morning shade and sun all afternoon. The rock and routes are not pictured. For approach directions, see page 375. Map, page 374.

1762. **Hollywood Boulevard** (5.5) Take thin cracks up to a right-facing corner near the left end of the rock. **Pro:** To 2 inches. **FA:** Todd Swain; 11/89.

1763. **Sunset Strip** (5.9) Start 15 feet right of *Hollywood Boulevard*. Climb a flake, go up a left-slanting crack, pass a horizontal, then go up and right on an easy face to the top. **Pro:** To 2 inches. **FA:** Alan Bartlett, Debbie Daigle; 3/88.

1764. **Good Friday** (5.10b) (TR) This is the steep face right of *Sunset Strip*. Difficulty depends on how much you use holds on the right edge. **FA:** Bob Gaines, Keith Brueckner; 3/97.

1765. **Rodeo Drive** (5.6) Start 12 feet right of *Sunset Strip*. Climb a crack left of a chimney, then go up the face. **Pro:** To 2 inches. **FA:** Todd Swain, Mark Bowling; 11/89.

The Wart

This small, square-ish formation is about 40 yards southeast of Sports Challenge Rock and about 20 yards north of Locomotion Rock; lying just east of the nature trail. All routes are located on the west face (morning shade, sunny all afternoon). For parking and approach directions, see page 375. From the trail fork, take the right-hand trail for about 50 yards, where it heads up steps blasted from the rock. Head right from here to the rock. Map, page 374.

1766. **Symbolic of Life** (5.11a) ★ Face climb up and left past four bolts on the left side of the west face. **Pro:** To 2 inches. **FA:** Todd Gordon, Todd Swain, Tom Atherton, Dave Mayville; 8/90.

1767. **Preparation H** (5.11a) (TR) Begin just right of the start of *Symbolic of Life,* and head straight up the face to a crack. **FA:** John Bachar, Kevin Powell; 12/79.

1768. **Compound W** (5.11b) (TR) Begin about 10 feet right of *Preparation H.* Go up cracks in a corner, then left under the roof to finish as for *Preparation H.* **FA:** John Bachar; 12/79.

1769. **Toad Warriors** (5.12b) ★★ Begin as for *Compound W,* but head straight up the face past four bolts. **FA:** Paul Borne; 1990.

1770. **The Good, the Bad, and the Ugly** (5.10a) Start to the right of the last two climbs. Go up over a roof to a right-slanting hand to off-width crack. **Pro:** To 4 inches. **FA:** Chick Holtkamp, John Lakey; 2/78.

Locomotion Rock

This small but tremendously popular crag lies in the extreme southeast corner of the Real Hidden Valley. For parking and approach directions, see page 375. From the trail fork, take the right-hand trail for about 25 yards (Locomotion Rock is off to the right). Turn right off the main trail onto a climbers' trail and follow this for 25 yards to the crag. Routes lie on the west face (morning shade, sun all afternoon). Rap anchors may be found on top of *Jumping Jehoshaphat* and *Leaping Leaner.* Map, page 374.

Advisory: It is not uncommon for groups to toprope one or more climbs in this area. If you place topropes on routes and leave them up for more than a short time, you must be prepared to either share the ropes with other climbers or pull them down. Totally dominating this crag with topropes and then being unwilling to share

or pull your ropes is not only extremely rude, but might justify the removal of your ropes. Be courteous instead.

1771. **Jumping Jehoshaphat** (5.7) ★ Begin on a round boulder; go up the left-slanting handcrack. **Pro:** To 2.5 inches. **FA:** Tim Powell, Dan Ahlborn; 4/77.

1772. **Grain Dance** (5.10c/d) (TR) ★ Begin as for *Jumping Jehoshaphat,* but move right to a crack/seam that parallels that route. **FA:** Bob Gaines; 1987.

1773. **Leaping Leaner** (5.6) ★★ Begin right of *Jumping Jehoshaphat* and climb up and right into another left-slanting crack. Originally (and occasionally) led with a leap across from boulders onto the rock (avoiding the start moves). A direct start is possible too; the farther left you start, the easier. **Pro:** To 3 inches. **FA:** Tim Powell, Dan Ahlborn; 1977.

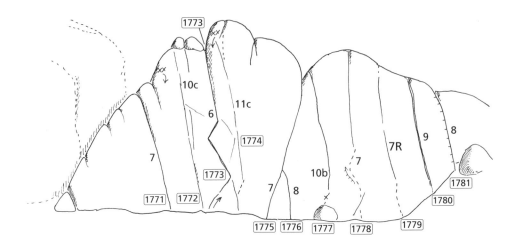

1774. **Slip and Slide** (5.11c) (TR) ★ Start down in the pit to the right of *Leaping Leaner*. Head up and right on a face to a seam; finish up the face to the summit. **FA:** Bob Gaines; 11/89.

1775. **Lumping Fat Jennie** (5.7) ★ Begin in the pit on the right. Go up the left-hand of two cracks that meet after 20 feet. **Pro:** To 2.5 inches. **FA:** Unknown.

1776. **Snnfchtt** (5.8) ★ (pronounced like a sniffling noise) Starts in the pit on the right. Climb the right-hand of two cracks that meet after 20 feet. **Pro:** To 2.5 inches. **FA:** Randy Vogel, Darryl Nakahira, Charles Cole; 1981.

1777. **Gunks West** (5.10b) ★ This route is just right of *Snnfchtt;* begin off a boulder. Climb the face past a hangerless bolt to a crack. **Pro:** To 2.5 inches. **FA:** Todd Swain, Thom Scheuer; 4/84.

1778. **Hhecht** (5.7) ★ (pronounced like clearing your throat) Begin 10 feet down and right of *Gunks West*. Face climb into a crack on the far right side of west face. **Pro:** To 2.5 inches. **FA:** Charles Cole, Randy Vogel, Darryl Nakahira; 1981.

1779. **Skippy the Mudskipper** (5.7) (R) Climb the crack right of *Hhecht;* it does not reach the bottom. **Pro:** To 3 inches. **FA:** Todd Gordon, Cyndie Bransford, Brian Stikes, Bruce Christie; 10/92.

1780. **Gritty Kitty** (5.9) The off-width right of *Jump Back Loretta*. **Pro:** To 4+ inches. **FA:** Todd Gordon, Cyndie Bransford; 10/92.

1781. **Jump Back Loretta** (5.5) Climb a handcrack in a right-facing corner on the southeast corner of Locomotion Rock. **Pro:** To 3 inches. **FA:** Todd Swain; 3/85.

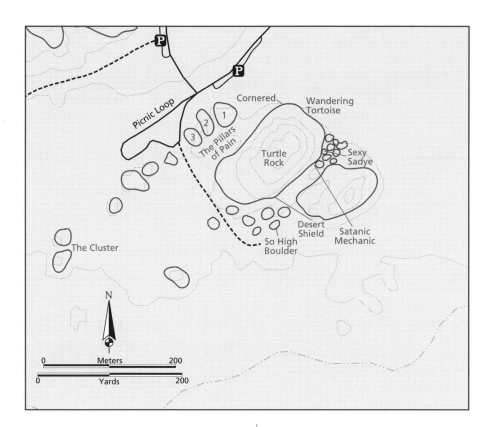

The map shows labels: Picnic Loop, Cornered, Wandering Tortoise, 1, 2, 3, The Pillars of Pain, Turtle Rock, Sexy Sadye, Desert Shield, Satanic Mechanic, So High Boulder, The Cluster, N, Meters 0 – 200, Yards 0 – 200, P, P

TURTLE ROCK

This very large formation lies south of the large Real Hidden Valley parking lot and immediately adjacent to (south of) the picnic areas. It features routes of the widest possible variance in grade of any formation in the Park (from 5.3 to 5.14a).

From the park's West Entrance, take Park Boulevard 8.6+ miles to a four-way intersection (Intersection Rock parking is to the east, and Hidden Valley Picnic Area is to the west). This intersection lies 0.1 mile north of the T intersection of Park Boulevard and Barker Dam Road (which provides access to Hidden Valley Campground). Turn west on the Hidden Valley Picnic Area road. After a few hundred yards, a large parking area lies adjacent to the trailhead for Real Hidden

Valley proper (to the northwest). To the southeast is a picnic area, and directly behind it is the large mass of Turtle Rock's north face. Map is above.

The descent for most routes is via the west end of the rock. The descent is not straightforward and several possibilities exist. You may want to scope the descent route ahead of time if your descent skills are not well developed.

Turtle Rock Bouldering

The area to the southwest of Turtle Rock sports some of the best bouldering in Joshua Tree. Many fine (and high off-the-deck) problems are found here. This is the site of the famous So High Boulder.

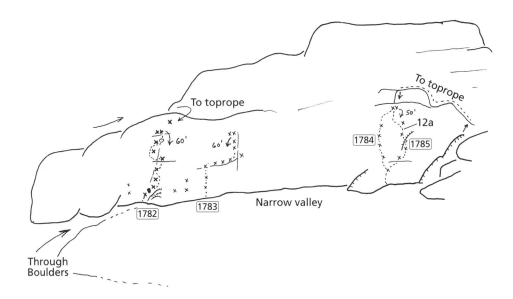

Through Boulders

Narrow valley

To toprope

To toprope

Turtle Rock—South Face

The south face lies in a sheltered corridor and is overhanging, with rock that ranges from good to poor. All routes are hard (5.12 to 5.14) sport routes. *Satanic Mechanic* (5.12a/b) and *Desert Shield* (5.13a) are the best known and most sought-after routes. *Integrity* (5.14a) is the hardest route on this wall, involving a long traversing section. To reach the south face, walk around the far right (west) side of the rock (west of the Pillars of Pain), then turn left at the So High Boulder and cut slightly left through boulders to reach the corridor along the base of the south face. Routes are encountered in the following order: *abandoned project; Desert Shield; abandoned project; Integrity; Jesus Lives;* and *Satanic Mechanic.* Map, page 421.

1782. **Desert Shield** (5.13a/b) ★★★★ (Sport) This steep endurance route is the first route encountered upon entering the corridor on the south side of the rock (an incomplete project lies to the left). Rock has broken off over the years. Seven bolts lead to coldshut hooks; one rope reaches on lowering. The

rock is loose in places and care should be taken not to pull key holds off. Setting up a toprope requires medium to 3-inch pro and a second rope (access from the far left). **FA:** Scott Cosgrove, 1/91.

1783. **Integrity** (5.14a) ★★★ (Sport) This lies about 50 feet right of *Desert Shield* (two incomplete routes lie between). Go up to a horizontal, make a long traverse right, then go up a shallow crack/seam. **Pro:** Nine bolts; two-bolt anchor/lower off; long draws/runners helpful. **FA:** Scott Cosgrove; 1995.

1784. **Jesus Lives** (5.12c) ★★ (Sport) This route and *Satanic Mechanic* both lie at the far eastern end of the corridor. Both routes start roughly in the same place; this route climbs up and left past bolts, ending at the *Satanic Mechanic* shuts. **FA** (TR): Rolland Shook. **FA** (Lead): Scott Cosgrove; 3/91.

1785. **Satanic Mechanic** (5.12a/b) ★★★★ (Sport) This fun route starts with *Jesus Lives,* but climbs up and right into a crack/flare, then heads out left (crux) and up to shuts. One rope lowers. To reach the anchors to set up a toprope, climb up and left along a diagonal crack/flake; a belay might be helpful. **FA:** Roy McClenahan, Doug McDonald; 2/88.

Turtle Rock— Corridor South Face

The following two routes lie on a separate formation parallel to the south side of Turtle Rock. This formation forms the "corridor" along the southern side of Turtle Rock. Approach by walking around the east end of Turtle Rock. The face and routes are not pictured. Map, page 421.

1786. **The Birds Flock to Turtle Rock** (5.5) (R) Begin near the right (east) end of the formation. Go up a seam/crack that curves somewhat left and up, past horizontals, until you can traverse right to a chimney. **Pro:** To 3 inches. **FA:** Tony Bird, Nick Bird, Erika Bird, Sue Ann Chapman et al.; 1/94.

1787. **The Three Bears Go to Turtle Rock** (5.5) (R) Begin as for *The Birds Flock to Turtle Rock.* Go up a right-leaning crack, then up past horizontals and bushes to reach a final chimney (same finish as *The Birds Flock to Turtle Rock*). **Pro:** To 3 inches. **FA:** Ben Chapman, Sue Ann Chapman, Catherine Reyes, Lupita Reyes et al.; 1/94.

Turtle Rock—South Face, Right End

The next three routes lie on the extreme right end of the south face. However, they are probably best approached by walking around the northeast face and then up the boulders lying against the south and southeast faces. If you are already in the corridor on the south face, continue right over the boulders. Map, page 421.

1788. **Kippy Korner** (5.9) (R) This route lies just above and right of the anchors on *Satanic*

Mechanic, beginning off a ledge system you reach from the right. This is the right-leaning crack that heads through a couple of horizontals. **Pro:** To 3 inches. **FA:** Charles Cole et al.; 1983.

1789. **Biskering** (5.9) (R) This crack begins off a ledge about 30 feet right of *Kippy Korner.* Go over a small roof, then up the obvious crack system that diagonals up and left (passing a larger roof). Above, head right then up. **Pro:** To 3 inches. **FA:** Charles Cole et al.; 1983.

1790. **OK Korner** (5.9) (R) This takes the curvy crack to the right of a right-facing corner/crack system to the right of *Biskering*. **Pro:** To 3 inches. **FA:** Charles Cole et al.; 1983.

Turtle Rock—Southeast Face

The following routes lie just right of the South Face, Right End routes. They are most easily reached by heading left around the northeast side of Turtle Rock, then up boulders against the base of the southeast face.

1791. **Lieback and Lingerie** (5.10d) (R) ★ This is to the right of and up from *Sexy Sadye.* Go up a right-leaning flake (two bolts), then go up to meet *Sexy Sadye* at its fourth bolt. **Pro:** To 2 inches; 50-foot rappel. **FA:** Bob Gaines; 11/90.

1792. **Sexy Sadye** (5.10d) (R) ★★ This four-bolt route heads up and left, beginning 20 feet right of *Lieback and Lingerie.* **Pro:** To 2 inches; 50-foot rappel. **FA:** Charles Cole, Steve Anderson; 1983.

1793. **Shut Up and Climb** (5.10a) (R) Chimney up a large flake 30 feet right of *Sexy Sadye;* then go up and right past a bolt to a right-leaning crack that leads to *Bisk.* **Pro:** To 2.5 inches. **FA:** Bill Cramer, Mark Uphus, Michelle Pinney; 5/89.

Turtle Rock—Northeast Face

The northeast face is somewhat broken and features a number of worthwhile, mostly two-pitch easy to moderate climbs. To reach the northeast face, walk left around the rock. Routes receive some sun in the morning and afternoon shade. To descend from lower pitches, belay anchors/rap stations can be found. To descend from the summit, head down the west end of the rock (somewhat tricky route-finding).

1794. **Bisk** (5.4) ★ Begin on the highest boulders/talus at the left side of the northeast face (above the initial part of *Shut Up and Climb*). **Pitch 1:** Go up crack and left-facing dihedral to a ledge (5.4; 100 feet). **Pitch 2:** Go up a chimney, then right and up. Straight up is a variation (5.7). **Pro:** To 3 inches. **FA:** John Wolfe, Rich Wolfe; 1965.

1795. **Ripples** (5.7) ★ Begin 20 feet down and right of *Bisk*. **Pitch 1:** Go up a right-slanting ramp/crack to a large ledge (5.5).

Pitch 2: Head up and right into a right-slanting slot (5.7). **Pro:** To 3 inches. **FA:** Hank Levine, Fred Lytle; 1973.

1796. **Luminous Beast** (5.10c) (R) Begin left of *Luminous Breast;* go up the face to the small left-slanting roof. Undercling it right to finish up *Luminous Breast*. **Pro:** Thin to 2 inches. **FA:** Dave Mayville, Keith Bruckner; 1995.

1797. **Luminous Breast** (5.8) (R) Begin below the large belay ledge of *Ripples.* Go up the face just right of a thin seam, passing just right of a small roof; finish on the *Ripples* ledge. **Pro:** Thin to 2 inches. **FA:** Dave Evans, Jeff Elgar; 2/77.

1798. **Rehab** (5.9) This route begins off a boulder about 20 feet right of *Luminous Breast.* Go up face past one bolt; then up flakes and cracks until you can head left to join *Luminous Breast* just below the belay ledge. **Pro:** Thin to 2 inches. **FA:** Dave West, Mark Harrell; 11/89.

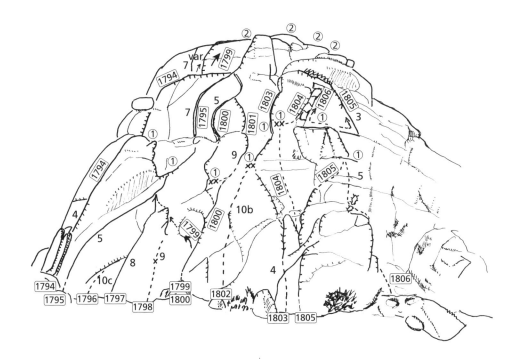

1799. **Wandering Tortoise** (5.3) Begin near the center of the northeast face. Go up easy rock to a ledge (20 feet); head left and up to join *Rehab* and *Luminous Breast*. **Pro:** To 2.5 inches. **FA:** Hank Levine, Fred Lytle; 1973.

1800. **Blistering** (5.5) ★ Begin as for *Wandering Tortoise* (near the middle of the northeast face). **Pitch 1:** Head up easy rock and a knobby face, staying right of an arch, then up and left to a belay ledge beneath a shallow chimney (5.5); two-bolt anchor. **Pitch 2:** Go up the chimney to easier rock (5.5). **Pro:** To 3 inches. **FA:** Chris Perez, Nelson Smith; 9/76.

1801. **Snapping Turtle** (5.9) (R) From the bolt anchor at the end of the first pitch of *Blistering,* traverse right, then head up a crack to a bulge to rejoin that route. **Pro:** To 3 inches. **FA:** Bob Gaines, Brian Prentice; 5/98.

1802. **Give a Mouse a Cookie** (5.10b) ★ Begin a bit up and right of *Wandering*

Tortoise/Blistering. Go up cracks to a small ledge; continue on the face past three bolts to bolt anchor atop the first pitch of *Easy Day.* **Pro:** Thin to 2 inches; two fixed pins. **FA:** Todd Gordon, Cyndie Bransford, George Armstrong; 10/93.

1803. **Easy Day** (5.4) Begin near the right side of the northeast face (just left of a chimney/gully and *Turtle Soup*) and behind a tree. **Pitch 1:** Go up a thin crack and left-slanting ramp to a ledge below and left of a slot; two-bolt anchor (5.4). **Pitch 2:** Go right then up a slot to easier ledges. **Pro:** Thin to 3 inches. **FA:** Chris Gonzales, John Wolfe; 2/77.

1804. **Ninja Turtle** (5.8) (R) ★ **Pitch 1:** Begin as for *Easy Day,* then head straight up the face with horizontal cracks right of *Easy Day* to a bolt anchor. **Pitch 2:** Move right, then up the steep headwall (5.8 R). **Pro:** To 3 inches. **FA:** Bob Gaines, Yvonne Gaines; 4/93.

1805. **Turtle Soup** (5.3) Begin near the right side of the northeast face at a chimney/gully. **Pitch 1:** Go up the chimney/gully about 50 feet until you can move right to a belay ledge around the corner. **Pitch 2:** Continue up and right until below the summit headwall; either go right or left around this. **Pro:** To 3 inches. **FA:** John Wolfe et al.; 1967.

1806. **Cornered** (5.5) Begin just around the right edge of the northeast face on a ledge below a corner. **Pitch 1:** Go up the corner to a ledge, then left and up to the belay ledge of *Turtle Soup.* **Pitch 2:** From atop a block above the ledge, traverse left on a small ledge (5.5) then go up the left side of the summit headwall. **Pro:** To 3 inches. **FA:** Chris Gonzales, John Wolfe; 2/77.

Turtle Rock—North Face

The routes on the north side of Turtle Rock face the Hidden Valley parking area and the picnic area.

1807. **Touché Away** (5.9) ★ This route begins off a ledge 25 feet right of *Cornered,* on the left side of the north face. Go up the right-hand of three cracks to a ledge, go left, then head up a right-tending crack to face climbing past horizontals. **Pro:** To 2.5 inches. **FA:** Dave Evans, Jim Angione; 1979.

1808. **'Nilla Wafer** (5.8) (R) Begin in a left-facing corner about 100 feet right of *Touché Away.* **Pitch 1:** Go up the corner, then up and left; belay at the bottom of a round flake (the Wafer). **Pitch 2:** Go up the right side of the Wafer; then make a long traverse left along horizontal cracks until you can head up just right of *Touché Away.* **Pro:** To 3 inches. **FA:** Bill Cramer et al.; 1993.

1809. **Pile in the Sky** (5.10c) Scramble up to and begin in a cave near the right end of the north face. Go up the right-leaning crack under a roof. Pro; To 2.5 inches. **FA:** Charles Cole et al.; 1979.

The Pillars of Pain

These rocks lie just north of the western end of Turtle Rock and next to the road/picnic area. Three pillars or towers can be seen. The name is a pun on the Towers of Paine, the impressive rock towers in the Patagonia region; these are a wee bit less imposing. The easternmost tower is Pillar 1, the middle Pillar 2, and the western Pillar 3.

To reach the pillars from Park Boulevard, turn west on the Hidden Valley Picnic Area road. After a few hundred yards, a large parking area lies adjacent to the trailhead for Real Hidden Valley proper (to the north). A picnic area is to the south and directly behind it is the large mass of Turtle Rock's north face. The Pillars of Pain lie in front of the right (west) end of the north face of Turtle Rock. The routes are not shown. Map, page 421.

Pillar 1—East Face

The east face of Pillar 1 features two cracks that look like a "V." A bolt is found between the cracks (placed on the first lead of *Super Spy*). The routes get morning sun and afternoon shade.

1810. **Super Spy** (5.11d) ★ This is the left-hand of the V cracks. **Pro:** Thin to 2 inches. **FA** (TR): John Bachar; 1980. **FA** (Lead): Jonny Woodward.

1811. **Secret Agent Man** (5.11c) (R) ★ The right-hand, right-slanting crack. **Pro:** Thin to 2 inches. **FA** (TR): John Bachar et al.; 1980. **FA** (Lead): Hidetaka Suzuki.

1812. **Mata Hari** (5.8) Begin just right of *Secret Agent Man;* go up the right-slanting crack. **Pro:** To 2.5 inches. **FA:** Unknown.

The Pillars of Pain

Pillar 1   Pillar 2   Pillar 3

1806 1807

1808

1809

Pillar 2—East Face

Other cracks have been climbed (aid and free) on this face, but no information is known. It sees some morning sun and is shady all afternoon.

1813. **Acid Rock** (5.11a) ★ This takes the leftmost right-diagonalling handcrack on the east face of Pillar 2. **Pro:** To 2.5 inches. **FA:** Mike Lechlinski, Gib Lewis, Charles Cole, Marius Morsted, Dean Fidelman; 11/79.

1814. **Danny Gore** (5.10d) Begin about 15 feet right of *Acid Rock,* off a boulder. This is the easiest looking crack on the right side of the east face. **Pro:** To 2.5 inches. **FA:** Dan McHale, Joe Brown, Greg Bender; 12/69. **FFA:** Unknown.

Pillar 2—West Face

This route gets morning shade, some sun in the afternoon.

1815. **West Face Route** (5.7) Begin on the west face of Pillar 3; go up the low-angled face to the notch between Pillar 2 and Pillar 3. Finish up a crack on the west face of Pillar 2. **Pro:** To 2.5 inches. **FA:** Mark Powell, Beverly Powell; circa 1965.

Pillar 3—East Face

This face sees some morning sun and is shady all afternoon.

1816. **Whatchasay Dude** (5.10d) ★ This route takes the very short, overhanging finger crack on the upper east side of the summit block of Pillar 3. **Pro:** Thin to 2 inches. **FA:** Mike Lechlinski et al.; 1981.

The Cluster

Take the Hidden Valley Picnic Area road (to Real Hidden Valley) west until it curves south toward Turtle Rock; here you can take a one-way loop road west to several parking spots with picnic tables. From the western terminus of the road, walk between the boulders to the south into an open area where you'll find very large boulders and singular, small formations. To the west is a small formation with a steep eastern face containing several solution holes. Map, page 421.

1817. **Gripped Up the Hole** (5.10a) (R) ★ Go up the east face past two bolts (one may be missing) using the "holes." No fixed anchors exist on top; a simul-rap is necessary to descend. **FA:** Dave Evans, Kevin Powell; 2/77.

1818. **Digitalis Destructi (aka Fingers of Frenzy)** (5.11b) ★ This right-slanting thin crack lies on the east face of the small formation to the right of the rock with *Gripped Up the Hole*. Go up the crack to a horizontal, exit right. **Pro:** Thin to 2 inches. **FA** (Solo): John Bachar; 1980.

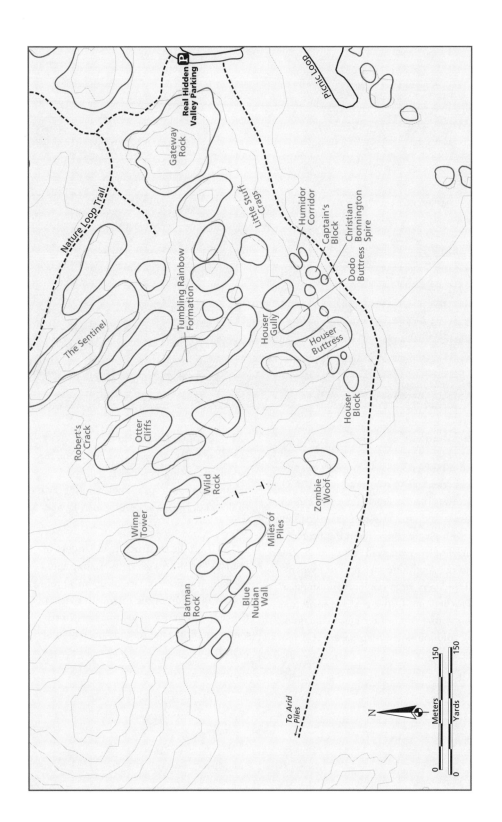

HOUSER BUTTRESS AREA

This area lies on the southern, outside perimeter of the Real Hidden Valley, west of the Real Hidden Valley parking area. From the park's West Entrance, take Park Boulevard 8.6+ miles to a four-way intersection (Intersection Rock parking is to the east, and the Hidden Valley Picnic Area is to the southwest). This intersection lies 0.1 mile north of the T intersection of Park Boulevard and Barker Dam Road (which provides access to Hidden Valley Campground). Turn west on the Hidden Valley Picnic Area road. After a few hundred yards, a large parking area lies adjacent to the trailhead for Real Hidden Valley proper (to the north). To the south is a picnic area, and directly behind it is the large mass of Turtle Rock's north face. From the western end of the Real Hidden Valley parking area a well marked trail heads west toward ridges of rocks and buttresses. The most prominent buttress of rock is Houser Buttress, which lies approximately 225 yards to the west. Map, page 430.

Little Stuff Crags

Several small formations rise high above the boulder fields/talus on your right (north) approximately midway between the parking area at Real Hidden Valley and Houser Buttress.

1819. **Short but Sweet** (5.9) ★★ This route is on the south side of a large boulder like formation located about 180 feet up the hillside. Go up the straight-in thin crack in brown rock; it has a slight S-shape to it. **Pro:** To 2 inches. **FA:** Alan Bartlett, Alan Roberts; 1983.

1820. **Sweet and Sour** (5.8) The chimney/off-width located about 20 feet left of *Short but Sweet*. **Pro:** To 4+ inches. **FA:** Todd Swain; 1/98.

1821. **Swisher Sweets** (5.9) A crack about 12 feet up and right from *Short but Sweet*. **Pro:** To 2.5 inches. **FA:** Todd Swain; 1/98.

1822. **Atonal Scales** (5.8+) (not shown on photo) This and *Fish Scales* lie on a rock up and left of from *Short but Sweet,* near the top of the hillside. Two short pitches; loose. **Pitch 1:** Go up a flake chimney to ledge. **Pitch 2:** Move left, then up a straight-in crack. **Pro:**

To 3+ inches. **FA:** Rob Kelman, Eric Wright; 3/92.

1823. **Fish Scales** (5.9) (not shown on photo) **Pitch 1:** Do the first pitch of *Atonal Scales.* **Pitch 2:** Go up fist crack in a corner off the back of the ledge. **Pro:** To 4 inches. **FA:** Alan Bartlett, Tucker Tech, Karlis Ogle; 10/00.

Christian Bonnington Spire

This is a small pinnacle of rock rising at the base of the hillside about 70 yards right of Houser Buttress. One route is on its east side and is not pictured. See photo on page 434. Map, page 430.

1824. **Christian Bonnington Spire** (5.8) Go up the wide crack on the east side of the pinnacle, then up and left on the face past one bolt. **Pro:** To 4 inches. **FA:** Todd Gordon, Alan Bartlett; 8/97.

Captain's Block

This large block lies immediately right (east) of the pointy pinnacle of the Christian Bonnington Spire and about 150 yards from the Real Hidden Valley parking area. See photo on page 434. Map, page 430.

1825. **Captain Stupor's Troopers** (5.9) (not shown on photo) Go up a crack on the west face, then up the face past one bolt. **Pro:** To 2.5 inches. **FA:** Alan Bartlett, Todd Gordon; 8/97.

1826. **Paul Petzl** (5.10a) Begin on the right (east) side of the block; go up the face past one bolt to a crack. **Pro:** To 2.5 inches. **FA:** Unknown.

The Humidor Corridor

The following route faces south and lies in a small east-west corridor about 50 feet right of the Captain's Block. See photo on page 434. Map, page 430.

1827. **The Humidor** (5.9) ★ Go up a right-leaning crack in dark rock. **Pro:** To 2.5 inches. **FA:** Alan Bartlett, Todd Gordon; 8/97.

Houser Buttress

Houser Buttress presents as a nice 80-foot tall, south-facing buttress of rock located about 225 yards west of the Real Hidden Valley parking area. From the park's West Entrance, take Park Boulevard 8.6+ miles to a four-way intersection, with Intersection Rock parking to the east and Hidden Valley Picnic Area to the west. This intersection lies 0.1 mile north of the T intersection of Park Boulevard and Barker Dam Road (which provides access to Hidden Valley Campground). Turn west on the Hidden Valley Picnic Area road. A large parking area is a few hundred yards down the road. To the west of the main parking area, a climbers' trail leads toward Houser Buttress, which is visible in profile as you approach it. Map, page 430.

Houser Block

This squarish block sits about 175 feet left of the main Houser Buttress. Descend off the back (north) side.

1828. **Chas' TR** (5.10d) (TR) (not shown on photo) Go up the face just left of *Grunge Rock* (a left-leaning chimney/off-width). **FA:** Chas Wilson; 1993.

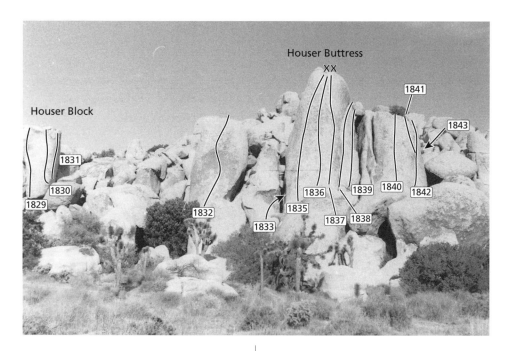

1829. **Grunge Rock** (5.9) This left-leaning off-width/chimney is on the south side of Houser Block. **Pro:** To 5+ inches. **FA:** Alan Bartlett; 11/00.

1830. **Badger's Choff Piece** (5.10d) ★ A three-bolt climb on the southeast arête that has a somewhat height-dependent crux. **FA:** Nick Conway, Stu Critchlow, Todd Gordon; 4/92.

1831. **Armageddon Tired** (5.11a) ★★★ This is a short three-bolt route on excellent rock just left of the northeast corner of this block. **FA:** Herb Laeger et al.

The following route is located on the south face of a large block located about 60 feet left of Houser Buttress.

1832. **Snap on Demand** (5.11d) (R) ★★ This four-bolt route has continuous climbing and is cruxy and runout past the last bolt. **FA:** Darrel Hensel, Jonny Woodward; 10/86.

Houser Buttress

The following routes lie on the large south-facing Houser Buttress.

1833. **Hidden Arch** (5.11d) ★★★★ A hidden gem, this faces west and is just around the corner from *Loose Lady* (morning shade/afternoon sun). Face climb past two bolts (5.10c) to a small ledge. Above, go up into a left-leaning flared dihedral with a crack that starts thin and becomes hands at the top. **Pro:** Many thin to 2 inches; fixed pin; two-bolt anchor/rap. **FA:** Herb Laeger, Rich Smith; 5/77. **FFA:** Mike Lechlinski, Lynn Hill, John Long.

1834. **Nasty Lady** (5.11c) ★★★ (TR) (not shown on photo) Climb *Hidden Arch* until you can exit up and right onto a steep enjoyable face, climbing to the *Loose Lady* anchor.

1835. **Loose Lady** (5.10a) ★★★★ A perennially popular steep friction route, and a good

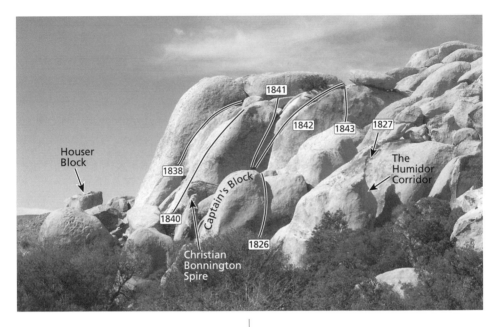

introduction to Josh slab climbing. Go up the
left side of the buttress; the crux is down low,
but there is sustained climbing to the top.
Pro: Seven bolts; two-bolt anchor/ 80-foot
rap. **FA:** Dave Houser, Jan McCollum; 11/77.

1836. **California Girls** (5.11b) ★★ (TR)
Toprope the face between *Loose Lady* and
Puss N' Boots. **FA:** Chris Miller; 1997.

1837. **Puss n' Boots** (5.11b/c) ★★ Begin
about 15 feet right of *Loose Lady;* go up the
steeper face to the same anchor. **Pro:** Seven
bolts; two-bolt anchor/80-foot rap. **FA:** Bob
Rotert, Kelly Carignan.

1838. **Dummy's Delight** (5.9) ★★★ This
right-curving crack is on the right side of
Houser Buttress (facing east). **Pro:** To 3
inches. **FA:** Randy Leavitt, Mike Waugh;
1978.

1839. **Ladyfingers** (5.10b) ★★★ A six-bolt
face route just right of *Dummy's Delight.* **Pro:**
To 2 inches for anchor. **FA:** Bob Gaines,
Yvonne Gaines; 11/98.

Dodo Buttress

This face/recessed buttress lies immediately
right of Houser Buttress, but is probably best
approached from farther right through large
boulders. Descend off the back (north), then
down the gully/boulders.

1840. **Lucky Lady** (5.8) ★★ Go up the middle of the south face past two bolts. **Pro:** To 2
inches. **FA:** Alan Bartlett, Alan Roberts; 1983.

1841. **Rock Out with Your Cock Out**
(5.10a/b) This and the next route *(Dodo's
Delight)* lie about 35 feet right and around
the corner from *Lucky Lady.* This route takes
the left-hand of two cracks that begin
together. Head pretty much straight up. **Pro:**
To 2.5 inches. **FA:** Todd Gordon, Pat
Brennan; 12/84.

1842. **Dodo's Delight** (5.10a) ★★ This climbs
the right-hand of the two cracks, which
slants well to the right. Ends atop *Herbie's
Hideaway.* **Pro:** To 3 inches. **FA:** Alan Bartlett,
Alan Roberts; 1983.

1843. Herbie's Hideaway (5.10d) (R) ★★
This short thin crack is about 40 feet to the
right of *Dodo's Delight*. Some tunneling is
required to reach it. It shares the *Dodo's
Delight* belay. **Pro:** Very thin to 2 inches. **FA:**
Herb Laeger, Eve Laeger, Bob Kamps; 1/87.

D–S Spire

This small pinnacle lies about 50 feet east of
Herbie's Hideaway; it has two cracks on its
southern face and a two-bolt anchor on its
summit. The spire and routes are not
pictured.

1844. Duebenkorn/Rothko Spire Route
(5.8) This is the right-hand thin crack that
heads straight up on the southern face of the
D–S Spire. **Pro:** To 2 inches. **FA:** George
Zelenz; 1997.

1845. Left Spire Route (5.4) The left-hand,
wide, and left-slanting crack on the south
side of the spire. **Pro:** To 4 inches. **FA:**
Unknown.

Houser Gully

Approach the following routes by heading up
through boulders to the right of Houser and
Dodo Buttresses. You will find yourself in a
gully of sorts that soon becomes a corridor.
The first four routes are found on the wall
on your left. This wall faces east. The remain-
ing two routes lie farther north, opposite
Todd's Hardcover (the back side of the Solosby
Face). The gully and routes are not pictured.
Map, page 430.

1846. The Albatross (5.10c) ★ This is a thin
crack above an alcove that widens to hands.
It begins above a yucca. **Pro:** Thin to 2.5
inches. **FA:** Mike Lechlinski et al.; 1980.

1847. All Booked Up (5.6) ★★★ This is a
nice hand-crack in a right-facing corner
about 50 feet right of *The Albatross*. **Pro:** To 3
inches. **FA:** Hank Levine, Dag Kolsrud; 1978.

1848. Sunday Papers (5.10b) This and
Todd's Hardcover are located about 200 feet
right (uphill) from, and somewhat behind, *All
Booked Up*. Start in a "pit," climb a short flake
to a slab, then go up and left to a fist crack.
Pro: To 3.5 inches. Rappel off a two-bolt
anchor to the right (on top of *Todd's
Hardcover*). **FA:** Alan Roberts, Todd Swain;
1/89.

1849. Todd's Hardcover (5.10b) (TR) Begin
off a boulder just right of *Sunday Papers* and
head straight up to bolt anchors. Rappel 40
feet. **FA:** Todd Swain; 1/89.

The next two routes lie on a face opposite
Todd's Hardcover (faces west); this is the back
side of Solosby Face.

1850. Thunderhead (aka Gaston's Groove)
(5.12a) ★ This is the thin crack in the back of
a groove that leads to face climbing on plates
above. **Pro:** Thin to 2 inches. **FA:** Paul
Turecki; 1988.

1851. Give the People What They Want
(5.10d) ★ This three-bolt route lies on the
left side of a chimney/corridor to the left of
Thunderhead. **Pro:** To 2 inches. **FA:** Dave
Griffith, Paul Turecki; 1988.

Zombie Woof Rock

Zombie Woof Rock is a small squarish tower located about 150 yards west and north of Houser Buttress. From the large Real Hidden Valley parking area (see page 431 for driving directions), hike west along a well-marked climbers' trail toward Houser Buttress (which is located about 225 yards west of the parking area). From below Houser Buttress, continue west for about 60 yards to where the trail heads northwest toward Arid Piles. Follow the trail northwest for another 90 yards; the back (west) side of Zombie Woof Rock is on your right (it has a dark section of rock in the middle). Routes are located on the east and north sides of the rock. There are no fixed anchors on top; simul-rappel off to descend. Map, page 430.

Zombie Woof Rock—East Face

The east side of this small rock sports a large roof and overhanging cracks. It gets morning sun and afternoon shade.

1852. **Poodle Woof** (5.10d) ★ Go up the slot/chimney to a handcrack on the left side of the east face. **Pro:** To 3+ inches. **FA:** Charles Cole, Mike Lechlinski, Rob Raker; 1982.

1853. **Zombie Woof** (5.12b) ★★ Begin just right of *Poodle Woof,* then go over the roof's left side via a thin crack. **Pro:** Thin to 2 inches. **FA** (TR): John Bachar; 1/80. **FA** (Lead): Jerry Moffat; 1983.

1854. **Roof Woof** (A3/A4) This is the crack/seam that heads straight over the roof to the right of *Zombie Woof;* a bolt is found near the top. **Pro:** Lots of thin aid gear; ground-fall possible. **FA:** Unknown.

Zombie Woof Rock—North Face

The north side of Zombie Woof Rock is a steep slab with some horizontal breaks. It is shady most of the day.

1855. **Bats with AIDS** (5.10b) Begin of the right side of the north face. Go up to a bolt, traverse right in a horizontal, then go up past a second bolt (crux; very height-dependent). **Pro:** Thin to 2 inches. **FA:** Todd Gordon, Dave Evans, Brian Elliott; 12/90.

Ringwinker Wall

This north-facing face lies behind (north) and above *Snap on Demand* (left of Houser Buttress) and somewhat east and above Zombie Woof. One five-bolt face route is located here. The best approach is to head up a rocky gully left of *Snap on Demand;* at its top, go left to reach the wall/route. From Zombie Woof Rock, look about 250 feet above the desert to a small pine; the wall lies just above. The wall and route are not pictured. Map, page 430.

1856. **The Ringwinker** (5.11b) The five-bolt face route. **Pro:** For anchors. **FA:** Nick Conway, Stu Crichlow, Todd Gordon; 4/92.

Miles of Piles Rock

This formation lies about 100 yards northwest of Zombie Roof Rock. The west face is overhanging and sports several fine crack routes. The east face is taller and has a number of longer, but lesser quality crack routes. From the Real Hidden Valley parking area (see page 431 for driving directions), hike west along a well-marked climbers' trail toward Houser Buttress (about 225 yards west of the parking area). From below Houser Buttress, continue west for about 60 yards to where the trail turns northwest. Zombie Woof Rock, a small square tower, is on your right after about 100 yards. Miles Of Piles Rock is the tall formation about 120 yards directly north. Map, page 430.

10c

1858

1859

11a

11a

10b

1860

1861

Miles of Piles Rock—West Face

From near Zombie Woof Rock, head north and scramble up a small valley. Near a large fallen tree go right, and after a bit of scrambling you will find yourself at the base of the west face. A large pine tree is near the base of *Winds of Whoopee*. Downclimb to the left (north). The routes see morning shade and sun in the afternoon.

1857. Breaking Wind (5.9) (not shown on photo) Begin about 35 feet left of the tree; just left of *Making Wind*. Go up and into the dogleg crack (crux). **Pro:** To 2.5 inches. **FA:** Todd Swain; 9/92.

1858. Making Wind (5.10c) ★ Begin about 30 feet left of the tree, below a "pod"-shaped alcove. Go up into the pod, then up double cracks to a small ledge. **Pro:** To 2.5 inches. **FA** (TR): Dan Hirshman. **FA** (Lead): Dave Mayville, Paul Borne, Dave Bengston; 1991.

1859. Flaring Rhoid (5.10b) ★ Begin about 30 feet left of the tree, as for *Making Wind*. Go up to the pod, then traverse right on a flake/face to the overhanging crack to the right. Follow this to where it joins the next route; continue to the top. **Pro:** To 2.5 inches. **FA:** Perry Beckham, Bill Ravitch; 1/84.

1860. Winds of Change (5.11a) (R) ★★ This is the overhanging crack system just left of *Winds of Whoopee;* joins *Flaring Rhoid* at the top. **Pro:** To 2.5 inches. **FA** (TR): Dan Hirshman. **FA** (Lead): Paul Borne, Dave Mayville, Dave Bengston; 1991.

1861. Winds of Whoopee (5.11a) ★★★ Begin just left of the tree and immediately right of *Winds of Change*. Go up the clean crack that varies from thin to fist. **Pro:** To 3+ inches. **FA:** Rob Raker, Perry Beckham, Randy Vogel; 1/84.

Miles of Piles Rock—East Face

From just past the north side of Zombie Woof Rock, head right (northwest) through a more open area. You will soon find a small dam; walk across this, then follow the wash north (passing another small dam). Scramble north across boulders until below the east face (on your left). Descend either left (south) or right (north) depending on the route (it should be obvious). The face sees morning sun and afternoon shade.

1862. Cruelty to Animals (5.10a) Begin on the left end of the east face; go up the straight-in hand crack in a rounded left-facing corner (5.10a), then up to a ledge. **Pro:** To 2.5 inches. **FA:** Alan Bartlett, Dave Evans, Pat Nay; 4/88.

1863. Rat Boy (5.10c) Begin at the same place as *Cruelty to Animals*. Go up a right-slanting crack (5.10c), pass a small bush, then go left and up a thin crack. **Pro:** Thin to 2 inches. **FA:** Dave Evans, Alan Bartlett; 4/88.

1864. Cripple Crack (5.10b) This two-pitch route lies on the center of the east face. **Pitch 1:** Go up a steep thin crack to a large ledge (5.10b). **Pitch 2:** Head up over a small roof, then move left into a chimney. **Pro:** Thin to 3 inches. **FA:** Alan Roberts, Tony Puppo, Alan Bartlett; 3/88.

1865. Liquid Rats (5.10d) Begin about 15 feet right of *Cripple Crack;* right of center on the east face. Go up a double overhanging lieback crack system (5.10d), then up a thin, slightly right-slanting crack above. **Pro:** Thin to 2 inches. **FA:** Todd Gordon, Brian Elliott, Jim Angione, Dave Evans; 12/90.

1866. Mickey Rat (5.10a) This and the next three crack routes are right of *Liquid Rats*. Go up a low-angled crack and slab to the

steeper left-hand crack. **Pro:** To 3 inches. **FA:**
Alan Bartlett, Pat Dennis; 2/92.

1867. **Feeding the Rat** (5.11b) Begin as for
Mickey Rat, but head up the crack second
from the left—a very thin crack just right of
Mickey Rat. **Pro:** Thin to 2 inches. **FA:** Brian
Elliott, Dave Evans; 12/90.

1868. **Rat Patrol** (5.10b) Begin as for *Mickey
Rat.* This is the third of the four crack systems and is just right of *Feeding the Rat.* **Pro:**
To 2 inches. **FA:** Todd Swain, Jeff Rickerl;
3/93.

1869. **Rat Up Your Alley** (5.10a) Begin as for
Mickey Rat. Go up the right-hand of the
four crack systems. **Pro:** To 2.5 inches. **FA:** Pat
Dennis, Alan Bartlett; 2/92.

Wild Rock

The following routes lie on the west-facing
rocks almost directly opposite the east face of
Miles of Piles Rock. Approach as for the east
face of Miles of Piles Rock, but stay a bit
right. The formation lies directly above a
wash and boulders, and about 100 feet west
of the west face of the Otter Cliffs.

Alternatively, you could easily approach
Wild Rock from the Otter Cliffs' west face
by walking a short distance southwest along
the wash. The rock gets morning shade and
afternoon sun. Map, page 430.

1870. **Wild Abandon** (5.11a) This route faces
the far right end of Miles of Piles Rock's east
face, roughly opposite *Rat Up Your Alley.* Go
up a crack until you can traverse right past

one bolt into another crack. Loose rock. **Pro:** To 2.5 inches. **FA:** Don Reid, Alan Nelson; 11/91.

1870A. **Unknown** (5.10/5.11?) Begin about 15 feet right of *Wild Abandon*. Go up discontinuous cracks past a bolt to the crack above. **Pro:** Thin to 2 inches. **FA:** Unknown.

1871. **Long-Necked Goose** (5.9) Begin about 75 feet right of *Wild Abandon*. Go up a left-slanting inverted corner, then up past two bolts to the top. Poor rock. **Pro:** Thin to 2 inches. **FA:** Alan Bartlett, Alan Roberts; 3/88.

Souvenir Rock

This formation lies in a narrow corridor between Miles of Piles Rock and Blue Nubian Wall. Approach as for Blue Nubian Wall, but about 80 feet before you reach *Momento Mori*, turn right and scramble along until you reach this corridor. The rock and route are not pictured.

1872. **Souvenir** (5.10c) Go up a thin crack/seam with two bolts. **Pro:** Thin to 2 inches. **FA:** Dave Bengston, Dave Mayville; 1991.

Blue Nubian Wall

This formation lies about 50 yards northwest of and below Miles of Piles Rock's west face, on the east margin of the open plains to the west. From the large Real Hidden Valley parking area (see page 431 for driving directions), hike west along a well-marked climbers' trail toward Houser Buttress (about 225 yards west of the parking area). From below Houser Buttress, continue west for about 60 yards to where the trail turns northwest. Follow the trail northwest for 200+ yards. This rock lies along the edge of the desert floor and faces west (morning shade, afternoon sun). It has several vertical and diagonal crack systems. Map, page 430.

1873. **Scream** (5.11a) (R) Begin on the steep face left of *Blue Meanie*. Go up the face past two bolts, then left and up an arête. **Pro:** Thin to 2 inches. **FA:** Rico Miledi, Ian Parker; 1990.

1874. **Blue Meanie** (5.10a) This is a right-slanting crack that passes a small pillar and then heads up a small dihedral. It is on the left side of the Blue Nubian face. **Pro:** To 3 inches. **FA:** Mark Bowling, Alan Bartlett, Cal Gerberding, Steve Gerberding; 11/00.

1875. **Blue Nubian** (5.10a) ★ Begin on the left side of the face. Go up a left-slanting finger-to-hand crack. **Pro:** To 2.5 inches. **FA:** Mike Lechlinski, John Long; 1/80.

1876. **Conceptual Continuity** (5.11c) ★ (TR) Begin immediately right of *Blue Nubian*. Go up the thin crack that peters out into a seam near the top; continue up the face. **FA:** Mike Lechlinski, John Long; 1/80.

1877. **Momento Mori** (5.11a) This is a thin crack on a separate buttress located about 30 feet right of *Conceptual Continuity*. There is a fixed pin at the start; the route stays in the left-hand crack. **Pro:** Thin to 2.5 inches. **FA:** Dave Evans, Pat Nay, Alan Bartlett; 4/88.

Batman Rock

This tall formation lies about 90 yards left of and up from Blue Nubian Wall, and is seen in profile from Blue Nubian Wall. Approach as for Blue Nubian Wall, then continue left (north). Map, page 430.

Batman Rock—North Face

Scramble up and around the right side of the formation to the north face. A large cave will be seen. This face can also be approached from Real Hidden Valley proper by heading west from near Wimp Tower.

1878. **The Bat Cave** (5.11c) ★★ (not shown on photo) Climb out of the cave on an over-hanging face past four bolts. **Pro:** To 2 inches; two-bolt anchor. **FA:** Dave Bengston, Paul Borne, Dave Mayville; 1991.

North Face

West
Face

1879
(hidden)

Batman Rock—West Face

Scramble up a rocky gully along the base of
the west face; the one recorded route lies
near the left side of the face.

1879. **Woodward Route** (5.10d) ★ Begin
on the left side of the west face; go up a discontinuous crack system over a bulge partially protected by bolts. **Pro:** To 2 inches;
four bolts. **FA:** Jonny Woodward, Darrel
Hensel, Kevin Powell, Greg Epperson; 3/89.

Arid Piles, Jimmy Cliff, Mount Grossvogel
(described on page 293)

Though these formations are described in the Lost Horse section of the guide, and are most commonly approached from the terminus of Lost Horse Road, they may be more easily approached from the Real Hidden Valley parking area.

From Park Boulevard, turn west on the Hidden Valley Picnic Area road. A large parking area is a few hundred yards down the road. From the main parking area, head west along a climbers' trail leading about 225 yards to Houser Buttress. From Houser Buttress, continue west along the trail for another 60 yards; the trail veers northwest from here. Follow this for several hundred yards until you can head directly west to Arid Piles, the obvious large "formation" sitting in the desert. Jimmy Cliff lies north of Arid Piles, and Mount Grossvogel across a dirt road to the northwest of Arid Piles. Map, page 282.

Candlestein Pass
(described on page 305)

Though these formations are described in the Lost Horse section of the guide, they may be more easily approached from the Real Hidden Valley parking area. This area is located west of Arid Piles, Jimmy Cliff, and Mount Grossvogel, and south of the large hillside containing the S Cracks Formation, in a canyon/wash that runs to the northwest. You can approach this area from either from Lost Horse Road (see page 305 for directions), or by heading west past Houser Buttress, then northwest, passing just south of Arid Piles (see approach description above). Map, page 305.

Hidden Valley Campground and the Outback

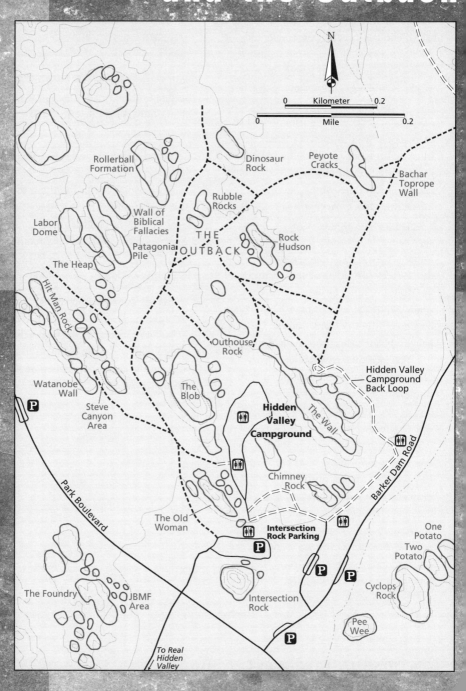

N

| 0 | Kilometer | 0.2 |
| 0 | Mile | 0.2 |

Rollerball Formation

Dinosaur Rock

Peyote Cracks

Bachar Toprope Wall

Rubble Rocks

Wall of Biblical Fallacies

THE OUTBACK

Rock Hudson

Labor Dome

Patagonia Pile

The Heap

Hit Man Rock

Outhouse Rock

Hidden Valley Campground Back Loop

Watanobe Wall

Steve Canyon Area

The Blob

The Wall

Hidden Valley Campground

Park Boulevard

Chimney Rock

Barker Dam Road

The Old Woman

Intersection Rock Parking

One Potato Two Potato

The Foundry

JBMF Area

Intersection Rock

Cyclops Rock

Pee Wee

To Real Hidden Valley

HIDDEN VALLEY CAMPGROUND

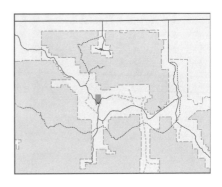

Since 1949, this campground has been the traditional center of the Joshua Tree climbing scene. Though it seems perpetually full throughout the climbing season, most climbers prefer to camp here as there is a lot of good climbing within walking distance, and the rocks surrounding the campground offer many good and popular climbs. Day users should park in the very large Intersection Rock parking area, located on the north side of Intersection Rock (immediately south of the campground). The Intersection Rock parking area is reached via a signed road located off Park Boulevard approximately 8.6 miles from the West Entrance; this is 11.7 miles from Pinto Wye (the Park Boulevard and Pinto Basin Road intersection). Toilet facilities and an emergency phone are located here. Climbers can post notes (must be dated) on the back of a bulletin board adjacent to the parking area.

To reach the actual Hidden Valley Campground, turn northeast off of Park Boulevard onto the Barker Dam Road (signed also for Hidden Valley Campground and Keys Ranch). The turn is located about 0.1 mile farther south of the Intersection Rock turn (8.7+ miles from the West Entrance). Drive east on Barker Dam Road for less than 0.1 mile and turn north (left) on the signed Hidden Valley Campground road. There is no day-use parking in the campground; thus, unless you are staying in the campground, you should park in the large Intersection Rock parking lot.

Formations in the campground are described in a clockwise manner, beginning with Intersection Rock. Formations lying outside Hidden Valley Campground proper (The Outback) are described next, also in a clockwise manner. Map, page 445.

Occupied Campsite Rule: Any route that begins out of or behind an occupied campsite may not be climbed without the occupants' permission. This rule applies to only a few locations in Hidden Valley Campground, particularly the west face of Chimney Rock, from West Face Overhang to Pinched Rib. Remember, courtesy goes a long way.

The guide does not refer to individual campsite numbers that lie adjacent to various rocks. The park service has regularly "reformatted" this and other campgrounds and thus changed the campsite numbers, rendering this information quickly obsolete and less than useless.

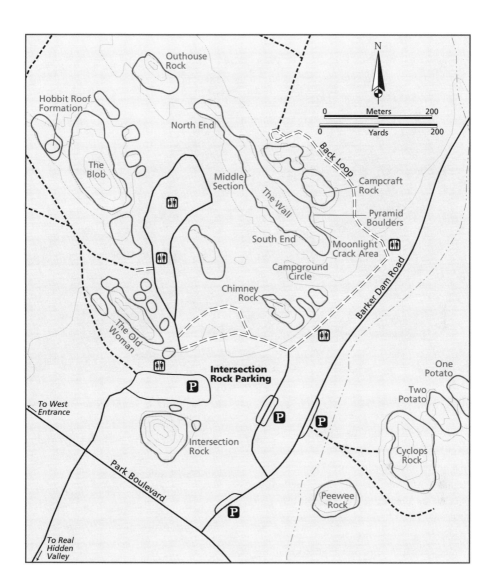

Intersection Rock

This large formation is located adjacent to (just south of) the large Intersection Rock parking area (toilets and emergency telephone here). Most climbs are either one long or two shorter pitches. This is a perennially popular crag with ultra-easy access. All the faces/aspects of Intersection Rock have climbing, providing route possibilities for all weather conditions.

Descents: Intersection Rock is one of several formations in the Hidden Valley Campground area that have no easy (less than fifth class) descent routes. There are several ways of getting off the top of the rock. All rappels can be done with a single 50-meter rope, and all have fixed anchors.

- Rappel route 1: *Mike's Books* (two rappels: 80+ feet, then 65 feet);
- Rappel route 2: Atop *Huevos,* just right of *Upper Right Ski Track* (80+ feet to ledge; walk off right).
- Downclimbs: Experienced climbers regularly downclimb either *Upper Right Ski Track* (5.3; exposed) to the ledge and walk off right; or *Southeast Corner* (5.3; more involved, but less exposed).

Intersection Rock—North Face

The routes on the north face lie directly adjacent to the Intersection Rock parking area. Most routes are in the shade all day. Rappel 80+ feet from atop *Huevos,* or downclimb *Upper Right Ski Track* (5.3, exposed!).

1880. **North Overhang** (5.9) ★★★ This route starts off the ledge that leads up to *Upper Right Ski Track.* Two short pitches. **Pitch 1:**

Climb a flake/crack to a sloping ledge just below the summit overhang. **Pitch 2:** Climb out and left around the overhang (one bolt), then up a crack to the top. **Pro:** To 2 inches. **FA:** John Wolfe, Howard Weamer; 5/69. **FFA:** John Long, Rick Accomazzo; 9/72.

1881. **Huevos** (5.11d) ★★ Start up the first pitch of *North Overhang,* then head out left onto the face. **Pro:** Seven bolts; medium pro. **FA:** Unknown; 1980s.

1882. **Upper Right Ski Track** (5.3) ★★ Begin near the left end of the large ledge on the right side of the north face. Go up the obvious deep crack/chimney system. Commonly used as an exposed descent route. **Pro:** To 3 inches. **FA:** Unknown; circa 1949/1950.

1883. **Lower Right Ski Track** (5.10b/c) ★★★ Tricky moves lead up holes past a bolt to a ledge (5.10b/c), then up the crack in the left-facing corner (5.9) to a large ledge. Walk off right. **Pro:** To 2.5 inches; one bolt. **FA:** Unknown; circa 1955. **FKFA:** John Long; 9/72.

1884. **Trapeze** (5.11d) ★★ There are four ways of doing this route (the next three are also listed below). This is the most commonly done variation. Begin off a boulder, head up and right past a bolt; after the fourth bolt, exit right over the roof. **Pro:** Four bolts; to 2 inches. **FA:** Bob Gaines, John Long; 4/87.

1885. **Fast Track** (5.11c) ★ After the first bolt, head right and finish up *Lower Right Ski Track.* **FA:** Bob Gaines, Bob Mallery; 1/87.

1886. **Trapeze Center** (5.12a) ★★ Head left at the roof to a fifth bolt, then climb over the center of the roof. **Pro:** 5 bolts; to 2 inches. **FA:** Bob Gaines; 4/87.

1887. **Trapeze Left** (5.12b/c) ★★ At the roof, go left past the fifth bolt to a sixth; go over the roof's left side. **Pro:** Six bolts; to 2 inches. **FA:** Bob Gaines; 4/87.

1888. **Left Ski Track** (5.11a) ★★★ The crux is actually getting to the bolt; higher up the route eases dramatically. After about 75 feet, either stay in the crack or head up and right on an easy but runout face. Can be done in one or two pitches. This is the route made "famous" in the short story *The Only Blasphemy* by John Long. **Pro:** To 3 inches; one bolt. **FA** (upper crack): Phil Johnson & others; 11/49. **FKA** (lower crack): Al Ruiz, Rich Wolfe; 1966. **FFA** (lower crack) Tom Higgins et al.; 4/68.

1889. **Kool Aid** (5.10d A4) (R) ★ **Pitch 1:** Super thin aid up seams/cracks right of *Half Track* past several horizontals to ledge (A4). **Pitch 2:** Go up a curving flake to join the last bit of *Left Ski Track* (5.10d). **Pro:** Thin aid stuff. **FA:** Tony Yaniro, Erik Burman; 3/77. **FFA** (second pitch): Lynn Hill; 1980.

1890. **Ignorant Photons from Pluto** (5.11a) ★ (TR) An obscure variation/route. Start up *Half Track,* head right on a horizontal, then go up the face to join *Left Ski Track.* **FA:** Mike Lechlinski, John Long; 1979.

1891. **Half Track** (5.10a) (R) ★ This is hard to protect at the bottom (crux); it joins *Zigzag* at the end of the first pitch. **Pro:** Thin to 2 inches. **FA:** Unknown. **FFA:** John Long, Royd Riggins; 10/72.

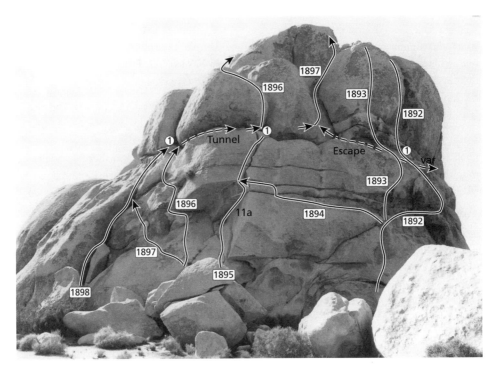

Intersection Rock—East Face

Located around to the left of the north face from the Intersection parking area, this face gets early morning sun and shade in the afternoon. To descend, rappel from *Mike's Books* or downclimb *Southeast Corner* (5.3!).

1892. **Zigzag (aka Phil's Folly)** (5.5 or 5.10b) This route was most likely the first technical climb established in Joshua Tree, and was originally named *Phil's Folly*. This routes starts as does *Static Cling* and *Gaz Giz*. **Pitch 1:** Head far right to a ledge at an over-hang, then go back left to the base of a chimney (5.5). **Pitch 2:** Go up the chimney (5.10b). **Pitch 2 variation:** Traverse straight right on a small ledge to meet and then climb the upper section of *Left Ski Track* (5.5). Alternatively, escape straight left. **FA** (via the second pitch variation): Phil Johnson and others; 11/49. **FA** (second pitch/5.10b): Steve Eddy, Rob Muir; 4/73.

1893. **Static Cling** (5.11a) ★ **Pitch 1:** Start as for *Gaz Giz* and *Zigzag,* but head over the roof at the left of two crack/flakes. **Pitch 2:** Face climb past a fixed pin and two bolts. **Pro:** To 3 inches. **FA:** Charles Cole, Rusty Reno, John Long; 1985.

1894. **Gaz Giz** (5.6) Start as for *Zigzag,* but head left to double horizontal cracks; follow these left to meet *Goldenbush Corner* above its roof. **Pro:** To 3 inches. **FA:** Craig Fry.

1895. **Goldenbush Corner** (5.11a) (R) Climb up the lower of two parallel roofs and traverse right to the corner (5.11a); continue up an easy crack to a ledge. **FA:** George Harr and others; 10/54. **FFA:** John Bachar; 1977.

1896. **Jungle** (5.9) **Pitch 1:** Start as for *Southeast Corner,* but head up to the left end of the roof; take the wide crack up to the ledge. **Pitch 2:** Tunnel right, then go up the chimney on the right side of the block. **Pitch 3:** Head left and up a short handcrack. **Pro:** To 3 inches. **FA:** John Wolfe, Don O'Kelley, Ken Stichter; 10/70.

1897. **Southeast Corner** (5.3) ★ **Pitch 1:** Go up and left on the face to the white pillar, then up and left to meet *Secovar* and finish on the ledge. **Pitch 2:** Head right behind the block, then up to ledges. **Pitch 3:** Take the crack left of a chute to higher ledges; head right, then up a short chimney. Rappel *Mike's Books.* **Pro:** To 2 inches. **FA:** Unknown.

1898. **Secovar** (5.5) **Pitch 1:** Go up a chimney and crack to ledge. **Pitch 2:** Head right and then tunnel up behind a block to a higher ledge. Finish as for *Southeast Corner.* **Pro:** To 3 inches. **FA:** Ed Zombro, John Wolfe; 1968.

Intersection Rock—South Face

This face is sunny most of the day.

Descent: Two rappels down *Mike's Books* or downclimb *Southeast Corner* (5.3!)

1899. **Shana Grant** (5.10d) ★★ This route lies on the face of a large boulder to the right of the large ledge atop the first pitch of *Mike's Books* (route 1902), almost directly above *The Waterchute.* **Pro:** Four bolts, two-bolt anchor/rap. **FA:** Bob Gaines, Todd Gordon, Todd Swain; 11/92.

1900. **The Waterchute** (5.10b) ★ The flared chimney. A difficult entry move is the crux (it's gotten harder/slicker over the years). **Pro:** To 2.5 inches; one bolt. **FA:** John Wolfe; 1968.

1901. **Elijah's Coming** (5.10b) (R/X) From the *Mike's Books* dihedral, move right and up an unprotected face. Above, climb a face with two bolts to the right of *Mike's Books'* second pitch. **Pro:** To 3 inches. **FA:** Bob Gaines, Bruce Christle; 10/86.

1902. **Mike's Books** (5.6) ★★ A popular easy multipitch outing. **Pitch 1:** Either make an unprotected traverse from the left (easy), or head up a flake/crack (5.8), to the large dihedral that is climbed to a big ledge (two-bolt anchor here). **Pitch 2:** From the big ledge, head left and climb another right facing corner to its end, then continue up the featured face past one bolt (two-bolt anchor). Rappel the route. **Pro:** To 2.5 inches. **FA:** Unknown; circa 1955.

1903. **Bongledesh** (5.11a) ★ **Pitch 1:** Go up and left past two bolts, the up the easy unprotected face above. **Pitch 2:** Climb the unprotected face just left of the second pitch of *Mike's Books.* **FA:** John Long, Terry Goodykoontz; 12/73.

1904. **Holy Smokes** (5.12b/c) (R/X) Apparently climbs the face left of the second pitch of *Bongledesh.* No pro. **FA:** John Long; 1990.

Intersection Rock—Southwest Face

This face gets early morning shade and sun all afternoon. To descend, make two rappels off *Mike's Books* or rappel off Bat Ledge. You can also downclimb either *Upper Right Ski Track* (5.3!) or *Southeast Corner* (5.3!).

1905. **Traverse of No Return** (5.11a) This route begins to the left and around the corner from *Bongledesh* and about 25 feet right of *Drawstring.* Go over the roof/bulge past a bolt to a short crack, then head left and up past another bolt; finish on the large ledge. **Pro:** Two bolts; cams. **FA:** Bob Gaines, Jeff Batten; 1/85.

1906. **Drawstring** (5.7) ★ **Pitch 1:** Go up the curving chimney to a ledge on the right. **Pitch 2:** Continue up the crack to the face with one bolt. **Pro:** To 3 inches. **FA:** Woody Stark, Dick Webster; 5/69.

1907. **Southwest Passage** (5.8) ★ This route lies just left of the chimney of *Drawstring.* **Pitch 1:** Go up and left along a crack system to Bat Ledge. **Pitch 2:** Go up and left until nearly at *Bat Crack's* second pitch, then head back up and right to join *Drawstring* at the bolt on that route's second pitch. **Pro:** To 2 inches. **FA:** Howard Weamer, John Wolfe; 5/69.

1908. **Pinnacle Stand** (5.7) ★ Go up and left in a flare and cracks until you reach Bat Ledge. One pitch; finish up another route or rap (45 feet) from Bat Ledge. **Pro:** To 2 inches. **FA:** Howard Weamer, John Wolfe; 5/69.

1909. **Filet of Sole** (5.11d) ★ Begin from Bat Ledge; stay right of the second pitch of *Southwest Passage,* joining that route higher up. **Pro:** Three bolts. **FA:** Bob Gaines, Cal McCullough; 3/94.

1910. **Let It All Hang Out** (5.10b) One pitch; ends on Bat Ledge. **Pro:** To 2.5 inches. **FA:** Herb Laeger, Herb Saume; 4/78.

1911. **Bat Crack** (5.5) ★ Two pitches. **Pro:** To 3 inches. **FKA:** Jerry Gallwas, Barbara Lilley and others; 11/52.

1912. **A Question of Masculinity** (5.12c) ★ (TR) (not shown on photo) The thin seam just right of *Billabong.* **FA:** Kevin Thaw; 2/88.

1913. **Sympathy to the Devil** (5.10b) ★ Climb first part of *Billabong* (or *Bat Crack*), then head up the face right of *Billabong* past one bolt to a crack. Finish up *Billabong.* **Pro:** To 3 inches. **FA:** John Bachar; 1976.

1914. **Billabong** (5.10c) ★★ **Pitch 1:** Three bolts lead to a horizontal; belay right at the pillar. **Pitch 2:** Go up then left on horizontals to a crack. **Pro:** To 3 inches. **FA:** John Wolfe, Al Ruiz; 3/69. **FFA:** John Long, Bill Antel, Rick Accomazzo; 12/73.

1915. **Death by Misadventure** (5.10c) (R/X) This variation goes straight up on the second pitch of *Billabong* (instead of traversing left). **FA:** Randy Faulk; 4/88.

1916. **Shovling-Cole** (5.10b) **Pitch 1:** Start as for *Billabong,* but move left at its first bolt. Go up to a second bolt, then continue up the crack/flake past a third bolt. **Pitch 2:** Go left on a horizontal and finish up *West Chimney.* **Pro:** To 2 inches. **FA:** Charles Cole, Marjorie Shovlin; 1982.

Intersection Rock—West Face

This face sees shade in the morning and sun in the afternoon. To descend, rappel atop *Huevos* then walk off or downclimb *Upper Right Ski Track* (5.3!).

1917. **Outer Limit** (5.6 A3) Take the left of two overhanging thin cracks. **Pro:** Aid rack. **FA:** John Wolfe, Dick James, Howard Weamer; 1969.

1918. **Outer Limit, Free Variation** (5.9) ★ (not shown on photo) Climb *Outer Limit* to the beginning of the aid section. Traverse left into *West Chimney,* then after about 20 feet go back right to finish up *Outer Limit.* Two pitches. **Pro:** To 3 inches. **FFA** (upper section): Dave Mayville; 12/00.

1919. **West Chimney** (5.6) **Pro:** To 3 inches. **FKA:** Jerry Gallwas, Barbara Lilley, and others; 3/53.

1920. **The Flake** (5.8) ★★ A popular route despite the wide section on the first pitch. **Pitch 1:** Go up the wide crack in the recess, then a crack/flake to belay atop the flake. **Pitch 2:** Go up the face past two bolts. **Pro:** To 4 inches. **FA** (first pitch): Dick Webster, Woody Stark; 1967. **FA** (second pitch): Jim Wilson, Dick Shockley; 1971.

1921. **Marooned** (Variation to *The Flake*) (5.10c) (not shown on photo) From about halfway up the first pitch of *The Flake,* head right and up past a bolt to a wide crack. This finishes at the first belay on *The Flake.* **FA:** Todd Gordon, Cyndie Bransford; 4/92.

1922. **When Sheep Ran Scared** (5.10c) (R) ★ This route lies on the face between *Overhang Bypass* and *The Flake.* Begin in the right-hand of three closely spaced crack systems; traverse right at the horizontals. Go up the face past one bolt, angling up to the end of a right-slanting crack, then up past a second bolt to end on the sloping ledge belay of *Overhang Bypass.* **Pro:** To 2 inches. **FA:** Charles Cole, Dave Evans, Steve Anderson, Kelley Carignan, Craig Fry.

1923. **Overhang Bypass** (5.7) ★★★ Begin in the center of three closely spaced cracks. **Pitch 1:** Go up the crack, then up and slightly right to a roof/flake; pass this on the face to the right (5.7). Finish in a crack to a belay on a sloping ledge below the overhang. **Pitch 2:** Hand traverse right out the overhang, then go up the face (5.7) past one bolt. **Pro:** To 2 inches. **FA:** Unknown. **FKFA:** John Wolfe, Howard Weamer; 6/69.

1924. **Underpass** (variation) (5.6) ★ Begin in the crack/chute to the right of *Overhang Bypass* (as for *When Sheep Ran Scared*), then tunnel under the flake to meet *Overhang Bypass* at the roof. At the roof, head out left to easier ground, then go up the sloping ledge. **Pro:** To 2 inches. **FKA:** John Wolfe, Al Ruiz, Bill Briggs; 10/69.

1925. **Overpass** (variation) (5.8) ★ Begin in the crack/chute to the right of *Overhang Bypass* (as for *When Sheep Ran Scared*), then head right out a diagonalling crack. Before the crack ends, face climb up and left to join *Overhang Bypass* below the sloping ledge. **Pro:** To 2 inches. **FA:** Roy Naasz, John Wolfe; 1/70.

1880. **North Overhang** (5.9) ★★★ Description is on page 448.

1926. **Beginner's Three** (5.3) This is the second crack left of *Overhang Bypass*. This short handcrack finishes on the ledge to the left of the main face. **Pro:** To 2.5 inches. **FA:** Unknown.

The Old Woman

This formation lies just north and a bit west of the Intersection Rock parking area. It is directly west of the small parking areas (bulletin board) in Hidden Valley Campground. From the south, the profile of the formation vaguely resembles the face of—you guessed it—an old woman. Unless you are staying in Hidden Valley Campground, park in the Intersection Rock parking area. Map page 447; see page 446 for driving instructions.

Descents: There is no easy (less than fifth class) descent off the formation. The three different rappel descents all can be done with a single 165-foot (50-meter) rope. There is also one exposed and technical downclimb. Rappel anchors are found atop *Double Cross, Toe Jam,* and on a ledge below *Geronimo* (best for routes actually ending on the summit of the formation). Also, you can make an exposed (class 5) downclimb on the face below the anchor on the ledge below Geronimo, then traverse ledges off right.

The Old Woman—East Face

This face gets sun early in the morning, shade all afternoon. To descend, rappel either from the top of *Bearded Cabbage* or the ledge below *Geronimo.*

1927. **Toe Jam** (5.7) ★★ Start on the left side of the east face. Go up a short curving crack to a right-slanting crack system; then up a thin crack that ends just before reaching a large belay ledge (natural anchors). **Pro:** To 2.5 inches. Do not belay from the rappel anchor to the right (dangerous for second). **FA:** Jerry Gallwas, George Scheiff, Gary Hemming; 11/52.

1928. **Spider** (5.8) **Pitch 1:** Start just right of *Toe Jam,* join it in the right-slanting crack, but stay in that crack as it heads up and left (5.8) to the large ledge. **Pitch 2:** Head right to bolts atop *Spider Line,* then up and right along ledges to the summit overhang. **Pro:** To 3 inches. **FA:** John Svenson, George Karsh; 1968. **FFA:** Don O'Kelley; 1969.

1929. **Judas** (5.10b) ★ Go up a thin-hands crack to a face with two bolts. Finish up *Toe Jam* or *Spider.* **Pro:** To 2 inches; two bolts. **FA:** John Wolfe; 1967. **FFA:** John Long et al.; 4/72.

1930. **Buttered Croissant** (5.11b) ★ Begin on *Judas,* then head right past three bolts. **FA:** Bart Groendyke et al.; 1989.

1931. **Bearded Cabbage** (5.10c) ★★★ A perennially popular route, with a short crux that spits off many. Hand traverse left on a ledge/flake; reach left into a crack (crux), then go up into the easy crack above. More intimidating than difficult; great position makes it worth doing. **Pro:** To 3 inches; one bolt. **FA:** John Long, Richard Harrison; 12/73.

1932. **Spider Line** (5.11c) ★★★ Go up the overhanging and large leaning corner. Easily toproped off bolts atop the crack. **Pro:** Thin to 2.5 inches. **FKA:** Woody Stark, Dick Webster; 1967. **FFA** (TR): John Bachar; 1/78. **FA** (Lead/free solo): John Yablonski; 2/78.

1933. **Deviate** (5.10b) ★ Face climb past two bolts to a ledge, then follow the face or cracks to another ledge. Two–bolt anchor rap. **Pro:** To 2 inches. **FA** (to first ledge): Dick Webster; 4/69. **FA** (to second ledge): Dick James, John Wolfe; 5/69.

1934. **Geronimo** (5.7) ★★ A fun, easy roof crack that starts off the ledge with rap anchors. **Pro:** To 3 inches. **FA:** Phil Haney, John Mokri, Bob Dominick; 11/70.

1935. **Joint Effort** (A4) (R/X) A rarely done ultrathin aid seam. **FA:** Tony Yaniro, Randy Leavitt; 11/77.

1936. **Dynamic Panic** (5.12a) (R) Go up the pin-scarred crack to a flake and ledge. **Pro:** Thin pins, fixed copperhead; to 2 inches. **FA:** Bob Dominick, Phil Warner; 12/68. **FFA:** Tony Yaniro; 3/77.

1937. **Church Bazaar** (5.10d) ★ Begin off the ledge directly above the finish to *Dynamic Panic;* go up the face past three bolts. Approach from the right (class 5). **Pro:** To 2 inches. **FA:** Mike Waugh, Dave Houser; 11/77.

1938. **The Hintertoiser Traverse** (5.10c) ★ Begin off a ledge about 20 feet right of *Church Bazaar.* Go up a flake and face past two bolts to join *Church Bazaar* at its last bolt. **Pro:** To 2 inches. **FA:** Charles Cole, Bob Gaines; 1985.

1939. **Tabby Litter** (5.8) This very short handcrack lies on the far right end of the east face. **Pro:** To 2 inches. **FA:** Phil Haney; 1969.

1940. **Spinner for Dinner** (5.10b) (R) (not shown on topo) Located on the north end of the rock; about 45 feet right of *Tabby Litter.* Go up blocks, then face climb past one (old) bolt. **FA** (Aid): Unknown. **FFA:** Phil Bircheff, Alan Bartlett; 9/96.

The Old Woman—West Face

This face gets shade early in the morning and sun all afternoon.

Descents: For *Dogleg* and routes ending at the top of *Dogleg,* downclimb the back side of the rock to a large ledge below *Geronimo* and rap 80 feet from anchors here. For *Double Cross* and routes ending there, rap 80 feet from anchors.

1941. **Little Old Lady** (5.9) (not shown on photo) This, *Gladiator,* and *The Arena* are located on a face to the left of *Northwest Chimney.* Start on a ledge 30 feet up and left of *Gladiator;* follow a crack that turns to a left-facing corner. **Pro:** To 2 inches. **FA:** Unknown.

1942. **Gladiator** (5.9) (R) (not shown on photo) Located on the face left of *Northwest Chimney.* Climb a left-leaning crack to a grainy face. **Pro:** Thin to 2 inches. **FA:** Don McCleland; 1957. **FFA:** Unknown.

1943. **The Arena** (5.10b) (R) ★ (not shown on photo) Start *Gladiator,* then go right into a bowl and up thin cracks above. **Pro:** To 2 inches. **FA:** Unknown.

1944. **Northwest Chimney** (5.2) The chimney 50 feet left of *Dogleg.* **Pro:** To 3+ inches. **FA:** Unknown.

1945. **Northwest Finger Crack** (5.11a) This crack starts about 35 feet up *Northwest Chimney;* a thin crack on the right. **Pro:** Thin to 2 inches. **FA:** Dave Mayville, Steve Gerberding; 12/00.

1946. **Dogleg** (5.9) ★★★ This has a funky start and is a bit hard to protect at the bottom, but it leads to excellent crack climbing in back of a flare. Downclimb the back (east) side, then rap off a ledge (two-bolt anchor). **Pro:** To 2.5 inches. **FKA:** John Wolfe, Rich Wolfe; 12/65. **FKFA:** Dick Webster, Bill Briggs, Woody Stark; 2/67.

1947. **The Cavity** (5.11d) ★★ Go up the left side of the "Fang" flake (one bolt), then up the face past three more bolts to belay as for *Dogleg.* **Pro:** To 2 inches. **FA:** Bob Gaines, Dave Mayville; 1/94.

1948. **The Fang** (5.11b) (R) ★★ Go up past a bolt, then out the right side of the "Fang" flake, across a thin crack (5.11b R), and past a second bolt into a bowl. Exit right (third bolt) and finish up *Double Cross.* **Pro:** Thin pins; thin to 2 inches. **FA:** John Wolfe, Ken Stichter; 2/70. **FFA:** Tony Yaniro, Mike Waugh, Dave Houser; 12/77.

1949. **Bridwell-Sustad** (5.10d/5.11a) ★★ Start as for *Double Cross,* but head up and left past a bolt, then up past a horizontal crack *(Lower Band)* using the second bolt on *The Fang.* Above, head up and left to past a third bolt (10d) to finish on *Middle Band.* **Pro:** Thin to 2 inches. **FA:** Jim Bridwell, Steve Sustad; 1997.

1950. **Double Cross** (5.7+) ★★★ Easily one of the most popular routes in the park. However, you have to actually know how to jam the crack, otherwise it will seem much harder. There is virtually no pro until you reach the crack. Make sure you protect the first crack moves well. This climb has seen a disproportionate number of accidents in recent years—none, to my knowledge, on the runout section getting to the crack. **Pro:** To 3 inches. Rap from two-bolt anchor. **FKA:** John Wolfe, Rich Wolfe, Mike Wolfe; 3/67. **FKFA:** Woody Stark, Dick Webster, Bill Briggs; 1967.

1951. **Lower Band** (5.10b) (R) ★★ **Pitch 1:** Start as for *Double Cross,* but head left on a horizontal; belay at *Dogleg* (5.10a/b). **Pitch 2:** Drop down a bit then continue left on the horizontal (5.10b R). The crux is at the end of the second pitch, with a potential bad fall for the second. **Pro:** To 2.5 inches. **FA:** John

Wolfe, Al Ruiz; 2/69. **FFA:** Randy Vogel, Charles Cole; 1983.

1952. **Route 499** (5.11b) ★★ (TR) Go up the face and thin flake (past a bolt), then up the face past two horizontals. **FA** (Aid lead): Don O'Kelley, Dave Davis; 1971. **FFA** (TR): Unknown.

1953. **Double Start** (5.7) Go up either side into the wide chimney/flare. Rap from anchors atop *Sexy Grandma.* **Pro:** To 2 inches. **FA:** Dick Webster, Woody Stark; 2/67.

1954. **Sexy Grandma** (5.9) ★★ (Sport or sport-ish) Begin up the chimney flare of *Double Start,* then move right onto the face and higher up the arête, passing four bolts. **Pro:** Optional to 2.5 inches. Rap from bolt anchors. **FA:** Todd Gordon, Bob Gaines, Andrea Tomaszewski, Bill Russell; 12/98.

1955. **Band Saw** (5.10c) (R) ★★ Begin off a flake (5.10a R) to the first bolt; go up the right side of a small roof, then face climb past two more bolts. At a horizontal, head left. Alternatively, continue directly up to the next horizontal (5.11a R). Belay at/rap off *Sexy Grandma.* **Pro:** To 2 inches; three bolts. **FA:** Charles Cole, Gib Lewis; 1983.

1956. **Skill Saw** (variation) (5.10d) ★★ (TR) Start off a boulder to the right and head straight up to join *Band Saw* at the roof. **FA:** Bob Gaines; 1/00.

1957. **Middle Band** (5.10d) ★ **Pitch 1:** Go up a seam/crack in a small corner past an old bolt (5.10d) to a horizontal crack; follow this up and left. Belay at *Double Start.* **Pitch 2:** Continue left and up along horizontals to the belay atop *Dogleg.* **Pro:** To 3 inches. **FA:** John Wolfe; 1969. **FFA:** Bill Antel, Kim Cooper; 1973.

1958. **Treinte Anos** (5.10b) (R) ★ Start up *Orphan,* head up and left on seams, then up the higher of two left-diagonalling crack systems. Belay at/rap off *Sexy Grandma.* **Pro:** Thin to 2 inches. **FA:** John Wolfe; 6/69. **FFA** (TR): Bill Antel; 1973. **FA** (Lead): Unknown.

1959. **Orphan** (5.9) ★★★ Stem while jamming the handcrack (5.9), which leads into the chimney (right side in; 5.8). **Pro:** To 3 inches. Rap from atop *Toe Jam.* **FA:** Unknown; circa 1954.

1960. **Iron Man Traverse** (5.10c) (R) **Pitch 1:** Start in the arching crack right of Orphan, cross Orphan, traverse left (stay in the lower crack). Belay at *Double Start/Sexy Grandma.* **Pitch 2:** Drop down a bit and traverse left on horizontals ending atop Dogleg. **Pro:** To 3 inches. **FA:** Ken Rose, Rob Hershey; 2/72. **FFA:** Charles Cole, Randy Vogel; 3/86.

1961. **Dandelion** (5.10a) ★★ (not shown on photo) This route is located on the south end of the formation. Scramble up to and start off a ledge. Climb the right-arching crack to the vertical crack, then go up the face past one bolt. **Pro:** To 2 inches. **FA:** Don O'Kelley, Dave Davis; 9/71. **FFA:** John Long et al.; 12/73.

The Blob

This large, undistinguished formation lies north of the Old Woman, on the left (west) side of the campground near its north end. Unless you are staying in Hidden Valley Campground, park in the Intersection Rock parking area. See page 446 for driving instructions.

Descents: It is relatively easy to downclimb (class 3) from any of the routes. The easiest descents are either down the southern or northern ends of the formation. Map, page 447.

The Blob—Southeast Face

This face gets morning sun and shade in the afternoon. The best descent for all of the following routes is down a chimney and under blocks on the southwest side of the formation, roughly behind the top of *Papa Woolsey* and *Mama Woolsey.* No fixed anchors exist atop any of the face routes.

1962. **Death Flake** (5.11b/c) (not shown on photo) Start out of the boulder-filled gully. This is a two-bolt route just left of the dihedral of *The Wonderful World of Art.* **FA:** Richard Tucker et al.

1963. **The Wonderful World of Art** (5.10c/d) (not shown on photo) This ascends a wide crack in a right-facing dihedral just left of *Buissonier.* **Pro:** To 4+ inches. **FA:** Roy McClenahan, Todd Gordon; 3/88.

1964. **Buissonier** (5.7) ★★ This is the left-curving flake-thin crack. You can start either down in the boulders, or higher up by stemming off a block. **Pro:** Thin to 2 inches. **FA:** Mark Powell, Royal Robbins; 1965.

1965. **Junior** (5.10c) The two-bolt face just right of *Buissonier*. **Pro:** To 2 inches. **FA:** Alan Nelson, Sally Moser; 11/87.

1966. **Baba O'Reily** (5.10d) (TR) The arête between *Junior* and *Papa Woolsey*. **FA:** Bob Gaines; 12/02.

1967. **Papa Woolsey** (5.10a/b) ★★ One of the world's first "sport" bolted routes (but there is no fixed anchor on top). Go up the well-polished face past six bolts. **Pro:** To 2 inches for anchor. **FA:** Mark Powell; 1972.

1968. **Baby Woolsey** (5.11b/c) ★★ (TR) The face between *Papa Woolsey* and *Mama Woolsey*. **FA:** Chris Miller.

1969. **Mama Woolsey** (5.10a) (R) ★ Go up the right-slanting crack, which disappears. Make a move right into a bowl with a bolt; above a face and crack lead to the top. **Pro:**

Thin to 2 inches. **FA:** Mark Powell, Beverly Powell; 1965.

1970. **Pete's Handful** (5.10a) ★★ Nice (but short) crack in a corner. **Pro:** To 2 inches. **FA:** Craig Parsley, Mike Pope; 11/73.

The Blob—East Face

The face gets morning sun and afternoon shade. This steep and imposing face has only a handful of routes. Downclimb the southwest end.

1971. **Surrealistic Pillar** (5.10b) ★ Climb the crack on the left side of the dark-colored pillar. Loose blocks rest near the top. **Pro:** To 3 inches. **FA:** Craig Parsley.

1972. **Rotten Corner** (5.8) (R) The name tells all. **Pro:** To 3 inches. **FA:** Unknown.

1973. **Disco Sucks** (5.10c) (R) Go up cracks to a block/roof; go right until you can head up a right-facing corner, then head back left. **Pro:** To 2.5 inches. **FA:** John Yablonski, Charles Cole; 10/79.

1974. **I'm Not Afraid Anymore** (5.11b) ★ Go up and right on ramps past three bolts to

two-bolt anchor/rap. **Pro:** Thin to 2 inches. **FA:** Walt Shipley et al.; 3/89.

1975. **Perfidious** (5.6 C2+) (R) This thin overhanging crack begins to the right of *I'm Not Afraid Anymore*. Originally rated A4, modern gear lowers the rating. It also now sports four newer bolts that were added for

free attempts (clipping the bolts further lowers the rating and helps eliminate potential groundfall). Go up an easy ramp to this thin right-leaning crack (some fixed heads), which is followed to its end where two hook moves lead to the two-bolt anchor/rap (shared with the previous climb). **Pro:** Brass offsets; thin cams; various hooks, fixed heads. **FA:** John Wolfe, Ken Stichter; 5/70.

1976. **Zulu Dawn** (5.10d) (R) Start in a small corner to the right of the obvious left-facing dihedral; a bolt marks the start. Head up and right to a crack and then face climb past two bolts, staying right of the large corner system. **Pro:** Thin to 2 inches; three bolts. **FA:** Mike Law, Bob Gaines; 5/83.

1977. **The Persian Room** (5.13a) (TR) ★ This overhanging thin crack–groove starts down low between yucca plants. It is 100 feet right of and down from *Zulu Dawn*. **FA:** Dick Cilley; 1988.

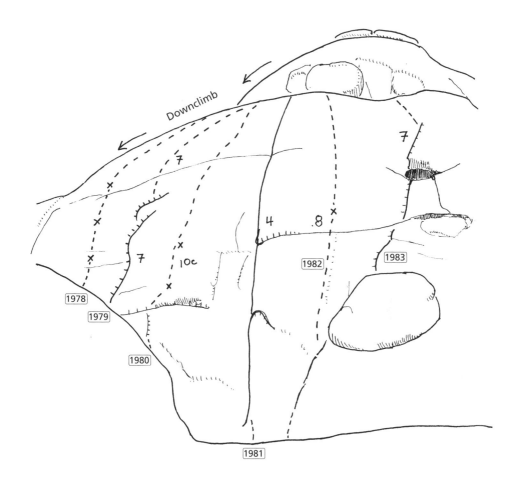

The Blob—North Face

The face sports mostly low-angled face and crack routes; it gets shade much of the day (sunny spring and fall afternoons). These routes are best approached from the east face by scrambling up and left on slabs and boulders. The most obvious climb here is *The Bong,* a long easy crack. Routes end below the actual summit. To descend, scramble down slabs to the left of the routes listed below.

1978. **A Walk on the Beach** (5.4) This is an easy three-bolt face on the left side of the north face. Start off a wedged flake (which forms the left side of the corridor). **Pro:** To 2 inches for anchor. **FA:** Unknown; circa 1979.

1979. **Ballbury** (5.7) Lieback a right-facing flake 30 feet left of *The Bong;* above, face climb past a horizontal. **Pro:** To 2 inches. **FA:** Unknown.

1980. **Use It or Loose It** (5.10c) This two-bolt face route is just right of *Ballbury* and 15 feet left of *The Bong.* **FA:** Rick Booth, Rick Ledesma.

1981. **The Bong** (5.5) ★★ The obvious and fun crack system; excellent for the grade. It passes a small roof (crux) lower down. Named for the wide pitons used to protect

the crack on early ascents. **Pro:** To 3 inches. **FA:** Unknown; circa mid-1950s.

1982. **The Bonglett** (5.8) (R) This is the face about 12 feet right of *The Bong*. Go up to and past a horizontal; a single bolt above protects the face to the top. **FA:** Unknown.

1983. **Hoblett** (5.7) This lies up and around the corner from the previous climbs. Go up a right-facing corner to a roof, then up the crack above. **Pro:** To 3 inches. **FA:** Dave Stahl, Rob Stahl, John Wolfe, Mona Stahl; 2/72.

The Blob—West Face

The low-angled and large west face of the Blob is best approached by walking west through the gap between the Old Woman and the Blob, then heading north in a wash. Scramble up easy slabs (class 3 to 4) to all the routes. The face gets shade in the morning and sun all afternoon. The routes all lie on the steeper upper half. Two vertical crack systems (*Beginner's One* and *Beginner's Two*) are the most obvious features. Descend by down-climbing either the southwest side (chimney at the bottom) or the northeast slopes (left of *On the Beach*) of the rock.

1984. **Return of the Blob** (5.10b/c) **Pro:** One bolt; to 2 inches. **FA:** Unknown.

1985. **Beginner's Two** (5.2) ★ The left-hand of two obvious crack systems. **Pro:** To 3 inches. **FA:** Unknown.

1986. **Dialing for Ducats** (5.10b) This two-bolt route is just right of *Beginner's Two*. **FA:** Alan Nelson, Alfred Randell; 12/87.

1987. **Safety in Numbers** (5.10a) (R) ★ Go up a water streak past a single bolt. **Pro:** To 2.5 inches. **FA:** Mike Waugh, Randy Vogel, Mike Lechlinski, Craig Fry, Dick Shockley, Jerry Garcia; 1/78.

1988. **Safety in Solitude** (5.9) Begin with *Safety in Numbers,* but head up and right under the arch, then up a crack. **Pro:** To 2.5 inches. **FA:** Alan Nelson; 12/87.

1989. **Smear Tactics** (5.10c/d) (R) ★ This two-bolt face begins right of stacked boul-ders. **FA:** Alan Nelson, Alan Bartlett; 1/84.

1990. **Frisco Knight** (5.10b) (TR) Toprope the face between *Smear Tactics* and *Berkeley Dyke*. **FA:** Alan Nelson; 11/89.

1991. **Berkeley Dyke** (5.8) (R) Go up a

right-slanting dike to a bolt, then up. **FA:** Alan Nelson, Alan Bartlett; 1/84.

1992. **Beginner's Luck** (5.9) (X) Start at *Beginner's One,* and head up and left (no pro) to join *Berkeley Dyke* near the top. **FA:** Alan Nelson; 12/85.

1993. **Beginner's One** (5.3) ★ The right-hand of two obvious crack systems on the west face. **Pro:** To 3 inches. **FA:** Unknown.

1994. **Reality Check** (5.9) (X) Start at *Beginner's One,* head up and right on a dike (no pro), then up. **FA:** Alan Nelson; 12/85.

1995. **Beginner's Twenty-Six** (5.10c/d) A single bolt protects hard moves up to a crack. **Pro:** To 2 inches. **FA:** Dave Davis, Don O'Kelley; 12/71. **FFA:** John Long, Rick Accomazzo, John Mokri; 1/73.

Hobbit Roof Formation

This small rock, with a large boulder balanced above, lies west and north of the west face of the Blob. To reach the Hobbit Roof Formation, park in the Intersection Rock parking area (unless you are staying in Hidden Valley Campground). See page 446 for driving instructions. From the Intersection Rock parking area, head north into the campground, then head west between the Old Woman and the Blob. Follow a wash north past the west face of the Blob; the route will be on your right. Map, page 447.

1996. **Hobbit Roof** (5.10d) ★★ The crux is a thin face past a single bolt, which leads to a nice thin crack that splits the roof/boulder above (5.10a). The crux face can be avoided by traversing in from the right. Easily and often toproped (extendo slings, etc., needed). **Pro:** To 2 inches. **FA:** Steve Godshall; 6/71. **FFA:** John Long; 1975.

Outhouse Rock

This formation lies just north of the apex of the main paved Hidden Valley Campground loop. Unless you are staying in Hidden Valley Campground, park in the Intersection Rock parking area. See page 446 for driving instructions. From the Intersection Rock parking area, head north into the campground to the apex of the paved loop road.

Descent: Rappel (70 feet) from bolts near the north end of the west face. Map, page 447.

Outhouse Rock—West Face

This is a fairly nondescript formation on this side that gets early shade and sun in the afternoon.

1997. **Clevis Multrum** (5.9) (R) ★ Begin left of *Northwest Chimney.* Go up a thin crack to an unprotected face up the northwest ridge; may be done in two pitches. **FA:** Todd Swain, Donette Smith; 1/93.

1998. **Northwest Chimney** (5.4) (R) ★ Go up a right-slanting chimney to face climb past one bolt. **Pro:** To 3+ inches. **FA:** Unknown.

1999. **Picking Up the Pieces** (5.10a) (R) Begin off a chockstone. Go up and right of *Northwest Chimney,* left and up to a flake, then up and left on a face, joining *Northwest Chimney* near the top. **Pro:** Thin to 2 inches. **FA:** Hank Levine, Fred Lytle; 12/76.

2000. **Five-Four-Plus** (5.8) ★ This is just right of *Picking Up the Pieces.* Go up and right the S-like crack. **Pro:** To 3 inches. **FA:** John Wolfe, Dick Webster; 4/69.

2001. **Frostline** (5.10a) This is the left-facing dihedral about 12 feet right of *Five-Four-Plus*. **Pro:** To 4+ inches. **FA:** Roger Linfield, Dave Woody; 2/79.

2002. **Outhouse Flake** (5.4) (R/X) ★ Go up a wide crack on the right side of the pinnacle (the left side is *Frostline*). **Pro:** Big. **FA:** Stew Harris, John Wolfe; 1965.

Outhouse Rock—East Face

For climbs on the east face, it is easiest to approach via a small "pass" between the north end of the Wall and the south end of Outhouse Rock. Alternatively, you can reach the east face from the end of the back campground loop. The face gets early sun and shade in the afternoon. Rappel off the west side.

2003. **Out for a Bite** (5.10d) ★ (TR) Climb the left-facing corner to a seam. Begin just left of *Diagonal Chimney*. **FA:** Tom Weldon; 1981.

2004. **Creamy Peanut Butter** (5.11c) ★ (TR) Begin with *Out for a Bite*. Go right at a horizontal, up a dike, then up and left on the face. **FA:** Scott Cosgrove; 1990.

2005. **Diagonal Chimney** (5.6) Go up the right-slanting chimney, then up the crack. **Pro:** To 3+ inches. **FA:** Many people; 1965.

2006. **Strawberry Jam** (5.9) ★★ Begin 10 feet right of *Diagonal Chimney.* Go up a thin crack to a ledge, cross *Diagonal Chimney,* then go up the crack above. **Pro:** To 3 inches. **FA:** John Long; 7/72.

2007. **The Loo Sanction (aka Mount Witness)** (5.10a) Begin right of a pine tree. Go up and right on flakes to a face, then up and left past three bolts. Finish up *Straight Flush.* **Pro:** To 3 inches. **FA** (TR): Todd Swain; 5/91. **FA** (Lead): Todd Gordon, Cyndie Bransford; 11/91.

2008. **Straight Flush** (5.8) ★★ This is a left-leaning crack system with the crux at the bottom. It is possible to traverse in from the left above the crux for a 5.6/5.7 variation. **Pro:** To 3 inches. **FA** (upper crack variation): Mike Loughman, Roger Hope; 1956. **FA** (from the bottom): Joe Herbst, John Long; 12/71.

2009. **Wise Crack** (5.9) ★ The crack system just right of *Straight Flush.* **Pro:** To 3+ inches. **FA:** Joe Herbst; 2/72.

The Wall

This very long and somewhat discontinuous formation lies on the east side of Hidden Valley Campground, lying just south of Outhouse Rock and extending to just east of Chimney Rock. It has several distinct sections, described from north to south (left to right). Unless you are staying in Hidden Valley Campground, park in the Intersection Rock parking area. See page 446 for driving instructions. Map, page 447.

The Wall—North End

This short and steep section of the Wall lies just south of Outhouse Rock, behind and right of the northern end of the paved Hidden Valley Campground loop. Routes face west, with shade in the morning and afternoon sun. Walk off left. Map, page 447.

2010. **Hands to Yourself** (5.11b) (TR) A 20-foot left-facing corner on the left end of the face. **FA:** Kurt Smith.

2011. **Hands Down** (5.11c) (TR) A hard boulder move reaches the crack. **FA:** John Bachar; 1976.

2012. **Two Scoops Please** (5.10d) (R) ★★ Begin just left of *Hands Off;* face climb up scoops. **Pro:** Two bolts; to 2 inches for anchor. **FA:** Herb Laeger, Dave Houser; 11/78.

2013. **Hands Off** (5.8) ★★★ The shallow crack/corner. **Pro:** To 2 inches. **FA:** John Long, Brian Portoff; 10/72.

2014. **Hands Up** (5.10d) Go up a curvy flake to a hard move up the summit boulder. **Pro:** To 2.5 inches; one bolt (needs replacing?). **FA:** Unknown. **FFA:** Todd Gordon; 1988.

The Wall—Middle Section

This small section of the Wall lies above the halfway point in main paved campground loop, after the loop road veers right. It gets shade in the morning, sun in the afternoon. Map, page 447.

2015. **Wallflower** (5.10a) Go up on the left face, past a horizontal and one bolt. **Pro:** For anchor. **FA:** Alan Nelson, Shartel McVoy; 1/87.

2016. **D. R. M. F.** (5.10b) (R) Go up the left-hand very thin crack and face. **Pro:** Thin to 2 inches. **FA:** Unknown.

2017. **C. F. M. F.** (5.8) Go up the right-hand thin crack. **Pro:** Thin to 2 inches. **FA:** Unknown.

2018. **Laserator** (5.11c) (TR) The face between *C. F. M. F.* and *Laid Back*. **FA:** Alan Nelson; 1/88.

2019. **Laid Back** (5.9) ★ The thin right-tending dogleg crack. **Pro:** To 2 inches. **FA:** Matt Cox, Dave Evans, Gary Ayres, Alan Lennard; 12/73.

Walk off back

The Wall—South End

The south end of the Wall presents a larger steep slab, split by a chimney/crack system, located behind and left of Chimney Rock. If you are not camping in Hidden Valley Campground, park in the large Intersection Rock parking lot (see page 446). From the Intersection Rock parking area, head over a flat rocky rise just left (north) of Chimney Rock into a wash, then up left along the base. It is also easily reached by walking up the wash from the Campground Circle area. Descend slabs on the back right, then down boulders to the right. Map, page 447.

2020. **Brown Squeeze** (5.10b/c) Climb the face to scoops and a dike. **Pro:** To 2 inches; two bolts. Belay anchors are located down the back side. **FA:** Mike Law et al.; 1983.

2021. **Good to the Last Drop** (5.9+) (R) ★★ Go up past two bolts to a horizontal, then up and left on a seam to face climb past one more bolt. Belay anchors are far down the back side. **Pro:** Thin to 2 inches. **FA:** Mike Waugh, Jan McCollum, Dave Houser; 1977.

2022. **Fatty Winds His Neck Out** (5.10d) (R) ★ Go up *Good to the Last Drop* to the horizontal, then go up and right past two bolts. Belay anchors are far down the back side. **Pro:** To 2 inches. **FA:** Roger Whitehead, Roger Hughes; 1984.

2023. **Don't Dick with Walt** (5.9) Begin up *Good to the Last Drop,* then head straight right on the horizontal to finish up *Damn Jam* chimney. **Pro:** To 4+ inches. **FA:** Dean Hart, Michael Dorsey; 2/85.

2024. Don't Let Me Down (5.11a) (TR) ★ Climb the face just left of *Damn Jam*. **FA** (bottom half/*Don't Waltz With Dick*): Mark Spencer, Shirley Spencer; 4/86. **FA** (top half): Bob Gaines; 10/99.

2025. Damn Jam (5.6) ★ The central chimney system. Gear can be placed in the back of the chimney, so bring runners to avoid rope drag. **Pro:** To 4+ inches. **FA:** Unknown; circa 1952/1953.

2026. Chalk Up Another One (5.10a) ★★★ Certainly the best and most popular route on this formation. Go up edges and smears past five bolts to a short crack. The crux moves (past the third bolt) can be slick. **Pro:** To 2.5 inches. **FA:** Jan McCollum, Hank Levine, Dave Houser; 1/78.

2027. Pumping Ego (5.10b) ★★ Begin to the right of *Chalk Up Another One*. Go up the face and flake to bolted friction climbing past four bolts. **Pro:** To 2 inches. **FA:** Alan Nelson, Mike Beck; 12/80.

Chimney Rock

Chimney Rock is the southernmost formation on the east side of the main Hidden Valley campground loop. It is located directly behind the point where the paved campground entrance road Ts at the (currently) unpaved entrance to the campground. It is named for the large chimney system splitting its west face, which is capped by a large block. As with other crags in the campground, unless you are camping here, you must park in the large Intersection Rock parking lot. See page 446 for driving instructions. Map, page 447.

Descents:

- Rappel 80 feet from an anchor atop *Blind Ambition* on the east face;
- Go down the easy chimney on the west face (fourth class); loose rock.
- Go down the southwestern end of the rock (5.1), below a small tree.

Chimney Rock—West Face

This side of Chimney Rock faces directly toward the main campground loop. The face is split by a large cleft (the "chimney"). It gets morning shade and afternoon sun.

2028. Dyno in the Dark (5.10b) ★ Approach via the corner, ledges, and face on the northeast corner of the rock (class 4/5) to a ledge above a great cave/hole (Space Station 27). Go up the overhang to a thin crack, then to a wider crack above. **Pro:** Thin to 3+ inches. **FA:** Charles Cole, Rusty Reno; 1/81.

2029. **Sunken Ships** (A2+/A3) This aid traverse begins out of the descent chimney and heads left under the roof. This was where a climb called *Loose Lips* (5.11a) existed before the entire section of the roof fell off in 1994. **FA:** Spencer Pfingsten, Gray Alexander; 1995.

2030 **West Face Overhang** (5.7) ★★ Go up the face to a crack and slot; above, head right and up, then right again to finish up the final summit crack. **Pro:** To 2.5 inches. **FA:** Unknown.

2031. **Ballet** (5.10a) (R/X) ★ Go up the unprotected face past two horizontals to a crack that is followed to the top. **Pro:** Thin to 2.5 inches. **FA:** John Wolfe, Dick Webster; 1/70. **FFA:** Tobin Sorenson, Gib Lewis; 1975.

2032. **Fear of Flying** (5.10d) (R) ★ Begin up a face past a loose flake, then go up and right on a dike to a face with two bolts to finish in the final crack of *West Face Overhang*. **Pro:**

Small cams to 2 inches. **FA:** Bob Gaines, Terry Ayers; 10/86.

2033. **Howard's Horror** (5.7) ★ Start up the easy crack, then traverse right to another crack. Alternatively, climb straight up the main crack from the bottom (5.10b R). **Pro:** To 2 inches. **FKA:** John Wolfe, Howard Weamer; 1/69. **FKFA:** John Wolfe, Al Ruiz; 1/70. **FA** (5.10b variation): Unknown.

2034. **Twisted Crystals** (5.11b) ★ The dike directly above finish of *Howard's Horror.* **Pro:** Three bolts; gear for an anchor. **FA:** David Estey, Alfred Randell; 1/87.

2035. **Break Dancing** (5.11a) ★ Begin between *Howard's Horror* and *Damper;* go up the face and horizontals past three bolts. **Pro:** To 2 inches. **FA:** Bob Gaines, Todd Gordon, Michael Paul, Walt Shipley, Rondo Powell, Bill Micklish; 4/88.

2036. **Dirty Dancing** (5.10b) Begin at *Damper*, then head up and left to a flake/corner. Above, a drill angle protects the face to the top. **Pro:** To 3 inches. **FA** (TR): Gene West, Bill Bloch; 3/87. **FA** (Lead): Bob Gaines, Yvonne McPherson; 11/87.

2037. **Damper** (5.9) ★★ The obvious hand-to-fist crack. **Pro:** To 4 inches. **FA:** Tom Higgins et al.; 4/67.

2038. **Pinched Rib** (5.10a) ★★★ Start at Damper, but head up and right to the dike with two bolts. Originally this route was rated 5.7, but sections of the dike have broken over the years. **Pro:** To 2 inches for anchor. **FA:** Roy Naasz; 3/73.

Chimney Rock—East Face

A two-bolt anchor is on the ledge where *The Flue, Flue Right, Blind Ambition,* and *Raven's Reach* end. Rappel 80 feet from the anchor. Alternatively, downclimb the cleft/chimney directly from the ledge on the west side of rock (loose and possibly dangerous). The face sees morning sun and afternoon shade.

2039. **Camouflage** (5.12b/c) ★ Head up and right on a ramp, then up a steep face past four bolts. **Pro:** To 2.5 inches for anchors. **FA:** Paul Borne; 10/88.

2040. **The Flue** (5.8) ★★★ Classic Josh for the grade. Go up a pod and horizontals to reach a right-diagonalling crack. **Pro:** To 2.5 inches. **FA:** John Wolfe, Dick James; 2/69.

2041. **Flue Right** (5.10b) (R) ★★ Begin at *The Flue,* then traverse right to discontinuous cracks and horizontals, staying right of *The Flue* at the top. **Pro:** To 2.5 inches. **FA:** John Wolfe, Dick James; 1/69. **FFA:** Gib Lewis, Tobin Sorenson; 1975.

2042. Blind Ambition (5.11a) ★★ Begin left of *Raven's Reach,* go up the face past horizontals and four bolts. **Variation:** The crux after the second bolt can be avoided by climbing the arête to the right. **Pro:** Thin to 2 inches; two-bolt anchor/80-foot rappel. **FA** (TR): Bob Gaines, Tommy Romero, 10/99. **FA** (Lead): Bob Gaines, Alan Bartlett; 10/99.

2043. Raven's Reach (5.10a) ★ This is the thin crack to a right-facing corner system; finish up and left at the *Blind Ambition* anchor. **Pro:** Thin to 2.5 inches. **FA:** John Long, Larry Brown; 3/71. **FFA:** John Long; 1979.

Hidden Valley Campground—Back Side

The following climbs are located west of the back loop of the campground. Most are on the back (east) side of the Wall. As with all Hidden Valley Campground routes, unless you are staying in the campground, you must park at Intersection Rock parking area (no day-use parking in the campground). Map, page 447.

Moonlight Crack Area

The following three toprope routes and *Red Hot Chile Pepper* are on a steep east-facing wall, behind a dual campsite located just before the campground road makes a sharp left and proceeds north. From the campground entrance, head right on the road past Chimney Rock, past the large open area, to where the rock comes close to the road on your left. The curving crack that doesn't reach the ground is *Moonlight Crack.* The area and routes are not pictured. Map, page 447.

2044. Major Threat (5.12a) (TR) Climb the face 12 feet left of *Moonlight Crack.* **FA:** Mark Wallace; 12/86.

2045. Moonlight Crack (5.10d) (TR) This is a shallow curving off-width that doesn't quite reach the ground; it starts with mantel moves. **FA:** Unknown.

2046. Minor Threat (5.11d) (TR) Climb the face/groove 6 feet right of *Moonlight Crack.* **FA:** Mark Wallace; 12/86.

2047. Red Hot Chile Pepper (5.10d) Begin behind a tree about 75 feet right of *Moonlight Crack.* Climb a seam to a handcrack. **Pro:** To 3 inches. **FA:** Mark Bowling; 3/92.

Pyramid Boulders

These two large boulders lie about 60 feet right of *Moonlight Crack.* The left boulder has a bolt anchor, the right does not. These lie somewhat in front and left of *Red Hot Chile Pepper.* The boulders and routes are not pictured.

2048. Pyramid of the Sun (5.11a) (TR) The northeast arête on the left boulder. **FA:** Bob Gaines.

2049. Pyramid of the Moon (5.9) (TR) The northeast arête of the right boulder. **FA:** Bob Gaines.

Campcraft Rock

This small formation sits up above the campsite found after you turn left (north) on the back loop. It has two obvious dihedrals on its south end. The rock and routes are not shown. Map, page 447.

2050. Wilderness Love Connection (5.9) The left dihedral/handcrack. **Pro:** To 2.5 inches. **FA:** Unknown.

2051. **Face of Music** (5.10c) (TR) This is the face/arête between the two dihedrals. **FA:** Unknown.

2052. **Campcraft** (5.9) (R) The right dihedral. **Pro:** To 2 inches. **FA:** Unknown.

The Wall—North End, East Face

The following routes are on the east side of the north end of the Wall. This face lies north of (beyond) the end of the back loop. Walk to the end of the back loop (a small turn-around here), and continue north about 120 feet.

2053. **Tyrannosaurus Rex** (5.9) Go up the wide, low-angled, left-leaning dike. **Pro:** Two bolts; gear for anchor. **FA:** Rex Pieper, Dog Benner; 12/88.

2054. **Tights, Camera, Action** (5.11a) (TR) This is the face 12 feet right of *Tyrannosaurus Rex,* beginning off a boulder. **FA:** Rex Pieper; 2/89.

2055. **Pyrannosaurus Next** (5.10a) This is the two-bolt route 65 feet right of *Tyrannosaurus Rex.* **FA:** Rondo Powell, Michael Paul.

CYCLOPS ROCK AREA

Cyclops Rock is the large rectangular formation that lies southeast of Hidden Valley Campground, about 100 yards south of Barker Dam Road. Cyclops, the Potato Head (two smaller formations immediately left/northeast of Cyclops), and Peewee Rock, a small isolated rock to the right (west) of Cyclops, are all just southeast of the entrance to Hidden Valley Campground. Unless you are staying in Hidden Valley Campground, park in the Intersection Rock parking area (see page 446). From Intersection Rock parking area, head east, crossing both the Hidden Valley Campground entrance road and then Barker Dam Road. There is also a large turnout on Barker Dam Road (at Cyclops Rock) with limited parking. Map, page 447.

The Potato Head

Two smaller formations lie immediately east of Cyclops Rock. They are from left (east) to right (west) One Potato and Two Potato. Routes are found on both faces of One Potato and Two Potato. See above for parking and approach directions. The Potato rocks and their routes are not pictured.

One Potato is the easternmost (left-hand) of the two Potato Rocks. Two Potato is the westernmost and is separated from One Potato by a north-south corridor. Its west face faces the east side of Cyclops Rock.

One Potato—East Face

The following routes are on the east face of One Potato, described from left to right. They get morning sun and afternoon shade.

2056. Spud Patrol (5.7) A left-arching corner is on the upper left end of the east face. Start 20 feet down and right of the corner, where a horizontal crack curves down. Climb to the crack, traverse left to a crack just left of the corner, then go up that crack to the top. **Pro:** To 2.5 inches. **FA:** Alan Nelson; 3/83.

2057. Ticket to Nowhere (5.8) Climb a left-leaning crack in the center of the face to a small ledge. Rappel off (no fixed gear) or downclimb the route. **Pro:** To 2.5 inches. **FA:** Alan Nelson; 3/83.

2058. Mr. DNA (5.11b) (TR) Start about 20 feet right of *Ticket to Nowhere,* at a flake 6 feet left of a patch of yellow lichen. Head straight up to the top. **FA:** Alan Nelson, Randy Burks; 3/83.

2059. Kidney Stone (5.10d) (TR) Start 5 feet right of the lichen patch (10 feet right of *Mr. DNA*) and climb straight to the summit. **FA:** Alan Nelson, Randy Burks; 3/83.

One Potato—West Face

The following two routes see morning shade and afternoon sun.

2060. The Real Thing (5.10d) (TR) This route is located near the right end of the west face; go up a juggy face along a seam. **FA:** Rich or Dave Tucker; circa 1989.

2061. Motor City (5.10c) (TR) Begin about 15 feet right of *The Real Thing* in a dark bowl; go up a steep face to a right slanting crack. **FA:** Rich or Dave Tucker; circa 1989.

Two Potato—East Face

The east face of Two Potato lies in the corridor separating One Potato and Two Potato. It gets morning sun and afternoon shade.

2062. Friend Bender (5.11b) This climb is located on northern end of the east face. Begin off small boulder; head up and right past horizontals on overhanging face moves. Escape right at the second horizontal. **Pro:** To 2 inches. **FA:** Alan Nelson, Tom Herbert; 1/87.

2063. Rick's Solo (5.10a) This is a wide crack in a right-facing dihedral that lies right and around from *Friend Bender* and left and around from *Tubers in Space.* **FA:** Rick Cashner; 1979.

Two Potato—West Face

This side of Two Potato faces the east side of Cyclops Rock.

2064. Tubers in Space (5.4) This route ascends a slab to a left-slanting handcrack. It is located directly opposite *Overnight Sensation* on Cyclops Rock. **Pro:** To 2.5 inches. **FA:** Todd Swain; 3/87.

2065. Masochism (5.8) A three-bolt face route just right of *Tubers in Space.* **FA:** Derrick Reinich, Todd Gordon, Tom Burke, Cyndie Bransford, Mike; 10/95.

2066. Commitments Are for Me (5.7) Start as for *Tubers in Space,* but head up and right on short ramp to a handcrack. **Pro:** To 3 inches. **FA:** Mark Harrell, Dave Harrell.

2067. Kyle's Nemesis (5.10c) This is the overhanging off-width crack to the right of *Commitments Are for Me.* **Pro:** To 4+ inches. **FA:** Josh Carlisle, Andy Thiel, Kyle Dahm.

Cyclops Rock

This formation lies about 100 yards south of Barker Dam Road, just east of the entrance road to Hidden Valley Campground (0.1+ mile from the Park Boulevard intersection with Barker Dam Road). Named for the natural rock "window" located near the top center of the northwest face; *The Eye* climbs up to this feature.

Unless you are staying in Hidden Valley Campground, park in the Intersection Rock parking area (see page 446). From the Intersection Rock parking area, head east, crossing both the Hidden Valley Campground entrance road and then Barker Dam Road. There is also a large turnout on Barker Dam Road (at Cyclops Rock) with limited parking.

Descents: Walk down slabs and boulders off the back (southeast) side of the formation; make a 100-foot rappel off the top of *The Official Route of the 1984 Olympics;* or make a 75-foot rappel off *Are We Ourselves.* Map, page 447.

Cyclops Rock—Northeast Face

This face lies around the corner and left of the main northeast face. It has a large dark roof feature that looks distinctly like a Volkswagen Bug. It is shady most of the day.

2068. **Overnight Sensation** (5.11b/c) ★★ Begin below the left end of the "Volkswagen Bug" roof. Go up the face and a left-diagonalling crack around the left end of the roof; higher, move right into one, then another, right-slanting crack. **Pro:** Three

bolts; small to 2 inches. **FA** (former name *Ajax*): John Wolfe, Rob Stahl; 11/70. **FFA** (TR): Rick Cashner; 1979. **FA** (Lead): Dave Mayville, Jodee Jondas, Mark Boline, Todd Gordon; 8/90.

2069. **Foul Fowl** (5.6) Go up to a corner system, then right on a face to a small cave and up to a ledge. **Pro:** To 3 inches. **FA:** Woody Stark, Bill Briggs, Pat Wiedman; 1966.

2070. **Carolyn's Rump** (5.4) This route climbs a chimney just left of the corner of the northwest and northeast faces; above, class 4 right and up. **FA:** John Wolfe, Carolyn Gilliland, Ed Zombro; 1967.

Cyclops Rock—Northwest Face

This large, steep face is clearly seen from Barker Dam Road and faces Hidden Valley Campground. A large central cleft in the face is capped by a small natural rock "eye" or hole near the summit, for which the formation is named. The route *The Eye* climbs the back of the deep cleft up to the "eye." This face receives morning shade and sun in the afternoon. Descend slabs down the back (southeast) side.

2071. **Ulysses' Bivouac** (5.8) This "route" climbs up to a sandy-floored cave about 25 feet above the north corner of Cyclops. Go up a crack to the left of the cave, then traverse into it; class 4 climbing takes you from the cave to the top. **FA:** Woody Stark, Dick Webster; 2/67.

2072. **Slim Jim (aka Nightmare on Angione Street)** (5.10c/d) The bolted face right of *Ulysses' Bivouac*. **Pro:** To 2 inches. **FA:** Todd Gordon, Jim Angione, Dave Evans.

2073. **Business Trip** (5.4) Begin just left of the cleft containing *Oversight*. Go up and left to the top of the block, then join *Carolyn's Rump* (class 4) straight up. **Pro:** To 3 inches. **FA:** Manfried Buchroilhuer; 1/90.

2074. **Oversight** (5.10a) This route climbs cracks in the back of a cleft just left of the face with *Thin Red Line*. At the ledge, go left and up. **Pro:** To 3 inches. **FA:** Alan Nelson, Randy Burks; 3/83.

2075. **Thin Red Line** (5.12b) (R) ★★ Climb the thin reddish stain/dike diagonalling up and left. Woodward refused to send up the drill to Hensel after Hensel climbed the crux above the second bolt, making the last section have groundfall potential. (See also *Brain Damage*/route 2805 in volume two of this guide.) **Pro:** Two bolts; to 2 inches. **FA** (TR): Ron Fawcett; 1985. **FA** (Lead): Darrel Hensel, Jonny Woodward.

2076. **Surface Tension** (5.10d) ★★★ Begin on the face right of *Thin Red Line* and left of the recess where *The Eye* begins. A funky (unprotected; 5.10a/b R) move into a hole and to the first bolt leads to face climbing diagonally up and left past three more bolts. **Pro:** To 2.5 inches, four bolts. **FA:** Charles Cole, George Willig, Randy Vogel, Steven Anderson; 1984.

2077. **The Eye** (5.3) ★★★ Always a popular outing. Start in the back of the deep cleft. Climb this, moving right on the face to avoid overhangs, then head directly up the face to the "eye." Walk through the "eye" and descend slabs on back of the formation. **Pro:** To 3 inches. **FA:** Dick Webster, Harold Webster; 1957.

2078. **Circe** (5.6) ★ Begin up *The Eye*, but at the first overhang move way right and stay near the arête to the top. **Pro:** To 3 inches. **FA:** Dick Webster, Harold Webster; 1967.

The following five routes begin off a large ledge located about 50 feet right of the deep cleft where *The Eye* is located. The ledge is about 45 feet off the ground. Class 4 climbing up the right side of a gully directly below *Fractured Fissure* brings you to this ledge.

2079. **Fractured Fissure** (5.10d) This route climbs the overhanging double crack system that heads up directly above the approach gully. **FA:** John Long, Brian Pohorff; 10/71. **FFA** (TR): John Long; 1981. **FA** (Lead): Todd Gordon, Don Reid; 5/98.

2080. **Telegram for Mongo** (5.10c) (R) ★★ Go up the face past two bolts, then up and left until you can traverse back right in horizontal cracks. **Pro:** To 2.5 inches. **FA:** Randy Vogel, Rob Raker; 1982.

2081. **Stairway to Heaven** (5.12a) (TR) ★★★ Toprope the face and overhang just right of *Telegram for Mongo*. **FA:** Peter Wautlich, Thomas Kraus; 11/86.

2082. **Leader's Fright** (5.8) (R) ★★★ This discontinuous and somewhat difficult-to-protect crack route begins off the right side of the ledge. **Pro:** To 2 inches. **FA:** James Foote, Woody Stark, Dick Webster; 1966.

2083. **Dino Damage** (5.11a) ★★ Begin off the extreme right end of the ledge. Go up and left on a face past four bolts, then up horizontals to a ledge (potential belay). Face climb past one more bolt to the top. **Pro:** To 2 inches; five bolts. **FA:** Randy Vogel, Todd Gordon, Sarah Vogel; 11/93.

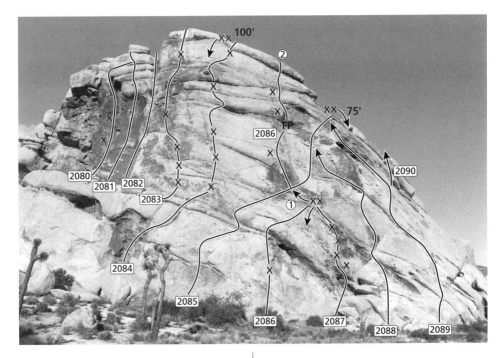

Cyclops Rock—Southwest Face

This face receives morning shade and is sunny most of the afternoon.

Descents:
- Walk down slabs on the southeast side of rock;
- Make a 100-foot rappel off the top of *The Official Route of the 1984 Olympics;*
- Make a 75-foot rappel off *Are We Ourselves.*

2084. **The Official Route of the 1984 Olympics** (5.10c) ★★★ Start in a recess; go up a diagonal crack to a horizontal. Above, climb a slab with three bolts to a small cave (fixed pin). Go left and then up past two more bolts to the summit. **Pro:** To 2.5 inches. **FA:** Randy Vogel, Charles Cole, Steve Anderson; 1984.

2085. **Are We Ourselves** (5.8) (R) Start about 12 feet right of *The Official Route of the 1984 Olympics.* Go up past a small flake, then

up and right along cracks, past plates, then up a final right-leaning crack. This can be done in one pitch or you can break it up into two pitches, belaying at the *Grey Cell Green* anchor. **Pro:** To 2.5 inches. **FA:** Dave Evans; 1984.

2086. **New Year's Day** (5.10b/c) ★★ Start 15 feet left of *Grey Cell Green.* **Pitch 1:** One bolt and one fixed pin protect the face to the upper ramp on *Are We Ourselves;* belay at *Grey Cell Green's* anchors. **Pitch 2:** Head up and left past three bolts and two fixed pins. **Pro:** To 3 inches. **FA:** Bob Gaines, Yvonne Gaines; 1/98.

2087. **Grey Cell Green** (5.10d) ★★ (Sport) Start in a cave and head up and left past four bolts to a two-bolt anchor/rap. **FA:** Don Wilson, Todd Gordon; 2/92.

2088. **Spaghetti & Chili** (5.7) Begin just right of *Grey Cell Green.* Head up a flake/crack to a left-diagonalling crack. Go left and up, joining *Are We Ourselves,* which is followed up and right to the top. **Pro:** To 2.5 inches; two-bolt anchor/rap. **FA:** Frank Avella, Jack Knox; 5/86.

2089. **Penelope's Walk** (5.5) This is about 30 feet right of *Spaghetti & Chili.* Go up a left-diagonalling crack to join *Are We Ourselves* where it heads up and right. **Pro:** To 2.5 inches; two-bolt anchor/rap. **FA:** John Wolfe, Dick Webster, Woody Stark; 4/69.

2090. **Goldilocks** (5.7) Begin as for *Penelope's Walk,* but then head straight up at an orange dike, passing small roofs near the top. **Pro:** To 2.5 inches. **FA:** Unknown.

Peewee Rock

This rather small formation, with less than stellar rock, lies just southwest of Cyclops Rock, about 30 yards south of Barker Dam Road and east of the entrance road to Hidden Valley Campground (0.1 mile from the Park Boulevard intersection with Barker Dam Road). Unless you are staying in Hidden Valley Campground, park in the Intersection Rock parking area (see page 446). From the Intersection Rock parking area, head east, crossing both the Hidden Valley Campground entrance road and then Barker Dam Road. There is also a large turnout on Barker Dam Road (at Cyclops Rock) with limited parking. Map, page 447.

Peewee Rock—East Face

This side of Peewee Rock faces the west side of Cyclops Rock. It gets morning sun and is shady all afternoon.

2090A. **The Reverend Dick Shook** (5.10a) Begin about 40 feet left of the start of *Belly Scraper,* below a lumpy, bucketed, and orangish face. Easy climbing leads to a large ledge, then go up past three bolts and one fixed pin to the top. Poor rock; OK climbing. **Pro:** Medium, plus a 4-inch piece for a hidden placement. **FA:** Todd Gordon, Tucker Tech et al.; 7/04.

Peewee Rock—North Face

This face sees shade most of the day.

2091. **Belly Scraper** (5.4) Go up a crack in a corner, then crawl right on a ledge (hence the name), then up a crack and face. **Pro:** To 3+ inches. **FA:** Dick Webster, Woody Stark; 2/67.

2092. **Pee Wee's Piton** (5.10a) ★★ (Sport) This route begins just right of the start of *Belly Scraper*, then crosses it to head up the featured face. **Pro:** Seven bolts; one fixed pin; two-bolt anchor/80-foot rap. **FA:** Bob Gaines, Todd Gordon, Dirk Addis; 12/98.

2093. **The Oui-Oui** (5.10d) ★★ Located to the right of *Pee Wee's Piton*, this route goes up the face past four bolts (also crosses *Belly Scraper*). Finish left to use *Pee Wee's Piton's* anchor. **Pro:** To 2 inches; four bolts. **FA:** Roy McClenahan, Jim Angione, Dave Evans.

2094. **Sand Castles** (5.11a) (TR) Climb the bulging face to a crack 40 feet right of *The Oui-Oui*. **FA:** Bob Gaines; 10/99.

Peewee Rock—West Face

This sees shade in the morning and sun in the afternoon. The face and route are not pictured.

2095. **Peewee's Big Bummer** (5.10a) This two-bolt route lies on the face of a boulder sitting about 45 feet off the ground. Stick clip the first bolt. **FA:** Richard Tucker et al.

Peewee Rock—South Face

A large boulder at the south corner of the rock has a large depression on its side. This face and its routes are not pictured.

2096. **Pull Before You Tie In** (5.10a) The obvious crack left of *Span-nish Fly*. **FA:** Unknown.

2097. **Span-nish Fly** (5.8) Lies about 50 feet right of *Peewee's Big Bummer*, behind a boulder with a section missing. Climb the face to a water chute to a corner, then go up the face and cracks. **FA:** Woody Stark, Dick Webster, Bill Briggs; 1968.

2098. **Tri-Step** (5.8) (R) Climb a shallow water chute to a ledge just left of the orange-colored face. Above, take the middle chute. A bolt in the final water chute has been removed. **FA:** Greg Fumaro, Steve Godshall, Richard Zito; 6/71.

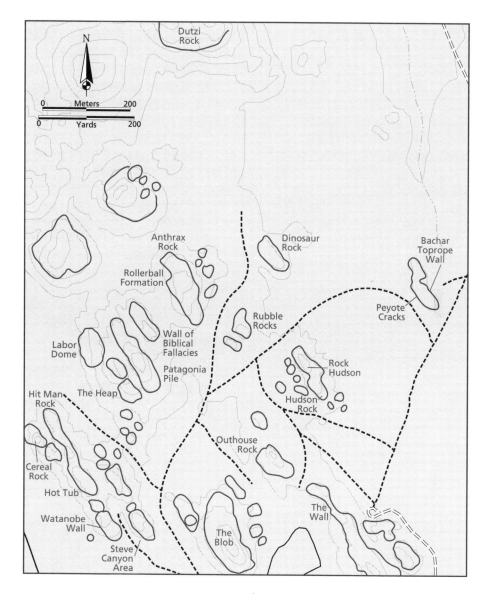

THE OUTBACK

The Outback is the area outlying the northern and eastern sides of Hidden Valley
Campground. It encompasses a variety of
crags including Steve Canyon and other crags
northwest of Hidden Valley Campground and
continuing east in an arc to the Peyote
Cracks and Bachar Toprope Wall, which lies

just west of the Echo Rock/Echo Cove area.
Though all of these crags can be easily
approached from Hidden Valley Campground,
unless you are staying in the campground,
the best parking and approach may vary. See
each specific rock/subarea for particular
parking and approach information. Map is
above.

STEVE CANYON AREA

This group of rocks lies about 200 yards northwest of the gap between the Old Woman and the Blob formations in Hidden Valley Campground. The Steve Canyon formations form a north-south canyon. Routes lie both within the canyon as well as on the east and west faces "outside" the canyon. The outside west faces (Watanobe Wall, the Hot Tub, and Cereal Rock) have their own names, which are different from the names of the faces inside the canyon (the Orc Face, Super Roof Wall, etc.). The outside, western-facing wall, are covered first; they directly face Park Boulevard. Next covered are the faces within Steve Canyon proper. Map, page 490.

Unless you are staying in Hidden Valley Campground, park in the Intersection Rock parking area. The Intersection Rock parking area is reached via a signed road off Park Boulevard approximately 8.6+ miles from the West Entrance and 11.7 miles from Pinto Wye (the Park Boulevard/Pinto Basin Road intersection). Toilet facilities and an emergency phone are located here. Climbers can post notes (must be dated) on the back of a bulletin board located in the Hidden Valley Campground parking lot. From the Intersection Rock parking area, head north into the main campground loop, then walk west between the Old Woman and the Blob. A rough trail heads northwest from here to Steve Canyon.

Alternatively, park at turnouts located on both sides of Park Boulevard 0.3 miles north of the Real Hidden Valley/Intersection Rock intersection; these are 8.3 miles from the West Entrance. The turnouts are about 75 yards west of the west-facing Watanobe Wall.

Watanobe Wall Area

The following routes lie on the west face of the rocks that form west side of Steve Canyon, and face Park Boulevard. Map, page 490.

Watanobe Wall—Left Side

The left side of Watanobe Wall lies above the desert floor atop boulders, and is characterized by a steep brownish face with several cracks. To descend, downclimb left, then down an rocky gully (just below *Amanda* and *Elixir* on the Hot Tub).

2099. **Wataneasy Route** (5.7) The easy crack just left of Watanobe Wall. **Pro:** To 3 inches. **FA:** Unknown.

2100. **Watanobe Wall** (5.10a) ★★★ Go up an arch to a crack; go left where the crack splits. Belay at horizontals below the top; walk off left. **Pro:** To 3 inches. **FA:** Tobin Sorenson, Jim Wilson, Guy Keesee; 1975.

2101. **Watasillywall** (5.11b) (TR) ★ Begin just right of *Watanobe Wall;* go up the face and seams. **FA:** Scott Cosgrove.

2102. **Yei-Bei-Chei Crack** (5.9) ★ Start 40 feet right of *Watanobe Wall*. Go up then left in a crack to a horizontal; finish left. **Pro:** To 3 inches. **FA:** Todd Gordon, Dave Evans, Kelly Carignan; 4/86.

Watanobe Wall—Right Side

This section of Watanobe Wall lies to the right of the more broken center section of this crag. Routes start near the desert floor.

To descend, either rap from anchors on the back (east) side of crag atop *Candelabra,* or downclimb (class 5) down the southern end of the crag.

2103. **Open Season** (5.9+) (TR) Once a lead with three bolts, this arête is currently a toprope. **FA:** Brad Singer et al.; 3/88.

2104. **Season Opener** (5.8) ★★ Crack to face. **Pro:** To 2.5 inches. **FA:** Alan Bartlett, Dave Black; 1/83.

2105. **Come-N-Do-Me** (5.10b) ★★ Climb a face past a bolt, go right to a roof and a horizontal, then go up the face past two more bolts. **Pro:** To 2.5 inches; three bolts. **FA:** Herb Laeger, Kevin Wright; 10/88.

2106. **I'm Already Bored with the New Millennium** (5.8) ★ This crack begins 30 feet right of *Come-N-Do-Me*. **Pro:** To 2.5 inches. **FA:** Dave Haber, Sheryl Haber; 12/99.

2107. **Do Do** (5.10a) (TR) Start up *I'm Already Bored with the New Millennium,* then head up and left to last bolt on *Come-N-Do-Me.* **FA:** Bob Gaines, Yvonne Gaines; 11/97.

2108. **Bored of the Rings** (5.7) Start at *I'm Already Bored with the New Millennium,* but head up and right along a ramp to a vertical right-facing flake. Go up the flake. **Pro:** To 2.5 inches. **FA:** Todd Swain, Donette Swain; 2/03.

2109. **Without a Trace** (5.8) (X) Essentially a highball boulder problem up an arête. **FA:** Rex Pieper, Doug Benner; 3/88.

The Hot Tub

This formation is located on the east side of Park Boulevard, just left (north) of Watanobe Wall. It faces the road. It is actually the back (west) side of the Super Roof Wall. Park either in the Intersection Rock parking area (8.6+ miles from the West Entrance; 11.7 miles from Pinto Wye), or at turnouts located on both sides of Park Boulevard (0.3 mile north of the Real Hidden Valley/Intersection Rock intersection; 8.3 miles from the West Entrance). With the exception of *Elixir, The Dharma Bums,* and *Amanda* (which have bolted rap anchors), descend to the left. Map, page 490.

The Hot Tub—West Face

This gets morning shade and is sunny all afternoon. Descend to the left.

2110. **Cyndie's Brain** (5.10a) (R) ★ Climb disjointed cracks up desert varnish 40 feet left of *From Here to Infirmary.* **Pro:** To 2 inches. **FA:** Todd Gordon, Todd Swain; 11/89.

2111. **From Here to Infirmary** (5.9) ★ Climb the fist crack out of a roof. This is located directly behind a pine tree left of *Hot Tubs from Hell.* **Pro:** To 2 inches. **FA:** Todd Swain, Todd Gordon; 11/89.

2112. **Hot Tubs from Hell** (5.9) Climb a right-facing corner/groove to a ledge 20 feet left of *Hot Tub of Death,* then go up a right-facing corner left of a chimney. **Pro:** To 2.5 inches. **FA:** Todd Gordon, Todd Swain; 11/89.

2113. **Jacuzzi of No Return** (5.10b) Start as for the above route. At the roof, take a flake and thin crack left. **Pro:** To 2 inches. **FA:** Todd Swain, Todd Gordon; 11/89.

2114. **Hot Tub of Death** (5.10a) Climb the right-slanting crack through the roof 100 feet left of Watanobe Wall. **Pro:** To 2 inches. **FA:** Todd Gordon, Todd Swain; 11/89.

The Hot Tub—South Face

The following climbs all lie on the south end of the Hot Tub which lies directly above the walk off gully for Watanobe Wall. They are sunny most of the day.

2115. **Belly Button** (5.11a) (TR) Begin off the left end of a large squarish block/flake on the left side of the south face (about 5 feet left of *Elixir*). Go up the face over a bulge (crux), then left to a crack at the top of *Hot Tub Of Death.* **FA:** Bob Gaines; 1/03.

2116. **Elixir** (5.10a) ★★ Begin off the right end of a large squarish block/flake on the left side of the south face. Go up the face and horizontals past three bolts. Ends on a ledge with two-bolt anchor/rap. **Pro:** Optional cams. **FA** (TR): Todd Swain. **FA** (Lead): Bob Gaines, Yvonne Gaines; 2/96.

2117. **The Dharma Bums** (5.8) The hand-and-fist crack right between *Elixir* and *Amanda;* it ends on a ledge (as does *Elixir*) with a two-bolt anchor/rap. **Pro:** To 4 inches. **FA:** Alan Bartlett, Dave Haber; 11/91.

2118. **Amanda** (5.10a) ★★★ Begin to the right of *The Dharma Bums* crack. Go up a face past a bolt to horizontals; above, continue up the face past four more bolts to a two-bolt anchor/rap. **Pro:** Thin to 2 inch cams. **FA:** Todd Gordon, George Armstrong; 10/95.

2118A. **We Never Get the Girls** (5.10a) ★★ This is another five-bolt route. Begin as for *Amanda,* but after that route's first bolt, head up and right to a ledge, then up the face past four more bolts. **Pro:** To 2 inches. **FA** (TR): Steve Powers; 2004. **FA** (Lead): Steve Powers, F. Haney, T. Pinar; 5/04.

Cereal Rock

This is the nondescript jumble adjacent to (left/north) of the Hot Tub. It is separated (barely) from the Hot Tub by a small gap. It is the northernmost extension of the west-facing rocks constituting Steve Canyon/Hit Man Rock. Hit Man Rock lies around the corner and a bit east and south of Cereal Rock. Park either in the Intersection Rock parking area (8.6+ miles from the West Entrance; 11.7 miles from Pinto Wye); or at turnouts located on both sides of Park Boulevard (0.3 mile north of the Real Hidden Valley/Intersection Rock intersection; 8.3 miles from the West Entrance). Map, page 490.

Cereal Rock—East Face

The following climbs lie on the eastern side of the formation (facing away from Park Boulevard) and gets some morning sun; shade in the afternoon. Descend to the left. The face and routes are not pictured.

2118B.   **Queerios** (5.8) This route begins on the left end of the east face, on a high ledge. Go up the featured face immediately left of a double crack system *(Dice Krispies)*. **Pro:** Cams to 2.5 inches. **FA:** Alan Bartlett, Rick Briggs, Mike Wilson, Mike Cross; 2/92.

2118C.   **Dice Krispies** (5.8) This route begins on the left end of the east face, on a high ledge. Go up the double crack system. **Pro:** To 2.5 inches. **FA:** Alan Bartlett, Rick Briggs, Mike Wilson, Mike Cross; 2/92.

2118D.   **Gruel and Unusual Punishment** (5.11a) (R) Begin about 12 feet right of *Dice Krispies*. Go up the face to a curving crack, then face climb (5.11a) past a horizontal to the top. **Pro:** Small to 2 inches. **FA:** Mark Bowling, Todd Swain; 2/92.

2119. **Oat Cuisine** (5.10c) (R) Begin near the right end of the east face. Climb a left-leaning discontinuous crack and face past a horizontal. **Pro:** Thin to 2 inches. **FA:** Todd Swain, Todd Gordon; 11/89.

2120. **Cereal Killer** (5.6) Begin near the right end of the east face (same spot as *Oat Cuisine*). Head up and right to a crack and face above. **Pro:** To 3 inches. **FA:** Todd Gordon, Todd Swain; 11/89.

2121. **Bran New** (5.5) Start at a right-facing flake/chimney on the north end of Cereal Rock (about 20 feet right of the last routes). Go up the flake/chimney, then up a knobby face past a horizontal. **Pro:** To 3 inches. **FA:** Todd Swain, Steve Inman; 11/89.

Cereal Rock—West Face

This side of Cereal Rock faces Park Boulevard and gets morning shade and sun all afternoon. Descend to the right.

2121A. **Wheat Czechs** (5.10b) This climb lies on the northwest end of the formation. Climb up to a ledge; above, go up a crack past two bushes to a roof, then up a crack to the top. **Pro:** To 3 inches. **FA:** Todd Swain, Cyndie Bransford; 2/92.

2122. **The Oat Route** (5.8) Begin on the left end of the west face. Go up past horizontals, then right and up into a short crack. **Pro:** To 2 inches. **FA:** Todd Swain, Kip Knapp; 3/91.

2123. **Raising Bran** (5.8) Begin about 20 feet right of *The Oat Route*. Go up ledges to a short dihedral capped by a roof, then up cracks. This is near the left end of the west face, very low to the ground. **FA:** Todd Swain, Kip Knapp; 3/91.

2123A. **Alfalfa** (5.8+) The left-hand crack on a rib of rock. FA: Dave Trevino, Todd Swain; 2/92.

2123B. **Quaking Oats** (5.10a) The thin crack/corner just right of *Alfalfa*. FA: Todd Swain, Cyndie Bransford, Alan Bartlett; 2/92.

2123C. **Cream of Weak** (5.11b) Face climb past two bolts, then go right into a crack. **FA:** Jeff Rickerl, Todd Swain; 2/92.

2124. **Buckwheat** (5.10a) (R) Start on the left edge, go up to an alcove, then right, then up past a bolt. **FA:** Todd Swain, Dick Peterson, 10/91.

2124A. **Puttin' on the Grits** (5.9) R Go up a crack to a corner, then left and up. **FA:** Todd Swain, Cyndie Bransford; 2/92.

2124B. **Morning Chunder** (5.7) Begin as for *Puttin' on the Grits,* but head right to a thin crack. Finish left. **FA:** Alan Bartlett, Kate Duke; 1/92.

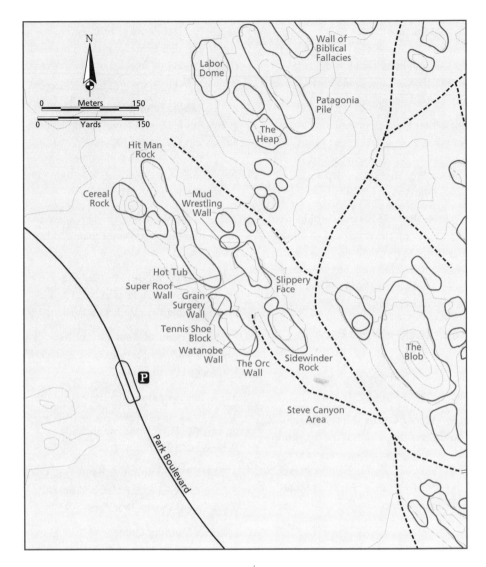

STEVE CANYON PROPER

This popular canyon lies about 300 yards northwest of the gap between the Old Woman and the Blob in Hidden Valley Campground. It is known for being relatively sheltered from the wind; the routes on the right side of the canyon (facing west) being warm on colder days. It was named for an old-time comic strip.

The rocks form a canyon that runs in a north/south direction. Routes lie both within the canyon as well as on the east and west faces "outside" the canyon. The outside west faces (described previously) have their own names (Watanobe Wall, the Hot Tub, and Cereal Rock).

Unless you are staying in Hidden Valley Campground, park in the Intersection Rock parking area, which is reached via a signed road located off Park Boulevard (approxi-

mately 8.6+ miles from the West Entrance
and 11.7 miles from Pinto Wye). From the
Intersection Rock parking area, head north
into the main campground loop, then walk
west between the Old Woman and the Blob.
A rough trail heads northwest from here to
Steve Canyon.

Alternatively, park at turnouts located on
both sides of Park Boulevard 0.3 mile north
of the Real Hidden Valley/Intersection Rock
intersection and 8.3 miles from the West
Entrance. These turnouts are located about
75 yards west of the west facing Watanobe
Wall.

The Orc Wall

This is the first face on your left as you enter
the canyon from the south. It gets sun in the
morning and is shady all afternoon. To
descend, make a 60-foot rappel from bolt
anchors atop *Candelabra,* or downclimb the
south end (5.5). Map, page 490.

2125. **Grand Theft Avocado** (5.7) This crack
is located on the right-hand side of the
southern end of the face. Named after some
young climbers who got busted for helping
themselves to this fruit. **Pro:** To 2.5 inches.
FA: Dave Evans; 10/78.

2126. **Candelabra** (5.10a) (R) (X if the
entire flake comes off!) ★★ Climb a right-
facing corner to an undercling/lieback. This
is usually toproped as the entire flake on the
upper section seems a bit precarious, as the
name would suggest. Two-bolt anchor/rap.
Pro: To 3 inches. **FA:** Dave Davis, Don
O'Kelley; 11/71. **FFA:** John Long; 4/72.

2127. **The Orc** (5.10a) ★★ This is the nice crack route about 45 feet right of *Candelabra*. At the bulge (crux), go either straight up or left and up. **Pro:** Thin to 2.5 inches. **FA:** Bob Dominick.

2128. **Orc Sighs** (variation) (5.10c) ★ Climb *The Orc* to just below the bulge (crux), then traverse straight right on a horizontal to finish up a crack (joining *The Troll*). **Pro:** To 3 inches. **FA:** Mike Tupper, Craig Reason; 1/83.

2129. **The Troll** (5.11b/c) ★★ Begin about 20 feet right of *The Orc;* best done in two short pitches to avoid rope drag. **Pitch 1:** Go up the thin face past two old bolts to a horizontal; go right and up a crack to a ledge. **Pitch 2:** Go up the face above the center of the ledge past one bolt. **Pro:** To 2.5 inches. **FA:** Tom Herbert.

Tennis Shoe Block

This small block lies atop the rock immediately right of the Orc Wall. It has a short handcrack on the right side of the block (*Tennis Shoe Crack*). It is the backside of the Watanobe Wall—Left. Approach from and descend to the right. It gets morning sun and afternoon shade. The block and routes are not pictured.

2130. **Wingtips** (5.11b) (TR) Climb up past a horizontal to a flake just left of *Tennis Shoe Crack*. **FA:** Bob Gaines; 11/89.

2131. **Tennis Shoe Crack** (5.8) ★ This handcrack curves up and left above a ledge where the block sits. **FA:** John Long; 6/72.

Super Roof Wall

The left (west) side of Steve Canyon is broken into two main parts (the Orc Wall and Tennis Shoe Block being the lower part). The upper part is distinguished by large roofs about halfway up the face. To approach, stay on the left side of the canyon were it gets rocky, scrambling up slabs and boulders to the base of the Super Roof Wall. Map, page 490.

2132. **Let's Get Horizontal** (5.11b) ★★ Begin just left of *Super Roof* and climb up and right, then up past horizontals. The route has three bolts. **FA:** Kelly Rhoads, Jeff Rhoads; 10/82. **FA** (Lead): Unknown.

2133. **Super Roof** (5.9) ★★★ This is the left-hand crack splitting the roof. **Pro:** To 3 inches. **FA:** Dave Ohlsen, Jon Lonne, Martin McBirney; 4/75.

2134. **Comfortably Numb** (5.11b/c) ★★ This is an off-width roof 20 feet right of *Super Roof.* **Pro:** To 5 inches. **FA:** Randy Leavitt et al.; 1980.

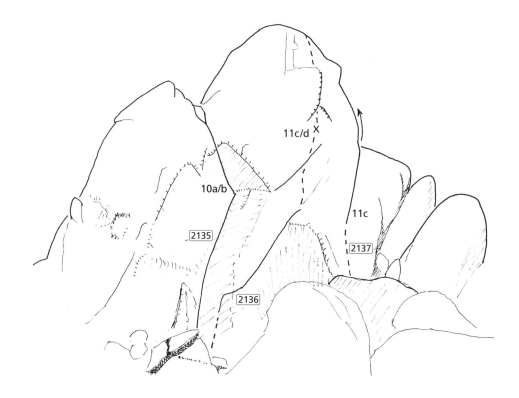

Mud Wrestling Wall

This west- and southwest-facing rock lies on the right side of Steve Canyon, directly past the Grain Surgery Wall and across from the Super Roof Wall. Where the canyon gets rocky, scramble up the left side of Steve Canyon, toward the base of the Super Roof Wall, then head right to the base of this face. Descend left (north). Map, page 490.

2135. **Female Mud Massacre** (5.10a) Begin at a wide, light-colored, overhanging corner across from *Super Roof.* Above, follow a left-slanting crack above a roof. **FA:** Todd Gordon, Marge Floyd (?) or Russ Eyles, John Strand, Tom Callaghan (?); 10/83.

2136. **Frigidity** (5.11c/d) Begin just right of *Female Mud Massacre.* Go up a crack to a bolt, then up and right on the arête.

2137. **Frigid Dare** (5.11c) (TR) The over-hanging and leaning lieback/groove 30 feet right of *Female Mud Massacre.* **FA:** Matt Oliphant, Bill Lebens; 1984.

Downclimb
XX
X
X
X
X
X
Downclimb
X
X
X
X
X
2145
2138
2139
2140
2141
2143
2142
2143
2144

Grain Surgery Wall

This west-facing formation lies on the upper right side of Steve Canyon, just beyond Sidewinder Rock. The main face is broken into two sections by a chimney up the middle of the wall. See page 490 for approach/parking info. Map, page 490.

Descents:

- Downclimb the north end of the formation (down the right side of the wedged block), then down the gully;
- Rappel off the top of *Grain Surgery* (70 feet);
- Rappel off *The Decompensator of Lhasa* (85 feet).

2138. **Grain Surgery** (5.10b) ★★★ Begin up the central crack in the middle of the left-hand section of the wall. Where this crack ends, move up and left past a bolt to a horizontal. Above, a bolt protects somewhat runout face climbing to the top. **Pro:** To 2 inches; two bolts/two-bolt anchor. **FA:** Randy Vogel, Brian Rennie, John Long; 3/80.

2139. **Super Monster Killer** (5.11a) (R) ★ Begin in the shallow crack system just right of *Grain Surgery*. Go up discontinuous cracks and an unprotected face (5.10c R) to the first of three bolts. **Pro:** Thin to 2 inches. **FA:** Eric Andersen, Chris Clark; 2/87.

2140. **Fist Full of Crystals** (5.10c) (R) ★★
Begin out of the bottom of the *Hoopharkz* chimney, heading up a small corner and crack system just to the left. Finish with the face. **Pro:** 0.5 to 2 inches. **FA:** Jonny Woodward, Mike Lechlinski, Randy Vogel; 10/82.

2141. **Hoopharkz** (5.4) ★ This is the obvious central chimney with one bolt about halfway up. **Pro:** To 4 inches. **FA:** Don O'Kelley, John Wolfe; 2/71.

2142. **Deflowered** (5.6) ★★ A fun easy climb up cracks that begin off a boulder about 10 feet right of *Hoopharkz*. **Pro:** To 3 inches. **FA:** Don O'Kelley, Dave Davis; 10/71.

2143. **The Decompensator of Lhasa** (5.10c) ★★★ This climb has two starts. Most climb the direct left-hand start: Begin off a large boulder and make a move right on a horizontal to a left-arching thin crack to horizontals. Above, go up and then right on thin friction, finishing up the right–hand arête (four bolts). **Right-hand variation:** Begin about 20 feet down and to the right, and go up a right-arching corner/flake (5.10a) to a horizontal (you might want to belay here). Head left on the horizontal to reach the bolted face above. **Pro:** Several 0.5 to 2 inches; two-bolt anchor. **FA** (via right-hand start): Charles Cole, Randy Vogel; 2/80. **FA** (left-hand start): Unknown; 1981.

2144. **Phineas P. Phart** (5.10b/c) ★ The short flared handcrack beginning off a ledge above and right of the main face. **Pro:** To 2.5 inches. **FA:** Unknown.

2145. **Lov'in Kohler** (5.9) Below and left of *Phineas P. Phart*. **FA:** Mark Harrell, Dave Harrell.

2145A. **Phineas Pinnacle** (5.5) This short route lies on the east (back) side of the small block; go up past one bolt. One-bolt anchor. **FA:** Unknown.

Sidewinder Rock

This squarish formation is the first rock on the right side of Steve Canyon as you enter from the south. It has a bowling pin shaped free-standing pinnacle (the King Pin) adjacent to its north end. To descend, either rappel (70 feet) from a two-bolt anchor atop the King Pin (you have to jump over to it from the top of the main formation), or make a fifth-class downclimb (or long jump down to a ledge) on the east side of the formation as shown on the photo of the east face. See page 490 for approach/parking info. Map, page 490.

Sidewinder Rock—West Face

This side of the rock is clearly visible from Park Boulevard and sports a prominent left-diagonalling dike that is utilized by several routes. The pinnacle on the north side of the rock is the King Pin. It gets morning shade and sun all afternoon.

2146. **Skinny Dip** (5.7) ★★★ A totally unique, must-do route. Begin on the north side of the King Pin pinnacle at the north end of the formation. Follow a short handcrack to an improbable tunnel-through, then go up the unprotected chimney of *Skinny Pin* (5.4 R) to the top (see the photo of the east face for the route line). **Pro:** To 2 inches. Two-bolt anchor/rap. **FA:** John Long, Phil Warrender; 9/72.

2147. **Invisible Touch** (5.10d) ★★ Begin up the northwest corner of the King Pin pinnacle; head up past three bolts, then right into a thin crack. Two-bolt anchor/rap. **FA:** Bob Gaines, Yvonne MacPherson; 3/87.

2148. **King Pin** (5.11a) ★ Head up the face past three bolts just left of the southwest corner of the King Pin pinnacle. Two-bolt anchor/rap. **FA:** Alan Bartlett, Scott Cole; 2/88.

2149. **Skinny Pin** (5.4) (R) ★★ This fun but unprotected wide chimney is formed by the gap between the King Pin and the main Sidewinder formation. **Pro:** None; two-bolt anchor/rap. **FKA:** Chuck Wilts and others; 10/54.

2150. **Jumping Jack Crack** (5.11a/b) ★★★ Go up the chimney (5.9 R) to a roof with a thin hands crack above. One of the first 5.11s in the park. **Pro:** To 2 inches. **FA:** John Long; 11/72.

2151. **Venucian Fece** (5.11a) ★ This is best led in two pitches. **Pitch 1:** Go up the chimney of *Jumping Jack Crack,* then right on a horizontal (5.10b/c) and belay in an alcove/wide crack. **Pitch 2:** Head up and right on a thin crack (5.11a), finishing as for *Sidewinder.* **FA** (TR): John Long, Eric Ericksson; 3/80. **FA** (Lead): Unknown.

2152. **Sidewinder** (5.10b) ★★★★ A fun and somewhat exciting route. Go up a flake to a bolt; thin face climbing (5.10b) leads to easier climbing up and left in a crack under an arching roof. Go up a crack to the dike; make an exhilarating foot traverse on the dike (one bolt protects) to its end (5.9+!). Move the belay to climber's right to better protect the second on the traverse. **Pro:** Medium to 2.5 inches. **FA:** Kevin Worrall, Eric Schoen; 6/74.

2153. **Diamondback** (5.10c) ★★ Go up *Sidewinder* to the crack/roof, then head up and right over the roof (5.10c) past three bolts to reach the dike; traverse left to join and finish up *Sidewinder.* **Pro:** To 2.5 inches. **FA:** Scott Cole et al.; 11/88.

2154. **Kingsnake** (5.12b) ★ Begin near the southwestern end of the main formation. Head up and left to a roof, then up and left past three bolts (crux) to the lower end of the *Sidewinder* dike, which is followed up and left to the top. **FA:** Paul Borne; 6/89.

2155. **Rattle and Hum** (5.11d) ★ An improbable friction route on the southern end of the main formation. Start left of *Rockwell 41C* (route 2157), then head up and left, then up past three bolts. **FA:** Bob Gaines, Yvonne MacPherson; 12/89.

2156. **Munchkin Land** (5.10d) (not shown on photo) This rather short route lies on a separate block to the right of the main west face. Go up a crack to a face (one bolt). **Pro:** To 2 inches. **FA:** Bob Gaines, Scott Cosgrove; 11/89.

Sidewinder Rock—East Face

This side of the formation seldom sees climbers, and offers a couple of as of yet unclimbed crack routes. It gets morning sun and is shady all afternoon.

2157. Rockwell 41C (5.11a) (R) ★ This route climbs a short thin dike past two bolts on the southeast corner the rock. Scramble up boulders on the south side of the rock to reach it (it could be combined with next route for a 2-pitch climb). **Pro:** To 2 inches for anchors. **FA** (TR): Rich Littlestone, Rick Booth, Rick Ledesma. **FA** (Lead): Todd Worsfold, Will Worme; 10/84.

2158. Jack Grit (5.10a) ★ This right-facing flake/block with a hand-and-fist crack is on the left (south) end of the east face. Probably better than it sounds. **Pro:** To 3+ inches. **FA:** Steve Emerson; 1978.

2159. Land of the Long White Cloud
(5.10c) Go up the right-facing corner/crack with a large bush about halfway up. **Pro:** to 2.5 inches. **FA:** Todd Gordon, John Madgwick; 9/87.

2160. Double Chili (aka Kiwi Route)
(5.10d) ★ Located just right of the last climb. Go up a crack to a horizontal; move right and up the thinning crack to the large block. Exit right. **Pro:** Thin to 2 inches. **FA:** Roy McClenahan, Mike Lechlinski; circa 1989.

2161 2162 2163 2164 2165 2166

Slippery Face

This is actually the east side of the Grain Surgery/Mud Wrestling Walls. Several fun moderate to easy routes are found here. It gets morning sun and is shady in afternoon.

2161. **Ice Climbing** (5.10a) Begin at a wide crack on the left side of the main face; go up this crack (which narrows) to a shelf, move right, then go up a thin crack (crux, 10a). **Pro:** To 2.5 inches. **FA:** Alan Bartlett, Alan Roberts; 11/82.

2162. **Mixed Climbing** (5.10a) Begin about 12 feet left of *Free Climbing's* large dihedral. Go up thin cracks/seams, around the left side of the roof, then up horizontals to a right-facing corner. **Pro:** Thin to 2.5 inches. **FA:** Todd Swain, Donette Smith; 10/93.

2163. **Free Climbing** (5.10a) Begin about 20 feet right of *Ice Climbing* at a large left-leaning, left-facing dihedral. Go up the corner, then around the right side of the roof

(5.10a) to face climbing past horizontals. Either traverse left to finish the right-facing corner of *Mixed Climbing,* or continue more or less up via horizontals and thin cracks. **Pro:** To 2.5 inches. **FA:** Unknown.

2164. **Slippery When Dry** (5.7) Begin between *Slippery When Wet* and the dihedral of *Free Climbing.* Go up to and over a roof to a handcrack and face climbing past horizontals. **Pro:** To 2.5 inches. **FA:** Todd Swain; 7/92.

2165. **Slippery When Wet** (5.7) This route starts about 30 feet right of the large dihedral of *Free Climbing.* Go up a curving crack to a ledge; move right and up a final corner. **Pro:** To 2.5 inches. **FA:** Craig Fry; 1978.

2166. **Slippery Arête** (5.5) Begin to the right of *Slippery When Wet* and to the left of an arête. Go up the face to a crack that leads to the large ledge on *Slippery When Wet;* finish up that route. **Pro:** To 2.5 inches. **FA:** Todd Swain; 7/92.

Hit Man Rock

This short formation is actually a northern continuation of the west side of Steve Canyon, lying on the east side of a formation that is just around the corner from the east face of Cereal Rock. Hit Man Rock lies about 150 yards north of the Super Roof Wall. The best approach for this formation is to park at the turnouts located on both sides of Park Boulevard 0.3 mile north of the Real Hidden Valley/Intersection Rock intersection and 8.3 miles from the West Entrance. These turnouts are located about 75 yards west of the west-facing Watanobe Wall. Walk north along Park Boulevard until you can head right (east) around the north (left) end of Cereal Rock.

From the Hidden Valley Campground or the Intersection Rock parking area, go west through the gap between the Old Woman and the Blob, then proceed straight north along a wash, staying to the right (east) of Steve Canyon (walking past the east face of Sidewinder Rock and the Slippery Face). A trail continues north (just east of these faces), heading over boulders, before dropping back down into a small valley containing Hit Man Rock on your far left, the Heap on your right, and Labor Dome farther north on your right. Map, page 490.

Descents:

- For routes 2167 to 2173, downclimb to the left (you may have to go up and then left).
- For routes 2174 to 2177, head down and right (behind the block and down the chimney).

2167. **Teflon Don (aka Oswald)** (5.8+) This route lies on the far left end of the formation beginning from a flat boulder; go up thin discontinuous cracks. **Pro:** Thin to 3 inches. **FA:** Todd Swain, Greg Bender; 1992.

2168. **Wiseguys** (5.7) Begin in a right-facing corner; go up the wide crack. **Pro:** To 3+ inches. **FA:** Brandt Allen, Laurel Colella, Alan Bartlett; 11/00.

2169. **The Hit** (5.9) Begin off a ledge to the right of the corner of *Wiseguys;* go up the obvious crack. **Pro:** To 2.5 inches. **FA:** Unknown.

2170. No route.

2171. **The Enforcer** (5.9) ★ The straight thin- to hand-size crack. **Pro:** To 2.5 inches. **FA:** Alan Bartlett, Alan Roberts; 1983.

2172. **Sniper** (5.11a) ★★ The three-bolt face and thin cracks route to the right of *The Enforcer.* **Pro:** To 3 inches. **FA:** Bob Gaines, Yvonne Gaines, Tommy Romero; 3/96.

2173. **Biscuit Eater** (5.10a) ★ Begin in twin cracks about 18 feet to the right of *Sniper;* continue straight up to where the twin cracks converge. **Pro:** To 2.5 inches. **FA:** Dave Evans, Todd Gordon, Kelly Carignan; 4/86.

2174. **Skinwalker** (5.10c/d) ★ Begin about 10 feet right of a pine tree. Go up a seam to a roof; above go up the left crack. **Pro:** Thin to 2 inches. **FA:** Todd Gordon, Dave Evans; 4/86.

2175. **Silencer** (5.11a) (TR) The face between *Skinwalker* and *The Bruiser.* **FA:** Bob Gaines, Tommy Romero; 3/96.

2176. **The Bruiser** (5.10c) ★★ This is the thin crack on the right side of the formation, to the right of *Skinwalker* and *Silencer.* **Pro:** Thin to 2 inches. **FA:** Alan Bartlett, Alan Roberts; 1983.

2177. **The Mechanic** (5.10c) (TR) This is the face on the right end/arête of the formation. **FA:** Todd Swain, Dana Bartlett; 10/89.

2178. **The Allnighters** (5.10b) (TR) (not shown on photo) Begin on the right end of a block to the right and below the right end of Hit Man Rock. Go up the overhanging crack. **FA:** Dimitri Barton, Al Swanson, Steve Gerberding, Mark Bowling; 11/00.

2179. **Acuity** (5.7) (not shown on photo) This is a large V-slot/corner on the northwest corner of Cereal Rock, which lies to the right of Hit Man Rock. It is visible from the Park Boulevard. **Pro:** To 2 inches. **FA:** Alan Nelson; 12/87.

Labor Dome

This small, dark-colored formation lies directly opposite (east of) Hit Man Rock. Approach as for Hit Man Rock (see page 501). To descend, downclimb right or rap off anchors atop *Working Overtime*. It sees morning shade and sun in the afternoon. Map, page 490.

2180. **Working Overtime** (5.9) ★ Begin on the left side of the formation. Go up a thin crack on the right to a ledge, move left and up a flake. **Pro:** Thin to 2 inches; two-bolt anchor. **FA:** Alan Bartlett, Alan Roberts; 1983.

2181. **Blue Collar** (5.4) ★ Begin just right of *Working Overtime*. Go up over the left side of the roof to a crack heading right and up. Go up loose flakes and a face. **Pro:** To 2 inches. **FA:** Bob Gaines; 1/00.

2182. **Corn Flakes** (5.6) ★ Begin as for *Woman's Work Is Never Done;* after about 15 feet traverse left on a horizontal, then go up the face to loose flakes, joining *Blue Collar*. **Pro:** To 2 inches. **FA:** Kim Heidel, Nicole Toner; 1/00.

2183. **Woman's Work Is Never Done** (5.10c) ★★ Go up the obvious diagonal thinning crack, then face climb when the crack disappears. **Pro:** Thin to 2 inches. **FA:** Maria Cranor; 1980.

2184. **Time and a Half** (5.10d) ★ Go up to, then over, the inverted V-shaped roof to the right of *Woman's Work Is Never Done*. **Pro:** Thin to 2 inches. **FA** (TR): Randy Leavitt; 1986. **FA** (Lead): Tony Walker; 12/90.

The Heap
Patagonia Pile
Wall of
Biblical Fallacies
Rollerball
Formation

The Heap

This blocky, squarish rock lies across (east)
from Hit Man Rock about 75 yards above
and to the right of Labor Dome. Approach as
for Hit Man Rock (see page 501). It gets
morning shade and afternoon sun. Descend
off the back.

2185. **Pinch a Smelly Scrutinizer** (5.10c)
Go up the face past three bolts (may not
have hangers) to join *Chicago Nipple Slump.*
Pro: To 2.5 inches. **FA:** Paul Borne et al.

2186. **Chicago Nipple Slump** (5.11c) ★★★
(TR) Go up a blunt arête to right-slanting
cracks, then left and up. **FA:** Mike Law; 1983

2187. **Bad Fun** (5.11a) ★ (TR) Go up seams
and cracks over an M-shaped roof, then up
and right to a crack. This was a lead route,
but bolts were removed for unknown reasons. **FA:** Mike Law; 1983.

2188. **More Bad Fun** (5.11b) ★ Begin about
6 feet right of *Bad Fun;* go up a crack and
face with one bolt to join *Bad Fun* above the
roof. **Pro:** Thin to 2 inches. **FA:** Paul Borne.

Patagonia Pile

Patagonia Pile is approximately 325 yards
north-northwest of the apex of the main
paved Hidden Valley Campground loop.
Unless you are staying in Hidden Valley
Campground, park in the Intersection Rock
parking area, which is reached via a signed
road off Park Boulevard approximately 8.6+
miles from the West Entrance and 11.7 miles
from Pinto Wye (the Park Boulevard and
Pinto Basin Road intersection). From
Intersection Rock parking area, head north
into the main campground loop, staying left
on the loop road where it splits. Just before
the northernmost point of the paved loop,
head a bit left where a deep campsite just
east of the Blob (containing a large, squarish
boulder) is located. Pass to the right of the
boulder and then out a wash into an open
area. Patagonia Pile is seen in profile a couple
hundred yards directly ahead. Patagonia Pile
is the square-looking formation with an
overhanging northeast face. Map, page 483.

Patagonia Pile—West Face

Just before you reach Patagonia Pile, head up
and left over boulders to the west face of the
formation. The routes here are not particularly noteworthy; they get shade in the
morning and sun all afternoon.

2189. **Student Unrest** (5.6) This straight
crack lies on the far left side of a separate
section of the rock uphill and left (north) of
the west face of Patagonia Pile. **FA:** Lotus
Steele, CriusAnn Crisdale et al.; 10/91.

2190. **King of the Mountain** (5.8) This lies
on a separate section of the rock uphill and
left (north) of the west face of Patagonia Pile.
This route climbs a curving thin crack. **FA:**
Unknown.

2191. **Couch Potato** (5.7) This is the crack
just right of *King of the Mountain*. **Pro:** To 2
inches. **FA:** Unknown.

2192. **Sultan of Sweat** (5.8) Begin in the
gully separating the upper face from

Patagonia Pile; go up left-slanting cracks. **Pro:** Thin to 2.5 inches. **FA:** Unknown.

2193. **Etta** (5.7) Begin farther up the gully from *Sultan of Sweat* (right of *King of the Mountain*); go up the short, steep wall on the left to a crack. **Pro:** To 3 inches. **FA:** Bob Gaines, Keith Breuckner; 3/96.

2194. **Tellurode** (5.8) (TR) The face left of *Patagucci.* **FA:** Bob Gaines, Keith Breuckner; 3/96.

2195. **Patagucci** (5.5) This is the left-hand crack system on the far left end of the main Patagonia Pile formation's west face. **Pro:** To 2.5 inches. **FA:** Lotus Steele, CriusAnn Crisdale et al.; 10/91.

2196. **Synchilla Burgers** (5.7) This is the right-hand crack system on the far left end of Patagonia Pile's west face. **Pro:** To 2.5 inches. **FA:** Unknown.

2197. **Telluride** (5.11a) (TR) The face between *Synchilla Burgers* and *Peabody's Peril.* **FA:** Bob Gaines; 3/96.

2198. **Peabody's Peril** (5.9) ★★ Two prominent cracks rise just right of the center of the west face of the main Patagonia Pile formation. This is the left crack, which has a fixed pin about 30 feet up. **Pro:** Thin to 2.5 inches. **FA:** Unknown.

2199. **Nobody's Right Mind** (5.9) This is the right crack; go up this past a bolt, then move right into another crack that finishes at boulders on the right top. It is a bit loose. **Pro:** Thin to 2.5 inches. **FA:** Unknown.

2200. **Filet of Rock Shark** (5.10b) ★ Begin about 15 feet right of *Nobody's Right Mind;* go up a thin left-leaning crack past a roof to bulging double cracks above. **Pro:** Thin to 2 inches. **FA:** Two locals, a surf bum, one Aussie, and a gentleman from Philadelphia; 3/91.

2201. **Sitting Around the Campfire Telling Fishy Stories** (5.10a) (TR) The crack/seam 20 feet right of *Filet of Rock Shark;* the farthest right crack on the west face. **FA:** Two locals, a surf bum, one Aussie, and a gentleman from Philadelphia; 3/91.

Patagonia Pile—Northeast Face

The northeast face of Patagonia Pile has several fun, steep routes on the dark brown rock at the left end of the face. The descent for these routes is to the left. The larger middle section of rock is of lesser quality; the far right end has a few worthwhile harder climbs. The face gets morning sun and afternoon shade.

2202. **Shirt for Brains (aka Wet Rock Day)** (5.11c) ★★ This route surmounts the roof on the far left end of the east face. Either start up the left-facing corner of *Male Exotic Dancers* then go left on a horizontal (best way), or traverse in from the left (loose). Go up flakes/corners to roof. Two bolts protect crux moves above the roof. **Pro:** Thin to 2 inches. **FA** (TR): Unknown. **FA** (Lead): Bob Gaines, Tommy Romero, 10/96.

2203. **Male Exotic Dancers (aka Shirt Heads)** (5.11d) ★★ Go up a left-facing corner to a ledge, then up a seam (5.10c; pro funky) to a roof. Go over the roof past one bolt and up the face/horizontals above. **Pro:** Thin to 2 inches. **FA** (TR): Mark Robinson, Will Chen; 10/86. **FA** (Lead): Paul Borne.

2204. **No Shirt Needed** (5.10d) ★★ Begin either as for *Male Exotic Dancers,* but move to the right end of the ledge, or go up *Jugline* past the first bolt to the ledge (5.11a). Go up the face (5.10b/c; pro: thin cams at the ledge) to a roof; then up the obvious thin-hands crack (5.10c/d). **Pro:** Thin to 2 inches. **FA:** John Yablonski, Kevin Worrall, Mark Chapman, Ed Barry; 1979.

2205. Jugline (5.11c) ★★★ Begin down and right of the ledge of *No Shirt Needed.* Go up then right past a bolt to a horizontal; go right, then up past a second bolt over a bulge (5.11c). Above, head up and left past horizontals and three more bolts. Two-bolt anchor/rap. *Jugline* and *Wet T-Shirt Night* share the same crux, but start and finish differently. **Pro:** Thin to 2 inches. **FA** (TR): Unknown. **FA** (Lead): Paul Borne.

2206. Wet T-Shirt Night (5.11c) (R) ★★★ Begin on the right edge of the face; go up a right-facing corner, then traverse left on the horizontal to the bolt protecting the moves up over the bulge (5.11c). Above, head up and right past horizontals and a second bolt. **Pro:** Thin to 2 inches. **FA** (TR): John Bachar, John Long, Lynn Hill, Mike Lechlinski; 1979. **FA** (Lead): Paul Borne.

2207. Dangerous Curves (5.11b/c) ★★ (TR) Climb the arête to the right of *Wet T-Shirt Night.* **FA:** Chris Miller.

2208. I Fought the Ants and the Ants Won (5.10b) (R) The left-slanting crack right of *Dangerous Curves,* past one bolt up high. **Pro:** To 2.5 inches. **FA:** Todd Gordon, Rick Briggs; 5/92.

2209. Ship of Fools (5.11a) ★ This crack route begins about 60 feet right of *Wet T-Shirt Night,* near the center of the broken face and to the left of a large "cave." Go up the crack past one bolt. **Pro:** Thin to 2.5 inches; one bolt. **FA:** Walt Shipley, Dave Bengston, Michael Paul, Steve Gerberding.

2210. Dead Man's Eyes (5.11b) (R) Begin out of the "cave" to the right of *Ship of Fools,* then go up and left on a slanting crack system. **Pro:** Thin to 2.5 inches. **FA:** Rob Robinson, Dane Sorie; 4/88.

2211. The Flying Dutchman (5.12a/b) ★★ Begin off a stack of rocks about right of the "cave" and climb straight up a thin crack on pin scars past two bolts and a fixed nut. **Pro:** Thin to 2 inches. **FA:** Unknown. **FFA:** Mike Paul; 10/88.

2212. The Yardarm (5.11b/c) ★ Begin about 10 feet right of *The Flying Dutchman* (as for *Walk the Plank*); go up seams to a bolt, then angle left and up past a second bolt to join *The Flying Dutchman* higher up. **Pro:** Thin to 2 inches. **FA:** Mike Paul; 10/88.

2213. Walk the Plank (5.11b/c) ★ Begin as for *The Yardarm,* but continue straight up past two bolts into the wider crack system above. **Pro:** Thin to 2 inches. **FA:** Mike Paul; 10/88.

2214. The Poopdeck (5.10a) The groove/cracks about 8 feet right of *Walk the Plank.* **Pro:** To 2 inches. **FA:** Dave Bengston, Steve Gerberding.

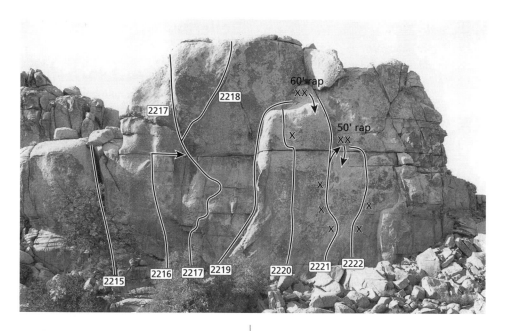

Wall of Biblical Fallacies

The Wall of Biblical Fallacies lies about 375 yards north-northwest of the apex of the main paved Hidden Valley Campground loop, and to the right (east) and a bit back from (north of) Patagonia Pile. Unless you are staying in Hidden Valley Campground, you must park in the Intersection Rock parking area, which is reached via a signed road off Park Boulevard approximately 8.6+ miles from the West Entrance and 11.7 miles from Pinto Wye (the Park Boulevard and Pinto Basin Road intersection). From the Intersection Rock parking area, head north into the main campground loop, staying on the left side of the loop road where it splits. Just before the northernmost point of the paved loop, head a bit left, where a deep campsite just east of the Blob (containing a large, squarish boulder) is located. Pass to the right of the boulder and then out a wash into an open area. The Wall of Biblical Fallacies is the small squarish formation atop a hill of boulders. It is just to the right and

back from Patagonia Pile (a large squarish formation), a couple hundred yards ahead. See photo on page 504. All routes are on the steep northeast face, which faces the Rollerball Formation and gets morning sun and afternoon shade. Approach the face via a trail in the small valley to the formation's right. Map, page 483.

2215. **Fissure of Men** (5.4) (R) This is the easy chimney on the left side of the wall. **Pro:** To 4+ inches. **FA:** Randy Leavitt, Doug Englekirk; 1/87.

2216. **Nailed to the Cross** (5.13a) (R) ★ Begin about 15 feet right of *Fissure of Men,* off a block. Go up the thin crack to a horizontal, then move right to finish on *Resurrection.* **Pro:** Many thin to 2.5 inches. **FA** (TR): Kevin Thaw, John Reyher, 2/88. **FA** (Lead): Kevin Thaw; 1989.

2217. **Resurrection** (5.12a/b) ★★★ Begin about 25 feet right of *Fissure of Men* at a small left-facing corner that goes to a small roof. Go up this corner, then out right past three pins (5.12a); head up and left on the face to a horizontal, then up the left crack (5.11a) in the upper headwall. **Pro:** Thin to 2 inches. **FA:** Randy Leavitt, Paul Schweizer; 1/87.

2218. **Medusa** (5.12c) ★★★ Climb the lower section of *Resurrection* to the horizontal, then take the right-slanting crack (5.12c) in the upper headwall, finishing on a face. **Pro:** Thin to 2.5 inches. **FA:** Hidetaka Suzuki.

2219. **New Testament** (5.10a) Begin at the large, left-facing corner system about 12 feet right of *Resurrection*. **Pro:** To 2.5 inches. **FA:** Randy Leavitt, Glen Svenson; 1/87.

2220. **Walk on Water** (5.12b/c) (R) ★★ Begin at a thin seam about 18 feet right of *New Testament;* Go up the seam past a pin and two fixed copperheads and a hangerless bolt above the horizontal. Make a 60-foot rap off a two-bolt anchor on the ledge. **Pro:** Very thin to 1.5 inches. **FA:** Randy Leavitt, Paul Schweizer; 2/87.

2221. **Blood of Christ** (5.12a/b) ★★★ Begin 12 feet right of *Walk on Water*. Face climb past three bolts to a two-bolt anchor/rap (or continue up the crack and rap off the *Walk on Water* anchor. **Pro:** To 2 inches. **FA:** Randy Leavitt, Paul Schweizer; 2/87.

2222. **Burning Bush** (5.12c/d) ★ Begin just right of *Blood of Christ*. Head up and right past two bolts to horizontals, finish up and left to the two-bolt anchor/rap of *Blood of Christ*. **Pro:** Thin to 2 inches. **FA:** Randy Leavitt, Paul Schweizer; 2/87.

2223. **Manna from Heaven** This route at the far right side of the wall (5.9) was destroyed by the 1992 earthquake. Guess those blocks were kinda loose.

Rollerball Formation

The Rollerball Formation lies about 400 yards north of the apex of the main paved Hidden Valley Campground loop; about 150 yards right (east) and back (north) from Patagonia Pile. Unless you are staying in Hidden Valley Campground, you must park in the Intersection Rock parking area. Make your initial approach as for Wall of Biblical Fallacies (see page 509).

The Rollerball Formation is not very obvious (it appears as a large rubble strewn hillside), but it lies to the right and back from the Wall of Biblical Fallacies (photo, page 504. Most routes are on the rocks on the western side and face the Wall of Biblical Fallacies; a few climbs lie on an east-facing wall at the southern end of the formation; and one route is on the formation's northeast corner. Map, page 483.

Rollerball Formation— West Face

Approach the west-face routes via a trail in the small valley between the Wall of Biblical Fallacies and Rollerball Formation. The face gets morning shade and afternoon sun.

2224. **Roller Coaster** (5.11c) ★★★ (Sport) Begin at the far left end of the formation. This fun route climbs the blunt arête and face past nine bolts to a two-bolt anchor/rap. **FA** (TR): Vaino Kodas, Herb Laeger. **FA** (Lead): Chris Miller; 1997.

2225. **Rollerbrah** (5.12a) ★★ (TR) (not shown on photo) Climb the face immediately right of *Roller Coaster* and stay independent of both *Roller Coaster* and *Rollerball*. **FA:** Randy Leavitt, Chris Hubbard, Glenn Svenson; 11/00.

2226. **Rollerball** (5.10b) ★★★★ A classic Josh crack that some find stiff for the grade. Go up ledges to a left-leaning corner/thin crack with a bolt at its top; then up to a roof with a handcrack splitting it. **Pro:** To 2.5 inches. **FA:** Jon Lonne, Dave Ohlson; 1976.

2227. P. O. S. Arête (5.9) (TR) Begin about 15 feet right of *Rollerball;* go up the arête between *Rollerball* and *Keep the Ball Rolling.* **FA:** Chris Miller; 5/98.

2228. Keep the Ball Rolling (5.9) ★ This route lies about 25 feet right of and around from *Rollerball;* go up horizontals and discontinuous cracks. **Pro:** Thin to 2.5 inches. **FA:** Jeff Rhoads, Lyle Schultz; 4/88.

2229. Naughty Boy (5.10c) (not shown on photo) The right-hand of two corner systems left of *Bamboozler.* **Pro:** To 2 inches. **FA:** Paul Borne, Rob Stockstill; 1999.

2230. Bamboozler (5.11b) ★★★ (not shown on photo) This steep face route is located about 70 feet left of *Rollerball.* Go up the face and seam past three bolts to a ledge with a two-bolt anchor/rap. **Pro:** Mostly thin cams. **FA:** Dave Mayville, Jodee Janda; 7/90.

2231. Romeo (5.11a) (TR) (not shown on photo) Toprope off the *Bamboozler* anchor. Begin just right of *Bamboozler;* head up and a bit right on the face, then back left. **FA:** Paul Borne, Rob Stockstill; 1999.

2232. Curveball (5.10b) (TR) Begin off a boulder 25 feet right of *Bamboozler.* Climb the face to a headwall with a right-slanting crack. **FA:** Bob Gaines; 12/99.

Rollerball Formation— Southeast Face

The following routes lie on a small east facing wall located near the southern end of the Rollerball Formation (facing the west face of Dinosaur Rock). Make your initial approach as described on page 510, but **do not** head up the small valley between Rollerball Formation and Wall of Biblical Fallacies. Rather, when you enter the wash that runs

east just before this point, follow it eastward until you can head around the southern end of the jumbled hillside that comprises the Rollerball Formation. The following routes are found on your left. There are two fairly obvious thin cracks on the east-facing wall. The face and routes are not pictured.

2233. Bolt Revolt (5.10a) (R) Begin to the left of the two thin cracks. Go up the face past an oval section of desert varnish and horizontals. **Pro:** Thin to 2 inches. **FA:** Chris Miller, George Armstrong, Dave Sharp; 10/92.

2234. Gesslerberg (5.10a) This is the left-hand of the two thin cracks. **Pro:** Thin to 2 inches. **FA:** Unknown Austrian climbers; 10/92.

2235. Wildkirchli (5.8) This is the right-hand of the two thin cracks. **Pro:** Thin to 2 inches. **FA:** Unknown Austrian climbers; 10/92.

Rollerball Formation— Northeast Corner (aka Roof Rock)

The following route lies near the northeast corner of the Rollerball Formation (facing toward Dutzi Rock to the northeast). The best way to approach this climb is to walk around left from Rollerball for about 100 yards to the northeast corner of the formation. Alternatively, you can reach this route by walking north past the west face of Dinosaur Rock, then angling west about 150 yards along the eastern edge of the Rollerball Formation until you reach the northeast corner. The face and route are not pictured.

2236. The Living Conjunction (5.11d) ★★ (TR) This route climbs the large (low) roof crack, beginning about 30 feet back in a deep cave. **Pro:** To 2.5 inches. **FA** (Lead with aid): Hank Levine; 1976. **FFA** (TR): Richard Cilley; 1981.

Rubble Rocks

This 40-foot tall formation lies northwest of Rock Hudson, midway between that formation and the Rollerball Formation. Approach as for either one of those formations. The sole known route lies in a small corridor that splits the formation. Map, page 483.

2237. **Toprope Conversion** (5.12a/b) ★ This route is on the east face of the narrow corridor splitting Rubble Rocks. Go up the face past two bolts. **Pro:** Thin to 2 inches. **FA** (TR): Skip Guerin. **FA** (Lead): Unknown.

Dinosaur Rock

This small rock lies directly north of the main Hidden Valley Campground loop, 350 yards north of Outhouse Rock and 160 yards north of Rock Hudson. Descend off the south end of the rock.

Unless you are staying in Hidden Valley Campground, you must park in the Intersection Rock parking area, which is reached via a signed road off Park Boulevard approximately 8.6+ miles from the West Entrance and 11.7 miles from Pinto Wye (the Park Boulevard and Pinto Basin Road intersection). From the Intersection Rock parking area, several approaches are possible:

- Head north into the main campground loop and walk into a small wash just right of a huge square boulder below the east side of the Blob. Once on the more level desert floor, head right (northeast), passing north of Rock Hudson (Dinosaur Rock is off to the left (north).

- Head north into the main campground loop and scramble through a gap between the north end of the Wall and the south end of Outhouse Rock. Walk north past the west side of Rock Hudson, then a bit northeast to Dinosaur Rock.

- Walk around the back (east) dirt loop of the campground and head more or less straight north past the west face of Rock Hudson, then a bit northeast to Dinosaur Rock. Map, page 483.

Dinosaur Rock—West Face

This short face is characterized by a short slabby face with a headwall above split by two wide cracks. It gets morning shade and afternoon sun.

2238. **Go 'Gane** (5.9) Go up easy cracks/blocks to a roof split by the left-hand wide crack. **Pro:** To 3+ inches. **FA:** Unknown.

2239. **Too Loose to Trek** (5.10b) ★ Go up the center of the slab past one bolt (5.10b), then go up a wide crack in the headwall above. Not really loose anymore. **Pro:** To 3 inches. **FA:** Randy Vogel, Howard King; 1976.

2240. **The Impressionist** (5.10c) (TR) This route begins about 18 feet right of *Too Loose to Trek*. Go up a crack to a horizontal/roof, then up the groove above. **FA:** Bob Gaines; 12/02.

Dinosaur Rock—North Face

The north side of the formation is taller and steeper with featured face climbing. It is shady most of the day.

2241. **Gorgasaurus** (5.7) This route begins at the northeast corner of the rock, near a pine. Go up a crack to a small roof, then head up and right along a diagonalling crack system to its end. **Pro:** To 2.5 inches. **FA:** Kevin Pogue, Elisa Weinman; 3/86.

2242. **Dyno-Soar** (5.12a) ★ Begin about 15 feet right of *Gorgasaurus*. Go up the face and seams to a steep face past two bolts. Cross *Gorgasaurus* and continue up an easier face to a horizontal crack high on the face; above

this, finish up a vertical crack on *Negasaurus*. **Pro:** Thin to 2 inches. **FA:** Todd Swain, Peggy Buckey; 4/86. **FFA:** Kris Solem; 1/92.

2243. **Negasaurus** (5.9+) ★ Begin behind trees about 25 feet right of *Dyno-Soar* in a finger crack; up the crack to a ledge, then go up a left-slanting crack that ends near the end of *Gorgasaurus*. Move up and left on a horizontal and finish up a vertical crack in the summit block. **Pro:** To 2.5 inches. **FA:** John Bald, Hank Levine; 11/73.

2244. **Goolabunga** (5.10b) ★ Begin as for *Negasaurus* up to the ledge; move right and belay. Go up the face past four bolts. **Pro:** To 2.5 inches. **FA:** Dave Evans, Jim Angione, Cyndie Bransford, Todd Gordon; 5/89.

Anthrax Rock

This formation lies about 50 yards north of the northeast corner of the Rollerball Formation. Approach this as for *The Living Conjunction* on Rollerball Formation's northeast corner (see page 512). Routes are located on the southeast and northwest sides of the rock. The rock and routes are not pictured. Map, page 483.

2245. **Fistful of Bush** (5.4) The easy crack on the southeast corner of Anthrax Rock; it passes a bush about 10 feet up. **Pro:** To 2 inches. **FA:** Cameron Burns, Paul Fehlau; 3/90.

2246. **Mouthful of Gank** (5.10a) This is a two-bolt face route on Anthrax Rock's southeast corner. **Pro:** To 2 inches. **FA:** Cameron Burns, Paul Fehlau; 3/90.

2247. **Afternoon Tea** (5.7) (R) This route lies on the northwest face of Anthrax Rock; roughly facing Cave Man Crag. Go up a handcrack to a horizontal/roof; move left to pass the roof, then up and right of an easy but somewhat runout face. **Pro:** To 2 inches. **FA:** Alan Bartlett, Brandt Allen; 11/00.

Dutzi Rock

This formation lies on the southern side of a large rocky hillside (Mount Dutzi) located about 350 yards north of Dinosaur Rock. Approach as for Dinosaur Rock (see page 513), and head north to this formation. It is sunny most of the day. Map, page 483.

2248. **Suzie's Cream Squeeze** (5.6) Begin on the far left side of the rock below a small arch with a bolt. Go up the arch, then left to a crack heading up. **Pro:** To 2.5 inches. **FA:** Scott Stuemke; 12/76.

2249. **Suzie's Lip Cheeze** (5.9) Begin as for *Suzie's Cream Squeeze,* but above the arch head up and right on a face past three bolts. **Pro:** To 2 inches. **FA:** Cameron Burns, Paul Fehlau; 3/90.

2250. **Sushi Dip, Please** (5.9) (TR) Begin right of *Suzie's Cream Squeeze;* go up left-facing flakes, then the face above. **FA:** Todd Swain, Jeff Rickerl; 3/93.

2251. **Pretzel Logic** (5.10c/d) (R) Begin near the "corner" of the formation, just right of a roof. Head out left below the roof, then up a runout face above the roof's left end. **Pro:** Thin to 2 inches. **FA:** Dave Evans, Todd Gordon; 11/87.

2252. **Pinhead** (5.10a) (R) ★ Begin as for *Pretzel Logic,* but head up and right in a corner, to a face past two bolts to an easier crack. **Pro:** Thin to 3+ inches. **FA:** Scott Stuemke, Howard King; 12/76. **FFA:** Dave Evans, Jeff Elgar, Randy Vogel; 1/77.

2253. **Elusive Butterfly** (5.7) (R) ★★ Go up the right-slanting dihedral/ramp to the right of *Pinhead.* **Pro:** Thin to 2 inches. **FA:** Dave Evans, Randy Vogel; 12/76.

2254. **Elusive Butterfly Arête** (5.7) (TR) ★
Go up the arête/outer edge of the ramp on
Elusive Butterfly; join that route to finish. **FA:**
Dave Evans, Cyndie Bransford.

2255. **Papillon** (5.10b) (R/X) Begin as for
Elusive Butterfly Arête, then head up and right
under a small arch, then up a flake and the
face above. **Pro:** Thin to 2 inches. **FA:** John
Howe, Michael Dorsey; 12/84.

2256. **Fingers on a Landscape** (5.11b) ★
Begin about 15 feet right of the last three
routes; go up the right-leaning finger crack.
Pro: Thin to 2 inches. **FA:** Lynn Hill, Charles
Cole; 1/80.

2257. **Tequila** (5.10d) (TR) Begin just left
of *Shakin' the Shirts;* go up a thin crack to a
face. **FA:** Bob Gaines, Linh Nguyen; 3/88.

2258. **Shakin' the Shirts** (5.10a) ★ The
right-slanting handcrack near the right end
of the rock. Named for a Bonzo Dog Band
tune and the "solid" lead on the first ascent.
Pro: To 2.5 inches. **FA:** Randy Vogel, Dave
Evans; 1/77.

2259. **Elvis Leg** (5.11a) (TR) The short face
right of *Shakin' the Shirts.* **FA:** Bob Gaines;
1/93.

2260. **Butterfly Constipation** (5.7) Begin
above the main Dutzi Rock face, roughly
above the finish of *Fingers on a Landscape.* Go
up a left-diagonalling crack past a bush, then
up and right in cracks, ending near the top
of Mount Dutzi. **Pro:** To 2.5 inches. **FA:**
Unknown.

Rock Hudson

Rock Hudson is a prominent rock located about 250 yards almost directly north of the apex of the main paved Hidden Valley Campground loop. This is about 150 yards north of Outhouse Rock. Unless you are staying in Hidden Valley Campground, you must park in the Intersection Rock parking area, which is reached via a signed road off Park Boulevard approximately 8.6+ miles from the West Entrance and 11.7 miles from Pinto Wye (the Park Boulevard and Pinto Basin Road intersection). From the Intersection Rock parking area, two approaches are possible:

- Head north into the main campground loop, scramble through a gap between the north end of the Wall and south end of Outhouse Rock, and walk northeast directly to the west face.
- Walk around the back (east) dirt loop of the campground and head more or less straight north to the west face of Rock Hudson. Map, page 483.

Rock Hudson—Frontage Rocks

These rocks lie in front (west) of the left end of the west face of Rock Hudson. One route is known. The route is not pictured.

2261. Cary Granite (5.3) Climb a water groove and finger crack on the northwest face of the formation; it's about 30 feet high. The name may be the best thing about this route. **FA:** Todd Swain; 3/87.

Rock Hudson—North and Northeast Faces

Descent is a walk off the south end, then back left. The faces see some morning sun and are shady in the afternoon. None of the routes are pictured.

2262. Where Ees de Santa Claus? (5.10a) This route lies on a small block with a right-slanting dike on the left side of the northeast face of Rock Hudson. Climb this to a steep flake/crack leading to a bolt. Traverse left, then up above the bolt. **Pro:** To 2 inches. **FA:** Herb Laeger, Dave Ohlsen; 12/86.

2263. Stahl Brothers Chimney (5.9) (R) Begin at a crack just left of the central chimney system on the back (northeast) face of Rock Hudson. Go up and right into the chimney. **Pro:** To 4+ inches. **FA:** Rob Stahl, Dave Stahl; 1980s.

2264. Doing that Scrapyard Thing (5.10d) ★★ This route is on the north end of Rock Hudson. Go up a crack in a small left-facing corner, over a roof, then up a narrowing crack to finish just left of a right-facing corner. **Pro:** 0.5 to 4 inches. **FA:** Tim Powell, Dan Ahlborn; 1977.

Rock Hudson—West Face

This striking face is visible from the Intersection Rock parking area and contains several fine routes up to 85 feet high. The best approach is over boulders right of *Hot Rocks* (for full approach see page 518). The descent is either a walk off the right end, then back left, or for *Nereltne* and *Absolute Zero*, a 75-foot rappel from anchors atop *Less Than Zero*. The face sees morning shade and sun all afternoon.

2265. **Nereltne** (5.7) ★★ Go up the right-slanting ramp to a left-facing corner. **Pro:** To 3 inches; two-bolt anchor/rap. **FA:** Craig Fry; 1978.

2266. **Less than Zero** (5.8) (TR) The short face left of the upper *Nereltne* corner (directly below the rap anchor). **FA:** Bob Gaines; 12/02.

2267. **Absolute Zero** (5.10c) ★ Face climb past horizontals left of *Looney Tunes* past three bolts. Either finish up the corner, or down-climb a ramp *(Nereltne)*. **Pro:** To 3 inches. **FA:** David Rubine, Don Mealing, Michael Wells; 3/80.

2268. **Looney Tunes** (5.9) ★★ Go up the nice thin-to-hand crack to finish up an easy chimney. **Pro:** To 3 inches. **FA:** Tobin Sorenson, John Long, Eric Ericksson; 6/74.

2269. **Stand and Deliver** (5.12a) ★★★ This fine route originally had eight protection bolts (in addition to natural pro). For some completely inexplicable reason (at the time of this edition), the bolts have been removed by some petty vandals. This should be rebolted, but until it is, you can toprope it. **Pro:** 0.5 to 1.5-inch camming units for horizontals. **FA** (TR): Francisco Blanco; 1987. **FA** (Lead): Paul Borne; 12/88.

2270. **Hot Rocks** (5.11b/c) ★★★★★ This classic crack route splits the center of the west face. Begin either up an unprotected seam on the left and step right to the crack (5.10b/c), or go straight up past a bolt (5.10d). Go up the finger crack (crux) to a variety of thin to handcrack moves; head left at the top to finish. **Pro:** Thin to 3 inches. **FA:** John Long, Richard Harrison, Ging Gingrich; 2/73. **FFA** (TR): John Bachar; 1978. **FA** (Lead): John Bachar; 1979.

2271. **Bolt, a Bashie and a Bold Mantel** (A4 5.8) ★★★ This rarely done climb takes the crack system about 15 feet right of *Hot Rocks*. Keep in mind that hard aid in Josh usually has groundfall (R/X) potential. **Pro:** Aid rack with thin to 2.5 inches. **FA:** Charles Cole, Dave Evans, Todd Gordon; 1984.

Hudson Rock

This small formation is really the far right end of Rock Hudson (lies to south). Routes lie on the west face and get morning shade and afternoon sun. The rock and routes are not pictured. Map, page 483.

2272. **Wayne's New Tones** (5.10c) ★ This route lies on the left side of the west face, left of *Gem Nabors*. Go over a roof, then right and up past two bolts. **Pro:** To 4 inches. **FA:** Todd Swain, Donette Smith, Stuart Wagstaff, Helen; 12/92.

2273. **Gem Nabors** (5.9+) ★ A right-slanting crack on the right side of the west face. **Pro:** Thin to 2.5 inches. **FA:** Unknown.

2274. **Ipecac** (5.11a) This is the short, right-slanting wide crack above the finish of *Gem Nabors*. **Pro:** To 5+ inches. **FA:** Bruce Binder; 1985.

The Peyote Cracks

This small but oft-climbed formation is about 250 yards northeast of Rock Hudson, roughly midway between Hidden Valley Campground and Echo Cove. Its west face is less than vertical and has three prominent cracks (the Peyote Cracks). The east face is overhanging and contains a number of excellent and difficult routes.

If you are staying in Hidden Valley Campground or are already parked at Intersection Rock parking area, you can walk here on a good trail that heads northeast from the end of the back loop of the campground. If driving, turn east off Park Boulevard onto Barker Dam Road. Head east, past the Hidden Valley Campground entrance, for 0.6+ mile, then turn left (north) onto Keys Ranch Road, a road that immediately turns to gravel, then dirt. Head straight, past the massive Echo Rock parking area (on your right), continue a few hundred yards,

and park at a very small parking area (on both sides of the road) located before the larger Echo Cove Rocks lot. A trail leads straight west to the crag. Map, page 483.

Peyote Cracks—West Face

The face is popular for moderately difficult routes that are easily toproped. These routes see morning shade and sun all afternoon. Routes are about 40 to 50 feet tall.

2275. **Button Soup** (5.2) (R) Begin behind a boulder and trees. Go up a slot to the right side of a roof. **Pro:** To 3 inches. **FA:** Unknown.

2276. **Matt's Problem** (5.10c) (R) Begin just right of *Button Soup,* boulder up over an overhang, then go up and left to join *Button Soup.* The crux is getting started; more of a high boulder problem than a route. **FA:** Matt Cox; 1974.

2277. Colostomy (5.10b) (R) Start either up *Matt's Problem* or stem off a tree, then go up and right in a trough. **FA** (?): Woody Stark; 1998. **FA** (Lead/solo): Leo Houlding; 1998.

2278. Left Peyote Crack (5.10d) ★★ The left of the three cracks. The crux is getting started (careful with placing pro); pretty trivial after that. **Pro:** To 2 inches. **FA:** Unknown.

2279. Stand by Me (5.10a) (TR) Go up the small pine, then the face between *Left* and *Middle Peyote Cracks*. **FA:** Peggy Buckey, Todd Swain; 3/87.

2280. Middle Peyote Crack (5.9) ★★ The middle crack. **Pro:** To 2 inches. **FA:** Unknown.

2281. Right Peyote Crack (5.8) ★★ The right crack. **Pro:** To 2.5 inches. **FA:** Unknown.

2282. Face It (5.10a) (R/X) ★★ The runout face to the right of *Right Peyote Crack*. **Pro:** One bolt; gear for anchors. **FA** (TR): Unknown. **FA** (Lead): Unknown.

2283. When You're a Poodle (5.11c) (R) ★ (not shown on photo) The two-bolt route on the south-facing wall around the corner to the right of *Face It*. **FA** (TR): John Havens. **FA** (Lead): Unknown.

2284. Zygote (5.11a/b) (not shown on photo) This is located on a west-facing slab to the right of *When You're a Poodle*. Go up past a weird hole in the rock to one bolt and the face above. Height-dependent crux. **Pro:** 0.75 to 2 inches. **FA:** Todd Gordon, Dave Evans, Jim Angione; 5/89.

Peyote Cracks—East Face (aka Bachar Toprope Wall)

This short (50-foot) overhanging face contains many difficult and excellent routes. Several of these routes were toprope problems that have since been led; in some cases, bolts have been added to protect these leads. It is still common for climbers to toprope many of these climbs, and bolt anchors exist on top of most routes. Slings and extendos may be helpful to set up topropes from some of these anchors. The easiest way to the top (or to get down) is down the south end of the formation. It gets sun in the morning, shade most of the afternoon. See page 521 for approach directions.

2285. Dimp for a Chimp (5.11a) The very short, left-slanting crack on the far left end of the face. **Pro:** To 3 inches or toprope. **FA:** John Bachar; 1980.

2286. The Moonbeam Crack (5.13a) ★★★ An ultrathin left-leaning crack. This route has been led, but most prefer a toprope or highball boulder/solo. **Pro:** From 0.25 to 2 inches. Gear needed for a toprope. **FA** (TR): John Bachar. **FA** (Lead): Unknown.

2287. Baby Apes (5.12c) ★★★★ A classic and powerful route. Go up and right under a roof, then back left above; move left into the crack/seam, then up this to the top. **Pro:** One bolt (*Rastafarian's* first bolt); thin to 1.5 inches; two-bolt anchor. Most people toprope this route using a longish (6+-foot) sling from belay bolts. **FA** (TR): John Bachar; 3/80. **FA** (Lead): Hidetaka Suzuki.

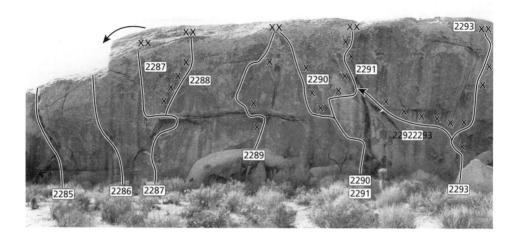

2288. **Rastafarian** (5.13b) ★★ Start as for
Baby Apes, but head straight up a left-leaning
seam above the roof. **Pro:** Four bolts;
optional to 2 inches. **FA:** Scott Cosgrove.

2289. **The Watusi** (5.12c) ★★★ Start off a
boulder, then go up over an overhang and
left to a right-leaning crack/flake. **Pro:** To 2
inches; three bolts. **FA** (TR): John Bachar;
1980. **FA** (Lead): Terry Ayers, Mike
Lechlinski, Tom Gilje; 12/88.

2290. **Dial Africa** (5.12c) ★★★ Start as for
Apartheid, but head left at a horizontal; go up
a thin seam to a crack. There is a poorly
located bolt for the crux. **Pro:** Three bolts;
thin to 2 inches. **FA** (TR): John Bachar. **FA**
(Lead): Scott Cosgrove.

2291. **Apartheid** (5.12a) ★★★★ (Sport) A
classic sport route with the crux down low,
but it doesn't relent 'til after you pull the
very last move. **Pro:** Four bolts; optional 1.5
inch; two-bolt anchor. **FA:** Scott Cosgrove.

2292. **Tribal Warfare** (5.13a) ★★★ (Sport)
Start up *Buffalo Soldier,* then after the second
bolt head up and left along a faint seam
(crux), until you join *Apartheid* for the last
three bolts. **Pro:** Nine bolts; two-bolt anchor.
FA: Scott Cosgrove; 11/96.

2293. **Buffalo Soldier** (5.12c) ★★ A very
bouldery start leads to a crack and easier
climbing. **Pro:** Four bolts (optional to 2
inches); two-bolt anchor.

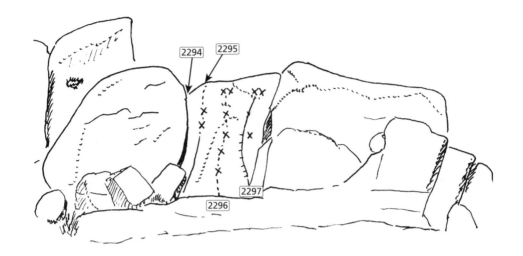

Peyote Cracks— East Face, Right End

The following routes lie on a separate section of rock lying to the right and a bit forward of the Bachar Toprope Wall. The rock quality is much coarser here. The face gets sun in the morning and shade all afternoon.

2294. **Hanging Turd of Babylon** (5.9) Offwidth crack. **Pro:** To 5 inches. **FA:** Todd Gordon, Andrea Tomaszewski; 10/99.

2295. **Handygland** (5.10a) ★ The crack to an arête with two bolts right of last climb. **Pro:** To 2.5 inches. **FA:** Todd Gordon, Andrea Tomaszewski, Nancy Sherber; 10/99.

2296 **Take the Pain** (5.13a) ★ (Sport) This four-bolt route lies on the overhanging face about 35 feet right of *Handygland*. The crux is by the third bolt; stick clip the first bolt. **FA:** Scott Cosgrove; 10/95.

2297. **Kalkowski Crack** (5.10d) Climb a corner past a bolt to a crack to the right of *Take the Pain*. **Pro:** To 2.5 inches. **FA:** Todd Gordon et al.; 9/00.

SPORT ROUTES INDEX

(route name, rating, quality, page number)

ROUTES BY RATING INDEX

(*Route name*, quality, page number)

5.0
❑ *The Gap* ★ 261
❑ *The Trough* 64

5.1
❑ *B-1* ★ 64
❑ *Balancing Act* ★ 336
❑ *Barney Rubble* 243
❑ *Simpatico* 65
❑ *Vogels Are Poodles Too* 301

5.2
❑ *Beginner's Two* ★ 464
❑ *Button Soup* 521
❑ *Decent Buckets* 410
❑ *Easy Buttress, Left* 126
❑ *Eyestrain* 65
❑ *Goeb's Goes Gecko* ★ 229
❑ *Mastering* ★★ 105
❑ *Northwest Chimney* 457
❑ *Three Swidgeteers* 350

5.3
❑ *B-2* ★ 64
❑ *B-3* 64
❑ *Beginner's One* ★ 465
❑ *California Burrito* 363
❑ *Cary Granite* 518
❑ *Chexquest Flemoids* 397
❑ *Dave's Ditch* 100
❑ *Easy Buttress, Right* 126
❑ *Epperson Groove* 149
❑ *First Little Pig* 150
❑ *Robaxol* 294
❑ *Scamp* 405
❑ *Shardik* 103
❑ *Southeast Corner* ★ 451

❑ *Tapeworm* 123
❑ *The Eye* ★★★ 479
❑ *The Perch Crack* 408
❑ *Third Little Pig* 150
❑ *Tucker's Tick List* 130
❑ *Turtle Soup* 426
❑ *Unknown* 58
❑ *Upper Right Ski Track* ★★ 449
❑ *Wandering Tortoise* 425

5.4
❑ *A Walk on the Beach* 463
❑ *Beatle Bailey* 275
❑ *Belly Scraper* 481
❑ *Bisk* ★ 424
❑ *Blue Bayou* 303
❑ *Blue Collar* ★ 503
❑ *Boost for the Beginner* 99
❑ *Borneo* 273
❑ *Business Trip* 479
❑ *Carolyn's Rump* 478
❑ *Carry the Water* 59
❑ *Easy Day* 425
❑ *Eschar* ★ 64
❑ *Eyesore* 65
❑ *Felix* 338
❑ *Final Act* ★ 337
❑ *Fissure of Men* 509
❑ *Fistful of Bush* 516
❑ *Fright Night* 122
❑ *Hoopharkz* ★ 496
❑ *Hueco Thanks* 284
❑ *Left Spire Route* 435
❑ *Look Mom, No Sweat* 105
❑ *Melanoma* 132
❑ *Mother Goose* 236
❑ *Muff Divers* 102
❑ *Northwest Chimney* ★ 465
❑ *Not Worth Your Pile* 402
❑ *Once in a Blue Moon* 302
❑ *Outhouse Flake* ★ 466
❑ *Pahrump* 102
❑ *Paint Me Gigi* ★ 105

5.6 continued

- Bush Driver 99
- Captain Standish 146
- Caw Caw 58
- Cereal Killer 489
- Chili Dog 333
- Chocolate Snake 341
- Circe ★ 479
- Cobs Wall 101
- Corn Flakes ★ 503
- Correct Me If I'm Wrong 137
- Cow Pie Corner 400
- Curtain Call ★ 337
- Damn Jam ★ 471
- Date Shake 334
- Deflowered ★★ 496
- Diagonal Chimney 467
- Dover Soul 73
- Escape from Wyoming 225
- Faith Healer 332
- Fake Foot 156
- False Classic Corner (aka Nolina Crack) ★★ 278
- Feline Pine ★ 339
- Filch 61
- Fixed Bayonets 146
- Fote Hog ★★ 383
- Foul Fowl 478
- Gaz Giz 450
- Glen's Crack ★★ 146
- H & R Block ★ 329
- Handicapped Zone 90
- Happy Helmet 150
- Hidden Taxes 329
- Iranian Party Hat 119
- It's Not Brain Surgery ★ 92
- Jack 146
- James Brown 95
- Karpkwitz 64
- Last Minute Additions 283
- Leaping Leaner ★★ 419
- Look Mom, No Hands 105
- Marmac's Crack 338
- Mike's Books ★★ 452
- Nolina Crack (aka False Classic Corner) ★★ 278
- Not the Clean Crack 137
- Now We Know 133
- Nuts and Cherries 334
- Outer Limit 453
- Penthouse Pet 222
- Perfidious 461
- Poodlesby 321
- Quo Vadis 106
- Ranger J. B. 413
- Ranger J. D. 413
- Rip Off 78
- Roach Roof 279
- Rodeo Drive 417
- San Rio Crack 339
- Self Abuse 268
- Shagaholic 277
- Silkworm 242
- Solar Technology 269
- Speed Bump 89
- Spinner 291
- Split 408
- Splotch 408
- Squirrel Attack 334
- Student Unrest 506
- Suzie's Cream Squeeze 516
- Swain in the Breeze ★★ 298
- Swiss Cheese ★ 250
- Talus Phallus 355
- The Chicken Ranch ★ 102
- The Great Thief 58
- The Key Knob 111
- The Playwright 337
- The Scythe 100
- The Stiffy 403
- Tower of Godliness—East Side 204
- Tulip 64
- Tyrone Shoelaces 135
- Underpass ★ 454
- West Chimney 453
- Yi 250

5.8 continued

5.8 continued

5.8 continued

5.8+

5.9

5.9 continued

- ❏ *Padded Handcuffs* 102
- ❏ *Peabody's Peril* ★★ 507
- ❏ *Penalty Runout* ★★ 283
- ❏ *Peruvian Power Layback* 252
- ❏ *Pick-a-Nick Baskets* 224
- ❏ *Pig in Heat* ★★ 320
- ❏ *Poetry in Motion* ★ 295
- ❏ *Poodle Jive* 322
- ❏ *Popular Mechanics* ★★★ 71
- ❏ *Progressive Lizard* ★ 228
- ❏ *Psycho Groove* ★ 337
- ❏ *Psycho II* 260
- ❏ *Pterodactyl Crack* 356
- ❏ *Pumpernickel Pickle* 95
- ❏ *Puttin' on the Grits* 489
- ❏ *Pyramid of the Moon* 474
- ❏ *Quit Doing Czech Girls* 286
- ❏ *Ravens Do Nasty Things to My Bottom* 325
- ❏ *Reality Check* 465
- ❏ *Red Eye* 133
- ❏ *Rehab* 424
- ❏ *Right Lizard Crack* ★ 228
- ❏ *Right S Crack* ★ 302
- ❏ *River Phoenix* ★ 124
- ❏ *Road Rage* 245
- ❏ *Rock & Roll Girl* 230
- ❏ *Rock Candy* ★★★ 250
- ❏ *Route 182* 325
- ❏ *Rubber Soul* 73
- ❏ *Runaway Truck Ramp* 357
- ❏ *Safety in Solitude* 464
- ❏ *Sexy Grandma* ★★ 458
- ❏ *Sgt. Saturn* 396
- ❏ *Short but Potent* 100
- ❏ *Short but Sweet* ★★ 431
- ❏ *Silent but Deadly* 248
- ❏ *Sine Wave* ★ 161
- ❏ *Slabulous* ★ 349
- ❏ *Smoke-A-Bowl* ★ 319
- ❏ *Snapping Turtle* 425
- ❏ *Solar Flare* ★ 69
- ❏ *Solo* ★ 377

- ❏ *Soul Research* 353
- ❏ *Spitwad* ★★ 249
- ❏ *Split Personality* ★★★ 250
- ❏ *Split Shift* 352
- ❏ *Spoodle* ★ 322
- ❏ *Spoonful* 340
- ❏ *Stahl Brothers Chimney* 518
- ❏ *Stemulation* ★ 66
- ❏ *Stepping out of Babylon* ★★ 190
- ❏ *Stolen Christmas* ★★ 159
- ❏ *Strawberry Jam* ★★ 467
- ❏ *Sunny Delight* ★ 91
- ❏ *Sunset Strip* 417
- ❏ *Super Roof* ★★★ 493
- ❏ *Sushi Dip, Please* 516
- ❏ *Suspect Rock* 325
- ❏ *Suzie's Lip Cheeze* 516
- ❏ *Swisher Sweets* 431
- ❏ *Take the Money and Run* 116
- ❏ *Tales of Brave Ulysses* 380
- ❏ *Tasgrainian Devil* 285
- ❏ *Teckno Sporran* 124
- ❏ *Teddy* ★★ 124
- ❏ *Teeter Totter* 51
- ❏ *Tender Flakes of Wrath* 91
- ❏ *The BMW Route* 378
- ❏ *The DMB* ★★ 195
- ❏ *The Enforcer* ★ 502
- ❏ *The Grinder* 160
- ❏ *The Hibiscus Shuffle* ★★ 76
- ❏ *The Hit* 502
- ❏ *The Humidor* ★ 432
- ❏ *The Jewel of Denial* ★ 195
- ❏ *The Lone Ranger* ★★ 285
- ❏ *The Magic Touch* ★ 360
- ❏ *The Mistake* 212
- ❏ *The Nose in a Day (aka Mano Negra)* 237
- ❏ *The Raccoon* 232
- ❏ *The Swidgeteria* 351
- ❏ *Thigh Master* ★ 242
- ❏ *Third World* 284
- ❏ *Three Friends and a Baby* 352
- ❏ *Tonto and the Great White Leader* 406

5.10/5.11
☐ *Unknown* 441

5.10a
☐ *7* 399
☐ *Aftermath* ★★ 121
☐ *Against the Grain* ★ 391
☐ *Alligator Lizard* ★ 228
☐ *Amanda* ★★★ 487
☐ *Ape Man Hop* ★★ 124
☐ *Arête #1* ★ 190
☐ *Ass Gasket* ★ 119
☐ *Ball Bearing* ★★★ 383
☐ *Ballet* ★ 472
☐ *Barley, Wheat or Rye (It's All Grain)* 287
☐ *Barn Dance* ★ 251
☐ *Barn Door Right* ★ 252
☐ *Barracuda* ★ 393
☐ *Basketball Jones* 135
☐ *Beef and Bean* ★ 364
☐ *Beefeater* 384
☐ *Berserk* ★ 295
☐ *Big Gulp* 109
☐ *Billy Barty Crack* 236
☐ *Bimbo* 64
☐ *Birdman from Alcatraz* ★ 353
☐ *Biscuit Eater* ★ 502
☐ *Blitzo Crack* ★★ 155
☐ *Blizzard* 332
☐ *Blue Meanie* 441
☐ *Blue Nubian* ★ 441
☐ *Blues Brothers* ★★★ 303
☐ *Bold Is a Four Letter Word* ★ 57
☐ *Bolt Revolt* 512
☐ *Broken Glass* ★ 377
☐ *Bubba Takes a Siesta* ★ 87
☐ *Buckwheat* 489
☐ *Bung Hole* 360
☐ *Burkulator* ★ 271
☐ *Buster Brown* ★★★ 95
☐ *Busy Beaver* ★ 240
☐ *Buyer Beware* 364
☐ *Calling All Swidgets* 351

☐ *Candelabra* ★★ 491
☐ *Carne Asada* 405
☐ *Cat Walk* 98
☐ *Celebrity Death March* ★ 384
☐ *Chalk Up Another One* ★★★ 471
☐ *Championship Wrestling* ★ 416
☐ *Charles in Charge* 358
☐ *Charley Horse* ★ 119
☐ *Chestwig* ★★ 231
☐ *Chicken* 364
☐ *Child's Spray* 358
☐ *Climbing Out of Obscurity* 98
☐ *Coming Up Short* 404
☐ *Cool Crack* ★ 117
☐ *Couldn't Wait* 348
☐ *Cruelty to Animals* 439
☐ *Crystal Deva* 210
☐ *Cyndie's Brain* ★ 487
☐ *Dandelion* ★★ 459
☐ *Death Before Lycra* 358
☐ *Desperado* ★ 406
☐ *Devine Wind* 267
☐ *Do Do* 486
☐ *Dodo's Delight* ★★ 434
☐ *Dos Chi Chis* ★★★★ (S) 149
☐ *Double Impact* ★ 360
☐ *Duncan Imperial* 105
☐ *Elixir* ★★ 487
☐ *Exiled* ★ 242
☐ *Face It* ★★ 522
☐ *Fantasy of Light* ★ 267
☐ *Female Mud Massacre* 494
☐ *Fissure King* ★★ 75
☐ *Fortune Cookie* 249
☐ *42N8 One* ★★ 201
☐ *Free Climbing* 500
☐ *Fresh Squeezed* ★★ S) 91
☐ *Frostline* 466
☐ *G. H. B.* 124
☐ *Gail's Dilemma* ★★ 75
☐ *Galumphing* ★ 267
☐ *Garden Path* 134
☐ *Gearhart–Spear* 98

5.10c/d

- Beginner's Twenty-Six 465
- Boogs' Route ★★ 200
- Child's Play ★★ 394
- Chute to Kill ★ 134
- Eddie Haskell Takes Manhattan ★ 414
- Ginger's Crack ★ 122
- Grain Dance ★ 419
- Hot Buttered Elves 270
- If 6 Were 9 ★★★ 276
- Lizard of Ahhs ★★ 272
- Nightmare on Angione Street (aka Slim Jim) 478
- Ohhh Dude 347
- Point Break ★ 100
- Pretzel Logic 516
- Quantum Jump ★★★ 329
- Skinwalker ★ 502
- Slim Jim (aka Nightmare on Angione Street) 478
- Smear Tactics ★ 464
- Start Fumbling 243
- The Importance of Being Ernest ★★★ 322
- The Mole ★★ (S) 88
- The Talking Fish ★★★ 245
- The Wonderful World of Art 459
- Too Thin for Poodles ★★ 134

5.10d

- Alcoholic Single Mothers 135
- Alexander's Salamander ★ 134
- Baba O'Reily 460
- Badger's Choff Piece ★ 433
- Barfing At Zeldas 316
- Be Good or Be Gone ★ 383
- Chas' TR 432
- Chemical Imbalance ★ 393
- Church Bazaar ★ 456
- Clive Live ★ 404
- Congratulations ★★ 394
- Cool Jerk 119
- Cranking Skills or Hospital Bills ★ 362
- Crescent Wrench ★★ 67

- Crimp or Wimp 362
- Danny Gore 428
- Direct Start ★ 275
- Doing that Scrapyard Thing ★★ 518
- Don't Be Nosey ★ 413
- Double Chili (aka Kiwi Route) ★ 499
- Dwindling Greenbacks ★★ 219
- Earth and Sky ★ 154
- Elbow Room 287
- False TKO 358
- Fatty Winds His Neck Out ★ 470
- Fear of Flying ★ 472
- Fractured Fissure 479
- Free Bubba John 362
- Gift Wrapped ★★ 321
- Girls in the Mist ★★★ 55
- Give the People What They Want ★ 435
- Gomma Cocida ★ 237
- Grain of Truth ★ 284
- Grey Cell Green ★★ (S) 480
- Grungy 203
- Gumshoe ★★★ 165
- Hands Up 468
- Hang and Swing ★★ 417
- Heaven Can Wait ★★★ 197
- Heavy Mettle ★★ 330
- Herbie's Hideaway ★★ 435
- High Anxiety ★ 71
- Higher Yield ★★ 108
- Hobbit Roof ★★ 465
- Hollywood and Bovine ★★ 400
- How 'Bout It ★★ 348
- How Spoilers Bleed 301
- Hyperventilation 201
- Imaginary Voyage ★★★★ 260
- Invisible Touch ★★ 498
- Janus ★★ 194
- Kalkowski Crack 524
- Kidney Stone 476
- King of Jesters, Jester to Kings ★★ 182
- Kiwi Route (aka Double Chili) ★ 499
- Kool Aid ★ 449
- Left Lizard Crack ★ 228

5.11a continued

- Cheese ★ 364
- Cheese Nip 365
- Cinnamon Girl ★★ 195
- Comic Relief ★ 411
- Crazy Climber ★★★ 295
- Daddy Long Legs ★★ 359
- Devil's Advocate ★★★ 186
- Dimp for a Chimp 522
- Dino Damage ★★ 479
- Direct Wrench ★ 67
- Don't Let Me Down ★ 471
- El Smear or Land 120
- Elvis Leg 517
- Enos Mills Glacier ★★ 254
- Full Metal Jacket ★ 367
- Girls in Our Mist 55
- Goldenbush Corner 450
- Green Chile ★ 364
- Gruel and Unusual Punishment 488
- High Interest ★★★ 107
- History ★ 65
- Honorable Hersheys ★★ 199
- Hooterville Trolley ★ 154
- Ignorant Photons from Pluto ★ 449
- Impulse Power ★ 359
- Ipecac 520
- Itty Bitty Buttress ★ 413
- Keith's Work 395
- King Pin ★ 498
- Lay Back and Do It 376
- Layaway Plan ★★ 326
- Left Ski Track ★★★ 449
- Lemon Lime ★ 264
- Limp-Wristed Faggot ★★ 347
- Liquid Confidence ★ 411
- Lizard in Bondage ★ 228
- Looking for Mercy ★ 211
- Me Mum Shit the Bed 382
- Mercy Road ★ 211
- Metal Shop ★ 367
- Midnight Oil 348
- Molten Mettle ★ 367

- Momento Mori 442
- Mussel Beach 117
- Natural Selection ★★★★ 203
- Northwest Finger Crack 457
- Off Night Backstreet ★ 356
- One Bolt Jolt 400
- Open Casket Funeral 296
- Papaya Crack ★★ 315
- Peanut Gallery ★★★ 286
- Popeye ★★ 292
- Preparation H 418
- Pyramid of the Sun 474
- Ratrace ★★ 287
- Roberts Crack ★ 392
- Rockwell 41C ★ 499
- Romeo 512
- Romper Room ★ 93
- Runaway ★★★★ (S) 380
- Sand Castles 482
- Scream 441
- Ship of Fools ★ 508
- Sigalert 245
- Silencer 502
- Slab Start ★★ 194
- Slow Mutants ★ 134
- Small Business 310
- Smarter Than the Average Ranger ★ 224
- Snap Crackle & Pap ★★ 276
- Sniper ★★ 502
- Spanuerism 225
- Static Cling ★ 450
- Stem the Tide 93
- Still Pumpin' 318
- Stop Making Sense 242
- Super Monster Killer ★ 495
- Swain Song ★★ 299
- Swift ★ 292
- Symbolic of Life ★ 418
- Tap Dancing ★★★ 54
- Telluride 507
- The Brontos or Us ★★ 284
- The Colossus of Rhoids ★★★ 371
- The Last Unicorn ★★★★★ 173

5.11c continued
- ❑ *Famous Potatoes* ★ 164
- ❑ *Fast Track* ★ 449
- ❑ *Flim-Flam Man* ★★★ 346
- ❑ *Frigid Dare* 494
- ❑ *Give a Hoot* ★ 358
- ❑ *Hands Down* 468
- ❑ *Hands of Fire* 210
- ❑ *Headbangers' Ball* ★ 259
- ❑ *Illicit Operations* ★ 311
- ❑ *Into You Like a Train* 227
- ❑ *It's Easy to Be Distant When You're Brave* ★★★ 202
- ❑ *Jingus Con* ★★ 302
- ❑ *Jugline* ★★★ 508
- ❑ *Laserator* 469
- ❑ *Max Factor* ★★ 358
- ❑ *Mitigating Damages* (aka O.W.) 220
- ❑ *Mulholland Drive* ★★★ 181
- ❑ *Nasty Lady* ★★★ 433
- ❑ *O.W.* (aka Mitigating Damages) 220
- ❑ *On the Back* (aka *Two against Everest*) ★ 50
- ❑ *Pitfall* ★★ 372
- ❑ *Rock Dog Candy Leg* ★★ 250
- ❑ *Roller Coaster* ★★★ (S) 510
- ❑ *Secret Agent Man* ★ 427
- ❑ *Shamrock Shooter* 229
- ❑ *Shin Bashers* ★ 166
- ❑ *Shit for Brains* (aka *Wet Rock Day*) ★★ 507
- ❑ *Slam Dance* ★ 381
- ❑ *Slip and Slide* ★ 420
- ❑ *Soviet Union* ★★★ 74
- ❑ *Spanking* ★ 168
- ❑ *Spider Line* ★★★ 456
- ❑ *Spontaneous Human Combustion* ★ 247
- ❑ *Telekinesis* ★★ 161
- ❑ *The 39 Slaps* ★★ 290
- ❑ *The Bat Cave* ★★ 442
- ❑ *The Houdini Arête* ★ 121
- ❑ *The Roadrunner* ★★★ 319
- ❑ *The Toothpick* ★ 308
- ❑ *Triathlon* 415
- ❑ *Two against Everest* (aka *On the Back*) ★ 50
- ❑ *Variation* ★★ 235
- ❑ *Wally Gator* ★ 228
- ❑ *Wet Rock Day* (aka *Shit for Brains*) ★★ 507
- ❑ *Wet T-Shirt Night* ★★★ 508
- ❑ *When You're a Poodle* ★ 522
- ❑ *Wheresabolt?* ★★ 205
- ❑ *Whistling Sphincter* ★ 236
- ❑ *Who'da Thought* ★ 247
- ❑ *Wokking the Dog* ★ 73
- ❑ *Women in Cages* ★ 102
- ❑ *Worms in Your Brain* ★★ 390
- ❑ *Yet Another Cilley Toprope* 129

5.11c/d
- ❑ *Frigidity* 494
- ❑ *Gravity Works* ★★★ 162
- ❑ *Hercules* ★★★★ 296
- ❑ *Hollow Dreams* ★ 309
- ❑ *If It's Brown, Flush It* ★ 397
- ❑ *The Crow's Nest* ★ 155
- ❑ *White Trash* ★★★★ 75

5.11d
- ❑ *Arms Control* ★★★ 205
- ❑ *Avante Guard-Dog* ★★ 206
- ❑ *Baby Huey Smokes an Anti-Pipeload* ★★ 236
- ❑ *Big Bad Bitch* 78
- ❑ *Black Hole* ★★★ 359
- ❑ *Blue Velvet* ★ 101
- ❑ *Cool but Concerned* 416
- ❑ *Dawn Yawn* ★★★ 195
- ❑ *Execution Time* ★★★ 326
- ❑ *Filet of Sole* ★ 453
- ❑ *Glory Road* ★ 350
- ❑ *Green Visitor* ★★★ 281
- ❑ *Hidden Arch* ★★★★ 433
- ❑ *High Tension* 73
- ❑ *Huevos* ★★ 449
- ❑ *Hyperion* ★★★★ 194
- ❑ *Landscape Crack* ★★ 125
- ❑ *Male Exotic Dancers* (aka *Shirt Heads*) ★★ 507

5.11d continued

- ❏ *Minor Threat* 474
- ❏ *Powered by Old English* ★★★★ 181
- ❏ *Ramming Speed* ★ 348
- ❏ *Rattle and Hum* ★ 498
- ❏ *Route of All Evil* ★★★ 56
- ❏ *Shake the Monster* 317
- ❏ *Shirt Heads* (aka *Male Exotic Dancers*) ★★ 507
- ❏ *Sideline* 75
- ❏ *Snap on Demand* ★★ 433
- ❏ *Super Spy* ★ 427
- ❏ *The Cavity* ★★ 458
- ❏ *The Centipede* ★★ 390
- ❏ *The Great Escape* ★★ 121
- ❏ *The Living Conjunction* ★★ 512
- ❏ *The Speculator* ★ 108
- ❏ *The Tombstone* ★★★ 196
- ❏ *Trapeze* ★★ 449
- ❏ *Up the Ante* ★★ 274
- ❏ *Warp Speed* ★ 359
- ❏ *Where Eagles Dare* ★★★ 386

5.11d/5.12a

- ❏ *29 Palms* ★★★★ 290
- ❏ *Unforgiven* ★★ (S) 68

5.12

- ❏ *Open Project* (S) 53
- ❏ *Unknown* 315

5.12a

- ❏ *Apartheid* ★★★★ (S) 523
- ❏ *Chief Crazy Horse* ★★★ 174
- ❏ *Dynamic Panic* 456
- ❏ *Dyno-Soar* ★ 515
- ❏ *Eagle Talons* ★★★★ (S) 185
- ❏ *Electric Free Gordon* ★★ 333
- ❏ *Fascist Groove Thing* 393
- ❏ *French Roast* ★★ 76
- ❏ *Gaston's Grove* (aka *Thunderhead*) ★ 435
- ❏ *Gravity Waves* ★★★★ 162
- ❏ *Great White Buffalo* ★ 386

- ❏ *Ionic Strength* ★★★★ 165
- ❏ *It's Easy to Be Brave from a Safe Distance* ★★★ 202
- ❏ *Jerry Smith Memorial Route* ★ 371
- ❏ *Leave It to Beaver* ★★★★★ 415
- ❏ *Light Touch* ★★ 351
- ❏ *Major Threat* 474
- ❏ *New Latitude* ★★★★ 390
- ❏ *No Rest for the Wicked* ★★★ 56
- ❏ *Nuclear Arms* ★★★ 165
- ❏ *Rap Bolters Are Weak* ★★★ 413
- ❏ *Rollerbrah* ★★ 511
- ❏ *Scary Monsters* ★★★ 261
- ❏ *Sideburn* ★★★ (S) 174
- ❏ *Stand and Deliver* ★★★ 519
- ❏ *Steel Pulse* ★ 366
- ❏ *Taxed to the Limit* ★★ 107
- ❏ *The Gauntlet* ★★ 360
- ❏ *The Last Stand* ★★★★ (S) 184
- ❏ *The Linden–Frost Effect* 120
- ❏ *The Lobster* ★★★ 415
- ❏ *The Mongolian Lieback* ★★★ 144
- ❏ *The Pit Slut* ★★ 373
- ❏ *The Tomahawk* ★★★★★ 179
- ❏ *Thunderhead* (aka *Gaston's Grove*) ★ 435
- ❏ *Tic Tic Boom* ★★★ 380
- ❏ *Toxic Waltz* ★★★ 333
- ❏ *Transfusion* ★★★ 193
- ❏ *Trapeze Center* ★★ 449
- ❏ *Waltzing Worm* ★★★ 261
- ❏ *Where Sheep Sleep* ★ 60

5.12a/b

- ❏ *Amionit* ★★ 362
- ❏ *Bikini Whale* ★★★★ (S) 391
- ❏ *Blood of Christ* ★★★ 510
- ❏ *Desert Tortoise* ★★★ 388
- ❏ *Resurrection* ★★★ 509
- ❏ *Satanic Mechanic* ★★★★ (S) 422
- ❏ *Slightly Sweating* ★★ 416
- ❏ *The Flying Dutchman* ★★ 508
- ❏ *The Sowsuckle* ★★★ 347

INDEX

Formations/walls are in roman.
Routes are in italics (*route name,* rating, quality, [S] for sport climb, page number)
Names starting with A, An, or The are alphabetized under the second word:
Acid Crack, The.

Arresting Rock 213
Arrowhead, The 183–84
Arturo's Arête (5.8) 344
As the Wind Blows (5.7) ★★ 123
Asian Fever (5.8) ★★★ 141
Asian Fever Buttress 140–41
Ass Gasket (5.10a) ★ 119
Assholes and Elbows (5.10b) 225
Astropoodle (5.10c) ★★ 324
Atlantis and Tire Tread Walls 265–67
Atlantis Approach Routes 265
Atlantis Area 265
Atlantis—Jimmy Cliff Area 265–75, 444
Atom Ant (5.11b) ★★ 165
Atom Smashers Area East 166–67
Atom Smashers Area, The 151–68
Atom Smashers Boulders 165–66
Atomic Pile (5.9) 328
Atonal Scales (5.8+) 431
Atrophy (5.9) ★ 54
Avalung (5.7) 59
Avante Guard-Dog (5.11d) ★★ 206
Aviary, The 352–53
Awfulwidth, The (5.8) 80

B

B Flat (5.7+) 219
B for Beers (5.10b) ★★★ (S) 55
B Sharp (aka *Lean-To*) (5.7) 219
B. A. S. E. Arrest (5.10c) 213
B-1 (5.1) ★ 64
B-2 (5.3) ★ 64
B-3 (5.3) 64
B52 Rock 92–93
Baba O'Reily (5.10d) 460
Baby Apes (5.12c) ★★★★ 522
Baby Banana (5.7) 316
Baby Blue Eyes (5.10b) 304
Baby Face (5.7) 120
Baby Face Slab 120
Baby Huey Smokes an Anti-Pipeload (5.11d) ★★ 236
Baby Roof (5.7) ★★ 120

Baby Roof Rock 120
Baby Woolsey (5.11b/c) ★★ 460
Baby-Point-Five (5.8/5.9) 64
Backdoor Santa, The (5.7) 271
Backstreets, The 108
Bad Boy Club (5.9) 283
Bad Czech Girl (5.11a) 285
Bad Fun (5.11a) ★ 504
Badger's Choff Piece (5.10d) ★ 433
Baffin Crack (5.8) ★ 117
Baggage Claim (5.9) 291
Bailey's Foster (5.10b) 213
Balance Due (5.10c) ★★★ 119
Balancing Act (5.1) ★ 336
Balcony Block, The 286–87
Balcony, The (5.11b) ★★★ (S) 286
Bald Women with Power Tools (5.10b) 80
Ball Bearing (5.10a) ★★★ 383
Ballbury (5.7) 463
Ballet (5.10a) ★ 472
Balloon that Wouldn't Die, The (5.7+) 182
Bamboozled Again (5.11b/c) ★ 236
Bamboozler (5.11b) ★★★ 512
Banana Cracks Formation 240, 314–16
Banana Peal (5.11b) ★★ 315
Bananas (5.9) 116
Band Saw (5.10c) ★★ 458
Bandersnatch (5.10b) ★ 355
Bank Note Blues (5.9) 116
Barbara Bush (5.10b) ★ 296
Barfing at Zeldas (5.10d) 316
Barley, Wheat or Rye (It's All Grain) (5.10a) 287
Barn Dance (5.10a) ★ 251
Barn Door Left (5.9) 251
Barn Door Right (5.10a) ★ 252
Barn Stormer (5.7+) 252
Barney Rubble (5.1) 243
Barracuda (5.10a) ★ 393
Baskerville Rock 66–67
Basketball Jones (5.10a) 135
Bat Cave, The (5.11c) ★★ 442
Bat Crack (5.5) ★ 453

Cheap Earthenware (5.7) 111
Cheap Thrills (5.11b) ★ 226
Cheese (5.11a) ★ 364
Cheese Grater, The (5.10c) 378
Cheese Nip (5.11a, A0) 365
Chemical Imbalance (5.10d) ★ 393
Chestwig (5.10a) ★★ 231
Chexquest Flemoids (5.3) 397
Chicago Nipple Slump (5.11c) ★★★ 504
Chick Hern (5.8) 412
Chicken (5.10a) 364
Chicken Lizard (5.10b) ★ 228
Chicken Mechanics (5.9) ★ 239
Chicken Ranch, The (5.6) ★ 102
Chicken Run (5.7) ★★ 74
Chief Crazy Horse (5.12a) ★★★ 174
Chief, The (5.5) ★★ 89
Child Proof (5.10b) ★ 144
Child's Play (5.10c/d) ★★ 394
Child's Play Crag 144
Child's Spray (5.10a) 358
Chile Willie (5.8) ★ 252
Chili Dog (5.6) 333
Chilly Willy (5.10c A1 or 5.11a) 283
Chimney (aka Satyriasis) (5.7) 399
Chimney Rock 471–74
Chocolate Decadence (5.7) 123
Chocolate Is Better Than Sex (5.9+) 394
Chocolate Mob Nobs (5.8) 260
Chocolate Snake (5.6) 341
Chop the Wood (5.8) 59
Chores of Yore Crag 59
Christian Bonnington Spire (5.8) 432
Christian Bonnington Spire 432
Chuckles (5.7) 373
Chuckwagon (5.8) ★ 119
Church Bazaar (5.10d) ★ 456
Chute to Kill (5.10c/d) ★ 134
Cinnamon Girl (5.11a) ★★ 195
Circe (5.6) ★ 479
City Council (5.9) ★ 311
City Slickers (5.11b) ★★ 256
Clamming at the Beach (5.9) ★ 117

Classic Corner (5.7) ★★ 278
Classic Corner Wall 278
Classic Country (5.10b) ★ 278
Clean and Jerk (5.10c) ★★★★ 415
Clean Crack (5.10a/b) ★★ 138
Clean Crack Formation 137–38
Clevis Multrum (5.9) ★ 465
Cliff Hanger (5.10b) ★★ 284
Climb of the Cockroaches (5.8) 279
Climb of the Sentry (5.5) 382
Climbing Out of Obscurity (5.10a) 98
Clive Live (5.10d) ★ 404
Cluster, The 429
Coarse and Buggy (5.11a/b) ★★★★ 346
Cobs Wall (5.6 or 5.8) 101
Cockroach Crag Area 276–81
Cockroach Crag Routes 278–79
Coffee Dome 160
Cohn Property, The 341
Cold Columbian (5.9) 252
Cold Cuts (5.9) 95
Cole–Lewis (5.8) 247
Cole–Lewis, The (5.10b) ★★ 171
Coliseum, The (5.10b/c) ★★ 199
Colossus of Rhoids, The (5.11a) ★★★ 371
Colostomy (5.10b) 522
Come-N-Do-Me (5.10b) ★★ 485
Comes Around (5.8) 361
Comfortably Numb (5.11b/c) ★★ 493
Comic Relief (5.11a) ★ 411
Coming Up Short (5.10a) 404
Commander Cody (5.7) 328
Commitments Are for Me (5.7) 476
Common Law Marriage (5.10c) ★ 193
Compact Physical (5.11a/b) ★★ 189
Compound W (5.11b) 418
Conceptual Continuity (5.11c) ★ 442
Confessional, The (5.10b) ★ 220
Congratulations (5.10d) ★★ 394
Conqueror Worm (A1/A2) 71
Conservative Policies (5.8) 394
Convenience Store, The 109
Cook the Dinner (5.5) 59

FALCON GUIDE®

HOW TO CLIMB!

The *How to Climb™* series includes the top instructional books on rock climbing technique.

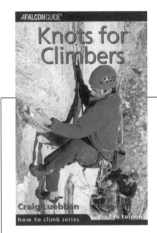

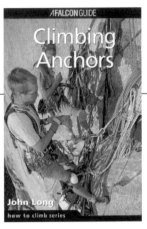

KNOTS FOR CLIMBERS, 2ND
Craig Luebben

HOW TO ROCK CLIMB, 4TH
John Long

CLIMBING ANCHORS
John Long

ADVANCED ROCK
CLIMBING
John Long &
Craig Luebben

BETTER BOULDERING
John Sherman

BIG WALLS
John Long &
John Middendorf

BUILDING YOUR
OWN INDOOR
CLIMBING WALL
Ramsay Thomas

CLIMB ON! SKILLS FOR
MORE EFFICIENT
CLIMBING
Hans Florine &
Bill Wright

CLIP & GO
John Long &
Duane Raleigh

COACHING CLIMBING
Michelle Hurni

GYM CLIMB
John Long

HOW TO ICE CLIMB!
Craig Luebben

HOW TO CLIMB 5.12, 2ND
Eric J. Hörst

RAPPELING
Scott Luebben

MORE CLIMBING
ANCHORS
John Long &
Bob Gaines

SELF-RESCUE
David Fasulo

SPORT CLIMBING, 3RD
John Long

TOPROPING
S. Peter Lewis

TRAINING FOR
CLIMBING
Eric J. Hörst

HIGH ROCKS AND ICE

The Classic
Mountain Photographs
of Bob and Ira Spring

Ira Spring
Foreword by John Harlin III

TOUCH THE SKY!

While other photographers were recording expeditions to distant places, Bob and Ira Spring were pioneers in photographing the remarkable climbers and peaks of the Northwest. Through stunning black-and-white photographs and personal accounts, HIGH ROCKS AND ICE chronicles the Spring brothers' life's work and along with it the history of mountain climbing in the Cascade and Olympic Mountains.

Areas covered include:

Mount Olympus · Mount Rainier · Tatoosh Range · Paradise Ice Caves · Sentinel Peak
White Rock Lake · Cowlitz Glacier · Alpine Lakes Wilderness
Glacier Peak Wilderness · Mount Eldorado

www.falcon.com

Climb Higher

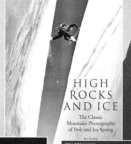

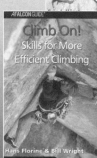

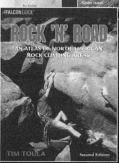

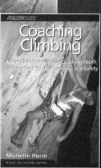

Train harder. Climb faster. Go farther.
Don't worry, we'll spot you.

▲▲ Beginner, intermediate, and advanced instruction

▲▲ Proper techniques for safe climbing

▲▲ Bouldering

▲▲ Ice climbing

▲▲ Mountaineering

▲▲ Training and coaching climbing

For a complete listing of all our titles, please visit our Web site at www.Falcon.com.

FALCON GUIDE®

Available wherever books are sold.

Orders can also be placed on the Web at www.Falcon.com, by phone from 8:00 A.M. to 5:00 P.M. at 1-800-243-0495, or by fax at 1-800-820-2329.

ACCESS: IT'S EVERYONE'S CONCERN

The Access Fund is a national nonprofit climbers' organization working to keep climbing areas open and conserve the climbing environment. Need help with a climbing related issue? Call us and please consider these principles when climbing.

- **ASPIRE TO CLIMB WITHOUT LEAVING A TRACE:** Especially in environmentally sensitive areas like caves. Chalk can be a significant impact. Pick up litter and leave trees and plants intact.
- **MAINTAIN A LOW PROFILE:** Minimize noise and yelling at the crag.
- **DISPOSE OF HUMAN WASTE PROPERLY:** Use toilets whenever possible. If toilets are not available, dig a "cat hole" at least six inches deep and 200 feet from any water, trails, campsites or the base of climbs. Always pack out toilet paper. Use a "poop tube" on big wall routes.
- **USE EXISTING TRAILS:** Cutting switchbacks causes erosion. When walking off-trail, tread lightly, especially in the desert on cryptogamic soils.
- **BE DISCRETE WITH FIXED ANCHORS:** Bolts are controversial and are not a convenience. Avoid placing unless they are absolutely necessary. Camouflage all anchors and remove unsightly slings from rappel stations.
- **RESPECT THE RULES:** Speak up when other climbers do not. Expect restrictions in designated wilderness areas, rock art sites and caves. Power drills are illegal in wilderness and all national parks.
- **PARK AND CAMP IN DESIGNATED AREAS:** Some climbing areas require a permit for overnight camping.
- **RESPECT PRIVATE PROPERTY:** Be courteous to landowners.
- **JOIN THE ACCESS FUND:** To become a member, make a tax-deductible donation of $35.

P.O. Box 17010
Boulder, CO 80308
303.545.6772

ACCESS FUND

your climbing future
www.accessfund.org